7,000 HUDSON–MOHAWK VALLEY (NY) VITAL RECORDS,

1808–1850

Fred Q. Bowman
and
Thomas J. Lynch

CLEARFIELD

Reprinted for
Clearfield Company by
Genealogical Publishing Company
Baltimore, Maryland
2008

Library of Congress Catalogue Card Number 97-73581
ISBN 978-0-8063-1530-0

Made in the United States of America

NOTE

In New York, town-filed vital records dated prior to 1880 are scarce. Fortunately from the early 1700's newspapers have covered marriage and death notices. All records in this book are drawn from microfilmed copies of newspapers filed at the State Library in Albany. Often these newspaper postings contain significant detail lacking in the more frequently sought cemetery, church and town record books. The records found in this book are by no means confined to the counties within which the newspapers were published. Among the more distant places mentioned are West Florida, Texas, Russia, Burma and the Sandwich Islands (Hawaii). Among the deaths at sea are those of persons who were enroute to southern states seeking cures for their various illnesses.

To maximize results here the reader should first check for the name sought in the left column of the text and secondly, regardless of the above results, scan the full contents of all the entries found in the surname of concern. For example the person seeking the father of George Guardenier (with the latter known to have been living in Albany County in the 1830's) finds no posting for George in the left column, but in the second phase search this entry is found:

GUARDENIER, Rynier V., son of Henry A., d 10/6/36 (friends of his father and of his brother, George Guardenier, invited to the funeral at 4 o'clock from the home of the latter, Ferry Street opposite St. Paul's Church) (6-10/7).

At the end of each vital record posting a parenthetical expression is found (6-10/7 above). The number preceding the dash identifies the newspaper from which the record is drawn (here the <u>Daily Albany Argus</u>) and the numbers following the dash reflect in order the month, day and, if needed, the year of issue of the newspaper. The newspapers' identities and other pertinent information are found on the map page immediately preceding the first page of record postings.

The time period of concern in this book (1808-1850) coincides with a massive migration wave westward from New England and New York into territories or states lying sequentially to the westward of New York. Not surprisingly therefore found within this book are frequent references to communities within New England and within the western region of reference above. The outline which follows, data drawn from Eleanor N. Myers' little known but extremely significant report,* (population totals here rounded to the nearest thousand) underscores the magnitude of this westward movement.

---

* <u>A Migration Study of the Thirty-Two States and the Four Organized Territories Comprising the United States in 1850, Based Upon the Federal Census of 1850</u>, Central New York Genealogical Society, Syracuse, 1977.

		but born in New York	but born in New England
Persons living in 1850 in	Ohio	84,000	66,000
" " " " "	Indiana	24,000	11,000
" " " " "	Michigan	134,000	31,000
" " " " "	Illinois	67,000	26,000
" " " " "	Wisconsin	69,000	27,000
" " " " "	Minnesota Terr.	500	700
	Totals	378,500	161,700

Persons born in New England but living in 1850 in New York   207,000

Prior to 1825 migrating persons from southern New England and southern New York in their travels to any of the six regions underscored above frequently traveled north along the Hudson Valley to Albany and from there westward along the Mohawk Valley to the vicinity of Rome. From this point many traveled a short distance north to Lake Ontario with transportation further west along the Great Lakes. In 1825 upon completion of New York's Erie Canal settlers bound for the west could board the canal boats at Albany, travel west as far as Rome along the Mohawk Valley, and after a trip of 350 miles debark at Buffalo on Lake Erie.

Entry 6 on the map page reveals that newspapers of Albany (then as now the capital city of New York) furnished cumulatively 2270 vital records for this book. These Albany newspapers are especially wide ranging both inside and outside of New York State (with heavy emphasis on New York City) in their vital record reportings.

Since 1985 I have compiled four other books and a journal article reflecting cumulatively more than 39,000 vital records drawn from newspapers published in New York statewide and dated prior to 1851. These five publications and others of genealogical concern are identified in the appendix to this book.

Fred Q. Bowman

HUDSON-MOHAWK VALLEY AREA COVERED BY THIS WORK

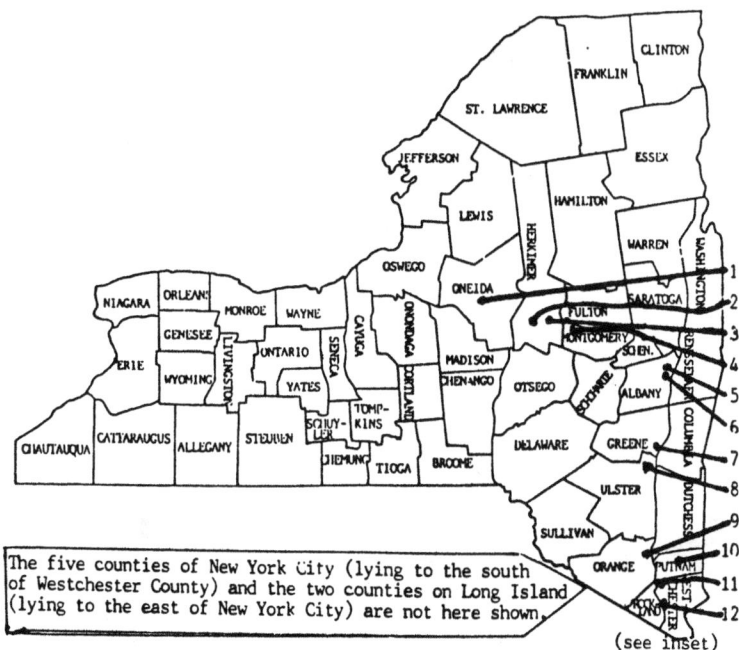

The five counties of New York City (lying to the south of Westchester County) and the two counties on Long Island (lying to the east of New York City) are not here shown.

(see inset)

Citation code number	Publication town	Newspaper title	Date span of review	Number of vital records secured
1	Rome	Rome Citizen	7/7/40-12/31/50	1050
2	Herkimer	Herkimer Herald	7/16/08-11/2/09	3
		Bunker Hill	11/30/09-2/1/10	9
3	Little Falls	Mohawk Courier	2/18/36-12/31/43	894
4	Fort Plain	Montgomery Phoenix and Fort Plain Advertiser	2/24/48-12/31/50	235
5	West Troy (in Watervliet)	West Troy Advocate and Watervliet Advertiser	10/4/37-12/30/50	963
6	Albany	Albany Advertiser	11/8/15-6/5/16	215
		Albany Gazette	1/1/26-12/31/26	296
		Daily Albany Argus	1/1/35-12/31/36	1759
7	Catskill	American Eagle	1/11/09-5/8/11	188
8	Saugerties	Ulster Telegraph	12/30/48-12/31/49	255
9	Newburgh	Newburgh Journal	10/9/41-2/18/43	260
10	Carmel	Putnam Democrat and Democrat Courier	6/27/49-12/31/50	32
11	Peekskill	Westchester Republican	3/5/33-12/3/35 also 1/1/39-2/27/44	312
		Highland Democrat	12/7/41-12/1/42	203
12	Sing Sing (in Ossining)	Hudson River Chronicle	10/23/38-4/14/40	386
			Total	7060

----- (surname blurred), Elias m 9/15/49 Margaret Simmons in Carmel; Rev.
    Henshaw (all of Carmel) (10-9/19)

-----, Ann - see JEWETT, David B.

-----, Isaac, (Capt.), distinguished brave of the Seneca Nation, d "in the cold a few
    evenings since") (from Buffalo Daily Star) (6-1/12/36)

-----, Julia - see TRED, Richard

-----, Toby, 63, "a colored man" d 11/6/95 at Kinderkook (his mother recently died
    at age 93). He refused to "touch, taste or handle ardent spirits" (alcohol).
    Data from an obituary in the Kinderhook Senate (6-11/28)

ABBEY, Dorephus of Albany m 1/9/16 Catharine M. Clark of Mount Pleasant in
    Troy; Rev. Butler (6-1/10)

ABBOT, Mary P. - see PALMER, Stephen

ABBOTT, Cornelia Ann - see KLOCK, Silas

ABBOTT, Elonzo E. of West Troy m 11/15/40 Catherine Morse of Watervliet in
    Albany; Rev. Starks (5-11/18)

ABEEL, Anthony m 4/13/11 Nelly Myer, dau. of Cornelius; Rev. Ostrander (all of
    Catskill) (7-5/8)

ABELL, F.A. - see RICHARDSON, A.J.

ABELL, Henry I. m 4/11/41 Betsey Near in Verona; Rev. Butler
    (1-4/27)

ABELL, James L. m 4/15/48 Jennett A. Gates in New London; C. Carroll, Esq. (all
    of New London) (1-4/21)

ABELL, Rev. J. - see BOGUE, Emily S.

ABELL, Sarah - see LOOMIS, Eli E.

ABELL, William, 36, of firm of Bristol & Abell of Utica d 6/30/35 at Cazenovia
    (consumption) (6-7/10)

ABLEMAN, Christian G., 89, d (date not given) at home of his son, Stephen R.
    (place not given) (6-3/6/37)

ABRAHAMS, David D., 35, d 4/1/44 in West Troy (5-4/3)

ACHESON, Joel of Utica m 6/13/38 Hannah Roper, dau. of Rev. J. Roper of Little
    Falls, in L.F.; Rev. G. Gary (3-6/21)

ACKEN, Margaret - see STILL, Charles H. (Rev.)

ACKER, Eliza A. - see BUCKBEE, Andrew

ACKER, John m 9/1/49 Rachael Vroman at the home of Mrs. Trumpbour; Rev.
    N.H. Cornell (all of West Camp) (8-9/8)

ACKER, Stephen m 2/20/40 Deborah Dingos(?) in Mount Pleasant, (both of
    Ossining); Charles Yos, Esq. (12-2/25)

ACKERLY, Obediah m 12/23/41 Sarah Daniels in Bedford; Rev. Romer
    (11-12/28)

ACKERMAN, Jacob m 7/4/49 Nancy Flanders at Fort Plain; Dr. C.G. Mc Lean
    (4-7/5)

ACKERMAN, John, d 7/9/49 in Saugerties (8-7/14)

ACKERMAN, Martha - see PERRIGO, John

ACKERMAN, Sarah Ann - see WOODWARD, J.M.

ACKERMAN, Thomas Jefferson, youngest son of Col. Samuel, m 6 8/39 Eliza
    Single, youngest dau. of William, in New Castle; Rev. Drake Waterbury
    (all of New Castle) (12-6/25)

ACKLEY, Abram, m 3/16/42 Betsey Morse, dau. of Stephen of Westmoreland, in
    M.; Elder Robinson of Vernon (1-3/22)

ACKLEY, Amelia - see STEVENS, John A., Esq.

ACKLEY, David, Esq. m 4/12/48 Mary Jane Montgomery in Westmoreland; Rev. Dunham (all of Westmoreland) (1-4/21)

ACKLEY, John D. m 3/21/44 Sally Ann Montgomery at Andover; Rev. Colburn (all of Westmoreland) (1-4/2)

ACKLEY, Lucinda (Miss), 19, d 7/14/37 in Springfield, Otsego County (3-7/20)

ADAMS, Allen, 43, d 8/19/39 in New Castle (12-9/17)

ADAMS, Ansel H. m 3/4/35 Ruth A. Nichols, both of Windsor; Rev. N.H. Adams (6-3/14)

ADAMS, Benjamin Augustus, 2, youngest child of Benjamin, d 3/21/48 (5-4/5)

ADAMS, Clara - see BANKS, Joseph

ADAMS, Edward of Little Falls m 12/5/37 Matilda Bartlett of Stratford, Montgomery County in S.; Rev. William Hogeson (3-12/14)

ADAMS, Eliza Ardine - see FREEMAN, John D.

ADAMS, Ezra, 29, d 8/3/40 at Lee Center (a brief illness) (1-8/11)

ADAMS, Frances, 24, wf of Sanford Adams, d 4/21/41 in Rome (1-4/27)

ADAMS, Franklin m 6/6/41 Juliet Wait, dau. of Job, in Little Falls; Rev. J.W. Olmstead (all of Little Falls) (3-6/10)

ADAMS, Franklin, 18, son of James C., d 4/13/48 in Fort Plain (4-4/20)

ADAMS, Gideon of Herkimer (German Flats) m (date not given) Orinda Hoskens of Cicero, Onondaga County in Cicero (1-12/29/40)

ADAMS, Hannah - see BUTTS, Daniel

ADAMS, John (President) - see JOHNSON, Abigail

ADAMS, John m 4/20/36 Maria Louisa Bills, both of Albany, in NYC; Rev. Spencer E. Cone (6-4/22)

ADAMS, John Quincy (President) - see JOHNSON, Abigail

ADAMS, Judith - see SEARS, William

ADAMS, Louisa (Miss), 24, d 6/23/37 (pulmonary consumption). Her brother-in-law, S.S. Vanderlip, is mentioned (funeral from 31 Church Street) (6-6/24)

ADAMS, Mary Ann - see RANDEL, William S.

ADAMS, Parker (Rev.) of Oneida Co. d 6/9/35 at St. Augustine, FL (consumption) (6-7/1)

ADAMS, Peter C. (Hon.) - see HALENBECK, Isaac A.

ADAMS, Pliny (Col.), 48, d 4/2/16 at Hampton, Washington County (buried with Masonic honors) (funeral procession was escorted by the corps of riflemen lately under his command) (nearly 3000 persons were present on this occasion) (6-4/17)

ADAMS, Rhoda - see HALENBECK, Isaac A.

ADAMS, Roland of Albany m (date not given) Lydia Webster of Schaghticoke in S.; Rev. Abram Switz (6-3/3/26)

ADAMS, Samuel W. of Cooperstown m 1/21/41 Maria Covenhoven of Herkimer at Frankford; Rev. L.G. Weaver (3-1/28)

ADAMS, Sarah - see LAWTON, J. Rathbun

ADAMS, Simon - see CADY, Nabby

ADAMS, Sophia - see STAGE, John (Rev.)

ADANCOURT, Francis, 15, son of Francis, d 5/12/26 in Troy (6-5/19)

ADDINGTON, Samuel H. of Paris m 5/27/46 Mary E. Foster of Whitestown at W.; Rev. B.G. Paddock (1-6/9)

ADES, Edward m 8/1/36 Sarah Gorham, both of Albany, in St. Peter's Church; Rev. Clement M. Butler (6-8/2)

ADRIANCE, Joseph T. of firm of Flagler and Adriance of Poughkeepsie m 5/19/36 Nancy G. Klapp, dau of James Grant of Dover, at D.; Rev. Andrus (6-5/26)

ADSIT, Sylvanus m 4/29/47 ____ Trenam, both of Rome, in R.; Rev. George Sawyer (1-5/7)

AGAN, Cornelia Ann, 19, wf of William and dau. (of J.H. Wells, d 6/10/47 in Rome (1-6/25)

AGANS, Stephen m 7/4/47 Mary Burns, both of Rome; H.C. Vogell (1-7/9)

AGATE, Harriet Ann - see CARMICHAEL, T.J.

AGATE, Harriet, 11 months, dau of Edward P. and Maria, d 2/21/42 in Sparta (scarlet fever) (11-3/8)

AGEE, Irena, about 32, wf of William, d 1/22/42 in Carmel (11-1/25)

AINSWORTH, Abigail, 69, wf of Nathan, d 2/28/40 in Herkimer (3-3/5)

AINSWORTH, De La F. m 11/3/36 Charlotte Kniffen in Middleville; Rev. William H. Waggoner (3-11/24)

AINSWORTH, Ira W. m 5/18/37 Parthenia I. Mosley; Rev. Dr. Welch (all of Albany) (6-5/20)

AINSWORTH, Marana L. - see LAMB, George W.

AKERMAN, Ann - see GUNSALLUS, Thomas

AKERMAN, John A. m 7/4/38 Catharine Fox in Danube; Ralph Simms, Esq. (3-7/12)

AKIN, Aaron B. - see DE FREEST, David M.

AKIN, Caroline - see ROSS, Elmer P.

AKIN, Hannah - see SMITH, Joseph G.

AKIN, John W. m 11/27/44 Harriet F. Parmelee in West Troy; Rev. William H. Peck (all of W.T.) (5-12/4)

AKIN, Martha T. - see TELLER, Jacob V.B.

AKIN, Sarah P., wf of Frederick W., d 5/17/36 at Greenbush (6-5/19)

ALBERTSON, William, formerly of Newburgh m 10/28/41 Margaret Hempfield of NYC, in NYC (9-10/30)

ALBRO, Elizabeth Ann - see MARTIN, Edward, Jr.

ALCOTT, Amelia, 20, eldest dau. of Elder D. Alcott, d 8/3/46 in Westmoreland (1-8/18)

ALDEN, A.O., Esq. of St. Albans, VT m 8/19/35 Elizabeth S. Lynde, dau of late Judge Lynde of Plattsburgh, in Keeseville; Rev. J.H. Coit. (6-8/26)

ALDEN, Enoch m 12/24/40 Milla Seymour, dau. of Rodney, at Redfield (all of R.) (1-12/29)

ALDEN, Mary A. - see FRENCH, Horace E.

ALDRICH, Mary - see GOODRICH, Cyrus

ALDRICH, Mary - see MERRITT, Charles W.

ALEXANDER, Edward M., about 3, son of Robert, d 9/1/41 in Little Falls (3-9/16)

ALEXANDER, Mary Jane - see SICKLER, William

ALEXANDER, Maurice S. m 8/25/36 Anastasia Lloyd, dau of late Col. William Duane, at Philadelphia; Rev. John Hughes (6-9/2)

ALEXANDER, Stephen (Professor) of Princeton College m 10/3/36 Louisa Mead, dau of John, Esq., of Albany, NY; Rev. Horatio Potter (6-10/5)

3

ALFORD, Amanda, 35, wf of Peletiah, d (date not given) at West Hartford
(7-5/31/09)

ALFORD, Cynthia - see PRIEST, Edwin

ALGER, Angelina - see RUSSELL, Edgar

ALGER, Elizabeth - see TYLER, Moses

ALICORN, Joseph, age blurred, d 5/18/49 at Rondout (8-6/2)

ALL, Henry of Danube m 12/6/38 Almira Dexter in Little Falls; Rev. T.W.
Olmstead (3-12/20)

ALLANSON, Harriet, dau. of J.S. Allanson, d (date not given) in NYC (6-8/22/26)

ALLANSON, Richard, Jr., Esq., 22, d 2/13/16 (severe illness of one month)
(6-2/14)

ALLARDS, Lucy Ann - see DURANT, Benjamin

ALLEN, Adaline - see REED, James

ALLEN, Adelaide - see DAYTON, Morgan

ALLEN, Adeline - see CLARK, L.D. (Dr.)

ALLEN, Ann M. - see WOODRUFF, Lauren C.

ALLEN, B.C. (male) - see LAWRENCE, William C.

ALLEN, Charles H. of Buffalo m 7/13/37 Melissa M. Kissam, dau. of Richard S.
Kissam, M.D., of NYC in NYC; Rev. Dr. Mac Auley (6-7/15)

ALLEN, Edward (Rev.), 50, d 10/6/46 at Fulton, Rock County, Wisconsin (illness
of six weeks). He was formerly a practitioner of law in Oneida Co., NY but
later became a minister of the Gospel in the Presbyterian Church (1-11/10)

ALLEN, Elihu of Augusta m 2/2/42 Mary A. Graves, dau of Benjamin, Esq., of
Westmoreland, in Augusta; Rev. Z. Paddock (1-2/8)

ALLEN, Eliza - see CARPENTER, Robert

ALLEN, Eliza - see WELLS, Leonard

ALLEN, Ervin m 2/5/45 Anna Mulfey, both of Rome, in R.; Rev. R.C. Vogell
(1-2/11)

ALLEN, Ethan B. - see WILKESON, Eli H.

ALLEN, Ezra C. Gross, 7, son of the editor of the Keeseville Herald, drowned in
the Au Sable River in Keeseville 7/4/37 (6-7/11)

ALLEN, G.E. of Rochester m 6/11/50 Lydia D. Rhodes of Bridgewater at B.; Rev.
C. Graves (1-6/26)

ALLEN, Horace d (date not given). Funeral from his late home at 3 o'clock at 551
South Market St. (6-11/3/36)

ALLEN, James B., 20, d 2/7/47 at home of his brother (not named) in
Westmoreland (1-2/26)

ALLEN, Jane - see FOX, Jacob

ALLEN, John, (Capt.), 53, d (date not given) in Brooklyn (6-11/28/26)

ALLEN, Julia - see WILKESON, Eli H.

ALLEN, Mabel (Miss), 76, d 8/12/50 in Fort Plain (4-8/15)

ALLEN, Mary M. - see MARSHALL, Lovinus

ALLEN, MAry, 81, relict of N---- (given name blurred) Allen of Fort Plain, d
11/10/48 at Battenville, Washington County at the home of J.H. Pitcher,
her son-in-law (she is dau. of Aaron Putnem of Pomfret, Conn.) (4-11/16)

ALLEN, Otis of the firm of Allen, Cary and Staubaugh of Buffalo m 4/17/35
Harriet Elizabeth, dau of late Thomas St John, of Delaware Co.; at the
home of A. Phelps, Esq. in Watervliet (6-4/22)

ALLEN, Penelope - see BALDWIN, Horace

4

ALLEN, Rebecca - see CALDWELL, Levi

ALLEN, Richard L. of Buffalo m at Northampton, Mass. 12/30/34 Sarah O. Lyman, dau of late Hon, J.H. Lyman and grand-dau of Judge Hinckley (6-1/8/35)

ALLEN, Russell W. m (date not given) Agatha Gardner Simons, youngest dau of William Simons, editor of the Republican Herald at Providence, RI, in P. (6-7/3)

ALLEN, Sarah - see SEELYE, Ambrose

ALLEN, Seneca m 9/26/50 Harriet E. Coonrad, both of Lee in Stevens Hotel in Rome; Rev. James Erwin (1-10/2)

ALLEN, Stephen m 10/13/37 Hannah Smith; Rev. C.R. Wilkins (all of Albany) (6-10/20)

ALLEN, Sylvia C. - see REES, Seth

ALLEN, Thomas J., 36, eldest son of Solomon Allen of Philadelphia d 5/9/35 at Louisville, Kentucky (6-6/3)

ALLEN, William - see SPARKS, Frances Ann

ALLEN, Z. of Westmoreland m 9/24/46 Emily Osborn of Rome; H.C. Vogell (1-10/6)

ALLENDORPH, Lewis W. of Sand Lake m 6/2/49 Hannah Hidley of Greenbush in Watervliet; Rev. T.F. Wyckoff (5-6/6)

ALLING, Matilda - see COLVIN, Andrew J.

ALLING, Sarah (Mrs.), 85, relict of late Stephen, d (date not given) ay New Haven (7-6/20/10)

ALLISON, Eliza, 33, wf of William N., formerly of Long Meadow, Mass., d 10/17/41 in Newburgh (9-10/23)

ALLISON, Elizabeth - see SNEDEKER(?), Edward

ALLISON, Jeremiah, about 36, d (date not given) in New Castle (consumption) (12-10/23/38)

ALMOND, Mary Ann - see WRIGHT, Timothy

ALMY, Clarinda - see SMITH, Ezekiel

ALRICH, Thomas - see HATCH, Sibyl

ALTER, Walley - see PRAME, John Henry

ALTON, Louisa I., infant dau. of William S. and Jane Ann, d 5/30/48 in NYC (4-6/8)

ALVERSON, Uriah, 99, 12/7/35 at his home in Madison (born in Johnson, RI; emigrated to Madison in 1789; a member of Baptist Church for 70 years) (from the Utica Observer) (6-12/19)

ALVORD, William - see WHITNEY, Emma

ALVORD, William, 36, of Albany d 12/17/37 at Savannah, Georgia (had sailed for that city from NYC with the hope of relief from a pulmonary complaint) (6-12/27)

AMBLER, Huldah - see FIELD, Amos

AMBLER, John V. (Rev.), pastor of baptist church in Lanesboro, Mass., m 6/29/41 Abigail Thomas of Frankfort in F.; Rev. T. Houston (3-7/1)

AMERMAN, John W, editor of the Norwalk Democrat Star, m 2/4/35 Mary Farnum of Bethel, CT at Bethel (6-2/10)

AMES, Ezra, 61, d 4/7/36 (his funeral at Albany 4/10) (6-4/9)

AMES, Ezra, 62, d 2/23/36 (funeral 3 o'clock from his late home, 41 South Pearl St.) (6-2/24)

AMES, Frances - see TEFFT, L.K.

AMES, John m 5/22/41 Achsal Foster, both of Somers, in West Somers; Rev. William H. Johnson (11-6/1)

AMES, John S., 20, son of Dr. Calvin Ames, d 1/7/38 in Columbia (papers in Oswego are requested to publish this) (3-2/15)

AMES, Matilda, 29, d 7/20/44 in West Troy (5-7/31)

AMES, Silas - see TEFFT, L.K.

ANABLE, Robert C., 20, son of Henry, d 12/10/36 in Hudson (6-12/17)

ANDERS, Rachael - see BRIGHAM(?), WIlliam

ANDERSON, David m 1/29/49 Gertrude M. Carey; Rev. O.H. Gregory (all of Werst Troy) (5-1/31)

ANDERSON, David m 2/28/44 Maria Smith in West Troy; Rev. Lane (all of West Troy) (5-3/6)

ANDERSON, Elizabeth - see MITCHELL, Josiah

ANDERSON, Hester - see BLAKELEY, Daniel

ANDERSON, Jane, widow of Peter, d (date not given) in NYC (6-12/26/26)

ANDERSON, Joseph (Hon.), 80, first Comptroller of the Treasury (for many years he held this assignment), d (date not given) at the home of his son in Washington, D.C. (6-4/21/37)

ANDERSON, Joseph m (date not given) Eliza Ann Le Count at Rochelle (6-5/25/16)

ANDERSON, S.H. m 5/8/36 Forilla North, both of Little Falls, in L.F.; Rev. Adams (3-5/12)

ANDERSON, William, 53, d 1/10/47 on College Hill 1-1/15)

ANDREAS, Sally M., 43, wf of Nelson Andreas d 2/9/50 in West Troy (5-2/13)

ANDREU, Pedro m 11/1/40 Helen J. Rawson of Rome in R.; Rev. H.C. Vogle (all of Rome) (1-11/10)

ANDREWS, Aaron, 52, of Catskill d 2/1/37 at St. Croix, West Indies (6-3/7)

ANDREWS, Alexander H., 30, formerly of Albany, d 8/27/35 in Louisville, KY (6-10/1)

ANDREWS, Charlotte Augusta - see CROSBY, Harrison W.

ANDREWS, Ephraim, 44, d 9/20/35 at his home in Coeymans (painful illness of 48 hours) (survived by a wife and six children) (communicated) (6-9/23)

ANDREWS, Jane Ann - see ROBERTSON, Robert (Capt.)

ANDREWS, John d 6/8/36 at Vienna, Pickens County, Alabama (born in Rochester, NY) (was enroute to Columbus, Mississippi) (6-7/9)

ANDREWS, John F. - see CROSBY, Harrison W.

ANDREWS, Maria - see BRIGGS, Albert N.

ANDREWS, P.C. Montgomery, foreman of the True American office, d 9/9/37 at New Orleans (he was from NYC and was formerly one of the proprietors of the New York Daily Sentinel) (6-9/22)

ANDRUS, Daniel, 89, a Rev. War soldier, d 8/9/40 in Allegany County (1-9/22)

ANGEL, Amanda (Miss), 24, only dau. of John and Martha, d 4/30/43 in Stark (consumption) (3-5/11)

ANGEL, Benjamin F., Esq., surrogate of Livingston County, m 6/1/36 Julia Jones, dau of Horatio at "Sweet-Brier", at Geneseo; Rev. Page (6-6/8)

ANGELL, Harriet - see WOLENCE(?), Nicholas

ANGEVINE, Susan M. - see SHADBOLT, Lafayette

ANNIS, Mary Eliza (Mrs.), 49, d 3/8/39 in Sing Sing (12-3/19)

6

ANTELL, Eliza P. - see ROUNDS, Hezekiah

ANTHONY, Harriet Amelia - see WOOLSEY, Thomas

ANTHONY, Harriet, 21, wf of William R., Esq., d 5/17/43 in Little Falls (severe illness of several weeks) (3-5/18)

ANTHONY, Jackson of Sharon Springs m 5/31/49 Mary Jane Colyer of Root in R.; Rev. C.H. Hervey (4-6/14)

ANTHONY, Mary Lucretia, infant dau. of William R., Esq., d 10/7/41 in Little Falls (3-10/14)

ANTHONY, Miss - see HAIT, Moore

ANTHONY, Samuel of West Troy m 11/21/38 Louisa Peck of Stockbridge, Mass. in East Troy (5-11/28)

ANTROT, Miss - see HOPPER, Edward

APLEY, Griswold, Esq., m 1/24/45 Ann Judd; Rev. H. Matteson (all of Rome) (1-1/28)

APPELBACK, Gotlip Frederick, printer, of NYC m 3/9/42 Sabina Patison of Yorktown at Shrub Oaks; Rev. Benjamin Curry (11-3/15)

APPLETON, James - see DOBERSON(?), Eliza

ARCHER, Margaret - see HALLOCK, Joel

ARCULARIUS, Margaret - see SNYDER, Henry W.

ARDEN, Elvira, 60, relict of Thomas B. and dau of late John Brotherson, Esq., d 12/6/42 in Putnam Valley (11-12/13)

ARMITAGE, Fletcher, 37, d 5/1/46 in Verona (consumption) (1-5/5)

ARMS, Charles of firm of Levi Cook & co. m 6/23/36 Harriet Morrell, dau of Hon. Abraham of Johnstown; Rev. Biman (6-6/27)

ARMS, Ebenezer W., counsellor at law, of Auburn, Cayuga County m 11/13/35 Lydia Avery, dau of Hon. Daniel Avery of Auburn; Rev. Cook (6-11/23)

ARMS, Guy, 47, broker, d 9/4/35 in Albany (6-9/7)

ARMSLY(?), Asenath (age not given), dau. of W.I., d 11/16/41 in Newburgh (9-11/20)

ARMSTRONG, Adna (Mr.), 38 d 4/4/36 in Springfield, Otsego County (survived by wife and three children) (3-4/14)

ARMSTRONG, Charles, 10, son of Jesse and A. Jane Armstrong, d 5/6/43 (1-5/16)

ARMSTRONG, Charles, 11, son of Jesse and A. Jane Armstrong, d 5/6/43 (1-5/9)

ARMSTRONG, Henry S. m 10/19/47 Harriet L. Briggs, dau. of Alva, Esq., of Rome; H.C. Vogell (1-10/22)

ARMSTRONG, James of Vernon m 9/14/42 Elizabeth Soliss of Verona in V.; Rev. D. Robinson (1-10/4)

ARMSTRONG, Letitia - see WILLIAMSON, Jason

ARMSTRONG, Samuel, 74, d (date not given) at his home in Lee (a short illness) (1-10/11)

ARNOLD, Almira - see SPALDING, Edwin

ARNOLD, Amey (Mrs.) - see VARNEY, Freelove

ARNOLD, Benedict - see MATTESON, Elizabeth

ARNOLD, Charlotte - see BELDING, Samuel

ARNOLD, Edward, Jr. m 12/30/41 Christina Mc Chesney, both of Little Falls; Rev. Loveys (3-1/6/42)

ARNOLD, Emma J. - see PERKINS, George R.

ARNOLD, Enoch, 61, d 12/3/38 at Fairfield (3-12/6)

ARNOLD, Lucinda - see HENDENDORFF, Abraham

ARNOLD, Marcelia S. - see BURLEY, Charles

ARNOLD, N.F. of 3rd Regiment NY State Artillery m 10/2/26 Hannah Maria
Brown of New Jersey in NYC; Rev. Eastburn (6-10/10)

ARNOLD, Rachel - see WELLS, Edwin

ARNOLD, Rebecca S. - see PATCH, O.R.

ARNOLD, Samuel G. Esq., editor of the Westchester Spy, pub. at White Plains, m
6/22/37 Sarah Jane Searles of Brooklyn at B.; Rev. S. Arnold (6-6/26)

ARNOLD, Susan Elizabeth, 15, dau. of Milo Arnold, d 4/4/41 in Rome
(consumption) (funeral "this day" at 12 o'clock at the Episcopal Church in
Rome) (1-4/6)

ARNOLD, Thomas - see PERKINS, George R.

ARNOLD, Thomas - see VARNEY, Freelove

ARONSEN, Catharine - see possibly OUTWATER, Jacob

AROSE, Samuel m 5/11/48 Phebe Ann Jacoby in West Troy; Rev. T.F. Wyckoff
(5-5/17)

ARROL, Mary (Mrs.), 43, d 2/24/35 at Albany (funeral from her home at 45
Beaver St. at 3 o'clock) (6-2/25)

ARTCHER, Edward, 1, youngest child of Edward, d 6/26/36 (funeral at 5 o'clock
from his late residence, 74 Eagle Street) (6-6/27)

ARTCHER, George, 42, d 1/27/36 in Albany (a short illness) (6-2/1)

ARTHUR, Caroline M. - see JOHNSON, Robert I.

ASHBURNER, Sarah - see SEDGWICK, Theodore

ASHBY, Henry, Esq., 40, one of the publishers of the Norfolk Beacon, d (date not
given) in Norfolk, VA (6-9/28/36)

ASHLEY, Mary Ann - see KERSLAW, Wright L.

ASPENWALL, Margaret - see HAMMOND, Abijah

ASPINWALL, George, lithographer, d 4/30/42 at West Point (9-5/7)

ASTOR, John Jacob, Jr. m 12/9/46 Charlotte Augusta Gibbes, dau. of Thomas S.,
Esq., at NYC; Rev. S.L. Southard (5-12/16)

ASTOR, William B - see WARD, Emily

ATHERTON, James H., 22, son of Hon. C.H. Atherton of Amherst, NH, d 6/13/37
in NYC (6-6/16)

ATKINS, Rebecca D., 36, wf of James, d 9/10/37 suddenly (funeral 9/11 from 36
Herkimer Street) (6-9/11)

ATKINSON, Mary E. - see PHILLIPS, Ralph

ATWATER, Ira, 52, d 2/23/35 in Homer (death the result of injuries in a fall from
a scaffold a few days previous) (6-3/11)

ATWATER, Thomas C. of the firm of J. & T.C. Atwater in Catskill m 4/22/35
Harriet Cooke, dau of Thomas B., Esq.; Rev. T.M. Smith (all of Catskill)
(6-4/27)

ATWATER, Zophet, 53, d (date not given) at Hamden (7-1/31/10)

ATWOOD, Emma Maria, 4, dau. of Anson & Mary A., d 10/1/43 in Troy (5-10/11)

ATWOOD, Leonora - see LAWRENCE, George

ATWOOD, Mary - see BURNSIDE, Robert

AUCHINHAUS, Agnes Lander - see STEVENSON, Matthew, M.D.

AUCHMOODY, Louis, 29, d 3/31/49 at Rosendale (8-4/14)

AUCHMUTY, H.T., 31, of US Navy d 10/5/35 at his home in Westchester County
(from the NY Times) (6-10/16)

AUREYONSEN, Catharine - see OUTWATER, Jacob

AUSTEN, Sarah Ann - see TOWNSEND, William H.

AUSTIN, Catherine Matilda - see CORNING, Edward

AUSTIN, Charles L., of Orwell, VT m 7/27/36 Frances L. Elliot, dau of Robert, Esq., of Albany (6-7/28)

AUSTIN, David, 65, d 5/7/42 in Somerstown (father of 19 children) (11-5/12)

AUSTIN, Elizabeth Jane - see KELLER, Michael J.

AUSTIN, John, merchant, of New Jersey m 7/27/42 Ann Matilda Wood, dau of Alfred in Bedford (11-7/28)

AUSTIN, Mary Seymour - see ELLICOTT, Andrew

AUSTIN, Mary Seymour - see GARY, Joseph

AUSTIN, Milo S., m 9/12/41 Cynthia Taylor, both of Oswego County; George Petrie, Esq. (3-9/16)

AUSTIN, Ruth Ann - see DYER, Thomas H.

AUSTIN, Silas, Esq., about 60, d 12/9/41 in Carmel (11-12/14)

AUSTIN, Stephen, merchant, formerly of Hartford, d (date not given) in NYC (7-8/2/09)

AUSTIN, Wilbur m 9/1/36 Mary Lewis of Little Falls at Rankin's Lock; Rev. Attwater (3-9/8)

AUTHISAR, Mary A. - see DICKERTY, Andrew W.

AVERILL, C. (Prof.) of Union College m 8/4/35 Julia Pomeroy, dau of Dr. Thaddeus, in Stockbridge, MA; Rev. Parker (6-8/7)

AVERILL, Chester, 33, A.M. Professor of Chemistry and Languages at Union College, d 8/10/36 at home of his father in Salisbury, CT (Schenectady Cabinet) (6-8/12)

AVERILL, Mary - see KNAPP, Thomas L.

AVERY, Austin m 8/30/40 Abby Barnard in Rome; Rev. James Barnard (all of Rome) (1-9/1)

AVERY, Charles H. m 9/8/50 Louisa Warner, both of Fort Plain, in F.P.; Rev. G.W. Gage (4-9/12)

AVERY, David m 11/20/38 Sally Hetherington in South Salem; Thomas Mead, Esq. (all of South Salem) (12-12/18)

AVERY, Eliza W. - see MORGAN, Richard

AVERY, George, late a midshipman attached to the US ship "Guerriere", d (date not given) at NYC (6-11/29/15)

AVERY, John H., Esq., 54, d 9/1/37 in Owego ("formerly practiced law in Tioga County and stood at the head of the profession")(for the past eight years spent most of his time in Washington and the states south of the Potomic River furnishing great improvements in the transportation of the mail) (from the Owego Advertiser) (6-9/14)

AVERY, Lydia - see ARMS, Ebenezer

AVERY, Samuel - see MORGAN, Richard

AXTELL, Daniel Cook (Rev.), 37, d 7/12/37 at Paterson, NJ (Rev. Axtell is the eldest son of the Rev. Dr. Axtell of Geneva, NY and was formerly pastor of the 2nd Presbyterian Church of Auburn, NY) (6-7/15)

AYER, Louisa, 37, wf of Robert, merchant, d 10/17/40 in West Troy (5-10/21)

AYERS, ---, wf of Dr. D. Ayers, formerly of Manheim, d 2/25/42 at Amsterdam (3-3/3)

AYERS, Daniel of Verona m 4/29/46 Abigail H. Dean of Rome in R.; Rev. C.M. Lewis (1-5/5)

AYERS, David, Jr., 32, d 10/1/49 at his home in Verona (dysentery) ("the deceased has left a family...", their names not given) (1-10/10)

AYLSWORTH, William, formerly of Canaan, Columbia County, d (date not given) in Clarence, Niagara County (6-9/26/26)

AYMAR, Benjamin m (date not given) Elizabeth Van Beuren, dau. of Cortland Van Beuren, Esq., at NYC (6-1/10/16)

AYRES, Adaline - see PLATT, George

AYRES, Ann, 17, dau. of late Sylvanus Ayres, d 11/16/43 in Buffalo (lingering consumption) (3-12/7)

AYRES, Charles of Verona m 12/18/47 Cecilia Clark, dau. of late Dr. John Clark of Rome; H.C. Vogell (1-1/7/48)

AYRES, Daniel (Dr.) of Amsterdam m 9/20/42 Mrs. Margaret Freeman of Manheim in M.; Rev. Myer of St. Johnsville (3-9/22)

AYRES, Hiram of Fairfield m 1/19/36 Ann Tuttle, dau. of Zopher M., Esq. of Salisbury, in S.; Rev. M. Weber (3-2/18)

AYRES, Mary - see TAGGART, Samuel

BABCOCK, George B. - see possibly BOBCOCK, George B.

BABCOCK, Henry S. of firm of Babcock & Baldwin of Cooperstown m 10/11/37 Lois Elizabeth Dixon, dau. of Archibald, Esq. of Gilbertsville, in Christ's Church, Gilbertsville; Rev. Hughes (6-10/20)

BABCOCK, Lydia E - see WILDER, Alfred

BABCOCK, Nathan m 3/26/43 Fanny Walrad; Rev. C.W. Leet (all of Little Falls) (3-3/30)

BABCOCK, Samuel m 12/24/43 Sarah Maria Simmons, dau of Alpheus; Rev. D. Westbrook (all of Peekskill) (11-12/26)

BABCOCK, Savina - see RAYMOND, Luzon

BABCOCK, Sophronia - see COOPER, John E.

BACHELDOR, Chester m 4/25/43 Olive Maria Chafy, both of West Troy, in W.T.; Rev. Z. Phillips (5-5/3)

BACKHART, Margaret - see HEM, John

BACKUS, ---- (Mr.) - see HOWK, Roswell

BACKUS, Elisha (Col.), 67, formerly of Utica and for 25 years a resident of Oneida County, d 8/12/50 at the home of his son-in-law, R.B. Chapman, Esq., at Morrison, St. Lawrence County (1-8/21)

BACKUS, Ezra - see TILLOTSON, Abigail

BACKUS, J. Trumbull (Rev.) of Schenectady m 5/1/35 Ann Eliza Walworth, dau of Chancellor Walworth, at Saratoga Springs; Rev. D.O. Griswold (6-5/6)

BACKUS, Ozias, 45, d (date not given) at Bozrah (7-6/20/10)

BACON, John F. of Albany m 10/24/37 Harriet E. Everett in Hudson; Rev. Waterbury (6-11/1)

BACON, Julia - see WOODRUFF, J.L.

BACON, Marshal J. of Michigan m 9/15/36 Belinda Graham, dau of David, Esq., in NYC; Rev. Dr. Brownley (6-9/19)

BADEAU, Georgianna, 4 months, dau. of Nathaniel and Huldah, d 1/27/45 in West Troy (5-1/29)

BADEU, Albert of New Rochelle m Phoebe Augusta Drake of East Chester at E.C.; Rev. Lawson Carter (11-2/4)

BADGER, Francis A. of Rome m 5/10/49 Mariette H. Inman of Lee in L.; Rev. H.C. Vogell (1-5/16)

BADGLEY, Cynthia - see FONDA, Tunis

BADGLEY, Philip m 11/2/37 Charlotte Mc Gregor, both of Waterford; Rev. Slingerland (5-11/8)

BAGG, Moses m 12/16/35 Susan Tracy, dau of late George G. Tracy of Whitesboro (both of Whitesboro) in Utica; Rev. Mandeville (6-12/18)

BAILEY, Aaron N. of Vienna m 4/14/46 Mary E. Cady of Verona in V.; Rev. H. Kendall (1-4/21)

BAILEY, Agnes (Mrs.) d 4/29/42 in Newburgh (9-5/7)

BAILEY, Charlotte - see TRUMBULL, George

BAILEY, Eliza - see PLACE, Ephraim D.

BAILEY, Eliza W. - see HOBBY, Charles

BAILEY, Harriet, 23, wf of Ervin A. of Potsdam, d 4/14/45 in Rome at home of her father, Egeliel Butler, Esq. in Rome (consumption) (1-4/22)

BAILEY, Henry, 24, son of Judge William Bailey of Plattsburgh, NY d 9/14/37 in Plattsburgh (yellow fever) (6-9/28)

BAILEY, Mary Ann - see DODGE, J.T.

BAILEY, Mary E. - see CHAMBERLAIN, William

BAILEY, Rowland (Dr.), about 70, d 7/9/34 at his home in Phillipstown (a long term resident there) (11-7/15)

BAILEY, Samuel P. of firm of Baily, Blake & Co. of Plattsburgh m 9/12/50 Ellen M. De Forris, eldest dau. of T. De Forris, M.D., of West Troy; Rev. Thomas W. Pearson (5-9/18)

BAILEY, Sarah D. - see HENDRICKSON, Thomas

BAILEY, Sarah M. - see GREEN, Jeremiah

BAILEY, Susan M. - see BLACK, C.B. (Dr.)

BAILEY, Thomas m 8/26/50 Anna Roth in Utica; Rev. Leeds (all of Utica) (1-8/28)

BAILEY,John (Hon.), formerly representative in Congress from Dorchester, MA and for several years previous a resident of Washington City, d 6/26/35 at home in Dorchester (6-7/10)

BAILY(?), Rhoda - see WETMORE, Justus

BAILY, Frances - see HAIGHT, William S.

BAILY, Thomas, 4, eldest son of Benjamin Baily, late editor of the Westchester and Putnam Democrat, d 1/31/42 in Carmel (11-2/2)

BAIN, Harriet E., 35, wf of James, d 2/18/48 at Pittsfield, Mass. (5-2/23)

BAIN, Maria - see DOOLITTLE, Andrew (Dr.)

BAIN, Peter H, about 53, d 5/31/35 at Kinderhook (6-6/3)

BAINBRIDGE, Sarah - see SAVAGE, Hiram F.

BAKEMORE, William of Peekskill m 2/23/35 Mary Halstead of Somerstown; Rev. D. Fly (11-3/3)

BAKER & WALBRIDGE - see WALBRIDGE, Romeo

BAKER, ----, 3, child of Adonijah, d 11/16/09 in Catskill (7-11/19)

BAKER, A.B. of Kirkland m 5/16/50 A.T. Loomis of Westmoreland in W.; Rev. S. Raymond (1-5/22)

BAKER, Albert L., Esq., attorney at law, m 1/31/37 Sarah Ann Miller, eldest dau. of James, Esq., in Buffalo; Rev. A. Chapin (6-2/3)

BAKER, Amanda - see QUINLAN, James E.

BAKER, Ann - see HOLT, Benjamin

BAKER, Ann - see TUCKER, Floyd

BAKER, Asa of Marcellus m 4/13/42 Huldah Hancock of Barre, Mass.; Rev. Rugs (1-5/3)

BAKER, Catherine Ann - see BURWELL, Elliott

BAKER, Hiram of Annsville m 4/20/48 Eliza M. Morrison of Rome in R.; Rev. F.W. Williams (1-4/21)

BAKER, Huldah Ann - see LOCKWOOD, Samuel E.

BAKER, Ichabod C., Esq., counsellor at law, of Whitesborough m (date not given) Mary Wells, dau of Sidney, Esq. of Cambridge, At C.; Rev. Hoyt (6-5/22/35)

BAKER, James - see VAN VORST, Elizabeth B.

BAKER, Mary Elizabeth - see CARPENTER, William F.

BAKER, Rachel - see SHATTUCK, Ira A.

BAKER, Susan, about 75, wf of William, d 2/17/39 in Sing Sing (12-2/19)

BAKER, Thomas m "in July", 1826 Elizabeth Hardiker, dau. of Richard Hardiker, merchant at Ancaster, Upper Canada (all of A.) (6-8/8/26)

BAKER, Whallinboro of NYC, 23, d 9/15/37 at Plattsburgh (from the prevailing epidemic) (6-9/28)

BALCH, Lewis H. m 12/22/44 Sarah Tucker, both of West Troy, at the Parsonage; Rev. John Fraser (5-12/25)

BALDING, Eliza - see DIBBLE, Jacob

BALDWIN, Alonzo C., 35, son of Ephraim, d 4/18/43 in West Troy (5-4/26)

BALDWIN, Catharine - see BUSH, Henry

BALDWIN, Charles, Esq., d suddenly 6/13/34 in NYC (an attorney at law there for many years) (11-6/17)

BALDWIN, Daniel, 64, d 1/24/42 at his home at Lake Mayopack, Carmel (for many years an honorable dealer in cattle) (11-1/25)

BALDWIN, Daniel, 64, d 1/24/42 in Carmel (11-1/25)

BALDWIN, Ebenezer m 11/30/09 Emma Waldring; Rev. David Porter (all of Catskill) (7-12/6)

BALDWIN, Ebenezer, formerly of Albany, d 1/26/37 at New Haven, Conn. (6-2/1)

BALDWIN, Eliza C., 21, wf of Lyman, d 8/4/48 in New London (1-8/11)

BALDWIN, Harriet H.G., 22, wf of Charles H. and dau. of Francis D. Grovenor of Utica, d 6/23/48 at West Boylston, Mass. (consumption) (1-6/30)

BALDWIN, Horace, merchant, of Norwich m 4/7/35 Penelope Allen, dau of late Samuel Dyer Allen, Esq. of North Kingston, RI in Sherburne, NY (6-4/15)

BALDWIN, James L. of West Troy m 10/14/41 Lucretia B. Montague of Troy in T.; Rev. Beman (5-10/20)

BALDWIN, Jesse - see VANDERPOEL, Rebecca G.

BALDWIN, John Abeel (Rev.) of Flatlands m 9/19/37 Elizabeth E. Van Kleeck, dau. of Lawrence L. Van Kleeck, Esq. of Washington City, at Flatbush, Long Island; Rev. Strong (6-9/22)

BALDWIN, John F., printer of Newburgh, m 12/5/41 Mary Cheney(?), 2nd dau. of Joseph of Paterson, NJ at the Methodist Episcopal Church in Paterson; Rev. David Kidder (9-12/18)

BALDWIN, John F., printer, of Newburgh m 12/19/41 Mary Cherry, second dau of Joseph of Patterson, NJ, in P. at the Methodist Episcopal Church; Rev. Daniel Kidder. (11-12/21)

BALDWIN, Lyman M. of Verona m 1/27/47 Eliza C. Thayer of Rome; Rev. R. Fox (1-2/26)

12

BALDWIN, Maria Woodward, 27, wf of Rodney N., Esq., d 6/21/49 in Kingston (8-6/30)

BALDWIN, Noah m 1/18/40 Fellica(?) Burroughs, dau. of Silas(?) in Petterson; Rev. Mc Leod (12-1/21)

BALDWIN, Samuel S - see YATES, Angelica

BALDWIN, Stephen W. (Col.), 41, d 1/16/37 in Baldwinsville (inflammation of the lungs) (6-1/24)

BALL, Alexander (Sir), the British Governor, d (date not given) at Malta (7-2/7/10)

BALL, Cynthia T. - see STEVENS, Charles

BALL, Flamen, Esq., counsellor at law and Master of Chancery, d (date not given) in Spartenburg District, South Carolina (a short and painful illness) (6-3/27/16)

BALL, Henry of the house of Marquand & Co. m 9/8/35 Frances Elizabeth Sistore, dau of late Joseph Sistore, in NYC; Rev. Cyrus Mason (6-9/11)

BALL, Jacob, 12, d 11/6/46 at Cohoes ("bilious fever") (5-11/11)

BALLAD, Julietta - see CARVER, Stephen W.

BALLARD, Eunice - see OBER, Tristram N.

BALLARD, John m (date not given) Laury Comstock at Glens Falls (6-6/1/16)

BALLEY, Michael (Capt.), 42, late of firm of Balley and Tufts of Greenbush, d 8/5/26 at his home in Washington City (born in Boston, Mass.; in War of 1812 was an officer in the 7th regiment of infantry) (6-8/22)

BALLOU, Eliza (Mrs.) d (date not given) in NYC (consumption) (6-5/22/16)

BALSTER, Eliza - see HEGEMAN, Adrian

BANCROFT, Anna B., 23 or 28?. wf of Dewitt C., Esq., d 10/21/44 in Rome (1-10/22)

BANCROFT, Charles H., 23, born in Salisbury, Conn., d 9/14/37 in Plattsburgh, NY (from the prevailing epidemic) (6-9/28)

BANCROFT, DeWitt C., attorney at law, of Rome m 3/21/45 Frances D. Bull, dau. of Joseph, Esq. of Westfield, Mass., at Meriden, Conn.; Rev. G.W. Perkins (1-4/8)

BANCROFT, Elizabeth A. - see FROST, Thomas G.

BANCROFT, Ephraim, 60, d 5/2/09 at Torrington (7-5/24)

BANCROFT, Senecva C., 1, son of William, d 7/19/40 in Little Falls (3-7/23)

BANGS, Cornelia - see HAWLEY, Nyrum

BANKER, Daniel d suddenly 8/10/33 in Carmel (11-8/20)

BANKER, Isaac m "a few evenings since" Eliza Van Ingen, both of Schenectady in S. (6-9/19/26)

BANKER, Joseph, 57, late of NYC, d 7/16/34 in Peekskill (11-7/22)

BANKINS, Maria Moore - see MILLS, Henry (Rev.)

BANKS, George W. m 10/16/39 Prudence Ann Smith, dau. of Henry, Esq., at Middle Patent; Rev. Travis, (all of M.P.) (12-11/5)

BANKS, Joseph m 10/2/39 Clara Adams, both of Bedford; Rev. R. Frame (12-10/8)

BANKS, Nathan O. "advanced in years" of New Fairfield, Conn., d 10/5/49 (fell off the plank and drowned while attempting to board the steamboat at Albany - "his remains were brought to Patterson, NY on the Harlem Rail Road for interment") (10-10/10)

BAR, John of Albion m 11/11/40 Mary Ann Rathbun of Rathbunville (Verone) in

R.; S.R. Stevens, Esq. (1-11/17)

BARBER, Bela, 75, d 9/17/36 ("very suddenly") at his home in West Troy (6-9/22)

BARBER, Electa (Mrs.) - see MILLER, William, Jr.

BARBER, Heman, 77, formerly of Herkimer County, NY, d 6/12/42 at Treemainville, Lucas County, Ohio (ill 5 days) (3-7/28)

BARBER, John, 87, father of William James of Albany, d 2/12/36 at his home in Montgomery, Orange County. (was an officer in the Rev. War) (6-2/18)

BARBER, Mary E. - see TAYLOR, William

BARBER, Olive H., 23, wf of Charles P., d 7/26/45 in West Troy (5-9/3)

BARBER, Sarah E., 8, dau. of Charles P. and Olive H., d 10/1/45 in West Troy (5-10/8)

BARCLAY, John (Dr.), the eminent anatomist, d 10/21/26 at his home in Argyle Square, Edinburgh, Scotland (6-12/22)

BARD, Eliza - see DELAFIELD, Rufus K.

BARD, Mary - see WILTSIE, Robert

BARD, Samuel (Capt.) - see BEADLE, Caleb

BAREMORE, Mary Ann - see HUBBELL, John A. Jr.

BARENGER, John, 50, d 6/23/33 in Peekskill (a lingering illness) (11-6/25)

BARING & BROS. - see BATES, William G

BARINGER, P.W., 40, "Thomsonian Physician", d 7/5/49 in Troy (5-7/11)

BARKER, Amelie E. - see TWING, A.T.

BARKER, Betsy Ann - see BURR, Oliver

BARKER, Charles, Jr. m 3/31/35 Frances Henrietta Dutcher, dau. of late Salem Dutcher, Esq.; Rev. George B. Ide; all of Albany (6-4/3)

BARKER, Clarissa, 59, consort of Eliasaph Barker, d 7/15/41 in Camden ("...a beloved mother and...loving wife") (1-7/20)

BARKER, Elizabeth - see JEFFERSON, Avery

BARKER, Harriet - see PATTERSON, Matthew

BARKER, Miss - see JONES, Jane

BARKER, Pierre A. - see BURWELL, Catharine Ann

BARKER, Pierre A. - see BURWELL, Catharine Ann

BARKER, Priscilla - see PIERCE, James M.

BARKER, Rhoda E. - see GREENE, John G.

BARKER, William of Carmel m 8/11/42 Mary Earley of Putnam Valley, in Putnam County; A.R. Austin, Esq. (11-9/22)

BARLOW, Harriet, 2, dau. of Elias, d 10/13/41 in Newburgh (9-10/16)

BARLOW, Nathan, 50, d 9/21/48 in Canajoharie (4-9/28)

BARLOW, William, Jr., about 33, of Easton, Mass., formerly of Haverstraw, NY, d 7/5/39 at sea on his return from the south where he had gone for his health (survived by a wife and child) (12-7/23)

BARNARD, Abby - see AVERY, Austin

BARNARD, James M., Esq., m 11/21/44 Lucina Gunnison, both of West Troy, in Albany; Rev. Z. Phillips (5-11/27)

BARNARD, James, 54, d 8/18/49 in Lima (cholera) (was for many years a resident of Rome) (1-8/29)

BARNARD, Mary G., 2, dau. of James and Mary, d 12/12/39 in West Troy (5-12/18)

BARNARD, Mary, 37, wf of James M., d 10/19/43 in West Troy (5-10/25)

BARNES, Abel S. of Holland Patent m 7/5/48 Margaret Jane Potter of NYC in

Holland Patent ("New York Sun please copy") (1-7/14)

BARNES, Anna, 70, wf of Rufus, Esq. and mother of Rev. Albert Barnes of
Philadelphia, d 2/25/45 in Rome (1-3/4)

BARNES, Caroline Matilda wf of Egbert W., d 6/21/50 in Albany at the home of
her father, Lewis Benedict (1-7/10)

BARNES, Chauncey, Esq., photographist, of Mobile, Alabama m 9/27/47 Lois
Clark, dau. of Asa, Esq., of Floyd, NY, in F.; Rev. L.I. Huntly (1-10/8)

BARNES, Eliza, 24, wf of Joseph, d (date not given) in NYC (6-11/28/26)

BARNES, Elizabeth - see CYPHER, Gabriel

BARNES, Elvira - see JOSLIN, David H.S.

BARNES, Erastus S. (Rev.) of Martinsburgh, Lewis County, m 9/22/41 Sarah
Miner of Northfield, Mass. in West Troy (5-9/29)

BARNES, Erastus, Esq., 44, d 9/11/36 at his home in NYC (repeatedly elected to
NYC's common council and was alderman of the 4th ward there) (6-9/14)

BARNES, Hezekiah (Deacon), 64, d 8/25/49 at Phoenix (consumption) (1-9/5)

BARNES, James, 52, killed (date not given) by falling from a load of wheat at
Benton (6-8/28)

BARNES, Lovina - see SANDFORD, Henry

BARNES, Lucy - see TUTHILL, Baldwin

BARNES, Richard of South East m 10/30/38 Margaret Kernan of New Castle at
N.C. (12-11/13)

BARNES, Richard of Utica m (date not given) Catharine Hughes of Deerfield;
H.C. Vogell (1-1/7/48)

BARNES, Rufus, father of Rev. Albert Barnes of Philadelphia, d 3/4/47 in Rome
(Rufus b. March, 1795) (1-3/12)

BARNES, William, Esq. m 7/17/49 Emily Weed, youngest dau. of Thurlow Weed,
Esq.; Rev. J.N. Campbell (all of Albany) (5-7/18)

BARNES, Zopher, 89, (a Rev. War soldier) d 9/20/42 in Camden (1-10/11)

BARNEY, Moreau, 26, d 3/30/35 in Warwick (consumption) (6-4/14)

BARNS, ----, about 7, child of "Mr. Barns", ship carpenter of Catskill, was
drowned 5/25/09 in the Catskill Creek (7-5/31)

BARNS, George W. m "recently" Jennett Hall, dau. of Ellis Hall, Esq. of Salisbury,
in S.; Rev. Fults (3-2/2/43)

BARNUM, ----, 3, a child of Clark Barnum, d 2/12/39 in Southeast (12-2/19)

BARNUM, Jonathan, 80 or older, d 10/7/49 in South East (10-10/10)

BARNUM, Mary - see RAYMOND, Daniel

BARNUM, Russel - see PADDOCK, Sarah

BARRET, Emily - see RUNDELL, John

BARRET, Samuel m 8/26/49 Catharine Light, both of Kent, in Carmel; William A.
Dean, Esq. (10-8/29)

BARRET, Z. - see RUNDELL, John

BARRETT, Elizabeth, about 28, wf of Moses, d 4/28/42, suddenly, in Bedford
(died in the night before the physician could arrive) (11-5/12)

BARRETT, Jeanette - see REYNOLDS, Alexander G.

BARRETT, Nancy, 30, wf of Abraham, d 1/7/42 in Bedford (11-1/18)

BARRETT, Phebe Angeline - see REYNOLDS, Ard

BARRINGER, Catharine - see GETMAN, Chauncey

BARRON, Samuel (Commodore) of the US Navy and late commander of a
squadron in the Mediterranean, d 10/28/10 suddenly in Hampton (7-11/14)

BARROW, Lewis m 8/7/40 Elizabeth Ofield in Rome; G. Wadsworth, Esq.
(1-8/11)

BARRY, Anable Irene, 2, only dau. of Rev. A.C. and Apelia Barry, d 10/28/48 in
Racine, Wisconsin (whooping cough) (4-11/9)

BARRY, Harriet - see MEEKS, J.C.

BARRY, John (Capt.) - see MEEKS, J.C.

BARRY, Mary Ann - see PORTER, Ephraim

BARRY, Standish, 3rd of Newport m 2/8/38 Almira Eliza Kniffen, dau. of John,
Esq. of Middleville, in M.; Rev. W.H. Waggoner (3-2/15)

BARSE, Charles of Herkimer m (date not given) Alvira Isaman, dau. of John of
Little Falls, in L.F. (3-6/22/37)

BARTHELEMY, M., the celebrated engineer and mechanist, d (date not given) in
Paris (death caused by a blow from the proboscis of an elephant) (6-5/4/16)

BARTLE, Almmelie Malaina - see TOWER, Charlemagne

BARTLE, David m 9/10/35 Ann Hendrickson at Binghamton; George Park, Esq.
(all of Binghamton) (6-9/29)

BARTLETT, Ann - see ELLIOTT, John

BARTLETT, Betsey Ann - see HAWLEY, Miron

BARTLETT, Henry, 21, d 11/24/42 at the home of his father in Newburgh
(9-11/26)

BARTLETT, Marcellus H. of West Troy m 7/15/48 Eliza A. Burns of Troy; Rev.
J.C. Burroughs (5-8/9)

BARTLETT, Matilda - see ADAMS, Edward

BARTLETT, Richard, Esq., 45, formerly Secretary of the state of New Hampshire,
d 10/23/37 in NYC (6-10/26)

BARTLETT, Susan Maria - see SMALLEY, George C.

BARTON, Benjamin Smith (Dr.), 48, (Professor of Theory and Practice of
Medicine and of Natural History and Botany at the University of
Pennsylvania), d 12/19/15 at Philadelphia (6-12/27)

BARTON, David (Hon.) d 9/26/37 at Boonville, Missouri (protracted insanity -
actually melancholy)(from St. Louis Republican) (6-10/24)

BARTON, Eliza - see ROTH, Nelson

BARTON, Samuel (Major), 36, postmaster in Lewiston, Niagara County, d 6/8/37
in Lewiston (6-6/20)

BARTOW, Maria - see COLE, Thomas

BASS, John, Esq., 66, d "lately" in Fairfield (3-3/31/36)

BASSETT, Abraham, 34, d (date not given) at New Haven (7-1/31/10)

BASSETT, Benjamin (Dr.) m 11/18/38 Juliet Strang, dau of late Underhill Strang
in Peekskill; Rev. Dr. Westbrook (all of P.) (12-11/27)

BASSETT, N.B. of West Troy m 11/3/37 Caroline Fisher, formerly of Springfield,
Mass., in West Troy; Rev. J. Learned (5-12/6)

BATCHELDER, Pamelia - see ROBINSON, Edward

BATCHELDER, Susan - see MC CAMMON, William

BATES(?), Jacob B., Esq., 27, late postmaster of Potter's Hollow(?) in the town of
German Flats, d "early part of last month" suddenly in Penfield, Monroe
County. While driving a heavy loaded wagon to Niagara Falls a barrel on
which he was riding fell and injured him fatally (3-2/25/36)

BATES, Antoinette A. - see DE SILVA, Robert P.

BATES, George C., Esq., counsellor at law m 5/25/36 Mrs. Ellen M. Wolcott in

Detroit at the home of Major R.A. Forsyth, US Army; Rev. B.H. Hockox (all of Detroit) (6-6/6)

BATES, Levina C. - see CLEAVELAND, J.M.

BATES, Sarah Ann - see PASINGER, Andrew

BATES, William G, 19, son of Joshua, Esq. of the firm of Baring & Bros. of England d 12/20/34 in England ("killed by an accidental discharge of a fowling piece at Northampshire") (6-2/5)

BATTLES, Mary - see JONES, Evans

BAUDER, Ezra m 1/15/50 Nancy Halstead; Rev. N. Can Alstlan(?) (4-1/17)

BAUDER, James of Wales Center m 12/31/48 Eliza Nestell of Frey's Bush at Fort Plain; Rev. B. Isbell (4-1/4/49)

BAUM, Chester m 12/24/41 Barbara Franklin in Schuyler; Elder Richards (3-1/13/42)

BAUM, Jacob H. m 5/22/49 Nancy Wilson in Minden; Bishop N. Van Alstine (all of Minden) (4-5/31)

BAXTER, Levi, Jr., (Hon) of Tecumseh, MI m 6/22/35 Elizabeth M. Orton of Delhi in Albany (6-6/25)

BAXTER, Maria - see BEALE, Joseph

BAXTER, Phebe, 21, wf of Cortland Baxter, d 9/13/42 (11-9/22)

BAXTER, Ruth F. - see PARKER, Melzar (Rev.)

BAY, ElIZA Treat, wf of John W., d 3/10/37 (funeral "at 4 o'clock") (6-3/13)

BAY, Mary - see WALSH, William

BAYARD, Eliza, wife of William P Van Rensselaer of Albany and dau of B.W. Rogers of New York City, d 3/20/35 near Matanzas (6-4/10)

BAYARD, William M., Esq., m 7/14/35 Romania Dashiel of Louisville, KY at Seneca Falls; Rev. George Dashiel (6-7/18)

BAYNHAM, Henry, 82, d (date not given) in NYC (6-11/3/26)

BAZEMANN, Philip H. of Troy m 2/24/45 Roseanne Palmer of West Troy; Rev. C.C. Burr (5-2/26)

BEACH, Eliza - see COLT, John

BEACH, Eliza W. (Mrs.) - see BEARDSLEY, John

BEACH, John H., Esq. of Saratoga Springs m 5/28/39 Mary Young, dau. of Hon. S. Young, at Ballston; Rev. D. Babcock (3-5/30)

BEACH, Miles, Esq., 62, postmaster of Saratoga d 2/20/37 (from the Saratoga Sentinel dated 2/21) (6-2/24)

BEACH, Orlando m 3/4/35 Julia Herring in Marcellus; Rev. Bierdsley (6-3/24)

BEACHUM, Polly, wf of W. Beachum, d (date not given) at New Canaan (7-6/13/10)

BEADLE, Caleb m 10/6/39 Mrs. Maria Inslee, dau of late Capt. Samuel Bard; Rev. Dr. Westbrook (11-10/15)

BEADLEY, Robert, 81, d 12/3/49 at home of James Benton in New Hartford (1-12/12)

BEAGS, Samuel m 5/9/49 Olive A. Scott, both of Cohoes, in West Day, Saratoga County; Rev. John Seage (5-5/6)

BEALE, Joseph, late of England, m 2/4/41 Maria Baxter, dau of Lebbeus Baxter of Delaware County, in Peekskill; Rev. Benjamin Curry (11-2/9)

BEALL, Robert Augustus (General), about 32, d 7/16/36 at Macon, GA (buried with military honors by the Macon Volunteers) (6-8/1)

BEALS, Elizabeth - see RICHARDS, James, Jr.

BEALS, Maria O. - see CURETON, John L.

BEAN, Daniel (Lieut.), 49, of Gilmantown, recently of Concord, NH, d 5/17/37 in Albany, NY (printers of New Hampshire are requested to print this) (6-5/20)

BEANYS(?), Samuel P. of Somers m 3/4/40 Elizabeth Lyon of Yorktown in Rye; Rev. Cancey (12-3/17)

BEARD, John m 7/23/40 Jane Petree, both of Little Falls, at Newport; J.M. Smith, Esq. (3-7/30)

BEARDSLEE, Elizabeth Frey, 27, wf of Augustus of Little Falls, d 10/27/37 at the home of her mother at Palatine Bridge, Montgomery County (consumption) (Survived by her husband "recently afflicted by the loss of their only child", her widowed mother and her last surviving brother) (3-11/4)

BEARDSLEE, Frances Emily, 5, dau. of John, d 6/9/39 in Little Falls (short illness) (3-6/13)

BEARDSLEE, John - see VAN ALSTINE, Mary

BEARDSLEE, John, infant son of John, Esq., d 9/10/41 in Little Falls (3-9/16)

BEARDSLEE, Mary Elizabeth, about 9 months, dau. of John, d 3/10/39 (3-3/14)

BEARDSLEE, Mary W., 28, wf of John, d 5/6/39 in Little Falls (3-5/9)

BEARDSLEY, ----, 11 months, only child of Augustus, d 6/20/37 in Little Falls (fever and cankered throat) (3-6/29)

BEARDSLEY, Catharine - see SHEPARD, George F.

BEARDSLEY, John, merchant, of Little Falls m 10/24/40 Mrs. Eliza W. Beach of NYC in NYC; Rev. Dr. Mc Arthur (3-11/5)

BEARDSLOE, Elizabeth, 27, wf of Augustus, Esq. of Little Falls, d 10/27/37 at the home of her brother (not named) in Palatine Bridge (6-11/8)

BEATTIE, Eliza - see HULSE, James W.

BEAUCHAMP, J.O. - see SHARP, Eliza

BEAUGRAND, Isedore D., sheriff of Sandusky County, Ohio m 1/1/38 Charlotte L. Symond of Watertown, NY in Lower Sandusky, Ohio; Rev. Reed (3-1/18)

BEAVER(?), ----, twin infant daughter of Edward, d 4/23/16 in Canandaigua (6-5/15)

BEAVER, John - see BOGARDUS, Maria D.W.

BECK, Catharine - see VAN CORTLAND, Pierre, Jr.

BECK, Edward, about 17, native of Engalnd, drowned 8/5/35 when he rode his horse into the water and, in trying to turn him, fell off. Was in the water about 15 minutes ("was not properly treated by (bystanders) as it is believed he might have been") (6-8/7)

BECK, Fayette S. m 9/8/50 Sally Wright, both of Oppenheim, in Fort Plain; Rev. G.W. Gage (4-9/12)

BECKER, Ann Maria - see RUSSELL, Jacob

BECKER, Henry, 86, d 7/16/36 in Little Falls (3-7/21)

BECKER, Jeremiah L. of Troy m 9/18/39 Margaret A. Macbeth, dau. of Daniel, in West Troy; Rev. Leonard of Albany (5-9/25)

BECKLEY, Susanna, 57, wf of James of Saugerties, d 11/24/49 in Troy (8-12/8)

BECKWITH, Eliza Ann - see KNICKERBACKER, Edwin

BECKWITH, Ira of Cairo m 8/10/40 Mary Haman of Little Falls in Cairo; Rev. Van Horn (3-8/20)

BECKWITH, James, merchant, late of Cairo, Greene County, m 4/7/36 Matilda

Hammond of Little Falls, in L.F.; Rev. David Morris (3-4/14)

BECKWITH, Jedediah - see RIGGS, Margaret

BEDIENT, Zadock (Capt.), 52(?), d 12/8/41 (1-12/21)

BEEBE(?), Hiram m (date not given) Marietta Snell, dau. of J.P., ESq., in
    Manheim; Rev. L. Swackhammer (3-12/24/40)

BEEBE, Abijah P. (Rev.) d 9/6/49 in Rome (was Presbyterian clergyman for "some
    time" in Oriskany. Through ill health moved to New York Mills where he
    lived 4 years. In 1848 moved to Illinois but, not recovering his health,
    moved to Rome, NY where he remained until his death) (1-9/19)

BEEBE, Abijah P. of York Mills m 12/23/41 Louisa Seymour of Westmoreland in
    W.; Rev. Pettibone (a double ceremony - see REMINGTON, John W.) (1-
    12/28)

BEEBE, Clarina, 38, wf of William N., d 3/2/47 in Vernon (consumption) (1-3/5)

BEEBE, Edmund (Capt.), 50, d (date not given) at Danbury (7-8/29/10)

BEEBE, Hannah, 97, widow of Samuel, d (date not given) at Waterford (7-2/7/10)

BEEBE, Lucy, 45, wf of Jared, d (date not given) at Lyme (7-3/8/09)

BEEBE, Mary Jane, 2, d 3/16/36 (dau of Asaph Beebe) (funeral at 3 o'clock from
    her father's home, 12 South Pearl St.) (6-3/18)

BEECHER, Abbie S. - see BUCKINGHAM, F. William

BEECHER, Harriet, wf of Rev. Dr. Beecher, d (date not given) at Walnut Hill near
    Cincinnati (6-7/18/35)

BEECHER, Jane, 21, wf of John, d (date not given) at New Haven (7-1/31/10)

BEECHER, Sally - see HUNT, Atvan

BEECHER, Sylvester - see CADY, Louisa M.

BEECKMAN, Helen S. - see GRAHAM, John A. Jr.

BEEDE, Ruth - see PEARL, Benjamin

BEEDLE, Jacob - see BROWN, Mary

BEEDLE, Sarah - see TRAVIS, Aaron

BEEKMAN, Anna Maria - see LEE, William

BEEKMAN, George Clinton m 4/8/35 Cornelia Ludlow, dau of late Jacob
    Mancius; Rev. Albert Smedes of Christ Church, NYC (6-4/10)

BEEKMAN, Peter Douw, Esq., 72, d 2/23/35 at Albany (a long time resident in A.)
    (funeral at 3 p.m. from his residence, 21 Van Schaick St.) (6-2/25)

BEEKMAN, Sarah H, age 9, dau of Theophilus, Esq. of Hudson d 12/31/34 (6-
    1/8/35)

BEEMAN, Philip of NYC m 7/24/44 Rosanna M. Wandell of Nyack, dau. of Evert
    G., in N.; Rev. Hopper (5-8/7)

BEERS, Wilbur(?) of Newburgh m 3/17/42 Jane Bradley of Marlborough in M.;
    Rev. Buel Goodsell (9-3/19)

BEERS, William m 7/25/45 Catherine M. Kipp, both of Albany, in West Troy;
    Rev. John Frazer (5-7/30)

BELDEN, Mary - see BIDWELL, Benson

BELDEN, Samuel, 17, d (date not given) in Newburg (6-5/15/16)

BELDING, Samuel, Esq. m 11/17/36 Charlotte Arnold, dau of Benedict Arnold, in
    Amsterdam, NY; Rev. Clancey (6-12/6)

BELEKNAP, James of Verona m 4/13/50 Mary Matilda Rockwell of Canastota;
    H.C. Vogell (1-5/8)

BELKNAP, Ann Maria, 10 or 16(?), dau. of James and Clarissa, d 12/9/42 in
    Newburgh (funeral 12/12 from her father's home on Colden Street)

(9-12/10)

BELKNAP, Augustus m 4/20/36 Hannah C. Holden, dau of Reuben; Rev. A.L.
Covel (all of Albany) (6-4/22)

BELKNAP, Chauncey F., Esq., attorney at law, of Newburgh m 11/20/42 Margaret
Anna Lane, dau. of Samuel of Newton, NJ, at Newton; Rev. Clarkson Dunn
(9-11/26)

BELKNAP, David, Jr., about 35, d 2/12/42 at the home of his father in Newburgh
(9-2/19)

BELKNAP, Henry C., about 11 months, son of Dr. Orran Belknap, d 11/21/42 at
the Quarantine, Staten Island (3-12/1)

BELL, Geo. D., Esq. of DePeyster, St. Lawrence County, m 2/12/45 Julia Ann
Moulton of Floyd; Rev. H. Mattison (1-2/18)

BELL, James C. m 1/16/45 Alida Pruyn, dau. of Casparus F., Esq. of Watervliet, in
W.; Rev. Duncan Kennedy (5-1/22)

BELL, John (Hon.), representative to Congress from Nashville m 9/25/35 Jane
Yeatman, widow of late Thomas Yeatman, Esq., in Nashville; Rev. Dr.
Edge of the Presbyterian Church (6-11/11)

BELL, Mary - see SKINNER, James

BELLINGER, Ann - see HOUSE, James

BELLINGER, Catharine - see CASLER, John

BELLINGER, Catharine - see SHOEMAKER, Matthew

BELLINGER, Christopher P. (Gen.), nearly 67, d 8/28/37 in Little Falls ("for more
than 40 years conspicuous in Herkimer County as a business man and as a
military officer) (3-8/31)

BELLINGER, Christopher, 75, formerly of Herkimer, d 6/9/39 in German Flats
(3-6/13)

BELLINGER, Frederick - see SHOEMAKER, Matthew

BELLINGER, Frederick, Esq. m 1/17/37 Eliza Myers, both of Herkimer County, in
NYC' Rev. Dr. Knox (3-1/26)

BELLINGER, Henry - SNELL, Reuben

BELLINGER, James of Little Falls m 1/10/50 Jane Green of Danube; Rev. N. Van
Alstlan(?) (4-1/17)

BELLINGER, John, 70, d 2/1/43 in Little Falls (a long term resident there) (his
funeral was from the Methodist Church) (3-2/9)

BELLINGER, Lawrence m 9/28/43 Elizabeth Fox, both of German Flats, in G.F.;
Rev. J.P. Spinner (3-10/5)

BELLINGER, Levi of Manheim m 8/23/43 Lovina Hall, dau. of Ellis Hall of
Salisbury, in S.; Rev. Devendorf (3-8/31)

BELLINGER, Mary - see SNELL, Reuben

BELLINGER, P.S. (son of Jacob) m 11/25/41 Nancy Casler (dau. of Major Peter B.
Casler), both of Little Falls (3-12/2)

BELLINGER, Peter F. - see CASLER, John

BELLOWS, Frances Augusta, 14, dau. of Charles H., Esq., d 3/1/42 in Newburgh
(9-3/5)

BELSHEW, Amelia - see BROWN, Miles H.

BEMENT, Caroline, wf of Caleb N., late proprietor of Bement's Hotel, Albany, d
10/13/36 at Three Hills Farm (a long and protracted illness) (6-10/14)

BENCHLEY, Angeline - see FORD, A.G.

BENCHLEY, Mary, consort of William S., Esq., d 5/24/36 in Newport (3-5/26)

BENCHLEY, William m 7/11/43 Catherine M. Haner in Herkimer; Rev. G.C. Woodruff (3-7/13)

BENCHLEY, William S., Esq. m 10/21/38 Roxey Ann Post, dau. of Dan Post, Esq. of Newport, in Newport; Rev. A.B. Grosh (3-10/25)

BENDER, Peggy Ann - see MOYER, Jacob

BENEDICT, Abigail - see HOYT, Linus

BENEDICT, Christiana, 39, wf of Micajah, Esq., d 3/16/43 very suddenly in German Flats (survived by her husband and children, not named) (3-4/6)

BENEDICT, Elizabeth - see RICKERD, George

BENEDICT, Isaac N. of South Salem m 11/13/39 Emily A. Keeler(?) of Wilton; Rev. Smith (12-11/26)

BENEDICT, Isaac N., 21, third son of Lewis, d 8/16/40 in Verona (ill eight days) (was about to enter the sophomore class at Hamilton College) (1-8/18)

BENEDICT, Jabez, 57, d (date not given) in Newburgh (6-8/22/26)

BENEDICT, James (General), about 63, d 7/23/41 in Tarrytown (11-8/3)

BENEDICT, Lewis - see BARNES, Caroline Matilda

BENEDICT, Lewis of Rockton, Illinois m 7/8/47 Martha D. Tyler, dau. of late Asa, Esq., of Holland Patent, at H.P.; Rev. J.F. Scovill (1-7/16)

BENEDICT, Mary Ann, 26, wf of Czar H., d 2/3/36 in Ballston Spa (a lingering illness) (6-2/15)

BENEDICT, Micajah, Esq. m 7/13/43 Catherine Harper of Cooperstown in Paine's Hollow; Rev. Huntington (3-8/3)

BENEDICT, Philena, 32, wf of John, d 9/5/42 at Newcastle Corner (11-9/15)

BENEDICT, Susan, dau of Hon. Jacob Lansing of Albany, d 5/4/35 (funeral from her late home, 292 North Market St.) (6-5/6)

BENEDICT, William, 10 months, son of Micaisah, d "lately" at Paine's Hollow (3-11/8/38)

BENHAM, Asahel m 5/28/36 Catharine Savage of Sauquoit, Oneida County, at S.; Rev. Kellogg (6-5/31)

BENHAM, Harriet A. - see BENNETT, D.S.

BENHAM, Harriet G. - see PRENTICE, George Dennison

BENJAMIN, A. Jane - see MESSINGER, Almon C.

BENJAMIN, Alansom of Rose, Wayne County, m 6/7/49 Mary Keeney of Rome in R.; Rev. W.E. Knox (1-6/13)

BENJAMIN, Ann Maria - see HOYT, Francis

BENJAMIN, Jerod A. m 12/25/41 Mary A. Dods, both of Lansingburgh, in West Troy; Rev. D. Starks (5-12/29)

BENJAMIN, Joseph L. of Livermore, Maine m 4/2/50 Emily M. Swan of Verona, NY at Watervliet; Rev. W.A. Miller (5-4/10)

BENJAMIN, Mary Judith (Mrs.) - see LANMAN, James (Hon.)

BENJAMIN, Park - see LANMAN, James (Hon.)

BENNERS, Miss - see WILLIAMS, Mary E

BENNET, Abigail - see MC DONNELS, Jerome

BENNET, Anna Catherine - see GREENE, William

BENNET, Eliza - see LITTLE, John

BENNET, Hiram A., 23, only son of Hiram, Esq. of Newburgh, d 12/23/42 in NYC (typhus fever) (9-12/31)

BENNETT, Alva (Rev.), 40, d 5/5/42 in Utica (1-5/10)

BENNETT, Ann Eliza - see SCHOONMAKER, Cornelius

BENNETT, Augusta Marsh, 18 months, only child of Asahel and Cordelia H., d
    7/19/45 in West Troy (5-7/23)
BENNETT, Catharine C. - see GROVENGER, Martin L.
BENNETT, D.S. (Capt.) of Camillus m 12/25/34 Harriet A. Benham, dau of
    Truman of Bridgewater, Oneida Co. at B. (Rev. Hough) (6-1/16/35)
BENNETT, Eliza M., 22, wf of A.B. Bennett, youngest child of Charles and Eliza
    Leffingwell of Rome, d 8/20/46 at Brockport (1-8/25)
BENNETT, Esther - see BRAYTON, William B.
BENNETT, Esther, 27 (?), sister of the proprietor of the Penn Yan Democrat, d
    1/10/36 in Starkey, Yates County (6-1/26)
BENNETT, George, M.D., m 2/19/47 Margaret Elizabeth Dutcher, dau. of John D.,
    Esq., both of West Troy; Elder William Sharp (5-2/24)
BENNETT, Hiram m 11/17/39 Catharine Price in West Troy; Rev. George Phippen
    (5-11/20)
BENNETT, James E of NYC m 3/21/35 Emeline Davidson of Albany in A.; Rev.
    J.D. Williamson (6-3/25)
BENNETT, James, Esq. m 1/13/38 Cynthia Stimson of Livingstonville, Schoharie
    County at L.; Rev. A.W. Bushnell (all of Livingstonville) (3 2/1)
BENNETT, Jane - see TODD, Horatio
BENNETT, Josephine, 8 months, only child of Asahel and Cordelia, d 8/23/47 in
    West Troy (5-9/1)
BENNETT, Martha, 5, dau. of R.O.K. Bennett, d 1/10/16 in Troy (xx16-2/14)
BENNETT, Melissa E., 26, wf of Adolphus, formerly of Rome, d 8/1/42 at
    Rockport, Monroe County (1-8/16)
BENNETT, Oscar of Rochester m 1/29/47 Paulina E. Lipe of Flemington, NJ at
    Oneida Depot, NY; Rev. James Nichols (1-2/26)
BENNETT, Thomas, Esq., 79, d (date not given) at his home in Rome (a
    Revolutionary War soldier; born in Western Fairfield Co., Conn. 18 March
    1761 (served during the War from age 16 in the militia, the Continental
    army and the "Coast Guards"; after the War lived in Montgomery County,
    NY until a few years before his death. Joined the Congregational Church in
    Conn. in 1782 and the Presbyterian Church in NY) (1-11/10/40)
BENNETT, William C. of Saugerties m 9/5/36 Catharine Chipman of Albany at
    Waterford; Rev. Stebbins (6-9/10)
BENOIT, Joseph m 4/22/42 Mary Lacque, both of Cohoes; Rev. Quinn (5-5/4)
BENSON, James of NYC m 10/5/26 Mary Sophia Jenkins of Albany in A.; Rev.
    Chester (6-10/6)
BENSON, Sarah Ann - see HEMPSTREET, John J.
BENTLEY, H.C. m 12/24/49 Elizabeth Simpson, both of Cohoes, in West Troy at
    the Tremont House; Rev. O.H. Gregory (5-1/9/50)
BENTLEY, Rosetta E. - see HAIKES, Franklin D.
BENTLY, William of Verona m 5/13/50 Loisa Gates of New York Mills at
    Whitesboro; Morris Wilcox, Esq. (1-5/22)
BENTON(?), Rosanna - see NICHOLS, William
BENTON, A.S., clerk of Orange County, d 8/1/49 at Goshen (8-8/11)
BENTON, Catherine, about 76, relict of Dr. Joseph Benton, late of Baldwin,
    Maine, d 10/30/42 at the home of her dau., Mrs. Mary Wadsworth in
    Hiram, Maine (newspapers in Niagara County, NY are requested to print
    this) (3-11/10)

BENTON, Charles, 2, son of Edward, d 9/25/39 in Little Falls (3-9/26)

BENTON, James - see BEADLEY, Robert

BENTON, Joseph (Dr.) - see HOWARD, Catharine

BENTON, Joseph (Dr.), 74, d 8/21/38 at his home in Baldwin, Maine (cholera) (was born in Tolland County, Conn. At age 20 commenced the practice of medicine and settled in Fryeburg) (3-9/20)

BERGEN, Alfred, M.D., 34, d 9/6/49 in Rome (had lived in Rome less than a year, member of the First Congregational Church there) (1-9/19)

BERGER, Catharine - see DE PAY, Bevier

BERLIN, Hunter, 22, d 12/27/41 in Mount Pleasant (11-1/11/42)

BERNARD, John Jr., son of John, Esq. of Albany m 3/18/16 Susan Coffon, dau. of Dr. Coffin of Boston; Rev. Bork (6-3/20)

BERRINGER, ----, dau. of Jacob - her funeral 11/1/37 from her father's home at 90 State Street (6-11/1)

BERRY, ---- (Mrs.), age blurred, wf of James, d 12/5/45 (place not given) (5-12/10)

BERRY, Abram (Col.) of Verona m 6/15/37 Sophia De Long, dau. of Major James De Long of German Flats, in G.F.; Rev. T. Houston (3-6/22)

BERRYMAN, Maria M., wf of E.U. and eldest dau of John G. Coster, Esq., d 12/16/35 in NYC (6-12/21)

BERTHRONG, James (Col.), 70, d 10/23/50 at Cazenovia (1-10/30)

BERTRAND, Lewis m 12/1/36 Catherine Capen; Rev. J.D. Williamson (all of Albany) (6-12/3)

BEST, Hannah F. - see YOUNGS, Isaac S., M.D.

BETHEL, Ann Eliza - see GIBBONS, George S.

BETTIS, William m 12/24/41 Mary Lounsberry in Sing Sing (both of Somers) (11-1/4/42)

BETTNER, James E., late of North Carolina m 11/7/37 Anna Carnochan, eldest dau. of John, Esq. of Savannah, Georgia in NYC at Trinity Church; Right Rev. Bishop Onderdonk (6-11/14)

BETTS, Carolyn, 3, dau of R.D. Betts, d 1/30/36 (funeral at 3 o'clock from her father's home at 101 Columbia St.) (6-2/1)

BETTS, Maria N., 25, wf of Capt. Silas, d 12/15/44 in Troy ("Connecticut papers please copy") (5-12/18)

BETTS, Sarah M. (Miss), about 16, d 4/27/50 in NYC (10-5/8)

BETTS, W. Wallace of NYC m 8/11/36 Cornelia Pearsall, eldest dau of late James of Brooklyn, at B.; Rev. Dwight (6-8/15)

BETTS, William, Esq. m 10/25/26 Anna Dorothea Robinson, dau. of Beverly, Esq., in NYC; Rev. Cornelius D. Dutlie (6-10/27)

BETTYS, George m 4/20/42 Sarah Ann Fulton, both of Fishkill in Newburgh at the Orange Hotel; Chauncey F. Bishop, Esq. (9-4/30)

BEVERLY, Jane - see HARRIS, Jesse

BEVIN, Mary Ann, wf of F.J., Esq., d 9/3/46 in Syracuse (was married 8/13/46 in West Troy; buried in the village cemetery in Syracuse) (5-9/16)

BEYEA, Reuben of Jefferson Valley m 11/24/36 Jane Collard of Yorktown at Y.; William Alley, Esq. of Carmel (11-12/3)

BEYES, Wright M. of Whitlockville m 11/6/39 Augusta Colyer of Bedford in B.; Rev. Travis (12-11/12)

BICKNELL, Charles, 6, son of James, d 6/6/47 in Westmoreland (1-6/18)

BICKNELL, Moses of Westmoreland m 3/1/42 Charlotte Cheeney, dau. of Chester of Vernon, in V.; Elder Martin Salmon (1-3/8)

BIDDLE, William, Esq., elder brother of Nicholas and Commodore James, d (date not given) in Philadelphia (after his retirement from the bar he had assumed his literary studies) (6-6/4)

BIDELMAN, Robert of Medina, Orleans County m (date not given) Harriet Louisa Cheever of Hickory Grove in New Haven, Oswego County; Rev. Allenson (6-8/16)

BIDWELL, Benson of East Hartford, Conn. m 9/17/48 Mary Belden of West Troy, NY in W.T.; Rev. T.F. Wykoff (5-10/4)

BIGELO, Sarah - see BOOTH, John H.

BIGELOW, Jackson of Brooklyn m 9/20/26 Elizabeth Briant of Albany; Rev. Leonard (6-9/26)

BIGGAM, Ruth, 33(?), wf of Andrew, d 8/25/42 in Newburgh (9-9/3)

BILL, Ann, wf of Earl of Sandusky, Ohio d 1/18/47 (1-1/29)

BILL, Caroline C., about 3, dau. of Chauncey C., d 1/1/47 in Vernon (scarlet fever) (1-2/5)

BILL, Caroline M. - see WILLIAMS, Elias L.

BILL, Chauncey C m 12/21/40 Anna E. Case, dau. of late A.E. Case in Vernon village; Rev. H.P. Bogue (all of V.V.) (1-1/5/41)

BILL, E. (Dr.) - see PUTNAM, George

BILL, Horace Earl, 11 weeks, son of H.N. Bill, former publisher of the Rome Citizen, d 3/31/49 in Rome (1-4/11)

BILL, Marcius E. m 12/19/47 Harriet A. Card in Rome; H.C. Vogell (all of Rome) (1-1/7/48)

BILL, Mary Ann Tredway, 33, wf of Charles E. Bill and dau. of John Tredway of Western, Oneida Co., NY, d 8/12/46 in Brooklyn (1-8/18)

BILL, Sarah M. - see PUTNAM, George

BILLINGS, Ellen Eliza - se TRAVIS, Nathaniel

BILLINGS, Hamilton m 5/8/48 Frances Vory, both of West Troy, in Albany; Rev. Dr. Wyckoff (5-5/17)

BILLINGTON, ---- (a stranger), a native of Montgomery County, d 10/12/36 at the house of Patrick Finn (3-10/13)

BILLINGTON, James C. m 2/18/41 Levina Perkins, both of Oriskiny, in Rome; E.C. Vogell (1-2/23)

BILLS, Maria Louisa - see ADAMS, John

BILLYES, John, 60, d (date not given) at Mount Pleasant (6-1/20/26)

BING, Edward F., 27, born in Sing Sing, d 3/20/39 at Georgetown, Randolph Co., Georgia (inflammation of the brain) ("at times he was subject to mental aberrations") (long time member of the Baptist church) (12-4/23)

BINGHAM, Maria Matilda - see DE BLAISEL, Le Marquis

BINGHAM, Moses M. m 8/11/42 Hannah Pitts, youngest dau. of late Capt. James Pitts, d 8/11/42 at Middlefield, Otsego County (9-8/20)

BINGHAM, Simon, Esq., "about 50," (formerly of Vernon) d (date not given) at Clinton, Michigan (short but painful illness) (6-9/3)

BINGHAM, William (Hon.) - see DE BLAISEL, Le Marquis

BINGLE, Eli m 7/3/49 Rosina Dunwoodie, both of Kingston, in Poughkeepsie; Rev. S.D. Cochrane (8-8/11)

BINNELL, Matilda - see COWLES, Oren

BIRCHALL, William m 10/3/49 Sarah Powell in Greenfield, Warwarsing; Rev. Thomas Newman (8-10/20)

BIRD, John - see FOSTER, Mason D., M.D.

BIRD, Romina - see FOSTER, Mason D., M.D.

BIRDSALL, Adelaide - see FENTON, William

BIRDSALL, Auburn(?), Esq., attorney at law, m 9/6/36 Louisa Amanda, adopted dau of Daniel S. Dickinson, Esq., at Binghamton; Rev. Edward Andrews of Christ Church (6-9/13)

BIRDSALL, Dorinda H. - see ROYCE, William

BIRDSALL, John (Hon.) m 8/4/36 Sally Peacock, adopted dau of Hon. William Peacock, in Mayville, Chautauqua Co.; Rev. J.G. Sawyer (6-8/16)

BIRDSALL, Sarah, 62, wf of Jonathan, d 3/5/39 in Yorktown (12-3/12)

BIRDSALL, Thomas, 26, d 1/20/40 in South Castle (12-2/4)

BIRGE, Chester B. m 10/18/48 Margaret C. Hake of South Schodack at S.S.; Rev. E.P. Stimson (5-11/1)

BISHOP(?), Harrison, 48, d 4/6 or 3/6/44 at White Water, Walworth County, Wisc. Territory (lived formerly in Verona, NY) (1-4/9)

BISHOP, Caroline - see MALLARY, George H.

BISHOP, George m 8/29/43 Levania Maria Spencer, dau. of John, in Salisbury; Rev. S. Northrup (bride & groom of Salisbury) (3-9/7)

BISHOP, Hosea E. m 7/14/49 Elizabeth Ann Short, both of Shandaken; Martin Schott (8-7/21)

BISHOP, Isaac - see MALLARY, George H.

BISHOP, Joseph A. of Stockbridge m 9/28/42 A. Maria Prentice in Vernon; Rev. D. Robinson (1-10/4)

BISHOP, William S., Esq., attorney at law, of Rochester m (date not given) Mary W. Sayles of Troy; Rev. Dr. Beman (6-9/18/35)

BISSELL, Mary Ann - see COIT, W.L.

BIXBY, Grace, 85, relict of Elias Bixby, an officer in the Rev. War, d (date not given) at Bridgeport, Conn. at the home of "Mrs. Hubbell", her niece (details are included concerning her husband. They were pioneer settlers in Oneida County, NY. Widow, Grace, after his death returned to Conn. where she was born) (6-9/15/37)

BLACK, C.B. (Dr.) of New Orleans m 2/7/42 Susan M. Bailey of NYC (and late of Newburgh) at New Orleans; Rev. Dr. Wheaton (9-2/26)

BLACK, William of Scotland d 12/18/35 at the Mansion House in Troy ("a lecturer on the country inhabited by the Jewish Nation and first Christians") (from the Troy Budget) (6-12/25)

BLACK, William, about 43, "a stranger but well known as the interesting lecturer on Palestine" d 12/18/35 ("has spent the last six months in this country lecturing") (born in Argyleshire, Scotland) (6-12/22)

BLACKMAN, Sarah - see PRATT, William

BLAIR, Arba (Dr.) - see DUDLEY, Frances M.

BLAIR, George T., Esq, attorney at law, m 9/15/36 Jane A. Pickells at home of Philip Heartt, Esq.; all of Troy (6-9/22)

BLAIR, James, 74, father of the editor of the Globe, d 1/7/37 at Port William, Kentucky (early in life he moved from Virginia to Kentucky; was Attorney General of Kentucky) (copied from the Globe) (6-1/25)

BLAIR, Jane B. - see MERRILL, Ardon

BLAIR, Mary S. - see FRASER, John O.

BLAIR, O.W., merchant, m 6/30/47 Emily E. Peckham in Verona; Rev. H. Kendall (1-7/9)

BLAKE, —— m 2/12/40 Harriet Mc Guire, both of Waterford, at Stillwater; Rev. Wescott (5-2/19)

BLAKE, Charles, 78, a Rev. War soldier, d 8/5/42 in Newburgh (was followed to his grave by members of the corporation of the village, the military and a large group of citizens (9-8/6)

BLAKE, James R. m 4/23/40 Elizabeth Woodruff, both of Waterford, at W.; Rev. Smith (5-5/6)

BLAKE, Robert, Esq. m 8/11/42 Sarah Van Dyke, dau. of late James of NYC, at Coldenham, Orange County; Rev. Robert H. Wallace (9-8/13)

BLAKE, Wealthy A. - see WEIST, Abram V.

BLAKELEY, Daniel m 6/19/39 Hester Anderson, both of Seneca Falls, in Little Falls; Rev. Blodget (3-6/27)

BLANCHARD, Caroline, infant dau. of Anthony, Esq. of Salem, Washington County, d 9/12/26 in Albany (6-9/15)

BLANCHARD, Dennis d 8/16/26 (place not stated) (6-8/22)

BLANCHARD, James, 22, son of Hon. Anthony I. of Salem, d 6/26/35 at Plattsburgh (6-7/13)

BLANCHARD, John, 28, d 4/4/37 at his home in Salem, Washington County (6-4/12)

BLANEY, George (Major), 39, of the US Corps of Engineers d 5/15 at Smithville, NC (his remains brought from the Fort 5/16 on board the Clarenden, attended by U.S. troops; buried at Wilmington with military honors) (6-5/30)

BLANY, John, 103, d 4/30/35 at Sandy Hill (6-5/7)

BLASHLY, Selah m 1/12/40 Ann Webb, both of Warren, in W. (3-1/23)

BLAUVELT, William W. (Rev.) pastor of the Presbyterian Church at Lamington, NJ m 9/12/26 Anna Maria Hutton, dau. of T. Hutton of NYC, at NYC; Rev. Dr. Matthews (6-9/19)

BLEECKER, Catharine W. - see VAN RENSSELAER, Cornelius G.

BLEECKER, G. & S. - see SHEPHERD, Phebe

BLEECKER, Henry (his funeral 11/14/37 from his late home, 41 North Pearl Street) (6-11/14)

BLEECKER, Henry, 74, d 11/11/37 (6-11/13)

BLEECKER, John, Esq. - see VAN RENSSELAER, Cornelius

BLEECKER, Mary - see SEYMOUR, Horatio

BLEECKER, Rachel, 79, consort of James, deceased, d 3/22/37 (funeral 3/24 from home of her son, G.V.S. Bleecker at 93 South Pearl Street) (6-3/23)

BLEEKER, Catharine Antoinett, 3, dau. of William E. and Lucy Ann, d 4/24/50 (4-5/2)

BLEVENS, Mary Ann - see TIRNEY, Peter

BLINDBURY, Charles of Detroit m 11/1/40 R. Ann Solice(?) of Vernon in V. (1-11/3)

BLINN, Sarah I. - see DOVE, Thomas P.

BLISS, Benjamin m 4/24/39 Ann Marie Merritt at New Castle (12-4/30)

BLISS, John m 6/3/39 Elizabeth Dickens, both of Little Falls; Rev. C.L. Dunning (3-6/13)

BLISS, Mary Ann - see HERSON, Alvah

BLISS, Oren of Salisbury m 12/23/40 Mary Ransom of Manheim in M.; Rev. F. Hawkins (3-1/21/41)

BLIZZARD, Mary H., wf of William, Esq., d 3/28/42 in Newburgh (9-4/2)

BLODGET, Luther P., Jr., merchant, of Bristol m 11/18/35 Pamela Chittenden, dau of Judge Truman Chittenden of Williston, VT in W.; George R. Mancer, Esq. (6-12/4)

BLODGET, Prudence Augusta - see BROWER, W. Henry

BLOODGOOD, Elizabeth M - see ROOT, Sheldon

BLOODGOOD, Francis, Esq., 71, of Albany d 3/6/40 in Albany (a lingering illness) (5-3/11)

BLOODGOOD, Gage m (date not given) Betsey Colegrove at Richfield (2-2/1/10)

BLOODGOOD, Lynott - see GRANT, Louisa

BLOOMER, Betsey, 38, wf of Henry d 1/30/40 in North Salem (12-2/11)

BLOOMER, Stephen of North Salem m 12/29/38 Ann Brundage of South East in S.E.; Rev. Warren (12-1/8/39)

BLOOMFIELD, John W., 82, d 10/12/49 in Rome (one of the oldest residents there) (1-10/17)

BLOORE, J., Esq. m 9/16/41 Katharine Livingston Turk, dau. of Dr. William Turk of the US Navy, at the Reformed Dutch Church in Waterford; Rev. Witbeck (5-9/22)

BLOUIN, Mary - see LEMNA, Andrew

BLOUNT, William, 67, d 9/10/35 at the home of W.B. Johnson, Esq. (lived in Tennessee since its formation) Governor there, 1809-1815 (from the Clarksville (Tennessee) Chronicle) (6-9/29)

BLOW, Catherine - see JACKSON, William

BLUER, Jeanette - see KETTERHOUSE, Anthony

BLYDENBURGH, Ruth - see CARLL, Timothy

BOAK, Maria - see DAVIS, James

BOARDMAN, John of Albany m 8/11/26 Maria C. Hulse of NYC in NYC; Rev. Dr. Mc Murray (6-8/18)

BOARDMAN, Sarah, wf of Rev. G.S. Boardman, d 7/18/49 at Cherry Valley (after an illness of thriteen hours - cholera) (1-7/25)

BOARDMAN, William G., merchnat, of Albany m 7/10/26 Amanda Parker, dau. of Joshua, Esq. of Buffalo, in B.; Rev. Crawford (6-7/21)

BOARDMAN, William, 63, d 4/24/35 (a short but painful illness); his funeral at 5 o'clock from his late home, South High St, near the Capitol (6-4/25)

BOBCOCK, George B., Esq. m 5/13/35 Mary B. Porter, dau of Herman B.; Rev. Parsons (all of Buffalo) (6-5/26)

BODINE, James Harvey, 7 months, son of John R., d 8/4/42 in Newburgh (9-8/6)

BOEKNOWEN(?), Egbert from Amsterdam m "lately" Margaret Borquin of Morehouseville at West Brunswick (town of Ohio), Herkimer County; G.A. Coppernall, Esq. (3-7/19)

BOGARD, Abraham, 113, d 7/14/33 in Maury County, Tenn. ("never drank spirits or was sick, nor took medicine of any kind") He was born in Maryland (11-8/13)

BOGARDUS, Aspasia S.J. - see SNOWDEN, J. Bayard

BOGARDUS, Maria D.W., 26, widow of Solomon, d 6/7/49 at the home of her brother, John Beaver in New Paltz (8-6/23)

BOGARDUS, Sally - see HENRY, Samuel

BOGART, Grandin Augustus, 22, son of John, Esq. of Albany, d 9/13/37 at New Orleans (6-9/26)

BOGART, John H m 4/8/35 Eliza Hermans, eldest dau of John Hermans; Rev. Dr. Sprague see also marriage of Erastus V. JOICE at same time (6-4/10)

BOGERT, Alida Ritzma - see WALKER, William F. (Rev.)

BOGERT, Helen Maria - see JERVIS, Timothy B.

BOGERT, Helen Mariah - see JERVIS, Timothy B.

BOGERT, Henry K. m 1/14/26 Mary E. Bogert, dau. of J.G. Bogert, Esq., in NYC at Grace Church; Rev. Wainwright (6-1/20)

BOGERT, Mary E. - see BOGERT, Henry K.

BOGERT, Rudolphus - see JERVIS, Timohty B.

BOGERT, Rudolphus - see JERVIS, Timothy B.

BOGUE, Emily S., 16, dau of D.P. Bogue, Esq. of St. Albans, VT, d 9/12/40 in Chittenango, NY at the home of Rev. J. Abell (short illness) (had left her home about a year earlier to attend the Female Academy at Utica, NY. One week before departure for her home she died.) (1-9/22)

BOGUE, Publius V. (Rev.), 72, d 8/28/36 at his home in Oneida County (extensively known in states of Conn., Vt., & NY as a minister of the gospel; was the oldest minister in the Presbytery of Oneida County) (6-9/3)

BOIES, Margaret E. - see DAYTON, Nathan

BOKE(?), William m 4/28/42 Agnes Burr(?); Rev. John Johnston

BOKEE, Catherine J. - see FLINT, Augustus

BOLLARD, Susannah (Miss) - see SAUNDERS, Samuel

BOLTON, James of Savannah m (date not given) Mary Ann Clay of Philadelphia at P. (6-5/8/16)

BOMFORD, George - see DERBY, Richard C.

BONAPARTE - see ROGE, ---- (Mr.)

BONCE, William of Lansingburgh m 11/25/44 Jane Shadboldt of West Troy in W.T.; Rev. Twing (5-12/4)

BOND, Cornelia, 23, d 11/5/46 at Buffalo (1-11/10)

BOND, William Grant m 1/6/41 Sarah Jane Wright, both of Verona; Rev. H.C. Vogell (1-1/19)

BONT, Samuel - see KNILL, Tiney

BOOKMASTER(?), Francis m 1/21/40 Jane Ann Mead, dau. of W. Letty Mead, in Southeast (bride and groom of Southeast); Rev. Mc Leod (12-2/4)

BOOM, Angeline - see MOORE, James M.

BOOMHOUSE, Mary Elizabeth - see HODGMAN, John H.

BOORAEM, Henry, 23, d (date not given) from injuries received in the fall of a house in a tornado at New Brunswick, NJ; formerly a midshipman in US Navy, son of Nicholas Booraem, Esq. (6-7/4/35)

BOORAEM, Thomas I. m 5/21/35 Georgiana Elizabeth Lyell, youngest dau of Rev. Thomas Lyell, in NYC at Christ's Church; Rev. Albert Smedes (6-5/28)

BOOTH, John H. m 1/1/39 Sarah Bigelo, both of West Troy, in W.T.; Elder F.S. Parke (5-1/9)

BOOTH, Joseph m 4/28/49 Emeline Hines; Rev. T.F. Wyckoff (5-5/2)

BOOTH, Laura, 49, wf of Gen. Walter Booth, d 4/4/41 in Meriden, Conn. (1-4/27)

BOOTH, Mary Elizabeth, 14 months, dau. of Thomas and Mary A. of Saugerties, d 9/13/49 at Wilbur (8-9/22)

BOOTH, Thomas H. of firm of Smith and Booth m 5/5/42 Maria C. Smith; Rev.
E.S. Griswold (all of Newburgh) (9-5/14)

BOOTH, Wheeler K. m 4/1/36 Charlotte Smith at Ballston Spa (6-4/4)

BORDEN, Angeline - see RENTOR, James

BORDEN, Hannah E. - see POWER, James

BORDER, Elizabeth - see NELLIS, James

BORDIN, Daniel m 12/4/25 Mrs. Catherine Fuller at Oppenheim (6-1/3/26)

BORLAND, William Henry, 8, son of William G., d 12/26/37 (funeral 12/28) (3-
12/28)

BOROUGHS, Maranda - see SHEARS, John

BORQUIN, Margaret - see BOEKNOWEN(?), Egbert

BORST, John B. of Middleburgh m 5/23/26 Marion Reid, oldest dau. of William
Reid, merchant of Amsterdam, in A.; Rev. Schermerhorn (6-6/20)

BORT, Margaret - see EDICK, David

BORTHWICK, H., merchant, of Albany m 11/23/35 Rachel Esmay, youngest dau.
of Peter of Bethlehem, in B.; Rev. Forte

BORTLE, Anna - see SHARP, John W.

BORTLE, Jane - see WALRADT, Charles

BORTLE, Robert m 1/1/41 Mary M. Lawrence of Durhamville in D.; Rev. Turner
(1-2/23)

BORTLES, Mary - see SOLUS(?), Benjamin

BOSEMAN, Philip H. - see possible BAZEMANN, Philip H.

BOSTWICK, Ella - see RAYMOND, William P.

BOSTWICK, Ichabod, 58, d 1/7/38 in West Troy (5-1/10)

BOSTWICK, John (Hon.) - see RAYMOND, William P.

BOUCK, Ann Eve - see SANFORD, Lyman

BOUCK, Austin of Whitesboro m 5/20/50 Rosetta O'Neil of Troy; Rev. T.W.
Pearson (5-5/22)

BOUCK, Caroline - see DANFORTH, V., M.D.

BOUCK, Catharine - see ORCUTT, Rice

BOUCK, Christian, 82, father of Hon. W.C., d 9/2/36 at Fulton (one of the early
settlers of Schoharie) (6-9/5)

BOUCK, Hermanus - see ORCUTT, Rice

BOUCK, W.C. (Hon.) - see SANFORD, Lyman

BOUGHTON, E.H. m 12/16/45 Olive Whitaker of West Troy, NY in North Adams,
Mass.; Rev. S. Pratt (5-12/24)

BOUGHTON, Edward m 1/1/40 Sarah Ann Grimp in New Castle; Charles Voe,
Esq. (12-1/7)

BOUGHTON, Joseph, Esq., attorney at law, m 9/17/36 Caroline L. Smith, eldest
dau of Samuel, Esq., at Binghamton; Rev. Peter Lockwood (6-9/20)

BOUGHTON, Marilla - see WEEKS, Ard

BOURDAGE, Louis, Esq. d 1/20/35 at St. Denis, River Chambly, Lower Canada.
Notary and member of the Assembly for Nicholet; was the "Dogen" or
oldest member of the house (30 year member; elected in 1804) (6-2/2)

BOUTEN, Gilbert m 1/21/39 Hannah Conklin, both of Bedford in Sounth Salem;
Rev. Frame (12-1/29)

BOUTON, Josephine, about 5, dau. of William S., d 9/15/41 in Little Falls
(3-9/16)

BOVEE, James (Capt.) m (date not given) Belphamer Scrivner in NYC (6-5/15/16)

BOVEE, Sarah Jane - see PITMAN, Thomas W.

BOWDISH, Rosa, wf of Gamaliel, d 9/20/49 in Root (4-10/11)

BOWE, Obadiah A., printer, formerly of Little Falls, m 6/24/37 Catharine Weaver, both of NYC, in NYC; Rev. C.K. True (3-7/27)

BOWEN, Benjamin - see ENOS, Catharine M.

BOWEN, Benjamin G., 57, of the Navy Commissioners Office, d (date not given) at Washington (6-12/26/26)

BOWEN, Catharine M. - see ENOS, A.W.

BOWEN, Elizabeth - see BROOKS, Calvin

BOWEN, Elizabeth - see BROOKS, Calvin

BOWEN, Elmina - see TUTTLE, Alanson

BOWEN, Henry L. of Homer m 4/20/46 Ann Elizabeth Wilgus of West Troy; Rev. Dodge (5-4/22)

BOWEN, James H. of Little Falls m 9/19/43 Caroline A. Smith, dau. of Dr. Ira A. of Evans Mills, in E.M.; Rev. Fish (3-9/21)

BOWEN, Joel m 1/1/38 Panthy Lewis in Salisbury; W. Avery, Esq. (all of Salisbury) (a double ceremony - see RICHARDSON, James)(3-1/11)

BOWEN, Levi - see HARINDEEN, Elmina

BOWEN, Louisa - see RICHARDSON, James

BOWEN, Mary A. (Miss), 18, formerly of Little Falls, d 2/17/42 at the home of A.W. E--- (surname blurred), Esq. in Michigan City, Indiana (above surname possibly Eams) (3-3/3)

BOWER, Nathaniel (Right Rev), D.D., Episcopal Bishop of South Caroline, d 8/25/39 at Charleston, SC (11-9/17)

BOWERS, Anne C. - see LEE, F.A.

BOWERS, Eunice - see SOPER, Charles C.

BOWERS, Sarah Stewart, dau of John M. of Cooperstown, d 11/1/36 at home of her brother-in-law, George B. Warren in Troy (6-11/3)

BOWMAN, Barbara, about 60, relict of Adam, d (date not given) (3-11/24/36)

BOWMAN, Jabez P. m 12/10/44 Frances H. Stevens; Rev. Dodge (all of West Troy) (5-12/18)

BOWMAN, James from Jamaica, West Indies m 9/3/39 Jemima Miller, dau. of Andrew of Cortlandtown, in C. (11-9/10)

BOWNE, Harriet - see PLATT, Isaac

BOWS, Amos, 13 months, son of the publisher of the Herkimer County Journal, d 8/29/40 at Herkimer (3-9/3)

BOYCE, Daniel D. m 12/25/38 Ellen B. Wendell, dau of Capt. Wandell in Sing Sing; Rev. S. Van Deusen (all of Sing Sing) (12-1/1/39)

BOYCE, Peter of Cooperstown m 2/14/37 Elizabeth Flansburgh of Albany; Rev. J.D. Williamson (6-2/16)

BOYD, David I., 49, of NYC d 7/28/37 (a protracted illness) (funeral 7/29 from home of P. Boyd, 71 Ferry St., Albany) (6-7/29)

BOYD, James A., Esq. m 1/17/38 Emily Stimson of Livingstonville, Schoharie County; Rev. A.W. Bushnell (all of Livingstonville) (3-2/1)

BOYD, Minerva J. - see HARRIS, Stephen

BOYD, Samuel, 30, painter d 10/3/35 at his home in Peekskill (11-10/6)

BOYD, William D. (Dr.), 45, d 9/12/42 at Cold Spring (11-9/22)

BOYER, Leonard m 9/1/41 Nancy Wiswell in Little Falls; Rev. Loveys (3-9/9)

BOYLE, Matthias m 4/22/45 Susan Switz, both of Schenectady, in West Troy; Rev.

O. H. Grady (5-5/7)

BOYNES, James m 6/6/48 Bridget Lue, both of Albany, at the West Troy
    Exchange; Rev. J.C. Burroughs (5-6/14)

BOYNTON, Calvin, 63, d 8/21/48 in West Troy (5-8/30)

BOYNTON, Lydia - see CORKINS, Dwight (Col.)

BOYNTON, Mary Jane, 43, wf of late Calvin Boynton, d 12/5/48 in West Troy
    (5-12/13)

BRACE, Julia - see FISH, Francis D.

BRACE, Sophelia - see HARVEY, Erriathan

BRACKNEY, Imagine - see GREEN, Elijah

BRADBURY, Amelia (Miss), 53, d 9/12/50 in Syracuse (1-9/18)

BRADFORD, Alexander W., Esq., m 12/17/36 Marianne Gray, dau of late
    Quartermaster General Andrew Gray, at Utica; Rev. Pierre A. Proal
    (6/12/21)

BRADFORD, Irene - see CRIST, Abram (Capt.)

BRADFORD, Susan - see PARMENTER, Gilbert

BRADISH, Luther (Hon.) Lieut. Governor of New York m 11/26/39 Mary E. Hart
    of NYC at the Church of St. Thomas in NYC; Rev. Dr. Hawks (5-11/27)

BRADISH, Luther (Hon.), Lieutenant Governor of NY, m 11/19/39 Mary E. Haft
    of NYC at the Church of St. Thomas in NYC; Rev. Dr. Hawks (12-11/26)

BRADLEY, Charles William (Rev.) m 5/16/36 Mary Hopper, dau of late James,
    Esq. of Utica, at Trinity Church in Utica (6-5/28)

BRADLEY, Daniel C. of Syracuse m 2/1/49 Sarah V. Dygert, dau. of John R. of
    Fort Plain, at F.P.; Rev. Dr. C.G. Mc Lean (4-2/8)

BRADLEY, Dimon, 48, d 11/7/35 at the home of Col. Leavenworth in Albany
    (6-11/10)

BRADLEY, Henry m 11/8/37 Sarah Harriet Tappan, dau. of George, at Catskill;
    Rev. Henry Ostrander (6-11/14)

BRADLEY, Jane - see BEERS, Wilbur

BRADLEY, Mary Spencer, 5, dau. of Amos A. & Caroline E. Bradley, d 6/16/42 in
    Little Falls (3-6/30)

BRADSHAW, Mary F., 19, wf of James Bradshaw, merchant of West Troy, d
    10/18/37 (5-10/25)

BRADT, ---- (Mrs.), wf of James F., d "a few days since" in Rotterdam (6-9/22/26)

BRADT, Catharine - see PILLINGS, Robert

BRADT, Eleanor - see OLIVER, James

BRADT, Margaret - see BURROUGHS, Charles

BRADT, Sarah - see RICHARDS, Ezra

BRADY, Cathrine - see SIMONS, George

BRADY, Jane - see SEYMOUR, William

BRAGUN, Samuel m (date not given) Ann Covenhoven at Rhinebeck (6-5/22/16)

BRAINARD, A.H. of Rome m 7/14/42 Lucy Segur of Taberg in T.; Rev. Mason
    (1-7/19)

BRAINARD, David Lewis, 28, only surviving son of Israel of Vernon, d 9/3/47 in
    Harrisville, Ohio (1-10/1)

BRAINARD, George H., Esq., of Buffalo m 9/6/49 Minerva Green of Rome in R.;
    Rev. James Erwin (1-9/12)

BRAINARD, Harriet M., infant and only daughter of A.H. and Lucy, formerly of
    Rome, NY, d 7/20/50 at La Prairie, Canada East (1-7/31)

BRAINARD, Israel W., 25, son of Rev. Israel of Verona, d 7/8/36 after a short but severe illness (funeral at 5 o'clock from Mrs. Courtney's, 26 Maiden Lane) (6-7/9)

BRAINARD, Margaret, 32, wf of A.H. and dau. of Jacob Gouge of Trenton, d 6/22/41 in Rome (consumption) (1-6/29)

BRAINARD, Mary (Miss), 47, formerly of Rome and sister of Rev. Thomas Brainard of Philadelphia, d 5/17/47 at Cayahoga Falls (1-6/25)

BRAINARD, Mary Elizabeth, 3, dau. of Alexander H., d 5/11/44 in Rome (scarlet fever) (1-5/21)

BRAINARD, Mary M., 32, wf of A.H. and dau. of Jacob Gouge of Trenton, d 6/22/41 in Rome (consumption) (1-7/6)

BRAINARD, Sabius of Litchfield m 1/15/40 Pamilla Day, dau. of Eli, Esq. of Winfield, in W.; Rev. Holcomb (3-1/23)

BRAINARD, Thomas (Rev.), editor of the Cincinnati Journal, m 11/29/36 Miss Mary Whiting, editress of the Microcosm, in New Haven, at N.H.; Rev. L. Bacon (6-12/3)

BRAINARD, W. Ann - see COMSTOCK, Waldo

BRAINERD, Daniel G., 17, son of A.H., d 5/16/48 in Rome (disease of the heart) (funeral at the Methodist Church) (1-5/19)

BRAINERD, Jeremiah (Capt.), 71, d 1/2/48 in Rome (in this region for more than 30 years) (an inventor of machines used on canal gates and in railroad construction) (1-1/7/48)

BRAKEFIELD, Thomas of Clinton m 2/26/40 Mary Ward of Norway, Herkimer County, at Clinton; Rev. William Thompson (3-3/19)

BRAMAN, Adam m 8/1/49 Jane A. Meehan; Rev. A. Fort (all of Esopus) (8-8/11)

BRAMHALL, Charles H., Esq. of Buffalo m 10/15/35 Eliza Hogeboom, youngest dau of Hon. Tobias L. of Ghent, in G.; Rev. J. Berger (6-10/26)

BRAND, Andrew, 15, born in Kentucky, d 9/18/50 in Albany, NY (came to Albany "about four weeks since", accompanied by his brothers and 2 friends "for the purpose of attending the State Fair in Albany "was prostrated by an attack of intermittent fever - every attention and care were taken of him") (5-9/25)

BRANDOW, Elizabeth - see PALMER, Reuben

BRANDRETH, Thomas of Newburgh m 10/26/38 Julia Gore of Watervliet in West Troy; J. Hart, Esq. (5-10/31)

BRANEN, Charles (Rev.), Roman Catholic pastor at Patterson, NJ, d 3/16/26 (6-3/21)

BRANT, Catherine, 78, relict of Captain Joseph Brant, celebrated leader of the Six Nations "who during the Rev. War carried terror into every border hamlet", d (date not given) at the Mohawk Village on the Grand River (5-1/10/38)

BRATHWAITE, Jane (Mrs.), 107, d (date not given) in Much Urswick, England ("Less than a year ago she could thread a needle with the naked eye") (6-7/21/26)

BRATT, Catharine, 20, second dau of George T., d 11/9/36 in Albany (inflammation of the brain) (funeral at 3 o'clock from her father's home, corner Lydius and North Market Sts.) (6-11/10)

BRAYMAN, Mason, Esq., formerly editor of the Buffalo Bulletin m 9/8/36 Mary Williams at home of H. case, Esq., in Buffalo; Rev. Chapin (6-9/19)

BRAYTON, Anna - see STERLING, John C.

32

BRAYTON, Hervey, Jr., nearly 3 years old, son of Hervey, Esq., d 2/8/45 at Westernville (scarlet fever) (1-2/11)

BRAYTON, S.V.R. m 11/4/45 M.L. Ring at West Troy; Rev. T.F. Wickoff (5-11/12)

BRAYTON, Wales of Litchfield m 8/7/36 Mary Strong of Cazenovia in C.; Rev. Barrows (3-8/11)

BRAYTON, William B. of Bethlehem m 9/18/39 Esther Bennett of Watervliet in West Troy; Rev. Leonard of Albany (5-9/25)

BREEN, Preston R., 22, nephew of William Roe, Esq. of Newburgh, d 12/18/42 near Canterbury (consumption) (9-12/31)

BREES(?), Eliza - see ODELL, Daniel

BREESE, Robert Lenox, 14, youngest son of late Arthur, Esq., of Utica, d 7/31/35 in Utica (6-8/6)

BREG, Isaac m 1/15/48 Lany Maria Limebeck, both former pupils in the NY Institution for the Deaf and Dumb, in Half Day, Illinois (4-3/2)

BREG, William, Jr., 23, "3rd assistant teacher of the Institution", d 5/15/49 at the Asylum for the Deaf and Dumb at Indianapolis, Indiana (born, mute from birth, in New York and raised at the Institution for the Deaf and Dumb in NYC (died of "congestion of the lungs") (4-5/31)

BREUSTER, Mary - see HAKES, Kaleb

BREWER, Laraine, 86, widow of late Col. Josiah of Tyringham, Mass. d 10/2/41 in Verona, NY at the home of her son, Artemas Brewer (1-2/15/42)

BREWSTER, Elizabeth - see MURPHY, Charles C.

BREWSTER, John m 5/3/45 Jane Dickson, both of West Troy; Rev. O.H. Gregory (5-5/7)

BREWSTER, John of Troy m 12/19/41 Jane B. Graham of West Troy in W.T.; Rev. D. Starks (5-12/22)

BREWSTER, Susan F. - see WILSON, Benjamin

BRIANT, Elizabeth - see BIGELOW, Jackson

BRICE, James, Esq., counsellor at law, of West Troy m 12/5/50 Ellen Nelligan of Albany in A.; Rev. P.Mc Closky (5-12/11)

BRICKELL, Susan - see SPALDING, Rowland E.

BRICKEN, William m 6/1/49 Harriet C. Nichols, both of West Troy, in W.T.; Rev. T.F. Wyckoff (5-6/6)

BRIDENBECKER, Isaac m 10/10/39 Catharine Folts in Frankfort; Rev. T. Houston (all of Frankfort) (3-10/24)

BRIDENBECKER, Jeremiah of Frankfort m 5/28/42 Margaret Harter, dau. of John, in Herkimer; Rev. J.P. Spinner (3-6/2)

BRIDGE, Matthew m (date not given) Mary Flagg in Beverly (6-5/8/16)

BRIDGER, ----, 6, dau. of Edward, d 2/6/39 in Sing Sing (12-2/12)

BRIDGES, Alida V. - see STRAIN, Henry (Major)

BRIGGS, Albert, merchant, of firm of A.N. Briggs & Co. m 5/14/36 Maria Andrews (dau of late Ephraim), both of Coeymans, in Durham; Rev. Phineas Cooke (6-5/17)

BRIGGS, Alfred of Rhode Island m 2/20/40 Jane Webb of Warren in W.; W.C. Crain, Esq. (3-3/12)

BRIGGS, Almira - see RANKINS, L.H.

BRIGGS, Anne Greene - see CRASSOUS, Joseph

BRIGGS, Cornelia E. - see CURTICE, William T.

BRIGGS, Cyrus m 1/31/47 Mrs. Joice, widow of late George of Rome; H.C. Vogell (1-2/5)

BRIGGS, David m 1/23/49 Ann Lamphere; H.C. Vogell (1-2/7)

BRIGGS, E.B. - see MAYNHOOD, Thomas

BRIGGS, Frances - see HINECEY, E.M.

BRIGGS, Harriet L. - see ARMSTRONG, Henry S.

BRIGGS, Jannette - see WILLIS, N. Judson

BRIGGS, Mary - see RANKIN, Sanford

BRIGGS, Mary - see ROBINS, William

BRIGGS, Mrs. - see WILCOX, Benjamin

BRIGGS, Philette - see CUSHMAN, John L.

BRIGGS, Samuel m 1/31/34 Phoebe Lyons in Peekskill, Rev. Marshall (all of Peekskill) (11-2/4)

BRIGGS, William S. m 10/10/35 Harriet Myers; Rev. John Nixon (all of Coeymans) (6-10/16)

BRIGHAM(?), William, merchant, of Albany m 1/14/16 Rachael Anders of Stockbridge, Mass. in S.; Rev. Jones (6-1/20)

BRIGHAM, Henry A. (Hon.) m 10/26/48 Mary A. Powell, both of West Troy, at the West Troy Exchange; Rev. G.C. Baldwin (5-11/1)

BRIGHAM, Lucius A. of Cincinnati m 9/23/50 Cornelia E. Taylor of Lenox, Mass. in L.; Rev. Neal(?) (5-10/2)

BRIGHAM, Oragen S., Esq., attorney at law, m 10/10/43 Frances E. Waterman, both of West Troy, in W.T.; Rev. Dr. Brigham of NYC (5-10/18)

BRIGHAM, Origen S., Esq., 35, postmaster in West Troy, d 12/24/50 (consumption) (5-12/25)

BRIGHAM, Stephen, 67, d 7/24/50 at Vernon (painful illness of 3 months) (1-7/31)

BRIGHAM, Stephen, Jr. (Capt.), 95, d 10/11/49 at Vernon (1-10/17)

BRIGHT, J. Huntington, Esq., formerly of Albany, d 6/15/37 at Manchester, Mississippi (6-8/9)

BRILL, John, Esq., of Western m 8/30/49 Cynthia Tibbitts of Rome; Rev. James Erwin (1-9/5)

BRIM, Emily - see CARD, Denison

BRINCKERHOFF, John - his relatives and friends invited to his funeral at 3 o'clock from his home at 4 Dean Street. (6-3/13/35)

BRINK, Adam, about 59, d 12/21/49 in Saugerties (8-12/27)

BRINK, Ann Maria - see ROSA, William

BRINK, Christina C. - see SNYDER, Jacob

BRINKERHOFF, Jacob - see VAN DEUSEN, Gertrude

BRINKERHOFF, T. - see VAN DEUSEN, Gertrude

BRINKERHOFF, Tunis of La Grange m 9/2/35 Susan Everitt, dau of Isaac of Poughkeepsie; Rev. Cornelius Van Kleef (6-9/12)

BRINSMADE, P.A. - see LITTLE, William Coffin

BRINTON, Catharine - see INGERSOLL, Edward

BRISBIN, Henry A., son of Rev. Brisbin, d (date not given) (funeral at 2 o'clock from Rev. Brisbin's home, 54 Church St.) (6-12/3)

BRISCO, Abigail, 64, wf of Nathan, d 5/13/39 in Pound Ridge (consumption) (12-5/21)

BRISLEY(?), (Mrs. Grant), 84, d 3/18/42 in NYC (9-3/19)

34

BRISTOL & ABELL - see ABELL, William

BRISTOL, David E. of West Troy m 2/8/44 Catherine L. Yates of Greenbush in G.; Rev. H.B. Knight (5-2/14)

BRISTOL, Harriet A. - see FORT, Simon

BRISTOL, Ira m (date not given) Sally Smith in Gorham (6-5/8/16)

BRISTOL, William (Hon.), US Judge for the district of Connecticut, d 3/7/36 at his residence in New Haven ("died suddenly while ordering a horse and sleigh from a domestic") (from the Hartford Times) (6-3/14)

BRITHWAIT, John of Syracuse m 1/22/47 Sarah Fitz Patrick of Utica; H.C. Vogell (1-1/29)

BRITT, Harriet - see MOORE, John

BRITTON, Eben - see MC RAY, H., Esq.

BRITTON, Susan M. - see MC RAY, H., Esq.

BROADBENT, Anna - see DAWSON, John

BROADHEAD, Rev. - see MC DOWELL, Margaret

BROCKETT, Calista L., 14, dau. of Alvah and Eunice, d 4/8/39 in Salisbury (3-5/2)

BROCKETT, Janette - see CROSBY, Allen G.

BROCKETT, Theresa - see DEMPSTER, James

BROMLEY, John Hallock m 2/9/37 Mary Malvena Mc Neil, dau. of Col. D.B., in Plattsburgh; Rev. J. Howland Coit (6-2/23)

BRONK, John L - see CONINE, Mary

BRONK, Leonard I, 17, only son of John L., Esq., d 3/15/35 at home of his father in Coxsackie (consumption 3 months) was a student at Union College (6-3/24)

BRONK, Robert (Rev.) m (date not given) Alida Lansing; Rev. Bogardus, all of Watervliet (6-6/1/35)

BRONSON, Abijah, 36, d 7/11/44 in Vernon (1-9/17)

BRONSON, Hannah, 71, relict of Daniel, d 10/16/36 in Warren (3-10/20)

BRONSON, Harriet, dau of Isaac of NYC, d 11/22/35 at Geneva, Switzerland (6-1/13/36)

BRONSON, Joel m 1/5/41 Eliza Hawkins, both of Lee Center, at L.C.; Rev. H.C. Vogell (1-1/19)

BRONSON, Prudence M. - see TUPPER, James

BRONSON, Zenas, 63(?), d 10/21/44 in Vernon (1-11/12)

BROOKER, Elizabeth N. - see SHEAR, Wallace B.

BROOKER, Isaac S. of Boston m 11/13/45 Catharine E. Little of West Troy in Albany; Rev. S.W. Fisher (5-11/26)

BROOKER, Margaret E. - see WEST, G.L.

BROOKER, Sarah, 43, wf of Samuel C., Esq., d 2/4/49 in Floyd (consumption) (1-2/14)

BROOKS, Calvin of Verona m 9/19/41 Elizabeth Bowen, youngest dau. of John, Esq. of Westmoreland; Rev. F.A. Spencer (1-9/28)

BROOKS, I. Lloyd of Maryland m 7/28/39 Angelina Whitney, youngest dau. of Shubel, Esq. in Sing Sing; Charles Yeo, Esq. (12-9/3)

BROOKS, Jonathan, Jr. m 6/10/35 Mary Elizabeth Keeler, dau of J.S. Keeler, Esq.; Rev. Dr. Ferris; all of Albany (6-6/11)

BROOMHALL, George m 11/29/38 Ann Owen, both of Mohawk in Little Falls; Rev. Thomas Towell (3-12/6)

BROTHERS, Angeline - see SMITH, Samuel

BROTHERSON, Eliza - see MC CLELLAND, William

BROTHERSON, John - see ARDEN, Elvira

BROTHERSON, Philip, Esq. - see MC CLELLAND, William

BROUWER, Mary - see HALL, Isaac

BROWER, Abraham, 31, d (date not given) in NYC (6-5/22/16)

BROWER, Eliza - see FISH, Moses W.

BROWER, Heshel m 12/2/47 Mary Elizabeth Waltz, both of Albany, in West Troy;
    Rev. J.C. Burroughs (5-12/8)

BROWER, John W., 15, son of William; Halenbake, Isaac Rue, 13, son of Isaac B.;
    Kidney, William, 12, son of Jonathan; and Clapper, Peter, 16, apprentice of
    Mr. Jonathan Kidney and son of Mr. ---- Clapper of Bethlehem drowned
    (date not given) while bathing in the Hudson River a little below Albany
    (from the Albany Gazette) (7-6/20/10)

BROWER, W. Henry of Rome m 1/28/43 Prudence Augusta Blodget, dau. of J.,
    Esq. of Stone Castle, at S.C.; Rev. Wilcox (1-2/28)

BROWER, William H. m 11/3/50 Isabella Bushnell, both of Albany; Rev. Thomas
    W. Pearson (5-11/13)

BROWN, ----, about 12 months, infant son of Dr. John R., d 3/26/36 at Salisbury
    (3-3/31)

BROWN, Almira - see VAN SCHUYLER, Joseph

BROWN, Andrew - see BROWNELL, Moses

BROWN, Andrew Edward, 11 months, son of Andrew E., d 6/3/37 (6-6/5)

BROWN, Ann Eliza - see CRANE, Joseph

BROWN, Annah H. (Mrs.) - see WILLMARTH, John L.

BROWN, Annis - see DAVISON, Joseph

BROWN, Benjamin, Esq., 57, d 10/6/47 in West Troy (5-10/13)

BROWN, Caleb - see MERRITT, John

BROWN, Celestia C. - see HEWETT, Richard

BROWN, Charles E. (Rev.) of Litchfield m 9/19/38 Lyon, dau. of late Dr.
    Benjamin Lyon of Little Falls, at the Baptist Church in Little Falls; Rev. A.
    Beach (3-9/27)

BROWN, Charles, merchant, of Albany m 6/15/37 Elizabeth Fries of Schoharie;
    Rev. J.M. Scribner (6-6/16)

BROWN, Daniel (Rev.) m 4/15/39 Susan Tompkins, dau of Isaac, Sr., in Carmel;
    Rev. Harrison (11-4/23)

BROWN, Daniel, 77, d 1/4/38 at Eatonville (born in Adams, Mass., but a pioneer
    settler in Fairfield, NY) (3-1/11)

BROWN, Edwin C. of V---(?) m 7/25/41 Mary J. Wells, dau. of J.Y. Wells of
    Rome, in R.; Rev. I.A. Eddy (1-7/27)

BROWN, Edwin m 2/25/35 Mary Ann Trumbull; Rev. J. Trumbull Backus; all of
    Schenectady (6-3/4)

BROWN, Eliza - see YOUNG, Truesdel

BROWN, Elizabeth - see MOE, Robert I.

BROWN, Emery W. of German Flats m 4/21/39 Betsey Graham of Columbia; Rev.
    Dr. Ash (3-5/2)

BROWN, Ester, 3, dau. of William C., d 11/13/41 in Newburgh (9-11/20)

BROWN, Esther - see CURTISS, Daniel

BROWN, Eunice - see SHERBURNE, Silas

BROWN, Eunice, 63, wf of Asael, d (date not given) at New Lebanon (7-5/10/09)

BROWN, Fanny Jane, 31, wf of Jackson T. Brown, d 4/1/42 in Newburgh (9-4/2)

BROWN, George (Col.) m 9/13/26 Hannah Hopkins, dau. of Judge enos Hopkins; Rev. Winter (all of North East, Dutchess County) (6-9/26/26)

BROWN, George Owen, 18, d 5/12/44 in West Troy (5-5/22)

BROWN, George, 1, son of Benjamin C., d 5/25/42 in Little Falls (3-6/2)

BROWN, George, Esq., 27, d 3/4/48 in the city of New Orleans (formerly of Rome and late of Syracuse) (1-3/17)

BROWN, Gerardus, about 90, d 2/25/39 in Sing Sing (12-3/5)

BROWN, Hannah - see COOK, Emanuel

BROWN, Hannah - see DEAN, Daniel

BROWN, Hannah Maria - see ARNOLD, N.F.

BROWN, Henry H. m 11/12/41 Almeda Wells in Albany; Rev. O.H. Gregory (all of West Troy) (5-11/24)

BROWN, Henry, 100, d 9/17/37 at Boston, Portage County, Ohio (a Rev. War soldier) (6-10/4)

BROWN, Horace, age indistinct, d 11/21/42 in Somers (11-11/24)

BROWN, Isaac D. of NYC m 6/29/36 Sarah C. Powell, dau of Henry, Esq., of Poughkeepsie, at P.; Rev. Van Ranken (6-7/1)

BROWN, J. Addison of Hammond, St. Lawrence County m 6/2/41 Mary Jane Daniels, dau. of Mahum of Poland, NY, in P.; Rev. Pierce

BROWN, J.M. (Dr.) of Florence m 6/22/47 Miss J.S. Coffin of Deerfield in D.; Rev. T.J. Whitcomb (1-6/25)

BROWN, J.P., 30, d 6/7/34 at Mobile (billious colic) (formerly of Somers, NY and son of Aaron Brown, sheriff of Westchester County) (11-7/15)

BROWN, James - see VAN SCHUYLER, Joseph

BROWN, Jane - see LENT, William H.

BROWN, Jeduthan of Chicago m 2/20/43 Ophelia C. Elmer of Rome, NY at Jefferson, W.I. (West Indies possibly intended here?) (1-3/14)

BROWN, John m 4/24/42 Eliza Murray; Rev. Quinn (all of West Troy) (5-5/4)

BROWN, John N. (Rev.) of Black River Conference m 1/1/45 Eliza Ann Steadman of Lee in church at Delta (1-2/4)

BROWN, John P., about 28, attorney at law, d 3/19/47 in Watertown (1-3/26)

BROWN, John, 104, born in Ireland, lived in US 50 years, d 6/22/36 in Warren County, New Jersey (6-7/11)

BROWN, John, d 8/9/49 in Saugerties (cholera) (8-8/11)

BROWN, Joseph m 12/26/36 Sarah Lord; Rev. C.P. Clarke (all of Albany) (6-12/28)

BROWN, Luther d 9/14/45 in West Troy (5-9/17)

BROWN, Luxana, about 28, wf of Eleazer, d 1/27/37 in Fairfield (3-2/16)

BROWN, Lydia Gaven, 80, relict of Elijah T., d (date not given) at the home of her son (not named) in Floyd (1-6/12/50)

BROWN, M. Moses, 97, patriarch of Providence (R.I.), d 9/6/36 (from the Providence Journal) (6-9/13)

BROWN, Major S. - see KNAPP, Tracy S.

BROWN, Maria Williams - see LOOMIS, Charles K.

BROWN, Mary - see BROWNELL, Moses

BROWN, Mary - see WOOD, George

BROWN, Mary Ann - see GOODROW, Francis

BROWN, Mary, 89, relict of Nathaniel, late of Peekskill, d 12/26/34 at Yorktown at the home of Jacob Beedle, deceased (11-2/3/35)

BROWN, Matilda - see FORT, James

BROWN, Miles H. m 3/10/36 Amelia Belshew in Warren; Rev. Whitman (3-3/17)

BROWN, Nancy - see HAILE, Amos

BROWN, Nancy - see WEST, Manton(?)

BROWN, Nathaniel W., 4, d 2/17/39 in Fairfield (3-3/7)

BROWN, Obadiah D., 53, d 9/21/35 at Gibbonsville (formerly of Bristol, RI) (apoplexy) (6-9/24)

BROWN, Oliver - see RUGER, Sophia

BROWN, Phebe A. - see MOORE, George F.

BROWN, Phebe W., 51, wf of Caleb, d 1/30/42 in Peekskill (consumption (11-2/15)

BROWN, Philander M., Esq. of Munnsville m 12/23/40 Cordelia Levina Horton(?) dau. of Daniel, Esq., at Vernon Center; Rev. S. Hastings (all of V.C.) (1-12/29)

BROWN, Robert, about 18, d 10/4/49 at Coxsackie (8-10/6)

BROWN, Roswell D. m 1/14/39 Elvira A. Eaton, dau. of John, in Eatonville; Rev. W.H. Waggoner (3-1/17)

BROWN, Samuel (Major) - see LOOMIS, Charles K.

BROWN, Samuel Jerome of West Troy m 7/18/44 Catharine Decker of Troy in T.; Rev. L. Howard (5-7/31)

BROWN, Sarah Ann, 28, wf of Abram I of NYC, d (date not given) at home of William Merrifield at Guilderland (consumption) (6-8/16/36)

BROWN, Sarah Jane (Mrs.), 23, d 10/28/48 in West Troy (2 weeks previously, with her back to the stove her clothes caught fire and she received severe burns resulting in her death) (5-11/1)

BROWN, Sarah M. - see HENRY, Calvin R.

BROWN, Sarah M., 3, dau. of Nathan, d 11/24/36 in Oppenheim (3-12/8)

BROWN, Sarah, 51, wf of David, d 8/23/42 in Newburgh (9-8/27)

BROWN, Thomas H.16 months, son of William H. and Catherine, d 12/5/38 in Sing Sing (12-12/18)

BROWN, Thomas J., 33, d 10/9/41 in Peekskill (11-10/12)

BROWN, Thomas Yardley (Col.) of Brownville m 3/6/37 Mary Ann Everett, dau. of late Professor Joel Everett of Sacket's Harbor, in Watertown at the home of George I. Knight of Prospect Hill; Rev. B.H. Hickox (6-3/13)

BROWN, William of Saugerties m 12/4/48 Mary Elizabeth Thomas of Albany in West Troy; Rev. Houghtaling (5-12/6)

BROWNELL, Moses m 1/1/16 Mary Brown, dau. of late Andrew Brown, Esq/

BROWNING, Robert d (date nor given) (his funeral at 3 o'clock from his late home, 33 Fulton St., Albany) (6-4/1/36)

BROWNING, Susan E. - see CHURCHILL, Albert W.

BRUEN, Harriet - see WHITEHOUSE, Henry

BRUNDAGE, Ann - see BLOOMER, Stephen

BRUNDAGE, Hackaliah, 70, d 2/26/42 in Bedford (11-3/15)

BRUNDAGE, Rachael, about 44, widow of John, d 9/26/39 in Bedford (12-10/8)

BRUNSON, Daniel, 73, (a Rev. War soldier), d 1/31/36 in Warren (3-3/17)

BRUSH, Electa J. - see BRUSH, William (Rev.)

BRUSH, William (Rev.), A.B., of New Haven, Conn. m 10/28/50 Electa J. Brush of Rome in R.; Rev. James Erwin (1-10/30)

BRUTON, Susan M. - see MC KAY, Henry

BRUYN, Sylvanus M. - see HASBROUCK, Elizabeth

BRYAN, Emily - see WATSON, Isaac

BRYAN, Francis, 76, d 11/5/36 at his late home, 219 North Market St. (6-11/7)

BRYANT, Evangelesta, 1, dau. of E.E. Bryant, d 4/23/41 in Vernon (1-5/11)

BUCHANAN, Boon, 113, d (date not given) at the poor House of Washington County, Penna. (better known as "Old Booty"; was a waiter in the army at Braddock's depot in 1755 (5-9/23/46)

BUCHANAN, Franklin (Lieut.) of the U.S. Navy, m 2/19/35 Nanie Lloyd, dau of late Gov. Lloyd of Maryland, at Annapolis, MD (6-3/4)

BUCHANAN, Thomas m 1/29/48 Esther Hubbard, both of Cohoes, at the West Troy Exchange; Rev. J.C. Burroughs (5-2/2)

BUCHANAN, William, about 55, d 3/16/42 in Newburgh (9-3/19)

BUCK, Harriet S. - PATTON, William Farley

BUCKBEE, Andrew of Peekskill m 4/16/39 Eliza A. Acker, dau of Jacob, Esq., of NYC, in NYC; Rev. Downers (11-4/23)

BUCKBEE, Catharine B. - see CLINTON, Benjamin

BUCKBEE, Levi of Whitlockville, Bedford m 4/25/39 Mary Cree(?) of North Salem; Rev. Rice (12-4/30)

BUCKINGHAM, F. William, Esq. of Boston m 6/30/47 Abbie S. Beecher, dau. of Mather Beecher, Esq. of Remsen, at R. (1-7/9)

BUCKLEY, Merriman L., 28, of firm of P.H. BUckley & Brother, d 2/8/37 in Troy (6-2/13)

BUCKLIN, ----, son of John C. d (date not given) (his funeral at 3 o'clock from 14 Columbia Street) (6-2/23)

BUCKLIN, Cynthia E. - see CHAPIN, E.G.

BUCKLIN, Edward A., about 12, d 2/24/39 in Fairfield (3-2/28)

BUCKLIN, Isaac B., M.D., of West Troy m 3/1/49 Urania Jennings of Troy; Rev. T. Seymour (5-3/14)

BUCKLIN, John - see CHAPIN, E.G.

BUCKLIN, John, 84, d 12/5/37 in Fairfield (an early settler in that town) (3-12/6)

BUCKLIN, Wesley m 1/3/50 Catherine L. Cole, both of West Troy; Rev. O.H. Gregory (double ceremony - see KNOWLES, William) (5-1/9)

BUDD, Eliza - see HAIGHT, Elijah

BUDDLE, William G., late of Canajoharie m 4/27/48 Charity Ann Dillenbeck, dau. of Daniel of Fort Plain, at F.P.; Rev. Isbell (4-5/4)

BUDLONG, Hiram, 2, son of Joseph, d 10/15/39 in Little Falls (by accidental scalding) (3-10/24)

BUEL, Charles, son of Jesse, Esq., m 2/21/35 Jane Anna Yates, dau of late John Cook, Esq.; Rev. Joseph H. Price, all of Albany. (6-8/22)

BUEL, Francis m 7/4/41 Wealthy Woodruff, dau. of Buckley Woodruff; Rev. F.A. Spencer (all of Westmoreland) (1-7/13)

BUEL, Leander R., infant son of Simon and Julia Ann, d 10/3/40 in Rome (1-10/13)

BUELL, Benjamin (Deacon), 82, d (date not given) at Hebron ("was for many years a member of the Legislature, and justice of the peace which office he resigned after he was 80 years of age") (7-6/13/10)

BUELL, Julia Ann, 21, wf of Simon, d 9/24/40 in Rome (1-9/29)

BUELL, Lucius of Torrington, Conn. m 4/1/45 Sarah Patten(?) of Rome; Rev.
Haynes (1-4/8)

BUELL, Mary A. - see MATHER, William, M.D.

BUELL, Olivia H., 21, eldest dau of Eli, d 7/1/36 in Hamilton (buried on her
birthday, 7/4) (6-7/19)

BUERLEY, Daniel m 9/29/41 Margaret Wilson (both of Oriskany) at Rome; Rev.
Charles Jones (a double ceremony - see PALMER, William) (1-10/5)

BULKELEY, Daniel (Capt.), 61, d (date not given) suddenly at Colchester
(7-8/1/10)

BULL(?), Harriet - see GRAY, James M.

BULL, Amy, (Mrs.), 89, mother of Archibald, Esq., of Troy, d 1/8/36 at home of
Josephine Dorr in Hoosick Falls (6-1/13)

BULL, David, 20, son of the Hon. Jonathan of Hartford, Conn., d (date not given)
at Augusta, Georgia (This is the fifth child Jonathan has lost within nine
months) (2-11/30/09)

BULL, Frances D. - see BANCROFT, DeWitt C.

BULLARD, Louisa, 1, dau. of Dr. David H. amd Julia S. d 7/16/47 in West Troy
(5-7/21)

BULLIONS, James Mc Naughton, 6, d 2/23/37 (deceased is son of Rev. Peter
Bullions of the Albany Academy (funeral 2/24 from the Albany Academy)
(6-2/24)

BULLIONS, Mary - see NELSON, W.G., M.D.

BULLIS, Frederick of Troy m 7/2/49 Sarah Cutting of West Troy in W.T.; Rev.
O.H. Gregory (5-7/4)

BULLIS, Permilia - see MAYNARD, Lyman

BULLITT, A.S. (Col.), late Lieut. Governor of Kentucky, d (date not given) at
Louisville (6-5/8/16)

BULLOCK, Adam B. (Rev.), 41, d 4/14/48 in --- (town name blurred) (4-4/27)

BULLOCK, Fanny - see RUNYAN, Henry B.

BULSON, Eliza - see MEAD, Henry

BUNCE, Alanson m 6/20/39 Cynthia Payn, dau. of Daniel, in Russia, NY; Asa
Vickery, Esq. (bride & groom of Russia) (3-6/27)

BUNCE, Jerusha E. - see PUTNEY, Nelson

BUNDY, Caleb, Esq. - see KELLOGG, George D.

BUNDY, Frances - see KELLOGG, George D.

BUNKER, Timothy (Capt.), 75, d in his sleep 12/19/35 at his home in Athens,
Greene County (6-12/29)

BUNNEL, Adaline - see VOSBURGH, Henry

BUNNER, Rudolph (Hon.), 58, d 7/31/37 at his home in Oswego (an early settler
there - "through his efforts in and out of Congress we are greatly indebted
for our noble piers and when the canal around Niagara Falls shall be added
his (efforts) will not be forgotten") (from the Oswego Palladium) (3-8/3)

BUR, Thomas (Colonel), about 50, d 9/2/42 (11-9/8)

BURCH, Aaron(?) m 12/15/39 Eliza(?) Pinckney, both of Southeast, in Patterson;
Rev. Mc Leod (12-1/21/40)

BURCH, Charles A., 14, son of Horace, d 9/6/38 in Little Falls (3-9/20)

BURCH, Eliza, 2, dau. of Thomas, d 11/24/38 in Little Falls (3-11/29)

BURCH, H.M., Esq. m 5/2/36 Frances A. Smith, both of Little Falls; Rev. Burtis
(6-5/5)

BURCH, H.M., Esq., merchant, m 5/2/36 Frances A. Smith, dau. of Samuel, Esq., in Little Falls; Rev. Arthur Burtiss (3-5/5)

BURDEN, Abraham - see HOLMES, A.H. (Dr.)

BURDEN, Sarah M. - see HOLMES, A.H. (Dr.)

BURDETT, John, 97, a Rev. War soldier, d (date not given) at Leominster, Mass. (5-1/17/44)

BURDICK, John of Oppenheim m 3/19/40 Mrs. Harriet Peacock of Manheim at Breckett;s Bridge; Rev. A. Blackburn (3-3/26)

BURDICK, John P. of Gardner, Mass. m 1/27/50 Ann M. Mc Gregor of West Troy; Rev. T.P. Wyckoff (5-2/6)

BURDICK, Lewis m 6/3/47 Salona Jenks, both of Troy, in T.; Rev. J.C. Burroughs (5-6/23)

BURDSALL, Mary Jane - see MERRITT, Henry

BURGE, Mary - see ROBERTS, P.J.

BURGESS(?), Abigail J. - see PURDY, Thomas

BURGESS, Isaac m 6/14/43 Hannah Halstead; Rev. Pease (all of Peekskill) (11-6/20)

BURGETT, Orpha - see WILLSON, Richard H.

BURGY, Emily Christiana, 6, infant dau of I.J. & Harriet Burgy and grand-dau of Elisha Cerwin, Esq., of Phillipstown, d 10/15/34 in NYC (11-10/21)

BURHANS, ---- (Col.) - see KIMMEY, David

BURHANS, John H. (Col.) m 10/21/26 Eleanor Waggoner at Bethlehem; Rev. Samuel Kissam (6-10/31)

BURHANS, Nelson H. m 7/4/49 Nelly Smith, 67, relict of late Lodowick Smith, in Saugerties (8-7/7)

BURHANS, Nicholas, about 50, d 3/27/49 at Glasco (8-3/31)

BURK, I.T., merchant, m (date not given) Sarah P. Farrar in Lawrence, St. Lawrence County (6-5/4/36)

BURK, Martha, 60, wf of Silas, d 10/21/35 at Manlius (typhus fever) (she was one of the earliest residents of the town and "has left an extensive family connexion") (6-10/31)

BURKE, Albert G. (Hon.), 31, lawyer, d 9/11/36 in Lodi (had represented that district in the state legislature; was appointed Supreme Court commissioner (6-9/27)

BURKE, John D., Jr., 9, d 8/8/48 in Fort Plain (4-8/17)

BURKE, Margaret - see SMITH, Robert

BURKETT, Rebecca (Miss), formerly of Hartford, Conn., d 4/3/16 at Cherry Valley (6-4/10)

BURLESON, Mary E. - see WATERMAN, Isaac V.

BURLEY, Charles of NYC m 6/10/43 Marcelia S. Arnold of West Troy; Rev. C.H. Hasken (5-6/21)

BURLINGAME, E.E. (Miss) - see CRAMER, J.A.

BURLISON, James H., 8, youngest son of John and Sarah, d 12/31/40 in West Troy (5-1/6/41)

BURLISON, John m 1/5/42 Mrs. Maria Devol, both of West Troy; Rev. D. Starks (5-1/12)

BURLISON, John m 12/12/46 Sarah Hill, both of West Troy, in W.T.; Rev. John Fraser (5-12/16)

BURLISON, Julia A. - see CONMARY(?), Prudent

BURNELL, Elizabeth - see WOODFORD, O.P.

BURNES, Lucinda - see HARRIS, J.F.

BURNES, Simeon of Kingston m 10/20/35 Elizabeth Cowel of Albany in A.; Rev. Leonard (6-10/22)

BURNET, Harriett - see CRANE, John (Rev.)

BURNET, Reuben of Rondout m 7/23/49 Josephine Lewis of Saugerties in S.; Rev. Dudley (8-8/4)

BURNETT, Charles P., 11, second son of William, d 11/15/40 in West Troy (see also BURNETT, Mary Ann) (5-11/25)

BURNETT, Margaret - see CUNNINGHAM, Hugh

BURNETT, Mary Ann, 9, dau. of William, d 11/17/40 (see also BURNETT, Charles P.) (5-11/25)

BURNETT, Sophia - see VANDENBERGH, John H.

BURNETTE, Katharine M. - see SOULE, Henry

BURNHAM, Eliza M - see THOMPSON, Alexander

BURNHAM, Mary L., 25, wf of James N., Esq. and dau of Cornelius Cuyler, Esq., d 6/19/35 (consumption) (6-7/2)

BURNHAM, Michael, 64, d 1/25/36 (was the original printer and publisher of the Evening Post and has left a large family) (from NY Commercial Advertiser) (6-1/26)

BURNHAM, Nathan, 74, d (date not given) at East Haddam (7-8/1/10)

BURNOP, Philip - see SHURS, Robert

BURNOP, Sarah M. - see SHURS, Robert

BURNS, Eliza A. - see BARTLETT, Marcellus

BURNS, Mary - see AGANS, Stephen

BURNS, Sarah M. - see DEVENBURGH, P.W. (Rev.)

BURNS, Thomas m. 12/24/34 Margaret Walker, dau. of James; Rev. H. Meeker (all of Albany) (6-1/3/35)

BURNSIDE, Andrew T. d (date not given) in NYC (6-5/15/16)

BURNSIDE, Robert of West Troy m 10/31/49 Mary Atwood of Troy in T.; Rev. Dr. Halley (5-11/7)

BURR(?), Agnes - see BOKE(?), William

BURR, Aaron (Col.), 80, formerly Vice President of the U.S., d 9/30/36 at Staten Island (an obituary included) (from NY Commercial Advertiser) (6-9/16)

BURR, Hannah, 21, wf of John d 8/21/39 in Sing Sing (12-8/27)

BURR, Jane Maria - see WILLIAMS, Rufus O.

BURR, Oliver of West Trot m 2/15/42 Betsy Ann Barker of New Lebanon in N.L.; Rev. J.G. Hall (5-2/16)

BURRALL, Charles, 73, d (date not given) in Goshen (6-5/12/36)

BURRELL, ----, infant dau. of M.B. and Catharine, d 1/13/49 in Canajoharie (4-1/25)

BURRELL, Jacob, merchant, m 3/10/36 Catherine L. Spinner, dau. of Rev. John P. of Herkimer, at H.; Rev. Spencer (3-3/17)

BURRELL, Lucina, 73, consort of late Jonathan, d 6/17/39 at Salisbury. At the same residence on the same day 10 hours later, Orenda Burrell, 37, wf of Harry, died (funeral 6/20) (3-6/20)

BURRELL, Oscar of Newark, NJ m 11/28/36 Mary Smith of Albany; R.C. Brisbin (6-12/1)

BURRELL, Thomas S. m 1/23/49 Louisa Wendell, dau. of Jacob, Esq., in Fort

Plain (bride & groom both of Fort Plain); Rev. B. Isbell (4-1/25)

BURRILL, L.W. (Miss) - see CARRYL, Lorenzo

BURRILL, Mary Rosalie - see IVES, Frederick

BURRILL, Nelson, merchant, of Herkimer m 12/13/38 Sophronia Campbell, dau. of Ethan, Esq. of Camillus, Onondaga County at C.; Rev. Harrington (3-12/20)

BURRILL, William F. of Salisbury, NY m 6/25/46 Harriet R. Hamlin, dau. of Joseph, Esq., of Holland Patent at H.P.; Rev. I.F. Scovill (1-6/30)

BURRILL, William, Esq. - see IVES, Frederick

BURROUGHS, Charles m 1/4/36 Margaret Bradt; Rev. C.L. Clark (all of Albany) (6-1/8)

BURROUGHS, Felicia(?) - see BALDWIN, Noah

BURROUGHS, Stepaen, Esq., nearly 80, one of the earliest settlers of the Eastern Townships of Lower Canada, d 1/23/40 at Three Rivers, Lower Canada (illness of "a few days only". Was well known in the US, had visited in New York State, 18 months prior to his death) (5-2/12)

BURROWS, Charles E. (Dr.), 43, d 9/1/44 in Mayville, Chautauqua County (5-9/18)

BURROWS, Julia Prudence, 11 months, dau. of Philander W., d 3/9/42 in Rome (inflammation of the lungs) (1-3/15)

BURROWS, Prudence H., 25, wf of Philander W. and eldest dau. of Cornelius Hollister of Rome, d 3/30/41 in Rome (a long term member of the Congregational Church in Rome) (1-4/6)

BURROWS, Sarah M., 14, dau. of P.W. of Milwaukie and grand-dau. of C. Hollister, formerly of Rome, d 5/13/50 in Beloit, Wisc. (scarlet fever) (1-5/29)

BURST(?), John m 9/23/41 Jemima Clute, both of Halfmoon, in Watervliet (5-9/29)

BURT, Benjamin, 46, eldest son of Hon. James Burt, d. 9/15/35 at Warwick (6-9/19)

BURT, Fanny - see HANER, Oliver

BURT, Fanny - see STANCEL(?), Oliver

BURT, Joshua of firm of Howe and Burt in Auburn m 1/6/36 Mary Amelia Relay, dau of late Henry, Esq. of Hudson in Albany; Rev. Potter (6-1/8)

BURT, Lansing m 10/25/41 Sophia Day in Danube; Zenas Green, Esq. (all of Danube) (3-11/4)

BURT, Rodolphus, formerly of Little Falls, d 9/17/39 in Lysander, Cayuga County (3-10/17)

BURTGOOD(?), Reed B., M.D. m 7/19/49 Susan Northrup, both of Troy; Rev. Pearson (5-8/1)

BURTON, Abram Sanford, Esq., editor of the Illinois Champion, d 9/1/35 at Peoria, Ill. (6-9/30)

BURTON, Amos T. (Dr.) m 6/30/36 Jane Patton, both of Albany; Rev. Holmes (6-7/4)

BURTON, Hannah - see SLOSSON, Augustus D.

BURTON, Hutchins G., Esq., ex. governor of North Carolina and for several years a congressman, d 4/21/36 in Lincoln County (6-5/5)

BURTON, J., Esq. - see NEWELL, Marcy B. (Rev.)

BURTON, James m 3/8/36 Margaret J. Hill; Rev. Dr. Campbell (all of Albany)

(6-3/10)

BURTON, Joseph d 5/31/33 in Peekskill (11-6/4)

BURTON, Maria Ann - see NEWELL, Marcy B. (Rev.)

BURTON, Thompson, M.D., of Charleston, NY m 2/7/36 Laura E. Royce of Orwell, VT at O. (6-2/18)

BURWELL, Ann, 40, wf of Dr. B. Burwell, d 9/13/38 in Buffalo (3-9/27)

BURWELL, Catharine Ann, 23, wf of Elliot Burwell, M.D., and eldest dau. of Pierre A. Barker, Esq., d 4/28/36 in Buffalo (3-5/5)

BURWELL, Catharine Ann, 23, wf of Elliott Burwell, M.D., and eldest dau. of Pierre A. Barker, Esq. d 4/25/36 at Buffalo (6-5/5)

BURWELL, Catherine A., wf of Dudley Burwell, Esq. and dau of Hon. Samuel Young, d 4/5/35 at Little Falls (6-4/9)

BURWELL, Catherine Ann, 24, wf of Dudley Burwell, Esq; and dau of Col. Samuel Young, d 4/5/35 at Little Falls ("an affliction of the brain") (6-4/11)

BURWELL, Elliott (Dr.) m 6/24/35 Catherine Ann Baker, dau of Pierre A., Esq., in Buffalo (all of that city); Rev. Shelton (6-6/29)

BUSH, Henry of Turin m Catherine Baldwin of Martinsburgh in M.; Rev. Erwin (1-2/16)

BUSH, John P. m 11/8/43 Elizabeth Hart, dau. of Martin, Esq. of Utica; Rev. Dr. Proal (3-11/16)

BUSH, Matilda - see WYBOURN, John O.

BUSH, Stephen, 35, d 1/6/16 at Palatine (6-1/13)

BUSHE, George Mc Cartney, M.D., 38, d 5/17/37 in NYC (consumption) (6-5/20)

BUSHER, Amanda F. - see SEATON, James W.

BUSHER, Sophia - see DAVIS, William H.

BUSHNELL, Frederick, Esq., president of the Bank of Rochester, d 11/7/37 at the home of his brother, Luther Bushnell, in Pittsford (6-11/13)

BUSHNELL, Ichabod Henry, only son of Lorin and Susan of Lee, d 4/19/45 in Lee (1-4/29)

BUSHNELL, Isabella - see BROWER, William H.

BUSHNELL, Mary (Mrs.), 89, d. (date not given) at Norwich (7-5/10/09)

BUSHNELL, Rebecca - see CARPENTER, Stephen F.

BUSHNELL, Semantha, 32, wf of Joseph, d 8/9/39 at Fairfield (3-8/22)

BUSSY, George O., 28, architect, d 12/27/46 at Lowell, Mass. (1-1/8/47)

BUTLER, ---- (Rev. Dr.) d 7/11/42 (presumably in Troy) (funeral at St. Paul's Church; funeral sermon by Rt. Rev. Bishop Doane of New Jersey; "one of the largest funeral processions ever witnesses in this city") from the Troy Whig (5-7/20)

BUTLER, Alvah M. m 4/17/48 Lorain B. Rowe, dau. of A. Rowe, of the American Hotel; H.C. Vogell (all of Rome) (1-5/12)

BUTLER, Caroline S. - see UTLEY, H. M.D.

BUTLER, Charles, 21, late of NYC and eldest son of Amos Butler, senior editor & publisher of the NY Mercantile Advertiser, d 8/11/36 at Raleigh, NC (6-8/18)

BUTLER, David (Rev.), D.D., 80, for many years rector of St. Paul's Church, d 7/4/42 (one of the oldest clergymen in the diocese of NY) (11-7/19)

BUTLER, Egeliel - see BAILEY, Harriet

BUTLER, Flora - see THOMAS, Amery

BUTLER, Harriet - see RHODES, Charles D.

BUTLER, Harriet C. - see WETMORE, Charles P.

BUTLER, John of Rome m 5/11/48 Delia A. Hibbard of Clinton in C.; H.C. Vogell (1-5/12)

BUTLER, Jonah, 55, d 8/23/41 in Newport (3-9/9)

BUTLER, Mary - see HILL, Hiland, Jr.

BUTLER, Mary Ann, 2, only dau. of Joseph Henry and Ann Maria Butler, d 9/16/39 in Troy (5-9/25)

BUTLER, Mary, 74, d 4/17/38 at Frankfort (3-5/3)

BUTLER, Nathan m 3/14/47 Almira Dunbar, both of Lee, at Kirkland; James Ormsbee, Esq. (1-3/26)

BUTLER, Ruth (Mrs.), 80, d 5/6/48 at Cassville in the town of Paris (1-5/26)

BUTLER, Ruth Ann, 23, dau. of Rev. Charles and Amanda, d 7/28/42 in Verona (1-8/30)

BUTLER, Sarah - see MC DONALD, George

BUTLER, Silas, 57, purser in the US Navy, d 3/9/37 (6-4/13)

BUTLER, William, 57, d 3/6/35 suddenly in Deposit while visiting S. Lusk, Esq. there; he "engaged for many years extensively in business" in Deposit (from Delaware Gazette) (6-3/14)

BUTMAN, Elizabeth, 46, wf of John, d 9/8/26 in Albany (6-9/12)

BUTRICK, G.H.G. m 1/7/42 Emily Granger in Vernon; Rev. Robinson (all of Vernon) (1-1/11)

BUTTERFIELD, John Lennebacker, infant son (age not given) of T.F. and C/A. Butterfield, d 8/21/50 in Utica (1-8/28)

BUTTRICK, Maria L. - see SPALDING, Alexander

BUTTS, Amy (Mrs.), 86, mother of Deacon Daniel, d 11/11/48 in Rome (one of the earliest settlers of Rome and among the first members of the Congregational Church - she was the only survivor of the original 34 members of that church) (1-11/17)

BUTTS, Daniel m 3/3/41 Hannah Adams, both of Rome, in R.; Rev. Theodore Spencer of Utica (1-3/9)

BUTTS, Henry of Western m 10/31/48 Emily Welch, dau. of Deacon Elisha of Clifton Park, at C.P.; Rev. Israel Keach (1-11/9)

BUTTS, Sarah A. - see CARROLL, Charles

BYCE, Susan - see WILKIE, William

BYINGTON, John m 10/17/49 Mary Ann Harrison, both of Danbury, Conn., in Carmel, NY; William A. Dean, Esq. (10-10/24)

BYNAM, Jesse A. (Hon), member of Congress, m 3/12/35 Maria Funston, dau of late Oliver, Esq. of Virginia; Rev. O. Brown (6-4/6)

BYRON, Elizabeth (Mrs.), formerly of Sing Sing, d 10/2/38 at the home of her son in the state of Ohio (12-10/23)

CABLE, Daniel, about 30, d 2/28/42 at Annsville (11-3/1)

CABLES, Rebecca Ann, dau of Widow Eliza, d 9/19/42 (11-9/22)

CADMUS, James H., 25, d 10/3/41 in West Troy (5-10/20)

CADWELL, Nehemiah, 79, d (date not given) in Hartford, Conn. (7-6/20/10)

CADY, Charlotte, wf of Jay Cady, d 3/4/37 at Minaville, Montgomery County (after a protracted illness) (6-3/8)

CADY, Freeman of Newport m 10/3/42 Frances Humaston of Vienna in V.; Rev. Hodges (1-10/11)

CADY, Louisa M., 25, wf of N.S. esq. and dau of Hon. Sylvester Beecher (killed when her clothes caught in a thrashing machine at Lenox, Madison County 11/6/35) (a detailed account of the accident included here) (6-11/23)

CADY, Mary E. - see BAILEY, Aaron N.

CADY, Nabby, 53, wf of Sylvester & dau of Capt. Simon Adams late of Columbia, Herkimer Co, formerly of New Marlborough, MA, d 7/7/35, after illness of 14 years, at Chatham, Columbia Co. (6-7/15)

CADY, Zilpha - see HOUGHTON, James

CAGWIN, Kezas(?)., Esq., 77, d 6/24/50 in Verona (dropsy) (1-7/3)

CAHILL, Margaret Anna - see WADLEY, E.S.

CAHILL, Margaret Mary, 3, dau of Thomas, d 10/21/36 (funeral 10/23 from 94 Water St.) (6-10/22)

CAIN, Mary - see GREEN, Joseph E.

CALDWELL, Amanda - see COMSTOCK, David

CALDWELL, Harman (Mrs.) - see JENKINS, Elisha (Col.)

CALDWELL, James - see SMITH, Thomas S.

CALDWELL, Levi of Rome m (date not given) Rebecca Allen of Trenton in T.; Rev. Nichols (1-3/16/41)

CALDWELL, Louisa, 19, formerly of West Troy, d 11/6/49 "near Lowell" (5-11/21)

CALDWELL, Margaret A., 28, wf of Joseph W., Esq. and dau. of Joshua Read, d 4/29/49 in Canajoharie (4-5/3)

CALDWELL, Mary - see SMITH, Thomas S.

CALDWELL, Mary - see SMITH, Thomas S.

CALDWELL, Mr. - see SCOTT, Moses Y.

CALDWELL, William m 11/23/40 Catherine Heman in Little Falls; Rev. J.W. Olmstead (3-11/26)

CALDWELL, William M. (Lt.) - see JENKINS, Elisha (Col.)

CALELEY, Patrick, 31, d 9/19/35 in Albany (a native of Newry, County of Down, Ireland ("editors of newspapers in Philadelphia" are asked to insert this notice) (6-9/22)

CALHOUN, Julia J. - see GATES, Le Roy L.

CALHOUN, Maria, wf of the editor of the Owego Advertiser, formerly of Canajoharie, d 10/14/49 in Owego (4-10/25)

CALLAHAN, S.T., editor of the Village Herald, m 8/10/36 Margaret R. Halstead of York (PA?) at Prince Ann, MD; Rev. Talbot (6-8/15)

CALWELL, Helen Jane - see YATES, William

CAMACE(?), James m 10/5/41 Hannah French at her home on Smith Street in Newburgh; Rev. E.E. Griswold (all of Newburgh) (9-10/9)

CAMACK, John, formerly of Newburgh m 1/5/42 Nancy E. Garret of Richmond, Virginia at R.; Elder B. Taylor (9-1/22)

CAMMET(?), Hillesha(?), 81, widow of late Thomas, d 4/2/42 in Cortlandt (11-4/7)

CAMP, Alfred W., son of Henry of Middletown, CT m 6/21/36 Clariss L. Cram, dau of John of Stockbridge, MA; Rev. Isaac Williamson of Albany (6-6/25)

CAMP, Clarissa L., 18, wf of Alfred W., d "this morning" (6-7/14/36)

CAMP, Sophia - see DAY, Edgar E.

CAMPBELL, Abbott m 5/8/37 Emily M. DeFoe; Rev. C.P. Clarke (all of Albany) (6-5/10)

CAMPBELL, C.M. (Miss) - see ETHERIDGE, Thomas

CAMPBELL, Cornelia - see VAN OLINDA, Cornelius

CAMPBELL, Emma (Miss), about 28, late of Massachusetts and sister of Catharine C. who is wife of John Simmons, Jr., d 8/28/49 at the home of John Simmons, Jr. in Saugerties (see also CAMPBELL, Lucy Ann) (8-9/1)

CAMPBELL, Ethan - see BURRILL, Nelson

CAMPBELL, Hermanus m 11/3/36 Cecelia Martin, both of Watervliet; Rev. Holmes (6-11/8)

CAMPBELL, John m 10/9/38 Eliza Jane Mc Gill, both of West Troy, in W.T.; Rev. Day (5-10/17)

CAMPBELL, Judith H - see GRANT, Asahel, M.D.

CAMPBELL, Lucy Ann (Miss), about 35, sister of Caroline C., who is wf of John Simmons, Jr., d 8/30/49 at the home of John Simmons, Jr. in Saugerties (see also CAMPBELL, Emma) (8-9/1)

CAMPBELL, Lydia Ann, 6, dau. of Gaylord and Lydia, d 4/23/39 (scarlet fever) (3-5/30)

CAMPBELL, Margaret (Widow), 75, of Albany d 11/11/35 at home of her son, Robert M. Campbell, in West Suffield, CT (6-11/19)

CAMPBELL, Margaret S. - see GOURLAY, W.B.

CAMPBELL, Niel, Esq. of Howard, Upper Canada m (date not given) Flora Johnston, dau of Malcolm, Esq. of Deerfield, in Russia, Herkimer Co.; Rev. W. Phelps (6-7/10/35)

CAMPBELL, Robert, 72, a Rev. War soldier, d 7/12/36 at his home in Cuba (born in Cherry Valley) (escaped massacre there in Nov. 1778) (6-8/12)

CAMPBELL, Sarah, 19, eldest dau. of William, d 7/25/37 (funeral from her father's home, 9 North Ferry Street) (6-7/26)

CAMPBELL, Sophronia - see BURRILL, Nelson

CAMPBELL, Sylvia D. - see COWLES, John A.

CAMPBELL, Timothy I., 51, of Little Falls, d 11/20/42 in Frankfort (3-11/24)

CAMPBELL, William (Hon.) - see GRANT, Asahel, M.D.

CAMPBELL, William of Rensselaerville m 1/11/10 Mary Gray of Catskill; Rev. David Porter (7-1/17)

CANDE, Jesse B. m 12/30/46 Mary R. Filtch, both of Vienna, in Rome; Rev. Gillett (1-1/8/47)

CANDER, Rebecca (Mrs.), 29, d (date not given) at New Haven (7-6/20/10)

CANFIELD, John - see HOWE, Fanny C.

CANFIELD, Louisa Cornelia, 34, wf of Mahlon D. and sister of Governor Seward, d 1/4/39 in Atlantic County, NJ (12-1/15)

CANFIELD, William of Troy m 1/19/43 Lydia Eaton, dau. of T.B. Eaton, Esq. of Hamilton County, in Little Falls; Rev. D. Towner (3-2/2)

CANNON, Martha - see STEWART, Joram N.

CANTINE, Misses - see TREMPER, Gertrude

CAPEN, Catharine - see BERTRAND, Lewis

CAPRON, Henry - see JONES, Jane

CAPRON, Nelson m 11/17/41 Emily Youngs; Rev. J. Loveys; all of Little Falls (3-11/25)

CAPRON, Sarah E. - see HARPER, Robert

CAPRON, Seth (Dr.), 74, d 9/25/35 at Walden (born in RI, served in the Rev. War "among the favorites of Gen. Washington"; settled in Whitesboro,

NY...erected the first cotton factory in operation in NY; established the Oriskany Wooden Factory) (6-9/29)

CARD, Denison, Esq., editor of the Clyde Gazette m 10/10/37 Emily Brim of Seneca Falls at S.F.; Rev. M. Rowley (6-10/17)

CARD, Harriet A. - see BILL, Marcius

CARDY, Joseph m 12/25/49 Mrs. Eliza Walker, both of West Troy; Rev. T.W. Parsons (5-1/9/50)

CAREY, Gertrude M. - see ANDERSON, David

CAREY, Hannah M. - see SUTHERLAND, Daniel P.

CAREY, Hester A. - se WARFORD, Joseph

CAREY, Josiah W. of Albany m 3/23/35 Calista Ann Ward of Penfield, Munroe Co. at St. Luke's Church in Rochester; Rev. Allen (6-3/31)

CARGEL, Zalman m 11/4/39 Susan Cree of North Salem in Owenville (12-11/12)

CARHART, ---- (Mr.) of Greenwich, CT m 4/10/42 Mary Flewelling of Bedford in B.; D. Olmsted, Esq. (11-4/14)

CARHART, Helena - see WINEHOOP, Jacob

CARL, Ada - see YOUNG, Ezeriah

CARLE(?), William m 9/29/49 Matilda Rosa; Rev. N.H. Cornell (all of Saugerties) (8-10/6)

CARLE, G. - see CROWNER, R.R.

CARLILE, Huldah (Mrs.) - see CROLIUS, John

CARLING, Sarah - see ELTING, John H.

CARLISLE, Eliza, 28, wf of Henry and dau. of late John Marshall of Lower Canada, d 5/17/41 at Salisbury (survived by her husband and three small children) (3-6/10)

CARLISLE, Henry m 11/17/41 Catharine Hummel at Brocketts Bridge; Elder H. Carrier (3-11/25)

CARLL, Timothy m 1/6/35 Ruth Blydenburgh, dau of Isaac, Esq., at Smithtown, L.I., NY (6-1/17)

CARMAN, Eliza - see GIBBS, William

CARMICHAEL, Caroline - see HAGEMAN, Jacob

CARMICHAEL, James, Jr. d (date not given) (funeral at 3 o'clock from his father's home, 48 Franklin St.) (6-11/17/36)

CARMICHAEL, T.J. m 5/6/35 Harriet Ann Agate, only dau of Thomas; Rev. Nathaniel Prime (all of Sparta, Mount Pleasant) (11-5/19)

CARNOCHAN, Anna - see BETTNER, James E.

CARNOCHAN, John, Esq. - see BETTNER, James E.

CARNRIKE, A.K. m 3/18/47 Sarah E. Harrison, both of West Troy, in Troy; Rev. Waggoner (5-3/24)

CARNRIKE, Fanny, 29, wf of Andrew K., d 2/26/45 in West Troy (5-3/5)

CARNRIKE, George T., 5, son of Andrew K. and Fanny, d 5/6/42 in West Troy (5-5/11)

CARNRIKE, Lany, 47, wf of J.G., d 8/28/44 in West Troy (5-9/4)

CARNRIKE, Margaret Ann, 2, dau. of Andrew & Fanny, d 3/24/44 in West Troy (5-3/27)

CARNY, John of NYC m 6/16/39 Margaretta H. Miller, only dau of late Henry N. of Cheraw, SC; Rev. Cooly (11-6/18)

CAROW, Eliza, 54, wf of Isaac, d 5/9/37 in NYC (6-5/11)

CAROW, Isaac, Esq. - see THOMAS, James P.

CAROW, Mary - see THOMAS, James P.

CARPENTER, A. (male) - see PENDILL, Morris M.

CARPENTER, Abraham m 9/28/42 Mrs. Tamer Frost, both of Somers, in Somers (11-9/29)

CARPENTER, Amanda Malvina - see SHERWOOD, James M.

CARPENTER, Benjamin, 62, d 12/17/38 in Somers (a member of the Friends Society) (12-12/25)

CARPENTER, C. of Somers m 1/18/40 Jane Waterbury on NYC in NYC; Rev. George Benedict (12-1/28)

CARPENTER, Charles S., 4, son of Henry and Mary A., d 2/21/45 in Rome (scarlet fever) (see CARPENTER, J. Wesley) (1-2/25)

CARPENTER, Chester of Hudson m 5/26/36 Jerusha Hall of Albany in A.; Rev. John N. Campbell (6-5/30)

CARPENTER, Deborah - see WASHBURN, Morgan

CARPENTER, Edward of Harrison m 2/27/42 Armona P. Smith of White Plains in Clayton, Ill.; Rev. Mc Coy (11-3/8)

CARPENTER, Eliza - see MOREY, William

CARPENTER, Hazel - see VARNEY, M.G. (Col.)

CARPENTER, Henry m 8/20/35 Elvira Hubbard; Rev. J.N. Campbell (all of Albany) (6-8/24)

CARPENTER, J. Wesley, 2, son of Henry S. and Mary A., d 2/15/45 in Rome (scarlet fever) (see CARPENTER, Charles S.) (1-2/25)

CARPENTER, Jane Eliza - see TERRY, Daniel

CARPENTER, Jane R. - see VARNEY, M.G. (Col.)

CARPENTER, Jane, 7, dau. of Stephen F., d 5/26/39 (3-6/27)

CARPENTER, Job, m 11/3/39 Maria Underhill in Sing Sing; Charles Yoe, Esq. (all of Sing Sing) (12-11/12)

CARPENTER, John of Fultonville m 2/20/48 Catharine Peeler of Stone Arabia at S.A.; Rev. A. Rumpf (4-3/2)

CARPENTER, Lucretia - see SMITH, Chauncey

CARPENTER, Mary Ann - see SMITH, Leonard

CARPENTER, Mary Ann - see SMITH, Leonard

CARPENTER, mary E. - see CONKLIN, Henry

CARPENTER, Mary M. - see PENDILL, Morris M.

CARPENTER, Matilda - see ROMER, John

CARPENTER, Nathaniel m 5/9/36 Margaret E. Lamphere of Madison County at Schenectady; Rev. Seymour (6-5/14)

CARPENTER, Robert m 3/19/39 Eliza Allen at the Chappequa Friends Meeting House; Joseph Hyatt, Esq. (12-3/26)

CARPENTER, Sarah - see CORNWELL, Charles H.

CARPENTER, Stephen F. m 5/29/39 Rebecca Bushnell at Fairfield; Rev. William Baker (3-6/13)

CARPENTER, Stephen F., m 5/29/39 Rebecca Harris; Rev. William Baker (3-6/27)

CARPENTER, Willet m 5/18/39 Sarah Chatterton at Greenburgh; Benson Ferris, Esq. (12-5/28)

CARPENTER, William F. of Mamoroneck m 3/25/40 Mary Elizabeth Baker of new Rochelle in N.R.; Rev. Abbot (12-3/31)

CARPENTER, William of Fairfield m (date not given) Delilah Spafford, dau. of

John D., Esq. of Manheim, in Salisbury; Rev. L.C. Rogers (3-4/14/36)

CARR, Denny(?) (Hon.), 63, one of the judges of the Court of Appeals, d (date not given) at his home near Richmond, Virginia (6-1/24/37)

CARR, Egbert E., Esq., printer of Rome m 4/6/49 Cornelia A. Loomis of Walesville in W.; Rev. F.H. Stanton (1-4/11)

CARR, Georgianna, 6, a twin child of Horatio M. and Harriet H., d 8/19/43 in NYC (5-9/6)

CARR, Mary - see LAWRENCE, Joseph

CARR, Sarah - see POTTER, Noah

CARRINGTON, Edward of firm of Goodwin, Carrington & Co., of NYC, m 8/4/35 Sarah Ann Terry, dau of Eliphalet, Esq., of Hartford City, at H.C.; Rev. H. Bushnell (6-8/10)

CARRINGTON, T. of Richmond m 12/13/48 Anna E. Whiteall, dau. of Benjamin G., formerly of Rome, NY, at White Plains, Henrico County, Virginia; Rev. Kepler (see RICE, M.M.) (1-4/11/49)

CARRIQUE, P. Dean, publisher and proprietor of the Hudson Gazette, m 5/12/36 Elizabeth Coleman, both of Hudson, at H.; Rev. William Whittaker (6-5/28)

CARROLL, ----, relict of late Anthony, d (date not given) in NYC (6-8/22/16)

CARROLL, A.B., 4, d 5/12/48 in Rome (scarlet fever) (parents names not mentioned) (1-5/19)

CARROLL, Arlando(?) of Concord, NH m 10/19/36 Catharine Quackenbush, dau of John N. of Albany; Rev. Vermilye (6-10/28)

CARROLL, Charles, Esq., of New London m 8/17/48 Sarah A. Butts, dau. of Daniel, Esq., of Rome, in R.; Rev. William E. Knox (1-8/25)

CARROLL, Louisa A. - see HALL, William C.

CARROLL, Lucyette - see NORTHRUP, Solomon J.

CARROLL, Phebe Calista - see THAYER, Stephen Van Rensselaer

CARRYL, Lorenzo, merchant, m 9/7/42 Miss L.W. Burrill, both of Salisbury, in S.; Rev. Dr. Chassel (3-9/8)

CARSON, Jane - see LOWERY, John

CARSON, John m 5/4/37 Sarah Caswell; Rev. C.P. Clark (all of Albany) (6-5/5)

CARSON, William C. of Albany m 11/30/36 Elizabeth A.W. Gardner dau of late Major Thomas Gardner of Louisa, Virginia, at L.; Rev. Fife (6-12/22)

CARTER, A. Jane - see PERRY, Stuart

CARTER, Henry M. m 8/10/50 Salome Goger (sic), both of Clayville in C.; Rev. John Waugh (1-8/14)

CARTER, Jane - see WOOD, Ancel

CARTER, Joseph A. of firm of Dow, Carter & Co. of Albany m 2/7/37 Esther K. Smith of Ogdensburg, in Buffalo; Rev. Church (6-2/16)

CARTER, Theophilus, 73, d 12/2/26 (funeral 12/5 at 3 o'clock from his late home at 94 North Pearl Street) (6-12/5)

CARVER, Richard m 9/23/49 Jane A. Van Allen, both of Danube, at the Hotel of Mr. Pier; Rev. J.B.Sax (4-9/27)

CARVER, Stephen W. m 4/8/39 Julietta Ballad, dau. of Zeba Ballad, in Carmel; Rev. Warren (all of Carmel) (12-5/14)

CARY, Abigail, 30, wf of John d 8/18/39 in New Castle. (also 8/19, an infant child of John (not named) died) (12-8/27)

CARY, John - see JOHNSON, Louise

CARY, John m 2/7/42 Margaret Maria Yearlsey, eldest dau. of Jonas, Esq., in Watervliet; Rev. Dr. Covel (5-3/2)

CARY, Sarah E. - see MACBETH, John

CASE, Anna E. - see BILL, Chauncey

CASE, Catharine, 78, wf of Elijah, Senior, a long resident of Little Falls, d 7/24/39 in German Flats while on a visit there (3-8/1)

CASE, Charlotte - see VAN DYKE, Henry

CASE, Eugene S., 1, son of Dr. J.H. Case, d 12/14/37 at Guilderland (funeral 12/16)(6-12/16)

CASE, Everett m 6/8/47 Eva Wilson, dau. of E. Wilson; Rev. Henry Emmons (all of Verona) (1-7/2)

CASE, Evert, 5, only son of Chauncey C. and Anna E., d 2/9/47 in Vernon village (scarlet fever) (1-2/12)

CASE, Henry R. m 6/30/44 Eliza N. Snell, both of Verona, in Hampton; Rev. F.A. Spencer (1-7/9)

CASE, Mary - see HAYNES, William B.

CASE, Newel M. m 10/13/50 Elizabeth Slackt(sic), both of Port Schuyler, in West Troy; Rev. O.H. Gregory (5-10/23)

CASEY, Dennis of Mobile, merchant, m 10/11/37 Sarah E. Day, dau. of late Russel Day, Esq. of Catskill, in C.; Rev. Joseph F. Phillips (6-10/24)

CASHDOLLAR, William m 12/25/47 Eliza Jane Grant, both of Albany, at the Exchange Hotel in West Troy; Rev. J.C. Burroughs (5-12/29)

CASLER, Amanda - see DE LONG, Cornelius C.

CASLER, Elizabeth - see PERRY, Henry

CASLER, Isaac of Little Falls m 5/1/39 Catharine Kilts in Herkimer; Rev. L.P. Badget (3-5/9)

CASLER, Jacob, 95, d (date not given) in German Flats (2-1/25/10)

CASLER, John H. of Little Falls m 6/4/43 Mary Covill of Danube in D.; George Petrie, Esq. (3-6/8)

CASLER, John m (date not given) Polly Evertson at German Flats (2-2/1/10)

CASLER, John m 10/13/38 Catharine Bellinger, dau. of Peter F., in German Flats; M. Benedict, Esq. (3-11/8)

CASLER, Lavinia - see HUNGERFORD, John F.

CASLER, Levi m 7/18/36 Maria Mc Lensley in Little Falls; Rev. Morris (3-7/21)

CASLER, Margaret, 23, dau. of Jacob, d 7/13/37 in Little Falls (3-7/20)

CASLER, Nancy - see BELLINGER, P.S.

CASLER, Nicholas R. of Little Falls m 7/9/48 Catharine Schuyler of Danube in Fort Plain; James W. Hamilton (4-7/13)

CASLER, Peter B. - see BELLINGER, P.S.

CASLER, Peter P. m 12/26/41 Elmira Folts; Rev. Loveys (all of Little Falls) (3-1/6/42)

CASLER, Rachel, nearly 72, relict of late Jacob, d 5/10/37 in Little Falls (3-6/1)

CASLER, Sabina - see HEATH, Henry Mc Lean

CASLER, Solomon of Little Falls m (date not given) Lovina Ricker of German Flats in Herkimer (3-9/5/39)

CASSIDY, Patrick, 47, d 7/22/35 at his farm near Albany (emigrated in his infancy with his parents from Cavan County, Ireland and arrived in Albany where he remained a lifetime. Was vice president of the Hibernian Provident Society. (a long obitiary is included) funeral from his late home corner

Maiden Lane and Chapel St. (6-7/24)

CASTLE, Sophia P. - see KNOWER, Benjamin

CASWELL, Edwin m 11/24/42 Maria Eaton, dau. of Parley Eaton, in Herkimer; Rev. G.C. Woodruff (all of Little Falls) (3-12/1)

CASWELL, George of Peekskill m 1/26/42 Alice Quick in North Salem; Rev. Fuller (11-2/8)

CASWELL, Jane - see PAVEY, A.A.

CASWELL, Sarah - see CARSON, John

CASWELL, William m 4/30/36 Harriet Harter in Hermiker; Rev. Wheeler (all of Herkimer) (3-5/5)

CATES, Margaret - see CROOKE, Philip S.

CATLIN, Charles T. m 3/27/42 Jane E. Morrison, both of West Troy, in W.T.; Rev. D. Starks (5-3/30)

CATLIN, Edwin R. of West Troy m Lucine Johnson of Auriesville, Montgomery Co., in A.; Rev. Hunt (5-8/11)

CATLIN, Marcus, 43, Professor of Mathematics at Hamilton College, d 10/14/49 at his home near Clinton (1-10/17)

CATLIN, Polly, 73, relict of Putnam Catlin, Esq. of Great Bend, Penn. and mother of Mr. Catlin, the artist now in England, d 7/15/44 at the home of her son-in-law, A. Hartshorn, in Delta, NY (1-7/16)

CATLIN, Samuel, Esq. of Wetrempke, Alabama m 12/22/36 Lucy M. Ryan of Troy, NY at Mount Pleasant, Newton County, Georgia; Rev. Bishop Andrew (6-1/25)

CATLIN, Theodosia Amanda, 25(?), d 1/2/45 in Pensacola, Florida (1-1/21)

CATON, John Dean of Chicago, Ill. m 7/28/35 Laura Sherrill, dau of Jacob, Esq., of New Hartford, Oneida Co., at New Hartford; Rev. Seares (6-8/6)

CATY(?), Elisha W. of Clifton park m 12/4/44 Esther Van Loon of West Troy in W.T.; Rev. John Frazer (5-12/11)

CAUDER, Peter m 8/2/37 Maria Maher, dau. of James; Rev. Kelly (all of Albany) (6-8/23)

CAULKINS, Abby, 19, wf of John L. and eldest dau. of C.L. Tompkins of Cohoes, d 5/24/42 in West Troy (survived by her husband and an infant child) (5-6/1)

CAULKINS, Adelia, 17, wf of John L. and eldest dau. of E. and C. Powell, d 4/1/40 in West Troy at the home of her father (5-4/8)

CAULKINS, Harriet (Miss), 16, d 11/22/37 in West Troy (5-11/29)

CAULKINS, John L. m 11/20/38 Adelia Powel, both of West Troy, in W.T.; Rev. Raymond (5-12/5)

CAULKINS, Russell (Dr.) of Little Falls m 6/25/39 Jane Helen Whitbeck, dau. of Peter of Avon, in A.; Rev. E. Marsh (3-7/11)

CAULKINS, Samuel N. of West Troy m 5/26/46 Julia Ann Marsh of Canastota in C.; Rev. Swan (5-5/27)

CAVIS, Desire - see JENNINGS, Royal

CERWIN, Elisha - see BURGY, Emily

CHABERT, Julius Xavier, M.D., of NYC m 6/8/37 Susannah Elizabeth Rapelje (relict of George Rapelje, Esq and only surviving dau. of late Bishop Provost) in NYC; Rev. James Coghlan (6-6/13)

CHADWAYNE, Jacob, about 40, d 9/28/39 at his home in New Castle (painful illness of 3 weeks) ("his late father-in-law" Stephen Conklin is mentioned.)

(survived by his wife and six children) (12-10/1)

CHAFY, Olive Maria - see BACHELDOR, Chester

CHAMBERLAIN, Merivale - see MANCHESTER, Stephen

CHAMBERLAIN, William m 10/16/49 Mary E. Bailey, both of Cherry Valley at Ames; Rev. C.H. Harvey (4-11/1)

CHAMBERLIN, Laura - see KING, Storrs L.

CHAMPLIN, Lovina E. - see THOMAS, Gilbert

CHANDLER, Anna H. (Mrs.) - see SMITH, Luke D.

CHANDLER, E.B. (Mrs.) - see EVERDELL, Robert (Rev.)

CHANDLER, Reuben, 18, d (date not given) at Homer (6-9/26/26)

CHANEY, Margarette - see KARR, S. Edward

CHAPIN, E.G. of Little Falls m 2/20/40 Cynthia E. Bucklin, dau. of late John, Jr. of Fairfield, in F.; Rev. C.I. Dunning (3-2/27)

CHAPIN, George S. m 4/14/41 Maria L. Garlock in Vernon; Elder D. Robinson (1-5/11)

CHAPIN, Josiah S. of Kingston, Upper Canada m 12/2/41 Amer Tompkins of Carmel at C.; Rev. Daniel Brown of Peekskill (11-12/6)

CHAPIN, Seth, 36, merchant, of firm of S. & C. Chapin, d (date not given) in Buffalo (6-11/21/26)

CHAPLIN, Louisa R. - see LAWRENCE, Windsor

CHAPMAN, Augustus m 1/9/42 Ann Matilda Ellis; Rev. Daniel D. Tompkins (11-2/15)

CHAPMAN, Augustus of Putnam Valley m 2/10/42 Mrs. Ann Matilda Ellis in Phillipstown; Rev. D.D. Tompkins (11-2/15)

CHAPMAN, Charles L., 35, son of William, d 9/10/37 (funeral 9/11 at the junction of the Mohawk and Hudson Railroad) (carriages available for transportation from 115 State Street) (6-9/11)

CHAPMAN, Elmira - see KEELER, J.B.

CHAPMAN, Frances A. - see WILLIAMS, H.C. (Major)

CHAPMAN, Hiram K. (Dr.), 31, d 4/27/42 in Newburgh (illness of about 24 hours) (9-4/30)

CHAPMAN, Jonas, Esq., 66, d 1/6/36 in Knox (6-1/21)

CHAPMAN, Lamira - see PERRY, Erastus B.

CHAPMAN, R.B. - see BACKUS, Elisha (Col.)

CHAPNEY, Henry C. of Rome m 3/22/49 Almira Reese of Western in Utica; Rev. E. Francis (1-3/28)

CHARLES, George - see DOWNING, James P.

CHARLES, George m 10/4/26 Mary Ann Nehemiah, both of Albany; Rev. Howard (6-10/10)

CHARLES, Sarah Ann - see DOWNING, James P.

CHASE, Beverly m 10/28/39 Mary Ann Green, both of Little Falls in L.F.; Rev. J.W. Comstead(?) (3-10/31)

CHASE, Cylinda - see GOODELL, George W.

CHASE, H.G., Esq., of Boston m 12/7/41 Elizabeth A. Schuyler, dau. of Capt. Peter of Boonville, in B.; Rev. Dr. Hunter (1-12/21)

CHASE, Henry I., son of Rt. Rev. Bishop Chase, m 11/7/41 in the chapel of Jubilee College, Illinois, Susan E. Ingraham, dau of Henry E., Esq.; Rev. Samuel Chase (11-12/7)

CHASE, Jacob - see CRANE, Jacob

CHASE, John D. m 1/12/39 Rebecca Peterson, both of Cortlandtown (ceremony at the house of Mr. John Peterson; Rev. Benjamin Curry of Shrub Oak, Yorktown (11-1/22)

CHASE, Nathan of Fly Creek m 10/3/49 Louisa Dinman of Newville at N.; Rev. J.S. (surname blurred) (4-10/18)

CHASE, Orlando P., 2, only son of Sylvanus G. and Mary Ann, formerly of Little Falls, d 5/16/42 in Albany (3-5/19)

CHASE, Sarah - see FAIRBANKS, William B.

CHASE, Stephen C. of Floyd m 3/17/42 Sarah Wiggins, dau. of Benjamin, Esq., of Rome, at R.; Rev. H.C. Vogell (1-3/22)

CHASE, Theron of Stratford m 4/5/39 Sally Demster of Ephratah in E.; Rev. Samuel Waters (3-4/25)

CHASSEL, David, Jr., 24, son of Rev. D. Chassel of Fairfield, d "recently" in NYC (hemorrhage of the lungs) (3-6/7/38)

CHASSELL, Catharine (Miss), 19, dau. of Rev. D. Chassell, d 9/6/36 in Fairfield (3-9/15)

CHASSELL, David (Rev.), principal of Fairfield Academy m 2/1/36 Eliza Griswold, dau. of William, Esq., at Fairfield; Rev. David Chassell (3-3/31)

CHATFIELD, Clinton of Fairfield m 2/12/40 Margaret White of Salisbury in S.; Rev. Loring (3-2/27)

CHATTERTON, Sarah - see CARPENTER, Willet

CHAUNCEY, Catharine M. (Miss), 22, only dau. of Commodore Isaac Chauncey, d 4/15/37 at Washington, D.C. (6-4/21)

CHAUNCEY, Charles - see WOOLSEY, William W.

CHAUNCEY, Sarah - see WOOLSEY, William W.

CHEETHAM, James, 38, editor and proprietor of the American Citizen and Republican Watchtower, d 9/19/10 in NYC (typhus fever) (survived by a wife, three sons and two daughters) (7-9/26/10)

CHEEVER, Harriet - see BIDELMAN, Robert

CHEEVER, Julia S.R., 13, youngest dau of Hon. S. Cheever of Albany, d. 8/13/35 (dropsey of the brain) (6-8/15)

CHELLIS, John C. m 9/12/47 Caroline Fields, both of Watervliet, in Troy; Rev. J.H. Walden (5-9/15)

CHENERY, Mary - see CROCKER, Franklin

CHENEY, Chester, 19, son of late William Cheney, Esq., of Newport, NH, d 3/19/35 at Matanzas (6-4/15)

CHENEY, Mary - see BALDWIN, John F.

CHENEY, Mary Jane - see GREELEY, Horace, Esq.

CHENEY, Mary Jane - see GREELY, Horace

CHERRY, Mary - see BALDWIN, John F.

CHESBRO, Huldah - see ROBINSON, George A.

CHESEBRO, Henry O. m 10/17/50 Frances A. Worden, dau. of Alvah, in St. John's Church, Canandaigua; Rev. Alfred Brach (all of Canandaigua) (1-10/23)

CHESEBROUGH, Lucia Louisa - see KEARNEY, Philip R.

CHESTER, Francis m 9/14/42 Chloe Luther in Little Falls; Rev. E.D. Towner (all of Little Falls) (3-9/15)

CHESTER, John (Col.), 60, a Revolutionary War officer who distinguished himself at the Battle of Bunker Hill, d (date not given) at Wethersfield, Conn. (2-11/30/09)

CHESTER, John m 6/14/37 Catharine Moreli, only dau. of Hon. William Moreli, in Detroit; Rt. Rev. Bishop Mc Croskey (all of Detroit) (6-6/23)

CHESTER, Joseph L. m (date not given) Catherine H. Hubbard, dau. of John, Esq., in NYC; Rev. Dr. Schroeder (all of NYC) (12-7/16)

CHEVALIER, Mary, 84, relict of late Peter Chevalier, merchant, of Albany, d 1/25/16 at Philadelphia (6-2/7)

CHEW, Elizabeth Anna, 23, wf of Anthony S., Esq. of NYC and dau of late John Van Vechten, formerly of Albany, d 9/5/35 at New Haven, CT (communicated) (6-9/9)

CHICHESTER, Elijah (Rev.) of Lansingburgh m 1/21/50 Mrs. Eddy of Waterford in W; Rev. Samuel Howe (5-1/30)

CHIDNEY, Lucy Ann - see TRUMBULL, Alonzo

CHILD, Elizabeth M., 5, dau. of Oliver and Edith S., d 2/12/37 at Le Rayesville, Jefferson County (dropsy on the brain) (6-2/21)

CHILD, John P., 2, son of Oliver and Edith S. of Le Rayville, Jefferson County, d 1/10/37 (consumption) (6-1/23)

CHILDS, David W., Esq., 45, of Utica, NY, d 7/27/26 in Pittsfield (6-8/15)

CHILDS, Jane S. - see GUITEAU, Hendrick N.

CHIPMAN, Catharine - see BENNETT, William C.

CHITTENDEN, Pamela - see BLODGET, Luther P.

CHITTENDON, A.H. m (date not given) Mary H. Risdon of Hopkinton In Lawrence, St. Lawrence County (6-5/4/36)

CHITTENDON, George W., M.D., of Westmoreland m 3/16/46 Charlotte A. Wellman of New York Mills at N.Y.M.; Rev. H. Colborn (1-4/21)

CHOLLAR(?), James, 63, d 4/20/47 in West Troy (funeral at home of his son, John B.) (5-4/28)

CHOLLAR, Caroline (Miss), 21, dau. of James, d/ 12/5/44 in Albany (5-4/16)

CHRISTIAN, John, 75, the blind Almanse(sic) seller m (date not given) Nelly Palmer, 64, both paupers ("a decent dinner was given by Mr Thornton, the overseer at the Poor House in Maryland") (6-6/16/26)

CHRISTIAN, Truman of NYC m 12/25/38 Catharine Wright of Sing Sing in S.S.; Rev. P. Van Deusen (12-1/1/39)

CHRISTIE, Ann, 66, 4/17/36 (funeral at 5 o'clock from 75 Green Street) (6-4/18)

CHRISTIE, Jane Angela - see KEEFER, Peter

CHRISTIE, Jane Angela - see KEEFER, Peter

CHRISTIE, Robert Andrew, Esq., 23, physician, only son of Robert, Esq. of Quebec, d 7/2/37 at the Quarantine establishment at Grosse Isle (6-7/11)

CHRISTIE, Samuel, 24, of Albany d (date not given) at Natchez, Mississippi (6-9/28)

CHRISTLER, Sylvester of Troy m 11/4/47 Elizabeth Stevens of West Troy; Rev. J.C. Burroughs (5-11/10)

CHRISTY, Margaret (Mrs.), about 77, d 4/24/43 in Manheim (3-4/27)

CHRYSTIE, Mary Ann - see CULVER, Lemuel

CHUBBUCK, Charles - see JUDSON, A. (Rev.)

CHUBBUCK, Emily - see JUDSON, A. (Rev.)

CHURCH, Jonathan, 96, d (date not given) at Granville, Mass. (7-5/10/09)

CHURCH, Luther m 2/16/42 Adelia Hitchcock in Utica; Rev. A.B. Grosh (1-2/22)

CHURCH, Maria - see STEADMAN, Willard

CHURCHILL, Albert W. of Little Falls m 9/5/39 Susan E. Browning, adopted dau.

of Joseph Rice of Salisbury, in S.; Rev. Dunning ("no wine was served as evidence of the march of temperance") (3-9/12)

CHURCHILL, Alida(?) (Mrs.), 51, formerly of Herkimer County, d 3/3/40 in Harmony, Chautauqua County (3-3/19)

CHURCHILL, Caroline - see WHIPPLE, Solomon

CHURCHILL, Emeline - see MC KINNEY, Erastus

CHURCHILL, George of Annsville m 5/10/46 Lucinda Monell of Rome; Rev. H. Mattison (1-5/12)

CHURCHILL, H.H. of Deerfield m 9/10/39 Cordelia Easterbrook of Manheim in Herkimer; Rev. Murphy (3-10/10)

CHURCHILL, Isaac P. of Manheim m 12/13/48 Mary Keller of Little Falls at Fort Plain; Rev. Dr. C.G. Mc Lean (4-12/21)

CHURCHILL, John, Jr. m 8/26/47 Louisa Rich at Alder Creek; Rev. Huntor (1-9/10)

CHURCHILL, Marlborough, formerly of the US Army, m 10/6/39 Elizabeth Louise Voris, only dau. of R.R. Voris, Esq., of Sing Sing, in St. Paul's Church; Rev. Dr. Creighton (12-10/8)

CHURCHILL, Nancy - see COLVIN, Harry D.

CHURCHILL, Roswell - see WHIPPLE, Solomon

CHURCHILL, Samuel H., 24, d 11/1/41 at New Windsor (9-11/13)

CHURCHILL, Sarah Ann - see FOX, Daniel C.

CHURTON, Mary - see WOOD, Gursham

CHURTON, Thomas, 58, d 7/17/46 in Vernon (1-7/21)

CINKLIN, Simeon, 80, d 6/11/50 in Van Hornesville (4-6/20)

CLAPP, Amasa of Lafayette m 6/12/48 Mary A. Hurley of NYC (both deaf mutes) in the chapel of the Deaf and Dumb Institution in NYC; Harvey P. Peet, President (4-6/29)

CLAPP, Delia - see HORTON, Stephen D.

CLAPP, Mrs. ----(?) E., 47, late consort of Philip, Esq., of Peekskill, d 10/4/42 (11-10/6)

CLAPP, Philip - see HORTON, Stephen D.

CLAPPER, Peter - see BROWER, John W.

CLAPSADDLE, Denas - see SPAULDING, Nathan

CLAPSADDLE, Denis, 67, d 1/10/42 in Columbia (3-3/17)

CLAPSADDLE, George, 15, youngest son of John, d 10/20/37 in Columbia (3-10/26)

CLAPSADDLE, Mary - see SPAULDING, Nathan

CLARE, Margaret - see CURRIN, William

CLARK, ---- (Mrs.), consort of Judge James Clark, governor-elect of Kentucky, d 8/27/36 in Winchester, KY (6-9/2)

CLARK, Aaron of Lewisboro m 12/22/41 Jane Fuller of Somers in S.; Rev. Jesse Hunt (11-12/28)

CLARK, Abijah H. m 11/6/39 Mary Ann Fisher, dau. of J. Fisher, Esq., in Mount Pleasant; Rev. Bullock(?) (12-11/26)

CLARK, Abner P. (Rev.), pastor of Presbyterian Church in Augusta, Oneida Co.; d 2/6/35 (6-3/26)

CLARK, Adam A. of Albany m 12/26/37 Almina Van Oestrand of Greenbush in G.; Rev. Dr. Welch (6-12/28)

CLARK, Adella, 14, dau of Joseph and Amy, d 10/18/38 at Pleasantville

(12-10/23)

CLARK, Allen of Steuben m 8/23/42 Mary Hill, dau. of David of Western, at W.;
Rev. Elisha Wheeler (1-8/30)

CLARK, Altie - see ST JOHN, Abijah

CLARK, Ambrose, 79, d 6/20/48 in Fort Plain (4-6/29)

CLARK, Andrew, 26, son of late Charles Clark of Catskill, d 7/13/35 in Toledo,
Mich. Territory (6-7/31)

CLARK, Asa S. m 10/3/49 Mary Moulton, dau. of Linus, Esq. of Floyd, in F.; H.C.
Vogell (1-10/24)

CLARK, Asahel ("supposed of the firm of Rawden, Wright, Hatch & Co. of NYC
and Rawdon, Clark & Co. of Albany") d 11/19/35 about 14 miles from
Columbus, Ohio. Died suddenly on the mail stage for Cleveland, reportedly
from "the rupture of a blood vessel" (1-11/28)

CLARK, Bernard, about 28, d 9/2/42 in Newburgh (9-9/3)

CLARK, Calvin (Rev.) of Westhampton, Mass. m 10/5/35 Evelina P. Greves, dau
of late Thomas Greves of Skaneateles at S.; Rev. Brace (6-10/17)

CLARK, Caroline - see HILL, Lafayette

CLARK, Caroline - see TELLER, De Witt C.

CLARK, Catharine M. - see ABBEY, Dorephus

CLARK, Catharine, 35, wf of Zephaniah, former proprietor of the Troy Budget, d
7/31/35 in Troy (6-8/6)

CLARK, Cecilia - see AYRES, Charles

CLARK, Daniel - see WHITNEY, William Wallace

CLARK, Darious, 90, d (date not given) at Colchester (7-3/8/09)

CLARK, Eliza F. - see TEN BROECK, H.W.B.

CLARK, George of Pleasant Valley m 3/25/48 Marianne Josephine Tarr(?) of West
Troy at the Baptist Church in W.T.; Rev. J.C. Burroughs (5-4/5)

CLARK, George R. of York, Montgomery County, m 11/19/38 Eunice Luceba
French of Watervliet in West Troy; J. Hart, Esq. (5-11/28)

CLARK, Jacob, 70, late of Peekskill d 11/13/43 in NYC (interred in the Methodist
Church yard in Peekskill) (11-11/21)

CLARK, James m 11/28/41 Lydia Riggs, both of Somers, in North Salem; Rev. S.J.
Hillyer (11-12/7)

CLARK, James of Bedford m 12/3/41 Nancy Northrup of Lewisboro; Rev. Dr.
Judson (11-12/21)

CLARK, John J., 33, d 7/24/47 in West Troy (5-8/4)

CLARK, John R. m 8/10/50 Nancy Sink in Rome; Rev. W.E. Knox (all of Rome)
(1-9/11)

CLARK, John, 97, d 2/22/36 at home of his son (not named) in Amsterdam (was a
major in the Rhode Island militia in the Rev. War)(in Feb. 1635 he had
living 6 ch., 61 grand ch., and 188 great grand ch. with one great-great
added since) (6-3/5)

CLARK, John, Esq., of Watertown m 10/18/41 Cornelia C. Romney, dau of Butler
Romney of Peekskill, at St. Peter's Chapel; Rev. Marcus, B.D., Rector
(11-10/19)

CLARK, L.D. (Dr.) m 11/24/44 Adeline N. Allen, dau. of Rev. E.W.R. Allen, at
the Methodist Church in Oriskany; Rev. E.W.R. Allen (1-12/3)

CLARK, Lewis m 11/5/46 Julia Ann Wheaton, both of West Troy, in Albany; Rev.
F.M. Hitchcock (5-11/18)

CLARK, Lois - see BARNES, Chauncey

CLARK, Luther, 35, attorney-at-law, d (date not given) in NYC (6-2/21/26)

CLARK, Major N. - see VAN CLEVE, Horatio

CLARK, Mariette - see TIBBITS, S.B.

CLARK, Martha A., 10 months, dau. of Oliver and Mehitable of West Troy, d
5/21/45 in Lansingburgh (5-5/28)

CLARK, Mary A. - see DIETZ, Adam

CLARK, Mary Ann - see PITTS, John M.

CLARK, Mary Garet - see WILSON, James, Esq.

CLARK, Mary, about 9, dau of Joseph, d 3/18/42 in Lewisburgh (11-3/21)

CLARK, Monmouth, 34, d 11/28/38 in Sing Sing (consumption) (12-12/4)

CLARK, Moses P. of firm of Clark, Weyman and Co. of NYC, d 9/12/37 at
Rahway, NJ (6-9/22)

CLARK, Mrs. - see FRANCISCO, James F.

CLARK, Nancy (Mrs.), 27, d 1/6/36 ("an affectionate wife and mother") (6-1/18)

CLARK, Orin P. m 9/6/38 Jane Ann Comstock in West Troy (5-9/19)

CLARK, Orselia M. - see TAVER, John W.

CLARK, Phila Marie - see HOWARD, R. Sumner

CLARK, Reymolds Greenman, about 6 months, d 4/22/39 in West Troy (5-4/24)

CLARK, Richard M. of NYC m 4/7/42 Sarah E. Felter, dau. of Theron, Esq. of
Newburgh, in N.; Rev. Charles A. Bleek (9-4/9)

CLARK, Robert (Hon.), 61, d 10/15/37 in Monroe, Michigan (born in Scotland).
Formerly a member of Congress from Delaware County, NY and prominent
member of the convention to review the Constitution of NY State. Served
as Register of the US Land Office when it was first established at Monroe
(from the Monroe Times) (6-11/4)

CLARK, S.S. of Italy (Yates County) m 12/27/38 Betsey Ann Nellis. eldest dau. of
Jacob of Fairfield, at Newport (3-1/3/39)

CLARK, Samuel H., editor of the Pennsylvania Intelligencer, Harrisburgh, PA m
6/1/37 Jane C. Van Valkenburgh, dau. of Jerorakim A. of Claverack, at C.;
Rev. M. Field (6-6/7)

CLARK, Sarah A. - see NICHOLS, Henry M.

CLARK, Sarah Ann - see PHILIPS, Ransom W.

CLARK, Sarah F. - see COLLINS, L.D.

CLARK, Sarah Jane - see WHEELER, David G.

CLARK, Sidney of Troy m 11/10/41 Eliza Vanderwerker of West Troy in W.T.;
Rev. John Cookson (5-11/17)

CLARK, Stephen (Hon.) canal commissioner of Rochester, m 7/22/45 Sarah L.
Phillips of Waterford in W.; Rev. Reuben Smith (5-8/13)

CLARK, Stephen of West Troy m 4/8/47 Eliza Ann Ives of Troy; Rev. Houghtaling
(5-4/14)

CLARK, Stephen, 67, of Buffalo, formerly of Newport, d (date not given) in
Onondaga County "while journeying to Herkimer to visit his friends"
(3-7/25/39)

CLARK, William H. of West Point m 9/9/41 Jane Emslie of Aberdeen, Scotland in
NYC; Rev. E. Everetts (11-9/28)

CLARK, William of Dansville m 6/23/49 Ann Eliza Fairfield of West Troy; Rev.
Houghtaling (5-6/27)

CLARK, William, about 70, d 4/24/42 in Newburgh (9-4/30)

CLARKE, Eliza - see RAYNER, Morris

CLARKE, George, Esq., 67, d 11/4/35 at his home at Hyde (Springfield) (died in 15 minutes - heart attack) ("He has left very large estates both in this country and in England") (from Cooperstown Free Journal) (6-11/10)

CLARKE, Isabella - see COCKRANE, Hubert

CLARKE, James Charles, about 45, d 11/16/41 in Newburgh (9-11/20)

CLARKE, William Jr., Esq., of firm of S. & M. Allen & Co. of New Orleans m 8/23/36 Anna P. Shellman, dau of Col. Shellman of Savannah, GA, in NYC at St. John's Chapel; Rev. Berrian (6-8/25)

CLARKSON, Ann - see LIVINGSTON, Robert

CLARKSON, John C. m (date not given) Louisa Lawrence Hicks, dau. of late Dr. John B. Hicks, at NYC; in St. Paul's Church; Right Rev. Bishop Hobart (6-5/4/16)

CLARKSON, Paul of Troy m 2/27/42 Mary Simmonds of West Troy in Troy; Rev. C.P. Clarke (5-3/9)

CLAY, Henry - see ERWIN, Ann B.

CLAY, John Randolph, Secretary of the American Legation m 4/2/35 Gibbs, Frances Ann Sophia, dau of Harry Leake Gibbs of St. Petersburg, at St. Petersburg, Russia (6-6/2)

CLAY, Mary Ann - see BOLTON, James

CLAY, Nathaniel m 8/4/49 Charlotte Ann Powers, both of Canastota, Oneida County; Rev. Houghtaling (5-8/8)

CLEAVELAND, J.M. m 2/20/41 Levina C. Bates, dau. of Eriemas Bates; Rev. William Green (all of Adams, Jefferson Co.) (1-3/9)

CLEAVELAND, Theodore N. of Constable, Franklin County, m 1/29/48 Emma Jane Sherman, dau. of S.H., Esq., of Floyd; H.C. Vogell (1-3/3)

CLEAVES, Mary (Miss), 54, formerly of New Windsor, d 10/19/41 in Elmira (9-11/6)

CLEETON, Samuel of England m 9/19/36 P----(?) Seeley of New Haven at St./ Paul's Chapel in New Haven (6-9/23)

CLELAND, Catharine, 93, relict of Samuel and mother of the Hon. Jonas Cleland, d 3/15/36 in Warren (survived her husband by about six months - they were originally from the neighborhood of Norwich, Conn. and among the earliest settlers in Warren (3-3/24)

CLEMENCE, Adaline - see WEST, Daniel D.

CLEMENS, John of Steuben m 2/18/47 Maria Cramer of Western; P.L. Fraser, Esq. (1-2/26)

CLEMENT, Jane - see STANTON, Egbert

CLEMENT, Mary - see FORT, John A.

CLEMENTS, William, 20, d 1/26/42 in Yorktown (11-2/8)

CLEMENTS, William, 89, d 12/20/41 in Yorktown (11-2/8/42)

CLEMONS, Lydia - see WILLIAMS, Warren B.

CLENCH(?), Benjamin V., 73, d 5/11/36 (funeral at 4 o'clock, 128 South Pearl St.) (6-5/12)

CLEVELAND, Elizabeth, 71, relict of Rev. Aaron Cleveland of Connecticut, d (date not given) in NYC (6-11/28/26)

CLEVELAND, James T. m 5/22/50 Mary Jane Stillman, both of Durhamville, at D.; Rev. James Nichols (1-6/19)

CLIDE, Sarah, 2 months, dau. of Robert, d 12/22/41 in Newburgh (9-12/25)

CLIFFORD, Susan - see MANSFIELD, Ralph

CLIFTON, Claiborn (Major), attorney at law and for many years a preacher in the Methodist Episcopal Church, d (date not given) in Fairfield District, South Carolina (6-10/27/26)

CLIMAKER, Augustus m 3/29/48 Harriet Cropsey, dau. of G., Esq., in West Troy; Rev. T.F. Wyckoff (5-4/5)

CLINTOD(sic), George, 15 months, only son of Charles A., d 8/19/35 in NYC (6-8/25)

CLINTON, Aaron m 4/16/40 Frances Juliet Hickock, dau. of Capt. James Hickock, in West Troy; Rev. O.H. Gregory (all of Troy) (5-4/22)

CLINTON, Benjamin, of firm of M.E. & B. Clinton, m 3/5/42 Catharine B. Buckbee in Peekskill; Rev. Daniel Brown (all of P.) (11-3/8)

CLINTON, De Witt (Governor) - see SPENCER, Catharine

CLINTON, DeWitt - see SPENCER, Ambrose

CLINTON, Dewitt (Col.) second son of late Gov. Clinton of NY, d (date not given) at Matansas, Col. (11-1/14/34)

CLINTON, Franklin (Lieut.) of US Navy, youngest son of late Governor Dewitt Clinton, d 2/19/42 (1-3/15)

CLINTON, Franklin (Liuet.) of US Navy, youngest son of late Gov. Clinton, d 2/19/42 in NYC (9-2/26)

CLINTON, Henry, 2, son of Alex., d 7/11/42 in Newburgh (9-7/16)

CLINTON, James (General) - see SPENCER, Catharine

CLINTON, James C. - see GUNSALES, Solomon

CLINTON, James m (date not given) Mary Ann Lockyear, both of Patterson, at Rhinebeck (6-5/22/16)

CLINTON, Maria DeWitt - see GOURLAY, Robert (Capt.)

CLINTON, Maria Gray, sister of Hon. J.G. Clinton, d "this morning" in Newburgh (funeral 5/22 from the house at the corner of Smith and First Streets) (9-5/21)

CLINTON, Morris m 10/21/41 Marietta Minor, dau of Truman Minor, all of Peekskill; Rev. Benedict of Patterson, Putnam County (11-10/26)

CLOSE, Margaret, wf of Ebenezer, formerly of North Salem, d 4/19/39 on Long Island (12-5/14)

CLOVES, Otis of Eaton, about 26, "but engaged upon the public works at Little Falls for some time past", d 9/21/37 (3-9/28)

CLOW, Harriet Maria, about 2, only dau. of Charles, d 5/20/39 at Frankfort (3-5/30)

CLOW, Jennett - see SHERMAN, Alonzo

CLUTE, Bersheba, about 86, d 9/13/47 in the town of Watervliet (she "was the oldest living inhabitant" of this town) (5-9/22)

CLUTE, Cornelia - see SUPPLY, F. Wilson

CLUTE, Derick, 79, d 1/29/39 in Watervliet (5-2/6)

CLUTE, Elizabeth, 57?, wf of Granton Clute, d 12/10/48 in Watervliet (5-12/20)

CLUTE, Ellen - see WILBUR, John W.

CLUTE, Jacob, 39, formerly of West Troy, d 2/13/45 in NYC (5-3/19)

CLUTE, Jemima - see BURST, John

CLUTE, Jonathan, 19 months, son of Peter, d 1/16/37 (funeral at 22 Beaver Street) (6-1/18)

COBB, ----- (indecipherable) (Mr.), 66, father of Dr. J.V. Cobb of Rome d 2/25/49 at his home in Rome (1-4/4)

COBB, Dean of firm of James & Cobb, merchants, of Troy m (date not given) Clarissa G. Lyman, dau of late Samuel, Esq., of Springfield, MA, at S.; Rev. Peabody (6-7/23/36)

COBB, J.P. m 6/14/49 Emma Osborne, dau. of George C., Esq., of Fredonia, in F.; Rev. Griswold (1-7/4)

COBB, Lucius J. m 10/19/42 Diantha P. Mills in Rome; Rev. C. (surname blurred) (all of Rome) (1-10/25)

COBB, Lucius J. of Blooming Grove, Orange County m 12/23/46 Catharine Scott of Hounsfield, Jefferson County, at H.; Rev. Lewis E. Shephard (1-1/1/47)

COBB, William S., 25, d 3/29/35 in Albany (funeral from his late home, 162 Washington Street, 2 o'clock, April 1) (6-3/31)

COBEE, Jane U. - see WITBECK, Isaac F.

COBOT, William H. of Massachusetts m 5/20/41 Amanda Traver(?) of NYC in Troy; Fayette Shipherd (5-5/26)

COBURN, Blansia - see DOUBLEDAY, Lewis M.

COCHRAN, Ellen - see LAWRENCE, Coonradt

COCHRANE, Hubert of NYC m 6/4/35 Isabella Clarke of Geneva in Trinity Church at G.; Rev. Dr. Mason, President of Geneva College (6-6/13)

COCKBURN, William m 2/15/49 Elizabeth Van Buren, dau. of Tobias, Esq., both of Kingston; Rev. J.C.F. Hoes (8-2/24)

CODMAN, Catherine - see HURD, John Russell

CODMAN, John - see HURD, John Russell

COE, David, 68, d 4/15/16 in Paris (6-5/4)

COE, Frances E. - see CONGER, Joseph O.

COE, John A. m 4/9/16 Johannah P. Musier, both of Albany; Rev. Dr. Niel (6-4/13)

COFFIN, ---- (Dr.) - see BERNARD, John Jr.

COFFIN, Alexander, Jr. m (date not given) Mrs. Polly Gelston in Hudson (6-5/22/16)

COFFIN, Alfred, son of Gorham Coffin, Esq., of Nantucket, MA m 3/1/41 Lellias Marcus in NYC by the Rev. Moses Marcus, B.D.; rector of St. Peter's Church in Peekskill (11-3/9)

COFFIN, George M., merchant of West Troy m 5/18/46 Sarah A. Harrington of East Troy at the home of Jacob S. Yost in Pottstown, Montgomery County, Penna; Rev. N.S.S. Beman, D.D. (5-5/27)

COFFIN, Miss J.S. - see BROWN, J.M. (Dr.)

COFFIN, Susan - see BERNARD, John, Jr.

COGSWELL, Moses P. - see VAN RENSSELAER, Cortlandt

COHEN(?), Sarah - see GRIFFIN, Nelson

COIT, W.L. of Montreal m Mary Ann Bissell, dau of late Josiah, of Rochester; Rev. Mack (6-9/15)

COLBURN, Walter, 56, d in the morning on 6/15/41 in Rome in consequence of being thrown from a horse (1-6/15)

COLBY, Moses, Esq., merchant of West Troy m 6/25/42 Sarah Westervelt of Bethlehem; Rev. Dr. Wyckoff (5-6/29)

COLDEN, Cadwallader D., Esq., formerly mayor of NYC d 2/7/34 at his seat in Jersey City (11-2/11)

COLDEN, Thomas, Esq., 72, grandson of late Governor Colden, d 3/27/26 at his seat in Coldenham (6-4/7)

COLDMAN, Joseph R., Esq, of Chatham m 8/12/35 Ann H. Coleman, eldest dau of Laban Coleman of Stanford, Dutchess Co., in NYC; Hon. Cornelius W. Laurence, Mayor of that city (6-8/17)

COLE, — (Rev.) of Tecumseh, Mich. m 9/18/39 Harriet Amelia Guion, dau. of James, Esq. of Bedford, at St. George's Church, NYC; Rev. Dr. Milnor (12-10/1)

COLE, A.J., 36, d 7/26/50 in Floyd (1-8/7)

COLE, A.W. of Rome m 4/23/50 Emeline R. Collins of Turin in T.; Rev. A.S. Wightman (1-5/8)

COLE, Catharine - see LIPPINCOTT, Thomas

COLE, David - see FAVELL, Daniel

COLE, Elizabeth - see SHEARMAN, Abraham

COLE, Elizabeth - see WARD, James A.

COLE, Elizabeth, 52, d 3/18/42 in Newburgh (funeral at home of her brother, Joseph Cole on Western Avenue) (9-3/19)

COLE, Eunice, 27, dau. of Chauncey and Eunice, d 5/31/50 at Lenox, Madison County (1-6/12)

COLE, Frederick W. m 6/20/36 Rebecca Fuller; Rev. Kirk (all of Albany) (6-6/23)

COLE, George H., 1 year, son of Eddy and Mary Ann, d 12/5/41 in West Troy (5-12/8)

COLE, Gideon P., M.D., of Potsdam m 1/29/38 Thirsa M. Gage, dau. of Sylvanus, Esq. of Fairfield; Rev. William Baker (3-2/1)

COLE, Gidron of Coonradt Settlement m 12/24/49 Ann M. Pierce of Rome; H.C. Vogell (1-1/9/50)

COLE, Hannah - see COLLINS, E.(?)

COLE, James P., 17, m 8/28/47 Laura J. Wheeler, 15, both of Nassau(?) at East Greenbush; Rev. Chase (5-9/8)

COLE, Jane - see NEWHOUSE, John

COLE, Jane - see SKINNER, W.H.

COLE, John L. (Lieut.) of Greenbush m (date not given) Elizabeth Phillips, dau of David, Esq., at Troy; Rev. Levings (6-11/6/35)

COLE, John, Esq., 75, a Rev. War soldier, d 8/13/37 in Wales, Erie County (6-8/22)

COLE, Lemuel m 7/4/47 Sarah West; Rev. H. Kendall (all of Verona) (1-7/9)

COLE, Levi m 10/6/49 Ann Hurst; Rev. T.F. Wyckoff (all of West Troy) (5-10/17)

COLE, Maria, wf of Elias, formerly of West Troy, NY d 3/2/46 in Hudson, Wisconsin Territory (5-3/25)

COLE, Mary - see FAVELL, Daniel

COLE, Mary - see LAWRENCE, John H.

COLE, Matilda J. - see KNOWLES, William

COLE, Spencer H. m 9/24/37 Eliza Liedew in Fairfield; Rev. W.H. Waggoner (3-9/28)

COLE, Spencer of Fairfield d 7/25/08 (was thrown from his wagon by his bolting horses "which dislocated his neck and he expired instantly" (2-8/9)

COLE, Susan - see DE PEW, George W

COLE, Thomas, 1st, 67, an early settler of Fairfield, d 8/6/36 in Fairfield (3-8/11)

COLE, Thomas, Esq., N.A. m 11/22/36 Maria Bartow, niece & ward of John Alexander Thomas, Esq., at Catskill; Rev. Joseph F. Phillips (6-11/26)

COLE, Catherine L. - see BUCKLIN, Wesley

COLE, William P. of Hurley m 10/10/49 Margaret B. Oliver of Marbletown in M.; Rev. C.I. Van Dyck (8-10/20)

COLEGROVE, Betsey - see BLOODGOOD, Gage

COLEMAN, A.H. of Whitestown m 6/5/42 Mrs. Caroline B. Jones of Little Falls in the Methodist Episcopal Church in L.F.; Rev. Loveys (3-6/9)

COLEMAN, Ann H. - see COLDMAN, Joseph

COLEMAN, Catherine K wf of Dr. A. Colman and dau of late Col. Rochester, d 4/7/35 in Rochester (comsumption) (6-4/14)

COLEMAN, Elizabeth - see CARRIQUE, P. Dean

COLEMAN, Elizabeth, about 70, widow of John, d 12/29/42 in Newburgh (9-12/31)

COLEMAN, John m 3/1/42 Martha Coleman in Newburgh; Rev. Young (all of Newburgh) (9-3/5)

COLEMAN, Martha - see COLEMAN, John

COLES, Louisa E. - see ROGERS, James H., M.D.

COLES, Sarah (Widow), 92, d (date not given) at Wilton (7-6/13/10)

COLEY, Huldah - see SEXTON, Frederick

COLFAX, Ebenezer of New Orleans m 3/2/46 Helen Louisa Sherman, formerly of Rome, NY, at New Orleans; Rev. Dr. Scott (1-3/31)

COLLARD, Jane - see BEYEA, Reuben

COLLENDER, John, d (date not given) at New Orleans (6-5/15/16)

COLLIER, Ann - see GOULD, Calvin

COLLIER, Frances - see RUGG, Joseph K.

COLLIER, J.A. Hon. - see RUGG, Frances

COLLINGS, Eleanor, 33, wf of Isaac, d 5/19/39 in West Troy (5-5/22)

COLLINS, ---- and ----, 10 and 9, "sons of Mr. Collins and Mrs. Sabra Hoyt" drowned at Grafton, NH. The parents of these youths within a few years have lost their only dwelling house and contents by fire, two promising sons after a few hours sickness, and two sons by drowning (6-8/15)

COLLINS, Alfred, Esq. of Albany, d 2/28/26 at Fort Howard, Green Bay, Michigan Territory (survived by his wife and children - not named) (6-5/30)

COLLINS, Caroline - see TORREY, Joseph W.

COLLINS, Charles - see TORREY, Joseph W.

COLLINS, Charles (Gen.) - see PRINCE, William

COLLINS, Charlotte Goodwin - see PRINCE, William

COLLINS, Clarissa G. - see WHIPPLE, Allen

COLLINS, E.(?) m 11/16/48 Hannah Cole, both of West Troy in W.T.; Rev. Seymour (5-12/6)

COLLINS, Edward, 21, eldest son of Hon. Ela Collins, d 11/6/35 in Lowville (consumption) (from the Lewis Republican) (6-11/16)

COLLINS, Emeline R. - see COLE, A.W.

COLLINS, L.D. m 1/13/48 Sarah F. Clark, both of West Troy, in W.T.; Rev. J.C. Burroughs (5-1/19)

COLLINS, Martha - see CRANDALL, Edward

COLLINS, Mary (Mrs.), 86, d 10/19/44 at Westmoreland (1-10/29)

COLLINS, Mary K., 21, wf of Daniel C., d 12/3/41 (consumption) (3-12/9)

COLLINS, Mary M. - see SWEET, Orlando J.

COLLINS, Sarah A. - see JUDSON, R.W.

COLLINS, Sarah Frances, 20, wf of Lorenzo D., d 12/10/48 in West Troy (5-12/13)

COLLIT, Joshua S. Feltus, 1, son of Dr. John Collit, d 4/21/41 at Yorktown (dropsey of the brain) (11-4/27)

COLLYER, William of Sing Sing m 10/7/39 Josephine G. Sanford of NYC; Rev. Dr. Bayard (12-10/22)

COLLYER, William, 61, father of Mrs. John Meacham of Albany, d (date not given) at Hartford, Conn. (6-1/6/16)

COLMITZ, George m 12/3/49 Margaret Stouse(?); John P. Foland, Esq. (all of Saugerties) (8-12/8)

COLT, John, Esq. of Pittsfield, Mass. m (date not given) Eliza Beach in Newark (6-5/22/16)

COLVAY, Margaret, 38, wf of James, d 3/27/49 at Rondout (8-4/14)

COLVER, John (Rev.), 72, d at his home in North East 7/23/35 (for 42 years a minister in the Methodist Episcopal Church) (6-8/6)

COLVIN, Andrew J. of Albany m 11/3/36 Rosina Matilda Alling, dau of P. Alling, Esq., of Newark, NJ, at N.; Rev. Henderson (6-11/8)

COLVIN, Harry D. m 2/3/37 Nancy Churchill, both of Little Falls, in L.F.; Rev. H.S. Attwater (3-2/9)

COLVIN, Henry, 22, son of James d 8/4/36 in Albany (6-8/8)

COLWELL, Margaret - see OLIVER, James

COLYER, Augusta - see BEYES, Wright M.

COLYER, Mary Jane - see ANTHONY, Jackson

COMMARY, Julia Elma, 1, dau. of Prudent and Julia A., d 8/25/45 in West Troy (5-8/27)

COMSTOCK, David m 6/30/41 Amanda Caldwell; Rev. I.L. Hunt (all of Rome) (1-7/6)

COMSTOCK, Edwin T. m 10/20/41 Sophia Huntoon in Newburgh; Rev. George Phinpen (9-10/23)

COMSTOCK, Henry m 10/16/40 Julia Pullman, dau. of E.C. Pullman, in Norway, NY; I. Comstock, Esq. (all of Norway) (3-9/24)

COMSTOCK, Jane Ann - see CLARK, Orin P.

COMSTOCK, Laury - see BALLARD, John

COMSTOCK, Luther, 22, d 10/7/41 at the home of his father in New Windsor (9-10/16)

COMSTOCK, Luther, 23, d 10/8/41 at New Windsor (9-10/9)

COMSTOCK, Permilia - see HINKLEY, Charles

COMSTOCK, Sophia, 21, wf of Edwin T., d 10/8/42 in Newburgh (9-10/22)

COMSTOCK, Waldo, Esq. of Fort Huron, Mich. m 11/10/49 W. Ann Brainard of Oriskany, NY at O.; Rev. E.C. Frischett (1-12/5)

CONANT, Daniel, 33, d 8/14/36 in Albany (6-8/16)

CONDICT, Lewis - see HALL, M.M.

CONDUKES, William of Buffalo m 6/27/37 Ann Eliza Dodge of Albany in A.; Rev. Campbell (6-6/29)

CONE, Bathsheba, 66, wf of Warren Cone, d 8/6/42 in Rome (1-8/9)

CONE, Betsey, 37, wf of Oliver, formerly of Leyden, Lewis County, d 4/22/41 in Verona (1-4/27)

CONE, John, 35, d 5/17/09 at Hebron, Conn. (7-5/31)

CONES(?), Evaline - see STANLEY, Matthew

CONEY, Joseph m 2/20/41 Eliza Tompkins of Putnam Valley; Rev. D.D.

Tompkins (11-2/23)

CONEY, Mary F. - see SHOLL, William N.

CONGDEN, Almira C., 21, wf of Nicholas S. and dau. of Charles Griffing of Little Falls, d 8/31/37 at Seneca Falls (a brief illness) (3-9/14)

CONGDON, Nathaniel S. m "lately at Seneca Falls" Almira C. Griffing, late of Little Falls (3-4/14/36)

CONGDON, Olivia (Mrs.) - see SMITH, Isaac S.

CONGER, James E., 24, formerly of West Troy, son of late Stephen M., Esq., of Newark, NJ, d 10/6/41 at Newark, NJ (5-10/20)

CONGER, Joseph O., formerly of West Troy, m 7/31/44 Frances E. Coe of Madison, Conn. in New Haven, Conn.; Rev. T.C. Teasdale (5-8/21)

CONGER, Samuel m 5/18/43 Almira Temple, both of West Troy, in Troy; Rev. O.H. Gregory (5-5/31)

CONINE, Mary, 86, relict of Peter, Jr. (dau. of Sybrant G. Van Schaick and sister of Col. Goshen Van Schaick, deceased, of the City of Albany) d 3/24/35 at Coxsackie at the home of her son-in-law, John L. Bronk, Esq. (6-3/31)

CONKEY, Frances M., 3 years, (parents' names not given) d 3/19/50 in Rome (scarlet fever) (1-3/27)

CONKEY, Mary E., 1, dau. of Charles G. and Angeline, d 3/11/50 in Rome (1-3/13)

CONKLIN, Annie - see MC CORD, David

CONKLIN, Derrick, about 50, d 7/17/41 in Peekskill (11-7/20)

CONKLIN, Drake, Esq., 69, d 2/10/39 in Yorktown (for many years was justice of the peace in Yorktown) (11-2/12)

CONKLIN, Drake, Esq., 69, d 2/10/39 in Yorktown (lived in Yorktown many years and was justice of the peace there for many years) (12-2/19)

CONKLIN, Hannah - see BOUTEN, Gilbert

CONKLIN, Henry m 7/12/49 Mary E. Carpenter in Milton; Rev. Hall (all of Milton) (8-8/25)

CONKLIN, J. - see PRATT, E.A.

CONKLIN, Jane, wf of Isaac of Peekskill, d 11/27/43 (11-11/28)

CONKLIN, John W., 24, son of late Gilbert, d 9/13/43 (11-9/19)

CONKLIN, John, about 60, a wealthy farmer, d 1/14/34 at his home in Yorktown (11-1/21)

CONKLIN, Jonas, 33, formerly of Buel, NY, d 1/21/49 in NYC (4-1/25)

CONKLIN, Margaret - see TUTTLE, Jacob

CONKLIN, Mary - see SLOAT, Daniel

CONKLIN, Mary J. - see RYDER, Jesse

CONKLIN, Mary, 57, wf of Eli, d (date not given) in NYC (6-8/22/26)

CONKLIN, Nancy - see FARQUHARMON, William J.

CONKLIN, Sally - see WETHERWAX, Sebastian

CONKLIN, Timothy, 96, a lieutenant in the Rev. War under General Washington, d 7/4/39 at Milan, Ohio while attending the celebration of the 4th - "taken with an apoplectic fit at the first discharge of cannon as the national banner rose to the top of the liberty pole on the public square at Milan" (5-8/28)

CONLY, Charles m 9/28/36 Mary King; Rev. R.C. Brisben (all of Albany) (6-9/30)

CONMARY(?), Prudent m 9/23/41 Julia A. Burlison in West Troy (5-9/29)

CONNELLY, John T., 17 months, son of John, d 6/4/36 (6-6/6)

CONNER, Lawrence, 40, d 8/23/36 ("lingering consumption") (friends and those of the Mechanics' Benefit Society and Albany Institute Society invited to his funeral at 5 o'clock from his late home, 262 Washington St.) (6-8/24)

CONNER, Mary Ann - see GOFF, John Edward

CONNERS, ——, son of L. Conners, d (date not given) (funeral "from his residence, 264 South Pearl St. 3 p.m. today") (6-1/22/35)

CONNORLY(?), Patrick, 31, d 2/20/37 at his home, corner of Pine and Chapel Streets (his friends and members of the Hibernian Provident Society are invited to his funeral) (6-2/21)

CONSTANT, Lucy Ann, infant dau of Capt. Lewis Constant, d 10/28/33 (11-10/29)

COOK, —— (Mrs.) - see RUSSELL, Joseph

COOK, Atwater, 80, a Rev. war soldier and father of Atwater Cook, Jr., Esq., d 6/29/39 in Salisbury (cancer of the throat) (born in Wallingford, Conn. In 1793 moved with his large family to Salisbury, NY then a wilderness. With a few others formed the Baptist Church at Salisbury (3-7/4)

COOK, Catharine - see ROSE, Garrett

COOK, Ella (Mrs.) - see COON, John

COOK, Emanuel, m 8/25/49 Hannah Brown, both of Westmoreland, in Rome; Rev. James Erwin (1-8/29)

COOK, Emily - see SMITH, George

COOK, Friend m 1/10/39 Emeline Hemstead, both of Little Falls, in Frankfort; Rev. Goo (3-1/17)

COOK, Gershom, Esq., 47, of firm of Cook, Lane, Corning & Co. of Troy, d 10/21/37 at Redford, Clinton County (5-10/25)

COOK, Gershom, Esq., 47, of firm of Cook, Lane, Corning & Co. of Troy d 10/14/37 at Redford, Clinton County (6-10/20)

COOK, Hannah, wf of George, Esq., formerly of Lebanon, Conn., d (date not given) at St. Armand, Lower Canada (7-5/24/09)

COOK, Henry - see MABIE, Margaret

COOK, Henry D. of Durhamville m 1/21/41 Joanna Hall of Verona at V.; Rev. Eddy (1-2/23)

COOK, Isabella - see RULE, James

COOK, James m 1/15/38 Mary Hitchcock, both of West Troy, in W.T.; Rev. J. Leonard (5-1/17)

COOK, Jane F. - see JORDAN, Allen

COOK, John - see BUEL, Charles

COOK, John L., 52, one of the editors of the <u>Richmond Enquirer</u>, d 4/23/36 at Richmond (6-4/28)

COOK, Joseph L. m 10/4/41 Elizabeth Smith, dau of Zopher; Rev. D. De Vinne (all of Peekskill) (11-10/5)

COOK, Julia Ann - see HYDE, Almond

COOK, Peabody, Esq., 81, d 9/4/49 in Springfield (4-9/13)

COOK, R.S. (Rev.), pastor-elect of the Presbyterian Church of Lanesboro, Mass. m 11/1/36 Ann Maria, eldest dau of Rev. Henry Mills, D.D., professor of Biblical criticism at the Auburn (NY) Theological Seminary, in Auburn; Rev. Dr. Mills (6-11/22)

COOK, Richard - see JORDAN, Allen

COOK, Richard m 3/1/49 Margaret Robinson, both of West Troy, in Warrensburgh; Rev. Spicer (5-3/14)

COOK, Julia Ann, infant dau of Hobart P. Cook, d 5/7/36 in Albany (6-5/9)

COOKE, Catherine E. - see VAN WAGENER, John H. (Rev.)

COOKE, H.G.P., A.M. (Rev.), 28, and only a few weeks after his brother John F Cooke, M.D., both younger brothers of Dr. Cooke of Albany, NY, d. "lately" in Gloucester, Engalnd (6-4/17/35)

COOKE, Harriet - see ATWATER, Thomas C.

COOKE, Richard - see VAN WAGENER, John H. (Rev.)

COOKINGHAM, Amy - see STEENBURGH, Henry

COOL, Catharine - see COOL, Henry B.

COOL, Henry B. m 1/19/37 Catharine Cool, both of Oppenheim, in Little Falls; George Petrie, Esq. (3-1/26)

COOLEY, Mary Burt - see CURTISS, H.H.

COON, Abby Jane, 37, late preceptress of the Female Seminary at Chicago, Ill., d 7/11/46 at the home of Mr. P. Fitzsimmons in West Troy (5-7/15)

COON, Abraham, about 50, d 8/30/49 in Saugerties (8-9/1)

COON, Elizabeth, 56, wf of John H., d 1/30/49 in Saugerties (8-2/10)

COON, Henry m 11/9/44 Elizabeth Davis in West Troy; Rev. Bissell (5-12/4)

COON, John H. m 11/16/49 Mrs. Ella Cook in Saugerties (8-12/8)

COON, Van Rensselaer, printer, m 12/31/35 Deborah Jane Tinkham, at the new Episcopal Church in Rochester; Rev. Allen A. Steele (6-1/12/36)

COONRAD, Harriet E. - see ALLEN, Seneca

COONRADT, Martha Ann - see HARRIS, Jeremiah

COONS, William H. m 5/13/49 Sarah M. Woodard, both of West Troy, at Wynantskill; H. Fraser, Esq. (5-5/23)

COONSHELL(?), Samuel P. m 9/5/49 Martha Knapp in Saugerties; Rev. C Van Santvoord (all of Saugerties) (8-9/8)

COOPER, A.L., M.D., of Auburn m 12/2/35 Georgiana Muir, eldest dau of late Gen. Alexander M. Muir, of NYC; Rev. Dr. Broadhead (6-12/7)

COOPER, Caroline (Miss), 55, dau. of late Obadiah Cooper of Albany, d (date not given)(her funeral from the home of Garret Yates in Greenbush 10/26) (6-10/25)

COOPER, Charles D., Esq. - see NOTT, Joel B.

COOPER, Charles m 4/15/35 Cornelia Sullivan, dau of Hon. Jacob; Rev. Dr. Sprague (6-4/16)

COOPER, Cyrus S., about 21, d 11/23/41 in Little Falls (3-11/25)

COOPER, Elias (Rev.) of St. James (or St. John's - record blurred) Church in Yonkers, d (date not given) at Yonkers (other death records this date are too blurred to be copied here) (6-1/24/16)

COOPER, Henry, 22, d 7/27/41 in Little Falls (3-7/29)

COOPER, John E. of Whitestown m 1/13/45 Sophronia E. Babcock of New Hartford at N.H.; Rev. Colburn (1-1/21)

COOPER, Margaret T. - see NOTT, Joel B.

COOPER, Miss - see COX, Valentine

COOPER, Thomas B. of Phillipstown m 3/4/34 Sarah Ferris, dau of Jonathan of Cortlandt Town in C.T.; Rev. Richard Wynkoop (11-5/6)

COOPER, William of NYC m 7/12/37 Sarah Wood, dau. of E. Wilson, Jr., Esq. of Troy, at T. (6-7/15)

COOS, Louisa - see POTTER, George I.

COOVENHOVEN, Ann - see BRAGUN, Samuel

COPLAND, Alexander m 10/15/26 Phebe Haines, dau. of Stephen & Katy Haines (see STEPHENS, Archibald, Jr.) (6-11/7)

COPPINS, Richard m 11/21/50 Mary A. Taft in Lee; A.A. Sinning, Esq. (all of Lee) (1-11/27)

COPPINS, Richard m 11/25/50 Mrs. Mary A. Taft in Lee; A.A. Stoning, Esq. (all of Lee) (1-11/27)

COPSEY, Mary Ann - see FINCH, Thomas

CORBIN, Laura M., 16, dau. of P.M. Corbin, Esq., cashier of the Bank of Lansingburgh, d 5/23/49 in L. (consumption) (5-5/30)

CORBITT, Robert, 39, late of Winfield, Herkimer County, d 6/3/39 at his home in Rome (3-6/13)

CORCORAN, Ellen - see HURLEY, J.

CORETHERS, Dorothy - see JOHNSON, William

CORKINS, Dwight (Col.) m 1/19/40 Lydia Boynton, dau. of General Boynton, in South Shaftsbury, VT; Rev. William Bell (This record is repeated with a poem added in issue dated 2/5) (5-1/29)

CORLISS, Albert H. of Western m 8/30/48 Susanna Lawson, dau. of George of Rome in R.; Rev. E.C. Pritchett (1-9/1)

CORNELL, ----, 3, son of Levi, d 10/26/37 (funeral 10/29 from his father's home - "foot of Pearl Street near the railroad") (6-10/28)

CORNELL, Edwin of Plattekill m 6/6/49 Fanny E. Pratt of the town of Lloyd, in L.; Otis Church, Esq. (8-6/16)

CORNELL, Mary A. - see YOUNG, Coe F.

CORNELL, Robert m 10/25/38 Mary Tyler, both of West Troy, in W.T.; Rev. Gregory (5-10/31)

CORNING, Asa, 62, father of Mrs. R. Winslow and Mrs. Elias Mather of Albany, d (date not given) at Hartford, Conn. (6-1/6/16)

CORNING, Edward of house of Shank and Corning of Albany m 6/19/26 Elizabeth Cowdry Stebbins, dau. of David of NYC; Rev. Dr. Spring (6-6/23)

CORNING, Edward of NYC m 1/6/35 at Brooklyn Catherine Matilda Austin, 2nd dau of late Daniel, Esq.; Rev. D.S. Carroll (6-1/12)

CORNING, Erastus - see SHERMAN, Watts

CORNISH, Louisa - see CRABB, Norman

CORNWELL, Charles H., m 10/3/41 Sarah Carpenter; Rev. Cornelius D. Westbrook (all of Peekskill) (11-10/5)

CORNWELL, Deborah (Miss), 49, dau. of late Jonathan, formerly of New Castle, d 9/6/39 in Henrietta, Monroe Co. (12-10/8)

CORRIGAN, Mary, 33, born in Monastereven, Kildare County, Ireland, d 7/22/36 in NYC (protracted consumption) (6-7/29)

CORSON, John O. m 5/4/41 Sarah Stroad, both of Canastota at Durhamville; W. Stillman, Esq. (1-5/11)

CORTELL, Emanuel, (Judge), Esq., 82, d 1/7/35 in Nichols, Tioga Co.; born in N.J.; Lived in Tioga Co. more than 40 years, an early settler there," served in the state legislature "several times"; judge of the court of common pleas for many years. (from Elmira Gazette) (6-1/24)

CORTELYON, Peter S., formerly sheriff of Kings County, d 4/16/26 at New Utrecht, NY (6-5/5)

CORTLAND, Harriet, 27, wf of Augustus F., d 3/10/36 at Yonkers (she the dau of late Peter Jay Muffin) (6-3/15)

CORWIN, William Bloomer (Capt.), 29, d 10/11/41 in Newburgh (9-10/16)

CORY, Rhoda, wf of Benjamin Cory, formerly printer of the <u>Herkimer Telescope</u>, d 6/28/40 in Stratford (3-7/9)

COSGROVE, Joseph m 11/21/38 Sarah Ann Ellison in Haverstraw; Rev. Canfield (all of H.) (12-12/18)

COSTELLO, Michael m 6/1/48 Ellen Higgins, both of West Troy; Rev. J.C. Burroughs (5-6/7)

COSTER, Adeline - see SCHERMERHORN, P.A.

COSTER, John G. - see BERRYMAN, Maria M.

COTRELL, J.G. of Albany m 5/28/36 Cornelia Wilkinson of Sauquoit, Oneida County in S.; Rev. Kellogg (6-5/31)

COTRILL, Peleg of Watervliet m 3/1/37 Mary J. Small of Albany in A.; Rev. C.P. Clark (6-3/4)

COUCH(?), Oliver W., 57, d 10/10/40 in Little Falls (formerly of Hartford, Conn.) (3-10/15)

COUCH, Franklin of Little Falls m 9/30/38 Sarah Wright of Lee, Mass. in New Canaan, Columbia County; Rev. J.B. Baldwin (3-10/11)

COUGHTRY, Joseph A. m 4/15/37 Margaret Lloyd, both of Albany; Rev. Brown of Fort Plain (6-4/21)

COUGHTRY, William (Capt.), 61, d 5/6/26 in New Scotland (town of Bethlehem), Albany County (survived by a wfie, 10 children and 19 grand children) (6-5/12)

COUGHY, Mary Boyd, 15, dau. of Mrs. Margaret Caughy, d 9/2/42 in Newburgh (9-9/17)

COUNHOVER, Emma C., wf of Rev. Counhover and dau. of Judge Watts of Carmel, d 5/3/50 in Bennington, VT. (interred in Carmel, NY) (10-5/8)

COUNTRYMAN, Alvan, 15, son of Solomon, Esq., formerly of Fort Plain, d 9/25/49 at Jasper Corners, Steuben County (4-10/4)

COUNTRYMAN, Daniel of Stark m 2/14/38 Sally Phillips, dau. of Peter W., formerly of Lisle, Broome County, in Stark; Rev. John Padgean (3-3/1)

COUNTRYMAN, David, Esq. of Danube m 3/9/41 Joanna Shoemaker of Minden (3-3/18)

COURTNEY, Isaac of Syracuse m 11/5/37 Julia Halenbeck of Troy; D. Russell, Esq. (6-11/8)

COURTNEY, Mrs. - see BRAINARD, Israel W.

COUSE, William m 4/12/46 Susan Matilda Ireland of Watervliet; Rev. Houghtaling (5-4/15)

COUTANT, Hannah - see KEATON, R.F.

COVELL, Alanson L. (Elder), 53(?), pastor of the First Baptist Church in Albany, d 9/20/37 in Albany (funeral 9/22 from the Baptist Meeting House - funeral sermon to be preached by Dr. B.T. Welch) (6-9/22)

COVELL, Ephraim (Deacon) of Verona (a Rev. War soldier), d 3/7/41 in Troy (he was the youngest of seven sons enlisting in the War) (1-3/23)

COVELL, John B., 24, d 4/28/46 in Vienna (1-5/5)

COVENHOVEN, Maria - see ADAMS, Samuel

COVILL, Mary - see CASLER, John H.

COWAN, Henry H. m 10/25/35 Eveline Huntington, both of Stephentown, In S.; Rev. William F. Hurd (6-10/29)

COWAN, Luther, 29, d (date not given) at Palmyra (6-9/26/26)

COWDER, Peter, 43, d 11/7/39 in Herkimer (consumption) (3-11/14)

COWDREY, Elizabeth - see PHELPS, Benjamin R.

COWDRY, John (Colonel) d 1/27/35 in NYC ("was one of the daring tea boys and was engaged in the storming of Stony Point") (11-2/3)

COWEL, Elizabeth - see BURNES, Simeon

COWELL, George, infant and only son of Charles, d 12/19/37 (funeral 12/21 from his father's home "in Rensselaer Street near the river") (6-12/21)

COWEN, Esek (Hon.), 57, Associate Justice of Supreme Court of New York, d 2/11/44 at his lodgings in the American Hotel in Albany (from the Albany Argus dated 2/12) (5-2/14)

COWLES, Catharine J. - see JACOCKEN, William

COWLES, Celestia Caroline, 1, dau. of Stephen H. and Angeline, d 7/22/47 in Rome (1-7/30)

COWLES, Elias, Esq. d 1/22/37 at Rhinebeck (6-2/3)

COWLES, John A. of Coburgh, Canada West m 7/4/44 Sylvia D. Campbell of Rome, NY in R.; Rev. H.C. Vogell (1-7/9)

COWLES, Junius A. m 11/9/48 Elizabeth Gardner, dau. of Richard, Esq., in Florence; Rev. S. Sweeney (bride & groom of Florence) (1-11/24)

COWLES, Oren m 4/1/44 Matilda H. Binnell; Rev. G.S. Boardman (all of Rome) (1-4/9)

COX, Eliza - see ELWOOD, Solomon

COX, Henry F. - see THUMMEL, Elizabeth M.

COX, Henry M. m 11/15/42 Catharine Westfall, both of Lee, Oneida County, in Little Falls; Henry Thompson, Esq. (3-11/24)

COX, Mary - see MORRIS, Benjamin

COX, Sarah - see WEMPLE, Walter V.

COX, Stephen of Peekskill m 12/6/43 Catharine L. Denike of Newark, NJ, in Newark; Rev. William Roberts (11-12/19)

COX, Valentine m (date not given) "Miss Cooper" at Northcastle; Rev. Dickenson (11-2/22/42)

COXE, Mary - see KNOX, J.R.

COYLES, Frederick, 32, formerly of Albany, d 2/14/37 at Romeo, Michigan (6-2/27)

COZIER, Eliza (Miss), 20, d (date not given) in Utica (6-8/22/26)

CRABB, Norman of Rome m 1/23/48 Louisa Cornish, dau. of Allen, Esq., of Lee Center; H.C. Vogell (1-3/3)

CRAFT, Ann Augusta - see SMITH, Lewis R.

CRAFT, John M., 45, d 2/16/39 at Pine Bridge (12-2/19)

CRAFT, Stephen, about 77, d 5/11/50 in Carmel (10-5/15)

CRAFTS, Griffin, Esq., 87, father of Alfred of Cherry Valley, d 11/26/35 at Hartwick (6-12/14)

CRAIG, Gordon, Esq., supervisor of the town of Oliver, Ulster Co., d 7/21/35 in Oliver ("an emigrant from the Emerald Isle") (an obituary follows from the Ulster (County) Sentinel) (6-7/25)

CRAIG, Jane, wf of Michael, merchant, and dau of Capt. John Mc Coy, d 11/22/33 at Annsville in the town of Cortland (11-11/26)

CRAIG, Laura M. - see RANDOLPH, W.B.F.

CRAIGHTON, Laura M - see RANDOLPH, William

CRAIN, Joel, 63, father of General Crain of the Assembly, d 1/14/35 in Pharsalia, Chenango Co. ("communicated") (6-1/27)

CRAIN, Rufus (Dr.) - see MARSHALL, Thomas

CRAM, Clariss L. - see CAMP, Alfred W.

CRAMER, Catharine - see GOVE, John F.

CRAMER, Hiram A. of Kingston m 3/4/49 Jerusha C. Nash of Hurley in H.; Rev. H. Wheeler (8-3/17)

CRAMER, J.A. of Glens Falls m 8/23/49 Miss E.E. Burlingame of Gerry, Chautauqua County, at Holland Patent; Rev. E. Buckingham (1-8/29)

CRAMER, Jason m 6/23/49 Catharine Heighron; Rev. Selah Ireland (all of Watervliet) (5-6/27)

CRAMER, John (Hon.) - see CURTIS, Edward

CRAMER, Maria - see CLEMENS, John

CRAMER, Mary - see CURTIS, Edward

CRANDALL, Edward of Verona m 8/1/42 Martha Collins, dau. of Deacon Joel Collins, at Westmoreland; Rev. Benjamin Paddock (1-8/9)

CRANDALL, Maria, 20, wf of Henry N.B., d 11/4/37 at Cohoes (5-11/8)

CRANE, Alcesta Flora, 24, recently from the south and wf of Rev. William Carey Crane of Montgomery, Alabama, d 6/23/40 at the home of her father in Rochester, NY (pulmonic consumption) (1-7/7)

CRANE, David B., 4, son of Alson Crane, d 1/20/42 in NYC (buried in Carmel) (11-2/8)

CRANE, Elizabeth Gardiner, relict of late Stephen and mother of Mrs. Eliza Parmenter of Newburgh, d 11/16/42 at Newton, Mass. (9-11/26)

CRANE, Elizabeth S., 24, wf of Isaac W. , Esq. (engineer on Chenango Canal) and adopted dau of Major Isaac Ledyard, d 6/26/36 in Schenectady at the home of Major Ledyard (6-7/1)

CRANE, Gilbert, 1, son of Gilbert, d 2/21/47 in West Troy (5-3/10)

CRANE, Jacob, 84, d 10/25/36 in Lee, Oneida County (a Rev. War soldier) born in what was called Narraganset (now Templeton), Mass. an obituary is included for him by Jacob Chase) (3-1/26/37)

CRANE, Jerusha, 25, wf of Almin B., d 1/20/42 in NYC (buried in Carmel) (11-1/25)

CRANE, John (Rev.) m (date not given) Harriett Burnet in Newark (6-5/22/16)

CRANE, Joseph H. of Carmel m 10/30/39 Ann Eliza Brown, dau. of Ferris Brown of Kent, Putnam Co., in K.; Rev. Warren (12-11/12)

CRANE, Mary Elizabeth, 7, only child of I.W. and Mary of Rome, d 9/30/49 at the Blossom Hotel in Utica (1-10/10)

CRANE, Polly, 67, wf of Ezra, d 2/11/26 in Cooperstown (6-2/17)

CRANE, Sarah - see JONES, Jabez

CRANE, Thaddeus, Esq., about 75, d 10/15/49 in Somers (had represented Westchester County in the State Legislature) (10-10/24)

CRANE, W. Carey (Elder) of Montgomery, Alabama m 8/23/41 Jane L. Wright, youngest dau. of William of Rome, in R.; Rev. S. Haynes (1-8/31)

CRANS, Moses m 10/17/37 Katharine Hainer; Rev. C.R. Wilkins (6-10/20)

CRAPO, Susan, wf of Seth d 2/8/36 (funeral at 3 o'clock from his home, 71 Hudson Street) (6-2/10)

CRARY, John S., 52, long-time merchant of NYC, d 10/31/37 in NYC (6-11/4)

CRARY, Roger, Esq., about 44, d 4/20/36 at Newburgh (born in Washington County) (6-4/23)

CRASSOUS, Joseph of Newburgh m 7/20/34 Anne Greene, dau of William H.

Briggs, Esq. of Peekskill in P.; Rev. Buck (11-7/22)

CRAWFORD, Amelia - see OAKLEY, John G.

CRAWFORD, Betsey (Mrs.) - see HARRIS, David

CRAWFORD, Cornelius - see SMITH, Amanda

CRAWFORD, Eliza B., 42, wf of George and dau. of late Walter P. Livingston of Clermont, d 9/6/36 in Hudson (6-9/14)

CRAWFORD, Richard H., m 11/21/36 Harriet L. Sickles, both of Albany; Rev. Holmes (6-11/23)

CRAWFORD, William m 11/21/49 Margaret J. Morell; Rev. T.F. Wyckoff (all of West Troy) (5-12/5)

CRAWLEY, James m 9/3/49 Mary Ann Mc Graw; J.P. Foland, Esq. (8-9/8)

CREE(?), Mary - see BUCKBEE, Levi

CREE, Susan - see CARGEL, Zalman

CREEMER, Adaline - see LEVERIDGE, John

CREGG, Jarvis (Professor) of Western Reserve College d 6/28/36 at Hudson, Ohio (scarlet fever) (6-7/13)

CREGO, Paul of Western m 4/26/42 Harriet Utter of Rome in R.; Rev. Haynes (1-5/10)

CREHAN, Harriet - see DRUM, Sylvester

CREIGHTON, Jane - see MEAD, Edward N. (Rev.)

CRESSEY, E.H., principal of Delaware Academy at Delhi m 8/5/35 Amanda Wilbur of Chatham at Chatham; Rev. Poor (6-8/7)

CRETSER, John m 12/11/42 Mary Flint, both of German Flats, in Little Falls; Rev. C.W. Leet (3-1/5/43)

CRIM, Delilah (Miss), 35, d 12/25/39 in Fairfield (3-1/9/40)

CRISSEY, William m 11/13/42 Harriet Roberts, both of Green Island, in Green Island in the town of Watervliet; Rev. R. Ballou (5-11/23)

CRISSY, Mills, merchant, m 5/24/42 Matilda Round(?) at Lewiston; Rev. A.F. Frame (11-6/9)

CRIST, Abram (Capt.) m 5/28/39 Irene Bradford in Fairfield; Rev. A. Gross (all of Fairfield) (3-6/27)

CRIST, Mary - see SMITH, Samuel C.

CRIST, Susan - see HARRIS, John S.

CRISTMAN, Ann Eliza - see MYRES, Abraham

CRISTMAN, Jacob - see MYRES, Abraham

CRISTMAN, Jacob F. - see POMEROY, Robert H.

CRISTMAN, Nancy (widow) - see SHOEMAKER, Richard L.

CRISTMAN, Sarah Ann - see POMEROY, Robert H.

CRISTY, Lydia - see TRENAM, Daniel

CROCKER, Franklin m 3/10/36 Mary Chenery; Rev. G.P. Clarke (all of Albany) (6-3/14)

CROFT, Hester - see ODELL, William

CROFTS, Alexander - see FRYER, William

CROFTS, Margaret Livingston - see FRYER, William

CROLIUS, John m (date not given) Mrs. Huldah Carlile in NYC (6-1/10/16)

CROMBIE, James of Bloomfield, Ontario County, m 8/23/49 Calista Adelia Page of Vernon Center at V.C.; Rev. M. Dunham (1-10/10)

CRONK, Stephen A. of Boonville m 2/17/47 Frances E. Thayer of Rome in R.; Rev. George Sawyer (1-2/26)

CRONK, Thomas P. m 5/23/37 Amelia Turner, both of Albany, in Troy; Rev. William D. Snodgrass (6-5/25)

CRONKHITE, Almira - see WHEELER, William

CRONKHITE, Caroline - see RACE, Richard M.

CRONKHITE, Hannah - see VAN NESS, Henry

CRONKHITE, John C. - see VAN NESS, Henry

CRONKHITE, Louisa - see PARR, John

CROOK, Almina, 17 years, wf of Thomas P., d 8/24/35 (friends of Thomas P. and of his brother-in-law invited to the funeral at 10 o'clock from the home of her mother, Mrs. Turner, at 36 Howard St.) (6-8/26)

CROOKE, Philip S., Esq. m 11/24/37 Margaret Cates of Flatbush, Long Island at F.; Rev. Strong (6-11/27)

CROPSEY, Harman, 37, builder, d "recently and very suddenly" at Brooklyn (6-1/28)

CROPSEY, Harriet - see CLIMAKER, Augustus

CROPSEY, William Henry, 2, only son of Gabriel, d 8/24/38 in West Troy (5-8/29)

CROSBY, Alexander H. (Rev.), 35, rector of St. John's Church, Yonkers, d 1/4/39 at the Island of St. Croix where he had gone for recovery of his health (His obituary in issue dated 2/19/39) (12-2/12)

CROSBY, Allen G. m 11/30/43 Janette Brockett, both of Salisbury, in S.; Rev. H.N. Loring (3-12/7)

CROSBY, Clarkson F. of NYC m 9/5/38 Angelica Schuyler, only dau. of J.C. Schuyler, Jr. Esq., of West Troy, in the town of Watervliet; Rev. Gregory (5-9/12)

CROSBY, Daniel, 61, d 7/18/44 at Hampton (1-7/23)

CROSBY, David G. m 10/31/39 Eliza Platt, widow of late William Platt and dau. of Ichabod Marvin, Esq., in Sodam, Putnam Co.; Rev. Mc Cleard (12-11/12)

CROSBY, Edward D., 4, son of Rev. Daniel Crosby of Charlestown, MA, d 5/30/35 in Albany "after a short but severe illness" (6-6/2)

CROSBY, Enoch, 87, d 6/26/35 at his home in Southeast ("his life...portrayed in the character of Harvey Burch in Fennimore Cooper's The Spy") 11-7/7)

CROSBY, Enoch, 87, d 6/26/35 at Southeast, Putnam Co. (was deacon and elder of the Gilead Presbyterian Church. (obituary included) (6-7/3)

CROSBY, Harrison W. of West Point m 4/12/37 Charlotte Augusta Andrews, dau. of John F. of Cold Spring, Putnam County at C.S.; Rev. Hugh Gibson (6-4/20)

CROSBY, James m 11/9/39 Maria Hodge, both of Otsego, in Herkimer; Rev. Murphy (3-11/14)

CROSBY, Louisa - see KEARNS, Louisa

CROSBY, O. (Dr.) m 10/20/35 Sarah B. Safford, dau of Nathaniel; Rev. Kirk (6-10/22)

CROSBY, Philura, 7, youngest dau. of Col. Stephen and Sarah, d 4/11/39 at Litchfield (3-5/2)

CROSEY, Mary - see HARTER, Nicholas

CROSS, David C. of Schuylerville (son of Lyman Cross, A.M., of West Troy) m 6/1/48 Elizabeth German of Schaghticoke at S.; Rev. Hutchins (5-6/7)

CROSS, Lawrence C. of West Troy m 7/30/43 Ellen Frances Moore of Albany in West Troy; Jonathan Hart, Esq. (5-8/9)

CROSS, Lucy Jane - see DAUCHY, Henry B.

CROSS, Statira - see SMITH, Hiram

CROSWELL, Eliza, 24, wf of William H. and dau of Alexander Hunt, Esq., d 9/3/35 at Woodstock (6-10/10)

CROSWELL, Mackay, father of the senior editor of the Albany Argus, d 7/7/47 at his home in Catskill (5-7/14)

CROTHERS, Mary Ann - see DAVENPORT, Henry

CROWELL, Keturah - see PEPPER, Elijah

CROWELL, Phebe W. - see SWEZEY, William W.

CROWELL, Robert, Esq., about 65, d 9/11/42 ar St. Andrews (9-9/17)

CROWLEY, Abia - see JACKSON, Thomas

CROWLEY, J.M. (Dr.), 43, ("long and favorably known as a practical Phrenologist") d 9/13/42 in Utica (a liver complaint) (1-9/20)

CROWNER, R.R., 63, d 4/15/48 at the home of G. Carle(?) (5-5/3)

CROWNER, William m 9/26/49 (in the morning) Elizabeth Thalhimer; Rev. O.H. Gregory (all of West Troy) (5-9/26)

CROWNINGSHIELD, George Casper, son of Hon. R.W. Crowningshield, late Secretary of the United States Navy, m 2/2/37 Harriet Elizabeth Stars, dau. of Hon. David of Boston, America, at Paris; Rt Rev. Bishop Luscombe (6-3/17)

CROWVEN(?). David(?) m 7/4/42 Phebe Hunter, both of Newcastle, in Pleasantville; Rev. Cornelius Montross (11-7/14)

CRUMBIE, Eliza, eldest dau of Robert, d 11/22/42 in NYC (heart disease) (buried in the Episcopal burying ground at Peekskill) (11-11/29)

CUDNEY, Hannah Jane - see SPRINGSTEAD, Daniel

CUDNEY, Nancy - see HALL, Jacob

CUDNEY, Rebecca - see GUMERE, Thomas

CULVER, Edward m 10/7/39 Sarah Teed, dau. of Samuel at Somers; Rev. Bangs (all of Somers) (12-10/15)

CULVER, Lemuel m 9/29/49 Mary Ann Chrystie of West Troy; Rev. Pearson (5-10/3)

CULVER, Mehitable B. (Mrs.) - see HASKIN, Whitman B.

CULVER, Oliver, Esq. - see HASKINS, Whitman B.

CUMMINGS, Catherine Ann - see ROCHESTER, Nathaniel T.

CUMMINGS, Frances - see WARDEN, Seymour

CUMMINGS, George E., Esq., of Winfield m 4/25/50 Jane A., Rowley of Rome in R.; Rev. Pratt (1-5/1)

CUMMINGS, Harrison, about 25, d 5/1/48 at the home of Mrs. Ann Joyce ("it is supposed that his parents live in Jefferson County, further information may be obtained by addressing a line to S.W. Moyer, Minden, Montgomery County or John Joyce, Manheim, Herkimer County") (papers in Jefferson and St. Lawrence Counties are alerted) (4-5/11)

CUMMINGS, M. Ann - see KLING, William

CUMMINS, Susan, 28, wf of Robert, d 12/26/48 in Putnam, Washington County (both persons - deaf mutes) (4-1/4/49)

CUMPSTON, Elizabeth G - see HACKLEY, Alexander

CUNNING, MAria - see ROUSE, Simeon

CUNNINGHAM, Edward m 2/18/41 Phebe Ann Sutton; Rev. Marshall (all of Peekskill) (11-3/2)

CUNNINGHAM, Edward m 6/15/46 Almeda Wells, both of West Troy; James M. Barnard, Esq. (5-6/17)

CUNNINGHAM, George, printer, m 9/19/49 Mary Elizabeth Miner in Saugerties; Rev. R.C. Crandall (all of Saugerties) (8-9/22)

CUNNINGHAM, Hugh of Thurlow, Canada m 4/28/16 Margaret Burnett of Albany; Rev. Dr. Blatchford (6-5/4)

CUNNINGHAM, Margaret (Widow), 76, mother of Henry, Esq., d (date not given) in Johnstown (6-4/25/26)

CUNNINGHAM, Nelson of NYC m 4/22/33 Frances Ellis of Peekskill; William H. Briggs, Esq. (11-4/23)

CUNNINGHAM, William J. m 5/22/39 Phebe Marshall, dau of Ezra, in Peekskill; David Lent, Esq. (11-5/28)

CURETON, John L. m 6/2/36 Maria O. Beals; Rev. T.E. Vermilye (all of Albany) (6-6/4)

CURRAN, Harriet Emeline, (age blurred), dau. of William, d 8/5/49 in Kingston (8-8/11)

CURRAN, Horace D. of Albany m 12/12/44 Elizabeth Worth, dau. of David of Watervliet, in Albany; Justice Garret Gates (5-12/18)

CURREY, Henry of Peekskill m 4/23/39 Elizabeth Ingersoll of Yorktown in NYC; Rev. Fowler (12-5/7)

CURREY, Henry of Peekskill m 4/23/39 Elizabethn Ingersoll of Yorktown in NYC; Rev. Fowelr (11-4/30)

CURRIE, John, 40, d 4/17/42 in Newburgh (9-4/30)

CURRIE, Richard, 85, d 7/5/35 at his home in Cortlandt Town, about 2 miles above Peekskill (a lingering illness) Interred at St. Peter's Church burying ground. (Funeral sermon by Rev. Marshall of Peekskill) (11-7/14)

CURRIN, William m 11/19/38 Margaret Clare in Sing Sing; Charles Yoe, Esq. (12-11/27)

CURRY, Ann Eliza - see MC KELLAR, Robert

CURRY, Justin E.B. of Oswego m 12/25/48 Mary R. Graves of Sand Bank at S.B.; Rev. J. Wallace (1-1/5/49)

CURRY, Mary Jane - see MUNSON, Henry J.

CURRY, William m 1/1/16 Mary Lynch, both of Albany; Rev. Mc Quade (6-1/6)

CURTICE, William T. of Groveland, Livingston County, m 10/17/50 Cornelia E. Briggs; dau. of N., Esq.; Rev. H.C. Vogell (of Rome) (1-10/23)

CURTIS, ---- (Mr.) m 7/2/42 Harriette Wager, both of Waterford, in West Troy; Rev. C.H. Hosken (5-7/27)

CURTIS, Amelia - see FULLER, Morris E.

CURTIS, Asa G. of West Troy m 5/31/44 Catherine Sisum of Guilderland in Troy; Rev. Bissell (5-6/5)

CURTIS, Asahel, 72, d 5/2/45 in West Troy ("newspapers in Vermont will please copy.") (5-5/7)

CURTIS, Daniel S. of West Troy m 2/16/42 Catharine Van Arnam of Troy in T.; E.S. Raymond (5-2/23)

CURTIS, Edward, Esq. of NYC m 2/6/26 Mary Cramer, dau. of Hon. John Cramer, at Waterford; Rev. Dr. Blatchford (6-2/17)

CURTIS, George of NYC m 11/16/36 Catharine Gansevoort, dau of late Leonard, Esq., of Albany, at Waterford; Rev. Dr. Stebbins (6-11/23)

CURTIS, James J., Esq., of Westmoreland d (suddenly) 4/16/49 at Albany (1-4/25)

CURTIS, Nancy - see HART, Gilbert

CURTIS, Newton M., about 34, "author of several popular fictions", d 2/20/49 at Charleton, Saratoga County (5-2/28)

CURTISS, Daniel m 10/17/26 Esther Brown, both of Albany; Rev. Ferris (6-10/20)

CURTISS, H.H. of Utica m 10/16/50 Mary Burt Cooley of Long Meadow, Mass. in L.M.; Rev. John Harding (1-10/23)

CURTISS, Hannah, about 40, wf of Isaac, d (date not given) at Trumbull (7-6/13/10)

CURTISS, Maria L. - see SEYMOUR, David L.

CURTISS, Mrs. Richard - see WASHBURN, William

CURTISS, Sheldon C. - see SEYMOUR, David L.

CUSHING, Helen M., 33, wf of Pyam Cushing of Medford, Mass. and dau. of late Thomas H. Whittemore, formerly of Utica, NY d 7/6/49 in Rome (consumption) (1-7/18)

CUSHING, Jonathan P., Esq., President of Hampton Sydney College, Virginia, d 4/26/35 at Raleigh, NC (6-5/13)

CUSHING, Nancy J. - see GRINNELLS, Josiah B.

CUSHING, S.B., Esq., m 8/17/36 Mary Woodcock, dau of late David, Esq., in Ithaca; Rev. A.M. Mann (6-9/2)

CUSHING, William, Esq., (Hon.), 75, Judge of the Supreme Judicial Court of the US., d (date not given) at Scituate, Mass. (7-8/26/10)

CUSHMAN, Augustus B., 11, youngest son of Alkanah and Mary E. Cushman, d 4/11/37 at Lebanon, NY (killed by falling from a horse)("Boston papers please insert the above") (6-4/15)

CUSHMAN, Charles T. (Dr.) of Columbus, formerly of Lairdsville, Oneida County, m 7/16/50 Jane A,W. Shaw, dau. of Capt. James of Wynton, Georgia, in W.; Rev. George F. Cushman (1-8/7)

CUSHMAN, Isaac (Hon.), 82, father of Hon. J.P. Cushman, d 6/2/42 in Troy (5-6/8)

CUSHMAN, John L. m 10/15/49 Philette Briggs, dau. of Mintis Briggs in Rome; Rev. H.C. Vogell (bride and groom of Lee) (1-10/17)

CUTLER, Lydia - see HOUGHTON, Daniel

CUTTING, Sarah - see BULLIS, Frederick

CUYLER, ---- (Dr.) - see PATTERSON, Joseph

CUYLER, Cornelius - see BURNHAM, Mary L.

CUYLER, Glen, Esq. - see SHEPARD, Catherine Ann

CUYLER, Isaac S., 34, d (date not given) His brother, Cornelius J. Cuyler is mentioned (funeral at 10 o'clock from the home of C.J. Cuyler, 123 Green St.) (6-9/29/36)

CUYLER, Jane - see PATTERSON, Joseph

CUYLER, Margaret, 39, wf of Cornelius, Esq. and dau of late Gen. Benjamin Ledyard, d 10/5/36 at the home of her husband in Aurora, Cayuga County (6-10/24)

CYPHER, Gabriel R. m (date not given) Elizabeth Barnes, both of New Castle, at N.C.; Rev. S. Van Deuson (12-11/27/38)

DAILE, Hugh of Mohwak m 11/20/41 Nancy Ann Riley of Frankfort; Rev. J. Loveys (3-11/25)

DAILEY, Harriet - see DUNN, Thomas

DAILEY, Thomas, 4, eldest son of Benjamin, late editor of this paper, d 1/31/42 in

Carmel (11-2/1)

DALE, _____ wife of W.A.T. Dale, d. (date not given), friends of W.A.T. invited
to attend her funeral "this afternoon" (6-1/28/35)

DALLIDA, James Edward m 9/4/44 Achna Swift, dau. of William P., at Utica;
Rev. Proal (all of Utica) (1-9/10)

DALTON, Alexander m 12/8/47 Elizabeth Melies, both of Albany, in West Troy;
Rev. J.C. Burroughs (5-12/15)

DAMF(?), Jane A. - see WOODARD, Caleb G.

DAMON, Susan A., 24, wf of Orlo R., d 4/29/49 at Waterville (born in Remsen,
NY 9/1/1824; survived by her husband and one child) (1-6/20)

DANA, Jane Ann Lansing, 3, dau. of J.C., Esq., d 4/19/37 in Little Falls (3-4/20)

DANA, Lorenzo D. m 10/26/47 Lucy A. Sandford, dau. of Robert of Chittenango,
in C.; Rev. James Abell (all of Chittenango) (1-11/5)

DANA, Richard P. of Boston m 7/21/35 Juliette H. Starr, dau of late Ephraim, Esq.
of Albany, in Hudson; Rev. Dana of Marblehead, MA 9 (6-7/23)

DANA, Samuel, 68, late of Groton, formerly president of the Massachusetts Senate
and afterwards chief justice of the common pleas, d 11/20/35 at
Charlestown (6-11/27)

DANA, Stephen A., about 60, d 8/7/46 in Troy (5-8/12)

DANFORTH(?), Olive Bradford (Miss), 16, d 4/1/42 in Danbury, Conn. (9-4/9)

DANFORTH, Angeline Hathaway, 31, consort of Hon. Thomas P. and sister of the
Messrs. Hathaway of Delhi, Delaware County, d 11/25/37 at Middleburgh
(6-12/4)

DANFORTH, Eliza J, about 29, relict of late John J Danforth and dau of Col.
Samuel Jackson, d 4/26/35 in Fonda (ill about 4 years) (6-5/8)

DANFORTH, John Jay, Esq., attorney at law of Middleburgh m 5/9/26 Eliza
Jackson, dau. of Col. Samuel Jackson of Florida, Montgomery County in
Florida; Rev. House (6-5/15)

DANFORTH, V., M.D., of Middleburgh m 10/4/42 Caroline Bouck, dau. of
William C. of Fulton, Schoharie County at F.; Rev. Dr. Lintner (9-10/29)

DANIELS, John of Bedford m 10/6/42 Laura Townsend of North Salem in S.S.;
Thadius Quick, Esq. (11-10/13)

DANIELS, John W., 12, son of Warner Daniels, d 4/22/26 (6-4/25)

DANIELS, Levi m 4/7/43 Mary Ann Shaw, dau. of Israel, in Holland Patent; Rev.
Marcus A. Perry (all of Trenton) (1-4/25)

DANIELS, Mahum - see BROWN, J. Addison

DANIELS, Mary Jane - see BROWN, J. Addison

DANIELS, Sarah - see ACKERLY, Obediah

DANIELS, Spencer m 5/18/37 Mary A.E. Lincoln; Rev. H. Potter (all of Albany)
(6-5/20)

DANIELSON, Peter m 4/28/10 Polly Meggs, dau. of Phineas (7-5/2)

DANN, Alanson m 12/30/41 Mary Hoyt; Rev. Patterson (a double ceremony - see
MATTHEWS, Robert) (11-1/4/42)

DANSKIN, Alma, dau. of William of Cuddebackville, d 12/24/41 suddenly near
South Middletown (9-1/8/42)

DARIUS, Matthew of Troy m 1/14/41 Jane Rogers of Watervliet in W.; Rev. J.
Leonard, Jr. of Albany (5-1/20)

DARLING, Benjamin (Capt.), 79, d (date not given) at Middletown (7-8/29/10)

DARROW, Erastus m 5/18/46 Susan R. Martin, both of Rochester, in R.; Rev.

Shaw (1-5/26)

DARROW, James S. of firm of Darrow & Van Namee m 3/1/36 Damarius Hazard, dau of Capt. Thomas Hazard, in Troy; Rev. S.D. Ferguson (all of Troy) (6-3/5)

DARROW, John F. of Catskill d 3/6/35 in NYC (6-3/9)

DASHIEL, Romania - see BAYARD, William M.

DASKUM, Charles A. of NYC m 9/25/39 Elizabeth Sniffin of Stamford, CT at Portchester; Rev. Elder D. Wilson (12-10/8)

DAUCHY, Henry B. of Troy m 5/17/48 Lucy Jane Cross, dau. of Lyman A. Cross, A.M., of West Troy, in the North Dutch Church in West Troy (5-5/24)

DAUCHY, Julia R. - see PATTISON, Edward

DAUSON, Robert, 50, d 4/24/42 in Bedford (11-5/19)

DAVENPORT, A. - see SHERWOOD, William

DAVENPORT, Dennis, 53, d 5/9/44 in Detroit, Mich. (apoplexy) (1-5/21)

DAVENPORT, Henry David, 17, d 6/27/49 in Detroit at the home of his mother, Mrs. Dennis Davenport, formerly of Rome, NY (consumption) (1-7/4)

DAVENPORT, Henry of Colesville, New Jersey m 10/10/41 Mary Ann Crothers, formerly of Newburgh, NY; Rev. B. Van Keuren (9-10/23)

DAVENPORT, Joseph, Esq., cashier of the Branch of the Commercial and Railroad Bank at Clinton, Mississippi, m (date not given) Susannah P. O'Keefe of Buffalo, NY, at St. PAul's Church, Buffalo; Rev. William Shelton (6-10/3/37)

DAVENPORT, Lewis of Bainbridge m 4/4/37 Mary Ann Seymour eldest dau. of Hon. William of Binghamton; Rev. John A. Nash (6-4/13)

DAVID, Almira - see RAYMOND, William W.

DAVID, David, 55, d 8/18/41 in West Troy (5-8/25)

DAVID, John m 6/7/42 Ruanhah Mould; Rev. Robert P. Lee (all of Montgomery) (9-6/18)

DAVIDSON, ---- (record mutliated) "... remains were brought to Saratoga Springs to be interred with those of his wife, daughter and son, Lieut. Davidson, in Green Ridge Cemetery" (5-12/22/47)

DAVIDSON, A (cadet) of Macklinburg County, North Carolina d 10/25/37 at West Point, NY (6-12/27)

DAVIDSON, Emeline - see BENNETT, James E.

DAVIES, C.C. (Lieut.), US Army, m 8/25/36 Louisa Elizabeth Vancleve, dau of late Dr. John of Princeton, NJ, at New Haven; Rev. Dr. Fitch (6-8/29)

DAVIES, Sarah Ann - see HILER, John

DAVIS, Belinda - see SMEDES, Abraham W.

DAVIS, Catharine - see SCHERMERHORN, Samuel

DAVIS, Charity - see SMITH, George

DAVIS, Charlotte - see PAYCHIN, Thadeus W.

DAVIS, Edward (Rev.) m 10/22/26 Belinda Emott, dau. of Hon. James, at Poughkeepsie in Christ's Church; Rev. Dr. Reed (all of Poughkeepsie) (6-10/27)

DAVIS, Edward H., 28, formerly of Kingston, d 1/22/49 at Poughkeepsie (8-1/27)

DAVIS, Elizabeth - see COON, Henry

DAVIS, Elizabeth - see RHODES, Samuel B.

DAVIS, George R. (Hon.) - see PAYCHIN, Thadeus W.

DAVIS, Ida Francis, 9 months, dau. of Joseph F. and Mary E., d 7/12/49 at

Rondout (8-7/21)

DAVIS, James of Elmira m 10/6/41 Maria Boak of Newburgh; Rev. Henry Conelly (9-10/16)

DAVIS, James, John and William - see GILBERT, Elizabeth

DAVIS, John Brazier, Esq., m (date not given) Laura Matilda Gay, dau. of Rufus, Esq. of Pittstown, Maine and grand dau. of Major Gen. Henry Dearborn (6-11/3/26)

DAVIS, John J., publisher of the American Intelligencer m (date not given) Ann M. Vedder of Schenectady in Albany; Rev. B.T. Welch (6-12/25/35)

DAVIS, John P. m 2/9/43 Lucinda Strough, dau. of John, Esq., in Manheim; Rev. C.W. Leet (3-2/23)

DAVIS, Laura S. - see EVARTS, Joseph

DAVIS, Leander of Warren m 10/4/49 Catharine Young of Springfield at S.; Rev. J.S. (surname blurred) (4-10/18)

DAVIS, Loren M m 2/3/35 Electa Pitts, eldest dau of Levi, Esq., at Chatham; Rev. Osborne (6-2/12)

DAVIS, Maria, (age blurred), wf of John P., d 7/20/49 in Rondout (8-8/4)

DAVIS, Mary M, 2, dau of Samuel, d 7/29/33 (11-7/30)

DAVIS, Moses of Fairfield m 1/11/38 Lovina Strough of Manheim in M.; Rev. J. Roper (3-1/18)

DAVIS, Nathaniel S., 28, eldest son of John of Floyd, d 5/18/48 at the home of his father (Elder Vogell delivered the funeral service attended by many) ("The New York Weekly Sun and Milwaukie papers please copy") (1-6/2)

DAVIS, Olive, 53, consort of John P., d 7/8/48 at Palatine Bridge (4-7/13)

DAVIS, Rachael - see GRANTS, Michael

DAVIS, Samuel Willard of Elyria, Ohio m 5/17/46 Louisa Jane Robinson of Rome; Rev. G.S. Boardman (1-5/19)

DAVIS, Sarah E. - see KING, Austin

DAVIS, Seymour C. m 7/8/46 Mary Sheldon, dau. of George; Rev. King of Westernville (bride & groom of Lee) (1-7/14)

DAVIS, Sylvia (Mrs.), 69, formerly of New Lebanon, Columbia County, d 2/1/36 in NYC (consumption) (6-2/9)

DAVIS, Theodore m 9/1/41 Mary Fults; Rev. Loveys (3-9/9)

DAVIS, Thomas of Troy m 12/7/47 Jane A. Farley of West Troy; Rev. Houghtaling (5-12/15)

DAVIS, William H, formerly one of the editors of the Petersburg Constellation, m 6/25/35 Sophia Busher of Richmond, at Richmond; Rev. Bowman (6-7/8)

DAVISON, Joseph, teacher at the Albany Classical School m 12/28/35 Annis Brown of Tinmouth, VT in T.; Rev. S. Williams (6-1/8/36)

DAWSON, ----, widow of John Dawson "of puppet show notoriety in these parts", d at Thornton in Craven ("although possessed of 100 pounds per annum she lived and died in the caravan in which Mr. Punch and his party used to travel") (6-1/27/16)

DAWSON, George W., 33, printer of the Cincinnati Advertiser and son of its editor, d 6/23/37 in Cincinnati (x6-7/8)

DAWSON, John m 11/9/50 Anna Broadbent; Rev. T.F. Wyckoff (all of West Troy) (5-11/13)

DAWSON, William m 2/11/36 Sarah Jay, dau of Peter A., Esq., in NYC; Rev. W. Richmond (6-2/18)

DAY, (given name lacking), 6 months, son of Francis Day, d 9/4/48 at Ames (4-9/14)

DAY, E. Bennet, 21, son of late Dr. J.B. Day of Fulton County, d 8/24/49 in Fort Plain at home of his brother-in-law, N.B. Wood ("typhus fever") (4-8/30)

DAY, Edgar E., Esq. of Catskill m 9/24/35 Sophia Camp, dau of Elisha, Esq., of Sacketts Harbor, at S.H. (6-10/3)

DAY, Eli - see BRAINARD, Sabius

DAY, Julia Ann - see HAWKINS, S.(?) C.

DAY, L. (Major) - see HAWKINS, S.(?) C.

DAY, Pamilla - see BRAINARD, Sabius

DAY, Philo, Esq., 30, of firm of Day and Whittelsey, d 8/24/09 in Madison (7-8/30)

DAY, Robert Henry, son of late Rodman O., drowned 11/29/36 in Nassau, Rensselaer Co. (6-12/5)

DAY, Rodman G., about 34, formerly of NYC and Catskill, d 10/12/35 at Nassau, Rensselaer Co. (6-10/19)

DAY, Russel, Esq. - see CASEY, Dennis

DAY, Sarah E. - see CASEY, Dennis

DAY, Sophia - see BURT, Lansing

DAY, William of Michigan m 7/7/36 Olive Haynes of Troy, dau of Rev. Lemuel of Washington County, NY, in Troy; Rev. B.M. Hill (6-7/26)

DAYTON, Daniel (Dr,) of Portage, St. Joseph's County, Indiana m 9/7/36 Catharine Pells at Syracuse, NY; Rev. H. Taylor of Salina, NY (6-10/3)

DAYTON, Morgan A. (Capt.) of Cortlandt Town m 8/12/39 Adelaide Allen of NYC in NYC; Rev. Foster (11-8/27)

DAYTON, Nathan of Lockport m 10/18/36 Margaret E. Boies(?) of Cortland in C.; Rev. J.I. Foot (6-11/8)

DE BLAISEL, Le Marquis, Chamberlain to the Emperor of Austria, m 4/17/26 Maria Matilda Bingham, dau. of Hon. William Bingham of the United States (6-6/13)

DE CAMP, Aaron, 65, d 8/1/39 in North Haverstraw (12-8/6)

DE COURVAL, Alphine - see OSWALD, Thomas H.

DE FOREST, Eliza F. - see DE FOREST, George B.

DE FOREST, George B. m 4/6/35 Eliza F. De Forest, dau of Benjamin, Esq., in NYC; Rev. Dr. Skinner (all of NYC) (6-4/12)

DE FOREST, Julia N. - see HILL, Frederick

DE FOREST, Mary - see EASTON, Isaac C.

DE FOREST, Pantora - see GRIFFEN, Charles A.A.

DE FORRIS, Ellen M. - see BAILY, Samuel P.

DE FREEST, David M. of Troy m 10/9/37 Mrs. Esther Garritson of NYC at the seat of Mr. Aaron B. Akin; Rev. Wyckoff (6-10/11)

DE GARMO, Abram of Stark m 2/7/50 Harriett Kling of Sharon; Rev. M. Kling (4-2/14)

DE GRAFF, Rhoda A. (Mrs.), 37, d 10/30/49 in West Troy (5-10/31)

DE LANCEY, Mary, relict of late Thomas J., Esq. and sister-in-law of Bishop De Lancey of Western New York, d 9/2/42 in NYC (9-9/17)

DE LONG, Cornelius C. m 10/30/36 Amanda Casler, both of Little Falls, in L.F.; George Petrie, Esq. (3-11/24)

DE LONG, James (Major) - see BERRY, Abram (Col.)

DE LONG, Peter J. of Covesville, Saratoga County, m 3/7/46 Susan Hays of
Warrensburgh; Rev. Dodge (5-3/11)

DE LONG, Sophia - see BERRY, Abram (Col.)

DE MONTROLOS, Charles Francis Frederick, attache to the French Legation, m
11/1/37 Mary Victoria Gratiot, dau. of Gen. Charles Gratiot of the US
Army, in Washington, D.C.; Rev. Dr. Hawley (6-11/7)

DE MOTT, Clarissa - see DEAN, Lewis A.

DE PAY, Bevier m 12/23/41 Catherine Berger of Rochester, Ulster County, at
Bloomingburgh; Rev. Connelly (9-1/1/42)

DE PEW, George W m 3/1/35 Susan Cole in Peekskill; Rev. Buck (11-3/3)

DE PEW, Henry W., Esq. m 1/30/42 Mrs Louise Elizabeth Hait; Rev. Dr.
Westbrook (all of Peekskill) (11-2/1)

DE PEYRONNET, Lewis Jules, only son of the Count de Peyronnet (ex-minister of
France and a prisoner in the Castle of Ham, m (date not given) Georgiana
Frances Whitfield, second dau of the late G. Whitfield, Esq. of St. Vincent
and Grenada on the Island of St. Vincents (6-6/8/35)

DE PUY, Hannah - see SMITH, Jacob

DE RITTER, Walter (Col.) drowned in the night in the Hudson River at the ferry
near Schuylerville. (6-9/2)

DE RUSEY, ---- (Lieut. Col.) of US Army Corps of Engineers m 4/11/37 Ann
Alida Denneston, dau. of Isaac, Esq., of Albany; Rev. Dr. Campbell
(6-4/13)

DE RUSSEY, Charles Edward, 21 months, son of Lt. Colonel R.E. De Russy, d
11/21/35 at West Point (6-12/3)

DE SILVA, Robert P., Esq. of Philadelphia m 5/6/35 Antoinette A. Bates, dau of
Barnabus of NYC; Rev. Orville Dewey (6-5/13)

DE VIRROYE, Francois Louis (Monsieur) of Canton de Vean, Switzerland m
9/22/40 Louise Mary Erline Pilet de Vich of the same place in Herkimer,
NY; Rev. J.P. Spinner (ceremony performed in French) (3-3/26)

DE VOE, John, Jr., formerly of Lewis County m 7/4/50 Eve Shaul of Stark in S.;
Rev. R. Smith (4-7/25)

DE WILDE, Cecelia De Moorson, 68, wf of Louis De Wilde, d 4/12/49 in West
Troy (funeral 4/8/49 left home of Mr. De Wilde for St. Patrick's Church)
(5-4/18)

DE WITT, Clinton, Esq., attorney at law m 10/22/35 Elsie Van Dyck, dau of late
Abraham, Esq., at Coxsackie; Rev. Sailes (6-10/31)

DE WITT, John, 30, d 12/6/35 (funeral from home of his brother, William H. at 6
Quackenbush St.) (6-12/7)

DE WITT, Susan Linn - see HUBBELL, Levi

DE WITT, Thomas of Fishkill m 10/11/26 Eliza Ann Waterman of NYC in NYC;
Rev. Mc Murray (6-11/7)

DE WOLF, Maria - see MANNERING, David

DE WOYCEYNEKI, Stanislaus, the Polish general, d at Dresden in May (was a
companion in arms of Washington and Kosiusko) (6-6/21)

DEAN, Abigail H. - see AYERS, Daniel

DEAN, Amee - see SMITH, Phillip T.

DEAN, Ann Elizabeth, 15, dau. of John, d 10/9/42 at Westmoreland (congestive
fever) (see also DEAN, Charlotte Electa) (1-10/25)

DEAN, Ann Elizabeth, 16, dau. of John and Lucinda, d 10/9/42 in Westmoreland (typhus fever) (1-10/11)

DEAN, Bradford C. m 4/21/46 Hannah Trip in Rome; Rev. G.S. Boardman (1-4/28)

DEAN, Charlotte Electa, 24, dau. of John, d 10/17/42 at Westmoreland (congestive fever) (see also DEAN, Ann Elizabeth) (1-10/25)

DEAN, Daniel of Ridgefield, CT m 1/2/39 Hannah Brown of Poundridge in P.; Rev. Patterson (12-1/29)

DEAN, F.A. (Lieut.) of US Navy, d suddenly 7/31/49 at Charleston, SC (8-8/11)

DEAN, George B., about 39, d 5/3/39 in West Troy (consumption) ("printers in Massachusetts please notice") (5-5/8)

DEAN, Hopkins of Delaware m 9/22/49 Elizabeth Gaming of Carmel, NY in C.; Rev. C.B. Keyes (10-9/26)

DEAN, Ira of Red Mills m 8/11/33 Harriet Haff of Sing Sing in S.S.; Rev. Dickison (11-8/13)

DEAN, James (Judge), 53, d 5/22/41 in Utica. (Judge Dean was the eldest son of the late James Dean of Westmoreland and the first white child born in Oneida County) (1-6/1)

DEAN, Lewis A. of Peekskill m 9/2/39 Clarissa De Mott, only dau of John H., Esq., of NYC, in NYC; Rev. Demerest (11-9/17)

DEAN, Sidney, 27, d 6/11/36 in Albany (funeral at 10 o'clock from her late home, 184 South Pearl St.) (6-6/16)

DEANE, Thomas m. of West Troy m 10/15/38 Frances E.C. Mc Gregor of Waterford at the house of Philip Badgley, Esq., in Waterford; Rev. Stebbins (5-11/28)

DEARBORN, Henry (Major General) - see DAVIS, John Brazier

DEARNSLEY, Elizabeth - see TINKER, Abel

DEARSTYNE, Catharine (Widow), 96, d 10/15/36 "in Bath, Rensselaer County" (Note: The State Dept. of Health's Gazeteer...., published 1980, lists a hamlet (no longer on maps) - Bath-on-Hudson, Rensselaer Co.) (6-10/18)

DECK, Catharine - see WRIGHT, Isaac

DECKER, Apollas m 10/19/49 Jane Westbrook, both of Rochester, Ulster County; Rev. E. Du Puy (8-10/20)

DECKER, Catharine - see BROWN, Samuel Jerome

DECKER, Daniel D. m 8/19/49 Lucretia Rogers, both of Shandaken, at S.; William Risley, Esq. (8-9/1)

DECKER, David B. (Capt.), about 40, of Westfield, Staten Island, d 12/2/42 in the night on board the sloop "Wasp" lying at Newburgh (9-12/10)

DECKER, Peter M., 78, d 7/4/49 in Rochester, Ulster County (8-7/14)

DEFOE, Emily M. - see CAMPBELL, Abbott

DEFOREST, James m 9/22/41 Eliza Green, both of Danube; Rev. Loveys (3-9/30)

DEFOREST, Leona - see WOODRUFF, Samuel

DEGARMO, Catharine - see TEFT, John

DEGRAAF, Peter V. - see FOX, Angelica

DELAFIELD, Charles m 8/11/36 Louisa M. Potter, eldest dau of Paraclete, Esq., at Schenectady; Rev. Dr. Knott (all of Poughkeepsie) (6-8/12)

DELAFIELD, Rufus K. m 11/8/36 Eliza Bard, dau of William, in NYC; Rev. John Mc Vickar (6-11/12)

DELAMANO, Catherine, 19, eldest dau of Andrew, d 11/18/35 in Albany (funeral 11/19 from 16 Van Schaick St.) (6-11/19)

DELAMANO, Samuel, son of Andrew, d 2/18/35 at Albany (funeral at 3 p.m. from his father's residence, 16 Van Schaick St.) (6-2/19)

DELANOY(?), Elizabeth - see WELCH, James

DELANOY, Emily B. - see STOW, Daniel B.

DELAVAN, Daniel (General), 79, a Rev. War Patriot, d 10/31/35 at Sing Sing (11-11/3)

DELAVAN, Edgar, 31, "for some time past" proprietor of the principal Hotel in this village", d 3/4/33, buried in Patterson, Putnam Co. (11-3/12)

DELAVAN, Edward Henry, 20, son of E.C., d 10/13/41 at Ballston Centre (5-10/20)

DELAVAN, H.A., merchant, m 12/8/35 Mary T. Leake, dau of Isaac Q., Esq., at Savoy, head of Seneca Lake (all of Savoy) (6-12/25)

DELAVAN, Henry W., Esq, 50, d (date not given) at his home in Ballston Centre (his funeral was 9/30/36 from the home of Mrs. Lockwood in Albany where he had lived many years) (6-10/1)

DELEHANTY, Catharine - see QUIN, Arthur

DELEHANTY, Terence, 20, d 2/15/36 (consumption) (funeral at 3 o'clock from his mother's home, 544 South Market St.) (6-3/17)

DEMAREST, Ann, 65, late of NYC, d 5/21/35 at home of her son-in-law, Gen. G.O. Fowler in Newburgh (6-5/26)

DEMENS, Henry m 12/14/49 Margaret Lyons, both of Factory Village, in Rome; Rev. Beecham (1-2/6)

DEMMING, Jesse m (date not given) Eliza Elsworth, dau. of John, at NYC (6-5/4/16)

DEMPSTER, James of Lascellsville m 12/30/40 Theresa Brockett of Bracketts Bridge at B.B.; Rev/ F. Hawkins (3-1/21/41)

DEMSTER, Sally - see CHASE, Theron

DENIKE, Catharine L. - see COX, Stephen

DENIKE, Isaac, Sr., 93, d 2/4/43 in Peekskill (born and raised in this neighborhood) (11-2/7)

DENIKE, Jacob m 11/7/35 Sarah Lent, both of Peekskill, at Albany; Rev. Sherman (grooms surname possibly intended for Ten Eyck) (11-11/17)

DENIKE, Jacob of Phillipstown, 76, brother of Robert and Isaac of Cortlandtown, d 7/17/41 (11-7/20)

DENIO, Cole H., Esq., attorney at law, of West Troy m 2/26/44 Jane Gleason of Troy in T.; Rev. L. Howland (5-2/28)

DENIO, Israel, 83, d 3/17/46 at his home in Rome (born in Greenfield, Mass., came to Rome area in 1795, to Rome in 1797; (an affectionate husband and father) (1-3/24)

DENISON, Ann Maria - see WISWALL, Thomas

DENISON, Mary (Mrs.), 60(?), late of Stonington, Conn., d 7/7/37 in Albany (interment in Stonington) (6-7/10)

DENISON, Mary Elizabeth - see WILSON, Alfred

DENISON, Sarah, about 40, wf of Abisha Denison, d 6/5/39 in Columbia (3-6/13)

DENNESTON, Ann Alida - see DE RUSEY, ---- (Lieut. Col.)

DENNESTON, Isaac, Esq. - see DE RUSEY, --- (Lieut. Col.)

DENNING, Charles, Esq., 48, d (date not given) in Catharinestown (6-5/15/16)

DENNISON, Latham, Esq., 76, d 10/3/47 at his home in Floyd (one of the earliest settlers there) (1-10/22)

DENNISON, Mary - see KEYSER, H.D.

DENNISTON, Eleanor, 71, wf of Isaac, Esq. d 3/26/35 in Albany (funeral 3/29 at 4 o'clock "from the mansion of Mr. Denniston") (6-3/28)

DENNISTON, Isaac - see MC KOWN, James

DENNISTON, Susan - see MC KOWN, James

DENTON, Martha Marie (Mrs.) - see MANDAVILLE, Isaac S.

DENTON, Sarah, about 76, widow of Nathaniel, d 7/12/40 in Newport (3-7/16)

DEPEW, Abraham, 75, d 12/26/38 (a long term resident of Peekskill) (11-1/1/39)

DEPEW, Charles A.C. (Capt.) m 4/21/33 Matilda Doty, both of Peekskill; Rev. William Marshall (11-4/23)

DEPEW, Henry W., Esq. m 12/30/41 Mrs. Louisa Elizabeth Hait; Rev. Dr. Westbrook (all of Peekskill) (11-2/1/42)

DEPEW, James of Peekskill m 5/19/41 Mary Gross of Phillipstown in P.; Rev. William H. Johnson (11-5/25)

DEPEW, Mary, 34, wf of Henry W., merchant, of Peekskill, d 3/3/39 (11-3/5)

DEPEW, Morris, 31, of firm of C.A.G. and M. DePew, merchants of Peekskill d 11/8/41 (11-11/9)

DERBY, Katharine - see SCOVILL, Ebenezer

DERBY, Richard C., Esq., of Boston m 9/8/35 Mrs. Louisa Lean, dau of Col. George Bomford, of the ordinance dept. at Kalorama near Washington; Rev. Dr. Laurie (6-9/12)

DEREVERE, Sophia - see JONES, James

DEUSLER, Eveline - see PERKINS, Emet K.

DEVENBURGH, P.W. (Rev.) of Florida m 2/18/50 Sarah M. Burns, dau. of G.P. Van Alstine of Canajoharie, at C.; Rev. M. Bellinger (4-2/21)

DEVENDORF, Cornelius, merchant of Fort Plain m 12/6/39 Caroline A. Merry, dau. of Ralph at Mohawk; Rev. Murphy (3-12/12)

DEVEREAUX, John, 87, father of Henry, Esq. of Salisbury, d 11/11/43 at his home in Richmont, Vermont (was a sergeant in Washington's army in the Rev. War) (3-12/14)

DEVINE, John of Little Falls m 9/24/38 Margaret Keating of Albany in A.; Rev. Kelly (3-10/4)

DEVOE, Jasper m 2/26/40 Eliza Ann Lefurgie, both of Greenburgh, at G.; Rev. George Walker (12-3/3)

DEVOL, Maria (Mrs.) - see BURLISON, John

DEWEY, Catharine - see VIELE, S.S.

DEWEY, Mary - see VAN ARNUM, William H.

DEWEY, Thomas, 54(?), d 4/17/49 in Kingston (8-4/28)

DEWING, Jared (Rev.), pastor of the united congregations of Greenbush and Nyack, m 12/9/35 Julia Ann Tuthill, dau of Selah Reeve, Esq., of Newburgh; Rev. Johnston (6-12/16)

DEWITT, Elizabeth, wf of Dr. William C., d 10/8/49 in Saugerties (8-10/13)

DEWITT, Matthew P. of Hurley m 11/7/49 Blandina Elting of Kingston in K.; Rev. J.C. Cruickshank (8-11/17)

DEWITT, Richard of Hopewell m 4/29/33 Jane Stoughtonburgh, dau. of late John; Rev. Thomas Dewitt (11-4/30)

DEXTER, Almira - see ALL, Henry

DEXTER, Gertrude, consort of Darius, Esq., formerly of Herkimer, and sister to Randolph J. and Robert Shoemaker, both of Herkimer, d 11/31/40 in Perry,

Pike County, Illinois (3-12/3)

DEXTER, Julia S. - see HALL, Adna

DEXTER, Laura, 50, wf of Hon. S. Newton Dexter, d 12/9/46 in Whitesboro, Oneida County (1-12/25)

DEXTER, Mary Frances - see NORTH, Edward

DEYO, Catherine - see STEWART, Samuel

DEYO, Daniel - see HALLOCK, Edward

DIBBLE, Carmi (?), esq., 57, merchant, d 4/30/35 near "Sandy Hill" leaving a wife and "youthful daughters" surviving him. (copied from the Sandy Hill Herald) (6-5/4)

DIBBLE, Frances M. - see GOODWIN, Stephen A.

DIBBLE, Jacob D. of firm of Dibble & Vedder m 8/6/35 Eliza Balding, dau of Isaac J., Esq., at Poughkeepsie; Rev. Thomas Reed of Schenectady, all others of Poughkeepsie (6-8/31)

DICKENS, Elizabeth - see BLISS, John

DICKENSON, Emily - see SEELY, Columbus W.

DICKERTY, Andrew W. m 3/19/49 Mary A. Authisar, both of Rome; H.C. Vogell (1-3/21)

DICKIE, John H. of Buffalo m 10/3/37 Ellen Sluyter, dau. of Rev. Sluyter, at Claverack; Rev. Richard Sluyter (6-10/11)

DICKINSON, Abel (Capt.) of Sandy Creek, Orleans County, m (date not given) Mrs. Margaret Wylie(?) of German Flats; Rev. J.P. Spinner (3-12/12/39)

DICKINSON, Daniel S. - see BIRDSALL, Auburn(?)

DICKINSON, Harriet N. (Miss), 25, dau. of David of Lewis County, d 6/2/46 in Vernon (1-6/23)

DICKINSON, Louisa Amanda - see BIRDSALL, Auburn(?)

DICKINSON, Lydia Ann - see HANY, Joseph

DICKINSON, Mary Ann - see HAINES, J.D.

DICKINSON, Susan M. - see HAVILAND, Bartlett

DICKSON, David (Hon.), member of House of Representatives from Mississippi, d 7/30/36 at Little Rock, Arkansas (6-8/26)

DICKSON, Jane - see BREWSTER, John

DICKSON, Robert of Whitestown m 12/27/48 Mary Patterson of Annsville at the American Hotel in Rome; H.C. Vogell (1-1/24/49)

DIEFENDORF, Catharine, 67, wf of George, d 6/3/49 at Frey's Bush (4-6/7)

DIEFENDORF, Cornelius H., Esq., 39, formerly of Minden, d 3/3/48 at Oregon City (Compiler's note: Present day maps of Oregon State show an Oregon City on the Williamette River near Portland. Settlers from the East settled along this river near Portland in the mid to late 1840's. There's no Oregon City in New York.)(4-8/17)

DIEFENDORF, Jeremiah m 5/22/49 Nancy Moyer in Minden; Bishop N. Van Alstine (4-5/31)

DIEFENDORFF, Lucy Ann - see SNYDER, Nathan M.

DIEFENDORFF, Solomon, 85, d 6/12/50 in Minden (4-6/20)

DIER, Peter m 6/2/49 Margaret Parker in Saugerties; Rev. P.C. Oakley (all of Saugerties) (8-6/16)

DIER, Susan - see MIDDAUGH, Alexander

DIETZ, Adam of Geines, Lewis County m 2/24/49 Mary A. Clark of Rome; H.C. Vogell (1-3/21)

DIEVENDORF, Henry I. - see RIGGS, Hiram
DIEVENDORF, Henry I. (Hon.) - see RIGGS, Hiram
DIEVENDORF, Margaret - see RIGGS, Hiram
DIEVENDORF, Margaret - see RIGGS, Hiram
DIEVENDORF, Maria, 42, wf of David, d 9/24/49 at Fort Plain (4-10/4)
DIGGS, Henson of Washington, D.C. m 12/11/39 Eliza Storms of Greenburgh at
     G.; Rev. George Walker (12-12/17)
DILLENBACH, Alexander of Palatine m 11/14/50 Magdelin Klock of St.
     Johnsville in S.J.; Rev. Rumpf (4-11/21)
DILLENBECK, Charity Ann - see BUDDLE, William
DILLON, ---- (Mrs.), d 6/20/49 in Saugerties (8-6/30)
DILLOW, Joseph, infant son of Richard, d 1/17/37 (funeral at 17 Hawk Street)
     (6-1/18)
DIMMICK, Lavenia - see THOMSON, Smith
DIMMICK, Samuel G. of Bloomingdale m 7/11/36 Eveline Hunter, dau of David,
     deceased, in Montgomery; Rev. Stockton (6-7/21)
DIMON, John P. m 9/5/41 Phebe Pierce, dau of Mathew L. in Fairfield; Rev.
     David Perry (all of F.) (11-9/21)
DINGEE, Catharine, about 73, wf of William, d 11/25/41 in Bedford (survived by
     "a husband and family") (11-12/7)
DINGEE, Roswell of Carmel m 11/26/33 Caroline Tompkins of Jefferson Valley at
     J.V.; Drake Conklin, Esq. of Yorktown (11-12/3)
DINGER, Hannah - see MC NEAL, Sylvester
DINGER, Harriet, 17, dau. of Robert, d 10/14/33 in NYC (interred in Yonkers)
     (11-10/22)
DINGMAN, Elizabeth E - see THOMPSON, Thomas Jefferson
DINGMAN, Gitty Ann - see SANDERS, Henry
DINGMAN, Julia - see MURPHY, Lawrence
DINGOS(?), Deborah - see ACKER, Stephen
DINMAN, Louisa - see CHASE, Nathan
DINWIDDIE, John W. of Porter County, Iowa m 8/19/44 Mary J. Perkins of Rome
     in Juliet, Illinois; Daniel Curtiss, Esq. (1-9/17)
DISABEL, Mary Delia, 2, youngest dau. of Francis and Abigail, d 6/20/47 (5-6/30)
DISBROUGH, Sally - see VAN VRANKEN, William
DIVEN, John H., 24, son of James Diven, deceased, formerly of Peekskill, d
     11/22/41 in Peekskill (funeral 11/24 at the home of his mother in
     Peekskill) (11-11/23)
DIX, Charles Edward infant son of Perry Dix, d (date not given) funeral at 3 o'clock
     from home of Mrs. Fuller, corner Maiden and Middle Lanes) (6-12/21/35)
DIXON, ----, 9 months, son of Levi, d 5/8/49 in Fort Plain (4-5/10)
DIXON, Archibald, Esq. - see BABCOCK, Henry S.
DIXON, Elizabeth - see BABCOCK, Henry S.
DIXON, Levi m 3/20/48 Margaret Freeman in Fort Plain; Rev. Dr. Mc Lean
     (4-3/30)
DOANE, Benjamin, 68, d 8/17/50 in South East (10-8/22)
DOBERSON(?), Eliza (Mrs.), 39, d 11/24/39 in Sing Sing (a lingering illness)
     (funeral from home of her brother-in-law, James Appleton) (12-11/26)
DOCKEY, ----, about 22, wf of Alexander, d 5/25/39 in Manheim (3-6/6)
DOCKSTADER, Frederick - see GRAY, A.M.

DOCKSTADER, Frederick - see VANDERBERG, Peter

DOCKSTADER, Henry F., Esq. - see MABEE, William H.

DOCKSTADER, Henry m 12/14/37 Rebecca Petrie, dau. of Adam, in Manheim; Rev. Swarthanmer (all of Manheim) (3-12/21)

DOCKSTADER, Jane - see PETRIE, Archibald

DOCKSTADER, Margaret - see MABEE, William H.

DOCKSTADER, Margaret - see VANDERBERG, Peter

DOCKSTADER, Marks L. - see PETRIE, Archibald

DOCKSTADER, Nancy - see GRAY, A.M.

DODGE, Ann Eliza - see CONDUKES, William

DODGE, Asa, about 44, late of Albany, d 6/13/26 in NYC (6-6/20)

DODGE, Henry, Esq. m 8/20/39 in New Castle Rebecca Kipp, dau. of Benjamin, Esq.; Joseph R. Hyatt, Esq. (all of New Castle) (12-8/27)

DODGE, J.T. m 9/1/40 Mary Ann Bailey of Westmoreland in W; Rev. William Pepper of Vernon (1-9/8)

DODGE, Julia Ann - see SIMMONS, Joseph A.

DODGE, Julia I. - see SPENCER, David

DODGE, Samuel of Rome m 4/16/46 Eliza Garret of Trenton in T.; Rev. N. Ferguson (1-4/28)

DODS, Mary A. - see BENJAMIN, Jerod A.

DOELL, Ann Eliza - see REYNOLDS, Ard(?)

DOHR, Charles H. m 12/12/43 Elizabeth B. Ethridge, both of Herkimer, in H.; Rev. William L. Dennis (3-12/14)

DOIG, Daniel of Oswego m 1/1/49 Julia M. Tibbits of Rome; Rev. F.H. Stanton (1-1/24)

DOLAN, James, about 35, d 6/14/49 in Saugerties (8-6/23)

DOLBEE, ---- (Mrs.), d (date not given) "at an advanced age" at Junius (6-9/26/26)

DOLE, "Aunt Bettie", age 135, d 3/23/42 at Troy (born in Africa, kidnapped to this country at age 13) (9-3/5)

DOLEN, Theron I., 30, d 12/15/42 in Newburgh (9-12/17)

DOLLARS, Ann - see LAINHART, George

DOLLARS, Sarah S - see VAN SLYCK, Anthony

DOLSEN, Ira V., 43, formerly of Newburgh, d 11/25/42 at Huntsville, Ill. (9-12/31)

DOLSON, Harriet - see MOORE, Emmett

DOLTON, James Henry of Cortlandt m 11/13/38 Emeline Haviland of Yorktown in Y.; Rev. Thompson (12-11/20)

DOMINICK, Peter, about 65, late of Danube, d (date not given) in Cicero, Onondaga County (3-6/13/39)

DONALD, Owen G. m (date not given) Barbara Hyde, both of Coonradt Settlement; H.C. Vogell (1-11/21/49)

DONALDSON, James C. of Utica m 1/27/41 Jane I. Wightman of Rome in R.; Rev. Selden Haynes (1-2/2)

DONAN, John m 8/18/48 Sarah Seage of West Troy in Albany; Rev. Dr. Sprague (5-9/6)

DONNELLY, Augustus, Esq., 67, attorney at law, d 9/10/37 at his home in Homer. Mr. Gregory delivered an address (at the funeral) in the Presbyterian Meeting House (from the Cortland Advertiser) (6-9/22)

DONOVAN, John m 10/28/50 Eleanor Fearon, both deaf mutes, in Brooklyn; Rev.

J. Addison Cary (4-11/7)

DOOLITTLE, ---, wf of C. Doolittle, d (date not given) (funeral at 3 o'clock from her residence, corner North Pearl and Van Tromp Street) (6-12/5/35)

DOOLITTLE, Andrew (Dr.) of Herkimer m 6/3/41 Maria Bain, dau. of Peter of Kinderhook, at K.; Rev. John C. Vandervoort (3-6/10)

DOOLITTLE, Charlotte P. - see NORRIS, James L.

DOOLITTLE, Hannah - see WHEELER, Robert B.

DOOLITTLE, Harvey (Dr.) - see TALCOTT, Enoch B.

DOOLITTLE, Henry, Esq., m 9/9/41 Delana B. Titus, dau. of Samuel, Esq., at Ballston; Rev. Murdock (5-9/15)

DOOLITTLE, Mary - see TALCOTT, Enoch B.

DOOUW, John D.P., Esq. d 2/22/35 at Albany (after a short illness) (6-2/23)

DOREMUS, Cornelius T. - see MESSLER, Abraham

DOREMUS, Elma - see MESSLER, Abraham

DORLON, Elizabeth - see RICHARDS, William

DORLON, Robert, Jr., formerly of Catskill, m 1/20/35 Jane Elting of Kingston at Columbus Point, Kingston; Elder Wyckoff (6-2/2)

DORMAN, Elizabeth C. - see PATCHIN, William

DORNE, Lewis (Col.) m 4/8/40 Julia Kniffin, both of Southeast, in S.; Rev. Mc Leod (12-4/14)

DORNNICK, Elizabeth, 80, wf of George, d (date not given) in NYC (6-11/3/26)

DORR, Josephine - see BULL, Amy

DORRAN(?), Horace m 8/19/35 Lydia Lounsberry, both of Peekskill; Rev. Kirkwood. (11-8/25)

DORRAS, Mary Jane - see WHIPPLE, J.W.

DORSET, Martin, 39, formerly of Ware, Mass. d 11/11/26 in Albany (6-11/17)

DORSETT, John m 11/15/35 Lavina Montross in Peekskill; Squire Purdy (11-11/17)

DORZERT(?), William Henry, 2, son of C. Dorzert, d 5/11/42 in Newburgh (9-5/14)

DOTT, Elizabeth, wf of Elisha, d 9/19/37 in Albany (6-9/21)

DOTT, Harriet - see RICE, Harvey

DOTY, Danforth, 73, a Rev. War soldier and father of Roland S. of Rome, d 3/23/41 at Adams, Jefferson County (1-3/30)

DOTY, Elvin, 9, son of Capt. Stephen H. of Bern, d 10/15/26 (the kick of a horse fractured his skull) (6-10/31)

DOTY, Fanny Antoinette, 2, dau. of Roland S., d 6/21/46 in Rome (1-6/23)

DOTY, Matilda - see DEPEW, Charles

DOUBLEDAY, Lewis M. of Cooperstown m 9/4/50 Blansia Coburn of Fort Plain in F.P.; Rev. G.W. Gage (4-9/12)

DOUBLEDAY, Ruth Maria - see EVERTS, Dudley, Jr.

DOUD, Elizabeth (Mrs.) - see SMITH, Thomas

DOUGHERTY, Addison, Esq. of NYC m 9/29/37 Ann Eliza Nicholson, dau. of late Hon. John Nicholson, at Trinity Church, Charles County, Maryland (6-10/17)

DOUGHERTY, John, 14, only son of John, d 6/19/49 at Rondout (8-7/7)

DOUGHERTY, Susan Hart, 14, dau of Wm. W., Esq. d 5/9/35 in Albany (funeral at 4 o'clock from her father's home, South Lansing St., near the corner of Green St.) (6-5/11)

DOUGHTY, —, "age not shown", consort of George W., d 5/14/50 at Farmers Mills, Kent (10-5/15)

DOUGHTY, E.T. (Lieut.) m 9/29/36 Hariett H. Hart, dau of Hon. R.P. Hart, in Troy; Rev. Dr. Snodgrass (6-10/3)

DOUGHTY, John D. m 3/2/37 Matilda Quarles, dau. of Francis, Esq., of Albany; Rev. Covell (6-3/4)

DOUGLAS, Charles of Buffalo, formerly of Columbia County, m 8/15/36 Harriet Rossiter, dau of N. Rossiter, Esq., of Buffalo, at Geneva (6-8/26)

DOUGLAS, Charles S. of Buffalo (formerly of Troy) m 10/21/35 Sarah A. Hollister, dau of Nathan S. Esq., of Troy, at St. Paul's Church, Troy; Rev. Dr. Butler (6-10/26)

DOUGLAS, Elisha M. of Waterford m 9/1/39 Lucy Martin of West Troy in W.T. (5-9/18)

DOUGLAS, Harriet L - see SMITH, Benjamin

DOUGLAS, Harriet S. - see GREEN, Horace, M.D.

DOUGLASS, John Jr. of Windsor, VT m 9/19/42 Synthia Douglass of Annsville, NY in Rome; Rev. David Morris (1-9/20)

DOUGLASS, Spearry, 72, d (date not given) in New London (6-5/8/16)

DOUGLASS, Synthia - see DOUGLASS, John Jr.

DOUGLASS, Warren, Senior, 55, d 6/18/42 in Annsville (1-7/19)

DOUW, Catharine Louisa - see TOWNSEND, John P.

DOUW, John D.P. of Albany, Esq., 79, d 2/22/35 at Albany. His Douw ancestor from Holland settled on the site of the present town of Greenbush, NY. He and his father served in the Rev War from Albany (an obituary) (6-2/26)

DOUW, John D.P., Esq.; friends & acquaintances of this person invited to his funeral at 3 p.m. from his residence on State Street, Albany (6-2/26/35)

DOUW, John DePeyster m 4/12/37 Margaret Schuyler, dau. of Stephen Van Rensselaer, Jr., Esq., in Albany; Rev. Vermilye (6-4/14)

DOUW, Lyntie (Mrs.) d (date not given) (her brother Jacob Ten Eyck is mentioned; funeral from her late residence, 32 Columbia Street, Albany) (6-2/4/36)

DOVE, Thomas P. of NYC m 12/8/36 Sarah I. Blinn of Albany in A.; Rev. Marshall (6-12/10)

DOW, Edward, Jr. (Dr.) d 8/25/35 at Chatham (6-8/29) also (6-8/31)

DOWD, Edwin R., 34, d 11/25/35 (funeral tomorrow at 37 Church St.) (6-11/26)

DOWE, Eliza - see EVENS, James

DOWNER, Esther - see SAULPAUGH, Charles E.

DOWNER, Mary L. - see MAYNARD, Eli

DOWNER, Mary L. - see MAYNARD, Eli

DOWNING, Benjamin of Montgomery, formerly of Washington, Dutchess County, m 1/2/42 Jane Mulliner of Little Britain at Bellville; William Jordan, Esq. (9-1/22)

DOWNING, James P., merchant, of NYC m 1/7/26 Sarah Ann Charles, dau. of George Charles of Albany, in A.; Rev. Weed (6-3/28)

DOWNING, William N., 32, d 9/12/42 in Newburgh ("Philadelphia papers please copy") (9-9/17)

DOWZER, Mary Ann - see MERRILLS, Lester

DOX, Peter P., Esq., postmaster of Albany and late sheriff of the City and County of Albany, d 11/21/15 (6-11/25)

DOXTATER, E.R. of Adams m 8/23/36 Abby M. Wardwell, dau of Hon. Danirl of

Mannsville, Jefferson County; Rev. G.S. Boardman (6-8/29)

DOYLE, James, d 8/5/49 in Saugerties (cholera) (8-8/11)

DOYLE, William, about 40, d "this morning" in Newburgh (9-5/21)

DRAKE, ― (Dr.) - see VANDERHOFF, David

DRAKE, ― (Dr.) - see VANDERPOOL, David

DRAKE, Gilbert, 50, of Catskill, d 6/4/09 (throat disease) (7-6/7)

DRAKE, Jane, 60, wf of Dr, Nathaniel, d 3/27/34 in Peekskill (a long and severe illness) (11-4/1)

DRAKE, Jolen J. (Esq.) of New Orleans m 6/17/43 Anna Van Amburgh of NYC; Rev. Moses Marcus (11-6/20)

DRAKE, Joseph (Col.), 99, a Rev. War veteran, d (date not given) in New Haven (6-9/17/36)

DRAKE, Nathaniel (Dr.) - see GOETSCHUS, Henry

DRAKE, Phebe, 79, wife of late Cornelius Drake, d 2/28/41 in Salisbury (3-3/11)

DRAKE, Phoebe Augusta - see BADEU, ____

DRAKE, Rachel - see MOSES, William

DRAKE, Samuel H., formerly lessee of the American Hotel in Albany and at time of his death a colonel in the Texas Army of Reserve, d 10/7/36 in Louisville, Kentucky (6-10/20)

DRAKE, William Henry, 24, of NYC d 10/3/46 at Port Schuyler (town of Watervliet) at the home of E.B. Stickney where he was visiting (dropsey of the chest) (5-10/7)

DRAPER, Ann Frances - see DUDLEY, Joseph H.

DRAPER, Mary B. - see HILL, Henry S.

DRAWYER, Hiram H. m 10/24/38 Addia Genning in Somers; Rev. George D. Sutton (12-11/6)

DRENNAN, Andrew, 46, d 7/14/48 in West Troy (5-7/19)

DRESSER, Horace B., Esq., counsellor at law of NYC, m 9/14/36 Lucy Pratt, dau of Erastus, Esq., of Spencertown at S.; Rev. Whitney (6-9/21)

DREW, Mary M. - see PUTNAM, Horace

DRIGGS, Chester, merchant, of NYC m 5/19/35 Angelina Reed, eldest dau of William of Albany; Rev. Dr. Sprague (6-5/21)

DRUM, Sylvester m 4/26/36 Harriet Crehan, both of Greenbush; Rev. L. Johnson (6-5/6)

DRUMMOND, Gertrude, 2, dau. of David G. and Sarah, d 5/20/45 in Lee (1-5/27)

DRURY, E.W., Esq., attorney at law, m 8/31/38 Evelyn T. Horton, dau. of Daniel, Esq. of Hubbardton, VT, in H.; Rev. Ayres (6-9/13)

DU BOIS, Barent (Capt.), 76, a Rev. War soldier, d 3/1/37 in Catskill (6-3/3)

DUANE, Anastasia - see ALEXANDER, Maurice S.

DUANE, Cornelius m 8/31/36 Gertrude Robinson at St. Paul's Church in Schenectady; Rev. Prof. Reed (6-9/2)

DUANE, William (Col.) - see ALEXANDER, Maurice S.

DUANE, William R m (date not given) Frances Eliza Prince, dau of William Walton, Esq. of Schenectady, in Schenectady (6-1/23/35)

DUBOIS, Catharine - see LOCKWOOD, Christopher S.

DUBOIS, Catharine, 52, wf of Benjamin, d 12/26/09 in Catskill (7-1/3/10)

DUBOIS, Gertrude (Mrs.), d (date not given) at New Paltz (6-6/5/16)

DUBOIS, H. (Miss) - see TERWILLIGER, Isaac

DUBOIS, Hannah Ann - see ECKERT, Isaac O.

DUBOIS, Henry Augustus, M.D., m 12/17/35 Catharine Helena Jay, dau of Peter A., Esq., Rev. Manton Eastburn (6-12/23)

DUBOIS, Jacob m 6/6/42 Jane Stewart, both of White Lake, at Wurtsburough; Rev. M. Roney of Newburgh (9-6/11)

DUDLEY, Charles E. (Hon.) formerly mayor of Albany and a member of the US Senate, d 1/23/41 in Albany (3-1/28)

DUDLEY, Charles N. of Pittsford m 1/24/41 Catharine Mc Chesney of Little Falls at L.F.; Rev. J.W. Olmstead (3-1/28)

DUDLEY, Frances M., 27, wf of Joseph A. of firm of D—(?) Roberts of Rome, d 9/2/44 at the home of her father, Dr. Arba Blair (funeral 9/4/) (1-9/3)

DUDLEY, Henry C of Greenbush, NY d 12/18/34 at Mr. Phillip Allen's at Buckingham County, Virginia (Asiatic cholera) (his physician called but could not arrive until collapse...") (6-1/10/35)

DUDLEY, James Whitin, 9 months, son of Joseph A. and Ann Frances, d 9/9/48 in Rome (1-9/15)

DUDLEY, Joseph A. m 9/1/46 Ann Frances Draper, dau. of Virgil, Esq., in Rome; Rev. Selden Haynes (all of Rome)(1-10/6)

DUER, Denning m 5/8/37 Caroline King, dau. of James G., at Highwood, New Jersey (6-5/11)

DUFFEY, Margaret - see HAGAN, Cain

DUFFIN, Eliza A. - see WHITE, Willard D.

DUFFY, Harriet - see PINNEY, Austin

DUFFY, William, 32, manager of the Albany Theater, d 3/12/36 (funeral at 3 o'clock from home of P.M. Morange, corner Maiden and Middle Lanes) (6-3/14)

DUKE, Ben, 97, m as his sixth wife, 12/6/45 Sylphia Matthews, 49, late of Philadelphia; Rev. C. Pirtle (from St. Louis Republican) (5-12/17)

DUKE, James, 78, d (date and place not given) (a short illness) (6-5/8/16)

DULSEN, June Clarissa, 11, dau. of Capt. Gabriel L., d 6/1/42 in Goshen (9-6/11)

DUMAUX, Eugenia - see EDMONDS, John Henry

DUMONT, —— T. - see WARFORD, James P.

DUNBAR, Almira - see BUTLER, Nathan

DUNBAR, Jonathan A. of Lee m 7/2/46 Harriet Patten of Rome in R; Rev. S. Haynes (1-7/7)

DUNBERGH, Augustus C. of Mohawk m 8/9/49 Amy E. Pine, of St. Johnsville in Fort Plain; Rev. Dr. Mc Lean (4-8/16)

DUNCAN, Mary - see FAUROT, L.B.

DUNCKEL, Lucinda - see WALRATH, William J.

DUNCKEL, Maria - see LAMBERT, John

DUNHAM, Josiah (Col.), 75, d 5/10/44 in Lexington, Kentucky (born in Connecticut, graduate of Dartmouth College, New Hampshire. Ten years officer in US Army and commander of the Fort and Garrison at Michillimacnac, then moved to Windsor, Vt., later secretary of State in Vt., established a Young Ladies Seminary in Windsor. Moved to Lexington, Ky in 1821 (this man an uncle to A.T. Dunham, Esq., President of West Troy)) (5-6/5)

DUNKIN, Ann - see VAN RENSSELAER, John S., Esq.

DUNKIN, Robert H., Esq. - see VAN RENSSELAER, John S., Esq.

DUNLAP, Andrew, Esq., late district attorney of the US for Massachusetts d

7/27/35 in Salem, MA (from <u>Boston Post</u>) (6-8/5)

DUNLOP, Alice, 10 months, dau. of A.A. and Jane, d 7/25/48 in West Troy (5-8/2)

DUNLOP, Archibald A. of West Troy m 6/2/45 Jane Hutton, dau. of late James, Esq., of Sheffield, England, in Sheffield, England (5-6/25)

DUNLOP, Helen - see MC CREEDIE, Thomas

DUNLOP, Janet, 64, wf of Robert, d 12/11/49 in Watervliet (5-12/19)

DUNLOP, Robert - see MC CREDIE, Helen

DUNN, Ann - see WOOD, Ross W.

DUNN, Ann Catharine - see HOLT, Jesse C.

DUNN, Anna Parker, youngest dau of Edward Dunn, formerly of Albany, d 10/7/36 at Little Rock, Arkansas (6-11/1)

DUNN, Chauncey of Rome m 12/29/47 Mary Jane Johnson of Lee; H.C. Vogell (1-1/7/48)

DUNN, Edward H., formerly of Albany, d 9/25/36 at his father's home near Little Rock, Arkansas (6-10/20)

DUNN, Edward m 10/12/38 Mary Milson, both of Little Falls, in Utica; Rev. Charles Quartros (3-11/8)

DUNN, John m 1/2/50 Mary Wight, both of Watervliet, at Albany; Rev. S.F. Morrow (5-1/9)

DUNN, Patrick, 47, d 3/14/36 in Little Falls (born in Ireland) (3-3/17)

DUNN, Thomas of England m (date not given) Harriet Dailey of Trenton, NY in T.; Rev. Parsons (1-10/2)

DUNNEL, Harriet - see VAN SCHAACK, Stephen

DUNNING, Ann Eliza, infant dau. of Rev. Charles L. Dunning, pastor of the Methodist Church, d 9/26/38 in Little Falls (3-10/4)

DUNNING, Cordelia - see TOWNSEND, James B.

DUNNING, Matilda, 17, dau. of Justus and Lucinda, d 2/12/48 (consumption) (1-2/18)

DUNNING, Sarah Durinda, 7, dau. of Richard and Sarah Ann, d 8/12/49 in Rome (1-8/15)

DUNSTAN, Peter, 70, d (date not given) in NYC (6-5/5/26)

DUNWOODIE, Rosina - see BINGLE, Eli

DUPONT, Gabrielle Josephine, relict of the late Victor DuPont, d 11/13/37 at her home on the Brandywine (6-11/27)

DURANT, Benjamin m Lucy Ann Allards, both of Lee, Mass. at Patterson's Tavern in Canaan (state not given) (6-3/12)

DURGY, George m 12/26/41 Emma Read in Rome; Judge Roberts (1-12/28)

DURHAM, Emeline - see INNES, William

DURHAM, Julia M., 20, dau. of late Eber Durham, Esq., d 6/15/41 at Durhamville (1-6/22)

DURHOLZ, John m 1/2/50 Theresa Kuhn in Fort Plain; Dr. C.G. Mc Lean (all of Fort Plain) (4-1/10)

DURIN, Oliver, 76, d 2/18/49 in West Troy (5-2/28)

DURKEE, Anna, 18 months, dau. of Rodney, d 9/21/37 (3-9/28)

DURKEE, Henrietta - see JONES, Benjamin R.

DURLAND(?), Sarah, 1, dau. of late Joseph, d 11/18/41 in Newburgh (9-11/20)

DURLAND, ----, infant child of Peter (given name not shown) d 12/1/42 (9-12/3)

DURLAND, Phebe E., age blurred, wf of Peter, d 9/26/42 in Newburgh (9-10/1)

DURNETT, Catherine Louisa, 4 weeks, dau. of W.R. and E.A. Durnett, d 1/9/41 in

Troy (5-1/20)

DURRIE, Horace (Capt.), 51, d 1/21/26 (funeral from his late home, 15 Liberty Street, Albany) (6-1/24)

DUSENBERRY, Charles, about 70, formerly a merchant of Peekskill, d 11/1/39 at Quincy, Putnam County (11-11/26)

DUSENBURY, Ann Eliza - see HORTON, Joseph S.

DUSENBURY, Richard J. (Dr.) of Albany m 4/6/37 Sarah Wood, dau. of late Daniel, Esq. of Boston, in Albany; Rev. Dr. Ferris of NYC (6-4/15)

DUSENBURY, Stephen T. of Brunswick m 11/4/47 Mary Elizabeth Robinson of West Troy; Rev. J.C. Buroughs (5-11/10)

DUTCHER, Charles Monteville, 2, son of Daniel B. and Margaret P., d 1/6/40 in Sing Sing (12-1/14)

DUTCHER, Frances Henrietta - see BARKER, Charles, Jr.

DUTCHER, John D., 41, d 11/22/47 in West Troy ("bilious fever") (5-11/24)

DUTCHER, Margaret Elizabeth - see BENNETT, George, M.D.

DUTTON, Rosina - see HALL, Fanny R.

DUXTATER, Almira - see GAINES, Willard O.

DUYCKINCK, Susannah, 81, relict of late Gerardus, Esq., formerly of NYC and sister of late Rev. Dr. John H. Livingston, d (date nor given) at Monticello, NY (6-7/22/36)

DWIGHT, ---- (Dr.), 73, Treasurer of Hamilton College, d 5/19/50 in Clinton (1-5/29)

DWIGHT, Thomas (Rev.) of Northampton, MA d (date not given) at Moscow, Livingston County (6-11/28)

DYCKMAN, William - see MANDAVILLE, Isaac S.

DYCKMAN, William N of Greensburgh, d. suddenly 1/17/34 in Peekskill (11-1/28)

DYER, Abraham V., 29, formerly of Albany d 7/17/35 at Russeltown (6-7/28)

DYER, Elias, 75, formerly of Albany, d (date not given) at Coventry, CT (6-3/5/36)

DYER, Elizabeth H., 30, wf of W.P. Dyer, d 4/2/41 in West Troy (5-4/7)

DYER, John L. m 11/3/45 Caroline Lyon at West Troy; Rev. T.F. Wickoff (5-11/12)

DYER, Jonathan H., 45, late coroner, d 3/22/44 in West Troy (5-3/27)

DYER, Ruth Ann, 20, wf of Thomas H., d 3/12/44 in West Troy (5-3/13)

DYER, Thomas H. of West Troy m Ruth Ann Austin of Troy; Rev. H.L. Starks (5-5/10)

DYER, Thomas H., 63, d 11/7/26 at Gibbonsville (born in Rhode Island) (6-11/17)

DYER, Thomas, 50, d 9/4/49 in Kingston (8-9/8)

DYGERT, Clarinda - see STARING, Charles

DYGERT, Daniel (Col.), about 47, formerly a member of the state assembly from Herkimer County, d 2/24/42 at his home in German Flats (3-3/3)

DYGERT, David, 29, grocer, d 7/28/38 in Little Falls at the home of James Mayer (had had frequent attacks of asthma) (3-8/2)

DYGERT, John W. of Little Falls m 12/9/38 Margaret M. Etheridge of Herkimer at Fort Plain' Rev. Belding (3-1/3/39)

DYGERT, John W. of Little Falls m 12/9/38 Margaret M. Ethridge of Herkimer at Fort Plain; Rev. Belding (3-1/3/39)

DYGERT, John, Esq., clerk of Herkimer County, m 9/13/37 Mary Lockwood, dau. of Solomon of Little Falls, in L.F.; Rev. Blodgett (3-9/14)

DYGERT, Joseph m 11/20/36 Louisa Van Slyke; Wm. Brooks, Esq. (all of Little Falls) (3-11/24)

DYGERT, Margaret - see WEBBER, David W.

DYGERT, Margaret, 51, consort of John Dygert, Esq., Clerk of Herkimer County, d 11/30/36 in Little Falls (member of the Presbyterian Church) (3-12/1)

DYGERT, Margaret, 51, consort of John, Esq., clerk of Herkimer County, d 12/1/36 at Little Falls (severe illness of several weeks) (6-12/6)

DYGERT, Mary E. - see MARSH, Ely T.

DYGERT, Polly, 49, wf of Denis, d "recently" in German Flats (3-4/20/43)

DYGERT, Sarah - see ELWOOD, Hiram

DYGERT, Sarah V. - see BRADLEY, Daniel C.

DYGERT, W.W. (Capt.) - see MARSH, Ely T.

DYGERT, Warner of Frankfort m 12/30/38 Eunice Harter of Mohawk in Herkimer; Rev. Murphy (3-1/3/39)

EACKER, George m 1/16/49 Ann A. Rich in Palatine; Rev. Pegg (all of Palatine) (4-1/25)

EACKER, Theodore Spencer, 8, only son of Abram & Laura d 9/18/48 in Rome (1-9/22)

EADY, A., 30, d (date not given) in Canandaigua (6-5/15/16)

EAGLESTON, Elizabeth - see GREENE, C.O.

EAGLETON, William m 10/30/39 Sarah Oakley at Annsville, Cortlandt Town; Rev. William H. Johnson (11-11/12)

EAMES, Caroline E. - see STOREY(?), Orvilla W.

EAMES, Hellen J. - see MC CLINTOC, Wilson

EAMS(?), A.W. - see BOWEN, Mary A. (Miss)

EARL, Eliza Marsh, 10 months, dau. of Robert & Caroline, d 10/25/49 in Rome (1-11/7)

EARL, Jonas - see SMITH, Caroline

EARL, Phebe A. - see SWEET, Henry L.

EARLE, Sophia (Mrs.), 22, d 10/14/39 in German Flats (3-10/24)

EARLE, William m (date not given) Hannah Mc Clure in NYC (6-5/15/16)

EARLEY, Mary - see BARKER, William

EARLL, Clarissa, 44, wf of Jonas Earll, Jr., d 4/2/35 at Onondaga (a communicant at the Episcopal Church) (6-4/15)

EASTBROOK, Lovelt, 28, d (date not given) in Concord, Mass. leaving a widow age 18. Her first husband was also age 28 when he died. She married both husbands on the same day in the same month (6-8/15/26)

EASTER, John C., 44, Adjutant General of the State of Georgia, d 7/11/35 in Hillsborough, Jasper Co., Georgia (6-7/31)

EASTERBROOK, Cordelia - see CHURCHILL, H.H.

EASTERBROOK, Jane - see HALL, Alexander

EASTMAN, Anna, 72, widow of Harvey Eastman, d 3/24/47 in Marshall (1-4/2)

EASTMAN, Obadiah, 87, d 11/14/36 in Littleton (died from a fall from a wagon about 2 weeks prior to his death) (6-12/6)

EASTON, Isaac C. m 9/15/40 Mary DeForest of Fairfield in Norway, NY; Rev. Burt (3-10/1)

EASTON, Sophronia, 19, wf of Dr. Charles D. Easton and only dau. of David Starkweather, d (date and place blurred) (3-12/29/36)

EATON, Allen m 6/14/37 Catharine Stebbins in Little Falls; J.W. Olmstead (all of

Little Falls) (3-6/22)

EATON, Eliza - see EHLE, James

EATON, Elvira A. - see BROWN, Roswell D.

EATON, Hellen M., 1, only child of Allen W., d 12/16/41 in Little Falls (3-12/23)

EATON, John - see BROWN, Roswell D.

EATON, Joseph D. of Troy m 10/8/45 Angeline Gue of Waterford in W.; Rev.
    Smith (5-10/15)

EATON, Lydia - see CANFIELD, William

EATON, Maria - see CASWELL, Edwin

EATON, Mary - see GRAHAM, Anson

EATON, Mary Ann - see YALE, T.G.

EATON, Parley - see CASWELL, Edwin

EATON, Rosanna - see HINE, Newell

EATON, Sally, 72, relict oF Elisha, d 2/1/39 in Little Falls (3-2/28)

EATON, Thomas H. m 9/6/40 Anna Webb, both of Frankford, in Little Falls; Rev.
    J.W. Olmstead (3-9/17)

EATON, Volney m 4/15/41 Alida Herkimer, both of Little Falls, in Trenton,
    Oneida County; Rev. Farley (3-5/20)

EBENSBERGER, John Frederick, 2, son of Frederick and Gertrude, d 9/18/42 at
    Herkimer (inflammation of the lungs) (3-9/22)

ECKER, William H. of Rome m 9/8/41 Catharine Knapp of Oriskany at Holland
    Patent; Rev. Mc Cue (1-9/28)

ECKERT, Isaac O., Jr., m 6/9/49 Hannah Ann DuBois at Olive; Martin Schutt,
    Esq. (all of Olive) (8-6/23)

EDDOWER(?), Anna - see WOODRUFF, Elias

EDDY, Eveline (Miss), 18, d (date not given) at Fort Edward (6-9/26/26)

EDDY, Isaac, "between 70 & 80 years old", d 7/23/47 in Waterford (5-7/28)

EDDY, Mrs. - see CHICHESTER, Elijah (Rev.)

EDDY, Nancy Ann - see WILDER, James L.

EDGERTON, Augustus m 2/22/49 Catharine M. Ham, both of Ava, at Stanwix
    Hall in Rome (1-2/28)

EDGERTON, James M. of West Troy m 1/7/40 Mary Martin of Albany in A,; Rev.
    Truman Seymour (5-1/15)

EDICK, Abigail V., wf of late George, d 5/26/40 in Columbia (consumption)
    (survived by two small childern) (3-7/30)

EDICK, David of Fort Plain m 5/6/49 Margaret Bort of Salt Springville at S.S.;
    Rev. A.E. Daniels (4-5/10)

EDICK, George, 30, d 5/20/36 in Columbia, Herkimer County (survived by a wife
    and two children) (3-5/26)

EDICK, Polly, 52?, consort of David, d 10/22/48 in Fort Plain (4-10/26)

EDMONDS, John Henry of Utica m 10/9/49 Eugenia Dumaux of NYC at the home
    of James Brown, Esq., in Clifton, NJ; Rev. George Leeds (1-10/17)

EDMONDS, Samuel (Gen.), 86, d 3/15/26 in Hudson (a Rev. War soldier; in War
    of 1812 was paymaster general of State of NY (6-3/24)

EDMUNDS, Samuel (General) - see HAILMAN, Lydia W.

EDWARD, Susan B., wf of James, Esq., d 4/8/35 at Ballston (6-4/10)

EDWARDS, Churchill m 2/5/40 Louise Wright of Warren in W.; W.C. Craine,
    Esq. (3-2/27)

EDWARDS, David G. m 12/3/42 Mrs. Mary Stanton in Newburgh; Chauncey F.

Bishop, Esq. (all of Newburgh) (9-12/10)

EDWARDS, Elemuel, 67, d 10/3/41 at Ross Ville (9-10/9)

EDWARDS, Elizabeth - see WILLIAMS, Hugh

EDWARDS, Ellen, 25, dau. of Anna Edwards, d 11/30/42 in Newburgh (9-12/3)

EDWARDS, Frances Ogden - see HOYT, William S.

EDWARDS, Francis m 10/30/46 P.D. Gleason, dau. of Jared, in Rome; Rev. H.C. Vogell (all of Rome)

EDWARDS, George C., first judge of Steuben County, d 11/18/37 at his home in Bath. (He was born in Stockbridge, Mass. 28 Sept. 1787 and was a lineal descendant of the late President Edwards of New England (6-11/27)

EDWARDS, Horace Armstrong, (age not given) son of Ward Armstrong, Esq., d 8/9/42 in Newburgh (9-8/13)

EDWARDS, John, about 4, son of John, d 8/7/49 in Saugerties (8-8/11)

EDWARDS, Maria - see PARK, Edward A.

EDWARDS, Milford, Esq. of London d December 1834 of a severe illness; "known for the last few years to many Americans residing in France." (6-3/26/35)

EDWARDS, Mrs. - see SOPER, Treadwell

EDWARDS, Nelson, about 30, d 10/10/41 in Newburgh (9-10/16)

EDWARDS, Thomas of Ephratah m 6/29/36 Anna Fox, dau. of C.C. Fox, Esq., of Palatine; Rev. C.A. Smith (6-7/4)

EGGABROAD, Peter, 92, d 11/1/48 at his home in Minden (4-11/2)

EGGER, Martina - see LANDON, John G.

EGLETON, Sarah - see VAN SECY, William C.

EHLE, James m 1/14/49 Eliza Eaton, both fo Fort Plain, at Ames; Rev. C.H. H--- (surname blurred) (4-1/18)

EIGABROAT, John (Hon.) of Minden m 3/7/41 Miss H. Myers of German Flats (3-3/18)

EIGHMEY, James, 24, d 8/13/42 in Newburgh (9-8/20)

EIGHMY, Albert m 2/18/47 Lydia Spore in West Troy; Rev. Houghtaling (5-2/24)

EIGHTS, Abraham, 17, son of Dr. Jonathan Eights, d 11/5/36 (6-11/7)

ELDER, Margaret - see WHITNEY, Richard J.

ELDERKIN, Rebecca, 88, relict of late John, d (date not given) at Lisbon (7-8/29/10)

ELINGER, Emburd, 75, of Bedford, Westchester County d 11/2/26 (consumption) (was an Ensign in the Rev. War) (6-11/10)

ELLICOTT, Andrew of firm of Grant and Ellicott, merchants, of Medina m 9/2/35 Mary Seymour Austin, dau of late David Fairman of Philadelphia, in Medina; Rev. J.O. Stokes (6-9/11)

ELLIOT, Edward, 22, son of Robert of Albany, NY, d 2/2/37 at St. Croix (had left Albany a few months prior to his death) (6-2/24)

ELLIOT, Elmira J. - see VAN CAMP, David

ELLIOT, Frances - see AUSTIN, Charles

ELLIOT, George (Deacon), formerly a member of the Legislature, d (date not given) at Killingworth (7-6/20/10)

ELLIOT, Jesse (Rev.) of the Baptist Church in Wyoming, NY m 5/10/41 Mary Willes of Western in W; Rev. H.C. Vogell (1-6/1)

ELLIOTT, John m 8/13/50 Ann Bartlett; Rev. T.F. Wyckoff (all of West Troy) (5-8/28)

ELLIOTT, Mary Ann - see RIVES, John C.

ELLIOTT, Robert, Esq. of Central Square m 10/22/46 Mary Ann Peckham of
Verona in V.; Rev. H. Kendall (1-11/10)

ELLIS, Ann Eliza, wf of Hon. Chesselden Ellis, d 5/25/45 in Waterford (5-6/4)

ELLIS, Ann Matilda - see CHAPMAN, Augustus

ELLIS, Catharine - see EVANS, Griffith

ELLIS, David of West Troy m 12/31/37 Maria Low of Poughkeepsie in West Troy;
Rev. Mann (5-1/3/38)

ELLIS, Edmund S., 64, d 2/26/38 (5-2/28)

ELLIS, Eliza R., 22, consort of Judge Powhatan Ellis of Mississippi, d 3/3/35 in
Washington at the home of her father, T. Winn, Esq. (6-3/16)

ELLIS, Frances - see CUNNINGHAM, Nelson

ELLIS, Mary, 13, dau of William, d 12/2/35 (6-12/3)

ELLIS, Thomas m 12/11/50 Eleanor Hughes in Utica; Rev. E. Griffith (all of Utica)
(1-12/18)

ELLISON, Sarah Ann - see COSGROVE, Joseph

ELLSWORTH, Sarah (Mrs.), 102, d 5/28/10 at East Windsor (7-6/13)

ELMENDORF, Edward, Esq., 46, attorney at law, d 10/2/35 at his home in
Ellenville, and 10/6/35 his brother, Sudam Elmendorf, 25, d in Kingston
(both died of typhus; sons of the late Conradt E., Esq.) (6-10/10)

ELMENDORF, Elizabeth LaGrange - see WYCKOFF, Theodore F.

ELMENDORF, Luther H., infant son of Dumond, d 3/13/49 in Kingston (8-3/31)

ELMENDORF, Peter Edward, Esq., 69, d 5/15/35 (a lingering illness) (6-5/21)

ELMER, Charlotte Huldah, 16 months, dau. of L.E., d at 5 a.m. 1/29/47 in Rome
(funeral 1/30/ at 2 o'clock from the Methodist Church (1-1/29)

ELMER, Eliza - see SMITH, Elijah

ELMER, Ischar, 54, wf of Theodorus and mother of Lebbeus E. and Charles W.
Elmer of Rome, d 4/8/47 in Columbia, Herkimer County (1-4/23)

ELMER, Ophelia C. - see BROWN, Jeduthan

ELMER, Sarah Ann - see ELY, Francis

ELMER, Wesley of Rome m 9/14/42 Elizabeth Marion Randall of Camden at C.;
Rev. H. Chapin (1-9/20)

ELMES, James Earnest, 14 months, son of Andrew, d 9/12/39 in Peekskill
(11-9/17)

ELSWORTH, Eliza - see DEMMING, Jesse

ELSWORTH, John - see DEMMING, Jesse

ELTING, Blandina - see DEWITT, Matthew P.

ELTING, Elizabeth (Mrs.), 52, d 12/25/49 in Saugerties (8-12/27)

ELTING, Jane - see DORLON, Robert, Jr.

ELTING, John H. m 11/6/49 Sarah Carling in Ellenville; Rev. Thomas Newman
(8-11/17)

ELWOOD, Daniel H. of Danube m 2/16/43 Joanna Jones of Stark in S.; Bishop
Ottman (3-3/2)

ELWOOD, Hiram of Herkimer County m 3/15/50 Sarah Dygert of Fort Plain in
F.P.; Rev. Dr. C.G. Mc Lean (4-3/28)

ELWOOD, Solomon, Esq. m 3/26/50 Eliza Cox in Minden; Bishop N. Van Alstine
(4-4/4)

ELY, Francis of Western m 5/4/43 Sarah Ann Elmer of Delta in Rome; Rev. R.C.
Brisbin (1-5/16)

ELY, John D., Esq. m 12/25/44 Almira Matthews; Rev. H. Matteson (1-12/31)

ELY, Moses, Esq., 52, d 9/11/42 at his home in New Windsor (9-9/17)

EMBLER, Ann Elmira - see WILSON, Henry

EMERSON, Oliver (Rev.) of the Troy Annual Conference m 4/30/48 Ann Eliza
 Williams in the Methodist Church at Canajoharie; Rev. J. Pegg (4-5/11)

EMERY, Catherine Maria - see SIMMS(?), Isaac

EMIGH, Mary Adelia, 20, wf of George W., d 7/5/49 in Kingston (8-7/21)

EMONS, Solomon, 82, father of the editor of the Keeseville Argus, d (date not
 given) at Fort Edward (6-10/19/35)

EMOTT, Belinda - see DAVIS, Edward

EMOTT, James (Hon.) - see DAVIS, Edward

EMSLIE, Jane - see CLARK, William H.

ENGELS, Jane - see RAMSAY, David D.

ENGLISH, Charles S. m 10/25/40 Ellen D. Miller, dau. of Franklin Miller, in
 Saugerties; Rev. Dr. Ostrander (8-10/27)

ENGLISH, Horace m 8/2/43 Sarah Authelda Weller at Newport; Rev. W.L. Wilson
 (all of Newport) (3-8/10)

ENGS, Elvira F. - see SNYDER, Henry

ENI, a native of the Island of Owhyhee (Hawaii?) in the Pacific Ocean, d 6/2/16 on
 board the sloop, "Charlotte" at Catskill (6-6/5/16)

ENOS, A.W., counsellor at law, m 4/19/36 Catharine M. Bowen, dau. of late
 Benjamin of Tennessee, at the home of R. Lockwood, Esq. in Little Falls;
 Rev. Attwater (3-4/28)

ENOS, Catharine M., 27, wf of A.W., Esq. and dau. of late Benjamin Bowen, d
 11/9/43 in Michigan City, Indiana (consumption)(was a member of
 Episcopal Church)(from Michigan Gazette)(3-11/23)

ENOS, Meigs, 22, only son of Hon. Truman Enos, d 10/2/44 at Westmoreland
 (1-11/12)

ENSIGN, Caroline - see SPRINGER, Martin

ENSIGN, Elizabeth Jane - see HART, George

ENSIGN, Thomas, 78, d (date not given) in Hartford, Conn. (7-6/20/10)

ENSIN, Jane (Mrs.) - see HOLMES, Morris

ERICKSON, Eleanor - see KERKER, George H.

ERWIN, Ann B., 28, d (date not given) "at Woodlands, the seat of her husband,
 James Erwin, Esq. (she, the last surviving dau of the Hon. Henry Clay)
 (surv. by her husband, 5 children and her parents) (from the Lexington
 Kentucky Int.") (6-1/8/36)

ESMAY, Rachael - see BORTHWICK, H.

ESPIE, James of NYC m 5/19/39 Agnes Martha Watson of Dobbs Ferry at D.F.;
 Rev. George Walker (12-5/28)

ESTES, Martha Ella, 4 years, dau. of Nathaniel and Sarah, d 11/17/50 in Utica
 (1-11/20)

ETHERIDGE, Margaret M. - see DYGERT, John W.

ETHERIDGE, Nancy, 57, consort of Nathaniel and eldest dau. of late Gen. Michael
 Myers, d 9/26/40 in Herkimer (3-10/1)

ETHERIDGE, Sally, 47, wf of Samuel, Esq., d 5/16/39 at Cold Water, Branch
 County, Mich. (Samuel was formerly a State Senator in Mich.) and
 formerly had lived in Frankfort, NY) (3-6/6)

ETHERIDGE, Thomas of Boylston m 2/14/49 Miss C.M. Campbell of Lee in
 Rome; Rev. W.E. Knox (1-2/21)

ETHRIDGE, Elizabeth B. - see DOHR, Charles H.

ETHRIDGE, Margaret M. - see DYGERT, John W.

ETHRIDGE, Nathaniel of Herkimer m 11/16/42 Mrs. Lydia House(?) of Columbia in C.; Rev. Elder M--- (surname blurred)

EVAN, Catharine - see WITBECK, James A.

EVANS, ---- (Mrs.), about 57(?), wf of Thomas d 12/4/45 in West Troy (5-12/10)

EVANS, David of Frankfort m 10/3/39 Mary Shorley(?) in Litchfield; Rev. T. Houston (3-10/10)

EVANS, Eliza - see FRANKLIN, Benjamin

EVANS, Eliza - see HENDRICKS, Albert B.

EVANS, Griffith of Rome m 11/2/41 Catharine Ellis of NYC in NYC; Rev. H. Chase (1-11/16)

EVANS, John - see ROBERTS, Edwin M.

EVANS, John - see THOMAS, John

EVANS, Margaret Ann, 27, wf of Richard, d 9/6/41 in West Troy (5-9/15)

EVANS, Mary - see ROBERTS, Edwin M.

EVANS, Mary Ann - see THOMAS, John

EVANS, Mary Augusta, 1, dau. of Thomas and Jane, d 11/26/46 in West Troy (5-12/9)

EVANS, Platt m 3/30/16 Eliza Ann Murray, both of Albany; Rev. Dr. Neill (6-4/3)

EVANS, Robert m 9/17/46 Ann Jones, both of Rome, in Camden; Rev. R. Richard Kirk (1-9/22)

EVANS, Silas S. - see HENDRICKS, Albert B.

EVANS, Thomas, Jr., 32, d 8/25/46 in West Troy (funeral from home of his father (not named) in the first ward in West Troy (5-8/26)

EVANS, Thomas, Sr., 68, d 6/1/49 suddenly in West Troy (5-6/6)

EVANS, William S. m 7/23/50 Cornelia Lewis in Remsen; Rev. Buckingham (all of Remsen) (1-8/7)

EVARTS, Joseph of Fairfield m 3/11/40 Laura S. Davis of Painted Post in P.P.; Rev. Smith (3-3/5)

EVCHANAU, Nancy - see PRESTON, James B.

EVENS, Crowell (Mr.), 53, d (date not given) in NYC (6-5/15/16)

EVENS, James of Cohoes m (date not given) Eliza Dowe of Troy in Albany; Rev. Allen Steele (5-10/22/45)

EVENS, John Westerly, 2, child of Cornbury Evens, d 10/6/41 in Newburgh (9-10/9)

EVERDELL, Robert (Rev.) of Danby, Tompkins County m 10/18/40 Mrs. E.B. Chandler of Hinesburg, VT in Little Falls; Rev. John Laveys (3-10/22)

EVEREST, Emily A. - see MORSE, Ebenezer

EVERETT, Harriet E. - see BACON, John F.

EVERETT, Joel (Professor) - see BROWN, Thomas Yardley (Col.)

EVERETT, Mary Ann - see BROWN, Thomas Yardley (Col.)

EVERILL, Mary B. (Mrs.) - see WILLIAMS, William

EVERIN, Philip Reynolds, 18 months, son of R. John and Elizabeth, d 12/23/35 in Peekskill (11-12/29)

EVERITT, Susan - see BRINKERHOFF, Tunis

EVERITT, Thomas T., M.D. m 10/19/35 Jane H. Thompson at the home of Hon. Smith Thompson; Rev. Samuel A. Van Vranken (6-10/22)

EVERSON, William D., Esq., about 40, d 4/17/39 in Peekskill (12-4/23)

EVERTS, Dudley, Jr. m 1/25/35 Ruth Maria Doubleday, eldest dau. of Hon. U.F.
Doubleday; Elder Wyckoff in Auburn; all of Auburn (6-2/2)

EVERTSEN, Barny E, 36, d 1/20/36 (friends of his mother and brother, Jacob Jr.,
invited to his funeral at 3 o'clock at home of his mother, 152 North Market
St.) (6-1/22)

EVERTSEN, John H. m 2/14/48 Finetta Sipperley, both of West Troy, in Troy;
Rev. Allen Steele (5-2/23)

EVERTSON, ___, wf of Martin Evertson. Her funeral at 10 o'clock from house of
William S. Staats, 43 Beaver St. (6-5/11/35)

EVERTSON, Polly - see CASLER, John

EVERTSON, William Henry, son of late William D. of Peekskill, d 8/31/39 at
home of Elijah Morgan in Yorktown (11-9/3)

EVSTAPHIEVE, Alexis Alexander, son of the "Russia Consul General" for the
United States m 11/7/35 Emily Wilson at Buffalo; Rev. Shelton (all of
Buffalo)(6-11/25)

EWING, ---- (Chief Justice) - see GREEN, Emily Augusta

EWING, John, Esq. d (date not given) at Philadelphia (6-5/8/16)

EWING, Letitia, 29, wf of Robert, d 2/20/39 in Haverstraw (12-2/26)

EYGABROAD, Lena M. - see MOYER, Simeon

EYGEBROT, Mary H. - see MYERS, Abram H.

EYNAMAN, John, about 53, d 12/4/38 in Little Falls (3-12/13)

FAIRBANKS, William B. m 11/3/36 Sarah Chase of Albany; Rev. Holmes (6-11/8)

FAIRCHILD, Harriet Elizabeth - see TEN EYCK, Anthony

FAIRCHILD, Robert of West Point, m 8/19/49 Sarah M. Place of Kingston, at K.;
Rev. C. Shook (8-8/25)

FAIRFIELD, Ann Eliza - see CLARK, William

FAIRFIELD, Jamin L., Jr., m 12/28/48 Harriet Rapp, both of West Troy; Rev.
Houghtaling (5-1/3/49)

FAIRLY, Alexander, 35, late resident of Peekskill, d 3/7/41 suddenly, at Elmira,
NY (11-3/9)

FAIRMAN, David - see ELLICOTT, Andrew

FAKE, Hannah - see FOX, Hiram

FAKE, Isaac, merchant of Paines Hollow m 10/18/37 Mary E. Hull of Little Falls
in Eatonville; Rev. W.H. Waggoner (3-11/4)

FALES, John W., about 30, late of Massachusetts, d 4/22/39 in North Haverstraw
("dropsey in the chest") (12-4/30)

FALK, Henry, about 49, formerly of Little Falls, d 2/17/39 in Steuben (3-2/28)

FANCHER, Susan - see HOLLY, Samuel

FANNING, Frances - see RUSHMORE, Elbert

FANNING, William Augustus, 1, son of Thomas C., s 3/12/42 in Newburgh
(9-3/19)

FARLEY, Jane A. - see DAVIS, Thomas

FARLEY, Martha - see PECK, Everard

FARLIN, Dudley (Hon.) d 9/25/37 at his home in Warrensburg ("has repeatedly
represented people in the State and General Governments") (6-10/2)

FARLIN, J. Warren (Rev.), son of Hon. Dudley Farlin and formerly pastor of the
Presbyterian Church in Saratoga Springs, d (date not given) in
Warrensburgh (6-4/20/37)

FARMER, Cornelia Ann, 324, wf of M. Farmer of Syracuse and eldest dau. of

Charles and Ann Mosely, d 5/6/41 at her father's home in Rome (1-6/1)

FARMER, Emma - see SMITH, Charles

FARMER, Henry, d 7/22/49 in Saugerties (cholera) (8-7/28)

FARMER, John - see WILLIAMS, Brown H.

FARMER, Maria - see WILLIAMS, Brown H.

FARMER, Sanford m 12/7/43 Elsie Petrie in Little Falls; Rev. C.W. Leet (3-12/28)

FARNSWORTH, Samuel (Capt.) d 11/22/26 in Schenectady (6-12/5)

FARNUM, Mary - see AMERMAN, John W

FARNY, Christian Charles m 3/19/49 Barbara Kasper, both of High Falls, in
    Rondout; Rev. C.H. Siebke (8-3/31)

FARQUARHANSON(?), William m 3/15/43 Priscilla Wheeler, dau. of H.
    Wheeler, in Rome; H.C. Vogle (1-4/4)

FARQUARSON, John, 52, d 8/14/49 (1-8/22)

FARQUARSON, N. Adaline - see SOPER, Asahel

FARQUARSON, Sarah M. - see JONES, Thomas, Jr.

FARQUERSON, Mary - see METTESON, Cyrus W.

FARQUHARMON, William J. of Fort Plain m 6/20/50 Nancy Conklin of Salt
    Springville in S.S.; Rev. H. Halstead (4-6/27)

FARR, Walter, 22, merchant, son of Asa of Manheim, d 7/24/37 at Pontiac,
    Michigan (a short illness) (3-8/17)

FARRAN, W.C. of St. Louis and of U.S. navy, d 2/24/35 (almost instantly when
    the horse he was riding "became unmanageable asnd struck a tree...")
    (6-3/21)

FARRAND, George C., 21, eldest son of David P., d 11/10/42 in Goshen (9-11/12)

FARRAR, Sarah P. - see BURK, I.T.

FASSETT, Amos - see STEWART, Mary (Mrs.)

FASSETT, Amos S. d 2/12/49 in Vienna (consumption) (came from Albany to
    Vienna about 1839) (from Rome Sentinel) (1-2/21)

FASSETT, Timothy - see STEWART, Mary (Mrs.)

FAULKNER, William, 54, late keeper of the Western Hotel, 9 Cortlandt St., and
    formerly keeper of the Geneva Hotel, d 11/9/36 in NYC (6-11/22)

FAUROT, L.B. of NYC m 9/12/42 Mary Duncan, dau. of Robert, Esq., at
    Cornwall; Rev. F.H. Vanderveer (9-9/17)

FAUROT, Stephen D. m 7/2/39 Ruth S. Prull "in the vicinity of West Point"; Rev.
    J.T. Perkins (11-7/9)

FAUTS, Allen m 4/30/49 Olesiene Fournier, both of West Troy, in W.T.; Rev. J.C.
    Burroughs (5-5/2)

FAVELL, Daniel m 2/1/43 Mary Cole, dau. of David, in Manheim; Rev.
    Diefendorf (all of Manheim) (3-2/23)

FAWBY(?), William H., Esq. of Albany m 10/5/36 Harriet H. Wilson, dau of late
    James, at Elizabethtown, NJ; Rev. Magin (6-10/8)

FAY, Catharine, wf of Ethan Allen Fay, d 7/12/37 at her home on Third Street,
    Farr's(?) Hall, Albany. Her brother (in-law?), Major H.A. Fay, is mentioned
    (6-7/13)

FAY, Edward m 5/20/16 Prescilla G. Price, both of Albany; Rev. De Witt (6-5/25)

FAY, Jonas (Dr.), 59, of Utica d 6/5/35 at Franklin, Herkimer Co. (a former
    surgeon in the U.S. Army) (6-6/13)

FAY, Lydia Lorraine - see WHITE, Horace T

FAY, Mary Eliza - see HARMON, Bronson

FAY, Sally, 45, wf of John, d 2/25/26 in Northampton, Montgomery County (survived by her husband and "a large family of children") (6-3/10)

FEARING, George B. (Capt.) of Chicago m 6/29/45 Sarah P. Tayler, dau. of Robert of Henry County, Illinois, formerly of West Troy, NY, in Henry County; Rev. M. Bliss (5-7/23)

FEARON, Eleanor - see DONOVAN, John

FEATHERLY, Mary Ann - see SHALL, Richard

FEATHERSON, James, 24, of Saugerties, d 6/16/49 on board the steamboat "R.L. Stevens" (8-6/23)

FEELOR, George H. - see RAWDEN, Freeman

FEETER(?), Benjamin A. , 1/19/37 Parmelia Heath, dau. of Henry, Esq., in Little Falls; Rev. Adams (all of Little Falls) (3-1/26)

FEETER(?), Benjamin, about 20, d 7/4/38 in Little Falls at the home of George H. Feeter(?) (3-7/5)

FEHER(?), John E. m 12/29/38 Phebe T. Johnson of Haverstraw in H.; Rev. Canfield (12-1/15/39)

FELLER, Alvina - see MOREY, Mason

FELLOWS, Fanny - see VIALL, Job G.

FELTER, Ann Eliza - see SUTHERLAND, Edmund

FELTER, Sarah E. - see CLARK, Richard M.

FELTHOUSE, Prime Fairly, 18 months, son of Henry of Peekskill, d 9/17/39 (11-9/24)

FEN, Betsey - see GURLEY, Phineas

FENNELL, A.J. (Rev.) of Groton, Tompkins County m 10/18/43 Racinia Augusta Hackley, dau. of P.M. Hackley, Esq., formerly of Little Falls, at home of Col. David Petrie in Little Falls; Rev. Bloodgood (3-10/26)

FENNELL, Mary Ann - see SINCLAIR, John P.

FENNER, Daniel, Esq. m 9/23/41 Almira Luther, both of Fairfield, in F.; Rev. A.D. Peck (3-9/30)

FENNER, Maria Louisa, 17, only dau. of Jeremiah of Newport, d 9/8/36 in Little Falls (3-9/15)

FENNER, William, 72, d 8/11/39 (3-8/22)

FENTON, Asa F. (Rev.), pastor of the Methodist Episcopal Church at Fort Plain, m 8/24/49 Sarah E. Fisk of Isle La Motte* at I.L.M.; Rev. N.B. West of Alburgh (Vermont)* *northern tip of Lake Champlain (4-8/30)

FENTON, Elizabeth T. - see LOOMIS, John B.

FENTON, J.P. m 11/5/48 E.A. Hubbard in Mechanicville; Rev. P. Cook (all of West Troy) (5-11/8)

FENTON, Rebecca W., 6, dau. of Dr. John and Rachael W., d 10/27/41 in Middle Hope (9-10/30)

FENTON, William M. of Pontiac, Mich., merchant, m 4/11/36 Adelaide S. Birdsall, dau of James, Esq., of Addison, Steuben Co., NY at A.; Rev. Betts (6-4/28)

FENWICK, John E. m 10/23/40 Elizabeth Field, dau. of Capt. John, in Saugerties; Rev. Dr. Ostrander (8-10/27)

FERO, Catharine, 10, dau. of Robert, formerly of Canajoharie, d 8/25/48 at Buffalo (4-10/5)

FERRELL, Catharine - see URANN, James R.

FERRIL, Andrew (Dr.) - see PRENTISS, Sarah (Mrs.)

FERRIS, Catharine Ann Hurcham, wf of Rev. Dr. Ferris, late of Albany, d 9/9/37 in NYC (a protracted illness) (6-9/14)

FERRIS, Elizabeth - see SANDS, Stephen T.

FERRIS, George, 77, d 4/29/39 in Yorktown (a long-term resident in Westchester County) (11-4/30)

FERRIS, Gould, a Rev. War soldier, d 6/8/35 in Pound Ridge (a long term resident there) (12-6/18)

FERRIS, J.H. m 10/4/42 Sarah Ann Nelson, dau of William, Esq.; Rev. Dr. Westbrook (all of Peekskill) (11-10/4)

FERRIS, J.H., Esq. m 10/4/42 Sarah Nelson, dau of William, Esq.; Rev. Dr. Westbrook; all of Peekskill (11-10/6)

FERRIS, Jane Eliza - see STRANG, Alsop H.

FERRIS, John Becker, 3, second son of William D., d 3/29/37 (6-3/31)

FERRIS, Joseph, Sr., about 80, d 11/24/41 in Peekskill. (11-11/30)

FERRIS, Julia - see MATTHEWS, Robert

FERRIS, Leonard m 2/6/42 Eliza Mc Gown ("both somewhat advances in years") (11-2/15)

FERRIS, Samuel m 3/20/39 Mrs. Esther Hopkins of Peekskill in P.; Rev. J. Youngs (12-4/2)

FERRIS, Samuel of Carmel m 3/20/39 Esther Hopkins of Peekskill in P.; Rev. J. Youngs (11-3/26)

FERRIS, Sarah - see COOPER, Thomas B.

FERRY, --- (Mrs.), wf of Heman, Esq., d 1/19/42 in Utica (1-1/25)

FERRY, Edward, 9, son of late Sylvester, d 8/25/42 in Newburgh (9-9/3)

FERRY, Irad, 64, d 1/4/37 at New Orleans (in discharging his duty he fell from the fourth story of a burning building) (6-1/24)

FESSENDEN, Thomas Green, Esq., editor of the New England Farmer, d 11/11/37 in Boston. was a candidate for Representative for Boston in the General Court (from the Boston Daily Advertiser) (6-11/16)

FETCHER, Joseph m 11/14/41 Catharine Smith; Rev. J. Loveys (all of Danube) (3-11/18)

FETTERLY, Agnes Helen, 2, dau. of Thomas, d 9/9/39 in Herkimer (3-9/12)

FIDLER, Nathan m 12/21/43 Elizabeth Tracy in West Troy; Rev. Z. Phillips (all of West Troy) (5-12/27)

FIELD, Amos m 12/25/38 Huldah Ambler; Rev. George D. Sutton (all of North Salem) (12-1/15/39)

FIELD, Elizabeth - see FENWICK, John E.

FIELD, Elizabeth (Mrs.) - see REGUS, William Clement

FIELD, James H., Esq., 39, son of late Daniel Field of Peekskill, d 1/21/43 in New Orleans (11-2/7)

FIELD, Jane - see GRIFFIN, Stephen C.

FIELD, Moses, 53, late of NYC, d 10/21/33 (a lingering illness) (11-10/29)

FIELD, Phebe, about 60, wf of James, d 3/7/39 in Greenwich (member of Society of Friends - Monthly Meeting of Purchase) (death was sudden "in a fit") (12-3/12)

FIELD, Samuel A.C. of North Salem m 9/26/42 Clara A. Lewis, dau of Garret C. of White Plains, at W.P.; Rev. Evans (11-9/29)

FIELDS, Caroline - see CHELLIS, John C.

FIERO, Christian C. m 10/15/49 Sarah J. Maxwell, both of Quarryville, in Q.; Rev.

B. Redford (8-10/27)

FIERO, Elizabeth - see VAN DER BECK, James J.

FIERO, Jane Ann - see O'BRIEN, Edward

FILD (sic), Mary - see TILLEY, William

FILER, De Loss L. m 3/8/40 Juliet Golden at Paine's Hollow (both of that place);
Rev. Richards (3-3/19)

FILER, Sally Amanda, 21, wf of Delos L. Filer, d 6/7/39 at Paine's Hollow (disease
of the heart) (survived by husband and an infant daughter) (3-6/13)

FILKINS, Henry of Herkimer m 8/20/49 Johanna Hurley of West Troy; Rev. T.W.
Pearson (5-8/22)

FILKINS, Sarah - see PAINT, Philander

FILLEY, Jonathan B., 21, d 9/14/41 in Vernon (obituary furnished) (1-9/21)

FILTCH, Mary R. - see CANDE, Jesse B.

FINCH, Aletha - see HILL, Uriah

FINCH, Henry m 10/13/46 Sarah M. Silliman, both of West Troy, in W.T.; Rev.
O.H. Gregory (5-10/21)

FINCH, John, 43, of Peekskill d "at half past five this morning" (11-7/20/41)

FINCH, Thomas of Frankfort m 12/4/50 Mary Ann Copsey of Willowvale in W.;
Rev. John Waugh (1-12/11)

FINDLAY, James, late candidate for governor of Ohio, d 12/28/35 at Cincinnati
(6-1/13/36)

FINE, John (Gen.) of Weedsport m 1/9/43 Mary Joslin, dau. of Nelson Joslin, Esq.
of Verona in V.; Rev. Torrey (1-1/17)

FINGER, Henry L. m 9/19/49 Ann Christina Snyder in Saugerties; Rev. P.C.
Oakley (all of Saugerties) (8-9/22)

FINK, Andrew A. - see SHELDON, Amelia

FINK, Charles, Esq., Teller of the Herkimer County Bank m 9/13/43 Nancy Anna
Mann, Eldest dau. of Hon. Abijah Mann, Jr. formerly of Herkimer County,
at Brooklyn; Rev. A.L. Bloodgood (3-9/21)

FINK, Henry of Manheim m 1/25/42 Catherine Van Alstine, dau. of Gen. C.N. Van
Alstine of Sharon, in S.; Rev. A.B. Chittenden (3-2/3)

FINN, Margaret - see PHILLIPS, Jacob

FINN, Maria - see IVES, Ambrose

FINN, Patrick - see BILLINGTON, ―――

FISH, Abby (Mrs.) - see LANING, Joseph

FISH, Almonzo D., Esq. m 3/9/37 Julia Ann Howell, dau. of Capt. William
Howell, in Herkimer (bride & groom, both of Herkimer); Rev. Wheeler
(3-3/16)

FISH, Amos - see TILLETSON, Gardner

FISH, Catharine - see KNAPP, Samuel

FISH, Francis D. of Little Falls m 3/15/38 Julia Brace of New Hartford, Oneida
County, in New Hartford; Rev. Palmer N. Way (3-3/22)

FISH, Mary - see MORRIS, David

FISH, Moses W. m 12/17/39 Eliza Brower, dau. of Jacob, Esq., in New Castle;
Rev. Travis (all of New Castle) (12-12/31)

FISH, Moses, Esq., 77, d 10/6/36 at Rome, NY (a native of Groton, Conn. and an
early settler in Little Falls) (3-10/13)

FISH, Nathaniel W. m 9/20/40 Harriet Howell in Herkimer; Rev. James Murphy
(all of Herkimer) (3-10/1)

FISH, Nicholas (Colonel), 74, d 6/20/33 in NYC (11-6/25)

FISHER, Barber m (date not given) Abigail Miller in Boston (6-5/15/16)

FISHER, Caroline - see BASSETT, N.B.

FISHER, Laus(?), about 50, of Kent, d 9/23/49 (10-9/26)

FISHER, Mary Ann - see CLARK, Abijah H.

FISHER, Phebe, wf of Jesse, d 1/11/39 in Sing Sing (12-1/15)

FISHER, Sarah - see JOCK, John

FISHER, Sarah Elizabeth - see RICE, William

FISK, ---- (Dr.) m in November 1841 Harriet Seranton at Kirkville (1-12/21)

FISK, Helen M. - see PROUTY, Lemuel D.

FISK, Joseph, Esq., Marshal of City of Albany m 5/21/35 Sarah Hurlbut of
Charlotte, VT at C.; Rev. Dr. Eaton (6-5/26)

FISK, Sarah E. - see FENTON, Asa F. (Rev.)

FISKE, George, 57, formerly of Claremont, NH, d 3/5/37 in Albany (funeral from
his late home at 30 Green Street) (6-3/6)

FISKE, Harriet (Mrs.) d 1/1/42 at Kirkville (1-1/11)

FITCH, Benjamin, 48, d 3/31/16 in Salem (death caused by a blow which fractured
his skull given by John Getty of Hebron about March (Mr. Getty jailed for
trial at the June circuit court) (6-4/6)

FITCH, J.P., Esq., editor of the Roman Citizen, m 12/16/47 Sarah M. Seymour,
dau. of Arden Seymour, in Rome; Rev. W.F. Williams (1-12/17)

FITCH, Jane H. - see PERKINS, D.W. (Dr.)

FITCH, Mrs. - see PARKER, Joanna (Mrs.)

FITCH, Samuel S., 61, d. (date not given) at Montville (7-5/10/09)

FITCHET, William Rockwell, 11 months, son of Harvey M. and Helen, d 10/22/47
in West Troy (5-10/27)

FITZ PATRICK, Sarah - see BRITHWAIT, John

FITZGERALD, Edmund (Col.), 66, d 12/4/38 in Halfmoon (5-1/4/39)

FITZGERALD, P. - see KELLY, ---- (Mrs.)

FITZSIMMONS, Catherine (Mrs.), 67 (?) d 7/17/35 (of consumption) in Albany
(funeral at 4 o'clock at home of her son-in-law, Peter Newman, at the two
mile house on the Great Western Turnpike) (6-7/18)

FITZSIMMONS, John, 26, d 1/13/35 at Albany (relatives and friends of the
deceased and his brother-in-law, Charles Quin are invited to his funeral
from Mr. Quin's home, 18 South Pearl St. at 3 pm 1/14 (6-1/14)

FITZSIMMONS, P. (Mr.) - see COON, Abby Jane

FLAGG, Mary - see BRIDGE, Matthew

FLAGG, Nancy - see WHITNEY, R.M.

FLAGLER, ----, child of Dr. John O., d (date not given - funeral 2/16/27 at 8 Van
Schaick Street) (6-2/16)

FLAGLER, Harvey L. m 11/20/35 Sarah J. Holden, both of Cold Spring, at
Williams Hotel in Peekskill; Rev. Marshall (11-11/24)

FLAGLER, Harvey N., 28, innkeeper, d 5/27/42 at Cold Spring (11-6/9)

FLANDER, Henry, 88, a Rev. War soldier, d 3/5/49 at St. Johnsville (4-3/8)

FLANDERS, Nancy - see ACKERMAN, Jacob

FLANSBURGH, Elizabeth - see BOYCE, Peter

FLANSBURY, Margaret, 51, wf of John, d (date not given) at her home in New
Scotland (6-3/26/36)

FLEMING, ----, wf of J.J., d 6/12/40 (5-6/17)

105

FLEMING, Augustus Jr., m 10/13/36 Euretta M. Moore, dau of late Benjamin of Claverack, at Christ Church in Hudson; Rev. Tiffany (6-10/21)

FLEMING, Augustus, Jr., m 10/13/36 Euretta U. Moore, dau of late Benjamin at Christ's Church, Hudson; Rev. W. Tiffany (6-10/20)

FLEMING, Cornelia Anne - see GRACIE, William

FLEMING, Julia - see NEWBOLD, Thomas R.

FLEUR(?), Andrew of Buffalo m 11/12/50 Mrs. Electa Thompson of Cohoes; Rev. Thomas W. Pearson (5-11/13)

FLEWELLING, Mary - see CARHART, ---- (Mr.)

FLEWELLING, Mary - see PUTNEY, William

FLEWWELLIN, Barnabas m 1/1/40 Jane Sutton, dau. of Robert of Yorktown, in Y.; William Hunt, Esq. of South Salem (12-1/7)

FLEWWELLING, Robert m 12/24/41 Elizabeth Putney in Yorktown; Johnh Greene, Esq. (all of Yorktown) (11-12/28)

FLINT, Amos of Rome m 3/20/41 Mrs. Susan Mc Guin of Sackets Harbor at Annsville; Rev. Isaac L. Hunt (1-3/23)

FLINT, Augustus of Amenia m 11/12/35 Catherine Bokee, dau of Hon. Abram Bokee, member of Congress from North East; Rev. William J.Mc Cord of North East (6-11/27)

FLINT, Henrietta - see KELLOGG, John (Dr.)

FLINT, Mary - see CRETSER, John

FLINT, Miss - see GREEN, Ira W.

FOARD, Hezekiah (General), 81, d 2/16/33 at home of his son on Bohemia Manor (a soldier throughout the Rev. War. Held rank of Captain by brevet at time of discharge in 1783) (11-3/5)

FOLGER, William H. (Capt.) m 12/26/36 Ophelia Olcott in Hudson; Rev. J. Waterbury (all of Hudson) (6-1/7/37)

FOLMSBEE, Mary E. - see GRISWELL, David

FOLTS, Catharine - see BRIDENBECKER, Isaac

FOLTS, Elmira - see CASLER, Peter P.

FOLTS, Fanny - see SMALL, William

FOLTS, J. Philo of Boonville m 2/21/42 Mary Fulmer of Steuben at S.; J. Covenhoven, Esq. (3-3/3)

FOLTZ, George of Frankfort m 5/1/37 Eliza Murray of Whitesboro at W.; Rev. A.B. Groat (6-5/3)

FONDA, Cornelia - see VANDERCOOK, John F.

FONDA, Douw I., 73, d 6/15/42 in Watervliet ("one of the oldest and most respected inhabitants") (5-6/22)

FONDA, Herman age blurred perhaps 74?, d lately in Michigan ("born and brought up in Watervliet, NY") (5-12/10)

FONDA, Lewis Henry, 20 months, only son of Tunis and Cynthia, d 1/2/45 in West Troy (5-1/8)

FONDA, Matilda Beekman, wf of Douw Fonda, Esq., d 10/3/37 in Albany (6-10/5)

FONDA, Olive Pamelia, 30, wf of Abram, d 6/2/49 in Troy (5-6/6)

FONDA, Sarah M. - see ROBINSON, Isaac A.

FONDA, Tunis, merchant, of West Troy m 11/9/40 Cynthia Badgley of Halfmoon in H.; Rev. Parks (5-11/18)

FOOT, ----, 81, relict of Jeremiah, d 2/7/09 at Colchester (left 9 children, 57 grand children, and 19 great grand children) (7-3/8)

FOOT, Abijah, 56, d (date not given) at Newtown (7-6/20/10)

FOOT, John (Capt.), 67, d (date not given) at Watertown (7-8/2/09)

FOOTE, Jeremiah, merchant, of Waterville, Delaware Co., m 5/17/26 Maria Wood, dau. of Jethro of Ledyard, Cayuga Co. in L. (6-6/23)

FOOTE, Lucia R. - see HAWES, Josiah L.

FOOTE, Thomas M, M.D. one of the editors and proprietors of the Daily Commercial Advertiser, m 8/10/36 Margaret St. John in Buffalo; Rev. William Shelton (all of B.) (6-8/15)

FORBES, William of NYC m 10/15/26 Jane Mc Lachlan of Albany; Rev. Ludlow (6-10/20)

FORCE(?), Bartholomew (Capt.) m 3/31/44 Laura Keeney of Rome in Clockville, Madison County; Rev. Lymon Wright (1-4/9)

FORCE, Alonzo m 8/25/36 Gertrude Ann Kittle; Rev. R.C. Brislin (all of Albany) (6-8/29)

FORD, A.G. m 1/2/40 Angeline Benchley, both of Fairfield, in F.; Rev. C.I. Dunning (3-1/30)

FORD, David (Col.), 74, d 11/6/35 at the Mansion house of the late Judge Ford near Ogdensburgh (Lived in New Jersey until 1804 "when he followed his brother Judge Ford, the pioneer of our settlement." Settled at Morristown. Served in the Rev. War from Morristown, NJ) (from Ogdensburgh Republican) (6-11/18)

FORD, Elizabeth K., 20, dau. of Simeon Ford, d 9/20/36 at Cleveland, Ohio (3-10/13)

FORD, Ellen - see MC VITHE(?), Mark

FORD, Emily C - see SHUMWAY, G.R.H.

FORD, Frances - see PETERS, Joram

FORD, Henry L. of Fairfield m 2/12/38 Lorain Root(?) of Little Falls in L.F.; Rev. Roper (3-3/1)

FORD, Jacob (Hon.), 93, a Rev. War soldier, d 7/24/37 at Austerlitz, NY (was formerly a first judge in Columbia County and a Baptist Church member 70 years) (from the Hudson Gazette) (6-8/9)

FORD, Mary, 5, d 2/21/35 and her sibling, Wesley, 7, d 2/24/35 (children of Linus E. Ford) at Fairfield (scarlet fever) (3-3/21)

FORD, Philip - see PETERS, Joram

FORD, S.E. - see MATTHEW, Penelope

FORD, Sally Ann - see KEITH, Stephen

FORD, Sarah - see LINZEY, John

FORD, Simeon, Esq., 63, d 10/12/39 at his home in Cleveland, Ohio (born in Berkshire County, Massachusetts, received his classical education at Williams College. In Herkimer County by 1798, attorney in Superior Court in 1801) (3-10/24)

FORHALL(?), Nancy - see JUDD, George W.

FORMAN, Catharine - see SUTTON, John

FORRESTER, Fanny - see JUDSON, A. (Rev.)

FORSEY(?). Charlotte - see HALL, ADAM

FORSHAY, Schuyler m 12/19/38 Catharine Van Cortlandt in Sing Sing; Rev. Van Deusen (12-12/25)

FORSTER, Ursula - see KELLY, James R.

FORSY, David m 1/5/35 Delia Mc Glashan; Rev. Potter (6-1/7)

FORSYTH, Clara C. - see MASON, Murray (Lieut.)
FORSYTH, John (Hon.) - see MASON, Murray (Lieut.)
FORSYTH, Major R.A. - see BATES, George C.
FORSYTH, Mary - see GLASS, Adam
FORSYTH, William W. of Albany m 9/6/36 Cornelia K. Strong, dau of late Rev.
    Purchal(?) N. of NYC, at NYC; Rev. Dr. Price (6-9/8)
FORT, A.P., 39, d 5/11/45 in West Troy (lingering consumption) (5-5/14)
FORT, Jacob of Stark m 10/9/49 Lucinda White of Springfield in S.; Rev. J.S.
    (surname blurred) (4-10/18)
FORT, Jacob S. m 4/27/16 Ann Merselis, both of Albany; Rev. Brunk (6-5/1)
FORT, James m 11/4/41 Matilda Brown in West Troy; Rev. O.H. Gregory (all of
    West Troy) (5-11/17)
FORT, John A. m (date not given) Mary Clement at New Orleans (6-5/15/16)
FORT, Simon m 3/24/44 Harriet A. Bristol in West Troy; Rev. Z. Phillips (all of
    West Troy) (5-3/27)
FOSHAY, John, about 75, d 10/25/50 in Kent Frances (10-10/31)
FOSHAY, Mary - see RYDER, Willett
FOSMIRE, Garett H. of Nassau m 2/27/36 Mary Ann Pitts, dau of Levi, Esq., in
    Chatham; Rev. William Hunt of New Lebanon (double ceremony see marr.
    of Hart Green) (6-3/21)
FOSMIRE, Sarah Ann - see GREEN, Hart
FOSS, Joshua, 100, d (date not given) at Barrington (7-5/10/09)
FOSTER, Abigail - see LAWSON, Laurence
FOSTER, Achsal - see AMES, John
FOSTER, Andrew m 1/30/44 Abigail Hitchcock, both of West Troy, in Troy; Rev.
    Ranford Wells (5-2/7)
FOSTER, Augusta Mariah - see REYMOND, George
FOSTER, Calvin, 35, d 1/28/37 at Pompey (consumption) (6-2/3)
FOSTER, Chandler of the City Hotel m 11/14/37 Catalina Lansing, dau. of A.F.
    Lansing; Rev. I.N. Wyckoff (6-11/15)
FOSTER, Elizabeth - see SHAFER, Peter B.
FOSTER, Emeline - see WAGNER, Chauncey
FOSTER, George Graham, 1, son of Junius G. and Helenora, d 4/5/45 in West Troy
    (5-4/9)
FOSTER, Hearty, consort of Ebenezer, Esq., d 7/18/38 at South Williamstown,
    Mass. after "a lingering and very painful illness" (3-7/26)
FOSTER, Horsa of Verona m 2/4/41 Cornelia Skadan, dau. of John C., of
    Durhamville, at D.; Rev. D.D. Ransom (1-2/23)
FOSTER, Jabez, Jr., Esq. m 5/24/36 Catharine J. Ten Eyck, dau of Hon. Egbert
    Ten Eyck; Rev. G.S. Boardman (all of Watertown) (6-5/30)
FOSTER, Mary E. - see ADDINGTON, Samuel
FOSTER, Mason D., M.D., m 9/21/37 Romina Bird, dau. of John, in Manchester,
    Ontario Co., Julius N. Granger, Esq. (all of Manchester) (6-9/29)
FOSTER, Rebecca - see WINTERS, William
FOSTER, Ruth (Mrs.), 79, d 1/21/42 (9-1/22)
FOSTER, Sarah A. - see MC COY, Edward
FOSTER, Timothy, 65, father of the Hon. Henry A. Foster of Rome, NY, d
    11/20/37 at Hartford, Conn. (6-12/
FOSTER, William, about 25, late of Crake Marsh, Staffordshire, England, d

7/13/26 at Stillwater, Saratoga County (was in the service of Dr. Elias
Willard. Drowned in attempt to swim the Hudson River) (6-7/21)
FOUNTAIN, Ezra, 18, only son of Tyler Fountain, Esq., d 11/25/38 at Peekskill
(severe and protracted illness) (12-12/11)
FOUNTAIN, J.H. of Manchester, Mich. m 12/24/40 Catherine Horton, dau of late
Cyrus of Putnam Valley; Rev. R.K. Thompson (11-1/5/41)
FOURNIER, Olesiene - see FAUTS, Allen
FOWLER, ---- and ---- (their names lacking), age 2 and 8, d 1/11 and 1/12/42 in
Yorktown (scarlet fever) (daughters of John Fowler) (11-1/18)
FOWLER, Ann Eliza, 35, wf of Dr. Charles G. Fowler, d 4/28/42 in Montgomery
(9-5/7)
FOWLER, Catharine, 61, widow of Caleb, d 12/14/41 (9-12/18)
FOWLER, Charles Augustus, 4, son of Egbert S., d 1/12/42 in Yorktown (scarlet
fever) (11-1/18)
FOWLER, Charles Augustus, about 5, eldest son of Egbert S., d 1/12/42 in
Yorktown (scarlet fever) (11-1/18)
FOWLER, David (Dr.), 79, father of Gen. G.O. Fowler, d 10/27/35 at his home in
Newburgh (6-10/31)
FOWLER, Dr. Charles G. - see FOWLER, Ann Eliza
FOWLER, Gen. G.O. - see DEMAREST, Ann
FOWLER, Jane, about 76, wf of Jesse, d 1/19/41 in Yorktown (11-1/26)
FOWLER, John, 92, late of Sing Sing, d 2/27/42 in NYC (11-3/8)
FOWLER, John, Jr. m 12/29/39 Sarah Ingersoll, dau. of Cornelius of Yorktown, in
Y.; Rev. Sloat (12-1/7/40)
FOWLER, Martha, 74, relict of late Reuben, d 1/1/34 in Peekskill (11-1/7)
FOWLER, Moses, about 75, d 1/10/39 in Yorktown (12-1/29)
FOWLER, Nathaniel D m 9/26/39 Elizabeth C. Hatluck, youngest dau of James B.;
Rev. J. Youngs (all of Peekskill) (11-10/1)
FOWLER, P.H. (Rev.) of Albany m 10/4/36 Jeanette, niece and adopted dau of
Hon. S.M. Hopkins, at Geneva; Rev. P.C. Hay(?) (6-10/10)
FOWLER, Sarah - see MOTT, Jacob
FOWLER, Thomas m 11/8/49 Ann Heustis; Rev. T.B. Phillips (all of Rondout)
(8-11/17)
FOWLER, William, 81, d 4/12/42 in Peekskill (11-4/14)
FOWLER, William, about 80, of Peekskill m 4/4/39 Amy Holmes, 25, of Carmel in
Carmel; Jacob Sunderland, Esq. (12-4/23)
FOWLES, Mary Elizabeth, 15, of Bangor, Maine d 10/5/45 in West Troy (typhus
fever) (5-10/15)
FOX, ----, 6, son of Daniel C. Fox, Esq., d (date and place of death not given)
(2-1/25/10)
FOX, Angelica, 31, wf of Peter, Jr. and dau. of Peter V. Degraaf, d 3/24/50 in
Herkimer (4-3/28)
FOX, Anna - see EDWARDS, Thomas
FOX, Ardon E., 25, son of Isaac of Rome, d 10/4/41 in Rome (consumption)
(1-10/12)
FOX, Catharine - see AKERMAN, John A.
FOX, Daniel C. m 10/12/43 Sarah Ann Churchill; Rev. C.W. Leet (3-10/19)
FOX, Elizabeth - see BELLINGER, Lawrence
FOX, Elizabeth - see FOX, Staats

FOX, Elizabeth - see LIPE, Joel

FOX, Frederick - see ORMSBY, Bethiah

FOX, George m 12/31/46 Sarah Geer, both of Troy; Rev. Houghtaling (5-1/6/47)

FOX, Helen, 4, dau. of Peter L., d 11/17/36 in Little Falls (3-11/24)

FOX, Hiram m 9/6/49 Hannah Fake, both of Danube; Bishop N. Valentine (4-9/13)

FOX, Jacob m 7/4/38 Jane Allen in Danube; Ralph Simms, Esq. (3-7/12)

FOX, Roland m 10/19/42 Susan J. Jefferson at Rome; A.C. Vogell (1-10/25)

FOX, Staats of South Carolina m 3/1/49 Elizabeth Fox, dau. of Archibald, Esq. of
   Palatine, in P.; Rev. Rumpf (4-3/8)

FOX, William W., Esq., 82, d 3/18/36 in Palatine (3-3/24)

FRAME, Solomon V. (son of Dr. William Frame formerly of Russia, NY) m
   2/20/39 Olive Wheeler of Russia, NY; Rev. A. Fish (3-3/14)

FRANCE, Hannah, about 73, relict of Philip, d 10/12/49 in Saugerties (8-10/27)

FRANCE, Richard m 3/19/49 Julia Hoovenburg, both of Saugerties, at Woodstock;
   Rev. Alexander Gulick (8-3/31)

FRANCIS, Daniel of Buffalo m 3/19/35 Alida Long of Albany; Rev. Dr. Sprague
   (6-3/21)

FRANCIS, John M., editor of the Troy Budget, m 12/8/46 Harriet E. Tucker, dau.
   of Pomeroy Tucker, Esq., of Palmyra, NY at P.; Rev. Harrington (5-12/16)

FRANCISCO(?), Cornelius, 77, "a volunteer soldier of the Revolution", d 1/12/37
   in Frankfort (3-1/26)

FRANCISCO, James F, m 1/15/26 "Mrs. Clark",; Rev. Dr. Chester (all of Albany)
   (6-1/20)

FRANE(?), Lawrence of Durhamville m 1/7/41 Charlotte M. Yale of Lenox at L.;
   Rev. Day (1-4/20)

FRANKLIN, Abraham, formerly of House of Franklin, Robinson & Co., d (date not
   given) in NYC (6-2/21/26)

FRANKLIN, Barbara - see BAUM, Chester

FRANKLIN, Benjamin m 10/31/45 Eliza Evans, both of Cohoes, at Troy; Elder P.
   Thomas (5-11/12)

FRANKLIN, John m 4/29/10 Meriam Jay, both of Catskill (7-5/2)

FRASER, Adam, formerly of Nova Scotia, m 10/21/35 Elizabeth L. Nugent of
   Albany; Rev. Kirk (6-10/23)

FRASER, Alexander, son of John, d (date not given and age lacking) (funeral
   2/2/37 from 20 Fox Street) (6-2/1)

FRASER, Harriet - seer MARVIN, Titus J.

FRASER, Harvey B. of Rome m 12/11/46 Harriet N. Hayden of Annsville in A,;
   Rev. William E. Holmes (1-12/15)

FRASER, Jane - see HUBBS, William

FRASER, John Henry, 28, d 4/20/16 in Montreal (born in Inverness, Scotland)
   (6-5/8)

FRASER, John O. m 10/2/44 Mary S. Blair, one of two oldest daus. of Abner B.;
   Rev. Button (all of Rome) (double ceremony - see MERRILL, Ardon)
   (1-10/8)

FRASER, Margaret (Miss), 25, d 3/26/35 in Albany (funeral "this afternoon" at 4
   o'clock from her late residence, 29 Dean St. (6-3/28)

FRASER, Robert H., 38, d 8/31/46 in West Troy at the home of his brother (not
   named) (formerly of Athens, Greene County where his body was taken for
   burial) (5-9/9)

110

FRASER, William B., 32, of firm of M.H. and W.B. Fraser, bookbinders, d
9/19/48 in Troy (5-9/27)

FRASER, William B.of Troy m 12/7/47 Mary Ann Roff of Albany; John Miles,
chaplain of Albany Bethel (5-12/15)

FRASER, William, 97, d (date not given) in Huntington, Conn. (6-12/1/26)

FRATT, Nicholas D.B., formerly of West Troy, NY, m Miss Mc Duffee of Racine,
Wisc. in R. (5-3/11/46)

FRAZER(?), William, M.D., of Darien, Georgia, d 7/1/37 at West Point, NY
(6-7/10)

FRAZER, C.E., M.D. of Delta m 1/26/42 Caroline White of Rome (1-2/1)

FRAZER, Delia Hedding, 3, dau. of John and Sarah, d 9/2/45 at the Methodist
Parsonage in West Troy (5-9/17)

FRAZER, Melinda - see MORAN, James

FRAZER, William, 67, d 1/23/45 at the Methodist Parsonage in West Troy
(deceased was the father of the Rev. William N. Fraser of Greenfield, NY,
both members of the Troy Conference of the Methodist Episcopal Church)
(5-1/29)

FREAR, Deborah (Mrs.) - see PECK, Allen

FREDENDALL, Jacob m 11/19/36 Catharine Eliza Griffin, dau of Richard; Rev.
Frederick O. Mayer (all of Albany) (6-11/23)

FREDENRICH, Philip m 3/15/36 Sarah Shaver; Rev. Welch (all of Albany) (6-3/7)

FREDERICKS, Sarah - see MEACER, Daniel

FREEMAN, Henry S., Esq., 27, d 8/24/35 in Attica (former editor and publisher of
the Attica Republican) (6-9/11)

FREEMAN, John D., Attorney General of the State (NY or Mississippi?) m
5/12/42 Eliza Ardine Adams, second dau. of Hon. George Adams, near
Jackson, Mississippi ("six years ago Mr. Freeman was a printer's boy in the
office of The Reflector, Schenectady, NY) (5-6/15)

FREEMAN, Lucinda - see WOOD, Robert

FREEMAN, Margaret - see DIXON, Levi

FREEMAN, Margaret (Mrs.) - see AYRES, Daniel (Dr.)

FREEMAN, Mary Elizabeth - see LOWRY, John

FREER, Richard m 10/9/49 Charlott Schoonmaker, both of Rosendale, in R.; Rev.
C.I. Van Dyxk (8-10/20)

FRELEIGH, ---- (Dr.) - see HASWELL, Joseph A.

FRELEIGH, Frances - see HASWELL, Joseph A.

FRENCH, Eunice Luceba - see CLARK, George R.

FRENCH, Hannah - see CAMACE(?), James

FRENCH, Horace E. of Floyd m 4/7/46 Mary A. Alden of Camden at Holland
Patent; Rev. J.F. Scovel (1-5/19)

FRENCH, James M. m 12/2/35 Sarah Ann Vanderpoel, dau of Hon. James; Rev.
Vermilye (6-12/4)

FRENCH, M. Holly of West Troy m 1/23/42 Lucinda Van Order of Troy in T.;
Rev. C.P. Clark (5-2/2)

FRENCH, Mary Elizabeth, 4, dau. of Joseph and Elizabeth, d 10/28/42 in
Newburgh (9-10/29)

FRENCH, Rachel - see SHUTTERS, John

FRENCH, Samuel m 11/7/48 Lydia A. Wheat, dau. of Grant Wheat of Rome in
Kalamazoo, Mich.; Rev. O.P. Hoyt (1-11/17)

FRIES, Elizabeth - see BROWN, Charles

FRINK, Luke, 82, d 9/22/41 in Rome (1-10/5)

FRINK, Susan - see HALL, J. Whitfield

FRISBIE, Elizabeth H. - see STEDMAN, David

FRISBIE, Seth B., formerly of Vernon, NY, d 1/8/42 at his home in Ohio
(inflammation of the lings) (1-2/8)

FRISBY, ----, (age not given) child of Edward Frisby, died (date not given) (funeral
10/5/37 from her father's home at 307 South Pearl Street, Albany) (6-10/5)

FRITCHER, Angelica - see PETRIE, Charles

FROST, J.C. of South Salem m 11/25/39 Tamer Ann Nelson, dau of Peter, Esq. of
Somers at S.; Rev. Bangs (12-12/3)

FROST, John (Rev.) of Whitesboro d 3/1/42 at Waterville (1-3/8)

FROST, Joseph C. of South Salem m 11/25/39 Miss ---- (name illegible), dau. of
Peter Nelson(?), Esq., of Somers in S.; Rev. Travis (12-11/26)

FROST, Joseph C., 23, youngest son of Stephen and Mary, d 3/20/40 at the home
of his father in South Salem (12-3/31)

FROST, Joseph C., about 24, d 3/20/40 in South Salem (survIved by a wife (not
named) (12-3/24)

FROST, Mary - see PURDY, Sylvanus

FROST, Tamer (Mrs.) - see CARPENTER, Abraham

FROST, Theodore Y. of Carmel m 12/30/49 Eliza Ann Scudder of New Fairfield,
Conn. in N.F.; Rev. Penill (10-1/2/50)

FROST, Thomas G. m 11/18/47 Elizabeth A. Bancroft, both of Rome, in R.; Rev.
Hall of New Berlin, Chenango County (1-11/19)

FROTHINGHAM, Lucretia, 11 months, dau. of William W., d 3/27/42 in Albany
(5-3/30)

FROTHINGHAM, Lucretia, 44, wf of W.W., Esq. d 2/26/42 in Albany (5-3/2)

FRY, Daniel m 12/14/37 Adelaide Hall, dau. of Green Hall; Rev. Dr. Campbell
(6-12/15)

FRY, Lydia B. - see PEASE, Erastus H.

FRYER, Hugh D. m 3/11/26 Clarissa Morell, both of Albany, at Troy; Rev.
Howard (6-3/14)

FRYER, Peter F. of Norwich m 10/28/26 Anna Russell of Albany; Rev. Wood
(6-11/3)

FRYER, William J. m 2/10/36 Margaret Livingston, dau of late Alexander Crofts,
Esq., at the Manor of Livingston; Rev. J.N. Wyckoff (6-2/13)

FUEHS, Emanuel m 8/14/49 Catharine Mecking; Rev. C.H. Siehks (all of
Rondout) (8-8/25)

FULLER, Amanda, 41, wf of Samuel P. Fuller, d 12/26/43 suddenly in Little Falls
(3-12/28)

FULLER, Asa, Esq. - see GROESBECK, William

FULLER, Catherine - see BORDIN, Daniel

FULLER, Daniel of Westmoreland m 3/21/43 Elinora R. Mursitroyd of Stockbridge
at Durhamville; Willett Stillman, Esq. (1-4/4)

FULLER, Ephraim D. of Peekskill m (date not clear) Ann Hunt of Whitlockville in
W.; Rev. Jesse Hunt (11-11/10/42)

FULLER, Ephraim D. of Peekskill m 11/9/42 Ann Hunt of Whitelockville in W.;
Rev. Jesse Hunt (11-11/22)

FULLER, George (Rev.) of "old Schoharie" m 9/24/39 Mary Miner of Round Hill,

Conn. at R.H.; Rev. Van Deusen (12-10/1)

FULLER, Henry m 11/8/49 Margaret Van Vlierden; Rev. C. Van Santwood (all of Saugerties) (8-11/10)

FULLER, Jane - see CLARK, Aaron

FULLER, John I., merchant, of Schenectady m 5/3/36 Louisa Gardner, dau of M. Gardner, Esq., of Wampsville in W.; Rev. Thomas B. Gregory (6-5/9)

FULLER, Juliette H. - see HITCHCOCK, J.H.

FULLER, Maria A. - see GROESBECK, William

FULLER, Morris E. of firm of Buell and Fuller, merchants, of Little Falls m 10/5/43 Amelia Curtis of Clinton, Oneida County; Rev. Norton (3-10/12)

FULLER, Orsaville - see SMITH, Lyman

FULLER, Phebe J. - see TUTTLE, Chauncy

FULLER, Rebecca - see COLE, Frederick

FULLER, Reuben m 4/26/43 Semerinus Matteson in Rome; Rev. Charles Jones (1-5/9)

FULLER, Richard, M.D., d 5/15/37 in Schenectady (6-5/18)

FULLER, Samuel (Rev.), 74, rector of Trinity Church in Rensselaerville, d 4/9/42 (1-5/10)

FULMER, Mary - see FOLTS, J. Philo

FULTON, Sarah Ann - see BETTYS, George

FULTON, Thomas m "this morning" Susan Soare, both of New Windsor, in St. George's Church; Rev. John Brown (9-10/23)

FULTS, Mary - see DAVIS, Theodore

FUNSTON, Maria - see BYNAM, Jesse A

FURMAN, Alma - see WOOD, Gilbert

FURMAN, Harriet A. - see GREEN, Joel

FURMAN, Harriet, 16 months, dau. of Jacob and Eliza Ann, d 4/23/47 in West Troy (5-4/28)

FURNAM, Polly, 31, wf of Asa, d 1/27/43 at Mohawk (3-2/2)

GAGE, Moses of Little Falls m 3/7/38 Mary Ann Putnam in Salisbury; Elder Thompson (3-3/22)

GAGE, Persis P., 26, wf of Ebenezer, d 12/31/38 in Little Falls (3-1/17/39)

GAGE, Phebe, 34, wf of Joseph D., d 12/8/41 in Rome (1-12/14)

GAGE, Thirsa M. - see COLE, Gideon P.

GAGER, Mrs. - see THORN, James Harvey

GAINES, Joseph, Esq. - see JACOBS, Horace

GAINES, Tabitha M. - see JACOBS, Horace

GAINES, Willard O. of Salisbury m 2/22/43 Almira Duxtater of Stratford in S.; Rev. A. Knapp (3-3/23)

GAINS, John (Capt.) of Newburgh m 12/12/41 Harriet Ten Eyck of Haverstraw in H.; Rev. Joseph Ashbrook (9-1/1/42)

GALE, Phebe Jane - see LUCE(?), William

GALLAGHER, Bridget - see HIGGINS, Matthew

GALLUP, John G., 20, eldest son of Gardner and Maria, d 8/2/46 in Rome (consumption of the lungs) (1-8/25)

GALPIN, Amos, a Rev. War soldier, 89, d (date not given) at Litchfield, Conn. (5-1/17/44)

GALUSHA, Ambrose P. m 1/1/42 Julia Mc Coy, both of Troy in West Troy; Rev. D. Starks (5-1/12)

GAMBLE, James M. (Col.) of US Marines and Commandant of the Marines in Brooklyn, d 9/11/36 at Brooklyn (6-9/14)

GAMBRELING, Churchill C. (Hon.) m 11/17/35 Phebe Glover, dau of late John J., in NYC; Rev. Eastburn (6-11/21)

GAMING, Elizabeth - see DEAN, Hopkins

GANONG, Daniel V., about 85, d 12/6/41 in Carmel (11-12/14)

GANSEVOORT, Catharine - see CURTIS, George

GANSEVOORT, Catharine E. Cooke - see HAZARD, John V.B.

GANSEVOORT, Conrad - see HAZARD, John V.B.

GANSEVOORT, Mary Isaacs, 11 months, dau. of Peter, d 10/10/37 (6-10/11)

GANSEVOORT, Mrs. Leonard - see ROSS, Evelyn

GARCIA, Maria Felicia - see MALIBRAN, Eugene

GARDINER, Daniel - see TERRY, Ann

GARDINER, Nathaniel, 40, d (date not given) in NYC (6-11/3/26)

GARDINER, Phoebe Jane - see HAZELTON, Platt S.

GARDNER, ----, 67, relict of late John, d 8/10/39 (3-8/22)

GARDNER, Andrew, son of Bailey Gardner, d 8/6/42 in Newburgh (9-8/13)

GARDNER, Ann Louisa - see HITCHCOCK, Milton E.

GARDNER, Benjamin (Deacon) - see ROGERS, Lucinda F.

GARDNER, Betsey A. - see KENT, Orrin S.

GARDNER, C.J. (Miss) - see VAN VALKENBURGH, J.Q.

GARDNER, Catherine, 5, dau. of Robert L. and Mary, d "this morning" in Newburgh (9-12/17/42)

GARDNER, Daniel (Hon.) of Troy m 6/23/35 Anne Terry, eldest dau of Seth Terry of Hartford, CT, at H.; Rev. Price (6-7/2)

GARDNER, Elizabeth - see COWLES, Junius A.

GARDNER, Elizabeth A.W. - see CARSON, William C.

GARDNER, Emeline - see SEE, Coles C.

GARDNER, Howell (Hon.) - see LOOMIS, Benjamin N.

GARDNER, James T. of Fitchburgh, Mass. m 3/12/46 Sarah Amelia Mulford of Watervliet, NY in W.; Rev. Houghtaling (5-4/15)

GARDNER, James V.P. of Utica m 7/29/46 Sophia W. Williams only dau. of William, at Rome; Rev. S. Haynes (1-8/4)

GARDNER, Louisa - see FULLER, John I.

GARDNER, Phebe Jane - see HAZELTON, Platt S.

GARDNER, Roby Maria - see GREENE, S.A.

GARDNER, Sarah Ann - see LOOMIS, Benjamin N.

GARDNER, Sarah Ann - see LOOMIS, Benjamin N.

GARDNER, Sarah Ann - see WARRELL, James

GARLOCK, Elijah, 9 months, son of John and Elcy (sic), d 5/10/37 in Manheim (3-5/18)

GARLOCK, Maria L. - see CHAPIN, George S.

GARNER, Ann - see RIECH, John Christian

GARNRYCK, Julia - see WENTWORTH, A.E. (Capt.)

GARNSEY, Nathan, 71, one of the oldest, wealthiest and most respected inhabitants of Clifton Park, d 7/30/43 in C.P. (5-8/2)

GARRET, Eliza - see DODGE, Samuel

GARRET, Lucius B. m 1/11/48 Gertrude Lawrence, both of West Troy, in W.T.; Rev. W.H. Waggoner (5-1/19)

GARRETT, Nancy E. - see CAMACK, John

GARRITSON, Esther (Mrs.) - see DE FREEST, David M.

GARRITSON, Maria - see LENT, Stephen

GARTNER, Mary - see WEST, George

GARVAN(?), William, about 3, son of William, d 12/17/38 in Little Falls (3-12/20)

GARVIN, Samuel B., Esq., counsellor at law, m 1/24/36 Julia Maria Mitchell, dau of Hon. Henry of Norwich, at N.; Rev. Wheeler of Butternuts (6-2/1)

GARY, Joseph, merchant, of Troy m 11/23/26 Mary Seymour Austin of Hudson in H.; Rev. Stebbins (6-12/1)

GARY, Julia - see LANE, Henry R.

GASTON, Louisa S, 18, wf of Norman I Gaston and dau of late Nicholas Thorne of Skaneateles, NY d 11/16/34 at Homer, Mich. (6-1/10/35)

GASTON, N.B., Esq. of Aurora, Cayuga Co m 2/8/35 Amelia C Tillinghast, only dau of John L, Esq. of Albany, at Albany; Rev. Price (6-2/20)

GATES, Amenia - see KELLOGG, Frederick

GATES, Eliza, 35, wf of Hon. Seth M., d very suddenly 8/22/40 (1-9/1)

GATES, Henry of Halifax, Vermont m 10/2/36 Jane Hawley of Rome, NY at R; Rev. D. Morse (3-10/13)

GATES, Jennett A. - see ABELL, James L.

GATES, Le Roy L. m 9/6/48 Julia J. Calhoun, both of Sauquoit, Oneida County, at S.; Rev. James C. Cordell of Paris (1-9/15)

GATES, Loisa - see BENTLY, William

GATES, Lydia Biddle, 18, only dau. of Col. William Gates of US Army, d 2/28/39 at Fort Columbus, Governor's Island (12-3/5)

GATES, Martin m 5/5/47 Louisa Owen; Rev. C.M. Lewis (all of Verona) (1-5/14)

GATES, Oliver m 12/18/37 Maria Lewis, dau. of Capt. Henry Lewis, formerly of Bridgeport, Conn., in Little Falls, NY; Rev. Roper (3-12/28)

GATES, Polly, 45, wf of Joseph, d 4/10/35 in Albany (funeral from her late home on South Pearl St.) (6-4/11)

GATES, Sarah Conant, 17, dau. of Luke and Mary, d 4/28/43 in Verona (1-5/9)

GATHWEIGHT, Ann (Mrs.), 67, d 6/29/43 on Fall Hill (3-7/13)

GAULKINS, John L. m 10/18/43 Jane Ann Learned in West Troy; Rev. C.H. Hosken (all of West Troy) (5-10/25)

GAWKE(?), Elizabeth Jane, 2 yrs., dau. of William and Elizabeth, d 5/16/45 in Westmoreland (1-5/20)

GAY, Adeline F. - see WRIGHT, James C.

GAY, Edwin D. of Ellenville m 8/5/49 Maria Goetschius of Kingston; Rev. C.F. Hoes (8-8/11)

GAY, Elizabeth - see TEN EYCK, Andrew

GAY, Horace, Esq. of Rochester m 8/17/36 Lucy Thompson, dau of late Joseph, in Riga; Rev. DeForest (6-8/22)

GAY, James Porter of Seneca Falls m 4/11/37 Martha A. Williams of Ballston Spa at B.S.; Rev. Babcock (6-4/13)

GAY, Laura Matilda - see DAVIS, John Brazier

GAY, Rufus, Esq. - see DAVIS, John Brazier

GAYLE, Sarah A, 31, wf of his excellency the Hon. John Gayle, d 7/30/35 in Tuscaloosa, AL (lock-jaw) (6-8/18)

GAYLORD, Chester, Jr. m 3/27/39 A.M. Smith(?) of Litchfield at L; Rev. Abram

Mills (3-4/4)

GAYLORD, Harriet - see MC CULLOUGH, William

GAZELAS, Roxana - see MORSE, Elijah H.

GAZLEY, Ward M., Esq., formerly editor and proprietor of the Political Index, formerly published at Newburgh, d 4/20/36 at Newburgh (6-4/23)

GEAR, Almira - see HOLTON, Amos

GEDDEN, Emma - see JACKSON, William

GEDNEY, John, 80, d 12/24/41 in White Plains (11-1/11/42)

GEER, Sarah - see FOX, George

GELL, William (Sir), antiquary and illustrator of the ruins of Pompeii and Herculaneum, d 2/4/36 at Naples (6-4/28)

GELSTON, Polly (Mrs.) - see COFFIN, Alexander, Jr.

GEMMEL, James m (date not given) Sarah Griffin in NYC (6-5/22/16)

GENNING, Addia - see DRAWYER, Hiram H.

GEORGE, Captain, 70, principal chief of the Onondaga tribe of Indians, d 6/13/37 at the Indian Castle in the town of Onondaga (he was one of the most able orators of the Six Nations "and was much esteemed by both the white and red man") (6-6/24)

GERE, Adeline E. - see MC CORMICK, George

GERE, Malinda, 27, dau of Hon. Isaac Gere, d (date not given) in Galway (6-6/4/35)

GERMAN, Elizabeth - see CROSS, David C.

GERMAN, William P. m 7/4/50 Maria Weaver, both of Watervliet, in Saratoga; Rev. P. Weaver (5-7/17)

GERMOND, Sarah - see HAZARD, Nathaniel

GEROW, A. m 11/3/41 Sylvia Lockwood, both of Jefferson Valley; Rev. D.D. Tompkins (11-11/9)

GEROW, Elizabeth, 10, dau. of Gilbert and Anna, d 11/7/42 in Hamptonburgh (9-11/12)

GESSNER, Jane - see REDDY, Michael

GETMAN, Anna Eliza (Mrs.) - see SMITH, Adam

GETMAN, Chauncey m 2/20/48 Catharine Lipe, dau. of John I.; Rev. Dr. Mc Lean (all of Fort Plain) (4-3/9)

GETMAN, Chauncey m 9/22/36 Catharine Barringer at Columbia; Rev. Devoe (3-9/29)

GETMAN, Sophrone - see MYERS, Jeremiah

GETTY, John - see FITCH, Benjamin

GIBBES, Charlotte Augusta - see ASTOR, John Jacob Jr.

GIBBONS, Elizabeth, 8 months, twin sister of Ann and dau. of W.P. and Mary R., d 8/7/49 in Poughkeepsie (8-8/25)

GIBBONS, George S., merchant, of Albany m 9/28/35 Ann Eliza Bethel, dau of late William, Esq. of NYC, at NYC; Rev. William Parkinson (6-10/2)

GIBBONS, Mrs. - see HALLENBAKE, Stafford

GIBBS, Frances Ann Sophia - see CLAY, John Randolph

GIBBS, George Clinton, Esq. m 11/3/35 Elmina Halsey, dau of Hon. J.H. Halsey; Rev. Thomas Lounsbury (all of Ovid) (6-11/10)

GIBBS, Maria L. - see MOSELT, Daniel

GIBBS, William m 3/10/36 Eliza Carman at Cohoes; L.V.K. Van Denmark, Esq. (6-3/15)

116

GIBSON, De Witt C. m 7/1/49 Esther Smith, both of Fort Plain, in F.P.; Rev. Dr.
    C.G. Mc Lean (4-8/2)
GIBSON, Elizabeth - see TITTARINGTON, David
GIBSON, Esther, 27, wf of De Witt Gibson and dau. of Joseph and Susannah
    Smyth, d 6/21/50 in Fort Plain (4-6/27)
GIBSON, Jane, 15, dau of Ira and Phebe, d 8/20/40 in Rome (1-9/1)
GIBSON, Phidelia H. - see SEALY, Thaddeus
GIDLEY, Timothy H. of Albany d 5/22/42 at Rome, Italy (5-7/27)
GIDNEY, Daniel J., 20, of Newburgh d 11/19/42 in NYC (pulmonary
    consumption) (9-11/26)
GIDNEY, Edward E., Esq. of Newburgh m 1/6/42 Sophroni Ryerson, dau. of John
    M., Esq., of Ringwood, NJ, in R.; Rev. H. Doolittle (9-1/8)
GIFFORD, Electa T. - see LEATHERS, Isaac
GIFFORD, George, formerly of New Paltz m 5/17/49 Eleanor Van Ranst; Rev. Dr.
    Lansing (all of NYC) (8-6/2)
GIFFORD, Joseph of Bern m 12/31/34 Ann Maranda Whitcomb of Bethlehem;
    Rev. Hiram Meeker (6-1/3/35)
GIFFORD, Marshall, 19, d (date not given) in Philadelphia (6-5/15/16)
GIFFORD, Robert, 41, d 4/14/49 in West Troy (consumption) (5-4/18)
GILBERT, Benjamin, 42, of firm of Gilbert and Worthington of Albany d 9/30/35
    in Albany (funeral 4 o'clock from his home 60 Howard St.) (6-10/2)
GILBERT, Clara - see POWELL, William
GILBERT, Elizabeth, widow of late Benjamin Gilbert deceased, d 6/2/36 in Albany
    (funeral from her late home, 55 Howard St.) survived by her mother, her
    three brothers: James, John and William Davis and a sister (not named)
    (6-6/4)
GILBERT, Minerva (Mrs.) - see MALTBY, John
GILBERT, Sarah A. - see HATHAWAY, Franklin
GILCHRIST, William of Springfield m 12/5/49 E.H. Johnson of Fonda in F.; Rev.
    Simmons (4-12/6)
GILDERSLEEVE, Ann - see MC GREGOR, William
GILES, Albert Henry, 5, son of Henry G. and Harriet H., d 1/2/50 in Rome (1-1/9)
GILES, Daniel m 3/28/37 Nancy Keith, dau. of James, in Newport; Rev. W.H.
    Waggoner (3-4/6)
GILES, Thomas, 22, d 8/12/42 in Rome (1-8/16)
GILL, Ann Read - see WILSON, James J.
GILL, Caroline - see NESSLE, William
GILL, Matthew, Esq. - see NESSLE, William
GILL, William, 3, son of Samuel S., d 12/14/42 in New Windsor (9-12/17)
GILLESPIE, Julia A. - see HALL, John H., Jr.
GILLESPIE, William, 24, student at law, d 7/11/08 in Herkimer (funeral sermon by
    Rev. Martin - at his interment a member of the Herkimer Law Society, to
    which he belonged, gave the eulogy (2-8/9)
GILLET, Electa, d (date not given) in Torrington (7-7/4/10)
GILLET, Jacob m 2/18/41 Emeline Mead, both of Putnam Valley; Rev. William H.
    Johnson (11-2/23)
GILLETT, Margaret (Mrs.), 70, of Troy, d 1/4/48 in West Troy at home of C.F.
    Selden (5-1/12)
GILLETT, Moses (Rev.), 72, d 6/5/48 in Rome (1-6/9)

GILLETTE, Julia, 49, wf of Richard of Rome, d 10/8/41 in Rome (1-10/12)

GILLINGHAM, George, 56, professor of music, d (date not given) in Philadelphia (6-9/26/26)

GILLINGHAM, Louisa - see TERRY, Adrian E.

GILLSON, Albert m 9/19/41 Elizabeth Laraby, both of Vernon, in V.; Elder James Blakeslee (1-9/28)

GILMORE, Caroline E. - see JONES, Andrew

GILMORE, Robert, 24, son of John, d 4/10/26 at Mentz (6-4/25)

GILPIN, Henry D of Philadelphia m 9/3/35 Eliza Johnston of Louisiana at Kentmore, near Wilmington, Delaware; Rev. H. Adams (6-9/11)

GILYEE, Anny - see WEEKS, William

GIRD, Richard S (Capt.), 29, late of Litchfield, Herkimer Co., d 7/18/35 at the home of his brother in Jackson, Louisiana (was for several years master of a trading vessel between New Orleans and Tampico) (6-8/28)

GIRVAN, Eliza A. - see MILLIGAN, William G.

GIRVAN, William, Esq. - see MILLIGAN, William G.

GISMER, Mary Catherine - see WATTERS(?), William

GLADDING, Edward W. m 5/15/42 Harriet L. Miller, both of Albany; Rev. C.H. Hosken (5-5/18)

GLASS, Adam m 11/30/50 Mary Forsyth; Rev. T.F. Wyckoff (all of West Troy) (5-12/11)

GLASS, Emma G. - see TABRAM, William G.

GLASS, H. Samuel m 7/1/41 Salome Trip, both of Rome, at the Public Square; E.C. Vogell (1-7/6)

GLASS, Ruth Ann - see SHELDON, S.H.

GLATT, Anthony, formerly of Canajoharie m 12/11/48 Catharine A. Swade of Utica at U.; Rev. Prole (4-12/28)

GLEASON, Jane - see DENIO, Cole H.

GLEASON, P.D. - see EDWARDS, Francis

GLEASON, Sarah C. - see HEMPSTEAD, Robert A.

GLENNON, John, 1, son of Thomas, d 11/19/42 in Newburgh (9-11/26)

GLEZEN, Oren - see HUBBARD, William

GLOVER, Phebe - see GAMBRELING, Churchill

GLOVER, Phebe - see JAYCOX, Enoch

GODDEN, David, Jr. m 4/24/36 ____ Slaly; Rev. C.P. Clarke (all of Albany) (6-4/27)

GODFREY, John of Auburn m 1/5/50 Eliza Martin of Albany, in Albany (both deaf mutes); Rev. John Clark

GODFREY, Margaret (Mrs.), 65, d (date not given) in NYC (6-4/3/16)

GODFREY, Nelson m 9/1/36 Eliza Miller, both of Albany; Rev. Martin (6-9/2)

GODFREY, Russell C., 36, formerly of Watervliet, d 2/2/44 in NYC (after a protracted illness) (5-2/14)

GOETCHIEUS, Henry m 11/20/42 Mrs. Jane Ann Vanderhoof; Rev. Dr. C. Westbrook (all of Peekskill) (11-11/29)

GOETCHIEUS, Margaret (Miss), 32, d 11/4/41 at the home of her brother, Col. Peter Goetchieus in Peekskill (11-11/9)

GOETSCHIUS, Maria - see GAY, Edwin D.

GOETSCHUS, Henry of Haverstraw m (date not given) Mrs. Jane Ann Vanderbilt, dau of Dr, Nathaniel Drake of Peekskill; Rev. Dr. Westbrook (11-12/1)

118

GOEWEY, U.I. - see HANAMAN, I.E.

GOFF, John Edward m 8/24/37 Mary Ann Conner, both of Albany, at Bethlehem; David Russell, Esq. (6-8/28)

GOGER (sic), Salome - see CARTER, Henry M.

GOGGILL, Mary Ann - see SMYTH, John W.

GOLD(?), Charlotte - see SHELDON, C.P. (Rev.)

GOLDEN, Almira, 37, wf of John, d 9/19/38 in Little Falls (survived by her husband and five small children) (funeral from her late home 9/21) (3-9/20)

GOLDEN, Hannah - see WILLIAMS, Henry B.

GOLDEN, Juliet - see FILER, De Loss

GOLDEN, Nancy - see GRIFFITH, Ira (Capt.)

GOLDSMITH, Elizabeth, 23, dau. of James, d 10/22/42 in Newburgh (9-10/29)

GOLDSMITH, Sarah, 78(?), d 12/14/42 in Coldenham (9-12/17)

GOLDWAYT, Jonathan, 41, d 6/8/37 (funeral from his late home, 124 State Street) (6-6/9)

GONSALIS, George m 7/20/47 Eliza Kirk, both of West Troy, in Waterford; Rev. B.F. Garfield (5-7/28)

GOODELL, Ellen, 26, wf of Richard, d 1/26/43 in West Troy (5-2/1)

GOODELL, George W. (Dr.) m 10/1/39 Cylinda Chase, both of Le Roy, in West Troy; John Hastings, Esq. (5-10/9)

GOODHUE, Ann - see LIVINGSTON, Robert

GOODING, William of Fall River, MA m 7/4/35 Augustina Vogel, late of Milton, NY, at the Legation of the United States at Bagota (6-8/28)

GOODMAN, Noah W., merchant of Delhi, Delaware County, m 6/26/38 Harriet N. Smith, dau. of Rev. R. Smith of Waterford, at W. (5-7/4)

GOODRICH, Adeline - see GRAY, George E.

GOODRICH, Allen, 84, father of Alpheus Goodrich, Esq., d 9/22/35 at Ballston Spa (6-9/25)

GOODRICH, Charity - see SEYMORE, Emory Tyler

GOODRICH, Charles, 61, d 4/20/35 in Albany (funeral at 3 o'clock from his late home, 2 Van Tromp St.) (6-4/22)

GOODRICH, Cyrus m 3/29/43 Mary Aldrich in Rome; Rev. Charles Jones (1-4/4)

GOODRICH, Joseph m 10/28/37 Angeline Newell, both of Waterford; Rev. Green (5-11/8)

GOODRICH, Sarah (Mrs.), 58, d (date not given) at Wethersfield (7-8/29/10)

GOODROW, Francis of Chazy Landing m 8/13/49 Mary Ann Brown of Schuylerville; Rev. Houghtaling (5-8/15)

GOODSELL, Thomas of Utica m 11/7/49 Henrietta Lieber, dau. of late Henry, in Canajoharie; Rev. W.N. Snell(?) (4-11/15)

GOODWIN, Anna, 86, consort of Deacon Solomon Goodwin, d 10/22/46 at the home of her son (not named) in Rome (1-10/27)

GOODWIN, CARRINGTON & CO. - see CARRINGTON, Edward

GOODWIN, Elizabeth, 38, wf of late Capt. Comfort Goodwin of Middletown, d (date not given) at Middletown (7-2/7/10)

GOODWIN, Helen R., 3 months, dau. of Charles and Maria, d 2/2/41 in West Troy (5-2/10)

GOODWIN, Jeremiah of Westmoreland m 2/3/41 Mary Delia Sedgwick, eldest dau. of Dr. P. Sedgwick of Andover, in A.; Rev. S.P.M. Hastings (1-2/9)

GOODWIN, Solomon, 80, a Rev. War officer, formerly of Williamstown, Oswego

Co., d 9/28/35 in Rome, NY (6-10/5)

GOODWIN, Stephen A., Esq. m 6/9/35 Frances M. Dibble in Auburn; Rev. James B/ Shaw (6-6/15)

GOOK, Rev. - see MC DOWELL, Margaret

GORDON, Arthur R. of Savannah m 10/17/36 Sarah Louisa Lyde, dau of late Edward of NYC, at the Church of the Assumption; Rev. Dr. Eastburn (6-10/21)

GORDON, Hugh (Capt.) m 4/20/26 Sarah Martin, both of Greenbush, in G.; Rev. Weeks (6-4/28)

GORDON, Sarah F. - see PRENTISS, Nathaniel L.

GORE, John, Esq. - see GREENOUGH, Horatio

GORE, Julia - see BRANDRETH, Thomas

GORE, Louisa I. - see GREENOUGH, Horatio

GORHAM, ----, "nearly 2 years old", son of John R. Gorham, druggist of Newburgh(?), d 8/15/42 from eating a poison which was placed on a plate for killing flies (9-8/20)

GORHAM, Nathaniel, one of the first settlers in Canandaigua, d (date not given) in Canandaigua (6-11/3/26)

GORHAM, Sarah - see ADES, Edward

GORHAM, Stephen, formerly of New Haven, CT, d 9/28/35 at Mobile (6-10/14)

GORMAN, John of Brunswick, Penn. m 3/14/46 Esther L. Meads of Verona, NY; Rev. H.C. Vogell (1-3/24)

GORMAN, Robert, Jr. m 5/30/35 Maria Hasbrouck m dau of Hon. Abraham, at Kingston; Rev. Dr. Gorman (all of Kingston) (6-6/13)

GORTON, Susan - see RIPLEY, J.W.

GOSMAN, Robert, Jr. m 5/30/35 Maria Hasbrouck, youngest dau of Hon. Abraham Hasbrouck of Rondout, at Kingston; Rev. Dr. Gosman (6-6/8)

GOUGE, Jacob - see BRAINARD, Margaret

GOUGE, Jacob - see BRAINARD, Mary M.

GOULD, Calvin m 4/28/46 Ann Collier; Rev. G.S. Boardman (all of Rome) (1-5/5)

GOULD, Catharine Darling, 45, of Sandusky, Ohio, sister of Mrs. William Gould, d 2/22/36 at the home of William Gould (friends of the families of William Gould and Anthony Gould invited to funeral at 3 o'clock from Mr. Wm. Gould's home, 104 State St. (6-2/23)

GOULD, Charles of Utica m 5/6/35 Henrietta S. Mumford, dau of late Thomas, Esq., at Utica (6-5/13)

GOULD, Cornelia - see NOBLE, Henry B.

GOULD, Delose m 6/27/37 Caroline Morrell, dau. of John, Esq., in Fonda; Rev. J.D. Fonda (all of Fonda) (6-7/11)

GOULD, Elizabeth - see MONK, Elizabeth

GOULD, James m 2/9/37 Mrs. Ann Petrie (relict of late Gen. Jost Petrie), both of Little Falls, at Herkimer; Rev J.P. Spinner (3-2/23)

GOULD, Jason, 40, d (date not given) in Stratford (7-7/4/10)

GOULD, John (Hon.) - see NOBLE, Henry B.

GOULD, Mary Elizabeth - see MORSE, George L.

GOULD, Richard m 2/7/42 Margaret Nixon(?); Rev. E.E. Groswold (all of Newburgh) (9-2/12)

GOUNDRY, George (Gen.) d 11/8/35 at Geneva (a short illness) (born in Wicliff in the north of England but "emigrated to this country in early youth. For the past 30 years he worked in the Pulteney Estate Land Office") (6-11/16)

GOURLAY, Robert (Capt.) m (date not given) Maria DeWitt Clinton at Newburgh (6-5/15/16)

GOURLAY, W.B. m 4/26/36 Margaret S. Campbell, both of Albany; Rev. Potter (6-4/28)

GOVE, John F. m 11/26/44 Catharine Cramer, both of Watervliet, in Troy; Rev. L. Howard (5-12/4)

GRACIE, Oliver C. m 10/10/26 Mary Ann Mc Kinney, dau. of A. .Mc Kinney; Rev. Dr. Chester (all of Albany) (6-10/20)

GRACIE, William m 7/16/36 Cornelia Anne Fleming, 2nd dau of John Boyce Fleming, in NYC; Rev. Bishop Onderdonk (6-7/18)

GRADY, Bridget Sophia - see HOTCHKISS, Alfred R.

GRAFT, Samuel of NYC m 6/7/42 Sarah E. Merrit of New Windsor in N.W.; Rev. Winslow (9-6/18)

GRAHAM, Anson m 3/10/36 Mary Eaton in Little Falls; Rev. Morris (3-3/17)

GRAHAM, Belinda - see BACON, Marshall J.

GRAHAM, Betsey - see BROWN, Emery W.

GRAHAM, Clementina E.J., dau of late John, Esq., d 1/15/36 in Washington (6-1/23)

GRAHAM, David Jr. m 6/3/35 Cornelia Matilda Hyslop, dau of Robert, Esq., in NYC; Rev. Dr. Anthon; all of NYC (6-6/6)

GRAHAM, Eliza - see WILLIAMS, Samuel

GRAHAM, Jane B. - see BREWSTER, John

GRAHAM, John A., Jr., m 11/22/36 Helen S. Beeckman, dau of Henry, Esq.; Rev. Dr, Skinner (all of NYC) (6-11/26)

GRAHAM, Margery - see VAN VRANKEN, Lyman

GRAHAM, William, 94, d 5/2/35 in Rutherford Co., NC (was a Colonelin the Rev. War, was for many years a member of the state assembly) (6-5/30)

GRANGER, Emily - see BUTRICK, G.H.G.

GRANGER, Francis, 2, son of Gideon R., d 12/7/40 at Vernon (scarlet fever) (1-12/22)

GRANGER, Harvey (Judge) - see SLOCUM, Catherine M.

GRANGER, James Harvey of firm of Bancroft and Granger m 8/29/36 Harriet Smith, youngest dau. of Jeremiah; Rev. Dr. Sprague (6-8/31)

GRANMAR, Thompson, 57, late of Western, d 9/22/47 at Dexter, Michigan (1-10/22)

GRANT, Asahel, M.D., of Utica m Judith H Campbell, adopted dau. of Hon. William Campbell, Surveyor General, at the Presbyterian Church at Cherry Valley; Rev. Lochead (sic). Doctor and Mrs Grant will sail from Boston to Constantinople as missionaries destined for Ourmiah in Persia joining Rev. Perkins and wife already in that country (more information included in newspaper but not copied here) (6-4/10)

GRANT, Eliza Jane - see CASHDOLLAR, William

GRANT, Gerdon, Esq., late of West Troy, m 5/18/43 Eliza Wolf of Troy in T.; Rev. N.S.S. Beman (5-5/24)

GRANT, James H. m 6/24/49 Jane Bedell, both of Albany, in West Troy; Rev. T.W. Pearson (5-6/27)

GRANT, Louisa, 24, wf of Henry Allen Grant and dau. of Lynott Bloodgood, Esq., of Albany, d 4/7/37 (funeral 4/9 from 212 North Market Street) (6-4/8)

GRANT, Mary - see WINNE, Aerian

GRANTS, Michael J. of Mohawk m 1/22/43 Rachael Davis of Little Falls in L.F.; Rev. C.W. Leet (3-1/16)

GRASSFIELD, John H. m 4/7/49 Lucinda Lasher, both of Saugerties, in Flatbush at the parsonage of the Seventh District; Rev. J.M. Hulbert (8-4/28)

GRATIOT, Charles (Gen.) - see DE MONTROLOS, Charles Francis Frederick

GRATIOT, Mary Victoria - see DE MONTROLOS, Charles Francis Frederick

GRAVES, Albert of Russia, NY m 1/27/40 Eliza C. Tuttle of Newport in Russia (3-2/6)

GRAVES, Charlotte - see LYNCH, Martin

GRAVES, Mary R. - see CURRY, Justin E.B.

GRAVES, Mary, 1, dau. of Ezra, Esq., d 2/1/39 in Herkimer (3-2/7)

GRAVES, Olive - see PHILLIPS, Drake H.

GRAWBARGER, Almira - see WITBECK, F.M.

GRAY, A.M. of firm of Smith & Gray m (date not given) Nancy Dockstader, dau. of Frederick; Rev. John P. Spencer (all of Herkimer) (3-4/26/38)

GRAY, Alexander m 3/22/49 Sarah Smith, both of Westmoreland, at the American Hotel in Rome; H.C. Vogell (1-3/28)

GRAY, Charles F. (Dr.), 24, d 12/10/42 in Newburgh (funeral attended by the members of the Society of Odd Fellows of which he was a prominent member. (9-12/17)

GRAY, George E. m 3/30/43 Adeline Goodrich in Rome; H.C. Vogle (1-4/4)

GRAY, Hannah E, 25, wife of the editor of the Lansingburgh Gazette, d. 2/4/35 in Lansingburgh (a lingering illness) (6-2/7)

GRAY, I.N., druggist, m 6/28/43 Catherine L. Hardy of Oppenheim in Little Falls; Rev. William L. Dennis (3-8/3)

GRAY, James M. m 1/28/38 Harriet Bull(?), dau. of Enos, in Little Falls; Rev. J. Roper, all of Gastown(?) (3-2/8)

GRAY, Marianne - see BRADFORD, Alexander W.

GRAY, Mary - see CAMPBELL, William

GRAY, Robert, 35, d 2/19/37 in Albany (was first librarian to the Young Men's Association and was employed by the United States Line of Forwarders on the Erie Canal. His funeral from hos late home at 9 Fox Street) (6-2/20)

GRAY, Willard A. m 3/6/36 Lucina Tanner; Allen S. Wheeler (6-3/9)

GRAY, William D., 67, d 4/3/41 in Little Falls (born in Smithfield, Rhode Island and moved to Fairfield, NY in 1793) (3-4/8)

GREELEY, Arthur Young, 8, only son of Horace and Mary Y.C. Greeley, d 7/15/49 in NYC (8-7/21)

GREELEY, Horace, Esq., editor of the New Yorker, m (date not given) Mary Jane Cheney, formerly of NYC, at Warrentown, North Carolina (3-7/21/36)

GREELY, Horace, Esq., editor of the New Yorker m 7/5/36 Mary Jane Cheney, formerly of NYC, in Immanuel Church, Warrentown, NC (6-7/14)

GREEN, Caleb m 1/6/42 Mary Ann House, both of Stockbridge, at Vernon Center; L.T. Marshall, Esq. (1-1/18)

GREEN, Catherine M. - see WELLS, Benjamin

GREEN, Daniel (Capt.), 85, a Rev. War soldier, d 11/1/40 in Rome (1-11/10)

GREEN, Edwin, about 1, son of Leonard and Lucy, d 9/2/39 at Paoli (12-10/1)

GREEN, Elijah m 5/25/48 Imagine Brackney in Rome; Rev. Stanton (1-5/26)

GREEN, Eliza - see DEFOREST, James

GREEN, Eliza (Mrs.) - see VAN SCHOONHOVEN, Ebenezer

GREEN, Elizabeth - see MURDEN, George

GREEN, Elizabeth - see STONE, William H.

GREEN, Emily Augusta, wf of Henry W., and eldest dau. of late Chief Justice Ewing, d 6/14/37 suddenly at Trenton, NJ (6-6/20)

GREEN, Enock, about 30, d 12/27/41 in Pound Ridge (11-1/4/42)

GREEN, Esther, 42, wf of T. Green, Jr., d (date not given) at New Haven (7-5/24/09)

GREEN, Hart of Chatham m 2/27/36 Sarah Ann Fosmire of Nassau; Rev. Wm Hunt of New Lebanon (a double ceremony; see marr. of Garett H. FOSMIRE) (6-3/21)

GREEN, Harvey of Somers m 12/23/40 Emily Strong, dau of Capt. John of Jefferson Valley and Yorktown; Rev. R.K. Thompson (11-1/5/41)

GREEN, Horace, M.D., of NYC m 10/27/41 Harriet S. Douglas, dau. of J.H., Esq., late cashier of the Saratoga Bank, at Waterford; Rev. R. Smith (5-11/3)

GREEN, Ira W. m 5/18/49 Miss Flint in Ames; Rev. C.H. Hervey (4-6/14)

GREEN, J., postmaster at Westerlo, m 6/25/37 Sally Mariah Stephens, dau. of Abel Stephens, deceased, and grand dau. of Hon. Archibald Stephens, late of Coeymans, at Coeymans; Rev. J. Gorman, D.D. (6-6/28)

GREEN, Jane - see BELLINGER, James

GREEN, Jane - see SCOFIELD, William A.

GREEN, Jared, 82, member of the Society of Friends, d 8/1/39 in Bedford (12-8/13)

GREEN, Jered Holly of Bedford m 11/26/38 Susan Weeks, dau of Silas of Somers, in S.; William Hunt, Esq. (12-12/4)

GREEN, Jeremiah m 10/20/41 Sarah M. Bailey, dau. of Isaac, Esq., in Waterford; Rev. Whitbeck (all of Waterford) (5-10/27)

GREEN, Joel m 11/4/49 Harriet A. Furman, both of West Hurley, in Woodstock; Rev. Voorhees (8-11/17)

GREEN, Joseph E. m 1/1/26 Mary Cain, both of Albany; Rev. Leonard (6-1/10)

GREEN, Joseph, 80, a Rev. War veteran, d 6/12/35 at Sodus, Wayne County (father of Hon. Byram Green of Sodus) (6-7/1)

GREEN, Julia E. - see KASSON, Henry W.

GREEN, Lewis of Danube m 2/28/39 Elizabeth James of Stark in S.; Rev. J.D. Lawyer

GREEN, Lucy, relict of John, Esq., d 8/21/35 at Galway, Saratoga Co. (6-9/1)

GREEN, Mary Ann - see CHASE, Beverly

GREEN, Minerva - see BRAINARD, George H.

GREEN, Nelson, merchant, m 1/30/41 Eliza More, dau. of Robert L., Esq., at Durhamville; Rev. D.D. Ransom (1-2/23)

GREEN, Robert m (date not given) Maria Toulau in NYC (6-5/15/16)

GREENE, C.O., Esq. of West Troy m 11/6/47 Elizabeth Eagleston of Danby, VT (5-11/10)

GREENE, John G. of Rome m 3/18/46 Rhoda E. Barker, eldest dau. of Capt. James of Madison, in M.; Rev. S. Platt (1-3/31)

GREENE, S.A. m 3/9/40 Roby Maria Gardner, both of Lowville; Rev. O. Wilbur (3-3/19)

GREENE, Stephen, about 70, d 3/18/42 in Poundridge (11-3/21)

GREENE, William of the house of Greene & Brothers of NYC m 8/25/35 Mrs. Anna Catherine Bennet in Philadelphia; Rev. Meyer (6-8/31)

GREENLY, Amelia Esther - see WEBSTER, Joseph

GREENMAN, Adley m 3/10/41 Lydia Ann Taylor, dau. of John of Boonville, in B.; Rev. Demming (1-3/16)

GREENMAN, Francis m 2/20/42 Clarissa E. Muscott in Western; Rev. Slee (all of Western) (1-2/22)

GREENMAN, Joseph of Albany m 1/15/10 Nancy Houd of Catskill; Rev. D. Porter (7-1/17)

GREENMAN, Thompson, 57, late of Western, d. 9/22/47 at Dexter, Michigan (1-10/15)

GREENOUGH, Aurelia (Mrs.) d 8/8; her husband, Epps Greenough, d 8/9; their son, Henry, 20, d 8/9; and their dau., Catherine, 18, d 8/10/34, all in Poughkeepsie, all of cholera (11-8/19)

GREENOUGH, Horatio, Esq. m 10/14/37 Louisa I. Gore, dau. of late John, Esq. (all of Boston) at Florence "at the English Minister's" (6-12/27)

GREENWOOD, Helen G. - se WILLIAMSON, Howard

GREENWOOD, Margaret M. - see POWELL, Elisha

GREENWOOD, Oliver, 85, d 5/27/47 in Lee (1-6/4)

GREGORY, —— (Mr.) - see DONNELLY, Augustus

GREGORY, Alvah, about 55, d 4/8/50 in Southeast (10-4/10)

GREGORY, Elizabeth - see SEARS, James

GREGORY, John R. (Dr.), formerly of Stamford, Delaware County, NY, d (date not given) on board the ship "Margaret" enroute from New Orleans to New York (Interred at the Quarantine Ground, Staten Island, NY) (6-6/5/16)

GREGORY, Lois - see PETERS, Isaac F.

GREGORY, Matthew - see WING, Mary

GREVES, Evelina P. - see CLARK, Calvin

GREY, Charles Mortimer(?), 9 months, son of Dr. Charles F. Grey, d 9/20/42 in Newburgh (9-9/24)

GREY, Pamela - see HALL, Hezekiah

GREY, Sarah, 40, wf of George, formerly of Newburgh, d 1/9/42 at Fishkill (9-1/15)

GRIDLEY, G. Thomson, Esq., m 5/4/37 Caroline W. Todd, dau. of John R., Esq., ar Verona; Rev. Lockwood (6-5/15)

GRIDLEY, Leander - see PATTEN, Lovina G.

GRIDLEY, Sylvester of Marshall m 9/10/46 Jane Elizabeth Smith of Vernon Center at V.C.; Rev. Raymond (1-9/15)

GRIFFEN, Charles A.A., Esq., of NYC m 10/20/36 Pantora J. De Forest, youngest dau of late David of New Haven, at New Haven; Rev. Dr. Cromwell (Double ceremony - see HILL, Frederick, Esq. (6-10/31)

GRIFFEN, Gilbert m 12/2/38 Mary S. Lane, both of Bedford, in B.; Rev. Thomas Brower of Greenwich (12-12/11)

GRIFFEN, James, 74, d 10/9/38 at North Street, White Plains (12-10/30)

GRIFFEN, James, about 73, d 10/26/38 in Harrison (12-11/6)

GRIFFETH, Janette, 2, dau. of Ariel and Sarah Griffeth, d 3/21/42 in Columbia (scarlet fever) (3-4/28)

GRIFFIN, Amanda F. - see GRIFFIN, Oscar F.

GRIFFIN, Angelica - see HUNTER, Augustus W.

124

GRIFFIN, Benjamin - see HALLOCK, Eliza

GRIFFIN, Catharine Eliza - see FREDENDALL, Jacob

GRIFFIN, David, 71, d suddenly 2/17/42 in Bedford while resting en route home on foot (11-2/22)

GRIFFIN, Electa Jane - see HARVEY, Charles

GRIFFIN, George, Rector of the Academy and a member of the class which graduated at Yale College in 1824, d (date not given) at Hilsboro, Georgia (6-11/28/26)

GRIFFIN, James W. of Little Falls m 11/19/48 Eunice Louisa Hedges of West Troy in Troy; Rev. G.C. Baldwin (5-11/22)

GRIFFIN, John R. m 10/2/39 Frances Carpenter Pugsley, both of Yorktown; James White, Esq. (11-10/8)

GRIFFIN, Joseph, 97, a Rev. War soldier, d 12/19/41 in Bedford (11-12/28)

GRIFFIN, Nelson, Esq. of Salisbury m 12/23/40 Sarah Cohen(?) of Little Falls in L.F.; Rev. William S. Bartlett (3-12/31)

GRIFFIN, Oscar F. m 9/24/35 Amanda F. Griffin; Rev. F.G. Mayer (all of Albany) (6-9/29)

GRIFFIN, Oscar F., 19, son of John, d 2/21/37 (6-2/23)

GRIFFIN, Rachael Laurence, 28, wf of David Griffin, d 12/1/49 in Flatbush (8-12/8)

GRIFFIN, Sarah - see GEMMEL, James

GRIFFIN, Stephen C. of Mamaroneck m 2/4/39 at the Friends Meeting House, Jane Field of Sawpit (12-2/26)

GRIFFIN, Theney, 27, wf of John d 12/27/41 in Bedford (member of the Methodist Episcopal Church for many years) (11-1/11/42)

GRIFFING, ----, consort of James Griffing, d 11/16/38 at an advanced age at Rocco Point (Southold, Long Island) (3-12/13)

GRIFFING, Almira C. - see CONGDON, Nathaniel S.

GRIFFING, Charles - see CONGDEN, Almira C.

GRIFFING, Honora - see WILCOX, ---- (Mr.)

GRIFFING, Lemuel, 72, d (date not given) at East Haddam (7-8/1/10)

GRIFFING, Peter W. m "lately" Mary Elizabeth Pratt, dau. of L. Esq., in NYC (3-7/21/36)

GRIFFISE, Francis d (date not given) in NYC (6-5/15/16)

GRIFFITH, Ira (Capt.) m 1/11/38 Nancy Golden; Elder Whiteman (3-1/25)

GRIGGS, Eliza - see LOOMIS, David

GRIMP, Sarah Ann - see BOUGHTON, Edward

GRINNELL, William H. of Cayuga County m 7/8/47 Charlotte Irving, dau. of Ebenezer, at Sunnyside, the home of Hon. Washington Irving; Rev. Dr. Creighton (5-7/14)

GRINNELLS, Josiah B. m 2/17/39 Nancy J. Cushing in West Troy; John Hastings, Esq. (all of West Troy) (5-2/20)

GRISWELL, David m 7/3/50 Mary E. Folmsbee, both of West Troy; Rev. P. Weaver (5-7/17)

GRISWOLD, Alma - see NEELY, Franklin

GRISWOLD, Chester - see TODRIO, E.T.

GRISWOLD, Eliza - see CHASSELL, David (Rev.)

GRISWOLD, George H., 3, son of Theodore, d 7/25/39 (3-8/1)

GRISWOLD, Harriet - see THERWILLAGER, Frederick

GRISWOLD, John, 84, d 2/20/48 at the home of his son (not named) in Annsville (1-3/3)

GRISWOLD, Mary T. - see WESSELLS, Henry W.

GRISWOLD, Mary, 86, relict of Dr. Elihu Griswold, formerly clerk of Herkimer County, d 7/15/41 at her home in Herkimer (3-7/22)

GRISWOLD, Rufus W. (Major), publisher of the Olean Advocate, m 3/20/37 Caroline F. Searles of NYC in NYC; Rev. Thomas Brentnall (6-4/20)

GRISWOLD, Samuel, 37, merchant, of Middleville, d 10/6/37 in M. (3-11/9)

GRISWOLD, Sylvester C., 47, d (date not given) at Suffield (7-6/20/10)

GROAT, Catharine - see SWART, Jacob N.

GROAT, Elizabeth - see TIMESEN, Eldert

GROESBECK, Jane - see OATHOUT, Jacob

GROESBECK, William, merchant of Little Falls m 2/8/41 Maria A. Fuller, dau. of late Asa Fuller, Esq., of Little Falls in Fairfield; Rev. Fowler (3-3/11)

GROESBEEK, John - see ODELL, Sarah Ann

GROFF, Catherine - see SERAM, Jacob

GROOM, Richard m 2/21/46 Sophia Shaver; Rev. Dodge (all of West Troy) (5-2/25)

GROOT, A.C. m 7/29/35 Sarah Knower in Auburn; Rev. D.C. Axtell; all of Auburn (6-8/10)

GROS, Elizabeth, 91, d 11/1/48 in Fort Plain (4-11/2)

GROSEBECK, Sarah - see KNICKERBACKER, Herman

GROSS, Maria M. - see MABEE, C.

GROSS, Mary - see DEPEW, James

GROSVENOR, Charles P. of Rome m 12/5/48 Abby R. Lyon, dau. of Samuel, Esq., of New Hartford at N.H.; Rev. Dolphus Skinner (1-12/8)

GROSVENOR, Harriet, 59, widow of Oliver C., d 1/13/50 in Rome (1-1/16)

GROSVENOR, Oliver C. - see HUBBARD, Zeruah

GROSVENOR, Oliver C., 58, d 4/8/42 in Rome (billious pluresy) (had lived in Rome more than 20 years and was a deacon of the First Congregational Church there) (1-4/12)

GROSVENOR, S.K. - see LEWIS, Daniel W.

GROSVENOR, Seth Heacock of Buffalo, merchant, m 6/29/36 Jane Grosvenor Wey, dau of William H., Esq., of Catskill; Rev. Joseph F. Phillips (6-7/9)

GROVENGER, Martin L. of Troy m 3/3/46 Catharine C. Bennett of West Troy; Rev. Dodge (5-3/11)

GROVENOR, Francis D. - see BALDWIN, Harriet H.G.

GROVES, Absolem L. (Major), 66, d 6/16/44 at Bridgewater (born in Brimfield, Mass. but settled in Bridgewater as early as 1804) (1-7/2)

GRUNDY, John R., Esq., 32, attorney at law and eldest son of Hon. Felix Grundy, d 6/6/36 at Columbus, Mississippi (6-7/7)

GUARDENIER, ----, infant son of George Guardinier, d (date not given). Funeral from his father's home in Ferry Street "opposite St. Paul's Church" (6-3/23/37)

GUARDENIER, Rynier V., son of Henry A., d 10/6/36 (friends of his father and of his brother, George Guardenier, invited to the funeral at 4 o'clock from the home of the latter, Ferry St. opposite St. Paul's Church) (6-10/7)

GUE, Angeline - see EATON, Joseph D.

GUE, Joseph V. of Lee m 7/2/50 Clarissa Reech of Western in W.; Rev. J.S. Kibbe

(1-7/10)

GUEST, ——— (Mrs.) - see STEELE, Abby (Miss)

GUEST, Mary (Mrs.), 69, d 7/7/36 at Lansingburgh (6-7/9)

GUEST, Mrs. - see STEELE, Tempe

GUEY, Louis Joseph, 31, d 11/2/09 in Hudson (7-11/8)

GUILD, Jane Elizabeth, about 4, dau. of Galen Guild of Little Falls, d 1/13/39
    (inflammation on the lungs) (3-1/24)

GUILE, Phebe Ann, 35, consort of Hon. Henry Guile, d 1/18/43 in Oppenheim
    (3-1/26)

GUINAND, Lewis m 4/5/26 Mary Ann Roy; Rev. Leonard (all of Albany)
    (6-4/25)

GUINN, Rebecca - see TALLMAN, Horace

GUION(?), Thomas Tompkins (Rev.) m 7/7/42 Catharine E. Holmes, dau of S.I.
    Holmes, Esq. in Bedford; Rev. A.H. Partridge (all of Bedford) (11-7/14)

GUION, Harriet Amelia - see COLE, ——— (Rev.)

GUITEAU, Hendrick N., m 8/20/50 Jane S. Childs; Rev. George Boardman (all of
    Cazenovia) (1-8/28)

GUIWITS, Mary, 34, consort of Jacob, d (date not given) at her home near
    Newville (3-5/4/43)

GUMERE, Thomas m 2/24/42 Rebecca Cudney in Mamakating; Rev. H. Connelly
    (9-3/5)

GUNNISON, Helen M. - see PECK, Abraham

GUNNISON, Lucina - see BARNARD, James M.

GUNSALES, Solomon, 52, d 4/29/42 in Newburgh (funeral 4/30 from home of
    James C. Clinton in First Street) (9-4/30)

GUNSALLUS, Thomas m 4/14/39 Ann Akerman, both of West Troy, in W.T.;
    Elder F.S. Parke (5-4/17)

GUNSALUS, Martha Jane, 2, dau. of Thomas and Emma Ann, d 6/9/44 in West
    Troy (see also GUNSALUS, Sarah Elizabeth) (5-6/19)

GUNSALUS, Phebe, 69, d 10/27/48 in West Troy (5-11/1)

GUNSALUS, Sarah Elizabeth, 4, dau. of Thomas and Emma Ann, d 6/9/44 in West
    Troy (see also GUNSALUS, Martha Jane) (5-6/19)

GURLEY, Phineas, Jr., m (date not given) Betsey Fen at Minden (2-2/1/10)

GURNEE, Matthew, Esq., about 48, merchant of Haverstraw d suddenly "a few
    days since" at the Barclay Street Hotel in NYC (12-3/31/40)

GUSSTEL(?), Julia M. - see RADDCLIFFE, William

GUSTIAN, Daniel W. of Johnstown m Nancy Snyder of Minden at Starkville; Rev.
    John I. Wendell (4-7/6)

GUTWITZ, David of Stark m 1/10/50 Lavina Wagner of Danube; Rev. N. Van
    Alstlan(?) (4-1/17)

GWADOH, Gaw-Heh, head chief of the Seneca Nation, d (date not given) at the
    Indian Reservation. "Distinguished for his bravery on the frontier in the late
    war, buried by the side of his ancient friend, Red Jacket. Known by whites
    as Young King" (6-5/21/35)

GWYNN, Jane, late of Ballyshannon, Ireland, d (date not given) in NYC
    (6-11/3/26)

GYPSON, William m 3/6/50 Mary Smith, both of Westmoreland, in Rome; Rev.
    James Erwin (1-3/13)

HAARBROUCK, Jansen(?), president of the Rondout Bank, m 10/9/49 Charlotte

Ostrander, dau. of J.D., Esq., in Kingston; Rev. C.F. Hoes (8-10/13)

HACKLEY, Alexander of Albany m 3/10/35 Elizabeth G Cumpston, dau of late John H. of Auburn; Rev. Josiah Hawkins (6-3/16)

HACKLEY, Archibald B., 29, son of Pluto M. of Little Falls, d 2/18/38 at Cincinnati while on a tour of the far west to find a home for himself and family (member of the Episcopal Church) (3-3/8)

HACKLEY, P.M., Esq. - see FENNELL, A.J. (Rev.)

HACKLEY, Philo - see PETREE, Charlotte

HACKLEY, Philo - see PETREE, Charlotte H.

HACKLEY, Racinia Augusta - see FENNELL, A.J. (Rev.)

HACKSTAFF, John L., Esq., editor of the Prattsville Advocate, m 3/24/47 Lydia M. Smith, dau. of Cyrus of Schoharie, in S.; Rev. Horam Chase (5-3/31)

HADDEN, James V., 16 months, son of Isaac, d. 12/11/41 in Peekskill (11-12/14)

HADLEY, James R. m 8/29/43 Alida Heermance, both of Albany, in West Troy; Rev. Z. Phillips (5-9/6)

HADSON, Rosa M - see HULL, Chester, Jr.

HAFF, Anthony, 29, deputy surveyor of the Port of New York, d 2/6/35 in New York City (6-2/13)

HAFF, Harriet - see DEAN, Ira

HAFF, Lawrence, 81, d (date not given) in Westchester County (6-2/21/26)

HAFT, Mary E. - see BRADISH, Luther

HAGADORN, Hannah - see MAYNARD, Dexter

HAGADORN, Mary Jane - see LAPE, William

HAGAN, Cain m 3/29/37 Margaret Duffey, both of Albany, at Bethlehem; David Russell, Esq. (6-3/31)

HAGEMAN, Jacob m 10/26/26 Caroline Carmichael, both of Sand Lake, at Blooming Grove; Rev. Dumont (6-10/31/26)

HAGEN, Eveline E. - see VOSBURGH, Peter

HAGER, Catharine - see REESE, Peter

HAGER, Daniel of Verona m 5/6/46 Elizabeth Kenton of Rome (or Verona?) in Verona; Elder Lewis (double ceremony - see REESE, Peter) (1-5/19)

HAIGHT, Caroline E., 22, wf of A. Haight, d 1/25/39 in Little Falls (3-1/31)

HAIGHT, Caroline E., 7 months, dau. of Alfred, d 7/31/39 in Little Falls (3-8/8)

HAIGHT, Daniel, 90, d 9/3/42 in Phillipstown (11-9/22)

HAIGHT, Elijah m 10/20/41 Eliza Budd, both of Philipstown, in P.; Rev. William H. Johnson (11-10/26)

HAIGHT, Elizabeth - see HARRIS, John (Dr.)

HAIGHT, Elizabeth, infant dau. of David of Bedford, d 5/31/39 in NYC (12-6/1)

HAIGHT, Emily, 11 months, dau. of Zener and Sarah Ann, d 2/28/40 in New Castle (12-3/3)

HAIGHT, Hiram, 31, brother of A. Haight of Little Falls, d 6/30/43 in Schenectady (3-7/6)

HAIGHT, Mary Ann - see SUTTON, Henry

HAIGHT, Mercy Ann - see LEE, James (Dr.)

HAIGHT, Pamelia of Peekskill, wf of Isaac d 2/26/39, "very suddeny" (12-4/2)

HAIGHT, Pamelia, wf of Isaac of Peekskill, d suddenly 3/25/39 (11-3/26)

HAIGHT, Phebe, 58, wf of David and mother of Alfred Haight of Little Falls, d 5/28/43 in Victor, Ontario County (3-6/8)

HAIGHT, R. Stewart m 11/28/43 Mary Elizabeth Wilson, both of NYC, in

128

Peekskill; Rev. Daniel Brown (11-12/5)

HAIGHT, William S. of Troy m 8/15/44 Frances Baily, dau. of N. Baily, Esq. of Waterford in W.; Rev. Witbeck (5-8/21)

HAIKES, Franklin D. m 2/17/47 Rosetta E. Bentley, dau. of late Rev. N. Bentley of Rome; H.C. Vogell (1-2/19)

HAIKES, Joseph M. of Westmoreland m 2/13/49 Eliza C. Tennant of Rome; H.C. Vogell (1-2/21)

HAILE, Amos m 5/20/38 Nancy Brown, dau. of E. Brown in Eatonville (bride and groom of Eatonville); John Hall, Esq. (3-5/24)

HAILE, Galen H., about 34, son of Nathan of Eatonville, d 2/24/37 in Jackson, Mississippi (a long and severe illness) (3-4/20)

HAILMAN, Lydia W., 42, wf of Dr. D. Hailman and dau. of the late General Samuel Edmunds of Hudson, d (date not given) very suddenly at Unity, Illinois (6-6/28/37)

HAINER, Elizabeth, 24, wf of Henry, d 10/11/47 in West Troy (5-10/13)

HAINER, Katharine - see CRANS, Moses

HAINES or HARRIS, Peter, about 36, d 2/22/42 in Bedford (11-3/1)

HAINES, Catharine, 2, dau. of Joseph, Jr. d 8/25/42 in Newburgh (9-9/3)

HAINES, Hannah (Mrs.), 65, d 12/27/42 in Newburgh (9-12/31)

HAINES, Harriet - see STEPHENS, Archibald Jr.

HAINES, J.D. m 5/4/48 Mary Ann Dickinson; Rev. T.F. Wyckoff (5-5/10)

HAINES, Julia Ann, 5, dau. of Joseph, Jr., d 8/26/42 in Newburgh (9-8/27)

HAINES, Katy (Mrs.) - see COPLAND, Alexander

HAINES, Katy (Mrs.) - see STEPHENS, Archibald, Jr.

HAINES, Nathaniel, Esq., 36, editor of the Eastern Republican, d 12/6/36 at Bangor, ME (6-12/17)

HAINES, Phebe - see COPLAND, Alexander

HAINES, Stephen - see COPLAND, Alexander

HAINES, Stephen - see STEPHENS, Archibald, Jr.

HAINS, Eliza - see TRAVIS, John

HAIT, Henrietta - see SIMONS, Nelson

HAIT, Louisa Elizabeth (Mrs.) - see DEPEW, Henry

HAIT, Louise Elizabeth - see DE PEW, Henry W.

HAIT, Moore (Dr.) of NYC, formerly of Peekskill, m 11/6/33 "Miss Anthony" of Fishkill at F. (Rev. Fisher) (11-11/12)

HAKE, Margaret - see BIRGE, Chester B.

HAKES, Kaleb m 2/15/49 Mary Breuster (sic), both of Watervliet; Rev. Burroughs (5-2/21)

HAKES, Sarah A. - see LADUE, Samuel

HALE, Alfred E. m 6/13/37 Julia Ann Post, dau. of Dan Post, Esq., in Newport; Rev. W.H. Waggoner (3-6/22)

HALE, Ammi m 11/18/40 Mary Ives in Vernon; Rev. William Pepper (all of Vernon) (1-12/1)

HALE, Caroline Alice, 10, eldest dau. of Rev. Dr. Hale, d 2/9/37 in Geneva (6-2/20)

HALE, Catharine, 79, relict of late Dr. Mordecai Hale, surgeon of the US Army, and sister of Hon. James R. Paulding, Secretary of the Navy, d 2/7/39 in Sing Sing (12-2/12)

HALE, Charles (Dr.), 36 (?), d 8/22/35 in Greenbush (New Hampshire newspapers are requested to insert this notice) (6-8/27)

HALE, Charles R. of Floyd m 3/14/49 Eliza E. Hinman, dau. of late Livingston Hinman of Stittville in S.; Rev. Walter R. Long of Whitesboro (1-3/21)

HALE, Elizabeth Myers, 9 months, dau. of Elizabeth A., d 2/3/39 in Herkimer (3-2/7)

HALE, Evelina - see JONES, William P.

HALE, Maria - see JOSLYN, Lewis W. (Dr.)

HALE, Mary Jane - see WELLER, Gideon

HALENBAKE, Isaac Rue - see BROWER, John W.

HALENBECK, Isaac A., merchant, m 2/11/16 Rhoda Adams, dau. of Hon. Peter C. of Coxsackie, at C.; Rev. Gilbert R. Livingston (6-2/17)

HALENBECK, Julia - see COURTNEY, Isaac

HALL, ---- (Mr.) - see TRAVIS, Stephen

HALL, ----, infant dau. of Jesse D. of Cassville (Paris), Oneida County, d 7/23/39 in Little Falls (3-8/1)

HALL, Abigail - see SANDERSON, Luther

HALL, Adam m 5/19/36 Charlotte Forsey(?); Rev. C.P. Clarke (all of Albany) (6-5/21)

HALL, Adelaide - see FRY, Daniel

HALL, Adna of West Troy, NY m 9/18/48 Julia S. Dexter of Portsmouth, NH in P.; Rev. Richards (5-9/27)

HALL, Alexander m 11/1/43 Jane Easterbrook in Herkimer; Rev. D. Chitester (all of Herkimer) (3-11/9)

HALL, Amelia, 5, only dau. of Lyman, d 3/1/09 in Catskill (7-3/8)

HALL, Arethusa - see TORREY, Elijah

HALL, Edward B. of Canaan, Columbia Co. m 9/27/37 Ann Maria Hotchkins of Albany; Rev. Holmes (6-9/29)

HALL, Edward of Ashfield, Mass. m 5/23/43 C.M. Mc Chesney of Little Falls at the American House in Utica; Rev. Hayes (3-6/1)

HALL, Elias, Esq. - see TORREY, Elijah

HALL, Ellis - see BARNS, George W.

HALL, Ellis - see BELLINGER, Levi

HALL, Fanny R., only child of T.F. Hall and the late Mrs. Rosina C. Hall, and only grand-child of Mrs. Rosina Dutton, late of Rome, d 3/9/41 at Rochester (1-3/16)

HALL, Green - see FRY, Daniel

HALL, Green - see TILLETSON, Gardner

HALL, Hellen H. - see WALRATH, Alfred

HALL, Henrietta - see WELLS, John A.

HALL, Hezekiah F. m 3/2/36 Pamela Grey, both of New Lebanon (6-3/9)

HALL, Isaac m 3/27/39 Mary Brouwer, both of New Castle, at N.C.; Rev. Van Deusen (12-4/2)

HALL, J. Whitfield of Mechanicville (formerly of Poughkeepsie) m 11/26/46 Susan Frink of West Troy in W.T.; Rev. O.H. Gregory (5-11/11)

HALL, Jacob m 9/9/41 Nancy Cudney, both of Oppenheim, in Little Falls; George Petrie, Esq. (3-9/16)

HALL, Jennett - see BARNS, George W.

HALL, Jerusha - see CARPENTER, Chester

HALL, Joanna - see COOK, Henry D.

HALL, John H., Jr. of Vernon m 6/9/44 Julia A. Gillespie at Clinton; Rev. B. Hawley of Utica (1-6/18)

HALL, John of Troy m 6/16/50 Mary Ann Hall of West Troy; Rev. J.C. Burroughs (5-6/26)

HALL, John W. of New Lebanon m 3/6/36 Emily Sikes of Nassau (6-3/9)

HALL, John Whitfield, 23, of Mechanicville, formerly of Poughkeepsie, d 12/22/46 in West Troy (typhus fever) (5-12/30)

HALL, Joseph, 53, d (date not given) at New Haven (7-6/20/10)

HALL, Julia - see SWEETLAND, Samuel

HALL, Julia - see VAN NORT, John

HALL, Lovina - see BELLINGER, Levi

HALL, M.M., wf of D.A., Esq. and dau of Hon. Lewis Condict of Morristown, NJ, d 8/5/36 at Washington, DC (6-8/15)

HALL, Martha - see SUTTON, Daniel B.

HALL, Martha Ives, 74, relict of late John, d 2/12/41 at Turin (1-3/16)

HALL, Mary - see PEAK, Samuel C.

HALL, Mary - see POWELL, Morton C.

HALL, Mary Ann - see HALL, John

HALL, Mary M. - see LEE, Charles

HALL, Mary M. - see LEE, Charles

HALL, Mr. - see TRAVIS, Stephen

HALL, Northrup of Peekskill m 1/1/43 Sarah Mekeel of Putnam Valley in P.V.; Rev. Daniel Brown (11-2/7)

HALL, Robert, nearly 65, postmaster of Hallsville, Montgomery County, d 12/7/41 in Minden after a short illness (3-12/23)

HALL, Sarah, 59, wf of Francis Hall, senior editor and proprietor of the New York Commercial Advertiser, d 9/5/46 at the British American Hotel at Kingston (Note by FQB: Mr. & Mrs Hall were on a Canadian trip when she had the fatal attack of apoplexy, so probably the above hotel was at Kingston, Ontario, Canada) (1-9/15)

HALL, William C. of Verona m 7/8/46 Louisa A. Carroll of Springfield in S.; Rev. S. Tracy (1-7/21)

HALL, William P. of Little Falls m 3/10/39 Ann Morcy of Fairfield in F.; Rev. A. Gross (3-3/14)

HALLACK, Sarah Elizabeth, 11 months, dau. of Joseph d 3/5/40 in Yorktown (12-3/10)

HALLADAY, James, 42, d 12/12/35 in Amsterdam (illness of 5 days) (6-12/18)

HALLAGH, James, 37, of firm of Strong, Hallagh & Co. of NYC d 10/11/37 in NYC (after a lingering illness) (6-10/13)

HALLECK, Almond, 49(?), d 11/22/38 in Little Falls (3-11/29)

HALLENBECK, Matthew of Guilderland m 11/12/26 Anna Morgan of Albany; Rev. Ferris (6-11/14)

HALLETT, Heman of Yarmouth, age about 46, d 11/22/35 at New Bedford suddenly ("in two or three minutes") (6-11/28)

HALLETT, Mary Elizabeth - see PICKETT, Charles

HALLOCK, Edward, 94, d 7/9/49 at home of his son-in-law, Daniel Deyo, in Newburgh (8-7/21)

HALLOCK, Eliza, 26, dau of Benjamin Griffin of Somers and widow of late Alexander Hallock, d 3/22/39 at the Nine Partners, Dutchess County (she was a member of the Society of Friends) (12-4/2)

HALLOCK, Joel of Long Island m 11/14/38 Margaret Archer, dau of Benjamin,
Esq. of New Castle, in N.C.; Chauncey Smith, Esq. (12-11/20)

HALSEY, Elmina - see GIBBS, George Clinton

HALSEY, John T. (Rev.), 45, d 7/2/42 at his late home in Elizabethtown, NJ
(9-7/16)

HALSEY, Nicoll - see MC DOWELL, Margaret

HALSEY, William A., about 35, formerly of Newburgh, d 9/23/42 at Chester
(9-10/1)

HALSTEAD, Hannah - see BURGESS, Isaac

HALSTEAD, John, 50, d 6/11/34 (for many years a resident of Peekskill and a
member of the Society of Friends) (11-6/17)

HALSTEAD, Margaret R. - see CALLAHAN, S.T.

HALSTEAD, Margaret, wf of Samuel of Peekskill, d 9/15/33 (consumption)
(11-9/17)

HALSTEAD, Mary - see BAKEMORE, William

HALSTEAD, Nancy - see BAUDER, Ezra

HALSTED, Elizabeth, about 70, wf of Philamon, Esq., d 8/27/39 in South Salem
(12-9/3)

HALSTED, Gilbert, 31, d 4/25/42 in Peekskill (11-4/28)

HALSTED, Ira m 10/21/38 Ann Young, both of Mount Pleasant; Rev. Moube
(12-10/30)

HALSTED, James D. of Rye m 10/20/35 Elizabeth S. Todd, dau of Eli M., Esq. of
Waterford, in W.; Rev. Smith

HALSTED, James D. of Westchester County m 10/20/35 Elizabeth S. Todd of
Waterford in W.; Rev. R. Smith (6-10/26)

HAM, Catharine M. - see EDGERTON, Augustus

HAM, Henry m 11/7/41 Mary Ann Miller in West Troy; Rev. D. Starks (5-11/17)

HAMAN, Mary - see BECKWITH, Ira

HAMBROOK, Mary - see SPENCE, George

HAMERSLEY, William, M.D., 71, senior consulting physician of New York
Hospital, formerly professor of the theory and practice of Physic and
Clinical Medicine in Columbia College and the College of Physicians and
Surgeons in NYC, d (date not given) in NYC (6-2/13/37)

HAMILTON, ---- (Mrs.), d 7/8/42 in Newburgh (9-7/16)

HAMILTON, David, 3, son of Dr. J.W. Hamilton, d 6/20/38 at Fort Plain (3-7/5)

HAMILTON, James - see MC INTOSH, Euphemia

HAMILTON, James, Senior, (Major), 82, d 11/26/33 in Charleston, SC (oldest
surviving field officer in the continental Army in Rev. War and father of
Gen. Hamilton, late governor of South Carolina) (11-12/17)

HAMILTON, Oliver, 27, d 6/30/49 in West Troy ("Binghamton papers please
notice") (5-7/4)

HAMLIN, Frances M., 29, wf of S.D. of Niagara Falls, d 9/2/46 in Annsville at the
home of her father (his name not given) (1-9/15)

HAMLIN, Hannah, 75, consort of Asa, deceased, d 7/4/41 in Rome (member of
First Presbyterian Church 35 years) (funeral at 2 o'clock at the home of S.
Goodwins) (1-7/6)

HAMLIN, Harriet R. - see BURRILL, William F.

HAMMOND, A. (Dr.) - see HOLMES, William (Dr.)

HAMMOND, Abijah, Esq. m (date not given) Margaret Aspenwall in NYC; Rev. Howe (6-2/28/16)

HAMMOND, Ammon, M.D., of West Troy d 7/21/49 at the home of his mother-in-law, Mrs. Marks (with his wife and two other persons he had visited Jonesville "to see his somewhat afflicted son" when he was stricken and died within 2 hours) (asiatic cholera) (5-7/25)

HAMMOND, Charles, Esq., editor of the Cincinnati Gazette, m 1/21/36 Elizabeth B. Morehead of Zanesville, Ohio at Z., Rev. Smallwood (6-1/27)

HAMMOND, Dr. (Mrs.) - see SPIER, Joseph

HAMMOND, Elisha, 88, a Rev. War Continental Army captain, d 2/27/39 at his home at Colinburgh near Croton (11-3/12)

HAMMOND, Elizabeth, 40, wf of Dr. A. Hammond d 9/7/45 in West Troy (5-9/10)

HAMMOND, Emma M. - see PLATT, Albertus H.

HAMMOND, George W., 24, d 5/20/41 in West Troy (5-6/9)

HAMMOND, John D., Esq., surveyor, d 8/7/36 at Carthage, Jefferson Co. (cholera) (6-9/20)

HAMMOND, Margretta - see HUESTIS, Harvey

HAMMOND, Matilda - see BECKWITH, James

HAMMOND, Walter, 11, son of John M., d 3/25/47 in West Troy (5-3/31)

HAMPTON, Harriet, oldest dau. of Gen. Wade Hampton, d (date not given) at Columbia, South Carolina (6-10/27/26)

HANAMAN, I.E. m 2/23/48 U.I. Goewey in West Troy; Rev. T.F. Wyckoff (5-3/1)

HANAY, Rosiana - see TRUMBULL, J. Abner

HANCOCK, --- (Mrs.), wf of Jotham. (her funeral at 4 o'clock 1/29/36 from 257 Washington St.) (6-1/29)

HANCOCK, Huldah - see BAKER, Asa

HANCOCK, John Jay, 5 months, son of W.J. and Sarah, d 3/25/47 in Rome ("cancer producing fits") (1-4/2)

HANCY, Nelson of Oswego m 8/20/36 Sarah Elizabeth Thomas of Albany (6-8/27)

HAND, Edward, merchant, of Buffalo m 4/18/37 Elizabeth W. Thompson at Durham; Rev. J. Thompson (6-4/25)

HAND, Ichabod (Capt.), 63, d 3/13/46 at Vernon (originally from Guilford, Conn. but lived the last 30 years in Verona and Vernon and was landlord of the Vernon Stage House) (1-3/17)

HANER, Catherine M. - see BENCHLEY, William

HANER, Jeremiah, 52, d 1/18/41 in Herkimer (3-1/21)

HANER, Oliver m 9/18/36 Fanny Burt in Stark; Rev. Sparry (3-9/29)

HANES, Henry P. of Sand Lake m 9/4/47 Mrs. Phebe Yorkes if Schodack at S.; Rev. Chase (5-9/8)

HANES, Sarah - see LOCKWOOD, William

HANKS, Mary D., 35, wf of Lucius B., Esq., d 5/23/45 at Hartford, CT (1-6/3)

HANN, Catharine - see ROSTIZER, Valentine

HANNUM, Leonard, Jr. m 7/4/49 Elizabeth Phelps, both of West Troy; Rev. T.W. Pearson (5-7/11)

HANSEN, Cornelia R. - see RHOADES, Lyman

HANY, Joseph, Esq. of Boonville m 4/18/43 Lydia Ann Dickinson of Rome in R.; Rev. H.C. Vogle (1-5/9)

HAPPY, Mary - see YERRY, Henry

HARD, Maria - see HATHAWAY, George C.

HARDENBERGH, Elmira - see MIDDAUGH, Jesse

HARDENBURGH, Peter (his age and date of death not given) d in Glen, Montgomery County (6-2/21/26)

HARDENDORF, William m 3/16/43 Margaret Palmer in Little Falls; Rev. C.W. Leet (3-3/23)

HARDENDORF, Zipporah F., 21, wf of William, d 12/2/41 in Little Falls (consumption) (3-12/9)

HARDER, Alexander, 2, son of Jacob and Emily of Danube, d 1/13/43 in Theresa, Jefferson County (3-1/26)

HARDER, Christina, 67, consort of John, d 7/13/42 in Danube (3-7/21)

HARDER, Isaac of Oneida County m 1/20/41 Mary Ann Hyser of Herkimer in H.; Rev. John P. Spinner (3-1/28)

HARDER, Jacob d 10/23/43 at Newville (after 2 weeks of fever) (survived by his wife and two children) (3-10/26)

HARDICK, Eliza - see VANCE, John

HARDIKER, Elizabeth - see BAKER, Thomas

HARDIKER, Richard - see BAKER, Thomas

HARDING, Helen, 4, dau. of Francis and Angelica S., d 5/20/45 in West Troy (5-5/28)

HARDING, Ira of San Hake (possibly intended for Sand Lake) m 8/18/44 Rebecca Van Volkenberg og the same place in West Troy; Rev. Benjamin L. Lane (5-8/21)

HARDING, Lucy, infant dau. of F. Harding, d 10/20/39 (5-10/23)

HARDY, Catherine L. - see GRAY, I.N.

HARDY, Marvin W. m 2/13/43 Frances E. North; Rev. C.W. Leet (all of Little Falls) (3-2/23)

HARE, John m 10/15/48 Esther Long in West Troy; Rev. T.F. Wyckoff (5-10/25)

HARFORD, M.E. - see PARDICAN(?), Gregory A.

HARGER, Hannah - see ROWBOTHAM, William

HARINDEEN, Elmina, 28, wf of Hon. Richard and dau. of Levi Bowen of Newport, d 4/29/41 at Newport (she is listed as a mother but her children not mentioned by name) (funeral sermon by Rev. Pierce of Trenton) (3-5/20)

HARKES, Phebe - see TERRY, George

HARMAN, Joseph, M.D., m 10/25/36 Sarah Michael, dau of Richard M., Esq., at Schenectady (6-10/26)

HARMON, Bronson, Esq., merchant, of Delmar m 4/3/36 Mary Eliza Fay, only dau of Major Eliza Fay of US Army; Rev. Professor Yates of Union College (6-5/4)

HARPER, Catherine - see BENEDICT, Micajah

HARPER, Nicholas, 72, d 1/29/43 at Washington (for nearly 30 years a clerk in the Treasury Department, had served in the US Navy aboard the frigates "United States" and "Boston." He was born in Ireland in 1798)(his obituary is included here) (5-2/8)

HARPER, Robert m 11/9/48 Sarah E. Capron, dau. of John; Rev. H.A. Raymond (all of Watervliet) (5-11/15)

HARRINGTON, Elzizabeth - see JEWELL, Merrett

HARRINGTON, Jane - see POLHILL, James

HARRINGTON, Juliet E. - see PEASE, William T.

HARRINGTON, Sarah A. - see COFFIN, George M.

HARRIS(?), William m 3/30/37 Madalena Keeler, dau. of Seth, in Fairfield; Rev. W. H. Waggoner (3-4/6)

HARRIS, Abigail - see HEMAN, ----

HARRIS, Albert G. of Little Falls m 8/23/38 Sophia E. Houghton of Fairfield in F.; Rev. J.E. Downing (3-9/27)

HARRIS, David of Montgomery m 12/1/41 Mrs. Betsey Crawford of Mamakating in M.; Rev. Connelly (9-12/18)

HARRIS, Ebenezer, 70, of Glastonbury was drowned 6/18/10 ("fell backwards out of a small boat "in the river opposite Rock Hill... he was subject to fainting spells") (7-7/4)

HARRIS, Edwin A., merchant, m 9/2/35 Christina P. Newlands, dau of Luke F.; Rev. Dr. Proudfit of Schenectady (bride & groom of Albany) (6-9/4)

HARRIS, Elizabeth - see HOWE, Amos

HARRIS, F.L., M.D., of Buffalo m 2/4/36 Mary Ann Mather, dau of Elias of Albany; Rev. Yates (6-2/5)

HARRIS, Frederick A., infant son of Albert G. and Sophia, d 2/7/42 in Little Falls (3-2/10)

HARRIS, J.F. m 4/14/42 Lucinda Burnes, both of New London, in N.L.; Rev. C.M. Lewis (1-5/3)

HARRIS, James d 5/3/36 (funeral at 4 o'clock from the home of his son, Robert, 556 South Market Street) (6-5/4)

HARRIS, Jane, 36, consort of Abraham, formerly of Middleville, d (date not given) in Utica (3-3/31/36)

HARRIS, Jeremiah m 11/20/44 Martha Ann Coonradt in Rome; Rev. Haynes (1-11/26)

HARRIS, Jesse of Root m 7/4/39 Jane Beverly in Herkimer; Rev. J. Murphy (3-7/11)

HARRIS, John (Dr.) of Greenwich, CT m (date not given) Elizabeth Haight, only dau. of Caleb of Bedford, in B.; Rev. Samuel Nichols (12-5/7/39)

HARRIS, John S. of Sherburne, Chenango County m 3/8/40 Susan Crist of Herkimer in H.; Rev. Murphy (3-3/12)

HARRIS, Maria - see WELCH, William

HARRIS, Peter - see possibly HAINES, Peter

HARRIS, Rebecca - see CARPENTER, Stephen

HARRIS, Sarah E., 21, dau. of late John Harris of Newburgh, d 10/14/42 in NYC (funeral 10/16 from Second Presbyterian Church in Newburgh) (9-10/15)

HARRIS, Stephen of town of Rowe m 11/25/47 Minerva J. Boyd of Watervliet, John Miles, "Chaplain of Albany Bethel" (5-12/1)

HARRIS, Thomas K. (Gen.), lately a member of Congress from Tennessee, d 4/18/16 "of wounds received in a rencountre with Col. Simpson" (6-4/24)

HARRISON, Clarissa B. (Mrs.), dau. and only child of Gen. Z.M. Pike and relict of J.C.M. Harrison, eldest son of Gen. Harrison, d 2/1/37 at her mother's home in Boon County, Kentucky (6-3/4)

HARRISON, Jane - see PAGE, William

HARRISON, Mary Ann - see BYINGTON, John

HARRISON, Robert, 16, d 10/17/36 in Albany (consumption) (friends of his brothers, John and Patrick, invited to the funeral at 4 o'clock from his late resdience, two doors west of the Scotch Presby. Church on Fox St.)

(6-10/18)

HARRISON, Sarah E. - see CARNRIKE, A.K.

HARRISON, William of England m 2/20/40 Louisa Van Buren of Warren in W.; W.C. Crain, Esq. (3-3/12)

HARRISON, William of Illinois m 4/14/46 Jenette Thayer, dau. of Ellery of Floyd, in F.; H.C. Vogell (1-4/21)

HART, Ann Elizabeth - see MUMFORD, George

HART, Asenath, 41, d 1/25/49 in West Troy (5-1/31)

HART, Azalia Ermesteen, 1, dau. of William and Rachael Eliza, d 3/25/50 in Rochester (Mrs. Hart was formerly of Fort Plain) (4-3/28)

HART, Elizabeth - see BUSH, John P.

HART, Emma - see WHITE, Howard

HART, George of West Troy m 4/5/49 Elizabeth Jane Ensign of Troy in T.; Rev. N.S.S. Beman (5-4/11)

HART, Gilbert B. m 10/6/41 Miss E.L. Taylor; Rev. D. De Vinne (all of Peekskill) (11-10/12)

HART, Gilbert, 73, m 7/8/39 Nancy Curtis, 56, in Carmel; Rev. Nimino (all of Carmel) (12-7/23)

HART, Hariett H. - see DOUGHTY, E.T.

HART, Hickson F., 29, d 9/21/42 in Yorktown (11-9/22)

HART, I.W. of Erie, Penna. m 5/4/43 Martha M. Mason, dau. of John, Esq., of West Troy in W.T.; Rev. Lane (5-5/10)

HART, James m 2/7/49 Mary Ann Mann, both of Sammonsville, in S.; Rev. Warner (4-2/22)

HART, Martin, Esq. - see BUSH, John P.

HART, Mary E. - see BRADISH, Luther

HART, Richard P., Esq., 64. d 1/2/44 at his home on Second Street, Troy (lived in Troy the past 40 years) (from Troy Daily Post) (5-1/3)

HART, William A., 27, d (date not given) at Tarrytown (6-1/20/26)

HART, William m 1/2/39 Nancy Hitchcock in Carmel; Rev. Sloat (all of Carmel) (12-1/15)

HARTER, Emily - see HEATH, Alfred

HARTER, Eunice - see DYGERT, Warner

HARTER, Harriet - see CASWELL, William

HARTER, James m 10/5/43 Charlotte C. Tibbets in Little Falls; Rev. C.W. Leet (3-10/19)

HARTER, John - see BREDENBECKER, Jeremiah

HARTER, Margaret - see BRIDENBECKER, Jeremiah

HARTER, Margaret - see PROUSE, Henry R.

HARTER, Maria - ROFFENOT, Augustus

HARTER, Mary - see PADDOCK, Samuel L.

HARTER, Nicholas, 60, m 8/27/41 Mary Crosey, 18, at Herkimer; Rev. Simeon Osborn (3-9/9)

HARTER, Phillip, 70, d 12/7/41 in Herkimer (3-12/16)

HARTFIELD, Jane Maria - see LUDLOW, Alfred

HARTFORD, Charles m 11/20/39 Sarah Lockwood, both of Poundridge, in P.; Rev. Paterson (12-12/3)

HARTMAN, Catharine - see VAN ANTWERP, Isaac

HARTNESS, Marcelline, 1, only dau of John and Huldah, d 12/2/36 in Albany

136

(friends of the family and of John's father-in'law, Nicholas Page, invited to the funeral, 12/4, at 195 North Market St.) (6-12/3)

HARTSHORN, A. - see CATLIN, Polly

HARTWELL, Nancy L. - see SAVERY, Hosea C.

HARVEY, Asahel, one of the proprietors of the Ontario Repository, d 7/12/35 in Canandaigua (6-7/28)

HARVEY, Charles m 12/25/39 Electa Jane Griffin; Rev. C.H. Underhill (all of Bedford) (12-12/31)

HARVEY, Erriathan m 1/14/41 Sophelia Brace, both of Camden, in C.; Rev. A. Graham (1-2/2)

HARVEY, Herman, 13, son of Obediah, d 3/2/10 at Durham (flung from a horse with one foot entangled in the bridle) (7-3/21)

HARWELL, Robert, Esq. of Hoosick m 9/12/37 Cynthia Haswell, dau. of late Arthur of Watervliet; Rev. Campbell (6-9/15)

HARWOOD, Nathan (Dr.) - see PRATT, Asenah H.

HARWOOD, Richard, Adjutant General of the State of Maryland, d 4/11/35 at Annapolis (6-4/15)

HASBROUCK, Elizabeth, 82, relict of James, d 9/29/49 at the home of her son-in-law, Sylvanus M. Bruyn in Shawangunk (8-10/13)

HASBROUCK, Israella - see PROUDFIT, David L. (Rev.)

HASBROUCK, Margaret - see JOHNSON, Joseph H.

HASBROUCK, Maria - see GORMAN, Robert

HASBROUCK, Maria - see GOSMAN, Robert, Jr.

HASBROUCK, Robert, 33(?), d 5/31/49 in Kingston (8-6/16)

HASBROUCK, Solomon, Esq., 84 yrs and 8 mo, d 12/17/34 at Kingston. (taught school at Kingston 42 yrs, justice of peace 20 years, collector of church rents 20 yrs, clerk of the village 20 yrs (copied from the Ulster Republican) (6-1/6/35)

HASCALL, Asa, Esq. of Malone m 7/19/37 Phebe A. Smith of Plattsburgh in P.; Rev. Halsey (6-7/28)

HASKINS, ----, infant son of L.G. Haskins, d (by drowning) 7/10/40 in Newport (3-7/16)

HASKINS, Alsa Clarrany, 25, eldest dau of William P., Esq., d 1/4/36 in Troy (a protracted illness) (survived by her parents, brothers and sisters") (from Troy Whig) (6-1/12)

HASKINS, Daniel Winton, 3, only son of Dr. Leonard G. and Elizabeth B. Haskins, d 7/10/40 in Newport by drowning (3-7/23)

HASKINS, Nathan Brown, 2, eldest son of Dr. Leonard G. and Elizabeth B. Haskins, d 8/3/38 in Manheim (3-8/9)

HASKINS, Whitman B. (formerly the host of the Ogdensburgh Hotel, now Mansion House, Albany) m 12/27/36 Mrs. Mehitable B. Culver at the home of Oliver Culver, Esq., near Rochester; Rev. Lyon (6-3/17/37)

HASLEHURST, James of NYC m 6/20/50 Irene E. Walcott, dau. of B.S., Esq., of New York Mills, at NYM; Rev. R.R. Kirk (1-6/26)

HASTINGS, Heman J., attorney at law of West Troy, m 11/13/41 Louisa H. Wood of East Troy in West Troy; Rev. D. Starks (5-11/17)

HASTINGS, Sarah M. - see KELLOGG, Edward

HASTINGS, Sarah Sophia, 4, youngest child of John, Esq., d 6/6/38 in West Troy ("Printers in Mass. are requested to print this") (5-6/13)

HASTINGS, Seth, Esq. - see KELLOGG, Edward

HASWELL, Arthur - see HARWELL, Robert

HASWELL, Cynthia - see HARWELL, Robert

HASWELL, Joseph A. of Watervliet m 12/6/26 Frances Freleigh, oldest dau. of Dr. Freleigh of Watervliet; Rev. Steele (6-12/12)

HATCH, Burrel, 53, d 7/5/48 in Rome (1-7/14)

HATCH, Burrett - see MORTON, Jane

HATCH, Hapsey - see OTT, George S.

HATCH, Heman, a Rev. War soldier, formerly of Centerville, NJ, d 12/26/43 at Newark, NJ (5-1/17/44)

HATCH, James M., Esq., attorney at law of Utica m 10/20/36 Julia Ann Sharpley, dau of late John of Hamilton, at H.; Professor Joel S. Bacon of H. (6-10/28)

HATCH, Jane - see MORTON, J.W.

HATCH, Melinda, 60, consort of Joseph, d 8/22/43 in Columbia (3-8/31)

HATCH, Philura Adeline - see STYLES, Robert S.

HATCH, Sibyl, 49, wf of Sylvanus, d 9/6/48 suddenly at the home of her husband in Rome (her first husband, Thomas Alrich, has died "a few years since") (1-9/15)

HATCH, Sylvenus m 2/5/45 Jane Roberts in Rome; Rev. H.C. Vogell (1-2/11)

HATCH, W.D., 17 months, only son of Joseph L., d 6/8/39 in Columbia (3-6/20)

HATFIELD, Joseph, d 9/22/42 in Greenburgh near White Plains (lived in Westchester County many years and was a prominent member of the Methodist Church.) (11-9/29)

HATFIELD, Richard, Esq., 47, late clerk of the courts of Oyer and Terminer and General Sessions of the Peace, d 7/16/33 in NYC (to be buried in White Plains) (11-7/23)

HATHAWAY, Franklin of Rome m 8/20/40 Sarah A. Gilbert of Hudson in H.; Rev. Parden (1-8/25)

HATHAWAY, George C. m (date not given) Maria Hard, both of Cleveland, Ohio, in NYC; Rev. D. Smith (1-4/28/46)

HATHAWAY, Joshua, (Judge), 75, d 12/8/36 in Rome (born in Suffield, CT 8/13/1761; a Rev. War veteran. Fought at Battle of Bennington) (a long obituary is included) (6-12/17)

HATHAWAY, Levantia - see PIXLEY, B.F.

HATHAWAY, Samuel, 20, d 8/28/39 in Sing Sing (short, severe illness) (12-9/3)

HATLUCK, Elizabeth C. - see FOWLER, Nathaniel D.

HATTER, Peter m 8/22/39 Souan Small, dau. of Melchior, in Herkimer; Rev. Spinner (all of Little Falls) (3-8/29)

HATTON, Benjamin, Esq., 73(?), d 12/1/36 in Catskill (6-12/10)

HAVELET, Elizabeth - see SETTLE, Jacob D.

HAVEN, Catharine Garrison, 19 months, dau. of Philander B., d 3/20/45 in Sangerfield (1-4/1)

HAVENS, Catharine A. - see TURNER, R.B.

HAVENS, George F., Esq. m 5/29/44 Clarinda J. Welton, dau. of Isaac of Paris, in P.; Rev. Isaac Swart (1-6/18)

HAVERLING, Henry, teller of the Steuben County Bank, d 1/7/35 at Bath (6-1/22)

HAVILAND, Bartlett of Dutchess County m 10/19/41 Susan M. Dickinson, dau of Gilbert of Cortlandt town (a Society of Friends marriage ceremony) (11-10/26)

HAVILAND, Emeline - see DOLTON, James Henry

HAVILAND, Esther - see HAVILAND, James

HAVILAND, Esther - see THOMPSON, B.

HAVILAND, James of Athens m (date not given) Esther Haviland, dau. of John of
Patterson, in P.; Benjamin Haviland, Esq. (12-1/21/40)

HAVILAND, Jane - see SUTTON, Leonard

HAVILAND, Roger m (date not given) Ruth Scisson at Glens Falls (6-6/1/16)

HAVILAND, William, 20, only son of Moses, d (date not given) in Somers
(12-2/18/40)

HAWE, Lydia W., 53, wf of Hezekiah, Esq., d 7/28/36 at Cohoes (6-8/2)

HAWES, John - see OPPIE, Theodore F.

HAWES, Josiah L. of Cobleskill m (date blurred) Lucia R. Foote of Franklin,
Delaware County, in Franklin; Rev. Charles Ingersoll (4-6/27/50)

HAWES, William, formerly preceptor of Canandaigua Academy, d (date not given)
in Lavonia (6-5/4/16)

HAWKINS, Eliza - see BRONSON, Joel

HAWKINS, Mary (Mrs.), 100, d (date not given) in Greenwich, Mass.
(descendants are 8 children, 82 grand children, 173 great grand children,
and 25 great great grandchildren) (5-12/22/41)

HAWKINS, S.(?) C. of Suffolk County m 9/14/37 Julia Ann Day, dau. of Major L.
Day of Canandaigua at C.; Rev. Philo E. Brown (6-9/25)

HAWKINS, Uriah, 82, (a Rev. War soldier) d 2/19/40 at Newport (served in the
Continental Army in the War six years) (his obituary is included) (3-2/27)

HAWKINS, William Frederick, 6, d 5/6/43 at the home of his father, David, Esq.
at Newport (illness of more than four years) (3-5/18)

HAWLEY, Charles m 10/18/48 Jane E. Walter, both of Canajoharie, in NYC; Rev.
John G. South (4-10/26)

HAWLEY, Elizabeth, 2, youngest dau of Gideon, Esq., d 8/8/36 (funeral at 5
o'clock from 210 North Market St.) (6-8/9)

HAWLEY, George W. of St. Louis, Missouri m 12/7/37 Catharine M. Payn of
Albany; Rev. A. Potter (6-12/8)

HAWLEY, Ichabod, about 70, d (date not given) at Trumbull (7-6/13/10)

HAWLEY, Jane - see GATES, Henry

HAWLEY, Miron m 1/1/45 Betsey Ann Bartlett, all of Rome; Rev. H. Mattison
(1-1/14)

HAWLEY, Nyrum m 1/20/47 Cornelia Bangs, both of Rome; H.C. Vogell (1-1/29)

HAWLEY, Ralph (Col.) m 10/12/36 Julia Frances Mallory, only dau of late Hon.
James, at St. Paul's Church, Troy (6-10/17)

HAWLEY, Rosanna - see SHELDON, John

HAWLEY, Thomas R. m 1/25/41 Lucretia Root, youngest dau. of Zalmon, Esq., in
Boonville; Rev. Deming (bride & groom of Remson) (1-2/23)

HAWLEY, William F. d 10/20/49 in Saugerties (consumption) (8-10/27)

HAWLS, Henry m 3/1/37 Julia R. Peck, dau. of Capt. Daniel; Rev. Welch (all of
Albany) (6-3/3)

HAWN, Conrad, 82, d 11/14/50 in Frey's Bush (4-11/21)

HAWN, MAria C. - see OLDS, William E.

HAWS, Elvin, grocer, m 4/15/41 Charlotte Dwight, dau. of Col. Solomon Sykes at
Durhamville; Rev. W. Turner (all of Durhamville) (1-4/20)

HAWSE, William H. m 5/21/43 Asenath Rerrington, both of West Troy; Rev. M.

Bates (5-5/31)

HAY, Thomas, 55, late mayor of Hudson, d 3/17/36 at Hudson (6-3/25)

HAYARD, Stephen (Col.), 67, (a Rev. War soldier from time of its commencement), d 12/13/15 (from the Pittsburg Gazetteer) (6-1/6/16)

HAYDEN, Anna W., 1, dau. of Cyrus and Mary, d 8/11/49 in Dresden (dysentery) (1-9/5)

HAYDEN, Aurelia - see HILLIARD, Lathrop

HAYDEN, Charles W. of NYC m 9/25/48 Cornelia C. Humphreys, dau. of late Dr. Humphreys of Utica, at Trinity Church in Utica; Rev. Dr. Proal (1-9/29)

HAYDEN, Cyrus, merchant, of Rome, m 9/15/41 Mary Veazie od Parma Center, Monroe County at P.C. (1-9/21)

HAYDEN, Harriet N. - see FRASER, Harvey B.

HAYDEN, Henrietta, 2, dau of Albert, d 3/11/36 in Albany (6-3/15)

HAYDEN, Henry, merchant, of Rome m 3/3/46 Helen M. Humphrey of Utica at Trinity Church in Utica; Rev. Proal (1-4/7)

HAYDEN, Lydia Ann - see VEAZIE, Henry

HAYDEN, Lysander W. of Western m 2/18/47 Laura E. Miles of Lee in L.; Rev. Tuller (1-2/19)

HAYDEN, Orange m 2/14/50 Mrs. Lydia B. Tredway of Rome in R.; Rev. William E. Knox (1-2/20)

HAYDEN, Seraphina - see PERRY, Robert

HAYDEN, Susan - see SANDFORD, Alfred

HAYES, isabella, 6, dau of late Timothy, d 11/21/36 (funeral at 3 o'clock from her mother's home, 29 Howard St.) (6-11/22)

HAYES, John m 4/24/42 Margaret Mc Carty; Rev. Quinn (5-5/4)

HAYES, Timothy, 49, d 5/29/36 at his home in Howard Street, Albany (for 20 years an Albany resident) (6-6/2)

HAYFORD, Harriet Elizabeth, 1, only child of Henry and Harriet J., d 9/18/47 in West Troy (5-9/22)

HAYFORD, Hilah Ann - see PODMORE, Joseph

HAYNES, Henrietta (Mrs.), 30, d 3/17/42 in Newburgh (9-3/19)

HAYNES, Martha Jane - see MABBOTT, Leonard

HAYNES, Olive - see DAY, William

HAYNES, S. (Rev.) - see SMITH, Abby Jane (Mrs.)

HAYNES, William B of Granville, NY m (date not given) Mary Case of New Lebanon at N.L.; Rev. Hazelton (6-1/12/35)

HAYNES, William Nevins, 21 months, only son of Rev. Selden Haynes, d 4/20/42 in Rome (1-5/3)

HAYS, John W., about 64, d 1/1/49 in Saugerties (8-1/6)

HAYS, Sarah E. - see TELLER, John A.

HAYS, Susan - see DE LONG, Peter J.

HAYWOOD, William, 42, of firm of W & J. Haywood, d 6/14/37 at Rochester (6-6/21)

HAZARD, Damarius - see DARROW, James

HAZARD, John V.B. m 9/20/37 Catharine E. Cooke, dau. of late Conrad Gansevoort; Rev. Vermilyea (all of Albany) (6-9/22)

HAZARD, Nathaniel M. m 8/5/35 Sarah Germond in Albany; Rev. Holmes (6-8/8)

HAZELHURST, William d 12/30/42 at Chambers Creek near Newburgh (funeral to be on 1/1/43) (9-12/31)

HAZELTON, Platt S. of Carmel m 1/2/39 Phoebe Jane Gardiner of Peekskill in P.;
    Rev. J. Youngs (11-1/8)

HAZELTON, Platt S. of Carmel m 1/3/39 Phebe Jane Gardner of Peekskill in P.;
    Rev. J. Youngs (12-1/15)

HAZELTON, William B. of Red Mills m 7/22/49 Mary Ann Strang, dau. of John,
    Esq., at Jefferson Valley; Rev. James B. Hyndshaw (10-7/25)

HAZLEHURST, William m 3/24/42 Ann Woodruff, both of New Windsor; Rev. J.
    Johnston (9-3/26)

HEARSEY, Harriet A. - see HOLMES, William B.

HEARSEY, Henry - see HOLMES, William B.

HEART, Philip T. (Dr.) of Schaghticoke m 4/8/35 Frances Cordelia Scott, only dau
    of William H. Scott, Esq., of Waterford, at W.; Rev. Smith (6-4/15)

HEARTT, Benjamin - see SMITH, Angeline

HEARTT, Diadama, age blurred, wf of Philip, d 12/11/50 in Troy (5-12/18)

HEATH, A.H. of Little Falls m 5/3/43 Mrs. Mary G. Mannering in Westmoreland;
    Rev. Edward Livermore (3-5/4)

HEATH, A.H. of Little Falls m 5/9/43 Mary G. Mannering of Westmoreland in W.;
    Rev. Edward Livermore (1-5/16)

HEATH, Alfred, merchant, m 7/13/42 Emily Harter, both of Little Falls, in Utica;
    Rev. William N. Pearce (3-7/21)

HEATH, Annette Elizabeth, 3, second dau. of H.(?) E., d 4/12/48 at Fort Plain
    (4-4/13)

HEATH, Benjamin - see STEVENS, Seth

HEATH, Charity - see SHARP, Phillip

HEATH, Henry Mc Lean, m 8/11/35 Sabina Casler, eldest dau of Richard N., Esq.,
    at Little Falls; Rev. Morris (all of L.F.) (6-8/18)

HEATH, Parmelia - see FEETER(?), Benjamin A.

HEATH, Sarah A. - see WING, D. Smith

HEATH, Stephen, 60, d 5/19/10 at East Windsor (7-5/30)

HEATH, Sylvia - see SMITH, Seth

HEATH, Sylvia - see STEVENS, Seth

HEAVELAND, Esther - see THOMPSON, Benoni

HEDGES, Eunice Louisa - see GRIFFIN, James W.

HEERMANCE, Alida - see HADLEY, James R.

HEERMANCE, Andrew W. of Hudson m 3/8/09 Rebecca Lines of Catskill at
    Athens; --- Park, Esq. (7-3/15)

HEERMANS, Eliza - see MONTGOMERY, George K.

HEESTREET, Alida - see KNIGHT, Peter

HEGEMAN, Adrian, Esq. m (date not given) Eliza Balster in NYC (6-5/8/16)

HEIGHRON, Catharine - see CRAMER, Jason

HEIMSTREET, Abram m 6/5/42 Caroline Outhout; Rev. O.H. Gregory (all of
    Troy) (5-6/8)

HEINARD, Alfred, about 23, d 10/31/41 at Collaberg (typhus) (11-11/9)

HEINGMANN, Charles August m 7/15/49 Catharine Elizabeth Kuhauft at
    Rondout; Rev. C.H. Subkie (all of Rondout) (8-8/11)

HELMER, Eliza, wf of Henry G., formerly from Herkimer, d 4/11/37 in Troy
    (3-5/4)

HELMER, Joseph W. m 8/19/41 Lovina Schuyler, dau. of Nicholas, Esq.; in
    Danube; Rev. J.W. Olmstead (all of Danube) (3-8/26)

HEM, John m 11/14/41 Margaret Backhart; Rev. J. Loveys (3-11/18)

HEMAN, ---- m 10/12/42 Abigail Harris at Floyd; A.C. Vogell (1-10/25)

HEMAN, Catherine - see CALDWELL, William

HEMAN, Martha, 82, widow of late David, d 9/11/36 (funeral from her late home in Schodack Centre "tomorrow at 10 o'clock") (6-9/12)

HEMENWAY, Rebecca Maria - see HOWSON, William

HEMPFIELD, Margaret - see ALBERTSON, William

HEMPHILL, Elizabeth - see HOLLISTER, Thompson B.

HEMPSTEAD, Robert A. m 11/29/49 Sarah C. Gleason, dau. of George, in Saugerties; Rev. C. Van Santvoord (8-12/1)

HEMPSTED, David L. of Buffalo m 9/2/35 Joanna E. King, dau of Dr. E. King of Palmer, MA at P.; Rev. Backhus (6-9/9)

HEMPSTREET, John J. of NYC m 11/27/26 Sarah Ann Benson of Albany in Troy; Rev. Benson (6-12/1)

HEMSTEAD, Emeline - see COOK, Friend

HEMSTREET, Anthony, formerly of Rome d 12/23/42 at Lyons (1-1/17/43)

HEMSTREET, Margaret Snyder, wf of Hiram, d 7/29/49 (survived by her husband and five small children) (5-8/1)

HENDE, A. - see LEE, Charles

HENDENDORFF, Abraham m 5/18/37 Lucinda Arnold, dau. of George of Fairfield, in F.; Elder Phelps of Eatonville (3-6/15)

HENDERSON, ----, 29, wf of John E., d 4/23/41 in Rome (was sick for several months) (1-4/27)

HENDERSON, 'J.E. m 12/6/46 Catharine Wiggins of Albion in Rome; H.C. Vogell (1-12/8)

HENDERSON, Daniel C., 1, son of N.S. Henderson, d 8/31/41 in Norway, NY (3-9/9)

HENDERSON, David m 4/24/42 Eliza Polhill; Rev. Daniel Brown (all of Peekskill) (11-4/28)

HENDERSON, Hannah Jane - see STEVENSON, Martin

HENDERSON, Hugh (Hon.) m 12/22/37 Helen A. Myers, dau. of Michael, in Juliet, Ill. (all lately of Herkimer County, NY); Rev. Prentiss (3-1/11/38)

HENDERSON, John Eaton (Lieut.) of 2nd US Artillery d 7/4/36 at Washington, DC (grad. with distinction from US Military Academy in 1834) (obituary included) (6-7/11)

HENDERSON, John, 49, d 11/7/45 in West Troy (5-11/12)

HENDERSON, Julia Ann - see SANFORD, James F.

HENDERSON, William m 3/11/35 Jane Kennedy; Rev. Webb (6-3/14)

HENDRICKS, ----, 51, wf of Benjamin, d (date not given) at Norwich (7-8/29/10)

HENDRICKS, Abraham (his age not given), d 4/23/49 in Saugerties (8-4/28)

HENDRICKS, Albert B. m 2/14/39 Eliza Evans, dau. of Silas S., in Fairfield; Rev. William Baker (3-2/21)

HENDRICKS, Nelly - see WOLVEN, James E.

HENDRICKS, Widow - see SYPHER, John

HENDRICKS, William, 25, d 3/12/49 at Glasco (8-3/17)

HENDRICKSON, Ann - see BARTLE, David

HENDRICKSON, Thomas (Lieut.) of US Army m 5/15/43 Sarah D. Bailey, sister of Dr. Joseph H. Bailey and dau of late Dr. Rowland Bailey of Kent, NY, at Fort Touson (Choctaw nation) (11-6/13)

142

HENDRICSON, Frances L. - see MC MANNUS, John

HENDRYX, Isaiah (Capt.), 79, formerly of Bennington, VT, d 11/30/35 in Troy (a
Rev. War soldier and father of I.J. Hendryx of Troy. (6-12/7)

HENINGER, H., 104, m Mrs. E.A. Park, 83, in Marion, the happy pair intend to
move to Texas where they mean to terminate their lives. (from the
Tallahasee Floridian) (6-12/19)

HENRY, Ann (Mrs.), 74, d 4/4/35 in Albany (friends of the deceased and her two
sons Joseph and James Henry invited to her funeral at 4 o'clock at her late
home, 31 Lafayette St.) (6-4/6)

HENRY, Calvin R. of Cleveland, Oswego County, m 11/19/45 Sarah M. Brown of
Mohawk; Rev. Samuel Thompson (1-12/2)

HENRY, Caroline P. - see LEE, Charles G.

HENRY, Catharine - see TATE, David S.

HENRY, Frances (Miss) - see MC ALLISTER, James M., M.D.

HENRY, Jacob m 10/5/41 Levina B. Mc Laughlin, dau. of James, Esq.; Rev. John
Johnston (all of Newburgh) (9-10/9)

HENRY, James m Caroline Morrow; Rev. J.N. Campbell; all of Albany (6-4/10)

HENRY, Margaretta C. - see SMITH, Erastus B.

HENRY, Peter Seton of Albany m Harriet C. Townsend, dau of Samuel of
Cornwall, Orange Co., ar C.; Rev. James C. Henry (6-9/5)

HENRY, Samuel m 1/2/10 Sally Bogardus in Catskill (7-1/10)

HEPINSTALL, Hannah S., wf of George, d 4/10/36 (funeral at 3 o'clock from 63
South Lansing Street) (6-4/12)

HERENDEEN, Thomas, 3, son of Richard, Esq., d 7/23/38 in Newport (3-9/6)

HERKIMER, Alida - see EATON, Volney

HERMANS, Eliza - see also BOGART, John H

HERMANS, Emeline S - see JOICE, Erastus V.

HERRICK, Mary E. - see SMEAD, Timothy

HERRING, Ann - see PRATT, E.A.

HERRING, John m 11/12/35 Polly Nye; Rev. Bronk (all of Watervliet) (6-11/14)

HERRING, John, 7 months, son of John and Polly, d 4/14/45 in West Troy (5-4/16)

HERRING, Julia - see BEACH, Orlando

HERRING, Moses, 33, d 5/24/48 in West Troy (5-5/31)

HERRING, William Henry, 3, son of John and Polly, d 9/18/43 (5-9/20)

HERRINGTON, Asenath - see possibly Rerrington, Asenath

HERRINGTON, Jeremiah d 3/24/48 in West Troy (5-4/5)

HERRON, James (Capt.), 61, late of US Army, d (date not given) at Zanesville,
Ohio (6-7/25/26)

HERSON, Alvah m 8/22/39 Mary Ann Bliss, both of Salisbury, in S.; Rev.
Augustus Beach (3-8/29)

HESS, Laura Louisa - see POWERS, T.W., M.D.

HESS, R.I. - see POWERS, T.W., M.D.

HESS, Solomon - see LEET, Huldah

HETHERINGTON, Sally - see AVERY, David

HETZEL, A.R. (Lieut.) of US Army m 11/19/35 Margaret P. Jack in Rochester;
Rev. Dr. Cutler (6-11/24)

HEUSTIS, Ann - see FOWLER, Thomas

HEWES, Mary Ann - see RAWSON, Erastus

HEWETT, Richard m 10/7/41 Celestia C. Brown, dau. of Nathan; Rev. A. Beach (all of Oppenheim) (3-10/2)

HEWLETT, Sarah - see MC CORD, Robert D.

HEYER, Mary - see VAN SCHAACK, Asa D.

HEYWARD, Hannah H. - see HONE, Henry

HIBBARD, Delia A. - see BUTLER, John

HIBBERD, Eunice, 24, wf of Truman, d 4/14/37 (funeral from 65 North Lansing Street) (6-4/15)

HICKEY, William m 6/9/43 Mary Ann Johnson (both of Salisbury) in the Old Church in Little Falls; Rev. John Shanahan (3-6/15)

HICKMAN, ----(?) Mrs., 59, d 8/16/36 in Albany (funeral at 4 o'clock from her late home, 15 Liberty St.) (6-8/17)

HICKOCK, Frances Juliet - see CLINTON, Aaron

HICKOK, Edgar, merchant, of NYC, m 10/7/35 Anna D. Reid, dau of James, Esq., cashier of the Bank of Lansingburgh in L.; Rev. Benedict (6-10/15)

HICKS, Carolyn, 21, dau. of late George A., d 10/11/48 in Brooklyn (1-10/20)

HICKS, Gerardus of Russia, NY m 5/3/37 Darcas Veston of Ohio, Herkimer County in the town of Ohio; Asa Vickery, Esq. (3-5/25)

HICKS, Jacob, 42, d 8/10/50 in Westernville (survived by a wife and 4 children) (1-8/21)

HICKS, James A., merchant, m 9/29/35 Eleanor H. Palmer, eldest dau of John, both of Plattsburgh, in P.; Rev. J.H. Coit (6-10/19)

HICKS, John B. (Dr.) - see CLARKSON, John C.

HICKS, Lousia Lawrence - see CLARKSON, John C.

HICKS, Maria - see YATES, William

HICKSON, James, 66, d 1/12/37 in Albany (6-1/18)

HIDLEY, Hannah - see ALLENDORPH, Lewis W.

HIGBIE, Eliza - see LEWIS, William E.

HIGBIE, Jennette Celestia (Miss), dau. of Robert, d 8/29/49 at St. Johnsville (4-9/6)

HIGGINS, Ann - see RICE, Combs D.

HIGGINS, C. - see RICE, Combs D.

HIGGINS, Desdamona - see SWEET, Martin L.

HIGGINS, Destimonia - see SWEET, Martin D.

HIGGINS, Ellen - see COSTELLO, Michael

HIGGINS, James Madison of Somers m 7/4/42 Mary Larkin of Sing Sing at Newburgh; Philip Clapp, Esq. (11-7/28)

HIGGINS, John P., M.D., 75, d 2/18/49 in West Troy (5-2/28)

HIGGINS, John Wilson of NYC m 4/13/36 Emily Mayhew, dau of A.W. Mayhew of Spencertown, at S.; Rev. Gould (6-4/19)

HIGGINS, Joseph m 7/12/41 Margaret Mc Cune, both of Rome; H.C. Vogell (1-9/7)

HIGGINS, Matthew m 8/16/41 Bridget Gallagher at Little Falls by George Petrie., at Utica 8/16/41 by Rev. --- (surname not given) and at Little Falls 8/30/41 by Rev. Joseph M. Burke of the Catholic Church (3-9/16)

HIGGINS, Morris R. m 10/23/45 Catharine D. Ward, both of Troy, in West Troy; James M. Barnard, Esq. (5-11/5)

HIGGLEY, Sylvia J. - see UFFORD, Daniel

HILDRICK, Thaddeus m 1/30/10 Betsey Willard in Herkimer (2-2/1)

HILDUS, H.K. of West Troy m 5/16/46 Martha A. Lewis of Remsen in R.; Rev. D.

Alcott (1-6/2)

HILER, John m 12/25/39 Sarah Ann Davies, both of NYC, in Ossining; Rev. Van Deusen (12-1/7/40)

HILERAN(?), William m 9/15/36 Mrs. Catharine Hoover in Little Falls; Rev. Martin (3-9/29)

HILL, Caroline E. - see KENDRICK, Edward E.

HILL, Cynthia - see PINTARD, John L.

HILL, Elizabeth, 34, wf of Samuel d 2/12/49 in Lowville (consumption) (1-2/21)

HILL, Frederick, Esq. of Catskill m 10/20/36 Julia N. De Forest, dau of late David of New Haven, at New Haven; Rev. Dr. Cromwell (Double ceremony - see GRIFFIN, Charles A.A. (6-10/31)

HILL, Gifford A. m 6/7/49 Harriet Lansing in Ames; Rev. C.H. Hervey (all of Ames) (4-6/14)

HILL, Henry S. m 4/25/50 Mary B. Draper, both of Rome, in R.; Rev. W.E. Knox (1-5/1)

HILL, Hiland, Jr. m 12/9/10 Mary Butler, both of Catskill (7-12/19)

HILL, Jane Eliza, 6 months, only dau. of William and Eliza, d 11/3/49 in Poughkeepsie (8-11/24)

HILL, Lafayette of Western m 6/16/46 Caroline Clark of Steuben at Holland Patent; Rev. I.F. Scoville (1-6/30)

HILL, Lorinda E. - see JONES, John S.

HILL, Margaret J. - see BURTON, James

HILL, Martha, 6 months, dau. of T.H. and Martha A. of West Troy, d 7/17/47 in Chesterfield, Mass. (5-8/4)

HILL, Mary - see CLARK, Allen

HILL, Nancy, about 9, second dau. of Cyrus S., d 3/24/41 in Constableville (1-3/30)

HILL, Nathaniel P. (Hon.), about 60, d 5/13/42 at his home in Montgomery (9-5/14)

HILL, O.P. of Holley m 8/12/35 Louisa James, dau of Hon. William James of Holley, at Albion; Rev. Metcalf (6-8/26)

HILL, Samuel, d 7/2/35 in Saratoga "at an advanced age." "manufacturer of ladies baskets, well known, sat for portrait suspended in the drawing room of the Union Hotel" (from the Saratoga Sentinel) (Note: This is the noted Sam Hill of "What in Sam Hill are you doing?" fame.) (6-7/10)

HILL, Sarah - see BURLISON, John

HILL, Sarah M. - see LOSEE, Cyrus

HILL, Susan, 24, wf of Eli and dau. of John Warner, d 6/27/09 at Burlington (7-8/2)

HILL, Thomas W of the firm of Hill and Glass of Canton m 12/24/34 Samantha Munro, dau of Daniel, Esq. of Camillus at C.; Rev. Harrington (6-1/16/35)

HILL, Uriah, merchant, m 4/10/42 Aletha Finch, dau of Reuben R., Esq., in Peekskill; Rev. William Marshall (all of Peekskill) (11-4/14)

HILL, Zacheus of Rome m 9/3/50 Susan L. Whipple, dau. of John H., Esq., of Adams, Jefferson County, in the Emanuel Church at Adams; Rev. H.B. Whipple (1-9/11)

HILLER, Celia Malvina, 1 yr, 9 mo, youngest dau of Jacob, Esq., d 3/21/35 in Sharon (6-3/31)

HILLEY, Jennett - see PARKER, Henry

145

HILLHOUSE, Thomas - see TEN BROECK, John C.

HILLHOUSE, William (Hon.), 36, for many years a member of the Council of the State of Connecticut, d 1/12/16 at Montville (6-2/3)

HILLIARD, Andrew J., 23, late of Little Falls, d 8/4/38 at the home of his brother, Oliver B., in Charleston, South Caroline (one week's illness) (3-9/27)

HILLIARD, Lathrop m 8/17/41 Aurelia Hayden in Delta; Rev. Bentley (all of Delta) (1-8/24)

HILLIKER, Fanny, 28 months, dau of William of Peekskill, d 2/27/42 (11-3/1)

HILLIKER, Harry of West Troy m 6/22/47 Eliza Parker in West Troy; Rev. T. Seymour (5-6/30)

HILLMAN, Elisha S of Lakeville, Livingston Co., m 9/24/40 Eretta M. Sippell, dau. of Col. William of Boonville, in B.; Rev. Demming (1-9/29)

HILLS, Asa W., 32, d 3/28/47 in Rome (1-4/2)

HILLS, Ira of Watervliet m 2/13/45 Adaline Van Patten of Albany; Rev. Alfred Saxe (5-2/19)

HILLS, Jane - see MC CORMICK, Andrew

HILLS, Russell D. of Plainfield, Ill. m 5/17/49 Lucinda B. Waterman, dau. of John E. of Lisbon, Ill. at Oneida Depot; Rev. P.S. Talmage (1-5/23)

HILLS, Samuel m 9/12/36 Margaret Van Vranken; Rev. Bronk (all of Watervliet) (6-9/21)

HILTON, James, 83, d 12/7/36 (funeral at 3 o'clock from his late home, 8 Plain Street) (6-12/8)

HILTON, Jemima, 54, wf of Benjamin, d (date not given) in Kinderhook (6-9/26/26)

HILTON, Joseph, 79, a Rev. War soldier seriously wounded at Bemis Heights ("a cannon ball was lodged in his body and cut out on the opposite side"), d (date not given) in Deerfield, NH (6-12/29/26)

HILTON, Peter W., 91, for 84 years an Albany resident, d 1/24/36 at his home in Guilderland (6-2/1)

HIMES, James, Jr. m 11/1/48 Martha Vanderwarken; Rev. J.H. Houghtaling (all of West Troy) (5-11/8)

HINCHMAN, Mary - see MORGAN, Roswell

HINCKLEY, Judge - see ALLEN, Richard L.

HINCKLEY, Minerva - see WAIT, George

HINDMAN, Louisa, 2, youngest dau of James and Margaret, late of Philadelphia, d 11/17/42 (11-11/22)

HINE, Newell of Little Falls m 5/2/41 Rosanna Eaton of Herkimer in H.; Rev. D----- (surname blurred) (3-5/6)

HINECEY (SIC), E.M. m 1/12/42 Frances Briggs, dau. of Lyman, formerly of Rome, in R.; H.C. Vogell) (1-1/18)

HINES, Emeline - see BOOTH, Joseph

HINKLEY, Charles m 8/28/42 Permilia Comstock in Lee; Daniel Twitchell, Esq. (all of Lee) (1-8/30)

HINMAN, ----, 37, wf of Nathaniel Hinman, d 7/23/10 (survived by her husband and four small children) (7-7/25/10)

HINMAN, Abner of Augusta m 1/10/47 Melory Perrin of Oneida at Vienna; Rev. Smith (1-1/15)

HINMAN, Eliza E. - see HALE, Charles R.

HIPWELL, Arabella, 40, relict of Abraham, d (date not given) in NYC (6-2/21/26)

HITCHCOCK, Abigail - see FOSTER, Andrew

HITCHCOCK, Abigail - see OSTROM, William

HITCHCOCK, Adelia - see CHURCH, Luther

HITCHCOCK, Angelica (Miss), 31, d 10/5/47 in West Troy (5-10/13)

HITCHCOCK, David (Capt.), 50, sloop master, d 1/12/39 in Sing Sing (lived a life-time in S.S.) (12-1/15)

HITCHCOCK, Edward Kirk, 3, youngest son of Robinson and Margaret, d 5/19/40 in West Troy (whooping cough) (5-5/27)

HITCHCOCK, Elmina J. - see WHEELER, George M.

HITCHCOCK, George Henry, d 1/19/49 (4 p.m.) at Schuylerville and his sister Sarah Jane d 1/20/49 ("20 minutes before 8") at Schuylerville. Both are children of Rev. V.M. Hitchcock, "late pastor of the Methodist Episcopal Church of Albany" (5-1/31)

HITCHCOCK, J.H. of West Troy m 9/9/46 Juliette H. Fuller, dau. of H.T., Esq. of Hebron, Conn., at H.; Rev. E.J. Doolittle (5-9/16)

HITCHCOCK, Jemima, 75, widow of Samuel and mother of Gilbert, d 8/3/37 at Schodack ("she was one of eleven persons in Gilbert's family recently piosoned by arsenic mixed in the butter by a negro servant girl") (6-8/10)

HITCHCOCK, John V. m 5/14/48 Mary A. Spencer, both of Cohoes; Rev. Houghtaling (5-5/24)

HITCHCOCK, Louisa, 13, months, youngest dau. of Daniel and Arsena, d 3/10/39 in Sing Sing (12-3/19)

HITCHCOCK, Margaret - see JACKSON, L.W.

HITCHCOCK, Mary - see COOK, James

HITCHCOCK, Milton E. of Oneida m 9/5/50 Ann Louisa Gardner, dau. of Charles L. of Oneida, in Albany; Rev. Howard (1-10/2)

HITCHCOCK, Nancy - see HART, William

HITCHCOCK, Sarah Jane - see HITCHCOCK, George Henry

HITE, Zilda - see HOWES, William

HIX, Amos, 76, d (date not given) at Augusta, Maine (6-5/4/16)

HIX, Sarah Jane - see OSGOOD, John

H---KEE(?), William m 10/8/50 Ruth Mc Clusky; Rev. T.F. Wyckoff (all of West Troy) (5-10/16)

HOAG, George of Otsego m (date not given) Clarissa Johnson at Hartwick (6-5/8/16)

HOAR, James m 11/24/42 Mary Ann June in Newburgh; Rev. John Brown (all of Newburgh) (9-11/26)

HOARD, John La Fayette m 9/11/42 Margaret Elizabeth Piper, dau. of James of Frankfort, at F.; Rev. Benedict (3-9/15)

HOBBIE, Selah R. m (date not given) Julia Ann Root, dau. of Gen. E. Root, ay Delhi (6-5/23/26)

HOBBY, Charles C., Esq., counsellor at law, m 10/10/39 Eliza W. Bailey, dau of late Dr. Rowland Bailey of Putnam County, at Peekskill; Rev. William Marshall (11-10/15)

HOBBY, Charles E., Esq., of White Plains m 10/10/39 Eliza W. Bailey of Peekskill at P.; Rev. William Marshall (11-10/22)

HOBBY, David R. m 6/29/39 Mary Purdy, both of Mount Pleasant, in Sing Sing; Rev. S. Van Deusen (12-7/9)

HOBBY, Mary - see HOYT, Lewis

HOBDAY, Anthony of Dutchess County m 12/24/41 Phebe Horton of Somers in S.;
Rev. Keeler (11-12/28)

HOCHSTRASSER, Ann Eliza - see TAYLOR, H.R.

HOCHSTRASSER, Louisa, 28, wf of Jacob, d 3/26/35 in Albany (consumption)
(funeral at 4 o'clock from 64 Howard St.) (6-3/28)

HODGE, David, 102, m (date not given) Elizabeth Raily, 40, both of Columbia
County, Georgia; John Dugald Smith, Esq. (Groom was at Braddock's
defeat and served throughout the Rev. War) (from Washington News)
(6-6/23)

HODGE, Maria - see CROSBY, James

HODGMAN, Henry L., 10 months, son of John H. and Mary E., d 9/25/49 in West
Troy (5-10/3)

HODGMAN, John H. of West Troy m 10/22/46 Mary Elizabeth Boomhouse of
Troy in West Troy; Rev. Houghtaling (5-10/28)

HOES, Catharine (Miss), dau of Peter, d 9/13/36 in Chatham (6-9/19)

HOES, Catherine Anne, 16, dau of Peter I., Esq. of Kinderhook, d 9/6/35 at the
Seminary for Young Ladies at Pittsfield, MA (an obituary) (from the
Pittsfield Sun) (6-9/12)

HOES, John C.F. (Rev.) of Chittenango m 9/15/36 Lucy Maria Rundell, eldest dau
of Gen. Roswell Rundell of Cortlandville, Cortland Co., at C.; Rev. Joseph
J. Foote (6-9/24)

HOFFMAN, Charlotte - see PRIME, Edward

HOFFMAN, Cornelia E. - see SANNAY, Edmund

HOFFMAN, Cornelius, 65, d (date not given) in NYC (6-4/3/16)

HOFFMAN, G.V.S. (his funeral 1/13/25 from his late home at 113 North Market
Street, Albany) (his father-in-law, Christopher Ruby is mentioned) (6-1/13)

HOFFMAN, Henry Eslence(?), 7, son of L.G. Hoffman, d 1/17/37 (scarlet fever)
(6-1/18)

HOFFMAN, Josiah Ogden, one of the judges of the Supreme Court of NYC and
formerly Attorney General of New York, d 1/24/37 in NYC (6-1/28)

HOGAN, Cornelius, 23, d 6/15/36 at the home of his father in Utica
(consumption). He was a member of the Catholic Church. Interred in the
Catholic burying ground 6/22 (3-6/23)

HOGAN, Naimo C. - see RODNEY, P.H.

HOGEBOOM, Catherine - see VAN BUREN, A.

HOGEBOOM, Eliza - see BRAMHALL, Charles

HOGLE, ----, infant, about 2 months, d 4/14/44 in West Troy ("accidental
administration of laudanum") (5-4/17)

HOKE, Peter m 7/4/49 Nancy Pickard at Starkville; Rev. Smith (4-7/12)

HOLBROOK, Daniel, Esq. m 12/1/41 Harriet L. Maynard, formerly of Little Falls,
in Amsterdam; Rev. Goodell (3-12/9)

HOLBROOKS, Lorena - see KING, John L.

HOLCOMB, N. of Massachusetts m 10/4/49 Elizabeth Pierce of Rochester, NY in
Rome; H.C. Vogell (1-10/24)

HOLDEN, Alvah m 12/18/34 Belinda Stevens; Rev. R. Kirkwood (11-12/30)

HOLDEN, Hannah C. - see BELKNAP, Augustus

HOLDEN, Sarah J. - see FLAGLER, Harvey L.

HOLDRIDGE, Delia, 27, wf of Robert C. d 11/23/49 in Kingston (12/1)

HOLENBECK, Sarah - see SECOR, John H.

148

HOLLAND, Robert of Redfield m 8/29/41 Hannah West of Western in W.; Joseph Halleck, Esq. (1-8/31)

HOLLENBAKE, Stafford d 3/14/35 in Albany (6-3/16)

HOLLENBAKE, Stafford his "relatives, friends and acquaintances" are invited to attend his funeral at 3 o'clock at the home of his mother-in-law, Mrs. Gibbons, 154 North Market St., Albany (6-3/17/35)

HOLLENBECK, John, 28, carpenter, late of Albany, d 9/22/34 "at Havanna" (6-1/9/35)

HOLLESTER, Louisa Clarissa (Miss), formerly of Hartford, Conn., d 1/16/37 in Albany (Conn. papers are requested to give this insertion) (6-1/18)

HOLLEY, Edward N., 32, eldest son of Edward O., d 3/19/36 at Hudson (consumption) (6-3/25)

HOLLIDAY, Robert - see KNOX, J.R. (Dr.)

HOLLISTER, C. - see BURROWS, Sarah M.

HOLLISTER, Cornelius - see BURROWS, Prudence

HOLLISTER, Cornelius - see SMITH, Abby Jane

HOLLISTER, David S. (Rev.) of the Oneida Annual Conference of the Methodist Episcopal Church d 3/4/48 at his father's home in Burlington, Otsego County (consumption) (4-3/16)

HOLLISTER, Frederick of firm of J. Williams & Co., Utica, m 6/28/36 Jane M. Stanton, dau of G.W., Esq. of Albany; Rev. Potter (6-7/1)

HOLLISTER, Sarah A. - see DOUGLAS, Charles S

HOLLISTER, Thompson B. of Baltimore m 10/12/36 Elizabeth Hemphill, dau of Robert, Esq., at Malta, Saratoga Co. (6-10/14)

HOLLY, Samuel m 6/11/39 Susan Fancher, both of Poundridge, in P.; Rev. Hobley (12-6/25)

HOLMAN, Sarah, about 2, youngest dau. of Perry and Sarah, d 6/2/41 in Little Falls (3-6/10)

HOLMES, ----, about 56, wf of Willet Holmes, d 2/13/40 in Sing Sing (buried in Bedford) (a member of the Society of Friends) (12-2/18)

HOLMES, A.H. (Dr.) of Danube m 5/15/41 Sarah M. Burden, dau. of Abraham of Frankfort, in F.; Rev. Thomas Houston (3-5/20)

HOLMES, Abijah, 81, d 12/27/41 in Bedford (11-1/4/42)

HOLMES, Abijah, Jr., 27, d 2/24/40 in Bedford (12-3/17)

HOLMES, Alexander, of firm of Mc Cafferty & Holmes m 9/2/35 Isabella Mc Navin; Rev. Campbell (all of Albany) (6-9/4)

HOLMES, Amanda, about 28, wf of Samuel, d 2/21/39 in Bedford (12-2/26)

HOLMES, Amy - see FOWLER, William

HOLMES, Ann Alida - see LA GRANGE, Conrad

HOLMES, Catharine E. - see GUION(?), Thomas Tompkins (Rev.)

HOLMES, Jacob P., "his friends and acquaintances invited to his funeral at 3 o'clock from his late residence, corner of Columbia and North Market Sts." (6-3/25/35)

HOLMES, John (Dr.), about 50, d 11/23/38 at his home in Danube (3-11/29)

HOLMES, John A. of Danube m 6/23/43 Charlotte Moak of Therese, Jefferson County in Compton, St. Lawrence County; Rev. Pettibone (3-6/15)

HOLMES, John W. m 7/13/37 Maria Town; John R. Manning, ESq. (all of Albany) (6-7/15)

HOLMES, Josiah S., 33, d 6/10/50 at West Troy ("Western papers please copy")

(5-6/19)

HOLMES, Lois, about 46, wf of Morris Holmes, d 5/18/36 (consumption) (3-6/2)

HOLMES, Mabel, 78, widow of Jeremiah, d 4/6/39 in Bedford (12-4/23)

HOLMES, Morris, formerly of Little Falls, m 10/1/37 Mrs. Jane Ensin of Buffalo in B.; Elder Mott (3-10/12)

HOLMES, Sarah (Mrs.), 86, d (date not given) at Salisbury (7-6/20/10)

HOLMES, Stephen, 45, d 3/16/40 in Bedford (12-3/24)

HOLMES, William (Dr.), partner of the late Dr. A. Hammond, d 7/26/49 (lived for several years in New Scotland where he had a large practice) (5-8/1)

HOLMES, William B., Esq., of Mohawk m 10/22/39 Harriet A. Hearsey, dau. of Henry of Cazenovia, in C.; Rev. Barrows (3-11/14)

HOLMES, William, M.D., m 2/6/38 Mary Ann Ward; Rev. Dr. Gosman (formerly of Philadelphia) (all of Westerlo) (5-2/14)

HOLT, Benjamin, merchant, m 10/8/38 Ann Baker in Little Falls; Rev. C.L. Dunning (all of Little Falls) (3-10/11)

HOLT, Daniel of Madison, Wisconsin m 6/24/41 Euphrasia S. Parkhurst of Middleville in M.; Rev. A.D. Peck (3-7/1)

HOLT, Jesse C., printer, m (date not given) Ann Catharine Dunn at Hudson; Rev. Wigton (7-2/15/09)

HOLT, John E - see MANNING, Frances Louisa

HOLT, William Johnson, Esq. "an old and highly respected inhabitant of this city (Albany)" d 11/19/26 at Montreal, Canada. (a Rev. War pensioner) (6-12/5)

HOLTENHOUSE, Katharine - see JONES, Henry

HOLTON, Amos of Lowville m 9/20/41 Almira Gear of Floyd in F. (1-10/12)

HOMER, Catharine - see PALMER, William

HOMMEL, Abraham m 9/13/49 Catherine Mower, both of Saugerties; Rev. Beers (8-9/22)

HONE, Henry, Esq. m 10/4/36 Hannah H. Heyward, dau of William, Esq., of South Carolina, in NYC; Rev. A. Maclay (6-10/7)

HONE, Samuel, 49, d 2/5/16 in NYC (6-2/10)

HOOFFER, Christopher N. of Ludwigburg, Suabia, Germany, a youth of 60 m (date not given) after a courtship of six hours, Miss Betsey Marrs, 76, of NYC (7-9/6/09)

HOOFT(?), Catharine - see MORRIS, William (Dr.)

HOOK, Thomas I. of NYC m 5/19/36 Margaret A. Van Ingen of Albany; Rev. E. Holmes (6-5/21)

HOOKER, Ann T. - see WOOD, William

HOOKER, James, Jr. of NYC m 5/24/36 Susan A. Watkins of Utica at U.; Rev. P.A. Proal (6-5/27)

HOOKER, William, merchant of Vienna m 11/4/41 Clarissa Hotchkins, dau. of Col Hotchkins of Vernon; Rev. Robert C. Brisbin (1-11/9)

HOOVENBURG, Julia - see FRANCE, Richard

HOOVER, Catharine (Mrs.) - see HILERAN(?), William

HOPCRAFT, Mary Louisa, 5, dau. of Henry and Elizabeth, d 8/13/48 in Fort Plain (4-8/24)

HOPE, Caroline - see SPEAR, William

HOPKINS, Elisha W., Esq., m 12/4/49 Amanda S. Parker, dau. of I.S., Esq., at the Presbyterian Church in Rome; Rev. W.E. Knox (all of Rome) (1-12/5)

HOPKINS, Emeline - see TRAVIS, Henry

150

HOPKINS, Enos (Judge) - see BROWN, George (Col.)

HOPKINS, Esther - see FERRIS, Samuel

HOPKINS, Esther - see FERRIS, Samuel

HOPKINS, Hannah - see BROWN, George (Col.)

HOPKINS, Harriet B. - see STEELE, Joseph (Rev.)

HOPKINS, Mary, 84, mother of William G. of Carmel, d 2/17/39 in New Castle (12-2/19)

HOPKINS, S.M. - see FOWLER, P.H.

HOPKINS, Samuel M. (Hon.) d (date and place not given), member of the NYC bar (had been a member of the House of Representatives in Congress and s Senator in the NY legislature - was a member of the Presbyterian Church (from the Geneva Courier) (6-10/13/37)

HOPKINS, William m 8/30/36 Mary Ann Richardson Tucker in Squam "This couple were married at 11 o'clock and the husband who was sick died at 4 p.m." (6-9/3)

HOPPER, Edward of Phillipstown m 2/20/41 Miss Antrot of Putnam Valley; Rev. D.D. Tompkins (11-2/23)

HOPPER, James (Capt.), d (date not goven) in Utica (6-5/25/16)

HOPPER, Joseph, 17, d 3/3/40 in Sing Sing (12-3/10)

HOPPER, Mary - see BRADLEY, Charles

HOPPER, Mary (Miss), 72, d (date not given) in NYC (6-2/21/26)

HOPSON, Eunice - see PRATT, Joseph

HORDICK, Jeremiah of Canajoharie m 5/10/48 Charlotte Zoller of Minden in M.; Rev. John I. Wendell (4-6/1)

HORN, Patrick m 2/25/39 Clarissa Knapp, both of Somers, in S.; Silas Gregory, Esq. (12-3/5)

HORNBLOWER, Mary, wf of Chief Justice Hornblower, of Newark, New Jersey, d 12/19/36 at the home of her son-in-law in Philadelphia while visiting her daughters (6-12/31)

HORNER, Catharine M. - see WARNER, Ezra T.

HORNING, Richard, Jr., 28, d 6/26/50 at Fultonville (4-7/11)

HORTON, Ann (Mrs.), 44, d (date not given) at the home of her son Cornelius N. Horton in Peekskill (11-10/1/39)

HORTON, Catherine - see FOUNTAIN, J.H.

HORTON, Catherine E. - see VAN ALEN, Samuel

HORTON, Cordelia Levina - see BROWN, Philander

HORTON, Daniel, Esq. - see DRURY, E.W.

HORTON, Elizabeth Jane - see MEAD, Isaac R. (Col.)

HORTON, Evelyn T. - see DRURY, E.W.

HORTON, Jacob (only son of Caleb) m 6/30/41 Charlotte Knapp, dau of Benjamin, all of Yorktown; Rev. R.G. Thompson of Crompound (11-7/6)

HORTON, James W. m 3/31/36 Alba C. Peck at Ballston Spa; Rev. D. Babcock (6-4/4)

HORTON, Jane M. - see VAN HOUSEN, Thomas

HORTON, Jesse m 3/3/42 Catharine Jaycox, both of Phillipstown, in P. (11-3/15)

HORTON, Joseph S. of Yorktown, of firm of Lane and Horton m 1/23/39 Ann Eliza Dusenbury, youngest dau of Charles Dusenbury of Phillipstown, in P.; Rev. J. Youngs (11-1/29)

HORTON, Louisa M. - see PIERSON, M. (Dr.)

151

HORTON, Mary A. - see TODD, Abraham H.

HORTON, Phebe - see HOBDAY, Anthony

HORTON, Philona - see KIRKUM, Thomas H.

HORTON, Stephen D., Esq., 33, d 3/5/42 in Peekskill (funeral at 11 o'clock from home of his father-in-law, Philip Clapp, Esq. (11-3/8)

HORTON, Stephen D., m 1/13/41 Delia Clapp, only dau of Philip, Esq.; Rev. Dr. Westbrook (all of Peekskill) (11-1/19)

HORTON, Virginia - see SCOTT, George E.

HOSFORD, Benjamin H., 38, d 9/9/49 in West Troy (5-9/19)

HOSFORD, Hannah J. - see SEWART, Robert G.

HOSFORD, Hiram of Buffalo m 6/25/49 Lucinda King of Oswego; Rev. Houghtaling (5-6/27)

HOSFORD, Selah m 1/6/42 Sarah Ann Lighthall, both of Albany; Rev. D. Starks (5-1/12)

HOSIE, John of Bloomingdale m 12/8/39 Eliza Storms of Greenburgh at G.; Rev. George Walker (12-12/7)

HOSIER, Elsey - see HUMBERT, Abraham B.

HOSKENS, Orinda - see ADAMS, Gideon

HOTALING, Martin C. m 10/9/49 Ann Lee; Rev. Phillips (all of Rondout) (8-10/20)

HOTALING, Mary Ann - see LITTLE, Dudley

HOTCHKIN, Catharine, 25, wf of Mark C., d 3/29/45 in Waterville (1-4/1)

HOTCHKIN, M.O. of Waterville m 1/14/47 Genett Hovey, dau. of Dr. Isaac of Morrisville, at M.; Rev. Harrington (1-1/22)

HOTCHKINS, Ann Maria - see HALL, Edward B.

HOTCHKINS, Clarissa - see HOOKER, William

HOTCHKISS, Alfred R. of Homer m 8/10/46 Bridget Sophia Grady of West Troy in Buffalo; James G. Dickie, Esq. (5-8/19)

HOTCHKISS, David m (date not given) Emily Palmer (both of Cherry Valley) at the "Hotel of Roswell Mallet in Ames"; Rev. C.H. Harvey (4-6/14/49)

HOTCHKISS, Eliphalet, 74, d 2/11/42 in Vernon (1-2/15)

HOUD, Nancy - see GREENMAN, Joseph

HOUGH, Huldah, 64, wf of Hon. Lemuel Hough, d 6/20/47 in Boonville (Ader Creek) (consumption) (1-7/2)

HOUGH, Martha A. - see WILLIAMS, Chauncey P.

HOUGHTALING, Amelia - see LAWTON, Charles D.

HOUGHTALING, Isaac of Esopus m 10/11/49 Eleanor Martin of Lloyd; Rev. A. Port (8-10/20)

HOUGHTALING, James, 58(?), master of the sloop, "Don Juan", d 8/31/49 in Rondout (cholera) (see RHODES, Erasmus) (8-9/1)

HOUGHTALING, James, M.D. - see LAWTON, Charles D.

HOUGHTALING, Jane Ann, 12, youngest dau of Barent, Esq., d 8/2/35 at Coxsackie (short but painful illness) (6-9/12)

HOUGHTON, Daniel m 1/19/26 Lydia Cutler; Rev. Leonard (all of Albany) (6-1/24)

HOUGHTON, James m 12/30/25 Zilpha Cady; Rev. Leonard (6-1/3/26)

HOUGHTON, John, near 50, d 4/29/39 in Herkimer (3-5/9)

HOUGHTON, Margaret - see RETALICK, Henry

HOUGHTON, Sophia - see HARRIS, Albert G.

HOUSE(?), Lydia - see ETHRIDGE, Nathaniel

HOUSE, ---- (Mrs.), 95, widow of George, d 7/30/47. Her brother, Jonathan Talcott, 93, was buried "last week" (1-8/6)

HOUSE, Charles of Fulton (town), Schoharie County m 5/17/37 Lucy Wheaton of Sunderland, VT; Rev. C.P. Clarke (6-5/18)

HOUSE, James m 9/27/37 Ann Bellinger in Little Falls; Rev. J.W. Olmstead (3-10/12)

HOUSE, Margaret - see LOOKER(?), Stephen

HOUSE, Maria - see VAN NESS, John

HOUSE, Mary Ann - see GREEN, Caleb

HOUSE, Mary L. - see TALCOTT, Jonathan, 2nd

HOUSEWORTH, Eleanor - see VALLEAU, Peter R.

HOUSTON, Thomas (Rev.), pastor of the Baptist Church in Frankfort, m 9/22/40 Maria Reed, dau. of Thomas, Esq. if Danube, in D.; Rev. J.W. Olmstead (3-9/24)

HOUSTON, Thomas m 5/8/26 Jane Anna Rowan, dau. of Rev. Dr. Rowan of NYC, in Schenectady; Rev. Brayton (6-5/19)

HOVEY, Genett - see HOTCHKIN, M.O.

HOVEY, J.P. (Rev.) m 8/22/36 in Auburn, Catherine M. Weed, eldest dau of Walter, Esq.; Rev. John Hovey (a double ceremony - see MURPHY, G.S.) (all of Auburn) (6-8/29)

HOVEY, J.S. of Rome m 2/10/47 Lydia C. Johnson of Frankfort at F.; Rev. J. Granis (1-2/12)

HOWARD, Almira M. - see STEVENSON, Eben

HOWARD, Catharine, about 40, consort of John and dau. of Dr. Joseph Benton of Baldwin, d suddenly (date not given) in Hiram, York County, Maine (3-3/8/38)

HOWARD, Harriet Cordelia - see WILLIAMS, Gibson T.

HOWARD, James of NYC m 6/5/44 Adelaide Seymour of Brooklyn in West Troy; Rev. Bissell (5-6/12)

HOWARD, John - see STEVENSON, Almira M.

HOWARD, Lucia, 37, wf of Ward B., Esq., late of Peekskill, d 3/8/34 in NYC (11-3/11)

HOWARD, Mary - see STERLIN, Jacob M.

HOWARD, Mary, 52, wf of Launcelot Howard, d 11/6/37 (funeral 11/8 at home of her son-in-law, H. Raymond at 75 Hudson Street (6-11/7)

HOWARD, R. Sumner of Lenox m 7/4/42 Phila Marie Clark of Stockbridge at the home of John Elliot; Rev. Ninde (1-7/12)

HOWARD, Robert H. - see STERLIN, Jacob M.

HOWARD, Rufus (Capt.) - see WILLIAMS, Gibson T.

HOWARD, Susan, 28, wf of Rev. O.R. Howard, d 8/8/43 in Fairfield (3-8/17)

HOWE, Amos m 5/18/48 Elizabeth Harris, both of West Troy; Rev. Houghtaling (5-5/24)

HOWE, Amos of New York City m 6/9/35 Catherine Montieth, dau of Capt. George Montieth of Albany; Rev. Dr. Ferris (6-6/11)

HOWE, Chauncey, formerly of Utica and late of Augusta, Georgia, d 9/14/37 at Farmington, Conn. after a short illness (6-9/22)

HOWE, Fanny C, 25, consort of Horace Howe, Esq. and dau of John M. Canfield, Esq. d 3/9/35 at Sacketts Harbor (6-3/14)

HOWE, Foster of Sandy Hill m 11/28/48 Mary Ann Murphy of West Troy in W.T.; Rev. Houghtaling (5-12/6)

HOWE, Harvey m 9/25/39 Jane Elizabeth Hoyt, both of North Salem; Rev. R. Frame (12-10/8)

HOWE, Hezekiah - see LELAND, David Warren

HOWE, John, 89, a Rev. War soldier, d 12/15/43 near Flemington, NJ (5-1/17/44)

HOWE, Margaret C., age blurred, wf of James, d 8/24/49 in Kingston (8-9/1)

HOWE, Martha P., 26, d 8/21/47 at the home of her father, the Rev. Samuel Howe, in Brunswick, Rensselaer County (5-9/1)

HOWELL, Ann - see MYER, Henry B.

HOWELL, Frances Minerva - see UNDERHILL, R.L.

HOWELL, Frances Minerva - see UNDERHILL, Robert L.

HOWELL, Harriet - see FISH, Nathaniel

HOWELL, Julia Ann - see FISH, Almonzo D.

HOWELL, Margaret A., youngest dau. of Maliby Howell, d 7/25/43 at Cohoes (5-8/2)

HOWELL, William (Capt.) - see FISH, Almonzo D.

HOWES, Eliza Anne, 45, wf of Dr. Fitch Howes, d 8/9/50 at Vernon Center (1-8/21)

HOWES, William m 6/1/42 Zilda Hite in Southeast; Rev. Mc Leod (11-6/9)

HOWK, Roswell of Rutland, Jefferson County, m 12/25/49 Sally Lighthall, dau. of George of Minden in M.; Rev. W.G. Anderson "a thoroughly educated couple of deaf mutes and the same will apply to all other deaf mutes presently among whom were Mr. Backus and Lady of Fort Plain (4-12/27)

HOWLAND, Emily, 2, dau of Capt. Egbert Howland, d 1/25/34 in Peekskill (11-1/28)

HOWLAND, Seth m 12/17/40 Adaline Monroe, dau. of Theodore, at Bridgewater; Rev. Holcom (all of Bridgewater) (1-12/22)

HOWSE, Harriet - see PLATT, Isaac

HOWSON, William m 3/10/36 Rebecca Maria Hemenway, both of Sand Lake; L.V.K. Van Denmark, Esq. (6-3/15)

HOXIE, Elizabeth A. - see LYON, William J.

HOXIE, H.C., Esq., merchant, m 3/4/40 Hannah Ward in Troy; Rev. Charles Pomeroy (all of West Troy) (5-3/18)

HOXIE, Maria - see OLENA, Francis

HOYT, Cornelia, about 21, wf of Stephen L., d 3/3/40 in Bedford (12-3/10)

HOYT, Eliza Jane - see RUSCO, Chancey

HOYT, Francis of NYC m 10/20/41 Ann Maria Benjamin of Bloomingburgh in B. at the Associate Reformed Church; Rev. Connelly (9-10/30)

HOYT, George Washington, 1, son of Curtis, d 1/1/49 in Saugerties (8-1/6)

HOYT, Henry d 12/28/36 in Albany (friends of the deceased and of his brother, George A. Hoyt, invited to his funeral at 3 o'clock from his late residence, 6 Liberty Street) (6-12/29)

HOYT, Jane Elizabeth - see HOWE, Harvey

HOYT, John, 44, d 9/2939 at his home in Cortlandt Town (11-10/1)

HOYT, Leger S., about 42, d 7/1/49 at Napanoch (8-7/14)

HOYT, Lewis of South Salem m 10/22/39 Mary Hobby, dau. of Guy Hobby, Esq., in Middle Patent (12-10/29)

HOYT, Linus m 10/1/39 Abigail Benedict; Rev. R. Frame (12-10/8)

HOYT, Mary - see DANN, Alanson

HOYT, William S. of NYC m 3/2/36 Frances Ogden, eldest dau of Gov. Edwards, in New Haven; Rev. Dr. Taylor (6-3/10)

HUBBARD, Catherine H. - see CHESTER, Joseph L.

HUBBARD, E.A. - see FENTON, J.P.

HUBBARD, Eleanor Augusta, 8 months, dau. of Isaac and Julia, d 12/27/42 in West Troy (scarlet fever) (5-12/28)

HUBBARD, Elvira - see CARPENTER, Henry

HUBBARD, Emeline Ermina, 8, dau. of Isaac and Julia, d 10/25/41 at West Troy (typhus fever) (5-10/27)

HUBBARD, Esther - see BUCHANAN, Thomas

HUBBARD, Gen. - see SIBLEY, George A.

HUBBARD, George W., 41, alderman of 2nd Ward and 1st assistant engineer of the fire department at Utica, d 1/20/42 at Utica (1-1/25)

HUBBARD, Grace H. - see LITCHFIELD, Edwin C.

HUBBARD, Grace, 38, wf of Solon W. Hubbard, d 12/13/42 in Russia, NY (funeral sermon by Rev, Fisk) (3-12/22)

HUBBARD, Jabez, 68, d (date not given) at Middletown (7-8/29/10)

HUBBARD, Mary E. - see PISHON, Marcellus

HUBBARD, Mary E. - see RUSSELL, William H.

HUBBARD, Mary Jane - see NORRIS, J.Q.

HUBBARD, William G. of Cato Four Corners m 10/7/47 Amelia Glezen, dau. of Oren Glezen of Vienna in V.; Rev. William B. Tompkins of Oneida Castle (1-10/15)

HUBBARD, Zeruah (Mrs.), 62, only sister of Oliver C. Grosvenor of Rome, d 4/7/42 at Cazenovia (billious plurisy) (1-4/12)

HUBBELL, ---- (Mrs.) - see BIXBY, Grace

HUBBELL, George C. m 12/31/35 Ann Eliza Pinkham, both of Hudson; Rev. Waterbury (6-1/1/36)

HUBBELL, John A., Jr., of Peekskill m 4/27/33 Mary Ann Baremore in Yorktown; Rev. William A. Hyde (11-4/30)

HUBBELL, Levi, Adjutant General, m 5/28/36 Susan Linn, dau of late Simeon De Witt, at Ithaca; Rev. A.M. Mann (6-6/3)

HUBBELL, Mary Ann, wf of John of Peekskill, d 2/2/34 in P. (consumption) (11-2/4)

HUBBELL, Nehemiah, 71, father of William S., Esq. of Bath, d 6/21/35 at Painted Post (6-6/29)

HUBBIRD(?), George W., Esq., 41 alderman of the 2nd ward in Utica, d 1/20/42 in Utica (3-1/27)

HUBBS, William m 2/7/38 Jane Fraser, both of Clifton Park, in West Troy; Rev. A. Judson (5-2/14)

HUDDLE, John G. of Canajoharie m 2/1/48 Lavina Laning of Stone Arabia at S.A.; Rev. A. Rumpf (4-3/2)

HUDLER, Lydia, (age blurred), wf of Edgar and dau. of Solomon L. (surname blurred), d 7/13/49 at Rondout (8-7/21)

HUDSON, Franklin A. of Utica m 11/1/48 Henrietta Webster, youngest dau. of Dr. Joshua, in Fort Plain; Rev. Dr. C.G. Mc Leod (4-11/2)

HUDSON, Harriet M. - see PECK, Darius

HUESTIS, Charles P. m 11/30/41 Elizabeth Owen in NYC; Rev. Grenell (all of

NYC) (11-12/7)

HUESTIS, Harvey m 2/5/40 Margretta Hammond, dau. of James, Esq.; Rev. Moore (all of Ossining) (12-2/11)

HUESTIS, John, Esq. of Millwaukin, VT, m 8/29/39 Laura Ann Ludington, oldest dau. of Lewis, Esq. of Carmel, NY, at C.; Rev. George Todd (12-9/3)

HUESTIS, Lafayette, 4, son of Peter, d 6/10/39 (town not stated - possibly Warren) (3-7/18)

HUESTIS, Lucy, wf of Samuel, Editor of the Sentinel, d 11/22/33 in Peekskill (11-11/26)

HUESTIS, Maria, 28, consort of Peter, d 5/1/39 (town not stated - possibly Warren) (3-7/18)

HUESTIS, Mary, 60, consort of Edward, d 3/18/39 in Warren (3-7/18)

HUFNALL, Betsey,wf of George, late of Fort Plain, d 6/6/49 in Racine Wisconsin (4-6/14)

HUGGINS(?), Henry T. m 7/2/37 Elizabeth Arthur, dau. of late John Hart Lynde, in Trinity Church at New Haven; Rev. Dr. Croswell (6-7/13)

HUGH, L.R. m 9/4/49 Miss E.M. Ryther, both of Nartinsburgh, at Stanwix Hall in Rome; Rev. W.E. Knox (1-9/5)

HUGHES, Catharine - see BARNES, Richard

HUGHES, Eleanor - see ELLIS, Thomas

HUGHES, Hugh of Herkimer m 3/12/40 Margaret Rowlings of Utica in U.; Rev. Griffith (3-3/19)

HUGHES, Robert, 39, d 12/2/43 (born in England) (11-12/5)

HUGHES, Roxy Ana - see MATTOON, C.C.

HULBERT, Jane Charlotte, 1, dau. of Isaac, d 4/1/26 in Geneva ("This is the third smiling little infant that, within a few days, has been carried from this house and family") (6-4/18)

HULBERT, Mary M. - see MERRIAM, E.N.

HULDER, Elizabeth - see LONGYEAR, Manassah

HULL, Amos G., M.D., 60, of NYC, inventor of the truss, d 9/8/35 at his home near New Haven, CT (after a short illness) (6-9/12)

HULL, Arael (?) B. of Utica m 6/30/40 Ruth Ann Newcome (?) of Rome in R.; Rev. Campbell (1-7/7)

HULL, Chester, Jr. editor of the Coxsackie Advertiser, m 2/17/35 Rosa M Hadson of Bainbridge; Rev. Adams of Unadilla (6-2/27)

HULL, Eliza Ann (Miss), 26, d 2/17/43 in Little Falls (3-2/23)

HULL, Esther Almira - see KELLOGG, Daniel W.

HULL, Eunice (Mrs.), 54, d 3/15/49 in Rome (consumption) (1-3/21)

HULL, John G, Esq. of Poughkeepsie, NY d 1/22/35 at St. Augustine, FL (6-2/23)

HULL, Joseph, about 64, formerly of Killingworth, Conn., d 6/10/38 in Fairfield (3-6/14)

HULL, Judson of Vernon m 9/25/46 Sophia F. Mills of Camden in C. (1-10/6)

HULL, Mary E. - se FAKE, Isaac

HULL, Mary M., 27, wf of Daniel S., d 11/25/38 in Litchfield (3-12/6)

HULL, William C. of New Haven m 11/21/26 Sally M. Staunton, dau. of George W., Esq., of Albany; Rev. Lacey (6-11/24)

HULSE, Andrew, sexton of the Presbyterian Church in Goshen m 11/18/41 Esther Smith; Rev. Dr. McCartee. "the parties, it is said, had not seen each other previous to the marriage." (from the Independent Republican, 11/26 - but

156

modified by this latter newspaper 12/3, acknowledging prior acquaintance) (9-12/4)

HULSE, James W. of Hamptonburgh m 12/6/41 Eliza Beattie of New Windsor in N.W.; Rev. William Blain (9-12/11)

HULSE, Maria C. - see BOARDMAN, John

HULSE, Silas, 63, d 1/17/42 in Newburgh (9-1/22)

HULSEY, William of Westmoreland m 4/26/16 Anna Tryon of Clinton, Oneida County, in C.; Rev. Dr. Norton (6-5/4)

HUMASTON, Frances - see CADY, Freeman

HUMBERT, Abraham B. m (date not given) Elsey Hosier in NYC (6-1/10/16)

HUMISTON, Ann - see WHITBECK, Henry R.

HUMISTON, Miranda - see SMITH, Alonzo

HUMMEL, Catharine - see CARLISLE, Henry

HUMMEL, Maria - see VALCK(?), Abraham

HUMMEL, Rhoda M. - see OWEN, Lemuel O.

HUMPHREY, Chauncy & Friend - see MITCHELL, ----

HUMPHREY, Christina Mary - see ST JOHN, Horace

HUMPHREY, George, formerly merchant of Albany, d 9/5/35 at his home in Chatham (apoplectic fit) (6-9/7)

HUMPHREY, Helen M. - see HAYDEN, Henry

HUMPHREY, Hugh - see VANSTEENBURGH, Elizabeth

HUMPHREY, James - see SLADE, Thomas

HUMPHREY, James m 1/13/16 Catharine Winne, dau. of Daniel I., Esq.; Rev. Bradford (6-1/17)

HUMPHREY, Martha (Mrs.), 88(?), d 1/7/37 (her son, William Humphrey and her brother James Lightbody, the latter of 330 Washington St., are mentioned) (6-1/9)

HUMPHREY, William (Dr.), 30, d 3/12/26 in Albany (funeral at home of his father, John Humphrey, 17 Washington Street, 3/15) (6-3/14)

HUMPHREYS, Cornelia C. - see HAYDEN, Charles W.

HUMPHREYS, Jane, 33, wf of Capt. James Humphreys, d (date not given) in NYC (6-8/22/26)

HUMPHREYS, Trevor, Esq., Capt., Royal Regiment, third son of Rear Admiral Sir J.P. Humphreys, C.B. & K.C.H. of Bramhall Hall in County Chester, England m 6/1/37 Frances Georgiana Sewell, third dau. of Hon. J. Sewell, L.L.D., Chief Justice of the Province and Speaker of the Legislative Council, at the Chapel of the Holy Trinity, Quebec; Rev. Henry D. Sewell (6-7/17)

HUNE, Margaret - see MORRELL, John

HUNGERFORD, John F. of Marshall, Oneida County m 7/15/38 Lavinia Casler of Little Falls; Rev. Thomas Towell, rector of Emmanuel Church, Little Falls (3-7/19)

HUNGERFORD, Nelson L., M.D., of West Troy, d 5/27/39 at the Falls of Niagara ("from the fall of a stone from the precipice")(had been a long-time resident of West Troy)(his obituary appears 6/12) (5-6/5)

HUNGERFORD, Paulina - see MINER, Isaac

HUNN, Jacob m (date not given) Sarah S. Willis in NYC (6-5/15/16)

HUNT, Albert De Lowe, 2, child of Mrs. Charity Hunt, d 5/8/47 at Westmoreland (scarletina) (see also HUNT, Charles Henry) (1-6/4)

HUNT, Alexander - see CROSWELL, Eliza

HUNT, Andrew J., 20, editor of the Times, d (date not given) at Little Rock, Arkansas Territory (6-1/12/35)

HUNT, Andrew Jackson, 20, editor of the Little Rock Times and a native of Ohio, d 9/16/35 at Little Rock, Ark. Territory (was ill six days) (6-10/14)

HUNT, Ann - see FULLER, Ephraim D.

HUNT, Atvan of Smyrna m 4/11/16 Sally Beecher of Denmark, NY at D.; Rev. Gerry of Denmark (6-5/4)

HUNT, Charles Henry, 6, child of Mrs. Charity Hunt, d 5/28/47 at Westmoreland (Hydrothorax the sequel of scarletina) (see also HUNT, Albert De Lowe) (1-6/4)

HUNT, David, M.D., the last of the family of the Hon. Ebenezer Hunt, M.D., d 7/15/37 at Northampton (6-7/19)

HUNT, Edward G., infant son of Rev. Jesse Hunt, d "lately" at Peekskill (3-11/24/36)

HUNT, Elijah, 46, d 11/21/45 at Andover (1-12/2)

HUNT, Jesse, 74, d 8/24/35 in Cincinnati (a pioneer settler in Ohio) (6-9/5)

HUNT, Montgomery, Esq., 60, late of Utica and formerly cashier of the Utica Bank, d 1/5/37 on the Island of St. Croix where he had gone for the benefit of his health ("his remains have reached New York on their way for interment at Utica") (6-2/21)

HUNT, Robert S. m 6/6/42 Juliett Wood in Newburgh; Rev. Elwin E. Griswold (9-6/11)

HUNT, Roxana - see RICHARDS, Thomas

HUNT, Ward, Esq., attorney at law m 11/8/37 Mary Ann Savage, oldest dau. of Hon. John Savage, in Utica; Rev. Mandeville (all of Utica) (6-11/10)

HUNT, William L., 73, d (date not given) in Westmoreland (1-5/2/43)

HUNTER, Augustus W. m 2/7/49 Angelica Griffin, both of Catskill, in Saugerties; Rev. B.S. Crandall (8-2/17)

HUNTER, Elijah, Esq., 67, (a Rev. War officer), d 12/22/15 at NYC (6-12/30)

HUNTER, Eliza - see STEWART, J.J.

HUNTER, Eveline - see DIMMICK, Samuel

HUNTER, George m 1/25/49 Jane Thornton, both of Watervliet, in W.; Rev. J.C. Burroughs (5-1/31)

HUNTER, Phebe - see CROWVEN(?), David(?)

HUNTER, William, Jr., Esq., of the State Department m 11/18/35 Sally S. Smith, dau. of Gen. W. Smith, all of Georgetown, in G.; Rev. Hawley of Washington (6-11/28)

HUNTINGTON, Benjamin, Esq., 73, formerly of Rome, d 8/3/50 in NYC (1-8/7)

HUNTINGTON, Edward of Rome m 9/4/44 Antoinny Randall, dau. of William of Cortland, at C.; Rev. Hoes of Ithaca (1-9/10)

HUNTINGTON, Elizabeth - see YOUNG, Charles C.

HUNTINGTON, Eveline - see COWAN, Henry

HUNTINGTON, Frances, wf of Dr. Nicoll H. and dau. of Henry Huntington, Esq., of Rome d 2/2/41 in NYC (1-2/9)

HUNTINGTON, George, Esq., 71, d 9/23/41 in Rome (member of the Congregational Church in Rome for almost thirty-three years) (1-9/28)

HUNTINGTON, Hannah, 74, widow of George Huntington, Esq., d 9/20/48 in Rome (funeral from her late home on Dominick Street) (1-9/22)

158

HUNTINGTON, Henrietta Amelia - see QUINLAN, Alfred F.

HUNTINGTON, Sophronia, 40, wf of James and dau. of late John Henry of Bennington, VT, d 11/9/41 at Rome, NY (was ill the past six months) (1-11/16)

HUNTOON, Sophia - see COMSTOCK, Edwin T.

HURCHAM, Catharine Ann - see FERRIS, Catharine Ann Hurcham

HURD, Ann Sophia - see VAN DEWATER, Robert J.

HURD, J.N. (Gen.) - see VAN DEWATER, Robert I.

HURD, John Russell m (date not given) Catherine Codman, dau. of late Hon. John Codman of Boston, at Boston (6-11/25/15)

HURD, Maria, 35, wf of Abram, d 3/7/39 at Newport (survived by her husband, a son, 2, and a dau., 5) (children's names not given) (3-3/14)

HURD, Richard M., 26, son of Gen. J.N.M. Hurd of Albany, d 11/25/36 at Natchez, Mississippi (6-12/22)

HURLBUT, George m 6/21/36 Sarah Louisa Smith, dau of Zachariah, Esq., at Brooklyn Heights; Rev. J.B. Waterbury (6-6/24)

HURLBUT, Sarah - see FISK, Joseph

HURLEY, J. m 4/23/42 Ellen Corcoran, both of West Troy; Rev. Quinn (5-5/4)

HURLEY, Johanna - see FILKINS, Henry

HURLEY, Mary - see RICE, Asa C.

HURLEY, Mary A. - see CLAPP, Amasa

HURST, Ann - see COLE, Levi

HUTCHINSON, Sarah B. - see SAMSON, Ichabod

HUTTON, Anna Maria - see BLAUVELT, William W. (Rev.)

HUTTON, Jane - see DUNLOP, Archibald A.

HUTTON, T. - see BLAUVELT, William W. (Rev.)

HYATT, Catherine, 73, wf of Major John Hyatt, d 9/10/41 at Yorktown (11-9/14)

HYATT, Elijah m 4/22/42 Sarah Maria Raymond in NYC (both of Peekskill) (11-4/28)

HYATT, Elizabeth, 59, relict of late Justus Hyatt formerly of Peekskill, d 5/27/39 at Troy (dropsy) (11-6/11)

HYATT, Jesse, about 80, grandfather of the editor of the Lockport Balance, d 7/19/35 at Danby, Tompkins Co., NY (6-8/10)

HYATT, John (Major), 78, a Rev. War soldier, d 5/13/42 in Yorktown (11-5/19)

HYATT, Mary, 47, wf of Joseph, formerly of NYC, d 3/5/41 at the home of Major John Hyatt in Yorktown (11-3/23)

HYATT, Warren, about 19, son of Nathaniel, Esq., d 10/21/38 at New Castle "very suddenly" (survived by a wife and one child) (12-10/23)

HYATT, William D., 25, d 11/7/41 at New Windsor (9-11/13)

HYATT, William, 25, d 2/18/42 in Newcastle (scarlet fever) (11-3/1)

HYDE, Abigail - see MOSIER, John

HYDE, Almond m 5/24/36 Julia Ann Cook in Vernon; Rev. H.P. Bogue (all of Vernon) (6-5/31)

HYDE, Barbara - see DONALD, Owen G.

HYDE, Catharine - see STEVENS, Frederick

HYDE, Eber (Deacon) - see MOSIER, John

HYDE, George C. (Rev.), late of Andover Seminary m 12/20/35 Henrietta M. Thatcher, dau of Judge Thatcher, at Mercer, Maine; Rev. George C. Hyde (6-1/13/36)

HYDE, Orrimal J. m 9/6/46 Caroline Park; Rev. D.P. Gorrie (all of Camden) (1-9/15)

HYSER, Aaron of Herkimer m 1/5/43 Laura Thum of Ellery, Chautauqua County in Herkimer; Rev. J. Spinner (3-1/12)

HYSER, Mary Ann - see HARDER, Isaac

HYSLOP, Cornelia Matilda - see GRAHAM, David, Jr.

HYZER, Michael T., 76, d 12/28/34 at Hyde Park (6-1/10/35)

INGERSOLL, Edward (Rev.) of Westport m 9/14/36 Catharine Seymour, dau of late Gurdon Seymour, Esq. of Savannah, GA at Trinity Church, New Haven; Rev. Dr. Cromwell (6-9/20

INGERSOLL, Edward m (date not given) Catharine Brinton at Philadelphia (6-5/25/16)

INGERSOLL, Edward of Philadelphia m 6/5/50 Anna C. Warren, dau. of late Stephen, in Troy; Rev. Robert B. Van Kleek (5-6/12)

INGERSOLL, Elizabeth - see CURREY, Henry

INGERSOLL, Elizabeth - see CURREY, Henry

INGERSOLL, Luther, 63, d 9/4/41 in Vernon (1-9/14)

INGERSOLL, Sarah - see FOWLER, John, Jr.

INGHAM, Anna, 31, wf of S.A. Ingham, M.D. and dau. of Hon. Edward Varney, Senator from the 4th District, d 1/3/42 in Russia, NY (3-1/27)

INGHAM, S.A. (Dr.) m 1/28/41 Anna Varney, dau. of Judge Varney; Rev. Elliot (all of Russia, NY) (3-2/4)

INGHAM, Samuel of Oswego m 1/31/48 Electa Jane Merrill, dau. of Pierpont Merrill of Utica, in U.; Rev. H.R. Clark (1-2/4)

INGHAM, Silas A., M.D., of Russia, NY m 11/27/42 Susan A. Todd of Norway, NY; Rev. William Baker of Fairfield (3-12/1)

INGLIS, Charles (Hon. Right Rev.), D.D., 81, Bishop of Halifax, Nova Scotia d (date not given) in the 58th year of his ministry (died instantly without pain) (6-3/23/16)

INGRAHAM, Mary - see WEST, John, Jr.

INGRAHAM, Susan E. - see CHASE, Henry I.

INMAN, Mariette H. - see BADGER, Francis

INNES, Harriete V. - see MUMFORD, S. John

INNES, William m 9/23/36 Emeline Durham in Albany; Rev. Horatio Potter (6-4/25/37)

INSLEE, Maria - see BEADLE, Caleb

IREDELL, Annie - see JONES, Cadwallader. Jr.

IRELAND, Francis A. m 10/19/48 Christina C. Ten Broeck in Watervliet; Rev. William Pitcher (5-11/1)

IRELAND, Susan Matilda - see COUSE, William

IRVINE, James (Rev.), 44, pastor of the 2nd Associate Presbyterian Church of NYC, d 11/24/35 in NYC (formerly from Hebron, NY) (6-11/27)

IRVING, Charlotte - see GRINNELL, William H.

IRWIN, James, formerly of Albany, m 12/26/36 Catharine Wilson, youngest dau. of James, in NYC; Rev. Spencer M. Cooke (6-1/6/37)

ISAMAN, Alvira - see BARSE, Charles

ISAMAN, John - see BARSE, Charles

ISBELL, William M., 11 months, son of Milo H. and Jane M., d 4/1/49 in Rome (1-4/4)

ISHEM, Alfred m 10/21/37 Delia Mandel, dau. of Henry, Esq., at Esperence; Rev.
J.D. Hicks (all of Esperence) (3-11/4)

ISMELL(?), Sevilla - see SARETT(?), E.R.

IVES, Ambrose m 2/13/49 Maria Finn, both of Halfmoon, in West Troy; Rev. J.C.
Burroughs (5-2/28)

IVES, Charlotte - see STEELE, Atwood

IVES, Chauncey of Norway, NY m 2/13/39 Harriet Tuttle of Salisbury, in S.; Rev.
C.E. Brown (3-4/4)

IVES, Cornelia Parker, 9, dau. of Caleb P. and Cornelia, d 1/15/49 in West Troy
(5-1/24)

IVES, Eliza Ann - see CLARK, Stephen

IVES, Frederick, merchant, m 9/28/42 Mary Rosalie Burrill, dau. of William, Esq.,
at Salisbury; Rev. Dr. Chassel (all of Salisbury) (3-9/29)

IVES, George Russell m 1/27/35 Mary Phelps Olmstead, dau of late Ralph, Esq.,
of NYC, in NYC; Rev. William Patton (all of NYC) (6-2/1)

IVES, Mary - see HALE, Ammi

IVES, Nancy - see TILLINGHAST, Thomas

IVES, Reuben (Rev.), 75, d 10/14/36 in Cheshire, CT (one of the oldest of the
Episcopal clergy of the diocese of Connecticut) (6-10/24)

IVES, Roxana, 46, wf of Truman Ives, d 3/12/39 at Salisbury (3-3/28)

JACK, Margaret P. - see HETZEL, A.R.

JACKSON, Agnes, 24, wf of William, d 5/14/41 in West Troy (5-5/19)

JACKSON, Ebenezer, Esq. d "lately at an advanced age" at Middletown, Conn.
(the survivor of 5 children, all sons, of Gen. Michael Jackson who
commanded a regiment of the Continental Line in the Rev. War) (6-11/21)

JACKSON, Edward B. - see UNDERWOOD, John C.

JACKSON, Edwin m 10/9/44 Mary S. King, both of Cooperstown, in Rome; Rev.
Haynes (1-10/15)

JACKSON, Eliza - see DANFORTH, John Jay

JACKSON, Joseph H m 2/16/36 Sarah Van Brunt, dau. of Theodore William, in
Fishkill; Rev. William S. Hyer (6-2/27)

JACKSON, Joseph I. - see TRIVETT, Sarah Jane

JACKSON, L.W. of Geneva, NY m 4/2/46 Margaret Hitchcock, dau. of Isaac, Esq.,
of West Troy, in W.T.; Rev. O.H. Gregory (5-4/8)

JACKSON, Maria Gloria - see UNDERWOOD, John C.

JACKSON, Minerva - see JOHNSON, ----

JACKSON, Peter, possibly age 122 but over age 100, (was born on the passage
from Africa and was a slave to a Dutchman in Kinderhook) d 5/19/49 at
Amherst, Mass. (5-5/30)

JACKSON, Ruth (Mrs.), 78, d (date not given) at Middletown (7-2/7/10)

JACKSON, Samuel - see DANFORTH, Eliza J.

JACKSON, Samuel - see SHELDON, Samuel J.

JACKSON, Samuel (Col.) - see DANFORTH, John Jay

JACKSON, Thomas m 12/21/46 Abia Crowley, both of Rome, in R.; Thomas
Dugan, Esq. (1-1/8/47)

JACKSON, William m 5/20/44 Catherine Blow, both of Rome; Rev. S. Haynes (1-
5/21)

JACKSON, William m 6/6/36 Emma Gedden, dau of late Isaac Jerome of
Onondaga, at Jeromeville; Rev. Francis T. Tedrig, rector of St. Paul's

Church, Syracuse (6-6/14)

JACOBS, Horace m 2/8/43 Tabitha M. Gaines, dau. of Joseph, Esq. of Vermont, in Salisbury, NY; Rev. A. Knapp (3-3/23)

JACOBS, Lucy, 66, sister of Ananias Platt, d 12/14/35 in Albany (funeral at 10 o'clock from home of Mr. Platt, 28 Jay Street) (6-12/16)

JACOBS, Roxyann - see SOPER, Hiram

JACOBUS, Samuel Jackson m 1/5/42 Eliza Marks, dau of Samuel, Esq., all of Peekskill; Rev. Moses Marcus, rector of St. Peter's Church, Courtlandt Town (11-1/18)

JACOBUS, Samuel Jackson m 1/5/42 Eliza Marks, dau of Samuel, Esq.; Rev. Moses Marcus, rector of St. Peter's Church in Peekskill (11-1/11)

JACOBY, Phebe Ann - see AROSE, Samuel

JACOCKEN, William m 10/10/48 Catharine J. Cowles, both of Rome, in R.; Rev. W.E. Knox (1-10/13)

JAMES, Catharine - see NEILSON, Samuel

James, Elizabeth - see GREEN, Lewis

JAMES, Hetley, wf of Daniel, M.D., d 8/12/36 at Utica (6-8/15)

JAMES, Louisa - see HILL, O.P.

JAMIESON, Malcolm, 21, printer, d 4/26/36 in Albany (consumption) (funeral at 3 o'clock from his late home, 3 Union Street) (6-4/28)

JAMISON, Mary - see SPILMEIER, Henry

JAMISON, William m 5/22/39 "Miss Laden", dau of Michael, formerly of Rockland County, in NYC; Rev. Powers (12-5/28)

JANES, Elisha B., 35, late principal of the Pearl Street Academy, d 5/21/37 in Albany (6-5/24)

JAQUITH, Jacob, 42, d 7/24/35 in Troy (6-7/30)

JARVIS, Huldah - see OSBORN, Charles

JARVIS, Mary (Mrs.) d 10/27/37 in Troy (5-11/1)

JAY, Catharine Helena - see DUBOIS, Henry

JAY, Meriam - see FRANKLIN, John

JAY, Peter A. - see PRIME, Mary Ruthford

JAY, Sarah - see DAWSON, William

JAYCOX, Catharine - see HORTON, Jesse

JAYCOX, Enoch m 1/15/42 Phebe Glover in Putnam Valley; Joel Bunnell, Esq. (all of P.V.) (11-1/25)

JAYCOX, James C. m 11/20/39 Rebecca Lounsberry in Peekskill; Rev. Richard Hopper (11-11/26)

JEFFERS, William m 5/15/41 Phebe Johnson, both of Oppenheim, in Little Falls; George Petrie, Esq. (3-5/20)

JEFFERSON, Avery m 5/3/50 Elizabeth Barker, both of Floyd; H.C. Vogell (1-5/8)

JEFFERSON, Susan J. - see FOX, Roland

JENKINS, Elisha (Col.) of Hudson, NY m 6/5/37 Mrs. Harman Caldwell, formerly of Boston, widow of Lt. William M. Caldwell of the US Navy, at Washington, D.C. at the home of General Touson (6-6/13)

JENKINS, John T. (Lieut.), 28, of US Navy, d (date not given) in NYC (6-2/11/36)

JENKINS, Mary Sophia - see BENSON, James

JENKINS, Sarah, wf of Col. Elisha (both formerly of Albany) d 1/10/35 at Hudson after a long illness (from the Evening Journal, prob. published at Hudson) (6-1/14)

JENKS, Achsah (Miss) - see JENKS, James M.

JENKS, James M., Esq., of Ashtabula County, Ohio m 9/19/49 Miss Achsah Jenks of Lee at Jenks Hotel, West Leyden) (1-9/26)

JENKS, Salona - see BURDICK, Lewis

JENNING, Abel m 5/4/42 Phebe Northrup in Ridgefield, CT; Rev. Fuller (11-5/12)

JENNINGS, Elijah, 40, d (date not given) at Newtown (7-8/29/10)

JENNINGS, John C., 30, of firm of Woodward, Otis and Terbell, d 2/22/42 in NYC (9-2/26)

JENNINGS, Nancy, 77, consort of late Hon. Joseph Jennings, d 9/10/42 at the home of William H. Talcott, Esq. in Fort Plain where she had gone to spend a few days with her niece (3-9/22)

JENNINGS, Royal m (date not given) Desire Cavis in NYC (6-6/5/16)

JENNINGS, Urania - see BUCKLIN, Isaac B.

JEREMIAH, John, d (date not given) in NYC (6-5/15/16)

JERMAIN, James B., Esq. of Newburgh m 11/17/42 Catherine Ann Rice, dau. of late Col. Clark Rice of Jackson, Washington County, at J.; Rev. Ephraim H. Newton (9-11/26)

JERMAIN, John P., 22, d 3/10/35 (friends of the deceased and of his father, S.P. Jermain, invited to John P.'s funeral from his late home, 73 N. Pearl St., Albany (6-3/11)

JEROME, Isaac - see JACKSON, William

JEROME, Mary - see SMITH, E.K.

JERVER(?), Mary, wf of Anthony. d 2/19/49 in Saugerties (8-2/24)

JERVIS, Timothy B., civil engineer, m 5/30/37 Helen Maria Bogert, dau. of Rudolphus of NYC, at NYC; Rev. Dr. Cox (6-6/2)

JERVIS, Timothy B., civil engineer, m 5/30/37 Helen Mariah Bogert, dau. of Rudolphus of NYC, in NYC; Rev. Dr. Cox (3-6/15)

JESSUP, William B. of Westport, CT m 9/13/36 Mary J. Wilson, dau of John Q., Esq., of Albany; Rev. Vermilye (6-9/16)

JEWEL, John, 72, a Rev. War soldier, d 12/4/38 in Greenburgh (12-12/11)

JEWELL, Elizabeth, 78, relict of late Nathaniel, d 3/2/49 in Rome (1-3/7)

JEWELL, Merrett m 10/24/49 Elizabeth Harrington at the Parsonage in Rome; Rev. James Erwin (all of Rome) (double ceremony - see SPENCER, George W.) (1-10/31)

JEWELL, Volkert, D. of Albany m 12/17/35 Gertrude Ring of Watervliet in W.; Rev. Meyerl (sic) (6-12/19)

JEWET, John, Esq., 92, d 4/17/49 in Tioga County "leaving a widow, age 90" (moved from Pawling, Dutchess County in 1795; lived in Carmel until 1818 when he moved to Tioga County; had been appointed a county judge but declined) (10-6/27)

JEWETT, Anna B., 30, wf of D.B., Esq., d 8/11/49 in Lansingburgh (5-8/22)

JEWETT, David B. of West Troy m 7/18/44 Ann ----, dau. of ---- at Trinity Church in West Troy; Rev. Bissell (part of this record indecipherable) (5-7/24)

JEWETT, David B., Esq., about 36, formerly of West Troy, d 11/30/50 in Middle Granville (consumption) (funeral 12/3/ from home of James Ray, Esq. in West Troy) (5-12/4)

JEWETT, Sarah - see PETRIE, Charles

JIMILTSON, Mary - see WHITE, Robert

JOB, Thomas of Troy m 12/25/44 Mary Sullivan of West Troy in W.T.; George

Coffin, Esq. (5-1/1/45)

JOCK, John of West Troy m 10/20/41 Sarah Fisher of Troy in West Troy; Rev. James Quin (5-10/27)

JOHNSON, ---- m 11/20/39 Catherine Miller of Bedford; Rev. Underhill (12-12/3)

JOHNSON, ---- of Depauville, Jefferson Co. m 9/24/40 Minerva Jackson, dau. of Timothy of Boonville, in B.; Rev. Demming (1-9/29)

JOHNSON, A.F. of Vienna m 4/20/48 Enfield Mc Corty of Lee in Vienna; Elder T. Martin (1-5/12)

JOHNSON, Abigail Louisa Smith, 37, wf of A.B., grand dau of late Pres. John Adams and niece of ex-President John Quincy Adams, d 7/4/36 at Utica (6-7/7)

JOHNSON, Agnes - see VAN EPS, Herman

JOHNSON, Andrew J. of firm of Ten Eyck and Johnson in Schodack m 5/24/36 Ida Van Dervoort of Brooklyn in B.; Rev. Meecker (6-6/1)

JOHNSON, Betsey (Miss), 19, d (date not given) at New Haven (7-1/31/10)

JOHNSON, Bryan, 19, formerly of Albany, d 10/28/37 in NYC (typhus fever). The deceased was the second son of A.B. Johnson of Utica (from the Utica Whig) (6-11/3)

JOHNSON, Chauncey m 4/7/50 Sarah Willard at Vienna; Elder Beckwith (all of Vienna) (1-4/24)

JOHNSON, Clarissa - see HOAG, George

JOHNSON, Daniel m 5/30/37 Levina White, dau. of Lyman, Esq., in Fairfield; Rev. E.W.R. Allen (all of Fairfield) (3-6/15)

JOHNSON, David Jr., 48, d 11/25/35 at his home in Lexington Heights, Greene Co. (6-11/28)

JOHNSON, David M.K., Esq. of Camden m 10/14/44 Frances J. Matteson, dau. of Simon of Rome; Rev. G.S. Boardman (1-10/15)

JOHNSON, E.H. - see GILCHRIST, William

JOHNSON, Ebenezer, Esq., ex-mayor of Buffalo m 12/7/35 Lucy E. Lord, dau of Rev. J. Lord, in Nelson; Rev. J. Lord (6-12/18)

JOHNSON, Edmund, 48, d (date not given) at New Hartford (7-6/27/10)

JOHNSON, Elizabeth - see WADLON, George W.

JOHNSON, F.M. of Rome m 9/2/48 Mary White of Lowville in L.; H. Miller, Esq. (1-9/22)

JOHNSON, H. of Schuyler m 10/7/47 Miss C.B. Shelley of Oneida Castle at O.C.; Rev. Goo (1-10/22)

JOHNSON, Horace H. m 9/24/35 Catherine M. Whiting; Rev. B.T. Welch (all of Albany) (6-9/28)

JOHNSON, Horace H. m 9/24/35 Catherine M. Whitney; Rev. B.T. Welch (all of Albany) (6-9/26)

JOHNSON, Jesse W. of Verona m 1/28/41 Caroline Matilda Shepard, dau. of David E., of Rome; Rev. Selden Haynes (1-2/2)

JOHNSON, Jonathan, 67, d 9/27/37 in Norwich, Chenango County (one of the earliest settlers in this county)(from the Norwich Journal) (6-10/7)

JOHNSON, Joseph H. m 1/26/43 Margaret Hasbrouck of New Paltz, at N.P.; Rev. D. Van O'Linda (9-1/28)

JOHNSON, Joseph R. m 10/10/37 Lucy Ann Skinner, both of Lansingburgh, in Waterford (5-10/25)

JOHNSON, Levina, 51, consort of Daniel, d 9/18/39 in Newport. Her husband,

Daniel Johnson, 50, d 9/19/39 (both were buried together) (3-9/26)

JOHNSON, Louisa, eldest dau of Thomas R Walker, Esq. d 1/5/35 at Utica (6-1/8)

JOHNSON, Louise, about 25, d 8/27/39 in New Castle at the home of her uncle, John Cary ("This is the third death which has occurred in Mr. Cary's family in the short space of ten days") (12-9/3)

JOHNSON, Lucine - see CATLIN, Edwin R.

JOHNSON, Lucy (Miss), 19, d (date not given) at Middletown (7-2/7/10)

JOHNSON, Lucy, 48, wf of Ward Johnson, d 4/18/09 at Wallingford (7-5/24)

JOHNSON, Lydia C. - see HOVEY, J.S.

JOHNSON, Margaret - see LANGDON, Allen

JOHNSON, Martin, 71(?), d 1/1/42 in Pound Ridge (11-1/18)

JOHNSON, Mary Ann - see HICKEY, William

JOHNSON, Mary J. - see PRIEST, Allen B.

JOHNSON, Mary Jane - see DUNN, Chauncey

JOHNSON, Mary S. - see WOOD, L. Sprague

JOHNSON, Phebe - see JEFFERS, William

JOHNSON, Phebe T. - see FEHER(?), John

JOHNSON, Robert I. m 10/8/39 Caroline M. Arthur, dau. of J.C., Esq., at Stuyvesant, Columbia Co. (12-10/15)

JOHNSON, Stephen W., 39, d 7/9/36 in Detroit (formerly of Albany) (6-7/21)

JOHNSON, Sylvester I., 57, (formerly of Remsen, Oneida Co.) d 8/30/46 at Penfield, Lorain Co., Ohio (1-9/15)

JOHNSON, W.B. - see BLOUNT, William

JOHNSON, Wesley m 9/20/42 Catharine Phillips, both of Watervliet, in Schenectady; Rev. Harwood (5-10/19)

JOHNSON, William H. of Troy m 11/27/41 Katharine Legal of Sand Lake in West Troy; Rev. D. Starks (5-12/1)

JOHNSON, William m 11/16/46 Dorothy Corethers in West Troy; Rev. Houghtaling (all of West Troy) (5-11/18)

JOHNSTON, Eliza - see GILPIN, Henry D.

JOHNSTON, Flora - see CAMPBELL, Niel

JOICE, Erastus V. m 4/8/35 Emeline S. Hermans, second dau of John Hermans; Rev. Dr. Sprague. See also marriage of John H BOGART at same time (6-4/10)

JOICE, Mrs. - see BRIGGS, Cyrus

JONES, Andrew m 2/3/39 Caroline E. Gilmore, both of Frankfort, in Utica; Ira Ckase, Esq. (3-2/21)

JONES, Ann - see EVANS, Robert

JONES, Benjamin R. m 2/17/39 Henrietta Durkee, both of Little Falls, in L.F.; Rev. J.W. Olmstead (3-3/21)

JONES, Cadwallader, Jr., Esq., of Hillsborough m 1/5/36 Annie Iredell, oldest dau of Hon. James. late senator of the US, in Raleigh, NC; Rev. George W. Freeman (6-1/23)

JONES, Caroline B. (Mrs.) - see COLEMAN, A.H.

JONES, Cyrenus of Eatontown, NJ m 10/12/45 Ann Stebbins of West Troy, NY; Rev. Dodge (5-10/15)

JONES, David O. m 1/5/48 Elizabeth Jones, both of Rome, at Floyd; Rev. Thomas F. Evans (1-1/14)

JONES, Eleanor M. - see NEWMAN, George H.

JONES, Elizabeth - see JONES, David O.

JONES, Elizabeth - see PRICHARD, Griffith

JONES, Evans m 5/4/36 Mary Battles in Herkimer; Rev. Roycer (3-5/19)

JONES, Ezekiel (Capt.), 50, d (date not given) at Boston (6-7/25/26)

JONES, Hannah (Mrs.) - see ZEIDER, George C.

JONES, Hannah M. - see MC DOUGAL, Isaac

JONES, Henry m 11/20/50 Katharine Holtenhouse, both of West Troy, in W.T.; Rev. C.F. Burdick (5-12/25)

JONES, Henry R. m 5/13/38 Caroline B. Page, dau. of William, Esq., in Little Falls; Rev. J.W. Olmstead (all of Little Falls) (3-5/17)

JONES, Henry W., 22, d 1/16/39 in Little Falls ("a mechanic by profession") (3-1/17)

JONES, Horatio, Esq., (Capt.), 72, d 8/18/36 at his home near Geneseo (born in Chester County, PA and with his parents emigrated to Bedford County, PA) (a long obituary not reported, is included from the Geneseo Livingston Register) (6-8/30)

JONES, Jabez, Esq., of Richmond, VT m 10/15/38 Sarah Crane, dau of Thaddeus, Esq. of Somers; Rev. A. Leadbeater (12-10/23)

JONES, James m 1/30/39 Sophia Derevere, both of Tarrytown, in Sing Sing; Rev. S. Van Deusen (12-2/5)

JONES, Jane, 24, consort of Nathaniel and dau. of Henry Capron, Esq., d 8/3/50 in Boonville (she had selected Miss Barker of Constableville to prepare her grave clothes. Her funeral service was conducted at the Presbyterian Meeting House near West Leyden, August 5) (1-8/21)

JONES, Jane, 64, wf of Thomas, d (date not given) at Steuben (1-3/25/45)

JONES, Jerard, 1 year, only son of Thomas and Margaret, d 3/11/50 in Rome (croup) (1-3/13)

JONES, Joanna - see ELWOOD, Daniel

JONES, John (Capt.) m 6/22/37 Rachel Thomas, dau. of David; Rev. Dr. Campbell (all of Albany) (6-6/28)

JONES, John m 1/4/42 Melissa Swift in Little Falls; Elder Richards (3-1/13)

JONES, John R. m 10/19/48 Anna Maria Williams, both of Rome, in R.; Rev. W.E. Knox (1-11/2)

JONES, John S. m 12/23/47 Lorinda E. Hill, both of Rome, at Whitesboro; Rev. Cole (a double ceremony - see NEWMAN, George H.) (1-1/7/48)

JONES, Julia - see ANGEL, Benjamin

JONES, Julia Chever, 1 yr old, only dau of Llewellyn Jones, Esq., teller of the Cayuga County Bank, d 7/20/35 "after a few hours illness" at Auburn (6-7/28)

JONES, Julia Mary, 14, eldest dau. of John R. and Amantha E., d 8/11/50 at Vernon (consumption) (1-8/14)

JONES, Lucina - see RENCHER, A.

JONES, Margaret, 42, wf of Benjamin, d 9/19/39 in Danube (funeral sermon by Rev. Charles L. Dunning of the Methodist Episcopal Church) (3-9/26)

JONES, Mary A. - see MILLER, Peter H.

JONES, Mary Eliza - see WILCOX, Henry W.

JONES, Merrick m 9/8/36 Ann Petrie in Fairfield; Rev. William H. Waggoner (3-9/15)

JONES, Nancy Louisa - see TAHASH, Isaac

166

JONES, Reuben, 70, of Stamford, CT m 8/11/39 Mrs. Lyon, 63, widow of late
     Daniel of Bedford, in Pound Ridge; William Lockwood, Esq. (12-8/20)
JONES, Robert W. (Lieut.) d 5/20/37 at the Naval Hospital in Brooklyn (his
     remains were removed to Newburgh for interment) (6-5/25)
JONES, Samuel, 84, d 7/9/36 at New Lebanon (a Rev. War soldier) (6-7/16)
JONES, Sarah - see WRIGHT, M——(?)
JONES, Thomas, Jr. m 8/16/47 Sarah M. Farquarson in Rome; Rev. F.H. Stanton
     (1-8/20)
JONES, William of South Trenton m 5/10/41 Elizabeth Waterbury of Holland
     Patent at Annsville; Rev. William A. Bronson (1-6/15)
JONES, William P. of Butternuts m (date not given) Evelina Hale(?) at St.
     George's Church in Newburgh; Rev. J. Brown (3-10/7/41)
JORDAN, Allen, Esq. of Hudson m 12/6/37 Jane F. Cook, dau. of Richard Cook of
     NYC, in NYC; Rev. Henry A. Rowland (6-12/28)
JORDAN, Catharine - see MANNERING, James
JORDON, Jane - see REYNOLDS, Elias
JOSLIN, David H.S. m 7/3/47 Elvira Barnes in Boonville; A.E. Chandler, Esq. (all
     of Boonville) (1-7/9)
JOSLIN, Isabel, 14, dau. of David and Ruth, d 8/18/38 at Frankfort (illness of 24
     hours) (3-8/23)
JOSLIN, Mary - see FINE, John (Gen.)
JOSLYN, Lewis W. (Dr.) of Cicero m 9/12/41 Maria Hale of Westmoreland in W.;
     Rev. F.A. Spencer (1-9/28)
JOY, Charles E., 36, d 2/14/49 in Kingston (8-2/24)
JOY, Hannah - see WEBSTER, George B.
JOY, Miles of Albany m 7/19/37 Eunice Penfield, dau. of Thomas, deceased; Rev.
     Dr. Lintner (ceremony in the brick church at Schoharie) (6-7/15)
JOY, Tjerck of Kingston m 8/27/49 Betsey Adaline Valck of Saugerties in S.; Rev.
     Redford (8-9/1)
JOYCE, Ann (Mrs.) - see CUMMINGS, Harrison
JOYCE, Garrett H., 28, printer, d 8/13/50 in NYC (1-8/21)
JUDD, Ann - see APLEY, Griswold
JUDD, Chester of Albany, 44, d 10/17/35 at Cherry Valley (6-10/22)
JUDD, George C., 4, son of George B., Esq., d 6/25/36 in Frankfort (3-6/30)
JUDD, George W. m 3/17/40 Nancy Forhall(?) of Frankfort at F.; Rev. Thomas
     Houston (3-3/26)
JUDSON, A. (Rev.) of the Congregational Church, West Troy, m 12/6/36
     Sophronia Mason, dau of John, Esq., formerly of Greenfield, MA, in Troy;
     Rev. Dr. Beman (6-12/17)
JUDSON, A. (Rev.), D.D., of Maulmain, Burmah, m 6/2/46 Emily Chubbuck
     (Fanny Forrester), dau. of Charles Chubbuck of Hamilton, Madison
     County, NY in Hamilton; Rev. N. Kendrick, D.D., Professor in the
     Madison University (1-6/9)
JUDSON, A. m 5/4/43 Emily S. Morton(?) in Vernon; R.C. Brisbin (all of Vernon)
     (1-5/16)
JUDSON, Charles m 3/16/35 Lavina Kromer in Albany; Rev. Kirk (6-3/18)
JUDSON, Esther - see PLATT, William
JUDSON, John Dean, 1, youngest child of Ard Johnson, d 9/18/50 in Vernon
     (1-10/30)

JUDSON, R.W., attorney at law, of Ogdensburg m 1/5/42 Sarah A. Collins, dau. of
Selden, Esq., of Collinsville, Lewis County, at C.; Rev. Lockwood of Rome
(1-1/18)
JULIA, Patience Amanda - see MIX, Warren
JULIAND, Frederick m 4/21/35 Jane Cameron Ringer in Zion's Church at Greene,
NY; Rev. Norman H. Adams (all of Greene) (6-4/27)
JUNE, Andrew m 1/1/43 Amelia E. Kingsland; Rev. E.W. Griswold (all of
Peekskill) (11-1/3)
JUNE, George m 12/8/38 Sarah Ann Lockwood, both of Wilton, CT, in South
Salem, NY; William Hupt, Esq. (12-12/18)
JUNE, Mary Ann - see HOAR, James
JUSLIN, Amy Ann - see NURSE, George
K----(?), Robert m 8/20/40 Catharine Snell, at St. Johnsville; Rev. Myers (all of
Little Falls) (3-9/3)
KALEY, George m 4/26/49 Margaret C. Ring in West Troy; Rev. T.F. Wyckoff
(5-5/2)
KANE, Anna - see RUSSELL, William Henry
KANE, Helen - see NICHOLSON, Samuel
KANE, Julian Ann - see LANSING, Evert
KANEVILLE, Maria - see LATOURETTE, John
KANPP, Martha - see COONSHELL(?), Samuel P.
KARKER, Jonas Y., 16, youngest son of Hannah, formerly of Watervliet, d (date
not given) in Jersey City, NJ (5-2/13/50)
KARR, S. Edward m 3/21/49 Margarette Chaney, dau. of Elder Chaney; Rev. John
Chaney (all of Whitestown) (1-3/28)
KASPER, Barbara - see FARNY, Christian Charles
KASSON, Henry W. m 1/5/50 Julia E. Green, dau. of John of Deerfield, at D.; Rev.
Corey (1-2/6)
KEARNEY, Philip R., m 11/17/36 Lucia Louisa Chesebrough, dau of Robert, Esq.,
in NYC Rev. Dr. Spring (6-11/22)
KEARNON, F. (Mrs.), 65(?), d 8/1/49 in Saugerties (8-8/4)
KEARNS, Louisa, 2, dau of John Kearns of Albany, d "this morning after a short
illness" (friends of the parents and of John's mother-in-law Mrs Louisa
Crosby, invited to the funeral at 4 o'clock from 515 South Market St.)
(6-8/16)
KEATING, Margaret - see DEVINE, John
KEATON, R.F. m 6/28/49 Hannah Coutant, both of Rosendale, in R.; Rev. Strong
(8-7/7)
KEEFER, Peter, Esq., postmaster of Therold, Upper Canada m 12/24/35 Jane
Angela Christie, only dau of James, Esq., of Geneva, NY, at the Mohawk
Church, Brantford, Upper Canada (6-1/13/36)
KEEFER, Peter, Esq., postmaster of Thorold (in Ontario, Canada), m 11/24/35
Jane Angela Christie, only dau of James, Esq., of Geneva, NY late of
England (at Mohawk Church, Brantford, Lower Canada); Rev. Lugger
(6-12/22)
KEEFER, Susan - see SNIDER, John
KEELER, Benjamin S., about 35, d suddenly 2/27/42 evening at Newport on his
way home from church (survived by a wife and children - their names not
given) (3-3/3)

KEELER, David, 90, a Rev. War soldier, d 12/16/43 at Brookfield, Conn.
(5-1/17/44)

KEELER, Emily A. - see BENEDICT, Isaac

KEELER, Floyd m 9/19/39 Jane G. Purdy, dau. of late Isaac, Esq., in North Salem;
Rev. Evans (12-9/24)

KEELER, J.B. of Buffalo m 5/14/39 Elmira Chapman of West Troy in W.T.; Rev.
Hopkins (5-5/22)

KEELER, Madalena - see HARRIS(?), William

KEELER, Marilla, 47, d 2/16/39 in Greenwich, CT at home of Thomas Carpenter
(12-2/19)

KEELER, Mary Elizabeth - see BROOKS, Jonathan, Jr.

KEELER, Nelson K., Esq., counsellor at law of Delhi, m 12/23/36 Emily H.
Ogden, dau. of late Abraham, Esq., in Walton; Rev. E.W. Maxwell
(6-1/2/37)

KEELER, Sarah Lucretia, 62, wf of James, d 12/11/36 (Friends of her husband, her
son (Charles A. Keeler) amd her son-in-law (S.M. Meigs) invited to the
funeral from her late home, 110 Green Street) (6/12/12)

KEENER, Elizabeth - see KLINE, Henry

KEENEY, Laura - see FORCE, Bartholomew

KEENEY, Maria Atwood, 1, dau. of Francis J. and Sarah D., d 10/1/43 (5-10/11)

KEENEY, Mary - see BENJAMIN, Alansom

KEENEY, Molly (Mrs.), 94, d (date not given) at New London (7-6/27/10)

KEESE, William Linn, 32, formerly of NYC and late associate rector of Trinity
Church, New Haven, d 2/19/36 in Cuba (6-3/10)

KEILL, Thomas, 81, d 9/20/37 in Stark (born in Germany and "one of those taken
prisoner with Burgoyne") (3-10/12)

KEITH, Eliza D., 37, consort of Aylmar Keith and dau. of Hon. Charles Wylie, late
of Rome, NY, d 5/28/41 at Naperville, Dupage County, Ill. (consumption)
(1-6/15)

KEITH, Nancy - see GILES, Daniel

KEITH, Stephen of Newport m 10/12/37 Sally Ann Ford, dau. of David of
Middleville, in M.; Rev. W.H. Waggoner (3-11/4)

KELLER, Henry I., 60, d 9/12/37 in Manheim (3-9/14)

KELLER, Jacob J., about 35, d 2/28/42 in Manheim (3-3/3)

KELLER, Jane - see REID, Charles

KELLER, Martha, about 18 months, only dau. of David, d 3/9/39 (3-3/14)

KELLER, Mary - see CHURCHILL, Isaac P.

KELLER, Michael J. m 7/9/36 Elizabeth Jane Austin in Albany; Rev. I.D.
Williamson (6-7/12)

KELLEY, Eunice (Mrs.) - see REED, Timothy

KELLOGG, Asa, 58, merchant of firm of Kellogg & Co. of Troy d 8/23/36 at Troy
(a long and painful illness) (one of the oldest and most extensive merchants
of Troy - from Troy Whig) (6-8/25)

KELLOGG, Chauncey P. m 10/20/36 Juliet Sherwood at St. Joseph, Mich.; John F.
Porter, Esq. (all of St. Joseph) (6-11/14)

KELLOGG, Cynthia - see ROCKWELL, James

KELLOGG, Daniel W, merchant of Ann Arbor, Mich. Terr. m 2/11/35 Esther
Almira, dau. of Archibald Hull, Esq., of Troy, in Detroit; Rev. Johnson
(6-2/28)

KELLOGG, Daniel, Esq., 56, president of the Bank of Auburn, d 5/4/36 at
    Skaneateles (6-5/14)
KELLOGG, Edward of NYC m 12/5/37 Sarah M. Hastings, dau. of Seth, Esq. of
    Albany; Rev. Dr. Sprague (6-12/6)
KELLOGG, Frederick of Westmoreland m 3/21/41 Amenia Gates, dau. of Deacon
    Warren of New Hartford, at N.H.; Rev. Searle (1-4/20)
KELLOGG, George D., merchant of Lowville m 3/29/37 Frances Bundy, dau. of
    Caleb, Esq. of Marcelula (sic) at M; Rev. Levi Parsons (6-4/10)
KELLOGG, Giles B, Esq, attorney, m 5/30/36 Adaline Kellogg, dau of Justin
    Kellogg, Esq., in Troy; Rev. Beman (all of Troy) (6-6/6)
KELLOGG, Henry Nelson m 8/15/42 Miriam Maria Moulton, dau. of David, Esq.,
    sheriff of Oneida County, at the home of N.S. Sleeper; Rev. W.W. Ninde
    (1-9/6)
KELLOGG, John (Dr.) m 7/23/48 Henrietta Flint, dau. of Henry, at Cherry Valley;
    Rev. Boardman (4-7/27)
KELLOGG, Maria, wf of Epenetas, formerly of Ulster County, d 7/18/49 in NYC
    (8-8/18)
KELLOGG, Palmer V. of firm of Kellogg & Sons m 9/6/36 Rachel Ann Shankland
    of Cooperstown at home of Col. John H. Prentiss in Cooperstown; Rev.
    Campbell (6-9/10)
KELLOGG, R.F. of Malone m 11/17/41 Mary Sherman of Floyd; H.C. Vogell
    (1-11/23)
KELLOGG, Spencer, Esq. - see ROCKWELL, James
KELLOGG, T.N. of firm of Bissell, Leonard & Co. m 5/23/49 A.L. Matteson, dau.
    of Jeptha, Esq., at Zion's Church; Rev. Gregory (1-5/30)
KELLS, John, 18, m (date not given) Mrs. Catharine Weaver, 40, at Livingston
    (7-8/1/10)
KELLY, ---- (Mrs.), 63, d 9/8/46 in West Troy after a lingering illness (funeral at 3
    o'clock 9/9 from the home of her son, P. Fitzgerald (5-9/9)
KELLY, James R. m 12/23/41 Ursula Forster in Southeast; Rev. Cloud (11-12/28)
KELLY, Jonathan S. m 1/22/16 Eleanor Paulding at Schenectady; Rev. Cumming
    (6-2/7)
KELLY, L.H. (Dr.) of Berkshire m 10/11/36 Angeline Rich, youngest dau of
    Ezekiel of Richford, at R.; Rev. D.S. Morse (6-10/17)
KELLY, Patrick m 9/14/42 Margaret O'Niel (sic) in Rome; Rev. Beecham (all of
    Rome) (1-9/20)
KELSY, Benjamin Alexander, 24, d 1/15/41 in Herkimer (consumption) (3-1/21)
KEMBLE, John C. (Hon.) of Rockford, Illinois m Charlotte M. Potts, dau. of Col.
    Henry Potts of Columbia County, NY, in Chicago, Ill; Rev. Blatchford
    (6-10/2)
KEMBLE, John C., formerly editor of the Troy Budget, and a member of the
    Assembly and the Senate of NY State, d 4/11/43 in the Insane Asylum in
    Worcester, Mass. (3-5/4)
KEMMY, Frederick, 60, d 9/27/35 at Bethlehem (6-11/2)
KEMP, Michael m 3/23/48 Mary Ann Rockenstein in Watervliet; Rev. S. Ireland
    (5-3/29)
KEMPTON, Sarah Ann - see TEALE, Sidenus
KENDRICK, Edward E., Esq., cashier of the Mechanics and Farmers Bank of
    Albany, m 11/22/36 Caroline E. Hill, dau of Rev. B.M. Hill of Albany;

Rev. B.M. Hill (6-11/28)

KENDRICK, Samuel, 21, d 3/13/45 in Hamilton (1-4/8)

KENEY, Nathaniel of Manchester, Hartford County, Conn. m 9/9/46 Clarissa J. Talcott of Rome in R.; Rev. Kendall of Verona (1-9/22)

KENNAH, Eleanor (Mrs.) d (date not given) in NYC (6-5/15/16)

KENNARD, Charles m 1/26/42 Phebe Parent in Somers; Jacob Ranet(?) (11-2/8)

KENNEDY, Hannah - see LAWRENCE, William

KENNEDY, Jane - see HENDERSON, William

KENNEDY, Lydia, 73, (relict of William who was a Rev. War soldier) d 9/21/39 at Bedford (12-10/1)

KENNEY, Charles M., 2 months, son of Rufus and Sarah Ann, d 8/25/41 in Rome (1-8/31)

KENT, Orrin S. m 11/9/40 Betsey A. Gardner in Rome; Rev. Vogle (all of Rome) (1-12/15)

KENT, Phineas of Boonville m 2/20/50 Maria Smith of Lee at the American Hotel (in Rome); H.C. Vogell (1-2/27)

KENT, William, 70, d (date not given) in NYC (6-9/26/26)

KENTON, Elizabeth - see HAGER, Daniel

KENYON, Abby S. - see WEST, Thomas F.

KENYON, John of Hopkinton, RI, d (date not given) (death caused by drinking a pint and a half of old spirits) (6-4/6/16)

KENYON, Mary Ann - see VIELE, Augustus, M.D.

KENYON, V.S. - see VIELE, Augustus, M.D.

KER(?), Delight, 27, wf of Dr. Robert Ker(?) d 12/10/40 at Mc Connellsville, Oneida County (typhus fever) (1-12/22)

KERKER, George H. of Albany m 5/21/26 Eleanor Erickson of NYC in NYC; Rev. Cowen (6-5/30)

KERKERS, William I. m 5/6/48 Olivia W. Raymond; Rev. T.F. Wyckoff (5-5/10)

KERMEYS, Elizabeth - see PRIME, Samuel

KERNAN, Margaret - see BARNES, Richard

KERR, Margaret Jane (Miss), 26, d 2/28/43 in West Troy (funeral at the house of her father (his name not given)) (5-3/1)

KERSHAW, Samuel m 1/1/42 Sarah Ross; C.T.E. Van Horne, Esq. (3-1/13)

KERSLAW, Wright L. m 10/28/41 Mary Ann Ashley, both of Washingtonville, in Newburgh; Rev. J.J. Strong (9-10/30)

KESSEGIUS, Alfred - see possibly RESSEGIUS, Alfred

KETCH, Mary E. - see SWARTWART, John

KETCHUM, Ezra, 94, d 8/27/42 at Ballston (a Rev. War soldier, one of the earliest settlers in the Ballston area) (one of the staff who captured the spy, Major Andre, "and rode him into camp") (5-9/7)

KETCHUM, J.T.E. of NYC, merchant, m 1/25/36 Lucy Ann Sweatland, dau of William, Esq. of Plattsburgh at Trinity Church in Plattsburgh; Rev. J. Howland Coit (6-2/4)

KETTERHOUSE, Anthony m 10/6/42 Jeanette Bluer, both of Watervliet; Rev. J. Rawson (5-10/12)

KEYES, Electa S. - see WAIT, Samuel C.

KEYES, Harriette - see WOOD, Gilmon

KEYSER, H.D. of Albany m 6/8/36 Mary Dennison, dau of Peleg, Esq., of Mystic, CT, at M.; Rev. Shaw (6-6/16)

KIDD, James m 11/9/36 Jane Maria Shepherd, dau of Robert; Rev. T.E. Vermilye (all of Albany) (6-11/11)

KIDDER, Mary E. - see MARTIN, William C.

KIDNEY, Jonathan - see VAN ZANDT, Sarah

KIDNEY, Maria, 56, wf of Henry, d 6/11/33 at Sparta (11-6/25)

KIDNEY, William - see BROWER, John W.

KIERGIUS(?), William D., about 50, d 2/13/39 in Sing Sing (12-2/19)

KIERSTED, Charles, 22, son of Jasper, Esq. of Broadalbin, d 9/19/35 at Watervliet (6-9/23)

KIERSTED, Maria, 20, wf of Luke and only dau. of Isaac Van Loon, Esq., d 4/28/16 very suddenly in Jefferson village, town of Catskill (6-5/4)

KILBORN, Elizabeth - see PARSONS, Spencer

KILBOURN, Judson d 4/7/46 in Vernon (1-4/14)

KILBURN, Delia J., 29, wf of U.C. d 7/29/49 in Rome (puepera convulsions) (1-8/8)

KILTS, Catharine - see CASLER, Isaac

KIMBALL, Mary - see MERRY, Orson

KIMBALL, Nancy, 21, d 11/9/26 in Albany (6-11/10)

KIMBALL, Norman (Major), formerly of Canajoharie and late of Livingston and Wells Express, d 5/18/48 in Silver Creek, Chautauqua County (4-5/25)

KIMBERLY, Horace of Augusta m 9/25/50 Esther L. Smith of Herkimer in H.; Rev. J.H. Harter of Rockton (double ceremony - see SCRANTON, Henry) (1-10/2)

KIMMEY, David m 4/28/16 Margaret Mabey, both of Bethlehem, at the home of Col. Burhans in Bethlehem; Rev. Holliday (6-5/8/16)

KINDELTON, Adam (Rev. Father, associate minister of the Catholic Church at New Orleans)(born in Ireland - founder and protector of the Catholic Association for male orphans comprising nearly 200 children)(from the New York Star) (6-10/27)

KING, Austin m 4/16/44 Sarah E. Davis, both of West Troy; Elder C.H. Hosken (5-5/1)

KING, Caroline - see DUER, Denning

KING, Edward, 40, son of late Rufus King, d 2/6/36 at Cincinnati (6-2/18)

KING, Elisha W., Esq., 55, d 12/3/36 in Brooklyn (6-12/6)

KING, Eliza (Miss), 26, dau. of late Capt. Thomas of Norwich, d (date not given) at Lisbon (7-2/7/10)

KING, Eveline, 1 yr., only child of Rev. George I. and Emily B., d 2/11/45 at Westernville (1-2/18)

KING, James G. - see DUER, Denning

KING, James R. m 7/21/41 Hannah Morgan, both of Albany, in Rome; Rev. I.I. Hunt (1-7/27)

KING, Joanna E. - see HEMPSTED, David L.

KING, John L. m 3/15/38 Lorena Holbrooks, both of West Troy, in W.T.; Rev. Leonard (5-3/21)

KING, John, 63, d 9/1/36 at his home in New Lebanon ("for nearly 40 years an active politician") (6-9/12)

KING, Joshua, 72, d (date not given) at Junius (6-9/26/26)

KING, Lucinda - see HOSFORD, Hiram

KING, Mary - see CONLY, Charles

KING, Mary - see NIGHTINGALE, P.M.

KING, Mary R. - see RUSSELL, Bartlett

KING, Mary S. - see JACKSON, Edwin

KING, Nathaniel Fitch, 45, d (date not given) at Newtown (7-6/20/10)

KING, Otillia, 30, consort of Gen. Nathaniel King, d 4/11/16 at Hamilton, Madosin County (6-5/4)

KING, Robert P. of Lowville m 11/29/49 Cornelia A. West of Rome in R.; Rev. W.E. Knox (1-12/5)

KING, Rufus A., M.D., 28, d 7/8/37 (severe attack of fever) at his home in Willow Spring, Claiborne County, Mississippi (grad. from Berkshire Medical Institution in Massachusetts in 1833). (from a Claiborne County newspaper, not named) (6-8/9)

KING, Salem T., District Attorney of Hillsdale County, Mich. (formerly of Rensselaerville, Albany Co., NY) m 5/2/37 Ellen J. Stevens, formerly of Litchfield, Mich., at Lima, Livingston Co., NY (6-5/10)

KING, Sarah, 75, d (date not given) at Junius (6-9/26/26)

KING, Storrs L. m 11/1/43 Laura Chamberlin in West Troy; Rev. Z. Phillips (all of West Troy) (5-11/8)

KING, William (Col.), an officer in the US Army "during the late war," d 2/1/26? (or 1/1/26?) near Mobile Alabama (6-2/3)

KING, Young - see GWADOH, Gaw-Heh

KINGMAN, Frances - see LYMAN, Huntington (Rev.)

KINGMAN, Leroy W., ESq. of Spencerville, NY m 5/8/37 Maria Livermore, only dau. of Col. William Livermore, in Spencer, Mass.; Rev. Packard (6-6/19)

KINGMAN, Michael, Esq. of Bristol, Wisc. m 5/15/49 Helen M. Smith, edlest dau. of John, Esq., of Delta, NY; Rev. Fraser (1-5/23)

KINGSBURY, Charles E. (Lieut.), son of Inspector General Jacob Kingsbury of reference below, d 6/8/37 at Fort Mellen, Florida (his long obituary is included) (3-10/12)

KINGSBURY, Fanny - see PARK, Stanton

KINGSBURY, Hannah, 67, wf of Levitt Kingsbury, d 1/7/50 at St. Johnsville (4-1/10)

KINGSBURY, Jacob, 81, formerly Inspector General of the US Army, d 7/1/37 in Franklin, Conn. (a Rev. War soldier) (see also Kingsbury, Charles) (3-10/12)

KINGSLAND, Amelia E. - see JUNE, Andrew

KINNE, Asa, 86, d (date not given) in Preston (7-2/7/10)

KINNEY, Adelaide, 8 months, dau. of A. Kinney of Vernon, d 4/15/41 in V. (see also Kinney, Mary Ann's death) (1-5/11)

KINNEY, Alden, 49, formerly of Vernon, NY, d 10/12/50 in Castalia, Sandusky County, Ohio (typhoid fever) (1-10/30)

KINNEY, John, Esq., m 12/31/40 Lucretia Melinda Mansfield, dau. of David, Esq., in Westmoreland; Rev. Nathaniel Herd (all of Westmoreland) (1-1/5/41)

KINNEY, Laura A. - see MALBURN, William P.

KINNEY, Leonard - his funeral at 9 o'clock 6/16/26 "from his residence in Beaver Street" (6-6/16)

KINNEY, Mary Ann, her age not given, dau. of A. Kinney of Vernon, d 4/25/41 in V. (see also Kinney, Adelaide's death) (1-5/11)

KINNEY, N. Maria - see WADE, Virgil

KINNEYS, D.J. - see MILLER, Clarissa

KINSLEY, Alonzo W. m 1/8/26 Eliza A. Simons; Rev. Dr. Chester (6-1/10)

KINSLEY, Julia and Joseph, ages 8 & 7, children of Lieut. Z.J.D. Kinsley d (date not given) at West Point (scarlet fever) (6-4/12/36)

KINSLEY, Mary, 9, eldest dau of Lieut. Kinsley, d 4/10/36 at West Point (scarlet fever - "she the third of five children victims to this desease within a fortnight") (6-4/16)

KINTER, Ann Maria - see SNYDER, Moses

KIPP, Betsey Mariah, about 29, wf of Reuben, d 3/19/40 in Somers (12-3/24)

KIPP, Catherine M. - see BEERS, William

KIPP, Eliza, 29, wf of Conklin Kipp, d 2/27/40 at New Castle (12-3/3)

KIPP, Isaac, Esq., counsellor at law, 69, d 1/20/37 suddenly in NYC (6-1/25)

KIPP, Jane - see RUSSELL, Thomas D.

KIPP, Rebecca - see DODGE, Henry

KIRBY, Elizabeth (Mrs.), 51, d 4/20/48 in Fort Plain (born in England and a resident of Fort Plain, NY for 19 years) (4-4/29)

KIRK, Andrew B. of Albany m 2/15/49 Mary A. Witbeck, youngest dau. of Thomas, Esq. of Watervliet; Rev. H.A. Raymond (5-2/21)

KIRK, Eliza - see GONSALIS, George

KIRKHAM, Eliza Jane - see PINCKNEY, Henry

KIRKHAM, Susan, 61(?), wf of Zopher Kirkham, d 4/6/42 in Carmel (11-4/7)

KIRKINSTOCK, Martin Armstrong, 3, son of Thomas and Agnes, d 4/5/42 in Newburgh (9-4/9)

KIRKLAND, Charlotte M. - see POST, Samuel

KIRKLAND, John Thornton, son of late General Joseph Kirkland of Utica and brother of Hon. Charles F. Kirkland, d suddenly 10/28/50 at Cleveland, Ohio (1-11/6)

KIRKLAND, Joseph (Gen.) - see TRACY, Charles

KIRKLAND, Joseph, 61, d 5/11/50 in Rome (tumor of the side) (1-5/22)

KIRKLAND, Joseph, Esq., about 50, d 5/11/50 in Rome (enlargement of the spine) (1-5/15)

KIRKLAND, Louisa - see TRACY, Charles

KIRKLAND, Melinda, 31, wf of George T., d 6/27/42 at State Bridge, Madison County (1-7/12)

KIRKPATRICK, ----, 83, d 8/25/42 in Newburgh (9-8/27)

KIRKPATRICK, John, 24, d 3/13/41 in West Troy (lingering illness of consumption) (5-3/17)

KIRKUM, Thomas H. of Carmel m 12/11/39 Philona Horton of Somers in S.; Rev. Nimmo (12-12/17)

KIRTLAND, Charlotte, 15, dau. of late C.P. Kirtland, d (date not given) in Vernon (1-4/17/50)

KIRTLAND, George W. (Col.), formerly of the provisional army, d (date not given) in Port-au-Prince (7-7/4/10)

KISSAM, Amanda K. - see SACKETT, John, Esq.

KISSAM, Elizabeth - see UNDERHILL, William

KISSAM, Melissa M. - see ALLEN, Charles H.

KISSAM, Richard S., M.D. - see ALLEN, Charles H.

KITCHEL, Josiah - see SWEZEY, Jane

KITTLE, Adam, 24, d 6/17/37 in Albany (funeral "this afternoon" from the home of his father, 32 Chapel Street) (6-6/19)

KITTLE, Ann, 20, wf of Adam, d 1/15/36 in Albany (6-1/18)

KITTLE, Gertrude Ann - see FORCE, Alonzo

KITTRIGE, George m Charity Welton, both of Rome; Rev. H.C. Vogell (1-1/11/42)

KLAPP, Nancy G. - see ADRIANCE, Joseph T.

KLINE, Henry m 9/15/49 Elizabeth Keener in Saugerties; Rev. P.C. Oakley (all of Saugerties) (8-9/22)

KLING, Anna Dorothy, 4, dau. of John L. and Eliza, d 12/8/49 in Fort Plain (4-12/13)

KLING, Elizabeth - see NUANS, Hiram E.

KLING, Harriett - see DE GARMO, Abram

KLING, Hiram H. of Utica m 9/22/47 Delphia U. Nurse of Frankfort at F.; P.C. Grosvenor (1-9/24)

KLING, William of Troy, Wisconsin m 9/18/47 M. Ann Cummings, eldest dau. of John of New York Mills, at N.Y.M.; Rev. N.D. Graves (1-9/24)

KLOCK, Magdelin - see DILLENBACH, Alexander

KLOCK, Margaret Ann - see MOYER, David Henry

KLOCK, mary C. - see LIPE, Rufus

KLOCK, Nancy - see ZIMMERMAN, John

KLOCK, Pamela - see WARNER, Bingham

KLOCK, Silas m 9/28/37 Cornelia Ann Abbott in Little Falls, George Petrie, Esq. (3-9/28)

KNAPP, Alvin, 33, d 12/26/41 in Newburgh (9-1/1/42)

KNAPP, Caroline P. (Miss) of NYC d (date not given) at the home of Rev. Marshall in Peekskill (11-8/24/41)

KNAPP, Catharine - see ECKER, William

KNAPP, Charlotte - see HORTON, Jacob

KNAPP, Clarissa - see HORN, Patrick

KNAPP, Edwin G. - see SYLVESTER, John R.

KNAPP, Emily - see SPRINGSTED, John

KNAPP, Ezra (Deacon), 62(?), d 12/7/41 in Westmoreland (1-12/21)

KNAPP, Jacob Frost, 42, d 11/13/43 in Yorktown (11-11/21)

KNAPP, Mary Hazins, 19, dau. of Hubbell Knapp of Albany, d 4/18/37 (funeral from home of her father at 52 Columbia Street) (6-4/20)

KNAPP, Moses, 64, d 7/7/39 at his home in Yorktown (12-7/23)

KNAPP, Nathaniel, Esq., 45, postmaster at Round Hill, Greenwich, CT, d 1/4/36 in NYC (6-1/13)

KNAPP, Ruth, about 50, wf of Reuben, d 1/7/40 in Bedford (12-1/14)

KNAPP, Samuel of Bedford m 1/1/39 Catharine Fish, dau of James of New Castle at N.C.; Rev. Rice (12-1/15)

KNAPP, Susan M. - see LYON, George

KNAPP, Thomas L., Esq. of Brownville m 3/24/35 Mary Averill, dau of James Averill, Esq. of Ogdensburgh, at St. John's Church in O.; Rev. F. Termaine (6-5/5)

KNAPP, Tracy S, Esq. of New Berlin m 3/3/35 Miss Ann Skinner, dau of Major S. Brown of Brownsville at St. Paul's Church, Brownsville, Jefferson Co; Rev. A.C. Treadway (6-3/14)

KNAPP, Urania C. - see SYLVESTER, John R.

KNEARKAM, ----, 18 motnhs, dau. of Peter of Russia, NY (scalded to death by the overturning of a tea kettle) (3-11/28)

KNICKERBACKER, Abram V., formerly of Troy, d 8/12/47 in Chicago (dropsey on the chest) (5-8/25)

KNICKERBACKER, Edwin, m 2/26/35 Eliza Ann Beckwith, eldest dau of Col. Nathan Beckwith, at Red Hook; Rev. A.N. Kittle (6-3/6)

KNICKERBACKER, Herman m 5/5/35 Sarah Grosebeck, dau of Capt. John W, in Schaghticoke, Rev. H.M. Boyde (6-5/14)

KNICKERBACKER, Margaret - see WALBRIDGE, Henry T.

KNIFFEN, Almira Eliza - see BARRY, Standish, 3rd

KNIFFEN, Charlotte - see AINSWORTH, De La

KNIFFIN, Alanson of Carmel m 1/16/39 Harriet Young, of Stamford, CT in S. (12-1/29)

KNIFFIN, David m 1/29/39 Unis Sarles, both of New Castle Corners, at N.C.C. (12-2/12)

KNIFFIN, John - see BARRY, Standish, 3rd

KNIFFIN, Julia - see DORNE, Lewis (Col.)

KNIFLIN, Amos, 87, d 2/6/42 in Southeast (11-2/15)

KNIGHT, Ann Maria - see LAWRENCE, William C.

KNIGHT, George I. - see BROWN, Thomas Yardley (Col.)

KNIGHT, Peter of West Troy m 4/10/41 Alida Heestreet of Cohoes in C.; Rev. J.M. Van Buren (5-4/14)

KNILL, Tiney, 27, wf of Rev. John Knill, pastor of the Episcopal Church in Little Falls and second dau. of Samuel Bont, Esq., d 9/19/37 at her father's home in Broadalbin (a severe and protracted illness of several months") (3-9/28)

KNOWER, B. - see VAN KLEECK, C.

KNOWER, Benjamin, 63, d 8/23/39 at his home in Watervliet (5-8/28)

KNOWER, Benjamin, Esq. of Albany m 6/23/36 Sophia P. Castle, dau of late William Shaw Castle of NYC, in NYC; Rev. Dr. Ferris (6-6/27)

KNOWER, Charles, 21, son of Benjamin, Esq. and brother-in-law and private secretary of Gov. Marcy, d 10/31 at Albany (6-11/1)

KNOWER, George Sidney, 20, d 4/1/37 (6-4/3)

KNOWER, Henry, 23, brother-in-law to the late Governor Marcy, d 11/20/41 at Albany (11-12/7)

KNOWER, Sarah - see GROOT, A.C.

KNOWLES, William m 1/3/50 Matilda J. Cole, both of West Troy; Rev. O.H. Gregory (double ceremony - see BUCKLIN, Wesley) (5-1/9)

KNOX, Eliza - see WARNER, Leonard R.

KNOX, Eliza A. - see WILLIAMS, Thomas, Jr.

KNOX, J.R. (Dr.) of NYC m 11/30/36 Mary Coxe, dau of late Robert Holliday of Fayetteville, NC, at the Astor House in NYC; Right Rev. Bishop Onderdonk (6-12/3)

KNOX, Mary, about 93, widow of John, d 5/3/50 in North Salem (10-5/8)

KNOX, Sarah Adelaide - see STRONG, William N.

KNOX, Sylvanus K., 18, son of Joseph of Floyd, d 6/6/41 in Rome (1-6/8)

KNOX, William Frederick, 1, son of Rev. W.E. and Alice of Knox, d 10/18/50 in Rome (1-10/23)

KNOX, William H. of Salisbury m 6/29/40 Louisa Leavett of Stratford in Little Falls; W. Brooks, Esq. (3-7/2)

KRAUSE, Christina - see ZIEGLER, Frederick

KRAZENBERG, Jacob m 11/21/41 Martha Elizabeth Shafer, both emigrants from Germany, now of Little Falls, at the Stone Church in Little Falls (3-12/2)

KROMER, Lavina - see WATSON, Charles

KRUM, Isaac B., 1, son of Isaac B., d 8/9/49 in Kingston (8-8/18)

KRUM, Maria - see SPARLING, George

KRUMBHAAR, Lewis, representative from Philadelphia, d 2/1/36 at Harrisburg, PA (6-2/9)

KUGLER, Mathew, 77, d 8/14/35 in Albany (6-8/17)

KUHAUFT, Catharine Elizabeth - see HEINGMANN, Charles

KUHN, Theresa - see DURHOLZ, John

KUMMEL, Henry E. of Cassel, Germany, merchant, m 5/12/36 Susan Mc kay of NYC in NYC; Rev. W. Crieghton (3-5/26)

LA GRANGE, Conrad of New Scotland m 3/9/35 Ann Alida Holmes of Albany; Rev. Webb (6-3/14)

LACEY, Maria A. - see SMITH, Horatio Hale

LACKEY(?), Catharine (Mrs.), 90, d 12/6/15 at Martinsburgh, Virginia (6-1/20/16)

LACQUE, Mary - see BENOIT, Joseph

LACY, Harriet - see MUDGE, Alva

LADD, Margaret - see WILLIAMS, Otis P.

LADEN, Miss - see JAMISON, William

LADUE, Samuel m 9/12/50 Sarah A. Hakes, dau. of J.H.; Rev. S. Frazer (all of Watervliet) (5-9/18)

LAGRILL, Louis m 12/24/39 Susan Purdy, dau. of Hunt Purdy; James Banks, Esq. (all of Sing Sing) (12-12/31)

LAINDELL, John A. of firm of Laindell & Fassett of Albany m 8/30/36 Mary Russell, dau of Thomas, Esq., of Pine Grove at P.G.; Rev. Dr. Sprague (6-9/1)

LAING, Thomas, 67, of Northumberland, Saratoga Co., d 3/7/35 (after a short but painful illness) (6-3/11)

LAINHART, George m 1/14/35 Ann Dollars, both of Guilderland; Rev. Dr. Ferris (see marriage of Anthony Van Slyck adjacent in same newspaper, same date) (6-1/17)

LAKE, Isaac m 1/6/42 Sarah W. Treadway in Warren; Job Bronson, Esq. (3-1/13)

LAMB, Frances - see LARNED, Allen G.

LAMB, George W. m 9/22/38 Marana L. Ainsworth at Cohoes; L.V.K. Vandemark, Esq. (5-9/26)

LAMB, Harriet P. - see STORES, Hiram M.

LAMB, William J., editor of the Lansingburgh Democrat m 3/25/46 Maria Low in Lansingburgh; Rev. W.W. Moore (all of Lansingburgh) (5-4/1)

LAMBERT, John m 6/21/49 Maria Dunckel, dau. of Abram, Esq., in Frey's Bush; Rev. Jacob I. Timmerman (all of Frey's Bush) (4-6/28)

LAMBERT, Sally - see REYNOLDS, Edward

LAMBY, F. of West Troy m 3/18/47 Rebecca Robbins of Troy in Cohoes; Rev. Frost (5-3/24)

LAMERAUK, Catharine - see RADLEY, James

LAMPHER, Robert, 60, d 10/19/39 suddenly in Ohio (heart disease) (father of 20 children, 15 living) (3-11/28)

LAMPHERE, Ann - see BRIGGS, David

LAMPHERE, Margaret E. - see CARPENTER, Nathaniel

LAMPHIER, Richardson m 2/18/41 Mary Roberts, both of Rome; E.C. Vogell (1-2/23)

LAMPMAN, Annis, 22, wf of A.P. Lampman, d 12/29/46 at Oneida Valley (1-1/8/47)

LAMPMAN, Betsey E. - see MERRILL, John

LANCASTER, Cyrus, late principal of Lyndon Academy, Vt., m 4/11/35 Mrs. Rebecca Wilson of Albany; Rev. R.T. Welsh (6-4/15)

LANDON, John G. m 6/24/49 Martina Egger, both of High Falls, in Rondout (8-7/7)

LANDT, Matilda - see LANDT, Montgomery

LANDT, Montgomery m 1/14/49 Matilda Landt; Rev. N.H. Cornell (all of Saugerties) (8-1/27)

LANE, Gilbert, 26, son of Cornelius M., d 11/15/50 in Canajoharie (4-11/21)

LANE, Henry R., M.D., m 9/15/36 Julia O. Gary, dau of Joseph, Esq., in Troy at St. Paul's Church; Rev. David Hutler (all of Troy) (6-9/22)

LANE, Julia M., wf of Matthew & dau. of Joseph Russell, Esq. of Troy, d 2/15/37 in Troy (6-2/13)

LANE, Margaret Anna - see BELKNAP, Chauncey F.

LANE, Mary S. - see GRIFFEN, Gilbert

LANE, Noah, 77, d 6/16/10 at Lyme, Conn. (7-6/27)

LANE, Phebe H. - see PURDY, Charles

LANE, Rowen Sears, 1, son of Andrew, d 12/22/36 in Ohio (fell into a kettle of boiling soap) (3-1/5/37)

LANE, Savrin E. of West Troy m 6/24/44 Elizabeth Tell, eldest dau. of Capt. Philip R., at Fawn River, St. Joseph's County, Michigan; Rev. Benjamin Ogden (5-7/10)

LANG, J. - see URTICK, Stephen C.

LANG, John, Esq., 66, proprietor of the New York Gazette, d 3/17/36 (from the Courier & Enquirer) (6-3/21)

LANG, John, Esq., 67, editor of the New York Gazette, d 3/17/36 in NYC (3-3/24)

LANGDON, Allen m 5/16/44 Margaret Johnson, dau. of Seldon Johnson, in Verona; Rev. Brainard (all of Verona) (1-5/28)

LANGFORD, Philip B. m 10/10/49 Mary A. Thomas, dau. of Briggs W. Thomas, Esq. of Utica in U.; Rev. Dickson (1-10/17)

LANGWORTHY, Abigail, 56, relict of late Rev. Elisha P. of Ballston Spa, d 11/16/36 in Rochester (6-11/22)

LANING, Joseph m 12/21/43 Mrs. Abby Fish in Little Falls; Rev. C.W. Leet (3-12/28)

LANING, Lavina - see HUDDLE, John G.

LANKTON, Polly, 74, widow of Joel, d 1/13/42 in Little Falls (This couple moved there from New Haven, Conn., 42 years earlier) (3-1/27)

LANMAN, James (Hon.) of Norwich, Conn. m (date not given) Mrs. Mary Judith Benjamin, widow of Park Benjamin, at Boston (6-11/3/26)

LANSING, A. Ten Eyck, 46, d 2/10/42 at his home in Manheim (3-2/17)

LANSING, A.F. - see FOSTER, Chandler

LANSING, A.Y. m 4/26/36 Eliza J. Van Alstyne, dau of M. Van Alstyne, Esq.; Rev. Kirk (all of Albany) (6-4/28)

LANSING, A.Y., Esq. m 4/26/36 Eliza J. Van Alstyne, dau of M. Van Alstyne,

Esq.; Rev. Kirk (all of Albany) (6-4/27)

LANSING, Alida - see BRONK, Robert

LANSING, Ann M., 28, dau. of Levinus A. Lansing of Watervliet, d 5/22/45 at her father's home (5-6/4)

LANSING, Catalina - see FOSTER, Chandler

LANSING, Catharine Ann - see ROSS, Jeduthan G.

LANSING, Cornelius T. of Watervliet m 6/30/46 Caroline Steer, dau. of Jacob of Albany, in A.; Rev. Dr. Wyckoff (5-7/8)

LANSING, Eleanor - see WILLIAMS, Henry

LANSING, Elizabeth - see RICHARDSON, John

LANSING, Elizabeth, 16, dau. of Garret I., d 8/4/48 (see LANSING, Margaret) (5-8/23)

LANSING, Evert m 9/29/42 Julian Ann Kane, both of Watervliet, at West Troy; Rev. Benjamin I. Lane (5-10/12)

LANSING, Hannah (Mrs.) - see LANSING, John I., Esq.

LANSING, Harriet - see HILL, Gifford A.

LANSING, Harriet, wf of Garret Lansing, formerly of Herkimer, d 2/21/39 in Albany (3-2/28)

LANSING, Helen Ten Eyck, 4 months, youngest child of Frederick, Esq., d 12/2/36 in Little Falls (3-12/8)

LANSING, Jacob - see BENEDICT, Susan

LANSING, Jacob A. (Rev.) of Watervliet m 9/28/42 Maria Lansing of West Troy in W.T.; Rev. O.H. Gregory (5-10/5)

LANSING, James, Esq. - see VEEDER, Henry

LANSING, Jane, 58, wf of Abraham, d 6/19/26 in Albany ("affectionate wife and tender mother") (6-6/23)

LANSING, John - his funeral "this afternoon at 3 o'clock from his late residence in Lawrence Street" (6-6/13/37)

LANSING, John Douglas, 6, son of A.T.F. Lansing, d 10/16/39 in Manheim (3-10/17)

LANSING, John I., Esq., 83, d 2/2/49 in Glen. His wife, Hannah, 77, d 2/11/49 in Glen (4-4/5)

LANSING, Levinus L., Esq. of West Troy m 11/17/46 Margaretta Lawrence, dau. of late Charles Kane Lawrence, d 11/17/46 at Waterford; Rev. Jacob A. Lansing (5-11/18)

LANSING, Margaret A. - see SIMS, William P.

LANSING, Margaret, 45, wf of Garret I., d 7/16/48 in Watervliet (see LANSING, Elizabeth) (5-8/23)

LANSING, Maria - see LANSING, Jacob A. (Rev.)

LANSING, Permelia - see MILLS, Deloss

LANSING, Rachael - see VEEDER, Henry

LANSING, Stephen m 10/17/50 Rebecca Wolfe, both of Pittstown; Rev. O.H. Gregory (5-10/23)

LANSING, William G., 9, only son of Garret T. and Lucy, d 2/24/38 in West Troy (5-3/7)

LANSING, William, 20, son of Abraham V.P., d 8/5/48 in Watervliet (5-8/16)

LANY, Mary - see SEGUR, J.W.B.

LAPE, William (Major), 26, d 8/27/36 at Greenbush (6-9/2)

LAPE, William m 4/22/47 Mary Jane Hagadorn, both of West Troy; Rev.

Houghtaling (5-5/5)

LAPPON, Maria, 3, dau. of William, Esq., d 11/22/09 in Herkimer (2-11/30)

LARABY, Elizabeth - see GILLSON, Albert

LARCOM, Amos, 72, d 11/21/48 in Troy (apoplexy) (5-11/29)

LARCUM, George Henry, 26, of firm of Larcum and Tucker of West Troy, d
8/9/48 in Troy (5-8/16)

LARKIN, J.W. m 6/10/46 Aleina Williams in Rome; Rev. H.C. Vogell (all of
Rome) (1-6/16)

LARKIN, Lucretia - see STEVENS, Jacob

LARKIN, Mary - see HIGGINS, James Madison

LARKIN, Mary Ann - see MONROE, Philetus

LARNED, Allen G. m 4/30/38 Frances Lamb, dau. of E.S. Lamb, at Salisbury
(3-5/3)

LARNED, Benjamin, 59, d 3/19/39 in Newport (severe illness of three months)
(3-3/28)

LARNED, George, Esq. of Detroit, son of Col. S. Larned, late of the US Army, m
3/12/16 Emily M. Watson, dau. of Elkanah Watson, Esq. of Albany; Rev.
Chester (6-3/16)

LARRABEE, Timothy, Esq., 79, d (date not given) at Windham (7-2/7/10)

LASHER, Catherine - see SWART, Chancy M.

LASHER, Eliza - see SNYDER, Elias

LASHER, Elizabeth - see SHOEMAKER, Henry

LASHER, Lucinda - see GRASSFIELD, John H.

LASSELS, Caroline - see MYERS, Reuben

LATHROP, Caroline A. - see REMINGTON, Philo (Col.)

LATHROP, Deloss, Esq., of Buffalo, 30, d 5/29/35 at home of Dyer Lathrop in
Albany (6-5/30)

LATHROP, John (Rev.), D.D., 76, Pastor of the Second Church in Boston, d (date
not given) in Boston "after a short illness" (6-1/13/16)

LATHROP, Samuel - see SPRAGUE, Mary L.

LATHROP, Stanton D., 4, son of Anderson and Marinda, d 9/18/49 at Van
Hornesville (4-9/27)

LATOURETTE, John of Newburgh m 3/19/42 Maria Kanevelle of White Lake at
W.L. in Sullivan County; Rev. Mc Laren (9-3/26)

LATOURETTE, John, 19, son of Jacob, d 11/10/41 in Newburgh (9-11/13)

LAVENDER, Thomas m 1/17/49 Alida Jane Vandemark in Watervliet; Rev.
Pitcher (5-1/24)

LAVOIR, John of Montreal, Canada East m Marie Liberte of West Troy in W.T.;
Rev. J.C. Burroughs (5-3/21)

LAW, Edward m (date not given) Lucy Williams in Canandaigua (6-5/15/16)

LAWPAUGH, Solomon m 11/23/37 Catharine Willsey, both of Westerlo; Charles
Hyndman, Esq. (6-12/21)

LAWRANCE, Coonradt m 12/7/49 Ellen Cochran, both of Rome; H.C. Vogell
(1-1/9/50)

LAWRENCE, Frances Maria, 1, youngest dau. of Lewis and Margaret, d 7/21/49 at
Fort Benjamin in Warwarsing (8-8/18)

LAWRENCE, Garret K., physician and botanist in the United Society called
Shakers, d 1/24/37 at New Lebanon after a severe and protracted illness
(6-1/28)

LAWRENCE, George m 10/25/37 Leonora Atwood, both of Lansingburgh, in L.;
Rev. E.B. Crandall (5-11/1)

LAWRENCE, Gertrude - see GARRET, Lucius B.

LAWRENCE, John H. m Mary Cole, both of West Troy; Rev. Houghtaling (5-9/12)

LAWRENCE, John Mc Dougal, Esq. of NYC d 5/22/35 at Clayton, Jefferson Co.
("probably apoplexy") (was owner of a tract of land near Clayton and had
arrived a day or two prior to his death) (from Sacketts Harbor Courier)
(6-5/30)

LAWRENCE, Joseph of West Troy m 5/14/48 Mary Carr of Cohoes; Rev.
Houghtaling (5-5/24)

LAWRENCE, Lewis H. (Major) m 10/24/38 Frances A. Vernan, dau. of William,
at Mechanicville, Saratoga Co; Rev. Reuben Hubbard (all of
Mechanicville) (12-10/30)

LAWRENCE, Margaretta - see LANSING, Levinus L.

LAWRENCE, Mary M. - see BORTLE, Robert

LAWRENCE, Stephen, 80(?), d 12/21/38 at Carmel (12-12/25)

LAWRENCE, William C. of Hyde Park m 12/13/26 Ann Maria Knight, step-dau.
of B.C. Allen, deputy sheriff of Albany County, in Albany; Rev. Leonard
(6-12/19)

LAWRENCE, William of Troy m 10/28/41 Hannah Kennedy of Schenectady in S.;
Rev. Dr. Nott (5-11/3)

LAWRENCE, Willliam of NYC m 1/7/39 Mary Ann Merritt, dau of Daniel of New
Castle, in N.C. (12-1/15)

LAWRENCE, Windsor m 12/29/41 Louisa R. Chaplin,dau. od Dr. J. Chaplin, in
Vernon; Rev. Adams (1-1/11/42)

LAWSON, John m 5/31/50 Margaret Patterson; Rev. T.F. Wyckoff (all of West
Troy) (5-6/5)

LAWSON, Laurence m 8/12/48 Abigail Foster, both of Waterford, in West Troy;
Rev. Seymour (5-8/16)

LAWSON, Susanna - see CORLISS, Albert H.

LAWTON, Andrew F., about 4 months, son of James C., d 10/9/39 in Herkimer (he
was the only surviving child) (3-10/17)

LAWTON, Charles D., counsellor at law, m 6/8/37 Amelia Houghtaling, dau. of
James Houghtaling, M.D., at Clyde; Rev. Joseph Fisher (all of Clyde)
(6-6/27)

LAWTON, Eliza Ann - see MERCER, Norman C.

LAWTON, Henry, Esq., of firm of Doty and Lawton m 7/2/49 Adelia Ann Parker,
dau. of I.S., Esq., in Rome; Rev. W.E. Knox (1-7/4)

LAWTON, J. Rathbun, of Great Barrington, Mass. m 3/12/46 Sarah Adams, dau. of
Horace of Rome, NY; Rev. G.S. Boardman (1-3/24)

LE BRETON, John, merchant, m 3/23/26 Eliza Sanford, eldest dau. of Hon.
Nathan Sanford; Rev. Proal (bride and groom of Albany) (6-3/31)

LE COUNT, Eliza Ann - see ANDERSON, Joseph

LE ROY, Herman - see NEWBOLD, Catharine A.

LEACH, James S. (Col.), attorney at law, m 10/20/36 Caroline White, dau of Asa,
Esq., at Cortland; Rev. J.I. Foot (all of C.) (6-11/8)

LEAKE, Mary T. - see DELAVAN, H.A.

LEAN, Louisa - see DERBY, Richard C.

LEARHARD, Charles of West Troy m 3/18/40 Ann M. Robinson of Sing Sing at

West Troy; Rev. O.H. Gregory (12-3/24)

LEARNED, Amaretta H. - see MATHER, Alfred

LEARNED, Charles G. of Waterford m 9/11/38 Maria Raymond of Troy (5-9/19)

LEARNED, Emily, 2, dau. of George and Emma, d 10/15/44 in West Troy (5-10/23)

LEARNED, Jane Ann - see GAULKINS, John L.

LEARNED, Jonas, about 15, son of Edward, Esq., d 12/2/38 in the town of Watervliet (5-12/5)

LEARNED, Mary Caroline, (age not given), dau. of Edward (Jr.) and Caroline, d 8/20/50 in Watervliet (funeral from the family residence) (5-8/21)

LEARNED, S.E. - see MC ALPINE, W.J.

LEATHERS, Isaac m 2/25/50 Electa T. Gifford, both of West Troy, in W.T.; Rev. J.C. Burroughs (5-2/27)

LEAVENS, Joshua, 84, formerly of Glens Falls, but for many years of Mobile, AL, d 6/23/35 in NYC (6-7/4)

LEAVENWORTH, Hannah, 78, wf of Col. Leavenworth, d 3/16/36 (funeral at 3 o'clock from the family residence in Bethlehem "near the M & M Rail Road") (6-3/18)

LEAVENWORTH, Jesse, Esq., 86, (father of Col. Henry Leavenworth of the 3rd regiment, US Infantry) d 11/21/26 at Sackets Harbor (was an officer in the French War and the Rev. War) (6-12/21)

LEAVETT, Louisa - see KNOX, William H.

LEDYARD, Benjamin (Gen.) - see CUYLER, Margaret

LEDYARD, Catharine - see VAN RENSSELAER, Cortlandt

LEDYARD, Isaac (Major) - see CRANE, Elizabeth

LEE(?), Elizabeth - see OWEN, Jehiel

LEE, Ann - see HOTALING, Martin C.

LEE, Augusta Isabella - see THOMPSON, John W.

LEE, Catharine - see STRANG, Fowler

LEE, Charles G. m 9/28/35 Caroline P. Henry, dau of Dr. J.D. Henry, at Rochester; Rev. T. Edwards (all of Rochester) (6-11/3)

LEE, Charles of Milo m 9/29/35 Mary M. Hall of Palmyra in Palmyra at the home of A. Hendee, Esq.; Rev. Shumway (6-10/10)

LEE, Charles, son of Hon. Joshua, of Penn Yan m 9/29/35 Mary M. Hall, eldest dau of late Ambrose Hall, Esq., of Palmyra, in P; Rev. G.R.H. Shumway (6-10/6)

LEE, Elizabeth - see OWEN, Johiel

LEE, F.A. m 9/24/35 Anne C. Bowers, dau of John, Esq, at Lakelands (near Cooperstown); Rev. Alfred E. Campbell (6-9/29)

LEE, Fanny - see TELLER, James W.

LEE, James (Dr.) of Troy m 12/6/40 Mercy Ann Haight of Malta; Rev. Poor of Saratoga (5-12/9)

LEE, John m Hannah Jane Taylor 12/24/34; Rev. H. Meeker (all of Albany) (6-1/1/35)

LEE, John, son of Ebenezer, d 9/16/42 at Annsville (11-9/22)

LEE, Mercy Ann, 31, wf of James Lee, M.D., d 9/8/49 at Mechanicville ("Poughkeepsie papers please copy") (5-9/12)

LEE, Oliver H. m 8/17/36 Jannette Parker, dau of late Philip S., Esq.; Rev. Dr. Springer (6-8/18)

LEE, Thomas J., Esq., formerly of Royalton, MA d (date not given) at Belfast, ME (died from poison of lead contained in brown sugar used in his family (other family members and several other families in Calais have thus died (sugar analysed and found to contain much acetate of lead mixed no doubt at time of manufacture) (from the Lowell Courier) (6-6/22)

LEE, William m 2/7/26 Anna Maria Beekman; Rev. Van Vechten (all of Schenectady) (6-2/21)

LEET, Huldah, 69, mother of Rev. C.W. Leet, Pastor of the Methodist Church in Little Falls, d 6/27/43 at home of her son-in-law, Solomon Hess in Verona (3-7/13)

LEFFERTS, Thomas, Esq., 49, counsellor at law, d 3/28/37 at Rochester, NY (6-4/10)

LEFFINGWELL, Charity (Mrs.), 73, d (date not given) at Norwich, Conn. (7-8/2/09)

LEFFINGWELL, Charles - see BENNETT, Eliza

LEFFINGWELL, Charles Lavius, 6 months, only child of N. Hyde and L. Zenana Leffingwell, d 11/18 41 in Rome (1-11/23)

LEFFINGWELL, Harriet - see SAYLES, Harriet

LEFURGIE, Eliza Ann - see DEVOE, Jasper

LEGAL, Katharine - see JOHNSON, William H.

LEGG, Maria, (age blurred), wf of Cornelius, d 8/7/49 at Flatbush (8-8/18)

LEGGAT, Jane Mc Dowall, infant dau. of W. Leggat, d 9/28/37 (funeral 9/29/from her father's home, 24 Beaver Street) (6-9/29)

LEGGETT, John N. m 12/31/38 Augusta Sophia Wheeler (dau. of Mead Wheeler, Esq.), both of Mount Pleasant, at the home of the bride's father; Rev. James V. Henry of Sing Sing (12-1/8/39)

LEGGETT, Reuben, 36, d (date not given) in NYC (6-8/22/26)

LEHMEIER, Benjamin of Rome m 6/13/49 Helen Oppenheimer of NYC in NYC; Right Rev. Dr. M. Lilienthal (1-6/20)

LEIGH, Mary Susan - see ROBINSON, Conway

LELAND, David Warren, Esq. of Charleston, SC m 10/21/35 Maria Wilkinson, dau of Hezekiah Howe, Esq. of Cohoes, NY at Trinity Church at Boston; Rev. D. Wainwright (6-10/30)

LELAND, Z.A. (Hon.) of Steuben County m 11/1/43 Abby E. Porter, dau. of late Elijah Porter, M.D., of Waterford, in W.; Rev. Smith (5-11/8)

LEMNA, Andrew m 1/7/47 Mary Blouin, both of Lansingburgh, in West Troy; Rev. Houghtaling (5-1/13)

LENT, Andrew Jackson m 3/27/42 Rosetta Lent, dau of Capt. Joseph, in Cortlandt; Rev. De Vinne (11-3/31)

LENT, Augustus m 11/9/35 Mariam Secor in Yorktown; Rev. Loring (11-11/17)

LENT, Elcy, wf of Abraham, d 11/10/33 (consumption) (11-11/12)

LENT, Hercules m 6/20/34 Hetty Montrose; Rev. R. Kirkwood (all of Cortlandt Town) (11-7/8)

LENT, Isaac, 36 (?), d 12/25/41 in Cortlandt (11-12/28)

LENT, Isaac, Senior, 99 d 12/25/1841 in Peekskill (11-12/28)

LENT, John, d 8/16/33 in Peekskill (consumption) (11-8/20)

LENT, Lavina - see MONTROSS, Ellison

LENT, Margaret - see STORMS, Abraham

LENT, Rachael, 18 months, dau. of Paul H., d 2/20/40 in Sing Sing (12-3/10)

LENT, Rachel - see THORP, Henry
LENT, Rosetta - see LENT, Andrew Jackson
LENT, Sarah - see DENIKE, Jacob
LENT, Smith, about 40, d 4/5/42 in Carmel (11-4/7)
LENT, Stephen, the 2nd, m 2/23/35 Maria Garritson; Drake Conklin, Esq. (all of
    Cortlandt) (11-3/31)
LENT, William H. m (date not given) Jane Brown, dau of Henry, deceased; Rev.
    Dr. Westbrook (all of Cortlandt Town) (11-9/22)
LEON(?), Winthrop, 11, son of Pedro, d 7/25/42 in Newburgh (9-7/30)
LEONARD, Asaph D. m 7/19/26 Julia Worden, both of Auburn, in St. Peter's
    Church; Rev. Lacey (6-7/25)
LEONARD, Benjamin of Rome m 5/30/44 Anna Maria Perry, dau. of late Isaac W.
    of Skaneateles, at the home of Dr. Morell at Borodino, Onondaga County;
    Rev. Clark (1-6/4)
LEONARD, Charles Van Vechten, 46, d 1/7/37 at Lansingburgh (friends of Maria
    Leonard are invited to attend her deceased son's funeral from the Phoenix
    Hotel in Lansingburgh (6-1/9)
LEONARD, Cholett (sic), 2 months, son of Alfred, d 6/30/48 in Fort Plain (4-7/6)
LEONARD, Edward A., formerly of Lansingburgh. d 8/26/37 at Fort Jessup,
    Louisiana (6-9/22)
LEONARD, F.B. of Lansingburgh m 5/25/35 Margaret Cornelia Nichols, dau of
    late Hon, John Nichols of White Springs, at Trinity Church in Geneva; Rev.
    Dr. Mason (6-6/11)
LEONARD, Helen L. - see WILLIAMS, E.
LEONARD, Helen L. - see WILLIAMS, E.
LEONARD, Jacob m 9/17/46 Jemima Veeder, both of Albany, in West Troy; Rev.
    Houghtaling (5-9/23)
LEONARD, Jemima - see RICHARDSON, James
LEONARD, Mary C. - see ORELUP, Azor(?)
LEONARD, Mary Elizabeth, 26(?), wf of Alfred, d 4/21/48 in Fort Plain (4-4/27)
LEONARD, Silas Wright, 9 months, son of Mr. and Mrs. Charles Leonard, d
    9/17/47 (5-9/22)
LEPAREUX, Alexander m 2/10/49 Mary Underhill, both of Bristol, in B. at the
    home of David Volk; Rev. N.H. Cornell (8-2/17)
LEROW, John m (date not given) Betsy Williams at Hartwick (6-5/15/16)
LEROY, Harriet Banyer - see WHITE, Campbell B.
LEROY, Jacob - see WHITE, Campbell B.
LESTER, Albert (Hon.) of Canandaigua m 9/17/50 Frances M. Morse of Grand
    Rapids, Mich.; Rev. F. Cummings (1-10/2)
LESTER, Charlotte Greenfeaf, 6, dau of Ezra, Esq., d 10/23/36 at Rensselaerville
    (6-10/28)
LEVE, James m 7/6/41 Margaret Petrie; Rev. Loveys (all of Little Falls) (3-9/9)
LEVENSON(?), Peter, 60, d 7/10/49 in Watervliet (5-7/18)
LEVERIDGE, John, about 80, d 10/29/41 in Cortlandt Town (11-11/9)
LEVERIDGE, John, Esq. of NYC m (date not given) Adaline Creemer of
    Woodbridge in Newark (6-5/22/16)
LEVERT, Henry s., M.D. m (date not given) Octavia V. Walton, dau of Col.
    George Walton, late of Florida, at Mobile ("the bride was celebrated belle
    at Saratoga last summer") (6-3/2/36)

LEVETT, J.C. of firm of Hyde & Leverett, Palmyra, NY m 6/8/37 Electa A.
Thayer, dau. of Joel E., Esq. of Buffalo, in B.; Rev. C.S. Hawks (6-6/14)
LEVINGS, ----, 35, wf of Peter B., d 3/20/46 in Watervliet (5-3/25)
LEVINGS, Catharine Jane - see SMITH, George
LEVINGS, Noah, Senior, 79, father of Rev. Noah Levings, D.D., of the Methodist
Church, Albany, d 11/17/41 at Lockport (5-12/8)
LEWIS, ---- (Mrs.), wf of Peter I., d 7/19/49 in Saugerties (8-7/21)
LEWIS, Amelia G., 24, wf of Wesley and eldest dau. of Joseph Mount, Esq., d
2/2/49 in Saugerties (8-2/10)
LEWIS, Amey, 48, formerly of Bristol. Conn., d 3/2/26 in Albany (lingering
consumption) (6-3/3)
LEWIS, Andrew of Athens m 6/26/36 Laura A. Raymond, dau of Elias of Athens,
at New Baltimore; Rev. Levi L. Hill (6-6/30)
LEWIS, Ann (Mrs.), 95, d 6/17/43 in Danube (3-6/22)
LEWIS, Ann Maria - see PEWTRESS, J.B.
LEWIS, Augustus m 10/4/49 Hannah Rich, both of Woodstock; Rev. Alex Goolick
(8-10/20)
LEWIS, Betsey (Mrs.), about 55, d 10/14/49 in Carmel (10-10/17)
LEWIS, Clara A. - see FIELD, Samuel
LEWIS, Cornelia - see EVANS, William S.
LEWIS, Daniel W., Esq., 75, late of Geneva, d 6/17/37 at the home of S.K.
Grosbenor, Esq., in Buffalo (6-6/24)
LEWIS, Edwin d 5/13/50 in Sullivan, Madison County (1-5/29)
LEWIS, George W., 1 year, youngest son of G.H. and A. Lewis, d 7/3/43 in West
Troy (5-7/5)
LEWIS, George, 4, only son of John and Elizabeth H., d 7/22/39 in Warren (scarlet
fever) (3-7/25)
LEWIS, Harriet Elizabeth, 14, only dau. of B. Lewis, d 9/24/37 in Little Falls
(3-9/28)
LEWIS, Henry - see GATES, Oliver
LEWIS, James m (date not given) Hepzibah Tarbox in Lynn, Mass. (married four
times in the same coat and "it is a pretty good coat yet" (from the Lynn
Mirror) (6-6/9/26)
LEWIS, Jane Vanderpool, wf of Peter I. Lewis, d 12/16/26 in Kinderhook (6-12/22)
LEWIS, Joseph m 7/6/43 Phebe Moralee in Little Falls; Rev. C.W. Leet (3-7/13)
LEWIS, Josephine - see BURNET, Reuben
LEWIS, L.D. of Little Falls m 10/3/42 Sarah J. Lyons of Hamilton, Upper Canada
in H.; Rev. J. Osborne (3-10/13)
LEWIS, Margaret M. - see WESSCHER, John H.
LEWIS, Maria - see GATES, Oliver
LEWIS, Martha A. - see HILGUS, H.K.
LEWIS, Mary - see AUSTIN, Wilbur
LEWIS, Morgan (General) - see LOUNDES, Rawline
LEWIS, Panthy - see BOWEN, Joel
LEWIS, Samuel, 90, a Rev. War soldier, d (date not given) in Hanover,
Chautauqua County (6-11/21/26)
LEWIS, Sarah Ann, wf of George E., formerly of Mount Pleasant, d 1/30/40 at
Herricks, Long Island (12-2/4)
LEWIS, William E. m 2/23/50 Eliza Higbie, both of Remson; H.C. Vogell (1-2/27)

LEYNE, Michael d 9/10/35 in Albany (funeral at 4 o'clock from his late home at
    301 North Market St.) (6-9/11)

LIBERTE, Marie - see LAVOIR, John

LIDDELL, John of Troy m 11/24/44 Jessie Munro of Montreal in West Troy; Rev.
    O.H. Gregory (5-11/29)

LIEBER, Henrietta - see GOODSELL, Thomas

LIEBER, John, Esq., 58(?), d 3/30/48 at Canajoharie (4-4/13)

LIEDEW, Eliza - see COLE, Spencer H.

LIFFINGWELL, Harriet - see SAYLES, George M

LIGHT, Catharine - see BARRET, Samuel

LIGHTBODY, James - see HUMPHREY, Martha (Mrs.)

LIGHTHALL, Sally - see HOWK, Roswell

LIGHTHALL, Sarah Ann - see HOSFORD, Selah

LILLYBRIDGE, Harrison, Esq. of Annsville m 9/30/50 Matilda Swartout of
    Detroit, Mich. at the Methodist Church in Rome, NY; Rev. James Erwin
    (1-10/2)

LIMEBECK, Lany Maria - see BREG, Isaac

LIMERICK, D. - see SUTHERLAND, William B.

LINACRE, Margaret Ann - see VAN SCHAACK, Nicholas

LINACRE, Thomas - see VAN SCHAACK, Nicholas

LINCOLN, Mary - see SACKETT, John B.

LINCOLN, Mary A.E. - see DANIELS, Spencer

LINCOLN, Sarah - see TUTHILL, Charles

LINDLEY, H.N. m 8/31/49 Hannah M. Phelps, both of Pocahontas, Ill.; Rev. J.
    Stafford (the bride is "one of the sweetest singers in our county") (from the
    Greenville (Illinois) Journal) (4-9/20)

LINDSEY, John (Rev.), 64, presiding elder of the Albany District, Troy Conference
    (presumably Methodist Episcopal Church), d 2/20/50 at Schenectady (was
    received into the Monmouth District in Maine in June 1809 (in M.E.
    church 40 years) (4-2/28)

LINDSEY, Jonas, 74, d 3/4/40 in Somers (12-3/10)

LINES(?), Julia F. - see WINCHELL, Alex.

LINES, Hannah, 41, wf of William of Mount Pleasant and dau of James Marshall
    of Dutchess County, d (date not given) in Mount Pleasant, Henry Co., Iowa
    Terr. (11-3/15/42)

LINES, Rebecca - see HEERMANCE, Andrew W.

LINK, Nancy - see SPOOR, Gilbert

LINN, Helen, 76, widow of Rev. Dr. William Linn, d 10/12/37 at Schenectady
    (6-10/13)

LINN, Susan - see HUBBELL, Levi

LINSEY, William, about 38, d 2/19/39 in Yorktown (12-2/26)

LINSLAY, William of Schaghticoke Point, m 12/25/44 Rebecca Witmarsh of West
    Troy in Albany (5-1/15/45)

LINZEY, John m 1/12/39 Sarah Ford, both of Little Falls, in L.F.; Rev. Thomas
    Towell (3-1/17)

LIPE, Catharine - see GETMAN, Chauncey

LIPE, Joel m 4/24/50 Elizabeth Fox in Fort Plain; Rev. G.W. Gage (4-4/25)

LIPE, Paulina E. - see BENNETT, Oscar

LIPE, Rufus of Fort Plain m 8/27/50 Mary C. Klock of St. Johnsville in S.J.; Rev.

Kneickson (4-8/29)

LIPPINCOTT, Thomas m (date not given) Catharine Cole in NYC (6-6/5/16)

LISHER, Thomas Jefferson D., 10, son of G.B. Lisher, Esq., d 12/10/37 in Albany (funeral 12/13 - corner of Schuyler and South Pearl St.) (6-12/12)

LITCHFIELD, Edwin C., Esq., of West Troy m 9/14/41 Grace H. Hubbard, dau. of Thomas H., Esq., of Utica, at U.; Rev. Dr. Prost (5-9/22)

LITCHFIELD, Mary S., 4 months, dau. of Edwin C. and Grace H., d 2/6/43 in West Troy (funeral at 3 o'clock 2/8) (5-2/8)

LITTLE, Catharine E. - see BROOKER, Isaac S.

LITTLE, Charles Augustus who d 4/6/35 at sea enroute from St. Croix; see a detailed account of his last days of life with the meeting of his brother at sea (6-4/28)

LITTLE, Charles Augustus, 24, of Albany d 4/6/35 at sea on the brig Gen. Trotter enroute from St. Croix (6-4/24)

LITTLE, Dudley m 6/22/35 Mary Ann Hotaling; Rev. Dr. Sprague (all of Albany) (6-7/2)

LITTLE, Elizabeth (Mrs.), 31, d (date not given) in NYC (6-12/26/26)

LITTLE, John of NYC m (date not given) Eliza Bennet of Bushwick, Long Island at B. (6-5/8/16)

LITTLE, Julia Ann, 17, dau. of Jonathan, Esq., d (date not given) in NYC (6-5/22/16)

LITTLE, Levi P. of Easton, Penn. m 5/8/39 Mary Smith, dau. of late John T., Esq., of Haverstraw, in NYC; Rev. C.F. Lefever (12-5/14)

LITTLE, Peter (Col.), late of the US Army, m (date not given) Catharine Lovely at Baltimore (6-5/29/16)

LITTLE, Robert, 80, d 5/30/35 in Hudson (a staunch Democrat through life; in Rev. War for 6 months hunted and watched the cowboys and was wounded in one of the skirmishes with them) (6-6/3)

LITTLE, William Coffin (Capt. of the brig Griffin) formerly of Boston m (date not given) Charlotte Augusta Wood of Augusta, Maine at the home of P.A. Brinsmade at Oahu, Sandwich Island (Hawaii); Rev. John Diehl (6-3/21/36)

LITTLEFIELD, Samuel, 17, son of Daniel, d 5/13/39 at Frankfort (3-5/16)

LIVERMORE, Maria - see KINGMAN, Leroy W.

LIVERMORE, William (Col.) - see KINGMAN, Leroy W.

LIVINGSTON, Cornelia, widow of late Philip., Esq., d 8/9/35 at home of her son Van Burgh Livingston, Esq., at Calender in the town of Greenburgh (dropsey of the heart) (6-8/12)

LIVINGSTON, Eliza D. - see THOMPSON, Smith

LIVINGSTON, Eliza Elliot, 61, widow of Alfred, d 4/9/37 in Poughkeepsie (6-4/13)

LIVINGSTON, Elizabeth Elliott (Mrs.), 61, d 4/9/37 at her home on Noxon Street in Poughkeepsie (died on her birthday) (6-4/20)

LIVINGSTON, Frances - see SILL, Rensselaer

LIVINGSTON, Frances - see SILL, Rensselaer

LIVINGSTON, George C., M.D., 27, late of Coxsackie, d 3/26/36 at New Orleans (pulmonary complaint) (6-4/25)

LIVINGSTON, Gertrude Laura - see LOUNDES, Rawline

LIVINGSTON, Hiram m 1/24/35 Susan Smith of Albany; Rev. Elder Welch

(6-1/26)

LIVINGSTON, James Allen, Esq., 24, youngest son of late Henry Walter Livingston, Esq. of the Manor of Livingston, NY, d 11/24/25 at Rouen, France (6-1/20/26)

LIVINGSTON, James B., M.D., son of Col. Henry A. Livingston of Poughkeepsie, d 10/29/37 at Balize Bay of Honduras (6-12/14)

LIVINGSTON, James Duane d 6/25/37 in NYC after a short illness (6-6/29)

LIVINGSTON, John (Rev. Dr.) - see DUYCKINCK, Susannah

LIVINGSTON, M., Esq. - see STEELE, Oliver

LIVINGSTON, Maria J. (Miss), 79, sister of late Col. James Livingston, d 9/22/39 at Stillwater (5-10/2)

LIVINGSTON, Mary - see OLMSTEAD, J.W. (Rev.)

LIVINGSTON, Mary Augusta - see STEELE, Oliver

LIVINGSTON, Mary, 3, dau. of V.R. and Jane S., d 12/5/47 in West Troy (scarlet fever) (5-12/8)

LIVINGSTON, Maturn, Esq. - see LOUNDES, Rawline

LIVINGSTON, Peter W., 57, d (date not given) in NYC (influenza) (6-2/17/26)

LIVINGSTON, Richard M., Esq., 50, counsellor at law, d 3/5/38 at his home in Schuylerville (5-3/14)

LIVINGSTON, Richard Montgomery, about 50, d 3/5/38 (a lingering and painful cutaneous disease) (member of the Baptist Church) (3-3/8)

LIVINGSTON, Robert of Clermont m 6/1/36 Ann Clarkson, only dau of Jeremiah Goodhue; Rev. William Richmond (6-6/4)

LIVINGSTON, V. Rensselaer m Jane M. Sutherland of Jackson. Mich. at J.; Rev. Marcus Harrison (5-2/2)

LIVINGSTON, Walter P. - see CRAWFORD, Eliza B.

LLOYD, Anastasia - see ALEXANDER, Maurice S.

LLOYD, Eliza - see ST. CLAIR, John

LLOYD, Margaret - see COUGHTRY, Joseph A.

LLOYD, Nanie - see BUCHANAN, Franklin

LOBDELL, Caleb, 63, d 3/28/43 in Clayton, Jefferson County (for 38 years a member of the Methodist Episcopal Church) (5-7/19)

LOBDELL, Harriet, 2, dau. of Alexander S. and Matilda, d 3/18/48 in West Troy (5-3/22)

LOBDELL, James - see TAYLOR, Maria

LOBDELL, James - see WILLIAMS, Francis Wells

LOBDELL, James O. of West Troy m 9/1/47 Alice P., dau. of Eli Person(?) of Johnstown, in J.; Rev. Chase (5-9/8)

LOBDELL, John B., 32, d 10/23/45 in West Troy (5-10/29)

LOBDELL, Maria - see TAYLOR, Morgan L.

LOBDELL, Maria, 1 yr., dau. of Alexander S. and Matilda, d 1/10/45 in West Troy (5-1/15)

LOBDELL, Perry m 12/19/41 Mary Reynolds in North Salem; Rev. N.J. Hillyer (11-12/28)

LOBGELL, Abigail - see OSBORNE, Clark

LOCKE, Frederick Augustus of NYC m 6/8/42 Sarah Ann Williamson of Poughkeepsie at Christ's Church in P.; Rev. Hiram Joliff (9-6/11)

LOCKERTY, Elizabeth (Mrs.), 76, d 2/23/37 in consequence of a broken arm in December (funeral from home of her son-in-law (not named) at 60 South

188

Pearl Street)(her son, W.C. Lockerty is named) (6-2/24)

LOCKWOOD, Alvah M, 23, d 2/10/35 at Albany (funeral tomorrow afternoon at 3
o'clock from his late residence, 65 Fox Street) (6-2/11)

LOCKWOOD, Christopher S. m 6/7/49 Catharine DuBois; at Olive; Martin Shutt,
Esq. (all of Olive) (8-6/23)

LOCKWOOD, Clarissa, 21, wf of Rev. L.R. Lockwood and dau. of John Tuttle,
Esq., d 4/16/37 at Windham (Rev. L.R. pastor of the First Presbyterian
Church there)(she had been married for one year) (6-4/24)

LOCKWOOD, Frances - see ST JOHN, George

LOCKWOOD, Hannah Jane - see PIERCE, Caleb

LOCKWOOD, Horatio - see REYNOLDS, Sophia

LOCKWOOD, Mary - see DYGERT, John

LOCKWOOD, Mary C. - see REYNOLDS, Horace

LOCKWOOD, Samuel E. of Bedford m 10/25/38 Huldah Ann Baker of Tarrytown
at T. (12-11/13)

LOCKWOOD, Sarah - see HARTFORD, Charles

LOCKWOOD, Sarah Ann - see JUNE, George

LOCKWOOD, Sarah, 74, wf of Stephen, d 12/12/39 in Sing Sing (12-12/17)

LOCKWOOD, Solomon, 79, d 12/31/41 in Little Falls (3-1/6/42)

LOCKWOOD, Sylvia - see GEROW, A.

LOCKWOOD, Uriah - see SAYRE, Edmund I.

LOCKWOOD, William of NYC m (date not given) Sarah Hanes, dau. of Horace of
Southeast, in S.; Rev. Warren (12-11/12/39)

LOCKYEAR, Mary Ann - see CLINTON, James

LODEWICK, Casper, 57, d 4/21/37 at his home in Schodack (6-4/24)

LODGE, James, senior, editor of the Cincinnati Gazette, d 12/19/35 at C.
(6-1/4/36)

LONDON, John, Esq., 70, late President of the Bank of Cape Fear, d 3/1/16 at
Wilmington, NC (6-3/27)

LONG, ----, 48, wf of Frederick, d (date not given) in NYC (6-5/22/16)

LONG, Alida - see FRANCIS, Daniel

LONG, Esther - see HARE, John

LONGYEAR, Manassah of Kingston m 7/12/49 Elizabeth Hulder of Woodstock at
W.; Rev. H. Wheeler (8-7/21)

LOOKER(?), Stephen m 7/5/38 Margaret House in Ohio, Herkimer County; G.A.
Coppernall, Esq. (3-7/19)

LOOMIS, ----, 83, wf of Timothy, d 7/28/39 in Warren (3-8/8)

LOOMIS, A. (Hon.) - see TODD, Bede(?)

LOOMIS, A.T. - see BAKER, A.B.

LOOMIS, Amasa, 75, d 6/10/37 at his home in East Windsor, Conn. (6-6/30)

LOOMIS, Anson C. of Seneca Castle m 11/2/35 Maria Pardy, dau of Stephen of
Benton, in B.; Rev. Iverson (6-11/23)

LOOMIS, Benjamin N., Esq., attorney at law of Binghamton m 10/10/37 Sarah
Ann Gardner, dau. of Hon. Howell Gardner of Greenfield, Saratoga Co., at
G.; Rev. T. Redfield (5/11/1)

LOOMIS, Benjamin N., Esq., attorney at law, of Binghamton, m 10/10/37 Sarah
Ann Gardner, dau. of Hon. Howell Gardner of Greenfield, Saratoga County,
at G.; Rev. Redfield (6-10/26)

LOOMIS, Charles K., Esq. m 10/17/37 Maria Williams, fourth dau. of Major

Samuel Brown (all of Brownville, NY) in Trinity Church at Newport, RI, by Rev. Dr. Wheaton (6-10/20)

LOOMIS, Charles m 3/12/45 Julia Sheldon in Lee; Rev. Downing (all of Lee) (1-3/17)

LOOMIS, Cornelia - see CARR, Egbert E.

LOOMIS, David B., principal of the Samsondale Academy m 10/21/39 Eliza Griggs of Tolland, Conn. at T.; Rev. Marsh (12-10/29)

LOOMIS, Dyer, M.D., of Louisville, Otsego County m 7/25/39 Mrs. Jane Willard of Little Falls in L.F.; Rev. T. Towell (3-8/1)

LOOMIS, Eli E. m 4/16/41 Sarah Abell; Rev. Butler (all of Verona) (1-4/27)

LOOMIS, Elizabeth - see STARKWEATHER, Rufus

LOOMIS, Emilia M., 22, consort of Dyer Loomis, M.D. and eldest dau of Cornelius Mabee, Esq. of Palatine, d 12/5/36 at Louisville, Otsego County. (interred in the family cemetery at Palatine) (6-12/13)

LOOMIS, Henry H., 29, formerly of Rome, d 9/23/41 in Fulton (1-10/5)

LOOMIS, Hezekiah H. (Rev.), 28, twin brother of late Rev. Henry H., formerly of Rome, d 1/6/42 at Cazenovia (1-1/18)

LOOMIS, John B., Esq., of Vernon m 10/28/41 Elizabeth T. Fenton, eldest dau. of A. Fenton, Esq., of Clinton, at C,; Rev. Clowes (1-11/23)

LOOMIS, Lebbeus (Col.), 79, a Rev. War veteran, d 1/10/36 at Cherry Valley (at age 17 was a volunteer at Battle of Bunker Hill. After the war settled in NYC. Lived in Cherry Valley about eight years) (6-1/28)

LOOMIS, Margaret, 5, dau. of Russel and Betsey, d 8/17/42 in Little Falls (3-8/25)

LOOMIS, Mary J. - see SAUNDERS, Edward D.

LOOMIS, Nathaniel S., Esq., 36, of Verona d 4/2/49 at Bath where he was acting magistrate (survived by a wife and 4 children) (1-4/25)

LOOMIS, Thaddeus, 1, youngest son of Arphaxed Loomis, d 11/9/41 in Little Falls (3-11/18)

LOOMIS, William G. m 10/14/44 Dorleson A. Wood, both of Vernon Center, at Lairdsville; Rev. Rockwell of Vernon Center (1-10/22)

LORD, Edmond J. of Albany m 4/17/47 Hester T. Thornton, dau. of Thomas, Esq., of Watervliet, in W.; Rev. Gregory (5-4/21)

LORD, Lucy E. - see JOHNSON, Ebenezer

LORD, Sarah - see BROWN, Joseph

LORMAN, Harriet - see SMITH, William H.

LOSEE, Cyrus of Greenville, Greene County m 10/19/36 Sarah M. Hill of Kingston in K.; Rev. Morris of Little Falls (3-10/27)

LOTHRIDGE, Jane - see PERRY, John

LOTTS, Eliza - see WETHERWAX, John M.B.

LOUCKS, Lany - see MANSFIELD, John

LOUCKS, Maria - see MILLEISEN, William

LOUCKS, Maria N,m 54, wf of A.P. of Peoria, Illinois and dau. of Gen. George H. Nellis of Canajoharie, NY, d 2/12/48 at Peoria (4-3/9)

LOUD, Samuel m 12/11/39 Eliza Wessels in Cortlandt; Rev. J. Youngs (11-12/17)

LOUD, Samuel of Verplank's m 12/7/42 Mary Jane Tice of Cortland Town; Rev. John Miles (11-12/13)

LOUDEN, Frederick, 75, the oldest inhabitant of Burlington, NJ, d 1/17/26 at Burlington (He fought with Wolfe in 1759 at the seige of Quebec. He was too old (above age 45) to serve in the Rev. War (survived by a large family of children, age range 17 to 50) (6-1/20)

LOUNDES, Rawline of US Army m 10/24/26 Gertrude Laura Livingston, second dau. of Maturin Livingston, Esq., at Staatsburg at the seat of General Morgan Lewis (6-11/7)

LOUNSBERRY, James, Esq., of Bedford m 8/24/42 Mrs. Ann Whitall of Peekskill; Rev. Moses Marcus (at the festival of St. Bartholemew the Apostle) (11-8/30)

LOUNSBERRY, James, Esq., of Bedford m 8/24/42 Mrs. Anne Whitall of Peekskill; Rev. Moses Marcus, B.D. (at time of the Feast of St. Bartholomew) (11-8/25)

LOUNSBERRY, Joseph, 24, d 9/19/41 in Peekskill (consumption) (11-9/21)

LOUNSBERRY, Joshua, about 50, a farmer, d 8/16/33 in Phillipstown (11-8/20)

LOUNSBERRY, Lydia - see DORRAN(?), Horace

LOUNSBERRY, Mary - see BETTIS, William

LOUNSBERRY, Rebecca - see JAYCOX, James C.

LOUNSBERRY, William, 27, son of John, d 9/18/42 (11-9/22)

LOUNSBURY, Nehemiah, about 30, d 1/25/44 in Cortlandt Town (11-1/30)

LOUNSBURY, Sarah Ann, 30 or 39?, wife of John and dau of Benjamin Merrill, d 2/28/42 in Cortlandt Town (consumption) (11-4/5)

LOUNSBURY, Sarah Ann, 30, wf of John and dau of Benjamin Merrill, d 3/28/42 in Cortlandt (11-3/31)

LOVEGROVE, William J. of Boston, 22, d 8/31/43 at the home of a friend in Poughkeepsie (the notice was sent from Oppenheim, Sept. 19) (3-9/28)

LOVELAND, Mary - see PALMER, Henry L.

LOVELAS, Lucretia - see RUSSELL, Samuel H.

LOVELY, Catharine - see LITTLE, Peter (Col.)

LOVETT, Henry, 47, d 10/12/47 in West Troy (typhus) (5-10/20)

LOW(?), Emily, 1, dau of Edward, d 7/3/42 in Ridgefield, CT (11-8/11)

LOW, Addison m 8/16/37 Elvira Steele, dau. of Samuel, Esq.; Rev. Wyckoff (all of Albany) (6-8/19)

LOW, David (Dr.), late of the US Army m 4/30/16 Juliet Mc Burney of Albany; Rev. Muirs of Galway (6-5/4)

LOW, David, d (date not given) in New Paltz (6-6/5/16)

LOW, Francis S. m 11/16/37 Hannah R. Wallace; Rev. Dr. Welch (all of Albany) (6-11/16)

LOW, John, 47, publisher of the Encyclopedia, d 4/23/09 in NYC after a short illness (7-5/31)

LOW, Maria - see ELLIS, David

LOW, Maria - see LAMB, William J.

LOWDER, William, weaver, d (date not given) in Newburgh (6-11/28/26)

LOWE, Charlotte - see NORRIS, Edward L.

LOWELL, Margaret Eliza Mansfield, wf of the Surgeon General of the Army, d 9/6/36 in Washington "leaving a large family of children, the youngest but twelve days old" (6-9/13)

LOWERY, John m 3/25/42 Jane Carson; Rev. J. Johnston (all of Newburgh) (9-3/26)

LOWREY, Deborah (Mrs.), 81, d (date not given) in NYC (6-1/10/16)

LOWRY, Agnes Maria - see SEEKER, John

LOWRY, John m 6/13/50 Mary Elizabeth Freeman, both of Oriskany, in Rome;

191

Rev. W.E. Knox (1-6/19)

LOYD, ---- (Mr.) d 8/8/49 in Saugerties (cholera) (8-8/11)

LOZER, Henry m 3/21/42 Eliza Ronck; Rev. Griswold (all of Newburgh) (9-3/26)

LOZIER, George of Hackensack, NJ m 8/18/39 Catherine Vervalen, dau. of
Richard, Esq. of Closter, NJ at Tappantown, Rockland Co., NY; Rev. I.D.
Cole (12-9/24)

LOZIER, Hildebrant, 71, a Rev. War soldier, d (date not given) at Herrington,
Bergen Co., NJ (served under Col. Henry Lee) (6-6/30)

LUCAS, Thomas, 62, formerly of Newburgh, d 7/13/49 in Kingston (consumption)
(8-7/21)

LUCE(?), William of Newburgh m 10/30/42 Phebe Jane Gale, dau of William of
Peekskill; Rev. Dr. Westbrook (11-11/3)

LUDINGTON, Laura Ann - see HUESTIS, John

LUDLOW, Alfred, Esq. of Utica m 7/18/35 Jane Maria Hartfield, youngest dau of
Saniel, Esq. of St. John N.B.; Rev. Dr. Gray (6-8/6)

LUDLOW, Charles (Capt.), formerly of the U.S. Navy, d 11/3/39 (attended
Episcopal Church Servive in Peekskill on the day of his death, returned to
his home in New Windsor and died suddenly that evening while talking
with his family) (11-11/5)

LUDLOW, Cornelia - see BEEKMAN, George Clinton

LUDLOW, Cornelia Ann - see WILLINK, John Abraham

LUDLOW, Ellen (Mrs.) - see SEDGFIELD, John, Esq.

LUDLOW, George W., 36, of NYC d 11/25/34, suddenly at Batavia, India
(6-7/1/35)

LUDLOW, Robert C. of US Navy, 39, d (date not given) at Windsor Hill, Orange
County at the home of his brother (not named) (6-5/26/26)

LUE, Bridget - see BOYNES, James

LUFFMAN, John D. of Waterford m 10/25/37 Jane Eliza Steenburgh of Halfmoon
in H.; Rev. Peer (xx5-11/8)

LUGAR(?), John Henry, son of Henry, d 8/5/42 in Newburgh (9-8/6)

LUSK, S. - see BUTLER, William

LUTE, John m 6/25/49 Catherine Sage, both of Sholem, at Ellenville; Milton
Shelden, Esq. (8-7/14)

LUTHER, Almina, 42, wf of Richard, d 7/20/49 in Kingston (see LUTHER,
Richard Francis and LUTHER, Richard) (8-8/4)

LUTHER, Almira - see FENNER, Daniel

LUTHER, Chloe - see CHESTER, Francis

LUTHER, Jeremiah m 8/6/43 Mary Ann Zielman, both of Albany; Rev. Z. Phillips
(5-8/9)

LUTHER, John, 87, a Rev. War soldier, d 6/4/36 (6-6/7)

LUTHER, Pathena, 27, wf of Moses H., d 10/30/42 in Butternuts, Otsego County
(3-11/10)

LUTHER, Richard Francis, 4, son of Richard Luther, d 7/25/49 in Kingston (see
LUTHER, Almina and LUTHER, Richard) (8-8/4)

LUTHER, Richard, about 55, d 8/1/49 in Kingston (see LUTHER, Almina and
LUTHER, Richard Francis) (8-8/4)

LYDE, Sarah Louisa - see GORDON, Arthur R.

LYELL, Georgiana Elizabeth - see BOORAEM, Thomas I.

LYMAN, _____ (Mr.) of Northampton, MA, d 1/24/35 at St. Augustine, FL

(6-2/23)

LYMAN, Clarissa G. - see COBB, Dean

LYMAN, Elizabeth, 68, wf of Dr. Micah J, d 2/3/35 in Troy (apoplexy)(6-2/5)

LYMAN, Harvey W. m 12/10/38 Almira Weber at Mohawk; Rev. James Murphy
    (3-2/7/39)

LYMAN, Huntington (Rev.) of Arcade m 4/25/39 Frances Kingman of Little Falls;
    Rev. Savage of Utica (3-5/2)

LYMAN, Martha. late consort of Jonathan Lyman of Albany, d 12/2/36 (funeral at
    3 o'clock from Jonathan's home, 96 Haw St.) (6-12/5)

LYMAN, Mary E., consort of Theodore, Jr. d 8/5/36 at Boston (6-8/22)

LYMAN, Orpha - see WYCKOFF, Samuel B.

LYMAN, Sarah O - see ALLEN, Richard L.

LYMAN, Sarah, 3, only dau. of Jonathan, d 5/9/37 (funeral from 26 Hawk Street)
    (6-5/10)

LYMAN, William A. of Constableville m 3/16/45 Catharine H. Powell of Lee in
    West Turin; Rev. C. Havens of Leyden (1-3/25)

LYMON, Rhoda H. - see SHEPARD, Charles O.

LYMON, William, D.D. - see SHEPARD, Charles O.

LYNCH, Alexander, 68, d 12/17/41 in Rome (lived in Rome "many years")
    (1-12/21)

LYNCH, Ellen, about 18, dau. of Patrick, d 8/5/49 in Saugerties (cholera) (8-8/11)

LYNCH, Lea, 9 months, son of Harrison and Louise F., d 1/10/50 at Brooklyn
    (whooping cough) (1-2/20)

LYNCH, Martin m 11/14/49 Charlotte Graves, both of Rome; H.C. Vogell
    (1-11/21)

LYNCH, Mary - see CURRY, William

LYNDE, Elizabeth Arthur - see HUGGINS(?), Henry T.

LYNDE, Elizabeth S - see ALDEN, A.O.

LYNDE, John Hart - see HUGGINS(?), Henry T.

LYNDE, Willoughbe, 27, one of the editors and publishers of the New York
    Transcript, d suddenly 7/14/35 in NYC (6-7/17)

LYNT, Catharine - see SUTTON, William

LYON, Abby R. - see GROSVENOR, Charles P.

LYON, Alvan A. of Sawpit m 4/28/39 Rebecca Lyon of Greenwich, CT at G.
    (12-4/30)

LYON, Amelia - see OGDEN, Joseph

LYON, Benjamin (Dr.) - see BROWN, Charles E.

LYON, Betsey, wf of Rev. Walter Lyon and dau of Rev. Hezekiah Sandford of
    Southeast, d 1/3/42 in Bedford (11-1/18)

LYON, Caroline - see DYER, John L.

LYON, Charles, merchant, m 12/19/36 Hannah Maria Vandenburgh; Rev. Dr.
    Sprague (all of Albany) (6-12/21)

LYON, Elizabeth - see BEANYS(?), Samuel

LYON, Elizabeth P. - see REQUA, Abram

LYON, Elizabeth, wf of Alexander D., d 11/22/38 at Utica (3-11/29)

LYON, Eunice, 66, wf of Samuel, Esq., d 6/1/49 at New Hartford (1-6/13)

LYON, Frances - see BROWN, Charles E.

LYON, George m 12/12/47 Susan M. Knapp; Rev. T.F. Wyckoff (all of West Troy)
    (5-12/15)

LYON, Martha - see LYON, Osman C.

LYON, Mary E., 3, only dau. of John N. and Jane, d 4/26/49 at New Hartford (1-5/2)

LYON, Mary W. - see PURDY, Isaac H.

LYON, Mrs. Daniel - see JONES, Reuben

LYON, Munson of Sing Sing m 1/1/39 Frances S. Mc Cord of Cortlandt in C.; Rev. Van Deusen (12-1/15)

LYON, Osman C. m 1/22/40 Martha Lyon, dau. of David, in North Castle; Rev. Dickerson (all of North Castle) (12-2/11)

LYON, Ransom m 9/27/46 Eliza J. Noland in West Troy; Rev. T.J. Wyckoff (5-9/30)

LYON, Rebecca - see LYON, Alvan A.

LYON, William J. m 5/29/45 Elizabeth A. Hoxie, both of West Troy, in Albany; Rev. Phillips (5-6/4)

LYONS, Margaret - see DEMENS, Henry

LYONS, Phoebe - see BRIGGS, Samuel

LYONS, Sarah J. - see LEWIS, L.D.

M----, Deborah - see WALSH, John

MABBOTT, Leonard m 10/29/40 Martha Jane Haynes, both of Salisbury, in S.; Rev. S. Northrup (3-12/3)

MABEE, C. of Palatine m 9/11/39 Maria M. Gross of Canajoharie in C.; Rev. Whiteman (3-9/12)

MABEE, Cornelius - see LOOMIS, Emilia

MABEE, Elizabeth, 42, consort of Cornelius, Esq., d 11/15/37 in Palatine, Montgomery County (a member of the Reformed Dutch Church) (6-11/24)

MABEE, William H. of firm of W.H. & J. Mabee of Fonda m 9/27/37 Margaret Dockstader, dau. of Henry F., Esq.; Rev. Alan Van Horne (6-10/2)

MABEY, Margaret - see KIMMEY, David

MABIE, Elias H., son-in-law if Isaac Martling of Haverstraw, d 10/29/41 at H. (11-11/9)

MABIE, Margaret (age blurred), wf of John and dau. of Henry Cook, formerly of Stone Arabia, d 1/27/37 at Manlius Centre, Onondaga County (6-2/2)

MABIE, Mary - see WHEELER, Walter

MAC CLATLIN, James m 2/5/48 Maria Vandusen of Fonda at F.; Rev. A. Rumpf (4-3/2)

MAC DONALD, Flora (Mrs.), 69, relict of Doctor Mac Donald, formerly of White Plains, NY, d. 4/2/35 in White Plains (member of the Episcopal Church) (6-4/28)

MACBETH, John m 6/8/43 Sarah E. Cary, both of West Troy; Rev. Leonard (5-6/14)

MACBETH, Margaret A. - see BECKER, Jeremiah L.

MACDONALD, Lancelot G. m 3/10/40 Lucy Mead of Bedford in B.; Rev. Card (12-3/17)

MACHIN, Nancy, 56, wf of Capt. Thomas Machin, d 4/20/50 in Charlestown, Montgomery County (survived by at least one child and a sister in addition to her husband) (4-5/2)

MACK, Elisha, Jr. of Albany m 12/23/37 Julia Ann Murphy of Watervliet at Troy; Rev. Hill (6-12/27)

MACK, Peter Dey, 1 yr, 8 mo, only son of Ebenezer Mack, d 4/15/35 in Ithaca

(6-4/27)

MACK, William H. m 10/13/36 Anna Shonts(?); Rev. Dr. Sprague (all of Albany) (6-10/15)

MACOMBER, Deborah, 77, widow of Pardon Macomber, d 9/2/41 in Western (1-9/14)

MACY, Robert J. (Capt.), 42, d 9/22/36 at Hudson (consumption) (Had been "a commander in the Havre and Liverpool packet lines") (6-9/27)

MADDEN, Susannah (Mrs.), about 60, d 1/18/42 in Montgomery (9-1/22)

MADDICK, Eliza - see WATKINS, D.C.

MADDOCK, Adelaide, 17, sister of Maria Maddock, 18, d 8/31/48 (see MADDOCK, Edward and MADDOCK, Maria) (1-9/15)

MADDOCK, Edward, 58, father of Adelaide and Maria, d 9/7/48 in Vienna (see MADDOCK, Adelaide and MADDOCK, Maria) (1-9/15)

MADOCK, Maria (Miss), 18, sister of Mrs. W.H. Pollard of Rome, d 8/23/48 in Rome (sse MADDOCK, Adelaide and MADDOCK, Edward) (1-9/15)

MAHER, James - see CAUDER, Peter

MAHER, Maria - see CAUDER, Peter

MAHON, Catharine, 76, wf of Hon. John Mahon, d 9/15/43 in Herkimer after a lingering illness (3-9/21)

MAIN, Thomas, Esq., 50, m 6/25/42 Rhoda Tucker, 13, dau of David of Stamford, CT, at the home of Alexander Lounsbury in North Castle (11-8/4)

MAIR, James H. of Argyle m (date not given) Martha B. Randol of Newburgh at Albany; Rev. Dr. Garfield (9-10/29/42)

MAITLAND, Martha C. (Miss) d (date not given) (was for a long time the principal and teacher of the Sunday school at the Wall Street Church, NYC) (from NY Daily Advertiser) (6-3/26/36)

MALBURN, William P. m 5/19/36 Laura A. Kinney in Albany; Rev. E. Holmes (6-5/21)

MALIBRAN, Eugene, Esq. m (date not given) Maria Felicia Garcia of the Italian Opera Company in NYC (6-4/7/26)

MALLARY, George H., Esq. of Poultney, VT m 2/2/37 Caroline Bishop, dau. of late Isaac of Granville, NY at G.; Rev. Reynolds (6-2/9)

MALLET, Roswell - see HOTCHKISS, David

MALLORY, James H. of Cohoes m 9/12/38 Sarah Jane Ryker at the home of John Ryker, Esq. in NYC; Rev. Hodgson (5-9/19)

MALLORY, Julia Frances - see HAWLEY, Ralph (Col.)

MALTAY, Norman m 9/16/41 Lovina M. Wright of Vernon at Vernon Center; Rev. R. Weed Gorham (1-9/21)

MALTBY, John of Lowell m 3/10/47 Mrs. Minerva Gilbert of Augusta in A.; Rev. J.M. Searling (1-3/19)

MANCHESTER, Bradford A., one of the publishers of the Buffalo Daily Commercial, m (date not given) Rachel Miller, third dau. of James, Esq.; Rev. William Shelton (6-2/3/37)

MANCHESTER, James T of Scipio m 3/18/35 Lucy Ann Thornton, dau of Stephen of Fleming, at F.; Rev. Ansel Clark (6-3/28)

MANCHESTER, Lester A. m 4/19/49 Henrietta K. Wordon, both of Lee; Rev. Chitester (1-4/25)

MANCHESTER, Stephen of Midway, Kentucky m 2/8/48 Merivale Chamberlain of Verona in V.; Rev. H. Kendall (1-3/17)

MANCIUS, Jacob - see BEEKMAN, George Clinton

MANCIUS, Margaret - see YATES, Richard

MANDAVILLE, Hannah, 76, wf of James, d 3/27/41 (11-3/30)

MANDAVILLE, Isaac S. m 2/14/44 Mrs. Martha Marie Denton, dau of late
    William Dyckman; Rev. Dr. Westbrook (all of Cortlandt Town) (11-2/20)

MANDEL, Delia - see ISHEM, Alfred

MANDEL, Henry - see ISHEM, Alfred

MANDERVILLE, (Mrs.), about 30, wf of Isaac, d 2/4/42 in Cortlandtown (11-2/8)

MANN, Abijah, Jr. - see FINK, Charles

MANN, J.M. (Dr.) - see RUMNEY, Elouisa

MANN, John Milton, 50, d 2/6/49 in Rome (1-2/21)

MANN, Mary Ann - see HART, James

MANN, Nancy Anna - see FINK, Charles

MANNERING, David of Hamilton m 5/3/42 Maria DeWolf of Bridgewater in B.;
    Rev. F.C. Brown (1-5/10)

MANNERING, James m 4/3/42 Catharine Jordan (both of Verplank); Rev. John
    Miles (11-4/7)

MANNERING, Mary G. - see HEATH, A.H.

MANNERING, Mary G. (Mrs.) - see HEATH, A.H.

MANNING, Frances Louisa, 19, (widow of Lt. David A. of US Army who d at Key
    West 7/21/35) d 9/18/35 at Edenton, NC in home of Lt. John Manning of
    US Navy (Frances Louisa was youngest dau of late John E Holt, Esq.,
    mayor of Norfolk, VA) (6-8/31)

MANNING, Hannah (Mrs.) - see MANNING, John

MANNING, John, Esq. of Mennington, Lower Canada m 10/1/37 Mrs. Hannah
    Manning of Poughkeepsie, NY at P.; Rev. James J. Ostrom (6-10/3)

MANNING, Maria D. - see WELLS, J.D.

MANSFIELD, Helen Maria - see WATERS, Chester W.

MANSFIELD, John m 1/21/49 Lany Loucks, both of Fort Plain, in F.P.; Rev. James
    Aplin, Esq. (4-1/25)

MANSFIELD, Lucretia Melinda - see KINNEY, John

MANSFIELD, Margaret Eliza - see LOWELL, Margaret Eliza

MANSFIELD, Ralph m 12/29/49 Susan Clifford, late of Carmel, in C. (10-1/2/50)

MANSFIELD, Samuel (Col.), 58, d (date not given) very suddenly in Hudson
    (7-2/14/10)

MANY, Walter C m 3/24/35 Catherine Mayer; Rev. Mayer; all of Albany (6-3/26)

MARCELLIS, Maria (Mrs.) d 1/5/16 in Albany (funeral 1/6 at 3 o'clock from home
    of John Voorhees, 27 Chapel St.) (6-1/6)

MARCELLUS, Garret N. - see SETTLE, Jacob D.

MARCELLUS, Margaret - see SETTLE, Jacob D.

MARCRAFT, Eunice Walker, 5, only child of William, d 12/7/37 (funeral 12/9
    from 318 State Street) (6-12/8)

MARCUS, Lellias - see COFFIN, Alfred

MARCY, Gov. - see KNOWER, Charles

MARCY, Governor - see KNOWER, Henry

MARDEN, Thomas W., 31, a deaf mute, d 9/4/49 in Argusville (was educated at
    the American Asylum for the Deaf and Dumb at Hartford, Conn.) (4-10/18)

MARIAN, Anthony (Capt.) m 5/4/41 Abigail Pratt, youngest dau. of Widow Pratt,
    in Verona; Rev. Lewis (1-5/11)

MARION, Marion H. - see STRANG, E.J.

MARK, Isaac, 29, d 4/18/50 in West Troy (5-4/24)

MARKELL, Irene, 40, wf of John, Esq., d (date not given) at Manheim (funeral sermon by Rev. Bloodgood of Little Falls) (3-7/1)

MARKELL, John, Esq. of Manheim m 2/23/42 Caroline Sherwood of Fairfield at F.; Rev. William Baker (a double ceremony - see SHERWOOD, Amos G.) (3-3/3)

MARKS, Edwin, of firm of A. Marks & Sons of Haverstraw m 5/22/39 Jane Ward, dau. of Thomas of Ramapo Valley in R.V.; Rev. Day (12-5/28)

MARKS, Eliza - see JACOBUS, Samuel

MARKS, Eliza - see JACOBUS, Samuel Jackson

MARKS, Isaac, 85, d 4/25/43 in Watervliet (5-5/3)

MARKS, Mrs. - see HAMMOND, Ammon, M.D.

MARKS, S. - see PHILIPS, Mary

MARRS, Betsey - see HOOFFER, Christopher N.

MARSH, Catharine - see UTLEY, David

MARSH, Ely T., Esq., attorney at law, m 9/15/42 Mary E. Dygert, dau. of Capt. W.W. Dygert in Frankfort; Rev. A.B. Grosh(?) (bride and groom of Frankfort) (3-9/22)

MARSH, Julia Ann - see CAULKINS, Samuel N.

MARSH, Lyman, son of Abraham, Esq., m 11/22/37 Achsa Munson, dau. of Jacob, in Salisbury; Rev. W.H. Waggoner (all of Salisbury) (3-12/7)

MARSH, Moses P., Esq., attorney and counsellor at law of Carrolton, Ill. m 11/21/36 Emeline Williams, dau of late Nathan, Esq. of Manlius at M.; Rev. J. Pound (6-12/6)

MARSH, Moses P., Esq., attorney and counsellor at law, of Carrolton, Ill. m 11/21/36 Emeline Williams, dau of late Nathan, Esq, of Manlius, at M; Rev. J. Pound (6-12/2)

MARSH, Seymour, 65, d 12/31/49 in Canajoharie (4-1/10/50)

MARSH, Ursula (Miss), 18, d 2/22/1835 in Pharsalia, Chenango Co (after 4 days' sickness); listed as "a daughter, a sister and a teacher" (6-3/17)

MARSH, William m 10/23/45 Sarah Jane Perry, both of West Troy, in Troy; Rev. L.A. Sanford (5-10/29)

MARSH, William, 40, d 2/4/42 in Newburgh (funeral 2/6/from his home on Fifth Street) (9-2/5)

MARSHALL, Abner, 79, d 9/18/41 at the home of Jacob M. Merrell in Westmoreland (1-9/28)

MARSHALL, Caroline (Mrs.), born in England, d 9/24/42 in Utica, NY (1-9/27)

MARSHALL, D.P. - see STEWART, Mary

MARSHALL, Eliza - see YOUNG, De Witt C.

MARSHALL, Eliza Preston, 1, dau. of James U. and Catherine, d 4/11/39 in West Troy (inflammation of the lungs) (5-4/17)

MARSHALL, Guy C. (Dr.), about 40, d 11/20/36 in Frankfort (3-11/24)

MARSHALL, Isabella, 40, wf of Daniel P., d 1/6/37 in Albany (long painful illness) (funeral from Daniel P.'s home, 368 South Pearl St.) (6-1/7)

MARSHALL, Isabella, 6 months, dau. of Francis, d 3/27/42 in Newburgh (9-4/2)

MARSHALL, James - see LINES, Hannah

MARSHALL, John - see CARLISLE, Eliza

MARSHALL, Lovinus of (town name blurred) m 3/22/48 Mary M. Allen of Vernon in V.; Rev. -.C.b---- (name blurred) (4-3/30)

MARSHALL, Phebe - see CUNNINGHAM, William J.

MARSHALL, Rev. - see KNAPP, Caroline P.

MARSHALL, Richard of Annsville m 8/17/50 Catharine Secor of Camden at the
Lee Centre House; Rev. J.S. Kibbe (1-8/28)

MARSHALL, Thomas, 72, d 7/31/39 at the home of his relative, Dr. Rufus Crain,
in Warren (deceased was one of the early New England pioneers in this
region) (3-8/8)

MARTIN, ----, child of Robert Martin, d (date not given) (funeral at 3 o'clock from
the father's home, 37 Maiden Lane, Albany) (6-2/12/36)

MARTIN, Cecelia - see CAMPBELL, Hermanus

MARTIN, Daniel, Esq., 58, President of the Mohawk bank, d 9/19/35 in
Schenectady (6-9/26)

MARTIN, E.T. Throop of NYC m 6/1/37 Cornelia Williams, only dau. of John,
Esq., at Utica; Rev. M. Fowler (6-6/6)

MARTIN, Edward m 8/31/44 Mary Mc Donald, both of Hartford; Rev. Quinn of
West Troy (5-9/11)

MARTIN, Edward, Jr. of NYC m 7/17/47 Elizabeth Ann Albro, dau. of John of
Stillwater, at the Church of St. Augustine in London (5-9/1)

MARTIN, Eleanor - see HOUGHTALING, Isaac

MARTIN, Eliza - see GODFREY, John

MARTIN, Frances H., 6, dau. of Homer and Sarah, d 6/18/37 (6-6/20)

MARTIN, George B. of Detroit m 9/3/35 Hannah H. Townsend, dau of Isaac of
Chester, Orange County, at C; Rev. Clark (6-9/9)

MARTIN, George, Esq. of Busti, Chautauqua County, m 1/29/37 Lucy Spalding of
Columbia in C.; Rev. Putman (3-2/9)

MARTIN, Harriet - see WILLIAMS, John, Jr.

MARTIN, Harvey of Johnstown m 1/1/49 Catharine Schuyler of Palatine Bridge at
P.B.; James Wagner, Esq. (4-1/4)

MARTIN, Henry H. m 10/8/35 Anna Townsend, dau of Isaiah; Rev. Dr. Campbell
(all of Albany) (6-10/9)

MARTIN, James (Rev.) m 1/5/26 Rebecca White, both of Albany; Rev. Peter
Bullions (6-1/10)

MARTIN, James, 75, d 11/2/35 in Albany (funeral at 3 o'clock from his late home,
32 Patroon St.) (6-11/4)

MARTIN, Lucy - see DOUGLAS, Elisha M.

MARTIN, Margaret (Miss), 75, d 8/11/42 in Montgomery (9-8/13)

MARTIN, Mary - see EDGERTON, James M.

MARTIN, Rebecca White, 29, wf of Rev. James Martin d 3/23/35 (funeral from
her late residence, 5 Fox near Pearl St.) (6-3/25)

MARTIN, Robert (his funeral at 3 o'clock from his late home corner South Pearl
and Herkimer Sts., Albany) (6-1/21/36)

MARTIN, Sarah - see GORDON, Hugh (Capt.)

MARTIN, Sarah Doty, 2, dau of Homer, d 7/27/36 (6-7/29)

MARTIN, Susan R. - see DARROW, Erastus

MARTIN, William Bond (Hon.), 65, chief justice of the fourth judicial district in
Maryland, d 3/31/35 at his home in Cambridge, Dorchester Co., MD
(6-4/16)

MARTIN, William C. m 1/5/45 Mary E. Kidder at Akron, Ohio; Rev. Kinny (all of

Akron) (1-1/28)

MARTIN, William M. of Mount Hope m 12/22/42 Sarah Westfall of Port Jervis at
P.J.; Rev. Burrows (9-12/31)

MARTLING, Isaac - see MABIE, Elias H.

MARVELL, Alfred m 9/1/36 Eliza M. Sanford; Rev. Covell (6-9/2)

MARVIN, Abbe, 3, dau of Alexander Marvin, d 6/12/35 (6-12/15)

MARVIN, Harriet Eliza, 2, dau of Henry, d 6/6/36 (6-6/8)

MARVIN, Harriet, 29, wf of Henry, d 11/13/35 in NYC (6-11/16)

MARVIN, Titus J. Esq. of Saratoga Springs, m 2/8/37 Harriet Fraser of NYC in
NYC; Rev. Bishop Onderdonk (6-2/13)

MARVIN, Walter, 8, eldest son of Henry, d 6/16/36 (6-6/18)

MARX, Louisa - see MYERS, Samuel

MASON, Ezra m 9/11/42 Lucy H. Seymour, both of Delta, in D.; Rev. W.W. Ninde
(1-9/13)

MASON, Frederick, formerly of Herkimer County, m 12/8/42 Clotilda Smith of
Harmony(?) in New York City; Rev. Dr. Balch (3-12/22)

MASON, Huldah, 70, wf of John formerly of West Troy, NY, d 4/15/50 at Erie,
Penna. (5-4/24)

MASON, John m 6/2/47 Charlotte Smith, both of Troy, in T.; Rev. William Sharp
(5-6/9)

MASON, Martha M. - see HART, I.W.

MASON, Murray (Lieut.) of the US Navy m 12/7/37 Clara C. Forsyth, dau. of Hon.
John, in Washington; Rev. Dr. Hawley (6-12/12)

MASON, Sophronia - see JUDSON, A. (Rev.)

MATHER, ---- (Mrs.) - see CORNING, Asa

MATHER, Alfred, Esq. m 12/26/48 Amaretta H. Learned, both of West Troy, in
W.T.; Rev. J.C. Burroughs (5-12/27)

MATHER, Heman, 10 months, son of Heman and Eliza, d 6/1/48 in West Troy
(congestion of the lungs) (5-6/7)

MATHER, Mary Ann - see HARRIS, F.L.

MATHER, William, M.D. m 5/24/36 Mary A. Buell in Fairfield; Rev. W. Tatham
(all of Fairfield) (3-5/26)

MATHEWS, Susan - see MILLER, Henry

MATHIOT, Susanna - see MILLESS, William

MATTESON, A.L. - see KELLOGG, T.N.

MATTESON, Barbary, 66, wf of Asa, d 6/28/41 at Floyd (a lingering and painful
illness) (1-7/13)

MATTESON, Catherine Amelia, 2 weeks, dau. of H.J. and Vernelia, d 7/20/47
(5-8/4)

MATTESON, Celestia, 11, dau. of Luther and Laura, d 9/28/47 in Rome (see
MATTESON, Charles F.) (1-10/8)

MATTESON, Charles F., 6, youngest son of Luther and Laura, d 9/26/47 in Rome
(see MATTESON, Celestia) (1-10/8)

MATTESON, D.J. - see WALWORTH, Aphelia (Mrs.)

MATTESON, Eliza - see MATTHEWS, Samuel

MATTESON, Elizabeth, 99, widow of Capt. Hezekiah, d 7/27/50 in Verona (she
was born,raised and married near New London, Conn. and "witnessed the
burning of that city by the British troops under the command of Benedict
Arnold the traitor") (1-8/7)

MATTESON, Frances J. - see JOHNSON, David M.K.

MATTESON, Harleigh J. m 1/21/46 Vernelia Smith; Rev. Dodge (all of West Troy) (5-1/28)

MATTESON, James of Rome m 9/2/40 Zenana Robinson of Vienna, Oneida Co. in Rome; Samuel B. Stevens, Esq. (1-9/8)

MATTESON, Jesse of Littlefield m 7/23/39 T. Angeline Streeter of Frankfort; Rev. Thomas Houston (3-8/1)

MATTESON, Louisa A. - see TAYLOR, Sylvester

MATTESON, Sarah, 94, wf of late David, formerly of Arlington, VT, d (date not given) in Fredonia, NY at the home of her son, D.J. Matteson, Esq., ("Bennington, Vt. papers please copy") (1-3/24/48)

MATTESON, Semerinus - see FULLER, Reuben

MATTESON, Silas m 6/20/44 Emely Stanford in Rome; Rev. Alley (all of Rome) (1-6/25)

MATTESON, Squire M., son of late Clark Matteson, d 1/20/42 in Lee (1-2/1)

MATTHEW, Penelope (Mrs.), 73, d 8/13/49 at the home of her son-in-law, S.E. Ford of West Troy (5-8/15)

MATTHEWS, Almira - see ELY, John D.

MATTHEWS, Charles, 1, son of Jared and Ann Amelia, d 5/16/50 in Rome (1-5/22)

MATTHEWS, Chauncey (Dr,), d 2/27/47 in Maumee City, Ohio (born in Camden, NY. For several years a student of Dr. Coleman of Rochester & graduated at the Seneca Medical College in 1837. A year later settled in Maumee (from the Maumee River Times) (1-4/9)

MATTHEWS, Eliza Shumate - see MC INTOSH, James (Lieut.)

MATTHEWS, Henry d 9/6/49 in Saugerties (consumption) (8-9/8)

MATTHEWS, James - see MC INTOSH, James (Lieut.)

MATTHEWS, Robert m 12/30/41 Julia Ferris in Pound Ridge; Rev. Patterson (a double ceremony - see DANN, Alanson) (11-1/4/42)

MATTHEWS, Samuel of Litchfield m 2/17/36 Eliza Matteson of Salisbury in S.; Rev. Rogers (3-3/17)

MATTHEWS, Sylphia - see DUKE, Ben

MATTICE, Joseph of West Troy m 5/5/42 Dorcas Taylor of Troy in T.; Rev. John Cookson (5-5/11)

MATTISON, Melissa - see MC GREGOR, George W.

MATTOON, C.C. m 8/1/50 Roxy Ana Hughes in Oswego; Rev. Almon Chapin (all of Oswego) (1-8/21)

MATTOON, Louisa, 31, wf of Richard, d 3/13/48 in West Troy (pulmonary consumption) (5-4/5)

MAXAM, Harden H., 16, d 10/7/42 at the home of his father (not named) in Rome (1-10/11)

MAXFIELD, Oliver H. m 10/12 45 Mary Malissa Parish, both of West Troy; Rev. Dodge (5-10/15)

MAXON, George G., grocer, of Durhamville m 2/4/41 Ann Marie Wood of Bergen, NJ, at Oneida Castle; Rev. Turner (1-2/23)

MAXWELL, Myles (Rev.), pastor of the Catholic Congregation in Rondout, d 9/1/49 in Rondout (consumption) (8-9/8)

MAXWELL, Sarah J. - see FIERO, Christian C.

MAY, Ann, wf of William L. of Chicago, d 7/19/36 at Chicago (Her husband had been 8 months in Washington and was expected home the evening she died) (Illinois Republican 7/26) (6-8/15)

MAY, William L. - see SPICER, Peter W.

MAYELL, John m (date not given) Lydia Wood; Rev. Ferris (all of Albany) (6-2/10/26)

MAYER, ----, about 80, relict of late Theobold Mayer, d 4/27/39 (3-5/9)

MAYER, Catherine - see MANY, Walter C

MAYER, Elizabeth Seeber, 72, widow of late Henry I., d 4/29/48 in Buffalo (4-5/4)

MAYES, Frederic J. m 7/1/50 Agnes McPhee in Rome; Rev. James Erwin (all of Rome) (1-7/3)

MAYHEW, Emily - see HIGGINS, John Wilson

MAYNARD, Dexter of New Hartford m 10/11/38 Hannah Hagadorn of Salisbury in S.; W. Avery, Esq. (3-10/18)

MAYNARD, Eli, 27, late proprietor of the Utica Observer d 10/1/41 at his home in Utica (1-10/12)

MAYNARD, Eli, proprietor of the Utica Observer m 5/18/36 Mary L. Downer of Kortright at Trinity Church at Utica; Rev. P.A. Proal (6-5/28)

MAYNARD, Eli, proprietor of the Utica Observer, m 5/19/36 Mary L. Downer of Kortright, Delaware County, in Trinity Church at Utica (3-5/26)

MAYNARD, Harriet L. - see HOLBROOK, Daniel

MAYNARD, Lyman S. of New Hartford m 3/15/49 Permilia Bullis of New York Mills at Stanwix Hall in Rome (1-3/14)

MAYNARD, Mary - see MC GUIRE, Michael

MAYNHOOD, Thomas of Saratoga m 10/22/35 (on board the canal boat "Genesee" at Jackson, E.B. Briggs, Captain) "a widow lady from Ohio. The lady came on board at Buffalo and the gentleman at Jordan strangers to each other. After a long courtship of 143 miles they proceeded to tie the nuptial knot - a magistrate at Fort Jackson officiating" (6-11/21)

MC ADAMS, Catharine, about 40, d 8/15/49 in Saugerties (cholera) (see MC ADAMS, John) (8-8/18)

MC ADAMS, John, about 45, d 8/13/49 in Saugerties (cholera) (see MC ADAMS, Catharine) (8-8/18)

MC ALISTER, Charles m 5/11/35 Margaret Vanderzee; Rev. Dr. Ferris, all of Albany (6-5/13)

MC ALLISTER, James M., M.D., m 9/14/37 Miss Frances Henry, youngest dau. of late John W. Rockwell' Rev. John N. Campbell (all of Albany) (6-9/15)

MC ALPINE, W.J., civil engineer, m 2/24/41 S.E. Learned, dau. of E., Esq., of Watervliet; Rev. Raymond (5-3/3)

MC BETH, ---- (Capt.), long a respected resident of West Troy, d 9/20/46 in West Troy (5-9/30)

MC BURNEY, Juliet - see LOW, David (Dr.)

MC CAFFERY, Joseph (age blurred) d 8/20/47 in West Troy at the home of his son-in-law, Mr. Whitbeck (5-9/8)

MC CALL, Henry S., Esq., counsellor-at-law, of Albany m 5/10/49 Rhoda W. Peasley of Bridgeport, Madison County; Rev. J.C. Burroughs (5-5/30)

MC CALL, James (Hon.) of Rushford m 6/6/36 Mrs. Lydia Washburn of Onondaga at O.; Rev. Griswold (6-7/9)

MC CAMMON, William m 6/29/36 Susan Batchelder, both of Albany, Rev. Dr.

Sprague (6-7/1)

MC CANNON, Ann (Mrs.), 105, d 8/20/46 (came to Paterson, NJ "a few months since" from the state of Illimois (from <u>Paterson</u> (NJ) <u>Intelligence</u>) (5-9/2)

MC CARTEE, Elizabeth (Mrs.), 78, d (date not given) in NYC (6-5/8/16)

MC CARTHY, Catharine, 15, dau. of John, d 6/18/49 in Saugerties (born in NYC) (see also MC CARTHY, Michael) (8-6/30)

MC CARTHY, Dennis, Esq., 57, d 7/28/35 in NYC (6-7/31)

MC CARTHY, John, 31 or 51(?), d 12/14/48 in West Troy (5-12/27)

MC CARTHY, Michael, 21, born in Saugerties, d 6/18/49 in Saugerties (son of John Mc Carthy) (see also MC CARTHY, Catharine) (8-6/30)

MC CARTHY, Michael, d 6/18/49 in Saugerties (8-6/23)

MC CARTY, Anna Maria - see VERMILYE, Robert G.

MC CARTY, Charlotte Elizabeth - see VAN PLANK, Isaac

MC CARTY, Margaret - see HAYES, John

MC CARTY, Martha - see VOUGHT, Isaac C.

MC CAUSLAND, Jefferson of Rondout m 5/16/49 Margaret Rause of South Rondout in S.R.; Rev. B.T. Phillips (8-5/26)

MC CHAIN, Ann, 20, dau of late James, d 10/18/39 in Cortlandt Town (11-10/22)

MC CHAIN, Lewis m 4/16/41 Ann Wood, dau of late George; Rev. Johnson (all of Peekskill) (11-4/20)

MC CHESNEY, C.M. (female) - see HALL, Edward

MC CHESNEY, Catharine - see DUDLEY, Charles N.

MC CHESNEY, Christina - see ARNOLD, Edward, Jr.

MC CHESNEY, Mary A. - see possibly MECHESNEY, Mary A.

MC CHESNEY, Robert I., 57, ("and the head of a large family") d 5/21/39 (his 17 children were present at the funeral) (3-6/6)

MC CLEARY, Daniel, about 32, d 12/21/15 in Clarence (was a member elect of the State Legislature for the counties of Niagara and Chautauqua) (6-1/17/16)

MC CLELLAND, ---- (Mrs.), age blurred, d 9/15/42 in Newburgh (9-9/24)

MC CLELLAND, William of Schenectady m 12/19/26 Eliza Brotherson, dau. of Philip, Esq., at Charlton; Rev. Kissam (6-12/26)

MC CLINTOC, Wilson, Esq. of Flag Creek, Cook County, Ill. m 10/26/41 Hellen J. Eames of Channahon, Will County, Ill. at C.; W.B. Peck, Esq. (1-12/28)

MC CLINTOCK, Helen Jane, 35, wf of Wilson, d (date not given) at Flagg Creek, Wills County, Illinois (formerly of Oneida County, NY) (1-12/25/46)

MC CLINTOCK, Mary - see ROCKWELL, George

MC CLINTOCK, Ralph - see ROCKWELL, George

MC CLURE, Hannah - see EARLE, William

MC CLURE, James, merchant, of Geneva m 8/21/26 Elizabeth Pohlman of Albany; Rev. Dr. Chester (6-8/22)

MC CLUSKY, Ruth - see H---KEE(?), William

MC COLLUM, Margaret (Mrs.) of Argyle d 5/4/36 at Albany (funeral at 4 o'clock at home of her son, Robert Mc Collum, 29 North Market St.) (6-5/5)

MC COLLUM, Robert m 3/4/35 Catherine Van Sandford; Rev. F.G. Mayer, all of Albany (6-3/10)

MC CONKEY, Alexander m 2/15/43 Julia Ann Parrot in Newburgh; Rev. E.E. Griswold (9-2/18)

MC CONNY, Ann (Mrs.), 58, d 12/4/48 in Rome (dropsy) (1-12/15)

MC COOL, Dennis, 49, d 10/11/41 in Newburgh (9-10/16)

MC COON, Samuel, Esq., counsellor-at-law, m 4/19/35 Adelia Perkins, dau of Capt. James Perkins in St. Paul's Church at Oxford, NY, all of Oxford; Rev. Leverett Bush (6-4/27)

MC CORD, David, Esq., of Mount Pleasant m 3/20/40 Annie Conklin of New Castle; Rev. Van Deusen (12-3/31)

MC CORD, Frances - see LYON, Munson

MC CORD, Henry T. m 3/15/42 Eliza Waring; Rev. Goodsell (all of Newburgh) (9-3/26)

MC CORD, Robert D. m 2/10/42 Sarah Hewlett, oldest dau. of William, Esq.; Rev. E.E. Griswold (all of Newburgh) (9-2/12)

MC CORD, Samuel of Sing Sing m 11/13/39 Anna Todd, dau. of Uel (sic) Todd of Greenburgh, in G.; Rev. L.M. Vincent (12-11/19)

MC CORIE, Mary Ann - see TILDEN, Barnard

MC CORMICK, Andrew m 4/5/26 Jane Hills; Rev. Leonard (all of Albany) (6-4/25)

MC CORMICK, Ann - see YOUNG, David H.

MC CORMICK, George of firm of Mc Cormick & Pelton, merchants, m 8/18/35 Adeline E. Gere, dau of Hon. Luther Gere; Rev. A.M. Mann, (all of Ithaca) (6-8/22)

MC CORMICK, Thomas m 8/15/48 Eliza Nugent, both of Fort Plain, in F.P.; Rev. Dr. C.G. Mc Lean (4-8/24)

MC CORTNEY, Agnes (Mrs.), 49, d 3/25/42 in Newburgh (9-4/2)

MC CORTY, Enfield - see JOHNSON, A.F.

MC COY, Ann, 55, wf of Capt. John, d 3/4/34 in Annsville (11-3/11)

MC COY, Charles W. (Capt.), 24, late master of the sloop "Ann Van Cortlandt", of Peekskill, and son of David Mc Coy of Annsville, d 12/20/41 at Annsville (11-12/21)

MC COY, Charles William (Capt.), about 25, son of David, d (date not given) at his father's home in Annsville, Cortlandt (11-12/21/41)

MC COY, Edward m 3/3/42 Sarah A. Foster, in Phillipstown; Rev. William H. Johnson (11-3/8)

MC COY, John - see CRAIG, Jane

MC COY, Julia - see GALUSHA, Ambrose

MC CRACKEN, Elizabeth, 59, widow of Rev. George Mc Cracken and dau. of William Snyder of Albany, d 5/13/26 in Troy (6-5/19)

MC CRACKEN, Samuel m 10/6/26 Sophia Van Tassell; Rev. Edwards (all of Albany) (6-10/10)

MC CREA, Thomas d 1/13/35 at Phillipsburgh, Orange Co. "leaving a large family" (6-1/22)

MC CREARY, Thomas, an elderly and respected person, d 3/1/42 in Newburgh (9-3/5)

MC CREDIE, Helen, 24, wf of Thomas and youngest dau. of Robert Dunlop, Esq., of Watervliet d 12/6/50 (5-12/11)

MC CREDY, Russilla - see WICK, Henry

MC CREEDIE, Thomas, late of Philadelphia, m 7/19/48 Helen Dunlop, dau. of R. Dunlop, Esq. of Watervliet, in Albany at the Delavan House; Rev. Dr. Kennedy (5-7/26)

MC CULLOUGH, William of Newburgh m 3/21/42 Harriet Gaylord of New

Windsor; Rev. J. Johnston (9-3/26)

MC CUNE, Jane - see MILLS, George

MC CUNE, Margaret - see HIGGINS, Joseph

MC DANIELS, Sally, 53, wf of James, d 6/7/37 at Danby, Conn. (a lingering illness) (6-6/22)

MC DERMOTT, Thomas, 27, son of Robert, Esq. of NYC d "a few days since" in NYC (pulmonary complaint) (6-1/24/26)

MC DONALD, Angus, 105, d (date not given) at his son's home in Knox, Albany County (born in Inverness, Scotland, "came to America as a private soldier with the army destined for the conquest of Canada - settled in Stonington, Conn. where he married." "Was a Rev. War soldier" (6-3/10/26)

MC DONALD, George m 7/7/47 Sarah Butler, dau. of Ezekiel, Esq., H.C. Vogell (1-7/9)

MC DONALD, Hugh m 12/4/37 Jane Ann Nelliger, both of Albany; Rev. S.V. E. Westfall of Union (6-12/5)

MC DONALD, James, 53, formerly of Canajoharie, d 8/19/48 in Clinton, Mich. (4-9/28)

MC DONALD, Mary - see MARTIN, Edward

MC DONNELS, Jerome of Fishkill m 11/30/39 Abigail Bennet of Quincy, Putnam County, in Q.; Rev. Daniel D. Tompkins

MC DOUGAL, Isaac of Ava m 6/18/50 Hannah M. Jones of Lee in L.; Rev. J.S. Kibbe (1-7/10)

MC DOUGALL, Peter, Esq. m 2/1/16 Jane Truesdale of Schenectady; Rev. Cumming (6-2/7)

MC DOUGALL, William, 43, printer, formerly of Albany, d 10/19/35 in NYC (consumption) (6-10/21)

MC DOWELL, Margaret (Mrs.), 73, d 4/28/35 at house of Hon. Nicholl Halsey in Ulysses, Tompkins Co., (Her biography "would be the history of the rise and progress of the Methodist Episcopal Church in the Lake Country." More than 40 years ago (she) accompanied the Rev.'s Valentine, Gook and Broadhead to Appletow (now Seneca Co.) (from Ithaca Journal) (6-5/15)

MC ELRATH, Anna (Mrs.), 75, mother of one of the publishers of the New York Tribune, d 3/11/47 suddenly at her home in Williamsport, Penn. (1-3/26)

MC ELROY, Jane - see MC NAUGHTON, Peter

MC ELROY, Jane (Mrs.), 27, d 1/2/42 in Newburgh (9-1/8)

MC ELROY, Jane, 75, wf of Alexander Mc Elroy of Trenton, NY, d 4/26/35 in Albany, at home of her son, Thomas Mc Elroy (6-4/28)

MC ELROY, Peter m 10/6/36 Ellen White; Rev. James Martin (all of Albany) (6-10/7)

MC EVERS, Eliza - see RAVENEL, John

MC EWAN, Elen Ann, 7, eldest dau. of John, d 10/9/39 in Little Falls (funeral sermon was preached in the Baptist Church) (3-10/10)

MC FADDEN, Archibald S. of Albany m 12/26/45 Nancy Pomeroy of West Troy in W.T.; Rev. O.H. Gregory (5-12/31)

MC FALL, William, 106, d (date not given) in Pelham, Westchester County (6-1/10/16)

MC FARLAND, John, 9, son of the late John Mc Farland, d 11/19/35 in Albany (funeral at 3 o'clock from the home of Mrs. Rose in Wendell St.) (6-11/20)

MC GEORGE, Philis - see NICHOLS, Alonzo

MC GILL, Eliza Jane - see CAMPBELL, John

MC GLASHAN, Delia - see FORSY, David

MC GLASHAN, Maria, 23, wf of William, d 1/26/26 in Albany (funeral from her late residence at 21 Store Lane) (6-1/27)

MC GOWN, Eliza - see FERRIS, Leonard

MC GRATH, Hugh, printer, d 5/29/36 in Albany ("funeral tomorrow at 5 o'clock from his late home, 247 South Pearl St.") (6-5/30)

MC GRAW, Mary Ann - see CRAWLEY, James

MC GREGOR, Ann M. - see BURDICK, John P.

MC GREGOR, Charlotte - see BADGLEY, Philip

MC GREGOR, Frances E.C. - see DEANE, Thomas M.

MC GREGOR, George W. m 11/1/44 Melissa Mattison, both of Schaghticoke, in West Troy; Rev. O.H. Gregory (5-12/4)

MC GREGOR, James, Esq., 35, of Napanee, Upper Canada d 1/27/1835 of consumption at the American Hotel in Albany while enroute to Scotland. Members of St. Andrew's Society invited to attend his funeral at 3 p.m. today at the American Hotel (6-1/28)

MC GREGOR, Melissa, 22, wf of George W., d 4/13/48 at Schaghticoke (Odd Fellows from Lansingburgh, Waterford and Cohoes attended the funeral "in large numbers" (5-4/26)

MC GREGOR, William m 6/16/49 Ann Gildersleeve; Rev. T.F. Wyckoff (all of West Troy) (5-6/20)

MC GUIGAN, Francis m 12/8/35 Sarah W. Southwick, youngest dau of H.C. Southwick; Rev. Welch (6-12/10)

MC GUIN, Susan - see FLINT, Amos

MC GUIRE, Harriet - see BLAKE, ----

MC GUIRE, Mary - see STOCKDALE, William

MC GUIRE, Michael m 6/5/37 Mary Maynard, both of Albany; David Russell, Esq. (6-6/7)

MC HARG, Jane Ann - see WOLCOTT, John P.

MC HATTON, Robert (General), a former member of Congress from Kentucky d 5/20/35 in Marion County, Indiana (a lingering illness) (6-6/11)

MC INTOSH, Euphemia Alston, wf of George and dau of James Hamilton of NYC, d 11/12/35 at General Mc Intosh's in St. Mary's, Georgia (6-12/4)

MC INTOSH, James (Lieut.), son of Gen. John Mc Intosh of Georgia, m 12/29/15 Mrs. Elizabeth Shumate, eldest dau. of James Matthews of Brooklyn, at B.; Rev. Woodhull (6-11/6/16)

MC INTYRE, Amelia O. - see SMITH, Edwin

MC INTYRE, Jacob, 9, son of Daniel, d 9/15/36 in Warren (3-9/29)

MC INTYRE, James, Esq., 59, d 7/24/35 at Broadalbin (6-7/31)

MC KAY, Henry, Esq., merchant, of Little Falls m 12/28/36 Susan M. Bruton, dau. of late Eben Bruton, of Little Falls, in Bethlehem; Rev. Horatio Potter (3-1/26/37)

MC KAY, Susan - see KUMMEL, Henry E.

MC KEE, Margaret, 58, wf of Thomas, Senior, late of NYC, d 6/14/36 (6-6/22)

MC KEE, Thomas, Sr., d 7/24/36 in Albany ("funeral tomorrow at 9 o'clock" from home of his son (not named) at 105 State St.) (6-7/26)

MC KEEN, Margaret - see SCRANTON, Henry

MC KELLAR, Robert m 12/15/41 Ann Eliza Curry, eldest dau of Rev. Benjamin

Curry, at Shrub Oaks; Rev. Benjamin Curry (11-12/21)

MC KIEFREY, ---- (Mrs.), wf of William, d 3/20/49 in Saugerties (8-3/24)

MC KIM, James, 27, first officer of ship "James Titcomb" and oldest son of John, Esq., of Washington, DC, d 10/18/48 at New Orleans (yellow fever) (4-11/2)

MC KINNEY, A. - see GRACIE, Oliver C.

MC KINNEY, Erastus of Albany m 12/31/34 Emeline Churchill, dau of Roswell of Albany; Rev. Hill (6-1/6/35)

MC KINNEY, Mary Ann - see GRACIE, Oliver C.

MC KINSTRY, Henry, about 2, only child of Henry, d 11/16/09 in Catskill (7-11/19)

MC KNIGHT, George, of the house of George McKnight & Co. m 1/11/35 Susan Wheeler at St. Paul's Church in Buffalo, Rev. Shelton. (bride & groom of Buffalo) (6-2/19)

MC KOON, Samuel, Esq., counsellor-at-law, m 4/19/35 Adelia Perkins, dau of Capt. James Perkins in St. Paul's Church at Oxford, NY; Rev. Leverett Bush (6-4/25)

MC KOWN, James m 4/25/16 Susan Denniston, dau. of Isaac of Albany; Rev. Dr. Neill (6-5/1)

MC LACHLAN, Jane - see FORBES, William

MC LACHLAN, Margaret - see MOFFATT, Hugh

MC LACHLAN, Robert, 27, d 5/28/37 (6-5/29)

MC LANE, Rebecca, consort of Judge Mc Lane of the Supreme Court and postmaster general during the administration of J.Q. Adams, d in early December in Louisville, Kentucky (she was a member of the Methiodist Church) (11-12/21/41)

MC LAREN, Mary E., 7, dau. of Rev. Malcom Mc Laren, d 4/5/42 at Hamptonburgh (9-4/9)

MC LAUGHLIN, Levina B. - see HENRY, Jacob

MC LEAH, Dorcas, 74, widow of John, d 3/21/47 in Waterville (1-4/2)

MC LEE, James P. m "lately" Margaret Smith in Minden (3-2/2/37)

MC LENE, Jeremiah, 70, of Columbus, Ohio, d 3/19/37 in Washington City (a painful illness that started 3/4). He had completed his second term in Congress - representative for the eighth Congressional District of Ohio (6-3/28)

MC LENSLEY, Maria - see CASLER, Levi

MC LEOD, Alexander, Esq. m 3/13/42 Helen Norman Morrison, eldest dau. of Capt. Morrison of Stamford, Upper Canada, at Stamford; Rev. W. Leeming (5-3/30)

MC MANNUS, John of NYC m 9/14/35 Frances L. Hendricson, dau of John of Albany; Rev. J.H. Tice(?) (6-9/16)

MC MANUS, William, 54, d 1/18/35 (pulmonary complaint) served as justice of the peace, surrogate and district attorney. In 1825 served one term in National Congress. In 1833 accompanied his dau. to Texas and returned home in spring 1834. Had intended to return to Texas in 1835. (from Troy Budget) (6-2/2)

MC MARTIN, Ann - see PEMBERTON, T.L.

MC MARTIN, Duncan, Jr. (Hon.) d 10/3/37 at Broadalbin ("had adorned the legislative halls and the judicial bench of the state")(from the Fonda

<u>Herald</u>) (6-10/10)

MC MULLEN, Andrew m 8/3/36 Alida Wendell, both of Albany, at Schenectady; Rev. Proal (6-8/12)

MC MULLEN, Jane - see MC NEAL, John

MC MULLEN, Thomas - see VAN BENTHUYSEN, Susan (Mrs.)

MC MURRAY, William, Rev. D.D., 51, d 9/22/35 in NYC (pastor of the Reformed Dutch Church, in Market Street, NYC) (6-9/28)

MC NAUGHTON, Dr. P. - see STEELE, Tempe

MC NAUGHTON, Peter, M.D., of Scottsville m 6/26/36 Jane Mc Elroy, third dau of late Samuel of Albany, in A.; Rev. C. Gates (6-6/30)

MC NAVIN, Isabella - see HOLMES, Alexander

MC NEAL, John of Minden m "lately" Jane Mc Mullen of Danube in D. (3-6/13/39)

MC NEAL, Sylvester m 10/17/38 Hannah Dinger, dau of Tyler Dinger, Esq., in Bedford, Cherry Street; Rev. Keyes (12-10/23)

MC NEESILE, George, 35, formerly of Kingston, d 7/12/49 in NYC (8-7/21)

MC NEIL, D.B. (Col.) - see BROMLEY, John Hallock

MC NEIL, Mary Malvena -see BROMLEY, John Hallock

MC NOAB, Grace (Miss), 20, d 6/19/37 (consumption) (6-6/21)

MC PARSONS, A., of Troy m 5/25/37 Mary Thorp of Catskill in C.; Rev. Thomas M. Smith (6-6/5)

MC PHEE, Agnes - see MAYES, Frederic J.

MC QUADE, Rosetta, 32 (or 52?), wife of Patrick d 8/22/36 (funeral at 5 o'clock from 38 Van Schaick St.) (6-8/23)

MC RAY, H., Esq., merchant of Little Falls m 1/19/37 Susan M. Britton, dau. of late Eben Britton of Little Falls, in Bethlehem; Rev. Horatio Potter (6-1/18)

MC VITHE(?), Mark, Esq. of Washingtonville m 7/2/42 Ellen Ford of New Windsor in Newburgh; Rev. Hill (9-7/9)

MEACER, Daniel, Esq. m 1/3/50 Sarah Fredericks of Rome in Taberg; Rev. Brown (1-1/16)

MEACHAM, John (Mrs.) - see COLLYER, William

MEAD, Amos of South Bethlehem m 11/29/38 Hannah M. Morehouse, dau of Aaron of Ballston, Saratoga Co., in B.; Rev. Fox (12-12/18)

MEAD, Angeline R - see TODD, William A.

MEAD, Benjamin, about 25, d 12/16/50 in Southeast (survived by a wife and 2 children) (10-12/19)

MEAD, Charlotte - see WICKSON, Alva

MEAD, David, a Rev. War soldier and brother-in-law of David Williams, one of the capturers of Major Andre, d 5/22/36 at Coeymans (6-5/27)

MEAD, Edward N (Rev.), rector of St. Paul's Church in Sing Sing, m 12/26/38 Jane Creighton, oldest dau of Rev. Dr. Creighton, at the home of her father; Right Rev. Bishop Onderdonk (12-1/1/39)

MEAD, Emeline - see GILLET, Jacob

MEAD, Henry m 7/4/48 Elizabeth Mosher at Pleasant Valley; Rev. A. Mosher (4-7/20)

MEAD, Henry of Philipstown m 11/21/35 Eliza Bulson of Peekskill; Rev. Daniel D. Tompkins (11-11/24)

MEAD, Isaac R.(Col.) m 3/11/40 Elizabeth Jane Horton, dau. of late James P., Esq.; Rev. Henry (all of Mount Pleasant) (12-3/17)

MEAD, Jane Ann - see BOOKMASTER(?), Francis

MEAD, Louisa - see ALEXANDER, Stephen

MEAD, Lucy - see MACDONALD, Lancelot G.

MEAD, Phebe Martha, 2, dau of John Mead, merchant, of Peekskill, d (date not given) (11-9/17/39)

MEAD, Sarah Emma - see WATERMAN, Henry P.

MEADE, Orlando of Albany m 4/14/35 Elizabeth Wilson, dau of the late James Wilson, of Elizabethtown, NJ at E. (6-4/21)

MEADS, Esther L. - see GORMAN, John

MECHESNEY, Mary A. - see PALMER, William M.

MECKING, Catharine - see FUEHS, Emanuel

MEEHAN, Jane A. - see BRAMAN, Adam

MEEKS, J.C. m 3/13/42 Harriet Barry, dau. of Capt. John Barry of NYC; Rev. Dr. Mc Asley (3-4/21)

MEETZ, J.Y. (Rev.), 76, d (date not given). Had 10 children with 4 sons and 5 daughters as well as 40 grandchildren and 12 Great grandchildren surviving him (11-6/4/33)

MEGGS(?), Caroline - see SINK, Robert

MEGGS, ----, 44, wf of Phineas, d 1/25/09 (very suddenly) (7-2/1)

MEGGS, Phineas m 4/26/10 Mrs. Morgan (7-5/2)

MEGGS, Polly - see DANIELSON, Peter

MEIGS, S.M. - see KEELER, Sarah Lucretia

MEKEEL, Sarah - see HALL, Northrup

MELICK, James O., Esq., formerly of Waterford, m 9/1/44 Sophia Norton of Huron, Mich. at H.; Rev. Alanson Fleming (5-9/25)

MELIES, Elizabeth - see DALTON, Alexander

MENEELY, Elizabeth Robinson, 5, dau. of James and Ann, d 3/8/38 in West Troy (5-3/14)

MENEELY, James Harvey, 18 months, youngest son of James and Ann, d 6/27/42 in West Troy (5-7/6)

MENEELY, James, 40, d 4/25/47 in West Troy (consumption) (funeral from his late home on Broad Street near Buffalo Street) (5-4/28)

MENEELY, Juliet Augusta, 6, dau. of Andrew and Philena, d 7/25/49 in West Troy (5-8/1)

MERCEBEAU, Lawrence (Rev.), late of West Troy m 9/30/46 Adelaide Stone, dau. of late Henry, Esq., of Rensselaerville, at R.; Rev. Marcus Smith (5-10/7)

MERCER, Norman C. m 9/20/37 Eliza Ann Lawton in Eatonville; Rev. J.D. Hicks (3-11/4)

MERCHANT, George W. m 8/8/37 Ann Walbridge, only dau. of E.W., Esq. of Lansingburgh, at L.; Rev. Phelps (6-8/10)

MERCHANT, Rosetta - see PARKSMAN, Robert H.

MERICK, Mary T. - see SEELY, James

MERITT, Helen Ann, about 20, d 9/24/42 in Lewisboro (11-9/29)

MERITT, Henry m 1/26/43 Mary Jane Burdsall at Marlborough; Rev. Oldren (9-1/28)

MERRELL, Jacob M. - see MARSHALL, Abner

MERRIAM, E.N., cashier of Lewis County Bank m (date not given) Mary M. Hulbert, dau. of Hon. R. Hulbert of Boonville, in B.; Rev. E.A. Renouf, rector of Trinity Church in Lowville (1-9/15)

MERRICK, Cecelia B. - see MERRILL, Charles

MERRIFIELD, William - see BROWN, Sarah Ann

MERRILL, Ardon m 10/2/44 Jane B. Blair, one of two oldest daus. of Abner B.;
Rev. Button (all of Rome) (double ceremony - see FRASER, John O.)
(1-10/8)

MERRILL, Benjamin - see LOUNSBURY, Sarah Ann

MERRILL, Benjamin - see LOUNSBURY, Sarah Ann

MERRILL, Charles (Dr.) of West Troy (formerly of Springfield, Maine) m 2/20/43
Cecelia B. Merrick of Troy in T.; Rev. Z. Phillips (5-2/22)

MERRILL, Edward, 7 months, youngest son of Edward A. and Jane Merrill, d
10/26/36 in Albany (6-11/1)

MERRILL, Electa Jane - see INGHAM, Samuel

MERRILL, Emeline N. - see WASHBURN, George E.

MERRILL, Emily, 42, wf of James and sister of publisher of the Herkimer Journal,
d "in April" in Jackson County, Michigan (long and painful illness)
(3-12/16/41)

MERRILL, James, 2, only son of Edward E. and Jane, d 7/20/37 in Albany (6-7/24)

MERRILL, John of Oneida Castle m 6/7/42 Betsey E. Lampman of Oneida Lake at
Oneida Depot; Rev. Ketchingman (1-6/14)

MERRILL, Sarah - see REXFORD, George R.

MERRILL, Timothy, Esq., 55, Secretary of State of Vermont, d 7/27/36 at
Montpelier, VT (was an officer of that state about 30 years) (6-8/15)

MERRILLS, Lester m 11/1/46 Mary Ann Dowzer in Lee; Squire Thorn (all of Lee)
(1-11/3)

MERRIT, Sarah E. - see GRAFT, Samuel

MERRITT, Ann Marie - see BLISS, Benjamin

MERRITT, Benjamin H. of Carmel m 11/21/49 Martha Jane Roney(?) of Somers in
S.; Rev. Mc Laughlin (10-11/21)

MERRITT, Caroline, youngest dau. of Jotham, d 8/10/39 at Greenwich, CT
(12-8/20)

MERRITT, Charles W. m 7/12/43 Mary Aldrich at Trinity Church, West Troy;
Rev. Bissell (5-7/19)

MERRITT, Elizabeth, (age blurred), widow of Gilbert, d 6/22/49 in Patterson
(10-6/27)

MERRITT, Isaac, about 40, son of James, d 11/22/38 in Sing Sing (consumption)
(12-12/4)

MERRITT, John, 9 months, son of John J. and Hannah B., d 1/24/42 in Peekskill at
the home of Caleb Brown (11-2/15)

MERRITT, Jotham m 11/12/38 Elizabeth Paige, dau of B. Paige, Esq., at Fairfield,
CT; Rev. Nicholl (12-11/20)

MERRITT, Mary Ann - see LAWRENCE, William

MERRITT, Solomon of Sing Sing, m 11/1/38 Adeline Travis of Cortlandtown in
C.; Rev. Youngs (12-11/6)

MERRY, Caroline A. - see DEVENDORF, Cornelius

MERRY, Orson m 2/5/39 Mary Kimball in Frankfort; Rev. L. Beach (3-2/21)

MERRY, Ralph - see DEVENDORF, Cornelius

MERSELIS, Ann - see FORT, Jacob S.

MERWIN, Hanford, 39, d 4/28/42 in Newburgh (9-4/30)

MERWIN, Samuel (Rev.), 62, of the Methodist Episcopal Church, d 1/12/39 at his home in Rhinebeck (12-1/29)

MESSINGER, Almon C. m 10/4/49 A. Jane Benjamin of Oneida Lake, Madison County, in Utica; Rev. William H. Spencer (1-10/10)

MESSINGER, Orson B., Esq., attorney at law, m 3/18 41 Margaret Moulthrop at Durhamville; Rev. W. Turner (all of Durhamville) (1-4/20)

MESSLER, Abraham, pastor of the Reformed Church at Ovid, m 9/11/26 Elma Doremus, only dau. of Cornelius T., at NYC; Rev. Dr. Matthews (6-9/19)

MESSLER, Cornelius, 83, a Rev. War soldier, d (date not given) near White House, Hunterdon County, NJ (5-1/17/44)

METCALF, Catharine, wf of William, d 8/27/48 in West Troy (5-9/13)

METCALF, Francis P. m 5/12/39 Mary Shaft, both of Little Falls in L.F.; Rev. Dunning (3-5/16)

METCALF, Lorenzo D. m (date not given) Rosanna Wood in Stratford; Rev. Elder Knapp (3-10/27/42)

METCALF, Luke - see SHERBURNE, Silas

METCALF, William of West Troy m 9/29/50 Esther Norton of Troy; Rev. Joshua Weaver (5-10/2)

METTESON, Cyrus W. m 11/17/46 Mary Farquerson, dau. of John, at Rome; Elder H.C. Vogell (bride & groom of Rome) (1-11/24)

MICHAEL, Sarah - see HARMAN, Joseph

MICHAELS, Mary Laura - see THROOP, Origin B.

MICHAELS, William G. - see THROOP, Origin B.

MIDDAUGH, Alxander m 6/3/49 Susan Dier in Saugerties; Rev. P.C. Oakley (all of Saugerties) (8-6/16)

MIDDAUGH, Jesse m 9/22/49 Elmira Hardenbergh in Saugerties; Rev. P.C. Oakley (all of Saugerties) (8-9/29)

MILES, Isaac, 69, d 9/1/42 in New Castle (11-9/15)

MILES, Laura E. - see HAYDEN, Lysander

MILES, Marcus W. m 12/20/48 Sarah Washburn; Rev. Chitester (all of Lee) (1-1/5/49)

MILES, Matilda M - see WASHBURN, David C.

MILES, Oliver C. of Lee m 11/17/50 Mary Jane Spkes (sic) of Remsen at the parsonage in Lee Centre; Rev. J.S. Kibbe (1-11/27)

MILLEISEN, William m 8/21/49 Maria Loucks; James W. Hamilton, Esq. (all of Fort Plain) (4-8/23)

MILLER, ---- (given name not shown), 10, dau. of James, d 11/18/41 in Newburgh (9-11/20)

MILLER, --- (Mrs.), 84, mother of Hon. Elijah Miller, d 10/3/35 at Auburn (6-10/17)

MILLER, A.D., 27, formerly of Richfield, Otsego County, d 6/29/36 at Harmony, Chautauqua County (3-7/21)

MILLER, Abigail - see FISHER, Barber

MILLER, Abraham Oakey, 24, son of late Peter of Albany, d 11/20/36 in NYC (consumption) (6-11/23)

MILLER, Andrew, 19, drowned 6/28/39 on the ship "John Howland" of New Bedford (born in Peekskill) (11-8/6)

MILLER, Ann Eliza - see QUICK, George

MILLER, Ann Eliza - see QUICK, George

MILLER, Ann Eliza - see STRATTON, Austin

MILLER, Benjamin F., 47, d 1/27/49 in Saugerties (8-2/3)

MILLER, Betsey, 70, wf of Caleb, d 2/2/38 in Little Falls (lingering and painful illness) (3-2/8)

MILLER, Catherine - see JOHNSON, ——

MILLER, Clarissa, dau of the widow Susanna Miller and sister of Erastus Miller of Albany, d suddenly 6/18/35 "while on a visit to Mr. D.J. Kinney's in Coeymans." (6-7/21)

MILLER, Cornelia - see WOOLLEY, Nathaniel C.

MILLER, David m 12/22/41 Emeline Miller; Rev. Hunt (all of Whitlockville) (11-1/4/42)

MILLER, David m 12/23/41 Emeline Miller in Whitlockville; Rev. J. Hunt (11-12/28)

MILLER, David, 76, d 2/16/43 in Newburgh (9-2/18)

MILLER, Delinda, 30, wf of James, d 3/14/39 in Bedford (12-3/19)

MILLER, Diana - see WALTZ, Gashere

MILLER, Elijah Jr., about 28, d 2/23/40 in Bedford (12-3/10)

MILLER, Eliphalet, 31(?), d 4/21/49 in NYC (buried in Saugerties) (8-4/28)

MILLER, Eliza - see GODFREY, Nelson

MILLER, Elizabeth, 38, wf of Samuel, d 2/5/38 in Little Falls (3-2/15)

MILLER, Ellen D. - see ENGLISH, Charles S.

MILLER, Emeline - see MILLER, David

MILLER, Francis - see MORKEE, Eli

MILLER, Gerrit m 11/2/36 Martha Seman, dau of late David; Rev. E.P. Stimpson (all of Schodack Centre) (6-11/3)

MILLER, Harriet L. - see GLADDING, Edward W.

MILLER, Henry m (date not given) Susan Mathews at Greenfield (6-5/15/16)

MILLER, Huldah (Widow), 98 or 38 (?), d 9/6/42 in Fairfield (3-9/15)

MILLER, James A., M.D., m 4/11/50 Harriet M. Weston at Stittsville; W. Ralph, Esq. (all of Trenton, Oneida County) (1-4/17)

MILLER, James, Esq. - see BAKER, Albert L.

MILLER, James, Esq. - see MANCHESTER, Bradford A.

MILLER, Jemima - see BOWMAN, James

MILLER, John Statts Lansing, 1, son of Dr. Jacob S. Miller, d 8/27/36 at Claverack (6-9/2)

MILLER, Luther, 73, d 9/5/46 in Rockford, Illinois (illness of five weeks) ("County papers please copy") (1-9/22)

MILLER, M.C.B. m 8/3/33 Sarah A. Verplank, dau of late Phillip, Esq., of Verplank's Point, at Trinity Church; Rev. Dr. Anthon (11-9/10)

MILLER, Margaret, 25, wf of George, d 6/5/49 at Ellenville (consumption) ("left three small children") (8-6/16)

MILLER, Margaret, wf of J.B., d 10/2/42 at New Windsor (9-10/8)

MILLER, Margaretta - see CARNEY, John

MILLER, Martin of Greenbush m 11/6/47 Mary Ann Van Olinda, eldest dau. of J.A., Esq., of Watervliet, in W.; Rev. William Pitcher (5-11/3)

MILLER, Mary Ann - see HAM, Henry

MILLER, Nancy Jane, 21, wf of John, d 7/30/42 in Ridgefield, CT (11-8/11)

MILLER, Peter H. of South Salem, NY m 12/18/38 Mary A. Jones of Ridgefield, CT in R.; Rev. Wheeler (12-12/25)

MILLER, Phebe, 55, wf of Luther, d 8/1/46 in Rockford, Illinois (a short illness) ("Papers in Oneida County please copy") (1-8/18)

MILLER, Rachel - see MANCHESTER, Bradford A.

MILLER, Renette C. - see THOMPSON, Nelson

MILLER, Sarah - see REED, Matthew

MILLER, Sarah Ann - see BAKER, Albert L.

MILLER, Sarah S. , wf of William C., d 12/28/37 (6-12/29)

MILLER, Stephen, about 22, son of Joseph, d 10/4/42 (consumption) (11-10/4)

MILLER, Thomas, eldest son of John, Esq., of Steuben, m 1/4/42 Nancy Vanderwacker of Western in W.; Rev. Charles Brooks of Steuben (1-2/1)

MILLER, William M., 29, second son of late Peter of Albany, d 12/7/36 at St. Croix (consumption) (xx15-1/2/37)

MILLER, William, Jr., m 2/13/48 Mrs. Electa Barber, both of West Troy; Rev. Houghtaling (5-2/23)

MILLESS, William m (date not given) Susanna Mathiot in Baltimore (6-5/15/16)

MILLIGAN, William G. of Utica m 9/16/41 (in the morning) Eliza A. Girvan, dau. of William, Esq. of Little Falls, in L.F.; Rev. Loveys (3-9/16)

MILLIMAN, Lewis I. m 6/7/45 Mary Porter, both of West Troy in W.T.; Rev. O.H. Gregory (5-6/18)

MILLIS, Elizabeth - see MOTT, Joseph

MILLS, Ann Maria - see COOK, R.S.

MILLS, Deloss of Lowville, Lewis County m Permelia Lansing of Ames in A.; Rev. C.H. Hervey (4-6/14)

MILLS, Diantha P. - see COBB, Lucius J.

MILLS, Dwight of Lewis County m 9/5/48 Hannahette White of Ames at A.; Rev. C.H. Harvey (4-9/14)

MILLS, George m 9/22/46 Jane Mc Cune, dau. of Alexander, Esq., of Rome; H.C. Vogell (1-10/6)

MILLS, Henry (Rev.) m (date not given) Maria Moore Barkins at Morristown, New Jersey; Rev. Henry Mills (6-5/25/16)

MILLS, Jonah T., 49, d 6/22/39 in Bedford (12-7/2)

MILLS, Louisa - see MITCHELL, A.H.

MILLS, Lucy, 72, consort of Deacon Samuel Mills of Guilford, d 11/9/26 at Guilford (6-11/28/26)

MILLS, Lyman m 12/9/42 Mary Schuyler; Rev. Mc Illvaine (all of Little Falls) (3-12/29)

MILLS, Martha, 85, relict of Isaac, d 2/7/35 at Chatham (6-2/13)

MILLS, Mary Ann - see WHITE, James

MILLS, Samuel John, 3, youngest son of Abram and Grace, d 4/1/39 at Litchfield (3-5/2)

MILLS, Samuel of Rome m 8/5/50 Mrs. Martha M. Usher of Saratoga Springs at S.S.; Rev. Chipp (1-9/18)

MILLS, Sarah - see WEST, John

MILLS, Seth D. of Penfield m 4/17/43 Julia A. Taylor of Lee at Lee; Rev. Bond (3-4/27)

MILLS, Sophia F. - see HULL, Judson

MILSON, Mary - see DUNN, Edward

MILWARD, Ellen - see THOMPSON, Joseph

MINER, Isaac of firm of Miner and Co. of Camden m 7/12/40 Paulina Hungerford of Vernon in Vernon Center; Rev. Seth Hastings (1-8/18)

MINER, Mary - see FULLER, George

MINER, Mary Elizabeth - see CUNNINGHAM, George

MINER, Sarah - see BARNES, Erastus

MINERLY, Joel m 9/26/41 Harriet Rhodes in Peekskill; Rev. William H. Johnson (11-9/28)

MINK, Stephen G. m 4/22/35 Hannah Wilkinson; Rev. Holmes (6-4/25)

MINN, David S m 1/6/35 Lucretia Weed; Rev. Price (all of Albany) (6-1/8)

MINNERLY, Joel, 32, d 5/19/39 in Sing Sing (12-5/21)

MINOR, Elizabeth M. - see YOUNG, Thomas Y.

MINOR, Marietta - see CLINTON, Morris

MINOR, Marvin of Cohoes m 11/21/47 Rebecca Ann Mitchell of West Troy in W.T.; Rev. Smith of Waterford (5-11/24)

MINOR, Russel(?) - see PADDOCK, Sarah

MINOR, Stephen (Major), President of the Bank of the Mississippi, d 10/20/15 (6-1/10/16)

MINTERN, Robert B. of NYC m 6/2/35 Anna Mary Wendell (dau of John L, Esq. of Albany, at St. Peter's Church; Rev. Horatio Potter (6-6/3)

MISSON, Moses m 5/5/48 Susan Spencer in Fort Plain; Rev. Dr. C.G. Mc Lean (4-5/11)

MITCHELL, ----, wf of William d (date not given) (friends of her husband and his brothers-in-law, Chauncy and Friend Humphrey are invited to her funeral at 9 o'clock from her husband's home, 109 South Pearl St.) (6-9/10)

MITCHELL, A.H. of Boonville m 1/1/50 Louisa Mills of Clinton in C.; Rev. Vermilye (1-1/9)

MITCHELL, Clinton, superintendent of the Canajoharie Deaf and Dumb Institution, m (date not given) Mary E. Rose, an assistant teacher in the NY Institution, in NYC (Miss Rose is a mute) (6-9/26/26)

MITCHELL, Edward, a soldier in the US Army "and one of the permament recruiting party of this station", d 5/12/37 in Albany (6-5/16)

MITCHELL, Elizabeth, 29, wf of William Mitchell, d 3/.30/26 in Albany (funeral from her husband's home at 48 Hamilton St.) (6-3/31)

MITCHELL, Hiram of Vienna m 12/11/49 Jan Rowbotham of Rome; H.C. Vogell (1-1/9/50)

MITCHELL, Josiah, Esq., of White Plains m 2/9/42 Elizabeth Anderson, dau of Joseph H., Esq., at Harrison; Rev. E. Wright (11-2/22)

MITCHELL, Julia Ann, 6, dau of William, d 11/24/36 in Albany (6-11/28)

MITCHELL, Julia Marie - see GARVIN, Samuel B.

MITCHELL, Rebecca Ann - see MINOR, Marvin

MITCHELL, Rowena (Mrs.), 42, d 6/8/35 in Norwich (consumption) (6-6/15)

MITCHELL, Stephen, about 70, d 9/27/46 in West Troy (5-9/30)

MITCHELL, william, about 32, d 7/17/26 in Albany (6-7/18)

MIX, Catharine - see SANFORD, Rodney (Col.)

MIX, Eli H. of Whitestown m Sarah Storms of Annsville in A.; Rev. Van Valkenburg (1-9/5)

MIX, James m 11/21/15 Elizabeth Vischer, both of Albany; Rev. DeWitt (6-11/25)

MIX, Warren of Camden m 1/1/42 Patience Amanda Julia of Utica at U.; Rev. W.N. Pearse (1-1/4)

MOAK, Charlotte - see HOLMES, John A.

MOAK, Nancy, 40, consort of John Moak, d 2/11/43 in Theresa, Jefferson County (typhus fever) (survived by her husband and four children) ("Albany editors please copy")(3-2/23)

MOE, Elizabeth, 28, wf of Robert I., d 3/16/48 in West Troy (5-3/22)

MOE, Robert I. m 1/18/42 Elizabeth Brown, dau. of Luther at West Troy; Rev. Hoskens (5-1/26)

MOFFATT, Hugh m 11/23/36 Margaret Mc Lachlan, both of Albany; Rev. T.E. Vermilye (6-11/26)

MOGER, Louise, 32, wf of David, d 10/29/39 in Bedford (12-11/5)

MOLAN, David, about 75, d 10/14/45 in West Troy (5-10/22)

MOLL, Andrew (Capt.) of Schodack m 1/6/35 Jane Nichols of Stuyvesant, Columbia Co, at Stuyvesant; Rev. John Gray (6-1/10)

MOLLENDORFF, ---- (Field Marshall), 92, d (date not given) at Havelberg in Prussia (he is believed to have been the oldest General in Europe) (6-5/8/16)

MONELL, Catharine Elvira, 11 months, dau. of Dr. Gilbert C., d 7/23/42 in Newburgh (9-7/30)

MONELL, John J., Esq. of Newburgh m 6/14/42 Mary Elizabeth Smith, dau. of N.B., Esq. of Woodbury, Conn., at W.; Rev. B.R. Andrew (9-6/18)

MONELL, Lucinda - see CHURCHILL, George

MONK, David, Esq., formerly of Fort Plain, d 4/23/50 at Mohawk (4-4/25)

MONK, Elizabeth Gould, 79, widow of late Hon. George Henty Monk d on the 53rd anniversary of her marriage (dates not given) in Montreal (born in Boston in 1759) (6-12/29/35)

MONROE, Adaline - see HOWLAND, Seth

MONROE, Philetus m 5/18/41 Mary Ann Larkin at Clinton; Rev. Gridley (all of Rome) (1-6/1)

MONROE, Sarah (Mrs.), 30, d 9/9/42 in Sing Sing (survived by a husband and several children) (11-9/15)

MONROE, Spencer N., formerly of Boston, m 5/16/44 Ann W. Morley, dau. of Deacon John of Van Buren, in V.B.; Rev. Brainard (1-5/28)

MONTAGUE, Lucretia B. - see BALDWIN, James L.

MONTGOMERY, Frances - see WYLIE, John

MONTGOMERY, George K, m 5/9/39 Eliza Heermans, both late of West Troy but now of Lansingburgh, in West Troy; Rev. Thomas Brand (5-5/15)

MONTGOMERY, Mary H. - see STODDARD, Edwin L.

MONTGOMERY, Mary Jane - see ACKLEY, David

MONTGOMERY, Sally Ann - see ACKLEY, John D.

MONTIETH, Catherine - see HOWE, Amos

MONTROSE, Hetty - see LENT, Hercules

MONTROSS, Ambrose m 9/8/42 Charlotte Tilley in Sparta, town of Mount Pleasant; Rev. Sidney A. Coney (11-9/15)

MONTROSS, Ellison m 12/6/41 Lavina Lent in Peekskill; Rev. Westbrook (11-12/7)

MONTROSS, James, 37, d 11/22/43 in Peekskill (11-11/28)

MONTROSS, Lavina - see DORSETT, John

MONTROSS, Mary Ann - see PETERSON, Thomas

MONTROSS, Mary Ann - see PETERSON, Thomas

MOONEY, Patrick, d 8/17/49 in Saugerties (cholera) (8-8/18)

214

MOORE, Cordelia - see PHILLIPS, Albert

MOORE, Cynthia S. - see NICHOLS, Moses H.

MOORE, Eliza, 5, oldest dau of O.J. Moore, Esq., d12/15/33 in NYC (scarlet fever) (11-12/24)

MOORE, Ellen Frances - see CROSS, Lawrence C.

MOORE, Emmet, merchant, of firm of Tuthill & Moore at Newburgh m 3/24/35 Harriet Dolson, dau of Samuel Dolson of Middletown, at M.; Rev. D.T. Wood (6-3/28)

MOORE, Euretta M. - see FLEMING, Augustus Jr.

MOORE, Euretta U. - see FLEMING, Augustus, Jr,

MOORE, Frances Sophia, dau. of John W. and Sarah of West Troy, d 5/4/48 in East Troy (5-5/17)

MOORE, George F. of Troy m 1/5/43 Phebe A. Brown of West Troy in Lansingburgh; Rev. O. Emerson (5-1/11)

MOORE, Gertrude (Mrs.) - see PATTERSON, Cornelius

MOORE, Harriet Amelia, 1, dau. of George F. and Phebe A., d 9/16/45 in West Troy (5-9/17)

MOORE, Horatio of Red Hook m 9/10/35 Marilla Snyder of Germantown at G.; Rev. Keeler (6-9/17)

MOORE, James M., ESq. m 6/11/37 Angeline Boom; Rev. Osborne (all of Albany) (6-6/13)

MOORE, John m 3/5/33 Harriet Britt; Rev. Bartlett (11-3/12)

MOORE, Maria O. - see PATTERSON, Cornelius

MOORE, Mary Ann - see SMITH, Lewis L.

MOORE, Mary, wf of Major Thomas P., late minister of the US in the Republic of Columbia, d 7/8/35 at Harrodsburgh, KY (6-7/31)

MOORE, William (Rev.), late of Oxbow, d 12/5/35 in Lisbon at the home of Robert G. Orr (6-12/29)

MOORES, Elizabeth Ann, 16, dau. of S.B. Moores, d 10/31/41 in New Windsor (9-11/6)

MORALEE, Phebe - see LEWIS, Joseph

MORAN, James m 11/17/48 Melinda Frazer, both of Cohoes, in West Troy; Rev. Houghtaling (5-11/29)

MORAN, Sarah, 71, widow of Edward, d (date not given) in NYC (6-11/28/26)

MORANGE, P.M. - see DUFFY, William

MORCY, Ann - see HALL, William P.

MORE, Eliza - see GREEN, Nelson

MORE, Eliza (Mrs.) d 7/14/49 in Saugerties (cholera) (8-7/21)

MORE, Iram, 7, son of John H. and Fanny, d 5/19/45 in West Troy (5-5/28)

MOREHEAD, Elizabeth - see HAMMOND, Charles

MOREHOUSE, Hannah - see MEAD, Amos

MOREHOUSE, John, 52, d 7/23/08 in Herkimer (2-7/16)

MOREHOUSE, Lydia - see STOREY, William

MOREHOUSE, Richard A., Esq., attorney at law, Utica, m 7/9/46 Elizabeth Rebecca Noyes, dau. of George, Esq., at Oriskany; Rev. S. Haynes (1-7/14)

MOREHOUSE, Richard H. m 7/9/46 Elizabeth Noyes, dau. of George at Oriskany; Rev. Haynes (1-7/21)

MORELI, Catharine - see CHESTER, John

MORELI, William (Hon.) - see CHESTER, John

MORELL, Clarissa - see FRYER, Hugh D.

MORELL, Dr. - see LEONARD, Benjamin

MORELL, Margaret J. - see CRAWFORD, William

MOREY, John H. of Albany m 9/8/38 Mary H. Tracy of West Troy; Elder F.S. Parke (5-9/12)

MOREY, Mason m 2/22/38 Alvina Feller in Middleville; Rev. W.H. Wagoner (3-3/1)

MOREY, William of Fairfield m 1/11/43 Eliza Carpenter of Norway, NY in N.; Rev. Smith (3-1/19)

MORGAN, Anna - see HALLENBECK, Matthew

MORGAN, Caroline Russell, 3, only dau of Samuel, d 11/12/36 (6-11/15)

MORGAN, Elijah - see EVERTSON, William Henry

MORGAN, George, 1, youngest child of Samuel, d 9/5/36 at 1:00 a.m. (6-9/7)

MORGAN, Hannah - see KING, James R.

MORGAN, Mrs. - see MEGGS, Phineas

MORGAN, Richard m 9/7/37 Eliza W. Avery, dau. of late Samuel H. of Oswego, at Aurora; Rev. James Richards, Jr. (6-9/25)

MORGAN, Roswell of West Winfield m 1/24/41 Mary Hinchman of Little Falls; Rev. J.W. Olmstead (3-1/28)

MORGAN, Sarah (Mrs.), 21, of Poughkeepsie d 1/30/35 leaving 2 children (age 21 and the other a few days old) Her husband, Henry B. Morgan, 27, house carpenter, had lived in Poughkeepsie, but left recently with his tools, etc. ("strong ground to suppose that he did not intend to return") He had left Springfield about 8 years ago, then worked for a time in Utica, NY. He is son of Samuel Morgan. Informants should contact the Poughkeepsie Telegraph of his whereabouts (11-2/10)

MORGAN, Sarah, 21, dau of widow, Maria Valentine, d 1/30/35 in Poughkeepsie leaving two children aged 13 months and a few days. Her husband, Henry B Morgan, left 10/10/34 to visit his parents and friends at Springfield, MA intending to visit Boston, Portland, Hartford and has not been heard from since. (printers requested to contact the editors of the Telegraph, Poughkeepsie (6-2/6)

MORGAN, Thomas C. m 4/17/38 Lyda Vandenbergh, both of West Troy, in Waterford; Rev. Slingerland (5-4/18)

MORGAN, William, "whose death was recently noticed" was born in South Wales; about 1800 emigrated to this country. (his obituary is extended herein) (6-7/11)

MORGAN, William, 58, d 7/2/35 at Buffalo (6-7/7)

MORKEE, Eli m 2/15/49 Francis Miller, both of Kingston; Rev. J.C.F. Hoes (8-2/24)

MORLEY, Ann W. - see MONROE, Spencer N.

MORRELL, Abbey, 43, wf of John, Esq., d 3/23/35 in Caughnawaga ("communicated") (6-4/21)

MORRELL, Caroline - see GOULD, Delose

MORRELL, Catharine - see SMITH, Nicholas J.

MORRELL, Harriet - see ARMS, Charles

MORRELL, James, 22, son of Hon. Henry Morrell of Greene, NY, d 10/25/37 at Mobile, Alabama (from the Binghamton Courier) (6-11/14)

MORRELL, James, his friends invited to his funeral ("at 4 o'clock today") at his late home, 12 South Lansing Street (6-9/25/35)

MORRELL, John - see GOULD, Delose

MORRELL, John, Esq., of Johnstown m 10/1/36 Margaret Hune of Waltham, MA at Claverack, NY; Rev. Richard Slyter (6-10/3)

MORRELL, Oscar, 16 months, youngest son of Capt. Thomas Morrell, d 12/4/41 in Newburgh (9-12/11)

MORREN, George of South Troy m 1/29/46 Mary Quick of West Troy in Troy; Rev. Stillman (5-2/4)

MORRIS, Alexander m 10/1/35 Juliette Ring, youngest dau of Nathaniel of Greenbush; Rev. James Walker (6-10/5)

MORRIS, Ann Maria - see NORTHRUP, Samuel A.

MORRIS, Benjamin H. of Oakland County, Mich. m 8/15/36 Mary Cox, youngest dau of Lewis I. Morris, Esq. of Butternuts, Oswego Co., NY, in B; Rev. Orasmus H. Smith (6-8/23)

MORRIS, Catherine, 37, wf of I.D. Morris, d 2/12/45 in Rome (rheumatic consumption) (1-2/18)

MORRIS, Charles, 60, d 1/6/26 at Watervliet (6-1/10)

MORRIS, David Johnston, 16, of Oxford, Chenango Co., son of Richard Morris, Esq. of Upton Park, Butternuts, d 2/22/35 at Oxford (6-3/4)

MORRIS, David, pastor of the Baptist Church at Little Falls, m 9/23/35 Mary Fish, dau. of Moses, Esq., in Rome, NY; Rev. J.W. Gibbs (6-10/5)

MORRIS, F.V.B., son of late Capt. Statts Morris, m 8/28/34 Theodora Francoise, dau of Hon. D.F.W. Pietermaat, resident in Batavia, Java. (married at Batavia, Java) (6-2/7/35)

MORRIS, Lewis Walter, 13 months, son of W.R., d 11/15/36 at Troy (funeral at 2 o'clock from his father's home, 307 First Street, Troy) (6-11/19)

MORRIS, Richard H. (Lieut.), 35, of the US Navy, d 11/5/37 suddenly at Pindartown, Georgia (son of Hon. Lewis P. Morris of Vermont). He had left Pensacola, Florida, in feeble health (6-12/13)

MORRIS, Rufus (Deacon), 76, d 9/15/48 in Ames (4-9/28)

MORRIS, Simon m 5/15/49 Mrs. Permelia Palmer, both of Dushville (sic), Esopus; Rev. W.S. Mickels (8-5/19)

MORRIS, Walter R., son of Capt. Staats Morris of Lansingburgh, m 9/5/26 Elizabeth S. Willard, dau. of Dr. Elias Willard of Albany; Rev. Dr. Chester (6-9/8)

MORRIS, William (Dr.) of Utica m 3/17/39 Catharine Hooft(?) of Danube in D.; Rev. J.D. Lawyer (3-4/4)

MORRISON, Adaline, 3, youngest dau. of James T. and Maria, d 1/27/41 in West Troy (scarlet fever) (5-2/3)

MORRISON, Ann Eliza, 1, d 2/20/48 in West Troy (scarlet fever) (5-2/23)

MORRISON, Eliza M. - see BAKER, Hiram

MORRISON, George R., 3, eldest son of Robert and Hannah, d 12/31/44 in West Troy (5-1/8/45)

MORRISON, Helen Norman - see MC LEOD, Alexander

MORRISON, James T., 46, d 9/3/41 in West Troy (5-9/8)

MORRISON, Jane E. - see CATLIN, Charles T.

MORRISON, Mary L. - see WOOLSEY, Melancthon B. (Lieut.)

MORROW, Caroline - see HENRY, James

MORSE, Betsey - see ACKLEY, Abram

MORSE, Catherine - see ABBOTT, Elonzo

MORSE, Ebenezer m 12/28/15 Emily A. Everest, both of Albany, in NYC; Rev. Matthews (6-1/6/16)

MORSE, Elijah H. of Mohawk m 8/17/42 Roxana Gazelas of Vassellsburgh(?), Maine in V.; Rev. Tappan(?) (3-8/25)

MORSE, Elizabeth (Mrs.) - see WEBER, James

MORSE, Foster (Capt.), 61, d (date not given) after illness of 14 days (contained in an obituary) (6-3/11/35)

MORSE, Frances M. - see LESTER, Albert (Hon.)

MORSE, George L. m 11/16/41 Mary Elizabeth Gould, both of Mohawk, at the Parsonage House in Herkimer; Rev. James Murphey (3-11/25)

MORSE, George N. of Williston, VT m 3/8/48 Hannah Jane Relyea of Ulsterville, NY (both deaf mutes) in NYC; Rev. J. Addison Cary (4-3/16)

MORSE, Henry B., 24, formerly of Lee, NY, d. very suddenly 6/13/41 at High Prarie, Iowa Territory (1-8/3)

MORSE, James O. (Hon.) of Cherry Valley, d 12/4/37 at Little Falls (Had been in attendance at the Montgomery County circuit at Fonda (6-12/5)

MORSE, James O. (Hon.) of Cherry Valley, First Judge of the Otsego County Courts, d 12/4/37 at the home of his son-in-law, A.G. Story, Esq., in Little Falls (while in seesion in court at Fonda "he was seized with an affection of the brain") (3-12/7)

MORSE, James O. (Hon.), 49, d 12/11/37 at the home of A.G. Story, ESq. in Little Falls. (Judge Morse was born in Massachusetts and graduated at Union College in 1809)(an obituary from the Cherry Valley Gazette is included) (6-12/14)

MORSE, John, about 45, d 6/15/37 in Little Falls (liver disease) (born in Vermont, settled in NY State when young, lived in Little Falls many years) (3-6/29)

MORSE, Lydia A. - see SPENCER, Joseph O.

MORSE, Sarah - see STORY, Albert G.

MORTIMER, Sarah Ann, 26, wf of Joseph, d 6/14/36 in Albany (6-6/16)

MORTON, Emily S. - see JUDSON, A.

MORTON, George, 23, son of William of Collsburg, d 3/20/35 at C. (11-3/24)

MORTON, J.W. m 1/31/49 Jane Hatch, both of Rome, in R.; Rev. W.E. Knox (1-2/7)

MORTON, Jane, 27, wf of Jay W. Morton and dau. of late Burrett Hatch, d 5/2/50 in Rome (1-5/8)

MORTON, Oscar M. m 12/10/46 Amelia Petrie, both of Rome; H.C. Vogell (1-12/15)

MORTON, Samuel D., 61, a respectable citizen of Rome, d (suddenly) 7/30/46 (member of the Presbyterian Church) (1-8/4)

MORTON, Samuel m 6/21/48 Sarah J. Rowley, both of Rome, in R.; Rev. F.H. Stanton (1-6/23)

MOSELEY, Parthenia I. - see AINSWORTH, Ira W.

MOSELT(?), Daniel T., Esq. m 10/11/36 Maria L. Gibbs, dau of William, Esq., at Shaneateles; Rev. J.T. Clark (all of S.) (6-11/8)

MOSELY, Charles - see FARMER, Cornelia Ann

MOSELY, Jane, 41, wf of Flavel Mosely, d (date not given) at Hampton (7-2/7/10)

MOSES, William m 9/28/42 Rachel Drake in East Florence; Rev. B. Fuller (all of Florence) (1-10/11)

MOSHER, Andrew, 9, son of Joseph L., d 12/5/49 in Duanesburgh (4-1/10/50)

MOSHER, Charity - see WENDELL, Rufus

MOSHER, Elizabeth - see MEAD, Henry

MOSHER, John, Esq., 41, d 3/8/42 at his home in Oppenheim (had been a Magistrate for about 20 years besides holding other offices in this town) (3-3/17)

MOSHER, Phebe, 55, wf of John, d 12/30/40 at Croton (11-2/2/41)

MOSIER, Israel m 1/20/40 Hester Russell in North Castle; Nathan I. Green, Esq. (12-2/11)

MOSIER, John m 12/8/39 Abigail Hyde, dau. of Deacon Eber Hyde, at the Baptist Church in Jordanville; Rev. A. Caldwell (all of Warren) (3-12/12)

MOSIER, Phoebe Jane - see ODEL, Isaac

MOSLEY, Mary A. - see VAN BOSKIRCK, Simon

MOTT, Jacob, son of Jacob I. of Tarrytown, m 10/18/38, Sarah Fowler, dau of William of Newcastle (12-10/23)

MOTT, Joseph m 9/4/43 Elizabeth Millis, both of Lansingburgh, in West Troy; Rev. Z. Phillips (5-9/6)

MOTT, Louisa, widow of late Lieut, William H. of the US Navy, d 11/29/36 ("after a lingering illness") (6-12/2)

MOTT, Mary W., 38, wf of Jordan L. Mott, d 12/23/38 in NYC (12-1/1/39)

MOTT, Peter of Plattsburg m 5/17/49 Margaret Shakelard(?) of West Troy in W.T.; Rev. S.F. Morrow (5-5/23)

MOTT, Samuel, Esq., 38, d 7/31/35 in Geneva (6-8/3)

MOTT, Sarah, about 35, wf of Israel, d 10/15/38 in North Castle (12-11/27)

MOULD, Ruanhah - seee DAVID, John

MOULTHROP, Margaret - see MESSINGER, Orson B.

MOULTON, Germain, 21, d 6/13/50 in Floyd (consumption) (1-6/26)

MOULTON, Julia Ann - see BELL, Geo. D.

MOULTON, Mariam Maria - see KELLOGG, Henry Nelson

MOULTON, Mary - see CLARK, Asa S.

MOUNT, Joseph - see LEWIS, Amelia G.

MOUNT, Nancy, 40, consort of Enoch, d 8/25/42 in Stark (for many years a member of the Baptist Church) (survived by her husband and nine children) ("Herkimer paper please copy") (3-9/8)

MOUNTFORD, Henry m 2/4/49 Mrs. Susan Spring in Fort Plain; Rev. Bishop Isbell (4-2/8)

MOWER, Catherine - see HOMMEL, Abraham

MOWER, John, 41, formerly of Annsville, NY, d (date not given) "by falling from a wagon" 6/13/50 at Half Day, Illinois (1-8/7)

MOYER, Catharine - see ZOLLER, Josiah

MOYER, David Henry m 5/15/49 Margaret Ann Klock, both of St. Johnsville (or Minden?) in Minden; Rev. J. Knieskorn of St. Johnsville (4-5/17)

MOYER, Helen, about 19, dau. of Andrew, d 5/5/48 at the home of her father in Minden (4-5/25)

MOYER, Jacob m 1/10/50 Peggy Ann Bender, dau. of George U., Esq.; Bishop R. Smith (4-1/17)

MOYER, John, nearly 93, d 4/7/38 in Manheim (3-4/12)

MOYER, Ludowick m 10/20/42 Marinda Rimph in Fairfield; Henry Thompson, Esq. of Little Falls (3-10/27)

MOYER, Nancy - see DIEFENDORF, Jeremiah
MOYER, S.W. - see CUMMINGS, Harrison
MOYER, Simeon m 12/27/49 Lena M. Eygabroad in Fort Plain; Dr. C.G. Mc Lean
    (all of Fort Plain) (4-1/10/50)
MUDGE, Abram, 27, d 6/15/48 in Earlville (4-8/3)
MUDGE, Alva - see SMITH, Horatio Hale
MUDGE, Alva, Esq., of firm of Mudge and Doty, merchants of Rome, NY m
    12/22/41 Harriet L. Lacy, dau. of Hon. Isaac of Chili, at C.; Rev. Billington
    of Scottsville (1-12/28)
MUDGE, Isabella W.M. - see MUSSEY, Elbridge G.
MUDGE, Joseph, 53, d 2/18/41 at Cohoes ("from a shock of Palsy") (5-3/10)
MUDGE, Martha, 17, adopted dau. of Nathaniel, d 12/7/46 in Rome (funeral at the
    Methodist Church at 2 o'clock Dec. 8.) (1-12/8)
MUDGE, Mary, 33, wf of Alva, d 4/4/41 in Rome (had been confined to her room
    with consumption for most of the winter) (1-4/6)
MUFFIN, Peter Jay - see CORTLAND, Harriet
MUHLENBERG, Catherine, 85, relict of Hon. Frederick Augustus Muhlenberg, d
    12/4/35 at Philadelphia (6-12/14)
MUIR, Ebenezer, Esq. - see RICE, William Henry
MUIR, Georgiana - see COOPER, A.L.
MUIR, Mary Ann - see RICE, William Henry
MUIR, William - see NOAH, Jane M. (Mrs.)
MULFEY, Anna - see ALLEN, Ervin
MULFORD, Mary H. - see PALMER, Andrew
MULFORD, Sarah Amelia - see GARDNER, James T.
MULLANY, Erin A.A. - see SHUFELDT, William F.
MULLINER, Jane - see DOWNING, Benjamin
MUMFORD, George H., Esq. of Rochester m 5/25/36 Ann Elizabeth Hart, dau of
    Hon. Truman Hart of Palmyra, at P.; Rev. Clark (6-5/30)
MUMFORD, Henrietta S. - see GOULD, Charles
MUMFORD, James Anthony, 26, son of late Benjamin B. of Newport, RI, d 1
    25/36 in NYC (remains removed to Newport for burial) (6-1/29)
MUMFORD, S. John, Esq., m 9/27/36 Harriette V. Innes, dau of late John Innes of
    Bristol, England, in NYC; Rev. Dr. Hawkes (6-9/30)
MUMFORD, Samuel Jones, 47, d 9/9/50 at Hinsdale, Mass. (probably a resident of
    Schenectady, NY in a trip - a detailed obituary is included from the
    Schenectady Cabinet) (4-9/19)
MUNELL, Elvira - see SAYRE, William
MUNRO, Jessie - see LIDDELL, John
MUNRO, Samantha - see HILL, Thomas
MUNSON, Achsa - see MARSH, Lyman
MUNSON, Eneas, M.D., 92, d 6/15/26 in New Haven where he was born
    6/21/1734 (the oldest surviving graduate of the Yale College where he
    received his first degree in 1753) (6-6/27)
MUNSON, Hannah R. - see WIGHT, Jabez
MUNSON, Henry J., M.D., formerly of Herkimer County, NY, m 11/9/37 Mary
    Jane Curry of Koskiosko, Attala County Mississippi, at K.; Rev. G.E. Nash
    (3-12/21)
MUNSON, Levinus of Hobart m 3/23/36 Mary Parish of Roxbury at R.; Rev. A.

Bronson (6-4/2)

MURDEN, George m 3/7/41 Elizabeth Green; Rev. William Marshall (all of Peekskill) (11-3/9)

MURDEN, Talbot, printer of NYC m 5/18/42 Hannah Tait, dau of Samuel, in Cortlandt; Rev. William Marshall (11-6/2)

MURDOCK, Eliza - see SAMSON, George W.

MURDOCK, James (Rev.) formerly of Houseville, Lewis County, d 1/14/41 at Crown Point, at the home of his son (not named) (apoplexy) (1-2/16)

MURDOCK, Mary, 84, d 5/14/42 in Newburgh (9-5/21)

MURPHY, ----, about 40, wf of Thomas, formerly of Bedford, d 6/3/39 in Haverstraw (12-6/11)

MURPHY, Charles C., M.D., of East Bloomfield m 5/14/49 Elizabeth Brewster, only dau. of Dr. Bela Brewster of Florence in West camden; Rev. Sweeney (1-6/20)

MURPHY, Elenor, 72, relict of late Philip, d 8/15/50 in Watervliet (5-8/21)

MURPHY, G.S., merchant, m 8/22/36 in Auburn, Cornelia E.Weed, second dau of Walter, Esq.; Rev. John Hovey (all of Auburn) (see HOVEY, J.P. (Rev.))(6-8/29)

MURPHY, Julia Ann - see MACK, Elisha, Jr.

MURPHY, Lawrence m 7/4/36 Julia Dingman in Albany; Rev. C.P. Clarke (all of Schodack) (6-7/7)

MURPHY, Mary Ann - see HOWE, Foster

MURRAY, Ambrose S., Esq., cashier of the Bank of Orange County, m 2/18/36 Frances Wisner, dau of Henry G., Esq.; Rev. Clarke (all of Goshen) (6-2/23)

MURRAY, Andrew J. of Weedsport m 1/11/49 Jane E. Woodworth of Vienna at the California House, Coonradt Settlement; Rev. F.H. Stanton (1-1/24)

MURRAY, Eliza - see BROWN, John

MURRAY, Eliza - see FOLTZ, George

MURRAY, Eliza Ann - see EVANS, Platt

MURRAY, Patrick of Utica m 12/27/42 Louisa Smith of Troy at the Tremont House, West Troy; J. Hart, Esq. (5-1/4/43)

MURRAY, Sarah - see SUTHERLAND, William B.

MURSITROYD, Elniora R. - see FULLER, Daniel

MUSCOTT, Clarissa E. - see GREENMAN, Francis

MUSIER, Johannah P. - see COE, John A.

MUSSEY, Elbridge G. m 4/26/40 Isabella W.M. Mudge in Cohoes; Rev. Van Buren (all of Cohoes) (5-4/29)

MYER, Abraham J. m 5/12/49 Amanda M. Turner; Rev. N.H. Cornell (all of Saugerties) (8-5/19)

MYER, Henry B. of firm of Myer & Mc Clasan of Buffalo m 8/16/36 Ann Howell, dau of R.H. Howell, Esq. of Newburgh; Rev. John Johnston (6-8/22)

MYER, Nellie - see ABEEL, Anthony

MYER, Susan M.P. - see SUMMERS, Jameson

MYERS, Abram H. m 11/3/50 Mary H. Eygebrot, both of Fort Plain, in F.P.; Rev. G.W. Gage (4-11/7)

MYERS, Catharine, 81, widow of Gen. Michael Myers, d 9/4/39 in Herkimer (long term member of the Dutch Reformed Church in Herkimer) (3-9/12)

MYERS, Clarissa - see SMITH, J.

MYERS, Eliza - see BELLINGER, Frederick

MYERS, Frances Eugenia, 14 mos., dau of Abram, d 9/22/35 at Gibbonsville (newspapers in Poughkeepsie and NYC are requested to publish this) (6-9/24)

MYERS, H. (Miss) - see EIGABROAT, John (Hon.)

MYERS, Harriet - see BRIGGS, William

MYERS, Helen A. - see HENDERSON, Hugh (Hon.)

MYERS, Jeremiah m 10/20/36 Sophrone Getman in Columbia; Rev. David Devoe (all of Columbia) (3-10/27)

MYERS, Joseph of Schoharie m 11/17/45 Charity Williams of West Troy in W.T.; Rev. S.L. Stillman (5-11/26)

MYERS, Margaret Feeter(?) - see RAWDEN, Freeman

MYERS, Mary - see RASBACH, David

MYERS, Mary Jane - see POWERS, Sidney A.

MYERS, Matthew (Col.) - see RAWDEN, Freeman

MYERS, Matthew (Col.) - see RAWDEN, Mary Richards

MYERS, Michael - see HENDERSON, Hugh (Hon.)

MYERS, Michael (Gen.) - see ETHERIDGE, Nancy

MYERS, Michael E., 21, son of Michael, Esq., formerly of Herkimer, d 9/19/39 at Juliet, Illinois (3-10/10)

MYERS, P. Hamilton, Esq., counsellor at law, m 2/1/41 Margaret M. Swain, dau. of William, in St. Peter's Church at Auburn (all of Auburn) (3-2/4)

MYERS, Philip A. of Westerlo m 1/13/47 Emma Tracy of West Troy; Rev. Houghtaling (5-1/20)

MYERS, Reuben, Jr. m 1/8/45 Caroline Lassels; Rev. George T. King (all of Western) (1-1/14)

MYERS, Samuel, Esq. m (date not given) Louisa Marx at Richmond (6-5/29/16)

MYGATT, Eliza - see SANDS, William G.

MYGATT, Henry - see SANDS, William G.

MYGATT, Henry R., counsellor-at-law m 12/2/35 Maria Tracy, dau of Lt. Governot Tracy, at Oxford, NY; Rev. Bush. (6-12/8)

MYGATT, Henry, merchant, 51, d 5/5/35 in Oxford (moved from New Milford, CT in 1807 and has remained in Oxford since) (6-5/9)

MYNDERSE, Leah (Mrs.), about 71, d 1/19/49 in Saugerties (8-1/20)

MYRES, Abraham m (date not given) Ann Eliza Cristman, dau. of Jacob, (bride and groom of German Flats); Rev. J.P. Spinner (3-12/12/39)

NACK, Matthias, 60, d (date not given) in NYC (6-11/3/26)

NAFEW, David B. of NYC m 1/10/36 Sarah G. Schley, dau of Hon. John, at Augusta, Georgia (6-1/29)

NAGLE, Charles B. of Waterford m 7/11/36 Caroline Mary Rodgers of Troy; Rev. I.D. Williamson (6-7/12)

NASH, Jerusha C. - see CRAMER, Hiram A.

NEAR, Betsey - see ABELL, Henry

NEELY, Franklin m 2/12/36 Alma Griswold in Fairfield; Rev. M. Weber (all of Fairfield) (3-2/18)

NEHEMIAH, Mary Ann - see CHARLES, George

NEHMIRE, John H., 84, a Rev. War veteran, d 1/19/36 ("funeral tomorrow at 2 o'clock from home of his son G.H. Nehmire, North Lansing St.") (6-1/20)

NEILSON, Agnes, 33, (youngest dau. of John, Esq. and sister of late Samuel

Neilson, proprietor and editor of the Quebec Gazette who died at the
  Quarantine station, Staten Island on his return from Gibralter, June 17), d
  10/10/37 at Quebec (illness of three and a half months) (6-10/19)
NEILSON, Samuel, Esq. of Quebec m 5/28/36 Catharine James, dau of Thomas,
  Esq., of County Wexford, Ireland, at St. Joseph's Church; Rev. James
  Commasky (6-10/20)
NEILSON, Samuel, son of Hon. John Neilson of Quebec, B.C., d 6/17/37 at the
  Quarantine Ground, Staten Island. He had returned from the Mediterranean
  (on the ship "Empress") "where he had gone for the benefit of the voyage"
  (6-6/21)
NELLIGAN, Ellen - see BRICE, James
NELLIGER, Jane Ann - see MC DONALD, Hugh
NELLIS, Betsey Ann - see CLARK, S.S.
NELLIS, Catharine - see VEDDER(?), Herman
NELLIS, George H. (Gen.) - see LOUCKS, Maria N.
NELLIS, Horatio of St. Johnsville m 1/9/49 Catharine Sanders of Minden at the
  home of Jacob Sanders in Minden; Rev. Rumpf (4-1/11)
NELLIS, Jacob P. - see CLARK, S.S.
NELLIS, James m 1/17/50 Elizabeth Border in St. Johnsville; Rev. Knesborn (all
  of St. Johnsville) (4-1/17)
NELLIS, Malvina - see NELLY, Justus H.
NELLIS, Maria - see WALRATH, David H.
NELLIS, Sylvenus, 62, d 12/11/50 in Minden (4-12/19)
NELLY, Justus H. m 3/2/37 Malvina Nellis, dau. of Jacob P., in Fairfield; Rev.
  William H. Waggoner (3-3/23)
NELSON, Earl (Right Hon.), about 49, nephew of the hero at Trafalgar, d (date not
  given) at his seat near Salisbury, England (succeeded in his title by his
  eldest son, Viscount Trafalgar, age 9) (6-8/8/36)
NELSON, Laura Young, 4, youngest dau of William, Esq, d 4/2/39 in Peekskill
  (11-4/9)
NELSON, Laura Young, 4, youngest dau. of William, Esq., d 4/3/39 at Peekskill
  (12-4/16)
NELSON, Mary - see WHITE, James
NELSON, Miss --- - see FROST, Joseph C.
NELSON, Richard James, 3, son of William, Esq., d 10/29/33 at Peekskill.
  (11-11/5)
NELSON, Sarah - see FERRIS, J.H.
NELSON, Sarah Ann - see FERRIS, J.H.
NELSON, Tamer Ann - see FROST, J.C.
NELSON, W.G., M.D. of Barnet, VT m 3/14/39 Eliza Mary Bullions(?), dau. of
  the Rev. Dr, Bullions(?) of Cambridge, Washington County, NY, at
  Cambridge; Rev. Dr. A. Bullions (12-4/16)
NELSON, William, about 60, d 3/1/39 in Somers (12-3/5)
NESSLE, William m 6/6/37 Caroline Gill (dau. of Matthew, Esq.), both of Albany;
  Rev. Dr. Listner of Schoharie (6-6/8)
NESTELL, Albet Lipe, 5, son of Jonas, d 7/5/50 at Fort Plain (4-7/11)
NESTELL, Eliza - see BAUDER, James
NETTERVILLE, Elizabeth, 39, wf of John W., d 6/24/36 (funeral at 5 o'clock 6/25
  from 23 Westerlo St.) (6-6/25)

NETTERVILLE, John W. - see NOBLE, Walter H.

NETTERVILLE, John W. m 6/29/37 Mary Pratt; Rev. Kip (all of Albany) (6-6/30)

NEWBOLD, Catharine A., relict of late Thomas Newbold of Philadelphia and dau of Herman Le Roy of NYC, d 12/29/35 in Paris (6-2/18/36)

NEWBOLD, Thomas R. of NYC m 11/11/35 Julia Fleming, dau of James, Esq., at St. George's Church in Hudson; Rev. Pardee (6-11/23)

NEWCOME (?), Ruth Ann - see HULL, Arael (?)

NEWELL, Angeline - see GOODRICH, Joseph

NEWELL, Darius C. of Sing Sing m 7/22/39 Irene Barnum of Bethel, Conn., at B.; Rev. Greenwood (12-7/30)

NEWELL, Hervey - see PADDOCK, Sarah

NEWELL, Jesse, Esq., 62, d 4/19/43 in Utica (a paralytic affliction) (one of the oldest citizens and most active business men of Utica) (1-4/25)

NEWELL, Julia - see ROUSE, Ambrose

NEWELL, Marcy B. (Rev.) of Amsterdam m 12/24/37 Maria Ann Burton, dau. of J. Burton, Esq. of Burtonville, Montgomery County at the Universalist House in Duanesburg by the Rev. H. Belding (6-12/28)

NEWELL, Susan, 72, relict of Samuel, d 12/6/36 at Southbridge, Mass. (6-12/10)

NEWHOUSE, John m 3/5/45 Jane Cole, both of Rome; Rev. H.C. Vogell (1-3/17)

NEWKIRK, John W. d (date not given) in Schenectady (6-8/22/26)

NEWLAND, John, 16, d 6/6/36 in Albany (funeral at 4 o'clock from his residence, 333 North Market St.) (6-6/7)

NEWLAND, Luke F. of Albany m 9/6/35 Helen L. Proudfit, eldest dau of Rev. Dr. Proudfit of Schenectady, in S.; Rev. Dr. Proudfit (6-10/9)

NEWLANDS, Christina P - see HARRIS, Edwin A.

NEWMAN, Elizabeth - see STAATS, Henry

NEWMAN, Erastus, M.D., m 12/12/46 Harriet Raymond, dau. of N.B., Esq. of Rensselaerville, in R.; Rev. John Fraser (5-12/16)

NEWMAN, George H. m 12/23/47 Eleanor M. Jones at Whitesboro; Rev. Cole (a double ceremony - see JONES, John S.) (1-1/7/48)

NEWMAN, Henry - see STAATS, Henry

NEWMAN, Peter - see FITZSIMMONS, Catherine

NEWMAN, Peter d 10/26/37 in Albany (funeral 10/27 from home of his brother, Thomas Newman in Lydius Street) (6-10/27)

NEWMAN, Sarah (Mrs.), 62, d "this morning" in Newburgh (funeral from the home of her son, Hiram C. Newman, on Grand Street "tomorrow morning") (9-11/13/41)

NEWTON, Ezra, Jr. m 7/27/43 Maria Louisa Spencer in Newport; Rev. W.L. Wilson (all of Newport) (3-8/3)

NEWTON, George S., 5, son of Daniel F., d 9/15/36 (funeral at 5 o'clock from his father's home, 264 Washington Street) (6-9/16)

NEWTON, John M. of Albany m 8/17/37 Eliza C. Mc Intosh, dau. of William Mc Intosh of NYC, in NYC; Rev. S.H. Cone (6-8/19)

NEWTON, Sarah Thorndike, wf of Edward A., Esq., and dau of late Hon. John Chandler Williams of Pittsfield, MA, d 10/24/35 at Rouen, France. Interred in England "near the residence of some friends". (6-12/29)

NICHOLS, Alonzo m 4/18/49 Philis Mc George, dau. of William, in Kingston; Rev. C. Shook (8-4/28)

NICHOLS, Ebenezer, 60, d (date not given) at Greenfield (7-8/29/10)

NICHOLS, Harriet C. - see BRICKEN, William

NICHOLS, Henry M. of Middlebury, VT m 5/18/26 Sarah A. Clark of Schenectady in S.; Rev. Proal (6-5/23)

NICHOLS, Isaac, 87, Rev. War officer, d. 11/23/35 in Brooklyn (born in Newark, NJ, served in War nearly 7 years, entered as private but was promoted to Lieutenant) (entry contains a long obituary) (6-12/7)

NICHOLS, Jane - see MOLL, Andrew

NICHOLS, Margaret Cornelia - see LEONARD, F.B.

NICHOLS, Moses H. of Newburgh m 10/24/42 Cynthia S. Moore of New Windsor in N.W.; Rev. Horace Winslow (9-10/29)

NICHOLS, Ruth A . - see ADAMS, Ansel

NICHOLS, Submitte (Mrs.), 66, d 5/17/48 at the home of her son George Nichols in the town of Watervliet (5-5/24)

NICHOLS, William m 9/18/36 Rosanna Benton(?), both of Litchfield, in Little Falls; Rev. Martin (3-9/29)

NICHOLSON, Ann Eliza - see DOUGHERTY, Addison

NICHOLSON, John (Hon.) - see DOUGHERTY, Addison

NICHOLSON, Redman, 42, formerly of Mago(?) County, Ireland d 4/12/37 in Little Falls (leaving an afflicted wife and 4 children in Ireland) (3-4/13)

NICHOLSON, Samuel m 6/1/36 Helen Kane, dau of Oliver, Esq., of NYC at NYC; Rev. W.R. Whittingham (6-6/4)

NICHOLSON, William d 11/19/35 on board the "steamboat Ohio" (funeral "this morning from 8 William Street" (6-11/20)

NICOLL, John, 69, d 3/3/42 at his home in New Windsor (9-3/5)

NIGHTINGALE, P.M. of Cumberland Island, Georgia m 11/16/36 Mary King, dau of John A., Esq., at Jamaica, Long Island; Rev. William L. Johnson (6-11/21)

NILES, Laura Frisby, 11, eldest dau. of Judge Niles of Rensselaerville, d 6/18/37 (6-6/22)

NINDE, W.W. (Rev.), 35, d 2/27/45 at Delta (a long obituary is included) (1-3/4/45)

NIVEN, George W., Esq., d 8/27/36 in NYC (was born in Orange County, NY; a brother of C. Niven, Esq., sheriff of Orange County) (from the Newburgh Telegraph) (6-9/3)

NIXON(?), Margaret - see GOULD, Richard

NIXON, Jonathan of West Point m 2/10/42 Mary Stewart of Newburgh in N.; Rev. Joseph Mc Carrell (9-2/12)

NOAH, Jane M. (Mrs.), 35, d 11/3/37 (her brother William Muir is mentioned) - funeral from 6 Van Tromp Street (6-11/4)

NOBLE, Henry B., merchant of Elizabethtown m 2/8/37 Cornelia Gould, dau. of Hon. John Gould, in Essex; Rev. Joel Fisk (6-2/13)

NOBLE, Nelson of West Troy m 3/12/44 Mary Pratt, dau. of Col. Chauncey Pratt of Covert, Seneca County, in Covert; Rev. O.H. Gregory (5-3/20)

NOBLE, Walter H. m 10/7/35 Margaret A. Reynolds adopted dau of John W. Netterville; Rev. Roberts (all of Albany) (6-10/9)

NOLAND, Eliza J. - see LYON, Ransom

NOONAN, Josiah A. of Madison, Wisconsin Territory ("formerly editor of this paper") m 9/21/40 Mary Louisa Tombling(?), dau. of late Dr. Abijah of Herkimer County, NY, at Waterford, NY; Rev. Stebbins (3-9/24)

NORRIS, Edward L. of Taberg m 4/29/41 Charlotte F. Lowe of Vienna in Rome; Rev. S. Haynes (1-5/4)

NORRIS, J.Q. m 7/1/48 Mary Jane Hubbard, both of West Troy, at Greenfield, NY; Rev. Charles Pomeroy (5-7/12)

NORRIS, James L. of firm of Doolittle and Norris m 9/19/48 Charlotte P. Doolittle, dau. of late James W. of Utica, in Utica; Rev. William H. Spencer (1-9/22)

NORRIS, Mary E. - see ROSE, Samuel L.

NORTH, Benjamin, 51, son of Robert, d 12/2/35 at Walton, Delaware County (a lingering illness) (6-12/17)

NORTH, Edward (Professor) of Hamilton College m 7/31/44 Mary Frances Dexter, only dau. of Hon. S. Newton Dexter of Whitesboro in W.; Rev. President North (1-8/6)

NORTH, Forrilla - see ANDERSON, S.H.

NORTH, Frances E. - see HARDY, Marvin W.

NORTH, Jane H. - see NOYES, Denison P.

NORTH, William (Gen.), 83, d 1/3/36 in NYC (was a Major in the Rev. War; in 1777 was appointed aide-de-camp to Baron Steuben; was Adjutant General of the American Army in 1797; for many years state assemblyman, speaker of the House and Senator in Congress (long obit included) (from the Schenectady Reflector) (6-1/13)

NORTHRUP, Cordelia - see PECK, George

NORTHRUP, Helen Maria, 3, dau. of Willet Northrup, d 4/23/38 at Frankfort (3-5/3)

NORTHRUP, Mary S. (Miss) d 5/17/49 in Perry (consumption) (1-6/13)

NORTHRUP, Nancy - see CLARK, James

NORTHRUP, Phebe - see JENNING, Abel

NORTHRUP, Polly - see STREVEL, Joseph

NORTHRUP, Samuel A. of West Troy m 9/10/45 Ann Maria Morris, eldest dau. of George of Troy; Rev. G.C. Baldwin (5-9/17)

NORTHRUP, Solomon J. of Lisle, Broome County m 1/10/49 Lucyette Carrol of Springfield in S.; Rev. H. Halstead (4-1/18)

NORTHRUP, Susan - see BURTGOOD(?), Reed B.

NORTHRUP, Susan - see YATES, J.M. (Rev.)

NORTHWAY, Mary Elizabeth, 2, only dau. of Rufus, d 6/27/50 in Utica (1-7/10)

NORTON, Abigail Maria - see WETMORE, Francis

NORTON, Burridge and Samuel - see SPENCER, Ambrose

NORTON, Elbert, 39, d 5/30/35 in Syracuse (6-6/5)

NORTON, Esther - see METCALF, William

NORTON, Hannah M. (Miss), 23, d 2/23/50 at the home of her brother, James M. Norton, Esq. in Buel(?) (4-2/28)

NORTON, Harriet M., 21, dau. of Dr. Ariel Norton, d 3/8/46 at Vernon (1-3/17)

NORTON, Helena - see PLATT, E.B.

NORTON, James Clinton, Esq. of NYC "in the prime of life" d 11/14/35 at East Hampton, L.I. (6-11/21)

NORTON, John, Jr., Esq., m 9/3/35 Mary Stuart, dau of late Lachian Stuart; Rev. J.N. Campbell (all of Albany) (6-9/4)

NORTON, Louise - see TODRIO, F.T.

NORTON, Mrs. - see SPENCER, Ambrose

NORTON, Sophia - see MELICK, James O.

226

NOTT, Eliphalet, D.D., President of Union College at Schenectady, m 8/10/42 Urania E. Sheldon, principal of the Utica Female Seminary (3-8/11)

NOTT, Joel B., Professor, of Union College in Schenectady, m 11/28/26 Margaret T. Cooper, eldest dau. of Charles D. Cooper, Esq. of Albany; Rev. Dr. Nott (6-12/1)

NOXON, William Edgar, 2, only son of William C. and Cornelia A., d 5/4/49 in Fort Plain (4-5/10)

NOYES, Celestine L. - see SMITH, William C.

NOYES, Denison P. of West Troy m 12/11/48 Jane H. North of Hancock, Mass. in West Troy, NY; Rev. J.C. Burroughs (5-12/20)

NOYES, Elizabeth - see MOREHOUSE, Richard H.

NOYES, Elizabeth Rebecca - see MOREHOUSE, Richard A.

NOYES, Isaac (Deacon), 61, d 10/19/25 in Edinburgh, Saratoga County ("Printers in Massachusetts will please notice this death") (6-11/21)

NOYES, Peleg, 83, d 1/17/47 at the home of his son (not named) in Watervliet (5-1/20)

NUANS, Hiram E. of Frankfort m 2/8/49 Elizabeth Kling of Whitestown in W.; Rev. N.D. Graves (1-2/14)

NUGENT, Eliza - see MC CORMICK, Thomas

NUGENT, Elizabeth - see FRASER, Adam

NURSE, Delphai U. - see KLING, Hiram H.

NURSE, George of Paris, Oneida Co. m 1/28/40 Amy Ann Juslin of Frankfort in F.; Rev. T. Houston (3-2/6)

NUTT, Elizabeth (Mrs.), 96, d 10/27/43 in West Troy (5-11/1)

NYE, Polly - see HERRING, John

NYE, Sarah, 61, widow of Timothy, d 10/30/48 in West Troy (a lingering illness) (5-11/8)

NYE, Timothy, 80, d 10/4/45 in West Troy (5-10/8)

OAKEY, Sarah (her age not given) d 6/4/47 at the home of her brother-in-law, William Vernon of Schaghticoke (5-6/9)

OAKLEY, Caroline G. - see PINGRY, John F. (Rev.)

OAKLEY, Daniel d (date not given) at Peekskill (6-1/20/26)

OAKLEY, John G. of Peekskill m 6/8/42 Amelia Crawford, oldest dau of George, of Yorktown; Rev. D. De Vinne (11-6/16)

OAKLEY, Sarah - see EAGLETON, William

OATHOUT, Jacob m 1/16/46 Jane Groesbeck in West Troy; Rev. T.F. Wyckoff (5-1/28)

OBER, Tristram N. m 10/18/47 Eunice Ballard, both of West Troy; Rev. Houghtaling (5-10/20)

O'BRIEN, Edward m 9/23/49 Jane Ann Fiero in Saugerties; Rev. C. Van Santvoord (8-9/29)

ODEL, Isaac m 1/8/39 Phoebe Jane Mosier at Collsberg; Rev. William Marshall (all of Cortlandtown) (11-1/22)

ODELL, Daniel m 2/12/39 Eliza Brees(?), both of Greenburg; Rev. George Walker (12-2/19)

ODELL, Evander of NYC m 1/9/39 Elizabeth Robins, dau of James of North Castle, in N.C.; Rev. S. Martindale (12-1/15)

ODELL, John (Col.), 79, a Rev. War veteran, d 10/26/35 at his home in Greenburgh (from Westchester Herald) (11-11/10)

ODELL, John (Col.), 79, d 10/26/35 at his home in Greenburgh (a Rev. War veteran served at the Battle of Long Island and "until the close of the war.") (from the Westchester Herald) (6-11/18)

ODELL, Phebe, 5, dau of John, d 11/20/39 in Peekskill (11-11/26)

ODELL, Sarah ANn (her funeral 7/11/37 at the home of her aunt, Mrs. Ira Porter at 15 Lancaster Street, Albany). The deceased is the dau. of John Groesbeek (6-7/11)

ODELL, Valentine m 3/27/39 Hannah Storms, both of Greenburg, at G.; Rev. George Walker (12-4/2)

ODELL, William m 1/11/35 Hester Croft; Rev. Isaac Lent (all of Philipstown) (11-1/20)

O'DONNELL, Sarah, 74, relict of Terence O'Donnell, formerly of Albany, d 8/19/36 at Stillwater (6-8/26)

OFIELD, Elizabeth - see BARROW, Lewis

OGDEN, Abraham, Esq. - see KEELER, Nelson K.

OGDEN, Abram, Esq., 75, d (date not given) at Berwick, Warren County, Illinois (acrofula of cancer) "emigrated from England when a young man, resided in Floyd (NY) where he married (wife's name not given) some 40 years since" (survived by wife and five children) (1-6/3/45)

OGDEN, Emily H. - see KEELER, Nelson K.

OGDEN, George B. of New Orleans m 8/29/36 Rebecca Ogden, dau of late David A., at Washington, St. Lawrence Co. (6-9/9)

OGDEN, Henry, Esq., formerly of Catskill, d 11/27/37 at Unadilla (6-12/8)

OGDEN, James m 6/25/39 Mary Ann Palmer, both of Mount Pleasant, in Sing Sing; Rev. S. Van Deusen (12-7/9)

OGDEN, John I. of NYC m 11/29/33 Mary Post, dau of Capt. Robert of Phillipstown, at P.; Rev. Daniel D. Tompkins (11-12/3)

OGDEN, Joseph m 2/6/45 Amelia Lyon, both of West Troy; Rev. Dodge (5-2/12)

OGDEN, Mordecai (Hon.) - see TILLOTSON, William

OGDEN, Rebecca - see OGDEN, George B.

OGDEN, Thomas W. of Mobile m 8/24/36 Ruth Schuyler, dau of Philip, Esq., at Schuylerville; Rev. May (6-8/29)

OGSBURY, David, 76, d 3/22/36 at his home in Guilderland (6-4/1)

O'HARA, Edward, Esq., 59, d 7/8/36 at home of his son in Esperence (born in Strabane, County Tyrone, Ireland; recently arrived to escape tyrannical laws of Engalnd) (6-7/15)

O'KEEFE, Susannah P. - see DAVENPORT, Joseph

OKIE, Abraham, Esq., 52, late president of the Western Bank, d 11/30/36 in Philadelphia (6-12/3)

OLCOTT, James H. of Lenox m 11/2/41 Eliza Teller of Rome in R.; Rev. S. Haynes (1-11/9)

OLCOTT, Jane Matilda d 4/9/37 at the home of her brother Theodore Olcott in Albany (her body removed to Hudson for burial) (6-4/11)

OLCOTT, Ophelia - see FOLGER, William H. (Capt.)

OLCOTT, Theodore m 5/6/34 Eliza Yates, youngest dau of John Van Ness Yates, Esq.; Rev. Dr. Sprague; all of Albany (6-1/21/35)

OLDS, William E. of Maryland, Otsego County, m 6/18/50 Maria C. Hawn of Albany in A.; Rev. S. Wheeler (4-6/27)

OLENA, Francis m 4/23/39 Maria Hoxie in West Troy; Rev. Leonard (all of West

Troy) (5-5/1)

OLIVER, Charles S. m 9/19/39 Adaline G. Robinson in West Troy; Rev. George
 Phillips (5-9/25)

OLIVER, James m 12/19/45 Margaret Colwell, both of West Troy; Rev. Dodge
 (5-12/24)

OLIVER, James m 5/30/35 Eleanor Bradt; Rev. Stebbins; all of Albany (6-6/1)

OLIVER, Margaret B. - see COLE, William P.

OLIVER, Robert, 76, d 12/17/34 at his home on Gay Street, Baltimore
 ("distinguished alike for his great wealth and enlarged liberality") (from the
 Baltimore American 12/20) (6-1/6/35)

OLIVIT, Hannah, wf of Jonathan, d 8/2/49 at Flatbush (8-8/18)

OLMSTEAD, Charles A m 1/27/35 Adelia D Wilkinson, dau. of David, Esq. (m. in
 St. John's Church at Cohoes); Rev. Stebbins (6-2/5)

OLMSTEAD, J.W. (Rev.), pastor of the Baptist Church in Little Falls, m 9/4/37
 Mary Livingston, dau. of R.M., Esq. of Schuylerville, in S.; Rev. J.W.
 Sawyer (3-9/21)

OLMSTEAD, John I. - see ROCKWELL, Mary (Mrs.)

OLMSTEAD, Mary Phelps - see IVES, George Russell

OLMSTED, Daniel Parker, 2, eldest son of John and Ann, d 9/28/45 in West Troy
 (croup) (5-10/1)

OLMSTED, Millicent, 5, dau of George D., d 7/19/36 (friends of George G. and
 his father David, invited to the funeral at 3 o'clock from her father's home,
 56 Division St.) (6-7/20)

OLMSTED, Thankful (Miss), 23, d (date not given) at Farmington (7-6/13/10)

ONDERDONK, Deborah, 76, relict of John, M.D., and mother of Rt. Rev. Bishop
 Onderdonk, d 4/20/37 at Hempstead, Long Island (6-5/1)

ONDERDONK, Letta Maria - see STYLES, John

O'NEIL, John, d (date not given) in NYC (born in Ireland) (6-6/5/16)

O'NEIL, Rosetta - see BOUCK, Austin

O'NIEL, Margaret - see KELLY, Patrick

OPPENHEIMER, Helen - see LEHMEIER, Benjamin

OPPIE, Theodore F., 27, of firm of Oppie and Nelson, merchants, of Peekskill, d.
 1/3/39 at Peekskill (consumption) (12-1/8)

OPPIE, Theodore F., merchant, of Peekskill, d 1/3/39 (consumption) (was First
 Lieut. of the Jefferson Guards which with Capt. John Hawes and others, he
 had organized) (11-1/8)

ORAM, James, 66, late printer and bookseller, d (date not given) in NYC (6-
 10/31/26)

ORCUTT, Charles A. m 10/18/47 Jane Ann Smith, both of West Troy; Rev.
 Seymour (5-10/20)

ORCUTT, Rice of firm of Gebhard and Orcutt m 1/11/37 Catharine Bouck, dau. of
 late Hermanus Bouck, in Schoharie; Rev. Dr. Lintner (all of Schoharie)
 (6-1/24)

ORELUP, Azor(?) of Rochester, son of Rev. H. Orelup, m 1/17/50 Mary C.
 Leonard, dau. of Rev. J. Leonard of Cohoes, in Cohoes; Rev. J. Leonard
 (5-2/6)

ORMSBY, Bethiah, 57, d 2/20/50 (of consumption) at home of her brother-in-law,
 Frederick Fox, in Canajoharie (formerly lived in Lebanon, Madison
 County) (4-3/28)

ORR, Harriet M., 21, wf of Edward and dau. of P. Randall, Esq., of Ames, d 8/21/49 in Detroit, Mich. ("the above sad notice was received yesterday by the family of Judge Randall..." - an obituary notice follows) (4-9/6)

ORR, Robert G. - see MOORE, William

ORSEN, Phebe, 83, widow of John, d 12/13/38 in New Castle (12-12/18)

ORSON, ---- (Mrs.) d at an advanced age (date not given) at Mount Pleasant (6-1/20/26)

ORTON, Abiram(sic) (Hon.), 61, d 3/29/37 in Arkwright. Judge Arkwright was an early settler in the territory of Arkwright before it was struck off as a town (was elected and re-elected to the board of supervisors)(from the Fredonia Censor) (6-4/13)

ORTON, Elizabeth M. - see BAXTER, Levi, Jr.

ORTON, Jane E. - see SHELLEY, Henry S.

OSBORN, Charles m (date not given) Huldah Jarvis in NYC (6-6/5/26)

OSBORN, Daniel m 9/15/49 Eliza H. Whitney; Rev. T.F. Wyckoff (all of West Troy) (5-9/19)

OSBORN, Emily - see ALLEN, Z.

OSBORN, Gideon H., about 47, a member of Dutchess Lodge No. 59, I.O.O.F., d 3/21/49 in Poughkeepsie (8-3/31)

OSBORN, Jacob - see PAIGE, William

OSBORN, Jacob, 41, d suddenly 2/27/35 at Little Falls (6-3/4)

OSBORN, Martha, 90, relict of Joseph, Esq., d 3/9/35 at her home in Somers (11-3/17)

OSBORN, Mary (Mrs.) - see PAIGE, William

OSBORN, Mary A. - see WOODWORTH, Benjamin

OSBORN, Selleck, the poet, formerly printer of the American Watchman in Delaware, d (date not given) in Philadelphia (6-10/31/26)

OSBORNE, Clark m 11/28/41 Abigail Lobgell, both of North Salem, in N.S.; Rev. S.J. Hillyer (11-12/7)

OSBORNE, Emma E. - see COBB, J.P.

OSGOOD, Erastus, 15, son of Daniel, d 7/11/39 in German Flats (3-7/25)

OSGOOD, John m 1/2/47 Sarah Jane Hix in Westmoreland; Elder J.P. Smith (all of Westmoreland) (1-2/5)

OSTERHOUDT, Jacob m 8/23/49 Maria Rider, both of Rochester, Ulster County, in R.; Rev. C.I. Van Dyck (8-9/1)

OSTERHOUDT, Mary Elizabeth, 2, only dau. of Jacob P. and A.M., d 8/7/49 in Kingston (8-8/11)

OSTERHOUT, Anna - see SIMMONS, Daniel

OSTERHOUT, Nelly Ann - see WHITAKER, Thomas V.L.

OSTRANDER, ---- (Mr.) m 7/4/36 Sarah Thorn, both of Albany; Rev. R. T. Brisbin of the Methodist P. Church (6-7/6)

OSTRANDER, Alexander m 9/17/37 Lovina Springer in Springfield; Rev. John D. Hicks (all of Springfield) (3-9/28)

OSTRANDER, Charlotte - see HAARBROUCK, Jansen

OSTRANDER, Eliza - see SPRINGER, Daniel

OSTRANDER, Mary Ann - see TUCKER, Joseph

OSTRANDER, Matthew m 7/4/36 Sarah Thorn, both of Albany; Rev. R.T. Brisbin of the Methodist P. Church (6-7/7)

OSTROM, Mary, 41, wf of late Joseph, d 3/10/39 in Little Falls (3-3/14)

OSTROM, William of Albany m 2/9/36 Abigail Hitchcock of Gibbonsville at Watervliet; Rev. Bronk (6-2/13)

OSTRUM, James, 48, d 2/17/39 in Little Falls (3-2/21)

OSWALD, John, 40, d 10/15/45 in West Troy (5-11/19)

OSWALD, Thomas H. (Col.) of Mississippi m 8/4/36 Mdslle. Alphine De Courval of Paris, France, teacher in the Troy Female Academy, at Troy; Rev. H.R. Judah (6-8/8)

OTIS, Oran G., Esq., counsellor at law, formerly of Little Falls, d suddenly (date not given) at Hartford, Conn. (apoplexy) (3-7/14/36)

OTIS, Oran G., Esq., counsellor at law, of Ballston d suddenly 6/27/36 at Hartford (apoplexy) (6-7/19)

OTIS, Sally, 68, wf of Hon. Harrison G., d 9/3/36 in Boston (6-9/13)

OTT, George S., Jr. m 11/3/49 Hapsey Hatch in Rome; Rev. W.E. Knox (all of Rome) (1-12/5)

OUDEN, Louisa - see TILLTOSON, William

OUDERKIRK, Margaret - see WHITBECK, Storm

OUISCONSIN, Charlotte - see VAN CLEVE, Horatio P.

OUSTERHOUT, Mary, dau. of Peter, Esq., d (date not given) in Catskill (7-7/26/09)

OUTHOUT, Caroline - see HEIMSTREET, Abram

OUTWATER, Jacob T., Esq., of Orange Town m 7/11/39 Catherine Aureyonsen of Closter, NJ in Tappan Town, Rockland Co.; Rev. Isaac D. Cole (12-7/16)

OVER----(?), William, 22, late of German Flats, NY d 6/16/38 at Louisville, Kentucky (his funeral discourse was to be delivered August 4, 1838 at the Fort Herkimer, NY Stone Church (3-8/2)

OVERACHE, Nancy - see RICH, David B.

OVERBACH, Lyman, about 32, d 9/1/49 in Quarryville (cholera) (8-9/8)

OVERBAUGH, Catherine (Mrs.), 18, d 1/5/09 in Catskill (7-1/11)

OVERSET(?), P.L., merchant, m 2/17/40 Alma L Start, dau. of Noah, Esq., in Little Falls; Rev. Clasel, Principal of Fairfield Academy (3-3/5)

OWEN, Ann - see BROOMHALL, George

OWEN, Edwin C.C., 1, youngest son of William and Mary, d 9/2/47 in West Troy (5-9/8)

OWEN, Edwin Meneely, 7 months, youngest son of William and Mary Ann, d 11/12/48 in West Troy (5-11/15)

OWEN, Elizabeth - see HUESTIS, Charles P.

OWEN, Jehiel of Phillipstown m 2/9/39 Elizabeth Lee(?) of NYC in Yorktown; Rev. J. Youngs (12-2/19)

OWEN, Johiel of Phillipstown m 2/9/39 Elizabeth Lee of NYC in Yorktown; Rev. J. Youngs (11-2/12)

OWEN, Lemuel O. m 4/8/50 Rhoda M. Hummel, both of Albany, in Rome; Rev. James Erwin (1-4/17)

OWEN, Louisa - see GATES, Martin

P-----(?), Mary Ann - see WILLIAMS, N. (M.D.)

PACKER, Lucretia, 26, youngest dau of William Packer, Esq., d 9/16/35 in Norwich (6-9/29)

PADDOCK, Alexander m 12/31/47 Lavanda Shaw, both of Western at Stanwix Hall in Rome (1-1/7/48)

PADDOCK, Samuel L. of Chautauqua m 10/21/39 Mary Harter of German Flats in

G.F.; Rev. Murphy (3-10/24)

PADDOCK, Sarah, 87, d 2/2/40 at Southeast in the home of her son-in-law Russel(?) J. Minor (she a member of Presbyterian Church in Southeast 59 years) (other sons-in-law mentioned: Hervey Newell and Russel Barnum) (12-2/11)

PADDOCK, Susannah - see STORM, James

PAGE, Calista Adelia - see CROMBIE, James

PAGE, Caroline B. - see JONES, Henry R.

PAGE, Jane - see SCOVELL, Jared

PAGE, John Chester, 11, youngest son of Nicholas and Huldah of Albany, d 7/31/37 suddenly at Athens, Greene County (6-8/3)

PAGE, Nicholas - see HARTNESS, Marcelline

PAGE, William - see JONES, Henry R.

PAGE, William m 12/27/47 Jane Harrison; Rev. F.H. Stanton (all of Oriskany) (1-12/31)

PAIGE, Elizabeth - see MERRITT, Jotham

PAIGE, James H., Esq., attorney at law, of Lewiston m 11/10/36 Mary S. Shepard, dau of Daniel, Esq., at Aurora; Rev. Amos G. Baldwin (6-11/21)

PAIGE, Susan, 42, wf of William, d 9/12/38 in Little Falls (3-9/13)

PAIGE, William of firm of Paige & Priest m 7/7/39 Mary, late consort of Jacob Osborn, deceased, in Little Falls; Rev. J.W. Olmstead (3-7/11)

PAIN, Samuel, 65, d 7/13/36 (6-7/18)

PAINE, Cornelius B. of German Flats m 2/13/43 Mary Ann Van Horne of Springfield in Cooperstown; Rev. Job Potter (3-3/2)

PAINE, Fanny Sophia, 13 months, dau. of Carlos G. of Nunda, d 5/24/39 in Paine's Hollow (3-6/6)

PAINE, John S, 22, from Plymouth, MA d (date not given) at Albany, NY (funeral at 4 o'clock from home of Amos S Westcott, 424 South Market St.) (6-3/26/35)

PAINE, Thomas, well known, d 6/8/09 in NYC (7-6/21)

PAINT, Philander A. of German Flats m 7/4/37 Sarah Filkins of Little Falls at East Richfield, Otsego County; Rev. Daniel Van Valkenburg (3-7/20)

PALAFOX, ---- (General) d (date not given) at Saragossa "a few days before the surrender of that city" (d "after some days illness") (7-5/10/09)

PALMER, Abigail (Mrs.), 69, d (date not given) at Windham, Conn. (7-5/10/09)

PALMER, Andrew, Esq. of Toledo, Ohio m 9/22/36 Mary H. Mulford, dau of Charles L. Esq., of Rensselaerville, at R.; Rev. Fuller (6-9/27)

PALMER, David, 13, son of Aaron and Lillie Ann, d 7/19/46 at West Troy (5-7/22)

PALMER, Dirck I., Esq., 41, d 1/11/37 at Saratoga Springs (6-1/23)

PALMER, Eleanor - see HICKS, James A.

PALMER, Emily - see HOTCHKISS, David

PALMER, Floyd m 11/20/39 Harriet Peck, both of North Castle, in Sing Sing; Rev. R. Van Deusen (12-12/3)

PALMER, Henry L., Esq., of West Troy m 5/18/43 Mary Loveland of Troy; Rev. N.S.S. Beman (5-5/24)

PALMER, James m (date not given) Catherine Van Vurste; Rev. Leonard (6-1/3/26)

PALMER, Margaret - see HARDENDORF, William

PALMER, Mary Ann - see OGDEN, James

PALMER, Mary Elizabeth, 5 months, only child of William H. and Mary A., d
9/11/50 at Galesville, Washington County (5-9/18)

PALMER, Mary, about 50, wf of Lewis, d 8/3/39 in Bedford (12-8/13)

PALMER, Nelly - see CHRISTIAN, John

PALMER, Permelia - see MORRIS, Simon

PALMER, Reuben m 3/5/09 Elizabeth Brandow; Rev. Limbaugh (7-3/8)

PALMER, Roseanne - see BAZEMANN, Philip H.

PALMER, S. Thompson of Middlefield, Otsego Co., m 10/5/37 Angeline
Raymond, dau. of Lewis of Sidney, in S.; Rev. Raymond (6-10/20)

PALMER, Stephen H. m 12/15/36 Mary P. Abbot, both of NYC, at Schenectady;
Rev. Albert Smedes (6-12/17)

PALMER, William M. of Waterford m 11/2/43 Mary A. Mechesney of Easton,
Washington County in E.; Rev. ----(?) (5-11/8)

PALMER, William of New Hartford m 9/29/41 Catharine Homer of Oriskany at
Rome; Rev. Charles Jones (a double ceremony - see BUERLEY, Daniel)
(1-10/5)

PAPSON, Elizabeth E., 65, widow of James, d 11/26/47 in West Troy (5-12/8)

PARDEE, Bela of Vernon m 9/23/40 Emily Thayer of Russia, Herkimer Co. in R.
(1-9/29)

PARDEE, Josiah, 75, d 9/13/46 in Vernon (1-9/15)

PARDEE, Mary Ann, about 49, wf of Phinas, formerly of New Salem, Esopus, d
5/12/49 in NYC (consumption) (8-5/19)

PARDICAN(?), Gregory A., a native of Greece, m 5/15/37 M.E. Harford of Society
Hill, South Carolina at Cheraw, SC; Rev. Ferne (6-6/6)

PARDY, Maria - see LOOMIS, Anson

PARENT, Phebe - see KENNARD, Charles

PARISH, Jasper, Esq., 69, d 7/13/36 in Canandaigua (b. Windham, CT March
1767 and emigrated with his parents to Lackawaxen, PA. In 1778 when the
British and Indians waged warfare on the Wyoming Valley he was captured
& remained a captive for 7 years. At treaty of 1784 at Fort Stanwix (now
Rome, NY) he was released. Lived in Canandaigua since 1792
(Canandaigua Repository) (6-7/28)

PARISH, Mary - see MUNSON, Levinus

PARISH, Mary Malissa - see MAXFIELD, Oliver H.

PARK, Caroline - see HYDE, Orrimal

PARK, E.A. - see HENENGER, H.

PARK, Edward A. (Rev.) Professor in the Theological Seminary at Andover, MA,
m 9/21/36 Anna Maria Edwards, dau of Col. William of Hunter at H.; Rev.
J. N. Lewis (6-9/27)

PARK, Eliza D. - see SLACK, Thomas W.

PARK, Stanton of Sangerfield m 4/17/16 Fanny Kingsbury at Cazenovia (6-5/4)

PARKE, Maria - see TEN BROECK, Samuel S.

PARKE, Mary - see YOUNG, David S.

PARKER, ---- (Gen.), 65, d (date not given) at Baltimore (6-7/25/26)

PARKER, Adelia Ann - see LAWTON, Henry

PARKER, Amanda - see BOARDMAN, William G.

PARKER, Amanda S. - see HOPKINS, Elisha W.

PARKER, Eliza - see HILLIKER, Harry

PARKER, Elizabeth (Mrs.), 51, d 5/28/37 (funeral from her late home at 63

Orchard Street) (6-5/30)

PARKER, Henry, Esq., A.M. of Albany m 9/14/37 Jennett Hilley of Pine Plains, in P.P.; Rev. Dr. Taylor (6-9/22)

PARKER, Jannette - see LEE, Oliver

PARKER, Joanna (Mrs.), 78, d 5/25/47 at the home of her daughter, Mrs. Fitch, in Vienna (born in Watertown, Conn. in 1769. In 1803 with her late husband, Eri, moved to Vienna, NY. They were among the first settlers in this region) (1-6/25)

PARKER, Joshua, Esq. - see BOARDMAN, William G.

PARKER, Margaret - see DIER, Peter

PARKER, Margaret Eyre - see UPPHOR, George

PARKER, Mary - see SHRIVES, Thomas

PARKER, Melzar (Rev.) of Elizabethtown, Essex County m 6/18/46 Ruth F. Baxter of North Annsville in N.A.; Rev. E.B. Baxter (1-7/7)

PARKER, Nicholas d suddenly 10/31/41 at Yorktown (11-11/9)

PARKER, Roxana - see SEATON, William L.

PARKHURST, Adeline - see WILSON, Moses

PARKHURST, Alpheus, 82, a Rev. War pensioner, d 10/29/42 in Little Falls (3-11/3)

PARKHURST, Euphrasia S. - see HOLT, Daniel

PARKHURST, Helen M. - see STARR, John R.

PARKINSON, Mary - see SOUTHWICK, Henry C.

PARKS, John J. m 9/24/41 Mary C. Shepard(?), both of Danube, in D. (3-10/7)

PARKS, Sarah - see WEEKS, Samuel

PARKSMAN, Robert B., editor of the Ashtabula Sentinel, m (date not given) Rosetta Merchant of Litchfield, Conn. at Ashtabula, Ohio (6-9/22)

PARMALEE, Harriet F. - see AKIN, John W.

PARMELEE, Howell, 49, d 9/17/43 in West Troy (5-9/20)

PARMELEY, Ira, 67, d 8/19/39 in North White Creek, Washington Co., NY (12-9/17)

PARMENTER, Anna Maria, 17, dau. of Hon. William Parmenter, d 11/8/41 at East Cambridge, Mass. (typhus fever) (9-12/25)

PARMENTER, Eliza (Mrs.) - see CRANE, Elizabeth

PARMENTER, Gilbert m 1/5/42 Susan Bradford in Fairfield (3-1/13)

PARMONTIER, Nicholas S., 58, professor of modern languages at Nashville University, d 7/15/35 in Nashville, TN (6-8/18)

PARNELL, James Henry, Esq. of Avondale, County Wicklow, Ireland m 5/31/35 Delia Tudor, only dau of Commodore Charles Stewart of U.S, Navy, at NYC; Rev. Dr. Taylor (6-6/5)

PARR, John m 11/13/49 Louisa Cronkhite at Frey's Bush; Rev. N. Van Alstine (all of Frey's Bush) (4-11/15)

PARRELL, Joseph, Esq., a Post Captain in the US Navy, d 11/25/15 in Washington City (6-12/6)

PARROT, Julia Ann - see MC CONKEY, Alexander

PARSON, Elijah of Skaneateles m 2/16 Eliza C Van Gaasbeek of Middleburgh at M.; Rev. J.B. Steele (6-2/23)

PARSONS, Anna (Mrs.), 53, wf of Major Joseph Parsons, d (date not given) at Enfield (7-5/24/09)

PARSONS, Armanda - see SOUTHWICK, Enoch M.

PARSONS, Elijah - see WILSON, James

PARSONS, Frederick T., editor of the Goshen Democrat, about 35, d 5/12/42 at his home (obituary copied from the Goshen Independent Republican) (9-5/14)

PARSONS, Spencer of Skaneateles m 10/13/36 Elizabeth Kilborn, dau of Gustavus, of New Hartford at N.H.; Rev. S.W. Brace (6-10/17)

PASCALIS, Felix A.O. (Dr.), 71, d 7/22/33 (from the NY Gazette) 11-

PASINGER, Andrew m 12/20/37 Sarah Ann Bates; Rev. C.R. Wilkins (all of Albany) (6-12/22)

PATCH, O.R., late of West Troy, m 11/21/44 Rebecca S. Arnold of Bremen, Maine in Waldsboro, maine; Rev. J. Dodge (5-12/11)

PATCHEN, Maria L. - see TIFFANY, L.F.

PATCHIN, William of Watertown m 8/21/39 Elizabeth C. Dorman at Little Falls; Rev. C.D. Dunning (3-8/29)

PATERSON, Sarah - see REED, Thomas

PATISON, Sabina - see APPELBACK, Gotlip Frederick

PATTEN(?), Sarah - see BUELL, Lucius

PATTEN, —— (Mr.) - see PICKET, Charles

PATTEN, Alexander, 4, son of Alphonse, d 1/6/37 (short illness) (funeral from Alphonse's home, 40 Liberty St.) (6-1/7)

PATTEN, Emeline Frances, 1, youngest dau. of Isaac and Sylvia, d 3/12/45 in West Troy (5-3/19)

PATTEN, Harriet A. - see DUNBAR, Jonathan A.

PATTEN, Lovina G., 32, wf of Franklin J. and eldest dau. of Leander Gridley, d 10/12/46 at her home in Spring Prarie, Walworth Co., Wisconsin (typhoid fever). Had moved with her parents from Vernon, NY in 1841 (survived by 5 children, the oldest age 10 and the youngest 7 weeks old (from the Chicago Western Herald) (1-2/5)

PATTEN, Mary E. - see TALCOTT, P.W.

PATTEN, Samuel, 31, d 4/5/42 at New Windsor (9-4/9)

PATTERSON, Albert C. of Buffalo m 1/7/36 Juliet C. Rathbone, dau of Samuel, Esq. of NYC, at NYC; Rev. Dewey (6-1/13/36)

PATTERSON, Alexander, 25, d (date not given) in NYC (6-8/22/26)

PATTERSON, C.E., Esq., son of Com. Patterson of the US Navy, d 1/15/37 at Cincinnati (6-2/3)

PATTERSON, Cornelius, formerly of Saratoga, m 11/8/37 Maria O. Moore of Red Hook, dau. of Mrs. Gertrude Moore of Dutchess County (6-11/10)

PATTERSON, Isabella - see TEESDALE, John

PATTERSON, Joseph of the house of Patterson and Waterman m 3/23/37 Jane Cuyler, dau. of Dr. Cuyler formerly of Poughkeepsie, at Philadelphia; Rev. John Brown (6-4/20)

PATTERSON, Margaret - see LAWSON, John

PATTERSON, Mary - see DICKSON, Robert

PATTERSON, Matthew A. m 3/2/35 Harriet Barker at New Lebanon; Rev. Silas Churchill (all of N.L.) (6-3/9)

PATTERSON, William, about 50, d 8/13/49 in Saugerties (consumption) (8-8/18)

PATTISON, Edward, Esq., m 1/11/49 Julia R. Dauchy, dau. of General Dauchy, at St. Paul's Church, Troy; Rev. R.B. Van Kirk (5-1/17)

PATTON, Jane - see BURTON, Amos T.

PATTON, William Farley, M.D., surgeon of US Navy, m 9/2/35 Harriet S. Buck, youngest dau of Anthony, Esq. at Fredericksburg, VA; Rev. E.C. Mc Guire (6-9/11)

PAULDING, Eleanor - see KELLY, Jonathan S.

PAULDING, James R. (Hon.) - see HALE, Catharine

PAVEY, A.A., Esq., merchant of Rome m 8/19/44 Jane Caswell of Lee; Rev. H. Mattison (1-9/17)

PAVEY, Frances Maria, 4, dau. of A.A. Pavey of Rome, d 5/29/44 in Henderson, Jefferson County (1-6/4)

PAWLING, Albert (Colonel), 87, an officer in the Rev. War, d 11/10/37 at Troy (was the first sheriff of Rensselaer County and the first mayor of Troy City (6-11/14)

PAYCHIN, Thadeus W., Esq., cashier of the Chautauqua County Bank, m 3/8/37 Charlotte Davis, dau. of Hon. George R. Davis of Troy, in T.; Rev. B.M. Hill (6-3/11)

PAYN, Catharine M. - see HAWLEY, George W.

PAYN, Cynthia - see BUNCE, Alanson

PAYNE, Noah, 77, a Rev. War veteran, d 11/24/36 near Fort Miller, Washington County (the full obituary details his experience in the War with attention on the Battle of Bennington) (6-12/2)

PEABODY, Betsey (Miss), 20, d (date not given) at Norwich, Conn. (7-8/2/09)

PEABODY, Ede Ann, 26, formerly of West Troy, d 5/24/44 at New Hartford, Oneida Co. (5-5/29)

PEABODY, James S., 43, formerly and for many years a resident of West Troy, d 5/30/50 at New Hartford, Oneida County (illness of 18 months) (5-6/12)

PEABODY, Williamn N., 29, eldest son of late William, d 7/26/42 in Newburgh (9-7/30)

PEACOCK, Harriet (Mrs.) - see BURDICK, John

PEACOCK, Sally - see BIRDSALL, John

PEAK, George, 104, d (date not given) in Rockport, Ohio (6-11/21/26)

PEAK, John (Rev.), 83, d 4/8/42 in Boston (5-4/20)

PEAK, Samuel C. m 11/27/42 Mary Hall, both of West Troy in W.T.; Rev. Z. Phillips (5-11/30)

PEAKE, Olive, about 52, wf of William F., d 3/31/48 in Fort Plain ("after a lingering illness - dropsy") (for 16 years a member of the Presbyterian Church) (4-4/20)

PEARCE, George W. m 7/3/39 Emeline Porter, both of Fairfield, In F.; Rev. Smith (3-7/11)

PEARL, Benjamin of Albany m (date not given) Ruth Beede in Danville, VT; Rev. White (6-7/21/26)

PEARL, Hiram - see SPAULDING, George W.

PEARL, Louisa - see SPAULDING, George W.

PEARSALL, Cornelia M. - see BETTS, W. Wallace

PEARSON, George - see TOTTEN, James G. (Lieut. Col.)

PEARSON, Oxiline - see TOTTEN, James G. (Lieut. Col.)

PEASE, Charles L., about 39, of firm of C.L. Pease & Co. of Albany d 8/12/36 in Rochester (while on a business trip) (Long obituary is copied from the Rochester Democrat not summarized here) (6-8/16)

PEASE, Erastus H. m 4/15/35 Lydia B. Fry, dau of Joseph; Rev. J.N. Campbell, all of Albany (6-4/17)

PEASE, Lydia, wife of Henry H., Esq., of Manchester, Mississippi and formerly of Utica, NY, d 12/1/36 at Manchester (6-12/22)

PEASE, William T., harbor master, m 11/18/35 Juliet E. Harrington, dau of I.R. Harrington, Esq. of the Eagle Tavern in Buffalo; Rev. William Shelton (6-11/24)

PEASLEY, Rhoda W. - see MC CALL, Henry S.

PECK, Abraham m 10/15/26 Elizabeth Ann Wood, both of Schaghticoke; Rev. Bronk (6-10/27)

PECK, Abraham m 11/30/49 Helen M. Gunnison, both of West Troy; Rev. T.W. Pearson (5-12/12)

PECK, Alba C. - see HORTON, James

PECK, Allen m (date not given) Mrs. Deborah Frear (6-5/22/16)

PECK, Charles Edgar, 4, son of Charles E., d 6/5/42 in Newburgh (9-6/11)

PECK, Daniel (Capt.) - see HAWLS, Henry

PECK, Darius, Esq., recorder of the City of Hudson, m 9/12/36 Harriet M. Hudson of Troy at Troy; Rev. Dr. Butler (6-9/24)

PECK, Everard, Esq., of Rochester m 9/21/35 Martha Farley of Waldoborough, MA at W; Rev. Mitchell (6-10/12)

PECK, George of Rome m 1/12/42 Cordelia Northrup of Utica in U.; Rev. Cooper of Wampsville (1-1/18)

PECK, Glorianna, 3, only dau. of Dr. Bethuel Peck, d 9/13/26 at Glens Falls (6-9/26/26)

PECK, Harriet - see PALMER, Floyd

PECK, Isaac, 63, d 4/3/41 in Danube (member of the Presbyterian Church) (3-4/15)

PECK, Jered, 69, d 5/27/ at Portchester, Westchester Co. (11-6/9)

PECK, Julia R. - see HAWLS, Henry

PECK, Louisa - see ANTHONY, Samuel

PECK, Maria - see PHILLIPS, James

PECK, Oliver, 56, d (date not given) at Newtown (7-6/20/10)

PECK, Reuben Camden m 7/4/44 Angeline Wing of Verona in New London; Rev. Alley (1-7/9)

PECKHAM, Emily E. - see BLAIR, O.W.

PECKHAM, John S. of firm of J.S. & M.Peckham of Utica m 6/8/36 Mary Townsend, dau. of Stephen Townsend, Esq. of Saratoga, at Saratoga (6-6/16)

PECKHAM, Mary Ann - see ELLIOTT, Robert

PECKHAM, Mary, 80, widow of Seth, d 7/13/50 in Utica (1-7/24)

PECKHAM, William N. m 11/3/41 Emily A. Reeskope, both of Verona, in V.; Rev. Vogell of Rome (1-11/9)

PEEBLES, Jane Adamson, wf of John, d 9/13/37 (funeral 9/14 from her residence at 493 South Market Street) (6-9/14)

PEEBLES, Tolbert m 10/2/45 Jane Sheldon of Cohoes in Troy; Rev. S.G. Spees (5-10/8)

PEEK, Keziah - see RENIVEE, Gilbert

PEELER, Catharine - see CARPENTER, John

PEER, Stephen H. of Troy m 4/13/42 Mary Temple of West Troy in W.T.; Rev. D. Starks (5-4/20)

PEET, H.P. Esq., principal of the New York Institution for the Instruction of the Deaf and Dumb m 8/18/35 Sarah Ann Smith, dau of Dr. Matson Smith of

New Rochelle, at N.R.; Rev. Isaac Lewis (6-8/22)

PEGG, Mary - see WETMORE, Alphonzo

PEGG, Mary, wf of John, d 9/16/38 in Sawpit (12-10/30)

PEGGS, Cynthia - see WILLIAMS, B. Whitman

PEGGY ("old Aunt Peggy") d 11/24/46 at Bloomingdale near Washington, D.C.
(was born in Virginia and claimed to be 120 years old. She could recall
interesting facts re Lower Virginia for a considerable time before the Rev.
War.) (1-1/8/47)

PELLET, Julia - see WEBSTER, Charles W.

PELLS, Catharine - see DAYTON, Daniel

PELLS, Mary Jane - see PIERSON, Calvin

PELTON, William S. (Dr.) of Ithaca m 9/13/37 Mary B. Tilden, dau. of Elam
Tilden, ESq. of New Lebanon, at N.L.; Rev. Silas Churchill (6-9/21)

PEMBERTON, Harriet, 15, dau. of late Ebenezer, d (date not given) (funeral at 4
o'clock from the corner of North Pearl St. and Columbia St.) (6-2/21/26)

PEMBERTON, Sarah (Mrs.), 58, d 12/4/37 after a protracted illness (her sons,
Ebenezer and John, are mentioned - funeral 12/5/37 from 59 Columbia
Street) (6-12/5)

PEMBERTON, Sarah, 3, youngest dau. of late Ebenezer, d 7/13/26 (6-7/18)

PEMBERTON, T.L., Esq., high constable of Albany, m 9/8/35 Ann Mc Martin,
formerly of Galway, Saratoga Co.; Rev. Kirk (6-9/10)

PENDELTON, Mercy L. (Miss), 24, dau. of Col. Benjamin C. and Aseneth,
formerly of Stonington, CT., d 4/21/46 in Verona, NY (1-5/19)

PENDILL, Morris M. of Byron m 12/8/36 Mary M. Carpenter, dau. of A. Carpenter
of Norway, NY, in N.; Rev. William H. waggoner (3-12/15)

PENDLETON, Jesse, 67, d 1/9/37 at Springfield, Mass. (6-1/14)

PENFIELD, Eunice - see JOY, Miles

PENFIELD, Harriet L., about 40, wife of Henry F., Esq., d 9/3/35 in Canandaigua
(6-9/7)

PENFIELD, Mary Elizabeth - see WHITE, James (Dr.)

PENFIELD, Thomas - see JOY, Miles

PENN, William - see WORDER, Savannah

PENN, William, 70, great grandson of the celebrated William Penn, founder of the
Province of Pennsylvania, d 9/17/45 at London, England (5-10/15)

PENNEL, Sally (Miss) d (date not given) at Buxton, Maine (hydrophobia) "was
bitten by a fox in the end of her thumb about five weeks since" (7-8/29/10)

PENNINGTON, William S. (Hon.), 64, Judge of the District Court of the United
States for the District of New Jersey, d 9/17/26 at New Brunswick, NJ
(6-9/26)

PENNY, Margaret, 71, widow of late Richard, d (date not given) in NYC (6-
6/5/16)

PENNY, Sarah (Mrs.), 103, d 1/20/16 in Spartanburg District, South Carolina
(born in County of Down, Ireland) (6-3/27)

PENNY, Sarah Adelia, 2, dau. of George, d 2/26/42 in Newburgh (9-3/5)

PENROSE, Catharine Howard only dau of Lieut. James W., U.S.A., d 10/13/36
(funeral from home of Horatio Potter, 68 Maiden Lane) (6-10/14)

PENSAIN(?), William Henry, 6 motnhs, son of John and Rhoda Jane, d 7/25/41 in
West Troy (5-7/28)

PENTRESS, Harriet, infant dau. of John and Martha of West Troy, d 8/10/48 in

W.T. (5-8/16)

PENTRESS, Martha G., 20, wf of John of West Troy, d 12/3/48 in Utica (5-12/6)

PEPPER, Elijah of Coldenham m 10/28/41 Keturah Crowell of Montgomery in M.;
Rev. J.B. Teneyck (9-10/30)

PEPPER, Isaac, 42, d (date not given) at Covington, Genesee County (note:
Covington now in Wyoming County - FQB) (6-8/11/26)

PEPPER, William (Elder), 50, formerly pastor of the Baptist Church in Vernon, d
3/12/46 at Vernon (1-3/17)

PERCIVAL, Asahel C., 10, only child of J.K. and Rosina, d 5/20/46 at Vernon
Center (1-6/2)

PERKINS (?), Edward M. of NYC m 8/17/36 Eliza Price, dau of William, Esq. of
Utica, at Trinity Church, NYC (6-8/20)

PERKINS, (Rev.) - see GRANT, Asahel, M.D.

PERKINS, Adelia - see MC COON, Samuel

PERKINS, Adelia - see MC KOON, Samuel

PERKINS, D.W. (Dr.) of Rome m 8/13/46 Jane H. Fitch of Williston, Chittenden
County, VT at W.; Rev. Bingham (1-9/1)

PERKINS, Emet K. m 2/13/40 Eveline Deusler, both of Little Falls, in L.F.; W.
Brooks, Esq. (3-2/27)

PERKINS, George R., professor of mathematics of the Clinton Liberal Institute m
5/3/37 Emma J. Arnold, dau. of Thomas, in Fairfield; Rev. William H.
Waggoner (3-5/4)

PERKINS, Hannah - see SMITH, Henry E.

PERKINS, Joseph, 71, d 1/31/49 in Rome (consumption) (1-2/7)

PERKINS, Levina - see BILLINGTON, James C.

PERKINS, Mary J. - see DINWIDDIE, John W.

PERKINS, Silas (Capt.), 82, "a Patriot of the Revolution", d 10/31/46 in Annsville
(1-11/10)

PERPIGNAN, Hannah, 22, wf of A.C., d 9/24/40 in Westmoreland ("an
affectionate wife and mother") (1-9/29)

PERRIGO, Joannah - see WARD, John

PERRIGO, John - see WARD, Ann (Mrs.)

PERRIGO, John m 1/15/45 Martha Ackerman, both of West Troy, in W.T.; Rev.
Dodge (5-1/22)

PERRIGO, Robert Henry, 15 months, son of John and Martha, d 2/24/49 in West
Troy (5-2/28)

PERRIN, Melory - see HINMAN, Abner

PERRINE, Augustus Freer, 2, son of George, d 9/2/49 in Kingston (8-9/8)

PERRY, Ann H. - see WILSON, Wilford L.

PERRY, Anna Maria - see LEONARD, Benjamin

PERRY, Anna Virginia, 4, dau. of Amos S., Esq., d 10/29/48 in Watervliet
(5-11/1)

PERRY, David G. (Dr.), "about 42", d 7/30/36 at Milan, Cayuga Co. (6-8/8)

PERRY, David, Esq. d (date not given) in Adams, Jefferson County (consumption)
(6-5/8/16)

PERRY, Ellen - see READER, S.

PERRY, Erastus B. m 9/12/37 Lamira Chapman, both of Pittstown, Mass., in
Albany; Rev. F.W. Smith (6-9/13)

PERRY, Henry m 12/26/41 Elizabeth Casler in Little Falls; Robert Casler, Esq.

(3-1/6/42)

PERRY, Henry, Esq., about 35, formerly of Orleans County, NY, d 9/14/42 at Bernadette County, Illinois (3-10/13)

PERRY, John m 10/19/41 Jane Lothridge in Newburgh; Rev. John Forsyth, Jr. (all of Newburgh) (9-10/23)

PERRY, John m 8/30/41 Catharine Rich in Rome; Rev. H.C. Vogell (1-9/7)

PERRY, Nehemiah (Dr.) od Ridgefield, CT m 11/14/38 Clarissa Purdy, dau of Isaac, Esq. of North Salem, NY; Rev. Dr. Wainwright (12-12/11)

PERRY, Robert of Lee m 1/8/45 Seraphina Hayden of Western in W.; Rev. King (1-1/14)

PERRY, Rosetta Maria - see SUNDERLAND, James

PERRY, Sarah Jane - see MARSH, William

PERRY, Stuart m 9/26/38 A. Jane Carter, dau. of Henry, Esq., at Newport; Rev. Roper (3-10/4)

PERSIVAL, ---- (Dr.) - see PRATT, William W.

PERSIVAL, Sophia - see PRATT, William W.

PERSON(?), Alice P. - see LOBDELL, James O.

PETERS, Abby, 44, wf of John R., d 11/23/37 in NYC (6-11/27)

PETERS, Harriet - see VAN HORNE, Fredus

PETERS, Isaac F., of Pleasant Valley m 11/25/35 Lois Gregory, dau of Joseph of Sand Lake, Rensselaer Co., at the hotel of Isaac N. Wooley in Pleasanr Valley; Rev. B.F. Wile (6-11/27)

PETERS, Joram, Esq., merchant of Little Falls m 6/13/38 Frances Ford, dau. of Philip, Esq. of Troy, in T.; Rev. N.S.S. Beman (3-6/21)

PETERSON, Mary - see WOOD, Jacob

PETERSON, Rebecca - see CHASE, John D.

PETERSON, Thomas m 12/24/38 Mary Ann Montross at the house of John Peterson of Cortlandtown, all of Cortlandt Town; Rev. Benjamin Curry of Shrub Oak (a double ceremony - see marr. of Jacob Wood same date) (11-1/8/39)

PETERSON, Thomas m 12/24/38 Mary Ann Montross of Cortland; Rev. Benjamin Curry of Shrub Oaks, Yorktown (a double ceremony see also marriage of Jacob Wood) (12-1/15/39)

PETREE, Charlotte H., about 33, consort of Col. David Petree and dau. of Philo Hackley, Esq., d 7/23/37 in Little Falls (a short illness) (member of the Presbyterian Scoiety) (survived by her husband, her parents, and brothers and sisters) (3-8/24)

PETREE, Charlotte, about 33, consort of Col. David Petree, d 8/23/37 at Little Falls (she is a dau. of Philo Hackley, Esq.) (6-8/28)

PETREE, Jane - see BEARD, John

PETRIE, Adam - see DOCKSTADER, Henry

PETRIE, Amelia - see MORTON, Oscar

PETRIE, Ann - see JONES, Merrick

PETRIE, Ann (Mrs.) - see GOULD, James

PETRIE, Archibald m 4/20/37 Jane Dockstader, dau. of Marks L. in Manheim; Rev. Swackhammer (3-5/4)

PETRIE, Barbara, nearly 90, (relict of Dr. Joseph Petrie, a surgeon in the army of the gallant but ill-fated "Herkimer" who like his brave commander, received his death wound in the sanguinary battle-field of Oriskany, 6

August 1777) d 3/11/38 in Little Falls (3-3/22)

PETRIE, Catharine M. - see WATERS, Sylvanus J.

PETRIE, Charles of Fultonville, Montgomery County m 6/4/46 Angelica Fritcher of Rome in R.; Rev. G.S. Boardman (1-6/16)

PETRIE, Charles of Lenox m 2/3/42 Sarah Jewett of Vernon in V.; Rev. E. Barber (1-2/15)

PETRIE, Daniel, 71, d 7/12/50 in Rome at the home of his son, Glen (1-7/17)

PETRIE, David (Col.) - see FENNELL, A.J. (Rev.)

PETRIE, Elizabeth - see SEGAR, Nelson

PETRIE, Ellen Maria, about 8 weeks, dau. of David, d 10/12/37 in Little Falls (3-10/19)

PETRIE, Elsie - see FARMER, Sanford

PETRIE, James, 29, d 8/20/36 in Manheim (3-8/25)

PETRIE, John D., 78, d 8/12/43 in Little Falls (3-8/17)

PETRIE, John L.M., 64, late of Manheim, d 10/20/39 at his home in Morristown, St. Lawrence County (3-11/14)

PETRIE, Jost (Gen.) - see GOULD, James

PETRIE, Margaret - see LEVE, James

PETRIE, Rebecca - see DOCKSTADER, Henry

PETRIE, Rufus m 10/4/36 Surina Richards in Columbia; Rev. David De Voe (3-10/13)

PETRIE, Woodbourne, 5 weeks, only son of Jacob D., Esq., d 5/27/36 at Columbia (3-6/9)

PETTETT, Hamilton, 1, son of Samuel, d 5/23/39 in Little Falls (3-6/6)

PETTIBONE, Chauncey (Hon.), one of the judges of St. Lawrence Co., d 2/24/35 at Stockholm (6-3/16)

PETTIBONE, Helen F. - see PORTER, Henry N.

PETTIT, John m 1/30/48 Catharine Prame of Stone Arabia at S.A.; Rev. A. Rumpf (4-3/2)

PEWTRESS, J.B. m 2/10/50 Ann Maria Lewis, dau. of George H., in the Church of the Holy Trinity; Rev. J. Weaver (5-2/13)

PHELPS, A. - see ALLEN, Otis

PHELPS, Azor, Esq., 75, d 4/3/37 at Shrewsbury, Mass. (was a Rev. War soldier, 1776-1777) (6-4/10)

PHELPS, Benjamin R. of the firm of Phelps and Son of Cincinnati m 5/28/35 Elizabeth Cowdrey, dau of Samuel, Esq. of NYC at Cincinnati; Rev. Dr. Beecher (6-6/6)

PHELPS, Clarinda, 24, wf of Ranny, d 7/11/41 at her home in Camden ("papers in Seneca and Ontario Counties please publish the above") (1-7/20)

PHELPS, Clarissa, 28, dau. of Samuel of Troy ("we believe formerly of West Troy") d 5/12/41 at Marion College, Missouri (5-6/2)

PHELPS, Elizabeth - see HANNUM, Leonard, Jr.

PHELPS, Elizabeth - see WABEN, Joseph H.

PHELPS, Hannah M. - see LINDLEY, H.N.

PHELPS, Joseph E., 9 months, son of Eli H. and Sylvia, d 1/25/45 in West Troy ("Greenfield, Mass. and Hartford, Conn. papers please copy") (5-1/29)

PHELPS, Lucy, 95, d 8/8/46 in Vernon (a member of one of the first three families who settled in Westmoreland, she was a member of the Presbyterian Church in Westmoreland) (1-8/18)

PHELPS, Lydia A. - see SYKES, Asaph

PHELPS, Martha A. - see SPARHAWK, Andrew

PHILIPS, Catharine Ann, 80(?), widow of James, d 2/11/49 at Wilbur (8-2/24)

PHILIPS, George (Dr.) d recently at his home in Dallas, Alabama (esteemed citizen of that state) (6-10/14)

PHILIPS, Mary, 69, wf of Rev. George Phillips and sister of S. Marks, Esq., editor of the Peekskill Republican, d 6/2/39 in NYC (12-6/11)

PHILIPS, Ransom W. of Franklin m Sarah Ann Clark of Rome; H.C. Vogell (1-1/29)

PHILLEO, Elizabeth (Miss), 24, dau. of Rev. Calvin Philleo of Canterbury, Conn. and grand dau. of Sarah Philleo, d 8/23/41 at the home of her uncle, Dr. P. Philleo in Newport, Herkimer Co. ("left her father's home last spring and commenced and continued a select school in Poland until her disease compelled her to abandon the pursuit") (3-9/30)

PHILLEO, Sarah, 84, widow of Enoch, d 4/29/41 at the home of her son, Milton Phillo in Russia, NY (born in New Milford, Conn. in 1757. after marriage she lived in Dover, Dutchess Co., NY until 1810 and then she & her family moved to Russia (member of Baptist church) (3-9/30)

PHILLIPS, Albert of Fishkill m 2/21/42 Cordelia Moore of NYC; Rev. J. Johnston (9-3/26)

PHILLIPS, Aleazer, Junior, 64, d 7/8/39 in Stratford (3-7/11)

PHILLIPS, Catharine - see JOHNSON, Wesley

PHILLIPS, Drake H. m 4/22/44 Olive Graves; Rev. Z. Phillips (all of West Troy) (5-4/24)

PHILLIPS, Elizabeth - see COLE, John L.

PHILLIPS, Elizabeth (Mrs.), 57, mother of Rev. Z. Phillips, pastor of the Methodist Episcopal Church in West Troy, d 9/11/42 in West Troy (5-9/14)

PHILLIPS, George W. - see UHLE, James H.

PHILLIPS, Jacob m 9/19/48 Margaret Finn, both of West Troy, in W.T.; Rev. Phillips (5-9/27)

PHILLIPS, James m 7/25/45 Maria Peck, both of West Troy, in West Troy; James M. Barnard, Esq. (5-7/30)

PHILLIPS, John E. Esq., about 40, counsellor at law, d 12/17/41 at Goshen (scarlet fever) (9-12/25)

PHILLIPS, John Jenkins, 11 months, son of Rev. B.T. and M.E., d 7/8/49 in Rondout (8-8/11)

PHILLIPS, Lana M. - see UHLE, James H.

PHILLIPS, Lurenda Malissa, 2 months, dau. of Joshua and Eleanor, d 5/19/37 in Stratford, Montgomery County (3-6/1)

PHILLIPS, Maria, 87, widow of Capt. Frederick Phillips, formerly of Phillipstown, Putnam Co., d 11/13/39 at Tarrytown (12-11/26)

PHILLIPS, Mariah, widow of Capt. Frederick Phillips of Phillipstown, d 11/13/39 at Tarrytown (11-11/26)

PHILLIPS, Mary, wf of George, d suddenly 6/9/39 in NYC (11-6/11)

PHILLIPS, Miss - see STORY, John

PHILLIPS, Peter W. - see COUNTRYMAN, Daniel

PHILLIPS, Ralph m 9/19/48 Mary E. Atkinson; Rev. T.F. Wyckoff (all of West Troy) (5-9/27)

PHILLIPS, Sally - see COUNTRYMAN, Daniel

PHILLIPS, Samuel J. m 9/19/50 Eliza L. Rudd, youngest dau. of Benjamin of Western in W. (1-10/2)

PHILLIPS, Sarah L. - see CLARK, Stephen (Hon.)

PHINNEY, Samuel (Rev.) - see VAN BENTHUYSEN, Sophia

PICKARD, James m 7/4/49 Salina Shoemaker at Starkville; Rev. Smith (4-7/12)

PICKARD, Nancy - see HOKE, Peter

PICKELLS, Jane A. - see BLAIR, George T.

PICKERT, Samuel m 3/30/37 Sally Porter, dau. of William Jr., in Fairfield; Rev. Lambert Swarthammer (3-4/6)

PICKETT, Charles m 1/20/45 Mary Elizabeth Hallett, both of Waterford, at Mr. Patten's Hotel in West Troy; Rev. O.H. Gregory (5-1/22)

PICKNEY, Caroline, 32, wf of Pierce and dau of Nathaniel Crane, d 2/16/39 in Carmel (12-2/26)

PICKNEY, John, 55, d (date not given) in NYC (6-11/3/26)

PIER, Mr. - see CARVER, Richard

PIERCE, Ann M. - see COLE, Gidron

PIERCE, Caleb m 3/17/41 Hannah Jane Lockwood; Rev. D.D. Tompkins (all of Putnam Valley) (11-3/23)

PIERCE, Elizabeth - see HOLCOMB, N.

PIERCE, James m. (Capt.) m (date not given) Priscilla Barker in Providence (6-5/15/16)

PIERCE, Phebe - see DIMON, John P

PIERCE, Richard m 3/4/26 Ann Vedder, dau. of Samuel A., esq., in Niskayuna; Rev. Jacob Van Vechten (6-3/7)

PIERCE, Sarah (Mrs.), 87, d 3/21/42 in Putnam Valley (11-3/29)

PIERCE, Schuyler R. of Warren, Herkimer County, m 10/10/42 Sarah Jane Prior of Fort Ann, Washington County, in West Troy; Rev. Benjamin L. Lane (5-10/12)

PIERSON, Calvin m 11/22/36 Mary Jane Pells; Rev. Covell (all of Albany) (6-11/26)

PIERSON, M. (Dr.) of Fishkill Landing, Dutchess County m 4/4/50 Louisa M. Horton, dau. of Deacon John W. of Adams Center, at A.C.; Rev. T. Bright (1-4/17)

PIETERMAAT, Theodora Francoise - see MORRIS, F.V.B.

PIKE, Alexander, Esq. m. (date not given) Sarah L. Roosevelt in NYC (6-5/8/16)

PIKE, Z.M. (Gen.) - see HARRISON, Clarissa B. (Mrs.)

PILET DE VICH, Louise Mary Erline - see DE VIRROYE, Francois Louis (Monsieur)

PILKINGTON, Martha - see WILBER, Jasper

PILLINGS, Robert m 6/30/49 Catharine Bradt, both of West Troy, in W.T.; Rev. O.H. Gregory (5-7/4)

PINCENEY, Maria ("who took an active part in the nullification struggles") d (date not given) in Charleston, South Carolina (6-5/21/36)

PINCKNEY, Charles, 66, d 10/16/34 in Carmel (11-10/21)

PINCKNEY, Eliza(?) - see BURCH, Aaron

PINCKNEY, Henry of Sing Sing m 4/17/34 Eliza Jane Kirkham of Carmel at C.; Uriah Hill, Esq. (11-4/22)

PINCKNEY, Louisa, 60, widow of James, d 11/22/37 in Catskill (member of Episcopal Church) (from the Catskill Recorder) (6-12/8)

PINCKNEY, William Henry, about 5 months, only son of Henry, d 3/23/40 in Sing Sing (12-3/31)

PINCKNEY, William m 5/30/44 Abigail Root of Vernon in V.; Rev. Hall (1-6/4)

PINE, Amy E. - see DUNBERGH, Augustus C.

PINGRY, John F. (Rev.) of Fushkill m 8/2/42 Caroline G. Oakley, dau. of James of Brooklyn, in B.; Rev. C.M. Oakley (9-8/6)

PINKERTON, Harriet - see WILLIAMS, John

PINKEY, Thomas, Esq., 72, d 10/28/36 in Knox (born in Westchester County & lived in northern part of this county during the Rev. War) (enlisted in militia at age 14) (6-11/3)

PINKHAM, Ann Eliza - see HUBBELL, George C.

PINKNEY, Harriet - see STRANG, John

PINNEY, Austin of firm of Chapin and Pinney, merchants of Buffalo, m 8/17/36 Harriet Duffy of Troy, in Buffalo; Rev. Rudd (6-8/22)

PINTARD, John L. m 3/1/48 Cynthia Hill, both of Westernville, at the American Hotel; H.C. Vogell (1-3/3)

PIPER, Alfred, about 10, son of Daniel (formerly of German Flats), d 10/22/41 in Orleans, Jefferson County (typhus fever) (3-12/2)

PIPER, Dolly Ann, about 12, dau. of Daniel, d 11/21/41 in Orleans (typhus fever)(3-12/2)

PIPER, Elizabeth (Mrs.), 33, d 11/11/41 in Orleans (typhus fever) (3-12/2)

PIPER, James - see HOARD, John La Fayette

PIPER, Margaret Elizabeth - see HOARD, John La Fayette

PIRNIE, Elizabeth (Mrs.), 73, d 1/2/42 "at the Purchase" (11-1/18)

PISHON, Marcellus R. of Clinton, Kennebec County, Maine m 2/28/48 Mary E. Hubbard, dau. of Jacob of Steuben, NY in S.; Rev. E. Buckingham (1-3/3)

PITCHER, J.H. - see ALLEN, Mary

PITCHER, Maria - see VOSBURGH, Isaac W

PITCHER, Samuel of Troy m 1/5/26 Maria Russell, dau. of Joseph, Esq. of Albany; Dr. Chester (6-1/10)

PITKIN, Epaphres, 84, d (date not given) at East Hartford (7-8/29/10)

PITMAN, Thomas W., merchant, of NYC m 10/27/36 Sarah Jane Bovee, dau of Hon. M.J. of Amsterdam, Montgomery County, in A.; Rev. J.D. Williamson of Albany (6-10/31)

PITTMAN, George Hubbard, 1, son of George W. and H.E., d 5/4/47 in NYC (5-5/12)

PITTMAN, Marietta, 2, dau. of George W. and Henrietta E., d 6/25/46 in West Troy (5-7/1)

PITTMAN, Mary Emma, 3, dau. of George W. and Henrietta E., d 11/13/42 in West Troy (scarlet fever - this is the second death from scarlet fever within this family within a week) (5-11/23)

PITTS, Electa - see DAVID, Loren M.

PITTS, Hannah - see BINGHAM, Moses M.

PITTS, John M. of Chatham m 5/22/37 Mary Ann Clark of Arcadia, in A.; Rev. Barrel (6-6/1)

PITTS, Mary Ann - see FOSMIRE, Garett H.

PIXLEY, B.F. of Vernon m 11/11/40 Levantia Hathaway of Stockbridge in S.; Rev. J.P. Simmons (1-12/1)

PLACE, Ephraim D. of Burlington, VT, m 3/25/37 Eliza Bailey of Salisbury, NH at

Cohoes; L.V.K. Vandenmark, Esq. (6-3/29)

PLACE, Sarah M. - see FAIRCHILD, Robert

PLACE, William of Utica m 9/8/47 Mary A. Shafer of West Troy; Rev. Seymour (5-9/15)

PLACIDE, Jane (Miss) d 5/16/35 at New Orleans (disease of the spine) (further details in this article) (6-6/4)

PLATNER, Anthony, 22, d 2/18/47 in Rome (consumption) (1-2/19)

PLATT, Albertus H. of Troy m 2/21/49 Emma M. Hammond, dau. of A. Hammond, M.D., of West Troy; Rev. Seymour (5-2/28)

PLATT, Ananias - see JACOBS, Lucy

PLATT, Catharine, 35, dau of Joseph Platt, deceased, and formerly of Poughkeepsie, d 7/11/36 at Blooming Grove (6-7/22)

PLATT, E.B. of Cohoes m 9/4/45 Helena Norton of Troy; Elder P. Thomas (5-9/10)

PLATT, Eliza - see CROSBY, David G.

PLATT, George m 3/13/36 Adaline Ayres, both of Manheim; John P. Snell, Esq. (3-3/17)

PLATT, Isaac, Esq., associate editor of the Poughkeepsie Eagle, m 10/1/37 Harriet Bowne of Montgomery, Orange County; Rev. Blaine (5-10/4)

PLATT, Isaac, Esq., senior editor of the Poughkeepsie Eagle m 9/19/37 Harriet Howse of Montgomery, Orange County in M.; Rev. Blain (6-10/5)

PLATT, William of Waverly Place m 8/6/45 Esther Judson of Waterford; Rev. R. Smith (5-8/13)

PLOUGH, John H., about 32, d 12/4/49 in Flatbush (8-12/8)

PLOUGH, John, about 63, d 10/29/49 in Saugerties (consumption) (8-11/3)

PLUMB, Abram, 20, d 1/2/41 in Camden (1-1/19)

PLUMMER, John H. d (date not given) in NYC (short and severe illness) (6-4/3/16)

PODMORE, Joseph m 8/30/49 Hilah Ann Hayford, both of West Troy, in W.T.; Rev. J.C. Burroughs (5-9/5)

POFT, John, 83, d (date not given) at Norwich (7-5/10/09)

POHLMAN, Elizabeth - see MC CLURE, James

POLHILL, Eliza - see HENDERSON, David

POLHILL, James of Peekskill m 3/5/41 Jane Harrington of Sing Sing at S.S.; Esquire Lea (11-3/6/41)

POLLARD, W.H. (Mrs.) - see MADOCK, Maria

POLOCK, John m 9/28/47 Mary Rebecca Swatling at Trinity Church in West Troy; Rev. Joshua Weaver (all of Watervliet) (5-9/29)

POMEROY, Charles - see STEEL, Rudolph N.

POMEROY, Jane - see STEEL, Rudolph N.

POMEROY, Julia - see AVERILL, C.

POMEROY, Nancy - see MC FADDEN, Archibald S.

POMEROY, Robert H. m 2/17/37 Sarah Ann Cristman, youngest dau. of Jacob F., Esq., in German Flats; Rev. Moon (all of German Flats) (3-2/23)

POMEROY, Theodore (Dr.) of Utica, NY m 11/5/26 Cornelia Voorhees of New Brunswick, NJ at N.B.; Rev. Hardenburgh (6-11/7)

POND, Eveline E., 21, wife of L.S. Pond and only dau of Dr. Abner Thurber, d 10/14/35 at Troy (6-10/19)

POND, Ira, 65, d 2/17/48 at Camden (survived by a wife and an aged infirm mother) (1-3/10)

POND, Sarah A. - see SPENCER, William H.

POPE, Resigned, 76, mother of H.H. and G.W. Pope, d 10/17/44 in Rome (1-10/22)

PORTER, Abby E. - see LELAND, Z.A. (Hon.)

PORTER, Ann Eliza - see SANDFORD, James S.

PORTER, Augustus (Hon.) - see TOWNSEND, Daniel J.

PORTER, Edwin W. of New Hartford m 5/30/50 Harriet Spencer of Waterville at W.; Rev. L. Hayhurst (1-6/12)

PORTER, Elizabeth, 69, wf of Stephen, d 6/1/50 in Lee (1-6/12)

PORTER, Emeline - see PEARCE, George W.

PORTER, Ephraim m (date not given) Mary Ann Barry in Boston (6-5/15/16)

PORTER, George Hale, 7 months, son of Rev. David Porter, d 9/27/10 in Catskill (7-10/3)

PORTER, Henry N., M.D., of Lee m (date not given) Helen F. Polson of Utica at New Hartford; Rev. Ira Pettibone (1-2/1/42)

PORTER, Ira (Mrs.) - see ODELL, Sarah Ann

PORTER, Ira m 8/2/37 Jane Eliza Rice(?); Rev. Buel (all of Albany) (6-8/3)

PORTER, Jane M. - see TOWNSEND, Daniel J.

PORTER, John K., Esq., counsellor at law, m 5/27/47 Sophia Topp in Waterford; Rev. Smith (all of Waterford) (5-6/9)

PORTER, Lucia Chauncey - see WADDELL, John

PORTER, Mary - see MILLIMAN, Lewis I.

PORTER, Mary B - see BOBCOCK, George B

PORTER, Nathan, son of Samuel, d instantly (date not given) at Berlin (7-5/10/09)

PORTER, Rachael, 66, wf of Deacon Noah, d (date not given) at Farmington (7-5/24/09)

PORTER, Sally - see PICKERT, Samuel

PORTER, Susanne, 32, wf of Selah, d (date not given) at Farmington (7-5/24/09)

POST, Anna M., 2, youngest dau. of Samuel M. and Nelly, d 10/22/49 in Saugerties (8-11/17)

POST, Dan - see BENCHLEY, William S.

POST, Dan - see HALE, Alfred E.

POST, Elizabeth, d 12/31/15 in NYC (6-1/6/16)

POST, Julia Ann - see HALE, Alfred E.

POST, Maria - see TAYLOR, James

POST, Mary - see OGDEN, John I.

POST, Mary I. - see ROBINSON, Sidney T.

POST, Mary L. - see ROBINSON, Sidney T.

POST, Mary, 92, widow of Garret Post of Sampton, NJ d 1/13/49 in Rome NY. (1-2/7)

POST, O. Rollo of New Hartford m 10/20/42 Rachel Watrous of South Coventry in S.C.; Rev. Chanucey Hoeth (1-11/22)

POST, Roxey Ann - see BENCHLEY, William S.

POST, Samuel of Oswego County m 9/3/46 Charlotte M. Kirkland of Rome; Rev. S. Haynes (1-9/8)

POST, Sarah - see VERMULE, Cornelius

POST, Sarah Ann (Mrs.) d 4/3/49 in Saugerties (lingering consumption) (8-4/7)

POTTER, Abel m 11/3/39 Rebecca Vibard; John Hastings, Esq., (all of West Troy) (5-11/6)

POTTER, Augustus S. m 9/24/46 Cornelia M. Putnam in Lee; Rev. Hathaway (all of Lee) (1-10/6)

POTTER, Elisha R. (Hon.) d 9/26/35 at his home in South Kingston, RI (anguina pectoris) (for many years a member of Congress and 25 years a member of Rhode Island's General Assembly from South Kingston) (from Providence Journal) (6-10/1)

POTTER, George I., Esq., attorney at law, m 4/24/49 Louisa Coos, dau. of late Judge Coos; Rev. W.H. (surname blurred) (all of Troy) (5-5/2)

POTTER, Horatio - see PENROSE, Catharine Howard

POTTER, Leighton Robert, 1 yr, only son of Rev. Horatio Potter, Rector of St. Peter's Church, Albany, d 8/1/35 at Schenectady (6-8/3)

POTTER, Louisa M - see DELAFIELD, Charles

POTTER, Martha J. - see RAPP, James A.

POTTER, Mary Jane - see BARNES, Abel S.

POTTER, Mary, wf of Hon. Elisha R., d 7/27/35 at Kingston, RI (6-8/3)

POTTER, Matilda Ann, 14, dau. of Tabor Potter, d 2/3/37 at Seneca Falls (died of arsenic pioson which had been spread on butter and bread for the killing of rats) (from the Ontario Republican and Freeman) (6-2/28)

POTTER, Noah of Troy m 2/18/35 Sarah Carr of Broadalbin in B.; Rev. Badger (6-3/20)

POTTER, Platt (Hon.) of Schenectady m 6/15/36 Mrs. L.A. Smith, dau of Rev. Paige of Fort Johnson, Montgomery Co. at Gilboa; Rev. Dr. Paige (6-6/24)

POTTER, R.D., merchant, 31, d 4/19/49 in West Troy (5-5/2)

POTTER, Thomas J., 20, of Hamburg, Erie Co., d 7/16/36 in Albany (6-7/21)

POTTER, William S. of Verona m 9/23/46 Esther M. Webster of Rome in Verona; Elder C.M. Lewis (1-9/29)

POTTS, Charlotte M. - see KEMBLE, John C. (Hon.)

POTTS, Henry (Col.) - see KEMBLE, John C. (Hon.)

POTTS, Jesse C. m 12/22/35 Eunice U. Walker, dau of Ashbel; Rev. H. Potter (6-12/23)

POTTS, Stacey, Esq., 85, d (date not given) at Trenton, NJ (6-5/8/16)

POUCHER, Lovina - see PULVER, John

POWARS, Joseph, 88, d (date not given) at Boston (6-7/25/26)

POWEL, Adelia - see CAULKINS, John L.

POWEL, James m 12/6/37 Loisa Row in Westerlo; Rev. Elbert Osborn (6-12/22)

POWELL, Catharine H. - see LYMAN, William

POWELL, E. (Mr.) - see CAULKINS, Adelia

POWELL, Elisha H m 1/20/48 Margaret M. Greenwood, both of West Troy, in W.T.; Rev. Joshua Weaver (5-1/26)

POWELL, Frances Augusta, 10, youngest dau. of Ebenezer and Chloe, d suddenly 1/12/43 at West Troy (5-1/25)

POWELL, James C., 35, son of the late Thomas Powell of Schenectady, d 7/16/35 in Albany (remains taken to Schenectady for burial) (6-7/20)

POWELL, Jane - see WILLIAMSON, James

POWELL, Mary A. - see BRIGHAM, Henry A. (Hon.)

POWELL, Morton C. m 9/16/40 Mary Hall at Waterford; Rev. O. Emerson (5-9/30)

POWELL, Sarah - see BIRCHALL, William

POWELL, Sarah C. - see BROWN, Isaac D.

POWELL, Thomas m 8/2/39 Ann Stratton at Bloomingdale; Rev. John Floy (sic) (all of Bloomingdale) (12-8/13)

POWELL, William m 1/7/41 Clara Gilbert, both of Peekskill; Rev. William H. Johnson (11-1/12)

POWER, James of Manchester m 2/24/39 Hannah E. Borden of Fairfield in F.; Rev. David Chassels (3-3/7)

POWERS, Charlotte Ann - see CLAY, Nathaniel

POWERS, Daniel of Halfmoon m 1/1/35 Maria Zebulon of Queensborough; Rev. Hiram Meeker (6-1/3)

POWERS, George Sr., 82, d (date not given) at his home "off Long Island" (6-5/5/26)

POWERS, Sidney A. of Summit County, Ohio m 10/5/47 Mary Jane Myers of Rome, NY in R.; Rev. F.H. Stanton (1-10/8)

POWERS, T.W., M.D., of NYC m 10/10/37 Laura Louisa Hess, dau. of R.L., Esq., of Syracuse at S.; Rev. John W. Adams (6-10/13)

PRAME, Catharine - see PETTIT, John

PRAME, John Henry m 2/2/48 Walley Alter, both of Palatine, at Stone Arabia; Rev. A. Rumpf (4-3/2)

PRATT, Abigail - see MARIAN, Anthony

PRATT, Asenah H., 26, wf of Capt. Edward W. and dau. of Dr. Nathan Harwood of Herkimer County, NY, d 5/25/39 in Newark, NJ (3-6/6)

PRATT, E.A. of the firm of Pratt & Treadwell m 6/17/35 Ann Herring, dau of late Thomas, Esq., at the home of J. Conklin, Esq., Brooklyn; Rev. D. Carroll (6-6/22)

PRATT, Fanny E. - see CORNELL, Edwin

PRATT, Hannah - see SPENCER, J.B.

PRATT, Huldah Maria - see TEN EYCK, George

PRATT, James R., Esq., of Covert, Seneca Co., m 11/8/43 Mary Rockwell of West Troy in W.T.; Rev. O.H. Gregory (5-11/15)

PRATT, Joseph of Salisbury m 10/31/41 Eunice Hopson of Mohawk at M.; Rev. T. Houston (3-11/25)

PRATT, Lucius of Buffalo m 8/17/36 Cynthia Harriet Weed, dau of Darius of Sawpit, at S.; Rev. Chauncy (6-8/29)

PRATT, Lucy - see DRESSER, Horace B.

PRATT, Mary - see NETTERVILLE, John W.

PRATT, Mary - see NOBLE, Nelson

PRATT, Mary Eliza - see SCOVILL, Alfred C.

PRATT, Mary Elizabeth - see GRIFFING, Peter W.

PRATT, Nicholas D.B. - see possibly FRATT, Nicholas D.B.

PRATT, Philo B, 42, d 2/23/35 at the home of his father in Kent, CT (typhus fever) (6-3/4)

PRATT, Sa----(?), 77, d 11/2/44 at Westmoreland (1-11/12)

PRATT, Sarah M. - see RUSCO, John H.T.

PRATT, Sarah, 28, wf of Orsamus, d 10/14/47 in Rome (consumption) (1-10/22)

PRATT, William of Lowell m 2/6/49 Sarah Blackman of Verona in V.; Rev. Johnson (1-2/21)

PRATT, William W., merchant, of Boston m 1/24/16 Sophia Persival, dau. of Dr. Persival of Greenbush, at G.; Rev. Clowse (6-1/27)

PRATT, Z. (Col.) of Prattsville m 3/16/35 Mary E. Watson, dau of Wheeler

Watson, Esq. of Rensselaerville, in Albany; Rev. Dr. Sprague (6-3/18)

PREBLES, Robert (Col.), 80, a Rev. War soldier and for four times a member of the State Legislature, d (date not given) at Chambersburg, Penna. (7-8/2/09)

PRENDERGAST, Martin (Hon.), one of the oldest citizens of Chautauqua County, d 6/26/35 in Mayville (6-7/1)

PRENTICE, A. Maria - see BISHOP, Joseph A.

PRENTICE, George Dennison, Esq. editor of the Louisville Journal, m 8/25/35 Harriet G. Benham, dau of Joseph S., Esq. at Louisville; Rev. Pearce (all of Louisville) (6-8/31)

PRENTICE, Marion I, 7, only dau of Ezra P., d 7/10/36 (6-7/12)

PRENTISS, John H. (Col.) - see KELLOGG, Palmer V.

PRENTISS, John H., 2nd, 24, d 5/2 7/38 in Little Falls (survived by his mother, a brother and a sister not named) (3-5/31)

PRENTISS, Nathaniel L. m (date not given) Sarah F. Gordon in NYC (6-5/22)

PRENTISS, Sarah (Mrs.), 61, formerly the widow of late Dr. Andrew Ferril, d 5/13/41 in Herkimer (3-5/20)

PRESCOTT, Daniel of New Hartford m 7/28/42 Mary Wood of Frankfort at F.; Elder John Miller (3-8/11)

PRESTON, Calvin, 84, a Rev. War pensioner, d 12/1/49 at North Gage in the town of Deerfield (1-12/12)

PRESTON, D.A. (Miss) - see RICHARDSON, J.M.

PRESTON, Francis, 69, of Virginia d 5/26/35 at the home of his son, Hon. W.C. Preston in South Carolina (6-6/11)

PRESTON, Irene - see WYMAN, Samuel

PRESTON, James B. of Verona m 4/18/49 Nancy Evchanau of Rome in R.; Rev. F.H. Stanton (1-4/25)

PRESTON, Jerusha - see WYMAN, Henry C.

PRESTON, Julia R. - see WILSON, George S.

PRESTON, Mary Elizabeth, 23, only dau. of Stephen, d 10/24/42 in Montgomery (9-10/29)

PRESTON, Mary, 23, dau. of Zera Preston of Lee, d 12/28/47 in Whitestown (1-1/14/48)

PRESTON, Nathaniel (Dr.), about 42, "a skilfull physician and postmaster", d 12/24/25 in Sheffield, Mass. (survived by his wife and a large progeny of children") (6-1/10/26)

PRESTON, Shandoney, Esq., m 9/6/42 Sally Ann Sheldon, both of South Dover, Dutchess Co., in Somers; Rev. Denton Keeler of North Salem (11-9/15)

PRESTON, Susan - see RHIND, William

PREVOST, William (Dr.), 25, son-in-law of Henry F. Yates, Esq. of Johnstown, d "about the 15th of July", 1826 near the village of Dexter in the territory of Michigan (survived by his wife and one child) (6-8/15)

PRICE, Catharine - see BENNETT, Hiram

PRICE, Eliza - see PERKINS, Edward M.

PRICE, Lavina (Mrs.), 23, d (date not given) in Brooklyn (6-5/15/16)

PRICE, Prescilla - see FAY, Edward

PRICE, Rhoda, 22, d (date not given) at Homer (6-1/20/26)

PRICHARD, Griffith, Esq., of Boonville m 8/17/49 Elizabeth Jones of Rome in R.; Rev. James Erwin (1-8/29)

PRIEST, Allen B. m 12/26/41 Mary J. Johnson, both of Little Falls; Rev. Loveys (3-12/30)

PRIEST, Edwin of Middletown, Conn. m 1/8/38 Cynthia Alford in West Troy, NY; Rev. A. Judson (5-1/17)

PRIEST, Eli - see WOODRUFF, Andrew

PRIEST, Sarah Jane - see WOODRUFF, Andrew

PRIME, Edward of NYC m 5/20/36 Charlotte Hoffman, eldest dau of late Dr. William, at West Farms; Rev. William Powell (6-5/26)

PRIME, Mary Ruthford, 25, wife of Frederick and dau of Peter A. Jay, d 9/9/35 in NYC (6-9/11)

PRIME, Samuel J. (Rev.), principal of Weston Academy, Conn. m 10/15/33 Elizabeth F. Kermeys, dau of Hon. Edward of Mount Pleasant, in M.P.; Rev. N.S. Prime (11-10/22)

PRIME, William Bard, 4, son of Edward, d 9/8/36 at New Brighton (6-9/13)

PRINCE, Frances Eliza - see DUANE, William R

PRINCE, Frederick(?), 76, d 3/25/45 at Bridgewater (lived in Bridgewater nearly 50 years) (1-4/8)

PRINCE, William, son of William Prince, Proprietor of the Linnaen Botanic Garden, m 10/2/26 Charlotte Goodwin Collins (dau. of Gen. Charles Collins, Lieutenant Governor of Rhode Island and grand-dau. of late Gov, Bradford of that same state) in Newport (6-10/10)

PRIOR, Sarah Jane - see PIERCE, Schuyler R.

PROUDFIT, Alexander (Rev.) of Amsterdam, Montgomery Co. m 6/28/42 Delia Williams, dau. of Richard B., formerly of Newburgh, at Cambridge, Washington Co.; Rev. T.C. Mc Laughey (9-7/9)

PROUDFIT, David L. (Rev.) of Schenectady m 10/9/37 Israella Hasbrouck, of Newburgh at N.; Professor Proudfit of Union College (6-10/17)

PROUDFIT, Helen - see NEWLAND, Luke F.

PROUSE, Henry R. of Little Falls m 5/17/41 Margaret Harter of Herkimer in H.; Rev. J. Murphy (3-5/20)

PROUTY, Lemuel D. of Brattleboro, Vt. m 1/14/45 Helen M. Fisk of West Troy, NY in Waterford; Rev. O.H. Gregory (5-1/22)

PROVOST, Bishop - see CHABERT, Julius Xavier

PRUDENCE, Diana, 26, wf of Lucius J., d. 5/3/46 in Rome (1-5/5)

PRULL, Ruth S. - see FAUROT, Stephen D.

PRUYN, Alida - see BELL, James C.

PRUYN, Casparus F., 53, d 2/10/46 at his home in West Troy (5-2/18)

PRUYN, Elmira - see SWIFT, Benjamin G.

PRUYN, Francis H. - see SWIFT, Benjamin G.

PRUYN, Helen, 32, wf of Samuel, d 10/28/36 in Albany (a lingering illness) (6-11/1)

PRUYN, Henry m 10/21/35 Ann Putnam, dau of Abram V. of Glen, Montgomery County at G.; Rev. Stephenson (6-10/24)

PUDDY, James (his funeral at 3 o'clock 2/10/36 from his late home, corner of Green and Beaver Streets) (6-2/10)

PUDNEY, Elizabeth (Mrs.), 72, d 1/13/48 in West Troy (congestion of the brain) (5-1/19)

PUGSLEY, Frances Carpenter - see GRIFFIN, John R.

PUGSLEY, Jane - see ROE, Cornelius

PULLMAN, E.C. - see COMSTOCK, Henry

PULLMAN, Julia - see COMSTOCK, Henry

PULTZ, David, about 60(?), d 6/10/49 in Saugerties (8-6/16)

PULVER, John m 3/19/36 Lovina Poucher, eldest dau of Henry, Esq., at Ghent (bride & groom of Ghent); Rev. J. Burger (6-4/2)

PURDY, Abigail, about 90, relict of Jacob, d 11/12/39 at Greenburgh (12-11/26)

PURDY, Abigail, nearly 90, relict of Jacob, a Rev. War Patriot, d 11/12/39 at Greenbush (formerly of White Plains) (11-11/26)

PURDY, Andrew, 71, d (date not given) in Yorktown (11-9/1/42)

PURDY, Charles of Mount Pleasant m 2/13/40 Phebe H. Lane, only dau. of Stephen of North Castle, at North Castle; Charles Yoe, Esq. (12-2/18)

PURDY, Clarissa - see PERRY, Nehemiah

PURDY, Henry, 74, d 10/14/41 in Newburgh (9-10/16)

PURDY, Isaac H. of North Salem m 9/16/39 Mary W. Lyon, dau. of Thomas, Esq. of Rye, in R.; Rev. Chancy (12-9/24)

PURDY, Jane G. - see KEELER, Floyd

PURDY, John G., 24, d 10/30/38 at New Castle Corners (12-11/13)

PURDY, Lewis, about 30, formerly of firm of Steers and Purdy of Sing Sing, d 2/12/39 at Croton (12-2/19)

PURDY, Mary - see HOBBY, David R.

PURDY, Mary, 30, wf of Robert, d 8/28/39 in New Castle (12-9/3)

PURDY, Susan - see LAGRILL, Louis

PURDY, Sylvanus of Marlborough m 7/6/39 Mary Frost of Yorktown at Y.; J.R. Hyatt, Esq. (12-7/9)

PURDY, Thomas of Smyrna m 4/6/45 Abigail J. Burgess(?) of Rome at Western in the order of the Society of Friends (1-5/6)

PUTNAM, Ann - see PRUYN, Henry

PUTNAM, Charles E., 4, only son of George, d 3/17/47 in Waterville (1-3/19)

PUTNAM, Cornelia M. - see POTTER, Augustus S.

PUTNAM, George of Waterville m 7/15/41 Sarah M. Bill, dau. of Dr. E. Bill of Vernon, in V.; Rev. R.C. Brisbin (1/7-20)

PUTNAM, Horace, Esq., m Mary M. Drew; Rev. H. Matteson (all of Rome) (1-12/31)

PUTNAM, Lucinda - see SHEPARD, Charles, M.D.

PUTNAM, Mary Ann - see GAGE, Moses

PUTNAM, Mary Elizabeth, about 2, only dau. of George and Sarah M., d 3/23/47 in Waterville (1-3/26)

PUTNAM, Mary, wf. of Horace, d 6/30/44 in Rome (consumption) (funeral at the Episcopal Church) (1-7/2)

PUTNEY, Elizabeth - see FLEWWELLING, Robert

PUTNEY, Nelson of White Plains, m 10/25/38 Jerusha E. Bunce of Sparta at S. (12-11/13)

PUTNEY, William m 11/27/38 Mary Flewelling in Somers; John Green, Esq. (all of S.) (12-12/4)

QUACKENBOSS, Anthony I., 39, son of Isaac A., Esq. late of Albany, d 12/7/36 at NYC (a lingering illness) (6-12/13)

QUACKENBUSH, Catharine - see SINSABAUGH, George W.

QUARLES, Francis of New Orleans m 8/25/35 Frances Ann Woodbridge, niece of Joseph Breed, Esq. of Norwich, CT, at Norwich (6-9/7)

QUARLES, Francis, Esq. - see DOUGHTY, John D.

QUARLES, Matilda - see DOUGHTY, John D.

QUICK, Alice - see CASWELL, George

QUICK, George m 1/12/42 Ann Eliza Miller in Bedford; Rev. Jesse Hunt (11-1/18)

QUICK, George m 1/12/42 Ann Eliza Miller in Bedford; Rev. Jesse Hunt (11-1/25)

QUICK, James (Capt.), 30, d 7/11/45 in West Troy (5-7/16)

QUICK, John R., 6, eldest son of Isaac, d 5/1/39 in North Salem (12-5/7)

QUICK, Mary - see MORREN, George

QUIN, Arthur, late of Troy, m 7/10/36 Catharine Delehanty, both of Albany; Rev. Urquhart (6-7/14)

QUIN, Charles - see FITZSIMMONS, John

QUINBY, Mileson, 89, widow of Josiah Quinby of New Castle d (date not given) at her home in NYC (12-3/26)

QUINBY, Moses, 80, d 1/23/40 at Middlesex, Conn. (12-2/11)

QUINBY, Underhill m 3/11/40 Ann Loomis Vorhis, only dau. of John; James Banks, Esq. (all of Mount Pleasant) (12-3/17)

QUINLAN, Alfred F., printer, of Binghamton, m 11/4/49 Henrietta Amelia Huntington, dau. of Joseph, Esq., of Thompson, Sullivan County; Rev. Bloomer (8-11/24)

QUINLAN, James E., editor of the Republican Watchman, m 4/6/42 Amanda Baker, dau of John of Westport, CT, at Westport; Rev. J. Hitchcock (11-4/28)

RACE, Catharine and Emeline, daus, and Marsden, son of Whiting and Rebecca Race, formerly of Catskill, d 12/14, 16 and 18 respectively in 1835 at Seneca Falls (scarlet fever) (6-1/1/36)

RACE, Richard M. of Canajoharie m 12/31/48 Caroline E. Cronkhite of Visscher's Ferry at V.F.; Rev. W.W. Halloway (4-1/18/49)

RADCLIFF, ----, 10, dau. of Thomas, recently of Poughkeepsie, d 8/12/49 in Kingston (8-8/25)

RADCLIFF, Edward - see VAN ESS, Sarah C.

RADCLIFF, Edward - see VAN NESS, Augustus Edward

RADCLIFF, William - see VAN ESS, Sarah C.

RADCLIFF, William Pitt, 49, d 6/8/49 at Rhinebeck Landing at the home of his father, John Radcliff, Esq. (8-6/23)

RADDCLIFFE, William of Albany m 3/27/49 Julia M. Gusstel (?) of Batavia; H.C. Vogell (1-3/28)

RADLEY, James, Esq. m 3/11/37 Catharine Lamerauk; David Russell, Esq. (all of Bethlehem) (6-3/17)

RAE, ---- (Miss) d "recently" at New Orleans (a talented actress) (from the New York Star) (6-3/14/36)

RAILY, Elizabeth - see HODGE, David

RAINBOW, Eliza - see VAN VOST, James

RAINEY, James, about 70, d 4/24/42 in Crawford (9-5/7)

RAMSAY, David D. m 9/9/36 Jane Engels, both of Albany, at Coeymans Landing; Rev. John M. Pease (6-9/27)

RANDALL, Antoinny - see HUNTINGTON, Edward

RANDALL, Elisha O. m 2/8/38 Maria E. Reynolds, eldest dau. of William, Esq., in Norway, NY; Rev. W.B. Curtiss (3-2/15)

RANDALL, Elizabeth Marion - see ELMER, Wesley

RANDALL, Fanny - see WILBUR, Solomon B.

RANDALL, George Roswell - see WARDEN, Satterlee (General)

RANDALL, Harriet E. - see WARDEN, Satterlee (General)

RANDALL, Margaret - see WHITE, Solon H.

RANDALL, Nicholas Norman, 14, son of N.P., Esq., d 7/15/35 in Manlius (6-7/23)

RANDALL, Nicholas P., Esq., 57, counsellor at law, d 3/7/36 at Manlius (a
    protracted illness) (from the Syracuse Chief) (6-3/14)

RANDALL, P. - see ORR, Harriet M.

RANDALL, P.N. of Feltonville, Mass. m 10/28/50 Louisa Wood, dau. of A.L.,
    Esq., of Mc Connellsville, at Mc C.; Rev. M.H. Hawkins (1-10/30)

RANDEL, William S. of Albany m 1/25/16 Mary Ann Adams in NYC (6-1/27)

RANDOL, Martha B. - see MAIR, James H.

RANDOLPH, Martha, widow of late Thomas Mann Randolph, and dau of Thomas
    Jefferson, d 10/10/36 suddenly at the home of Thomas Jefferson Randolph
    (6-10/20)

RANDOLPH, W.B.F. m 9/20/34 Laura M. Craig, dau of Hector, Esq., of NYC;
    Rev. Arbuckle (6-9/24)

RANDOLPH, William B.F. m 9/20/36 Laura M. Craighton dau of Hector, Esq.;
    Rev. Arbuckle (all of NYC) (6-9/27)

RANKIN, Sophia - see WARD, Edward

RANKINS, L.H. of Jacksonville (in the town of Little Falls) m 2/17/39 Almira
    Briggs in Newport; James C. Smith, Esq. (3-2/28)

RANKINS, Sanford m 7/8/41 Mary Briggs, both of Jacksonburgh (in Little Falls),
    in NYC; Rev. P. Harty (3-8/26)

RANNEY, Persis (Mrs.), 73, d 7/2/43 in West Troy (5-7/5)

RANSOM, Elizabeth, 27, wf of Barzilia Ransom, d (date not given) in NYC
    (6-2/21/26)

RANSOM, Isaac of Lansingburgh m 12/31/46 Caroline S. Rhynders of Waterford;
    Rev. Houghtaling (5-1/6/47)

RANSOM, Mary - see BLISS, Oren

RANSOM, Nicholas Huntley of Hudson m 10/15/35 Martha Ann Thompson of
    Philadelphia in P.; Rev. W.T. Brantly (6-10/22)

RANSOM, Owen (Brevet Major) of 9th Regiment, US Infantry, d suddenly 7/3/36
    at Fort Gratiot (6-7/23)

RAPELJE, George - see CHABERT, Julius Xavier, M.D.

RAPELJE, Susannah Elizabeth - see CHABERT, Julius Xavier, M.D.

RAPP, Harriet - see FAIRFIELD, Jamin L., Jr.

RAPP, James A. of Taberg m 8/8/50 Martha J. Potter of Floyd; Rev. James Erwin
    (1-9/11)

RAREY(?), Ammon d 5/17/36 at his residence at Rising Sun Tavern on South
    Pearl Street (6-5/19)

RASBACH, David, Esq., under-sheriff of Herkimer County, m 8/15/41 Mary
    Myers, both of Herkimer, in Mohawk; Rev. J. Murphy (3-8/26)

RASBERRY, Maxim m 11/19/48 Mary Ann Yates, both of West Troy; Rev. J.C.
    Burroughs (5-12/6)

RATHBONE, John (Rev.), 97, d 8/2/26 at Wallington, Conn. (Baptist
    denomination) (6-8/11)

RATHBONE, Juliet C. - see PATTERSON, Albert C.

RATHBONE, Sarah Buford, 2, youngest dau of J.H., Esq., counsellor at law in

Utica, d 7/3/36 (6-7/8)

RATHBUN, Mary Ann - see BAR, John

RATHBUN, William m 8/17/42 Mary Ann Willson(?) in Little Falls; Rev. C.W. L-
---(surname blurred) (3-8/25)

RAUSE, Margaret - see MC CAUSLAND, Jefferson

RAVENEL, John, Esq. of Charleston, S.C. m 2/5/35 Eliza Mc Evers, dau of
Charles, Esq.. in New York City; Rev. Dr. Berrian (6-2/10)

RAWDEN, Freeman of firm of Rawden, Wright and Hatch of NYC m 9/28/43
Margaret Feeter(?) Myers of Little Falls, dau. of Col. Matthew Myers of
Herkimer, in Little Falls at the home of George H. Feelor, Esq; Rev. J.P.
Spinner (3-10/5)

RAWDEN, Mary Richards, 30, wf of Freeman Rawden and dau. of Col. Matthew
Myers of Herkimer, d 5/28/42 in NYC (3-6/2)

RAWDON, MAry, 49, wf of Erastus, formerly from Connecticut, d (date not given)
in Windsor, Ohio (6-4/7/26)

RAWLINGS, Isaac (Dr.) d (date not given) in Calvert County, Maryland (formerly
an officer in the US Army) (6-4/7/26)

RAWNSLEY, Alice - see THORNLEY, Anthony

RAWSON, Erastus, Esq., merchant of Lockport m 1/25/36 Mary Ann Hewes of
Shelby, Orleans County, in S.; Rev. Gilbert (6-2/9)

RAWSON, Helen J. - see ANDREU, Pedro

RAWSON, Packard of Albany m 8/18/36 Frances M. Smith, dau of Roswell late of
Troy, at Brockport; Rev. Hunter (6-8/29)

RAY, James - see JEWETT, David B.

RAY, Richard, 36, son of late Cornelius, d "in March" at Paris (6-5/12/36)

RAYMOND, ----, infant dau of Stephen and Rachel, d 5/11/42 in Lewisboro
(11-5/19)

RAYMOND, Almira - see SEARS, Herman

RAYMOND, Angeline - see PALMER, S. Thompson

RAYMOND, Daniel of North Salem m 12/25/38 Mary Barnum of Danbury in
South East; Rev. Mc Leod (12-1/8/39)

RAYMOND, H. - see HOWARD, Mary

RAYMOND, Harriet - see NEWMAN, Erastus, M.D.

RAYMOND, Helen Wilson, 18 months, only child of Theodore and Rose Ann, d
12/29/44 in Boonville (1-1/14/45)

RAYMOND, Laura A. - see LEWIS, Andrew

RAYMOND, Lewis - see PALMER, S. Thompson

RAYMOND, Lucinda, 35, wf of Thomas, d 8/25/48 in Boonville (1-9/22)

RAYMOND, Lucinda, 35, wf of William H., d 8/25/48 in Boonville (consumption)
(1-10/6)

RAYMOND, Luzon m 11/21/50 Savina Babcock, both of Camden, in Rome at
Stanwix Hall; Rev. James Erwin (1-11/27)

RAYMOND, Maria - see LEARNED, Charles G.

RAYMOND, Olivia W. - see KERKERS, William I.

RAYMOND, Orissa A. - see SPENCER, George W.

RAYMOND, Sarah Maria - see HYATT, Elijah

RAYMOND, Uriah (Capt.) d 9/24/33 at Bedford ("an old inhabitant of that
village") (11-10/1)

RAYMOND, Vernon, 37, d 6/26/41 in Rome at the home of his brother (not named) (consumption) (1-6/29)

RAYMOND, William P. of Sidney m 10/4/37 Ella Bostwick, dau. of Hon. John Bostwick of Hamden, Delaware Co. in H.; Rev. Raymond (6-10/20)

RAYMOND, William W. of Ballston m 8/1/39 Almira David of West Troy; Rev. J. Poor of Saratoga Springs (5-8/14)

RAYNER, Morris m 12/1/41 Eliza Clarke, dau of Jabez; Rev. Devinne (all of Peekskill)(11-12/7)

RAYNES(?), Willit, merchant, of Syracuse m 9/1/35 Mary Van Kleeck, dau of late Teunis, Esq. of Poughkeepsie, at P.; Rev. Samuel A. Van Vranken (6-9/4)

RAYNOR, Reuben m 9/22/42 Charhille West at Fairfield; Rev. John Loveys (all of Fairfield) (3-9/29)

RAYNS, Henry m 11/1/36 Elen Vanduzen, both of Albany; Rev. B.C. Brisbin (6-11/3)

READ, Archer, d 5/29/33 at Mount Pleasant ("an old and responsible inhabitant of that town") (11-6/11)

READ, Emma - see DURGY, George

READ, Theodore of Southeast m 4/9/39 Mary Rundle, oldest dau. of Ezra of North Salem, in N.S.; Rev. George D. Sutton (12-4/23)

READ, William L., 28(?), formerly of Albany, d 6/22/37 at the home of his brother-in-law in Albion, Orleans County (survived by a wife and one child in Albany) (from the Orleans Republican) (6-7/11)

READ, William S. of New Haven, Conn. m 7/14/42 Nancy Vaughan of West Troy in Watervliet; Rev. M. Bates (5-7/20)

READER, S. m 11/12/48 Ellen Perry, both of Rome, in R.; George Barnard, Esq. (1-11/17)

READING, Joseph of West Troy m 9/8/47 Mary L. Weed of Albany at Cohoes; Rev. Cicero Barber (5-9/15)

RED JACKET - see GWADOH, Gaw-Heh

REDDY, Michael m 9/16/38 Jane Gessner in Little Falls; Rev. Thomas Towell (all of Little Falls) (3-9/20)

REDMOND, Margaret, 19, dau. of Samuel, d (date not given) in NYC (6-11/28/26)

REECH, Clarissa - see GUE, Joseph V.

REED, ----, 8, dau of "Mr. Reed", d (date not given) at Fonda (her clothes caught fire) (further information not given) (6-8/8/36)

REED, Angelina - see DRIGGS, Chester

REED, Cornelia - see WYCKOFF, (Rev. Dr.)

REED, David, 80, d 2/3/42 in Putnam Valley (11-2/15)

REED, Emeline - see TUTTLE, Henry B.

REED, Frances - see VAN PATTEN, Simon S.

REED, James W., Esq. m 4/17/37 Adaline Allen at St. Paul's Church in Oak Hill, Greene County; Rev. H.H. Prout (6-4/25)

REED, Margaret, 31, or 51(?), wf of James, d 3/20/49 in Saugerties (8-3/24)

REED, Maria - see HOUSTON, Thomas (Rev.)

REED, Mary Elizabeth, 17 months, dau. of Charles and Caroline H., d 6/16/50 at Chittenango (1-6/26)

REED, Matthew m 5/18/42 Sarah Miller, both of Somers, in Bedford; David Olmsted, Esq. (11-6/9)

REED, Newton of Amenia m 6/9/36 Ann Van Dyck, dau of Dr. Henry L. of

Kinderkook, at K.; Rev. L.H. Van Dyck of Cairo, Greene Co. (6-6/16)

REED, Roswell - see WYCKOFF, (Rev. Dr.)

REED, Thomas m 11/8/49 Sarah Paterson (both of Oriskany); H.C. Vogell (1-11/21)

REED, Thomas, Esq. - see HOUSTON, Thomas (Rev.)

REED, Timothy, a young man of Swanzey, New Hampshire, m 1/22/26 Mrs. Eunice Kelley of Danby "who at the wedding feast presented her partner with seven healthy children, the fruits of former marriages" ("the same justice reunited this lady 3 times in marriage") (6-2/7)

REEDER, Lydia - see WOODWORTH, Samuel

REES, Ambrose of Bristol, England m 3/3/42 Adah M. Tuttle of Poughkeepsie at Cold Spring (11-3/15)

REES, Seth of Green Bay, Michigan Terr. m 9/16/35 Sylvia C. Allen of Hinsdale, MA; Rev. S. Center (6-9/18)

REESE, Almira - see CHAPNEY, Henry C.

REESE, Peter of Rome m 5/6/46 Catharine Hager of Verona in V.; Elder Lewis (double ceremony - see HAGER, Daniel) (1-5/19)

REESE, Renett - see SCHOFIELD, Chester

REESKOPE, Emily A. - see PECKHAM, William N.

REEVE, Aaron Burr, Esq., 28, only son of the Hon. Tapping Reeve, Esq., of Litchfield, CT, d 9/1/09 at Troy (7-9/13)

REEVES, ---- (age not given), child of Mrs. Sally Reeves, d "last week" in Catskill (7-8/30/09)

REEVES, J. of NYC m 9/8/42 Dorothy Worth of Rome in R.; H.C. Vogell (1-9/13)

REEVES, James m 9/24/35 Caroline Sanford, dau of Luther; Rev. Merrit (6-10/6)

REGUS, William Clement, 22, eldest son of F.W., Esq. of Peekskill, d 12/19/41 at the home of Mrs. Elizabeth Field (11-12/21)

REID, Anna D. - see HICKOK, Edgar

REID, Catharine - see SCOTT, Charles

REID, Charles of Coeymans Landing m 2/21/35 Jane Keller of Albany; Rev. Charles Smith (6-2/26)

REID, Marion - see BORST, John B.

REID, William - see BORST, John B.

REIST, Nelson, about 2, son of Nelson, d 3/1/40 in Little Falls (3-3/5)

RELAY(?), Ann Eliza - see ROBERTS, N.W.

RELAY, Mary Amelia - see BURT, Joshua

RELYEA, Hannah Jane - see MORSE, George N.

REMBALDT, Louisa - see SPINDLER, Daniel

REMINGTON, ----, wf of Eliphalet Remington, Esq., d 8/18/41 in German Flats (3-8/28)

REMINGTON, Asa of Manheim m 7/3/37 Nancy E. Swift of Little Falls in L.F.; Henry Wick, Esq. (3-7/20)

REMINGTON, David (Rev.), 38, pastor of the church at Rye, d suddenly 1/25/34 at Rye. (11-2/4)

REMINGTON, Hannah S., 27, wf of John W. and dau. of Leverett Seymour of Westmoreland, d 12/8/47 at Oriskany (1-12/24)

REMINGTON, John W. of Oriskany m 12/22/41 Hannah Seymour of Westmoreland; Rev. Pettibone (a double ceremony - see BEEBE, Abijah

REMINGTON, Philo (Col.) of Herkimer County, m 12/21/41 Caroline A. Lathrop, dau. of John H., Esq., of Syracuse, at S.; Rev. Dr. Lansing (1-1/11/42)

REMSEN, Peter, Esq., 53, of NYC d 8/26/36 at his country seat at Newtown, L.I. (6-8/29)

RENCHER(?), A. (Hon) member of Congress from the Salisbury district, m 9/27/36 Lucina Jones, dau of Col. Edward, in Pittsborough, Chatham County, N.C.; Rev. Philip Wylie (6-10/24)

RENIVEE, Gilbert B. of Albany m 5/1/36 Keziah Peek of Schenectady in S.; Rev. Whetmore (6-5/5)

RENTOR, James of NYC m 4/17/43 Angeline Borden, dau. of James Borden of Fairfield; Rev. William Baker (3-4/27)

REQUA, ----, consort of James, d 8/21/36 at his home in Greene County (6-8/26)

REQUA, Abram of Newark, NJ, m 5/24/42 Elizabeth P. Lyon, sister of the principal, at the Irving Institute in Tarrytown (11-6/9)

REQUA, Joseph (Capt.), 81, a Rev. War soldier, d 4/30/39 at New Baltimore, Greene County (was a resident of N.B. many years) (12-5/21)

REQUA, Sarah A. - see SEELEY, Jeremiah H.

REQUA, William Clements, 22, eldest son of F.W. Requa, Esq., of Peekskill, d 12/17/41 at the home of Mrs. Elizabeth Field (11-12/21)

RERRINGTON, Asenath - see HAWSE, William H.

RESSEGINE, Mary, about 45, widow of William D. d 3/22/39 in Sing Sing (12-3/26)

RESSEGIUS(?). Alfred, 21, d 1/7/39 in Sing Sing (12-1/15)

RETALICK, Henry m 4/29/48 Margaret Houghton, both of West Troy, in W.T.; Rev. J.C. Burroughs (5-5/17)

REXFORD, George R of firm of L.M. & G.R. Rexford of Binghamton m 3/29/37 Sarah Merrill; Rev. Starkweather (6-4/13)

REYMOND, George m 5/14/39 Augusta Mariah Foster, dau. of Judge Foster, all of Southeast, in Southeast; Rev. Mc Leod (12-6/4)

REYNOLDS, Alexander G., principal of the Union Academy, m 10/30/39 Jeanette Barrett, dau. of Phineas; Rev. S. Nichols (all of Bedford) (12-11/12)

REYNOLDS, Ard of Stamford, CT m 1/12/39 Phebe Angeline Barrett, dau of Frederick, Esq. of Bedford, in B.; Rev. Patterson (12-1/15)

REYNOLDS, Ard(?) of Catskill m 12/12/10 Ann Eliza Doell of Albany in A. (7-12/19)

REYNOLDS, Betsey - see TRAVIS, William T.

REYNOLDS, Cynthia, 17, second dau. of Marcus T., Esq., d 3/25/37 at the home of her uncle (not named) in Amsterdam, Montgomery County (6-3/27)

REYNOLDS, Edward m 11/16/42 Sally Jay Lambert in Whitlockville; Rev. Jesse Hunt (all of Bedford) (11-11/24)

REYNOLDS, Elias of Somers m 3/10/39 Jane Jordon, dau. of James Jordan, Esq. at Croton (12-3/12)

REYNOLDS, Eliza, 36, wf of John, d 3/21/49 in West Troy (5-4/11)

REYNOLDS, Enos, Jr., m 12/24/41 Eliza Yorks in Unionville; Rev. William S. Moore (11-12/28)

REYNOLDS, Hannah, about 56, widow of Capt. Shubael Reynolds, d 3/7/39 at her home in Sawpit (12-3/19)

REYNOLDS, Horace m 11/1/38 Mary C. Lockwood, dau of Horatio, in Pound Ridge; Rev. Paterson(?) (12-11/13)

REYNOLDS, Margaret A - see NOBLE, Walter H.

REYNOLDS, Maria E. - see RANDALL, Elisha O.

REYNOLDS, Mary - see LOBDELL, Perry

REYNOLDS, Philip, 70, father of Philip, Jr., d 7/9/37 at Fonda (6-7/11)

REYNOLDS, Rufus m 6/9/39 Mary Jesup, dau of Samuel in Somers; Rev. Leadbetter (all of Somers) (12-6/25)

REYNOLDS, Ruth Ann, 17, d 3/4/42 in Southeast (11-3/15)

REYNOLDS, Sophia L., 2, dau of Horace and Mary C., d 8/14/42 at the home of Horatio Lockwood, Esq. in Pound Ridge (11-8/18)

REYNOLDS, Stephen Richard, 4 months, only child of P. Reynolds, Jr., editor of the Johnstown Herald, d 8/31/35 in Johnstown (inflammation of the brain) (6-9/5)

REYNOLDS, William Wallace, 23, son of James B., formerly of Newburgh, d 8/11/42 in NYC (funeral from the home of William E. Randall on First Street) (9-8/13)

RHIND, William m 8/25/49 Susan Preston, both of Saugerties; Rev. H. Ostrander, D.D. (8-9/29)

RHINEHEART, Francis, about 50, d 8/15/49 in Kingston (cholera) (8-8/18)

RHOADES, Lyman m 12/16/35 Cornelia R. Hansen, dau. of Cornelius; Rev. T.J. Sawyer (6-12/23)

RHODES, Charles D. m (date not given) Harriet Butler in NYC (6-5/29/16)

RHODES, Elizabeth, 29, wf of Robert R., d 1/5/35 in Utica (6-1/8)

RHODES, Erasmus, 30(?), of Milton, d 8/21/49 in Rondout (cholera) (he was a hand on the sloop "Don Juan" (see HOUGHTALING, James) (8-9/1)

RHODES, Harriet - see MINERLY, Joel

RHODES, Jane - see ROOSA, John T.

RHODES, Lydia D. - see ALLEN, G.E.

RHODES, Mary Ann - see SOUTHWORTH, Henry O.

RHODES, Samuel B. of Paris m 3/4/41 Elizabeth Davis of Bridgewater at B.; Rev. Page (1-3/23)

RHYNDERS, Caroline S. - see RANSOM, Isaac

RICARDSON (sic), Abel, 92, a Rev. War soldier, d (date not given) at Ashby, Mass. (5-1/17/44)

RICE, Asa C. of Hoosick m 4/24/47 Mary Hurley of West Troy; Rev. Houghtaling (5-5/5)

RICE, Catherine Ann - see JERMAIN, James B., Esq.

RICE, Combs D. of Whitesboro m 11/26/26 Ann Higgins, dau. of C. Higgins, Canal Insepctor of Albany; Rev. Leonard Combs (6-12/1)

RICE, Hamilton m 1/27/36 Catharine Thompson, dau. of Capt. Thompson; Rev. William M. Weber (3-2/18)

RICE, Harvey of Lowville m 1/28/45 Harriet A. Dott of Andover; Rev. A.G. Lathrop of Andover (1-2/4)

RICE, Jane Eliza - see PORTER, Ira

RICE, John Hartwell (brother of Hon. C.C. Rice of the legislature) born in the city of Limerick, Ireland, d 3/7/35 in NYC (6-3/11)

RICE, Joseph - see CHURCHILL, Albert W.

RICE, Lydia (Mrs.), 27, d (date not given) in NYC (6-5/15/16)

RICE, M.M., Esq. of Minnesota Terr. m 3/29/49 Matilda, dau. of B.G. Whitall, formerly of Rome, at White Plains, Henrico Co., Virginia; Rev. Kepler (see CARRINGTON, T.) (1-4/11)

RICE, William Henry of Ogdensburgh, NY m 9/20/37 Mary Ann Muir, second dau. of Ebenezer, Esq., at Willow Grove, Montreal; Rev. John H. Walden (6-10/3)

RICE, William of North Salem, Westchester County m 3/30/50 Sarah Elizabeth Fisher, dau. of John of Kent, Putnam County in K.; William A. Dent(?), Esq. (10-4/10)

RICH, Angeline - see KELLY, L.H.

RICH, Ann A. - see EACKER, George

RICH, Catharine - see PERRY, John

RICH, David B. of Warren, Mass. m 11/7/41 Nancy Overache of Danube; Rev. S. Ottman (3-11/11)

RICH, G.B., Esq. - see SPALDING, E.G.

RICH, Hannah - see LEWIS, Augustus

RICH, Jane Antoinette - see SPAULDING, E.G.

RICH, Louisa - see CHURCHILL, John Jr.

RICH, Riley, 42, d 8/28/49 in Kingston (8-9/1)

RICHARDS, Ezra of Troy m 8/2/38 Sarah Bradt of the town of Watervliet in West Troy; Rev. Lewis (5-8/8)

RICHARDS, Frances Louise, 2, only child of Albert and Frances C. of West Troy, d suddenly 8/21/44 in Darien, Conn. (5-9/4)

RICHARDS, Hawkins, 24, d (date not given) in Blanford, Mass. (7-7/4/10)

RICHARDS, James, Jr., late of Auburn Theological Seminary m 8/25/36 Elizabeth Beals, fifth dau of Thomas, Esq., at Canandaigua; Rev. Dr. Richards (6-9/2)

RICHARDS, Mary Eliza, 10, adopted dau. of Henry and Helen N., d 3/18/42 in West Troy (5-3/23)

RICHARDS, Nathan, 64, of Putnam County d 2/15/39 in Southeast (12-2/26)

RICHARDS, Ruth A. - see RIPLEY, Thomas C.

RICHARDS, Surina - see PETRIE, Rufus

RICHARDS, Thomas of New Hartford m 3/6/50 Roxana Hunt of West Leyden at the American Hotel (in Rome); H.C. Vogell (1-3/13)

RICHARDS, William of Apalachicola m 8/4/35 Elizabeth Dorlon, dau of Robert of Catskill, at C.; Rev. Prentiss (6-8/7)

RICHARDSON, A.J. m 1/30/48 F.A. Abell in New London; Rev. Josiah Arnold (1-2/25)

RICHARDSON, Abel - see possibly RICARDSON, Abel

RICHARDSON, Abel W., Esq., 34, one of the Justices of the town of Watervliet, d 12/25/38 in West Troy (5-1/2/39)

RICHARDSON, Amer, a native of England but long a resident of the County of Albany, d 7/12/37 (funeral from his late home at 303 South Pearl Street) (6-7/13)

RICHARDSON, Catharine Ann, 4, dau. of Israel P. and Sarah Ann, d 1/8/45 in West Troy (5-1/15)

RICHARDSON, Elizabeth, wf of John, d (date not given) in NYC (6-2/21/26)

RICHARDSON, Harriet Isabella, 5 months, dau. of John W. and Frances, d 2/25/45 in Rome (1-3/17)

RICHARDSON, J.M. of New London m 12/16/44 Miss D.A. Preston of Camden; Rev. D. Mason (1-2/18/45)

RICHARDSON, James m 1/1/38 Louisa Bowen in Salisbury; A. Avery, Esq. (all of

Salisbury) (a double ceremony - see BOWEN, Joel) (3-1/11)

RICHARDSON, James m 3/23/48 Jemima Leonard of Fort Plain in F.P.; Rev. Bishop Isbell (4-3/30)

RICHARDSON, John of Albany m 12/16/44 Elizabeth Lansing of Watervliet Centre; Rev. Dr. Welch (5-12/25)

RICHARDSON, Patience - see WEBBER, Arsenal

RICHERSON, Fanny - see WAIT, Daniel W.

RICHESTER, Nathaniel T., Esq., of Rochester m 6/15/36 Catherine Ann, dau of late James Cummings of NYC , in NYC; Rev. H.J. Whitehouse (6-6/28)

RICHEY, Margaret Ellen - see SLUYTER, Alfred

RICHMOND, Adelaide Elvireta, 4, dau. of Albert H. and Electa, d 8/9/49 in Saugerties (8-8/18)

RICHMOND, Ira D., merchant, m 10/3/37 Charlotte A. Skinner, dau. of David, Esq., in Ghent; Rev. Jacob Burger (all of Ghent) (6-10/10)

RICKER, Lovina - see CASLER, Solomon

RICKERD, George of Fulton (town) Schoharie County m 3/3/37 Elizabeth Benedict of Watervliet at Cohoes; L.V.K. Vandemark, Esq. (6-3/7)

RICKS, Jane - see ROMER, Henry

RIDER, Christopher (Mr.), 77, d 5/23/39 in Littlefield (paralysis) (one of the first settlers in Little Falls) (3-5/30)

RIDER, John Henry H., 18, son of John Rider of Rensselaerville, d 4/11/48 at the Institute for the Deaf and Dumb in NYC (smallpox) (4-4/20)

RIDER, Maria - see OSTERHOUDT, Jacob

RIDER, Mary (Mrs.), (age blurred), d 7/6/49 at Malden (8-7/7)

RIDER, Matilda, 16 months, dau. of Stephen J., d 6/12/26 (6-6/13)

RIDGEWAY, Isaac, 80, a Rev. War soldier and pensioner, d 3/4/40 in Putnam Valley (was a member of the Boston tea Party) (12-3/24)

RIDGEWAY, Susan - see ROTCH, Thomas

RIECH, John Christian, Esq., m 9/26/41 Ann Garner of Haverstraw; Rev. Moses Marcus, B.D., Rector of St. Peter's Church, Peekskill (11-9/28)

RIGGS, Frank, 2, only child of William H., Esq. (editor of the Mohawk Valley Gazette) d 5/20/48 at Canajoharie (4-5/25)

RIGGS, Hiram, Esq. of Jordan m 4/13/37 Margaret Dievendorf, dau. of Hon. Henry I. of Root, in R.; Rev. Paul Wiedman (6-4/24)

RIGGS, Hiram, Esq., of Jordan m 3/7/37 Margaret Dievendorf, dau. of Hon. Henry I., of Root, Montgomery County, at Root; Rev. Paul Weidman (6-3/13)

RIGGS, Lydia - see CLARK, James

RIGGS, Margaret, 101, relict of Joseph Riggs, D.D., d 10/10/42 at Saratoga at the home of her son-in-law, Jedediah Beckwith (5-10/19)

RIGHTMYER, John, 76, d 11/22/38 in Danube (3-11/29)

RIKEMAN, Mary Ann - see VAN VOORHIS, Charles

RIKER, Elizabeth - see SPRING, Edward

RIKER, Richard (Hon.), for many years recorder, d 9/26/42 in NYC (the courts adjourned as a mark of respect to the deceased) (11-9/29)

RILEY, Nancy Ann - see DAILE, Hugh

RILEY, Rosa, about 50, wf of Edward, d 8/5/49 in Saugerties (cholera) (8-8/11)

RIMPH, Marinda - see MOYER, Ludowick

RING, Gertrude - see JEWELL, Volkert D.

RING, Juliette - see MORRIS, Alexander

RING, Margaret C. - see KALEY, George

RING, Tamma, 40, wf of Philip G. of Rhinebeck d 1/2/35 after a short illness (6-1/10)

RING, Thomas C., ESq., cashier of the Highland Bank, m 3/29/37 Catharine Spear in Newburgh; Rev. John Brown (all of Newburgh) (6-4/4)

RINGER, Jane Cameron - see JULIAND, Frederick

RIPLEY, Charles, Esq., 40, of Albany, d 2/12/37 at Saugerties (severe illness of a fortnight) (6-2/21)

RIPLEY, J.W. of Rome m 7/9/50 Susan Gorton of Mayfield in M.; Rev. Richards of Broadalbin (1-7/17)

RIPLEY, Thomas C., Esq., formerly of Little Falls, m 11/14/37 Ruth A. Richards, dau. of Dr. William Richards of White Creek, at W.C.; Rev. Hagen (3-12/21)

RISDON, Mary H. - see CHITTENDON, A.H.

RIVES, John C., one of the editors of the Globe, m 1/12/36 Mary Ann Elliott of Washington City in W.C.; Rev. O.B. Brown (6-1/21)

RIX, Esther. 81, wf of Nathan, d 7/19/42 in Fairfield (3-8/11)

ROBBINS, ----, infant child of Jacob, d 4/17/39 in Herkimer (3-5/2)

ROBBINS, Caroline, wf of Hon. Silas W. and youngest dau of late Uriah Tracy of Litchfield, CT, d 1/25/36 at Mount Sterling, Montgomery County, Kentucky (6-2/12)

ROBBINS, Mary, 65, widow of late Ephraim, d 12/17/40 in Rome (1-12/29)

ROBBINS, Nathan, 60, formerly of West Troy, d 10/6/44 at Cohoes (5-10/9)

ROBBINS, Rebecca - see LAMBY, F.

ROBERSON, William H. of firm of L.W. Young & Co. m 4/4/42 Martha D. Tarbell in Newburgh; Rev. E.F. Griswold (all of Newburgh) (9-4/9)

ROBERTS, Benjamin S. (Lieut.) of the US Army m 9/18/35 Elizabeth Sperry, dau of late Anson (?) G., Esq. of Plattsburgh in P. (6-9/30)

ROBERTS, Benjamin, 67, d 11/16/49 in Plattekill (8-12/1)

ROBERTS, Edwin M. m 11/3/42 Mary Evans, youngest dau. of John, Esq., in Little Falls; Rev. Livermore (3-11/10)

ROBERTS, Esther (Miss), 22, dau. of Hiram, Esq., d 5/24/48 in West Troy (5-6/14)

ROBERTS, Harriet - see CRISSEY, William

ROBERTS, Harriet (Miss), 22, d 5/15/10 and Miss Lucy Roberts, 28, d 5/20/10 in Hartford, both daus. of John Roberts (7-5/30)

ROBERTS, James H., 23, formerly of Mohawk, NY d 10/21/39 at Galveston, Texas (yellow fever) (he had been recently married) (he was a son of Col. Amos Roberts) (3-1/9/40)

ROBERTS, Jane - see HATCH, Sylvenus

ROBERTS, Joseph Jr., 42, actuary of the Pennsylvania Company for Insurance on Lives, d 8/25/35 at Philadelphia (6-8/31)

ROBERTS, Lucy - see ROBERTS, Harriet

ROBERTS, Mary - see LAMPHIER, Richardson

ROBERTS. N.W., Esq. m 9/3/35 Ann Eliza Relay(?), both of Albany, in Albany; Rev. Dr. Sprague (6-9/4)

ROBERTS, P.J. m 5/28/37 Mary Burge; Rev. C.P. Clarke (all of Albany) (6-5/30)

ROBERTSON, Alexander, about 58, d 5/2/16 (place not given) (6-5/8)

ROBERTSON, Robert (Capt.) m 12/31/46 Jane Ann Andrews; Rev. O.H. Gregory (all of West Troy) (5-1/6/47)

ROBINS, Elizabeth - see ODELL, Evander

ROBINS, William of Floyd m 1/27/47 Mary Briggs, dau. of Nyrum of Floyd (1-1/29)

ROBINSON, Adaline G. - see OLIVER, Charles S.

ROBINSON, Ann M. - see LEARHARD, Charles

ROBINSON, Anna Dorothea - see BETTS, William

ROBINSON, Anna Maria, 24, niece of Hugh Robinson, Esq., of Schenectady, d 8/18/36 (6-8/22)

ROBINSON, Benjamin, d 3/27/42 in Newburgh (9-4/2)

ROBINSON, Beverly, Esq. - see BETTS, William

ROBINSON, Catherine Alexander - see STIDELL, Alexander

ROBINSON, Conway m 7/14/36 Mary Susan Leigh, dau of Benjamin Watkins Leigh, Esq. in Richmond; Rt. Rev. Bishop Moore (6-7/21)

ROBINSON, Dan (Capt.), 85, d (date not given) at Granville, Mass. (7-8/29/10)

ROBINSON, Edward, merchant, of Albany m 7/6/36 Pamelia Batchelder, dau of Nathaniel Sawyer of Bethlehem, at B.; Rev. C.P. Clark (6-7/8)

ROBINSON, Edwin W., 21, assistant civil engineer in the service of the United States, d 11/8/35 at Washington (illness of 18 days) (6-11/12)

ROBINSON, George A. of Troy m 7/18/50 Huldah Chesebro, dau. of M.P. of Whitestown in W.; Rev. R.R. Kirk (1-7/24)

ROBINSON, Gertrude - see DUANE, Cornelius

ROBINSON, Heman, Esq., 50, youngest son of Gen. David Robinson, d 2/26/37 in Bennington, VT (his death was sudden and unexpected) (from the Vermont Gazette) (6-3/4)

ROBINSON, Isaac A. of Buffalo m 10/24/47 Sarah M. Fonda of Batavia in Albany; Rev. T.F. Wyckoff of West Troy (5-11/3)

ROBINSON, Isaac D.W., 70, d 10/6/49 at High Falls (8-10/20)

ROBINSON, Louisa Jane - see DAVIS, Samuel Willard

ROBINSON, Margaret - see COOK, Richard

ROBINSON, Mary B. - see SLOCUM, Charles M.

ROBINSON, Mary Elizabeth - see DUSENBURY, Stephen T.

ROBINSON, Mary Elizabeth, 11 months, only dau. of William, d. 8/4/39 in Sing Sing (12-8/6)

ROBINSON, Mercy - see WEBSTER, Levi

ROBINSON, Phebe A. - see YOUNG, Henry G.

ROBINSON, Sarah 15, dau. of William and Elizabeth, d 8/18/37 in Toronto, Upper Canada (was mortally wounded by an unintended cut on her neck by the sickle she was using to reap wheat) (6-10/4)

ROBINSON, Sidney T (Major) of Catskill (formerly of Binghamton) m 9/22/35 Mary I. Post, dau of David, Esq., of Montrose, PA, in M; Rev. Worden (6-10/3)

ROBINSON, Sidney T. (Major) of Catskill (formerly of Binghamton) m 9/22/35 Mary L. Post, dau of David, Esq., of Montrose, PA at M; Rev. Worden (6-9/29)

ROBINSON, William, 60, d 11/21/47 in West Troy ("bilious fever") ("Ballston papers please copy") (5-11/24)

ROBINSON, Zenana - see MATTESON, James

ROBISON, Sarah - see VEDDER, John E.

ROBSON, William Alexander, 20, printer and publisher of the Reflector and
Democrat, d 1/21/38 at Schenectady after an illness of five days (born and
raised in Herkimer County) (3-2/15)

ROCHESTER, Col. - see BARNEY, Moreau

ROCKENSTEIN, Mary Ann - see KEMP, Michael

ROCKWELL, A. (Dr.), 40, physician and assistant surgeon of the United States
Arsenal at Watervliet, d 2/22/37 at his home in West Troy (after a lingering
illness). He was born Lanesborough, Mass. (survived by a wife, an infant
and three other children) (6-2/27)

ROCKWELL, George of Seneca Falls m 4/19/37 Mary A. Mc Clintock, dau. of
Ralph of Albany; Rev. Horatio Potter (6-4/20)

ROCKWELL, J.S. m 10/30/48 Elizabeth Wentworth, both of Rome; Rev. W.E.
Knox (1-11/2)

ROCKWELL, James, Esq. of Cleveland, Ohio m 10/3/37 Cynthia Kellog, dau. of
Spencer, Esq. of Utica at U.; Rev. Savage (6-10/7)

ROCKWELL, Jeremy, Esq. d 8/16/35 in Hadley, Saratoga Co. (6-8/27)

ROCKWELL, John W. - see MC ALLISTER, James M., M.D.

ROCKWELL, Julius (Hon.) of Pittsfield, speaker of the House of Representatives m
(date not given) Lucy Walker, dau of Hon. William P., in Lenox, MA
(6-12/6/36)

ROCKWELL, Mary - see PRATT, James R.

ROCKWELL, Mary (Mrs.), d (date and her age not given) (funeral this afternoon at
home of her son-in-law, John I. Olmstead, 74 Division Street, Albany
(6-1/10/37)

ROCKWELL, Mary Matilda - see BELEKNAP, James

ROCKWELL, Sarah, 68, wf of Nathaniel, d (date not given) at East Windsor
(7-6/27/10)

RODGERS, Caroline Mary - see NAGLE, Charles B.

RODGERS, Thomas, 2, son of Patrick and Rosana, d 4/16/41 in West Troy (5-4/28)

RODMAN, Anna C., youngest dau of late Daniel, Esq., of Albany, d 11/11/36 at
Cleveland (6-11/22)

RODMAN, Anna C., youngest dau. of late Daniel, Esq. of Albany, d 11/11/36 at
Cleveland, Ohio (3-11/24)

RODNEY, P.H. m 4/13/37 Naimo C. Hogan, both of Albany, at St. Mary's Church;
Rev. Mr. Schneller (6-4/24)

ROE, Cormelius m 9/13/39 Jane Pugsley; Rev. Loring (all of Cortlandt town)
(11-9/17)

ROE, Lucinda, 1, youngest child of Jefferson Roe, d 2/25/42 in Newburgh (9-2/26)

ROE, William - see BREEN, Preston R.

ROESIDE, James, Esq. d 9/3/42 in Philadelphia ("well known as an extensive mail
contractor and stage priprietor in many parts of the United States") (11-9/8)

ROFF, Mary Ann - see FRASER, William B.

ROFFENOT, Augustus m 11/16/43 Maria Harter in Little Falls; Rev. C.W. Leet
(3-11/23)

ROGE, ---- (Mr.) "the person who by order of Bonaparte administered poison to 500
sick and wounded soldiers in Syria", d (date not given) in Arabia
(7-1/31/10)

ROGERS, ---- (Mr.) of Western m 2/2/42 Harriet Wiggins of Rome; R.C. Vogell
(1-2/8)

ROGERS, B.W. - see BAYARD, Eliza

ROGERS, David H. m 9/13/41 Margaret Yerdon (or Verdon), both of Boonville; Rev. Charles Jones (1-9/21)

ROGERS, Edmund, of the firm of Rogers, Son & Co. of NYC d 6/1/35 in NYC at the home of his brother, James (apoplexy) (6-6/4)

ROGERS, George D., 3, only son of Daniel, d 6/21/39 in Little Falls (3-6/27)

ROGERS, Harriet M., 1, only dau. of Nelson and Lucy, d 8/4/48 in West Troy (whooping cough) (5-8/16)

ROGERS, Henry, 32, merchant, of firm of Rogers and Cowles, d 12/12/35 at Glens Falls (consumption) (6-12/19)

ROGERS, James H., M.D., m 7/7/35 Louisa E. Coles, dau of the late Jordan Coles, in NYC; Rev. Brentnell (all of NYC) (6-7/11)

ROGERS, John of firm of John Van Volkenburgh & Co. of Chatham Center m 1/28/36 Eliza Shipman, dau of late Stephen of Kinderhook, in K.; Rev. Heermance (6-2/6)

ROGERS, John of firm of John Van Vulkenburgh & Co. of Chatham Center m 1/28/36 Eliza Shipman, dau, of late Stephen of Kinderhook, at K.; Rev. Heermance (6-2/1)

ROGERS, John, 78, d 4/7/43 in West Troy, late of Huntington, Long Island (his remains temporarily placed in Troy to be sent to Huntington for burial when navigation will permit) (obituary included) (5-4/12)

ROGERS, Lucinda F., 24, wf of Rev. Thomas Rogers and dau. of Deacon Benjamin Gardner, d 9/2/41 in Pownal, VT. ("a few weeks previous (her health failing) she came to her father's house from West Troy, the place of her residence") (survived by her husband and "an infant" not named) (5-9/22)

ROGERS, Lucretia - see DECKER, Daniel D.

ROGERS, Jane - see DARIUS, Matthew

ROLLER, John, Jr. m 1/2/49 Mary C. Shill in Palatine; Rev. Pegg (all of Palatine) (4-1/25)

ROMER, ----, infant child of Henry Romer, d 2/15/39 in Sing Sing (12-2/19)

ROMER, Deborah (Mrs.), 41, d 9/13/42 (11-9/22)

ROMER, Elizabeth - see WATERS, Sylvester

ROMER, Henry of Cortlandt Town m 1/19/34 Jane Ricks of Yorktown; Rev. Buck (11-3/4)

ROMER, John of Pleasantville m 12/31/39 Matilda F. Carpenter, only dau. of Andrew G., Esq., of NYC, in NYC; Rev. Richardson (12-1/7/40)

ROMER, Rachel Ann - see SCHWARTSENBERG, Jacob

ROMNEY, Cornelia - see CLARK, John

RONCK, Eliza - see LOZIER, Henry

RONEY(?), Martha Jane - see MERRITT, Benjamin H.

ROOD, J. Hollis, 30, dentist, d 11/9/41 in Hamilton (a short illness - gastro enteritis) (survived by a wife and infant child) (1-12/7)

ROOF, John I. m 11/27/50 Emma N. Young, both of Canajoharie, in C.; Rev. G.W. Gage (4-11/28)

ROONEY, Mary, 18, wf of Patrick B., d 11/23/35 (funeral at 3 o'clock from her late home, corner Schuyler and Malcom Sts.) 11/25/36

ROORBACK, Horatio, 16, d 7/19/26 in NYC (6-7/25)

ROOSA, John T. (Capt.) of Kingston m 7/3/49 Jane Rhodes of Hempstead, Long Island in NYC; Rev. Wood (8-7/21)

ROOSEVELT, Sarah L. - see PIKE, Alexander

ROOT(?), Lorain - see FORD, Henry L.

ROOT, ---- Elwood, 4, and Anna Maria, 2, eldest children of Josiah and Nancy, d
8/31/48 in Frey's Bush (4-9/7)

ROOT, Abigail - see PICKNEY, William

ROOT, Anna Maria - see ROOT, ---- Elwood

ROOT, E. (Gen.) - see HOBBIE, Selah R.

ROOT, Joseph (Capt.), 79, d 4/30/16 at Oriskany (6-5/4)

ROOT, Julia Ann - see HOBBIE, Selah R.

ROOT, Lucretia - see HAWLEY, Thomas

ROOT, Mary - see STROPE, Cornelius

ROOT, P. Sheldon, Esq., of Utica m 10/12/36 Elizabeth M. Bloodgood, eldest dau
of Lynott Bloodgood, Esq. of Albany, at A. (6-10/13)

ROOT, William A., 27, d 6/14/35 at Port Byron, deaf, dumb and a botanical doctor
(a resident of NYC, 11 days from home enroute to Illinois with his 16 year
old brother) (kicked by a horse, died almost instantly) (6-6/20 & 6/22)

ROOT, William, Esq., 78, d 8/15/46 at Vernon (1-9/8)

ROOT, William, Esq., 78, d 8/15/46 at Vernon (Born in Great Barrington, Mass.
Came into Oneida County, NY nearly 50 years ago; one of the earliest
settlers in Vernon; member of State Assembly, 1821) (1-9/15)

ROPER, Hannah - see ACHESON, Joel

RORMAN, Henry, 25, of Bolivar, Allegany Co., d 8/26/36 in Saratoga (6-9/2)

ROSA, Matilda - see CARLE(?), William

ROSA, William m 7/4/49 Ann Maria Brink, both of Kingston; Rev. Hulbert
(8-7/21)

ROSCOE, Henry Hinsdale, about 15, only son of the editor of the Westchester
Herald, d 12/10/39 in Sing Sing (his funeral was 12/11 at the Presbyterian
Church) (obituary included) (12-12/17)

ROSE, Garrett m 5/7/42 Catharine Cook, both of West Troy; Rev. D. Starke
(5-5/18)

ROSE, Mary E. - see MITCHELL, Clinton

ROSE, Mrs. - see MC FARLAND, John

ROSE, Samuel L., attorney at law, m 8/5/46 Mary E. Norris, only dau. of Robert J.,
in Augusta; Rev. G. Bartholomew (bride and groom of Augusta) (1-8/11)

ROSEBOOM, Hester (Widow), 83, d 11/6/26 in Albany (6-11/7)

ROSECRANTZ, Anna, 39 or 89?, (indistinct), wf of late George, d 8/16/50 at Little
Falls (4-8/22)

ROSS, Elmer P., merchant, of Port Byron m 10/26/35 Caroline Akin of Johnstown
in J.; Rev. U.M. Wheeler (6-10/31)

ROSS, Evelyn, 20, dau of Thaddeus, Esq., d 12/14/36 (funeral from the home of her
grandmother, Mrs. Leonard Gansevoort, 42 Chapel Street at 3 o'clock)
(6-12/17)

ROSS, James, Esq., 59, formerly of Ulster County, d (date not given) at Mount
Pleasant, Westchester County (6-11/28/26)

ROSS, Jeduthan G. of Little Falls m 10/11/36 Catharine Ann Lansing of Salisbury
in S.; Rev. L.C. Rogers (3-10/13)

ROSS, Sarah - see KERSHAW, Samuel

ROSSITER, Harriet - see DOUGLAS, Charles

ROSSITER, Nathaniel (esq.), 72, d (date not given) at Albany (funeral "this afternoon" at 3 o'clock from his late home, 14 Columbia St.) (6-3/28/35)

ROSTIZER, Valentine m 12/24/46 Catharine Hann, both of Rome; B.P. Johnson, Esq. (1-1/1/47)

ROTCH, Thomas m (date not goven) Susan Ridgeway in Philadelphia (6-5/18/16)

ROTH, Anna - see BAILEY, Thomas

ROTH, Nelson of Utica m 10/28/50 Eliza Barton of Brooklyn in B.; Rev. John Stearns (1-11/6)

ROTHGANGAL, Mary Ann - see TIEMAN, Nicholas

ROUND(?), Matilda - see CRISSY, Mills

ROUNDS, Hezekiah of Seneca Falls m 10/1/44 Eliza P. Antell of West Troy; Rev. Dodge (5-2/9)

ROUSE, Ambrose of Fort Plain m 10/21/48 Julia Newell of Albany in Fort Plain; James W. Hamilton, Esq. (4-10/26)

ROUSE, Simeon m 9/8/50 Maria Cunning, both of Fort Plain, at Ames; Rev. Elliott (4-9/19)

ROVER, Charles m 5/3/49 Amelia Snyder, both of Port Benjamin, Warwarsing, in Ellenville; Rev. E.B. Ayers (8-5/12)

ROW, Keziah (Widow), 82, d (date not given) at New Hartford (7-5/31/09)

ROW, Loisa - see POWEL, James

ROWAN, ---- (Rev. Dr.) - see HOUSTON, Thomas

ROWAN, Jane Anna - see HOUSTON, Thomas

ROWBOTHAM, Jan - see MITCHELL, Hiram

ROWBOTHAM, William m 5/4/41 Hannah Harger, both of Lee, in Rome; Rev. H.C. Vogell (1-5/11)

ROWE, Caroline - see TALLMAN, John

ROWE, Lorain B. - see BUTLER, Alvah M.

ROWE, Rosina (Mrs.) of the theater, d 5/16/35 at New Orleans (over exertion) (further details in this article) (6-6/4)

ROWE, Sanford, 19, of Albany d (date not given) - (a long obituary is included) (6-11/28)

ROWLAND, Eliza (Miss), 38, d 4/25/46 in Rome (1-5/5)

ROWLEY, C.A. - see SHELLY, E.H.

ROWLEY, Hobart Hilton, 4, youngest son of late Martin Rowley, d 12/11/41 in Rome (1-12/14)

ROWLEY, Jane A. - see CUMMINGS, George E.

ROWLEY, Sarah J. - see MORTON, Samuel

ROWLINGS, Margaret - see HUGHES, Hugh

ROY, James - see SPENCER, David

ROY, James, Esq. of West Troy m 2/12/40 Caroline Spencer, dau. of David Spencer of Waterford, at W.; Rev. Reuben Smith (5-2/19)

ROY, John Spencer, 2, son of James and Caroline S., d 9/6/43 in West Troy (5-9/27)

ROY, John, 80, father of James and Andrew of West Troy, d 7/20/47 in Sterlingshire, Scotland (5-9/1)

ROY, Mary Ann - see GUINAND, Lewis

ROYCE, Laura E. - see BURTON, Thompson

ROYCE, William m 4/6/34 Dorinda H. Birdsall, dau of William, Esq., merchant; Rev. Buck (all of Peekskill) (11-4/8)

RUBY, Christopher - see HOFFMAN, G.V.S.

RUBY, Joseph, 48, d 2/21/38 at Jacksonville in the town of Little Falls (survived by a wife and nine children) (3-3/1)

RUCKEL, Mary (Mrs.), 62, d suddenly (date not given) in NYC (6-5/22/16)

RUCKEL, Phillip, 71, d (date not given) in NYC (6-5/8/16)

RUDD, Annie S. - see WILLIAMS, George

RUDD, Eliza L. - see PHILLIPS, Samuel J.

RUDES, John, 25, d 12/1/35 in Albany (friends of above and of his father, Jason, invited to his funeral at 3 o'clock from 43 Van Schaick St. (6-12/2)

RUE, Stephen D. m 5/8/49 Maria Young, both of Fort Plain, at Utica; Rev. P. Skinner (4-5/10)

RUFF, Miss M.L. - see VAN BUREN, J.

RUGER, Sophia, 36, wf of John Ruger and dau of Judge Oliver Brown, d 1/1/36 in Bridgewater ("leaves a husband and five infant children") (6-2/1)

RUGG, Frances, 25, wf of Joseph K. and dau of Hon. J.A. Collier, d 12/1/35 in Binghamton (obit from Broome Republican) (6-12/8)

RUGG, Joseph K, Esq. m 5/15/35 Frances Collier, dau of John A. Collier; Rev. John Fowler; all of Binghamton (6-5/22)

RULE, James m 2/9/45 Isabella Cook, both of West Troy, in Troy; Rev. C.C. Burr (5-2/12)

RULE, Sarah (Mrs.), 70, d 11/20/49 in Pittsfield, Mass. (5-12/5)

RUMNEY, Elouisa, wf of J.B. of Geneva and dau. of late Dr. J.M. Mann of Hudson, d 10/6/49 at Laurel Maryland (1-10/17)

RUMNEY, Gertrude, 28, wf of Robert, d (date not given) in Geneva (6-12/26/26)

RUNDELL, John of Erie, Penna. m "lately" Emily Barret, dau. of Z. Barret, at Salisbury Center; Rev. William Thompson (3-6/22/37)

RUNDELL, Lucy Maria - see HOES, John C.F.

RUNDLE, MAry - see READ, Theodore

RUNDLE, Solomon (Capt.), 61, d 6/4/39 in Peekskill (a long term resident there) (12-6/18)

RUNDLE, Solomon (Capt.), 61, d 6/4/39 in Peekskill (for many years sailed a market sloop from Peekskill) (11-6/11)

RUNYON, Henry B., of Haverstraw m 4/21/39 Fanny Bullock(?) of Horseneck, CT (12-4/30)

RUPERT, Barbara - see SHOLTUS, George H.

RUSCO, Chancey of Piffershire m 10/17/39 Eliza Jane Hoyt of South Salem in New Canaan; Rev. Smith (12-11/12)

RUSCO, John H.T. m 5/26/46 Sarah M. Pratt, both of West Troy, in Albany; Rev. Stephen Wilkins (5-6/3)

RUSH, George m 3/4/41 Frances Warren; Rev. D.D. Tompkins (11-3/23)

RUSHMORE, Elbert of Hempstead m 10/11/36 Frances Fanning of Albany; Rev. Marshall (6-10/12)

RUSSEL, ---- (Mrs.), 97, d 8/9/39 at Middleville (3-8/22)

RUSSEL, Charles S., 29(?), d 10/25/42 in Cold Spring (consumption) (11-11/3)

RUSSEL, Jacob, merchant, m 9/1/35 Ann Maria Becker, dau of Boyle (?) Becker, at Middleburgh; Rev. Lintner (6-9/8)

RUSSEL, Thomas (Hon.) - see TEMPLE, ----

RUSSELL, Anna - see FRYER, Peter F.

RUSSELL, Bartlett of Smith's Falls, Canada m 7/7/47 Mary R. King of Rome, NY at the home of Jesse Walsworth in Rome; Rev. Gilett (1-7/9)

RUSSELL, Charles, 68, formerly of firm of Seth Russell & Sons, merchants, in New Bedford, d suddenly 12/10/36 at the home of his son-in-law, Dr. P. Van O Linda in Albany (his funeral 12/13 from his son-in-law's home at corner of Green and Hamilton Sts.) (6-12/12)

RUSSELL, Edgar of Catskill m 8/2/35 Angelina Alger of Potter's Hollow at P.H.; C.F. Bouton, Esq. (6-8/7)

RUSSELL, Elizabeth - see SMITH, W.P.

RUSSELL, George - see WELLS, Hannah

RUSSELL, George, about 28, d 6/30/37 at Schenectady (came from Scotland, near Edinburgh, in 1831 and worked as foreman or superintendent of laborers on the Hudson & Mohawk Railroad (interred in St. Peter's Church burying ground at Albany) (6-7/5)

RUSSELL, Hannah - see WALCOTT, Proctor

RUSSELL, Hester - see MOSIER, Israel

RUSSELL, Joseph - see PITCHER, Samuel

RUSSELL, Joseph - see VOSBURGH, Isaac W.

RUSSELL, Joseph, 79, a Rev. War soldier, d 6/26/37 (funeral 6/27 from the home of his daughter, Mrs. Cook, at 265 State Street) (6-6/27)

RUSSELL, Joseph, Esq. - see LANE, Julia M.

RUSSELL, Maria - see PITCHER, Samuel

RUSSELL, Mary - see LAINDELL, John A.

RUSSELL, Samuel H. of Milan (Salina) m (date not given) Lucretia Lovelas of Youngsville in Y. (6-5/8/16)

RUSSELL, Thomas D. of Mount Pleasant m 1/22/40 Jane Kipp of New Castle in N.C.; Rev. B. Van Deusen (12-1/28)

RUSSELL, William H., tutor in Yale College, m 8/29/36 Mary E. Hubbard, dau of Dr, Thomas Hubbard of New Haven, CT, in Clinton, Oneida County (6-9/19)

RUSSELL, William Henry m 12/5/36 Anna Kane, dau of Oliver, Esq., in NYC; Rev. W.R. Taylor, Rector of Grace Church (6-12/12)

RUSSELL, William of firm of George Russell & Brothers m 10/14/35 Catherine Antoinette, eldest dau of John Van Valkenburgh, Esq.; Rev. Prindle (all of Albany) (6-10/16)

RUST, Elizabeth, 44, widow of Capt. Rust, d (date not given) in NYC (6-12/26/26)

RUST, Mary Ann, 9, eldest dau. of Nelson, d 5/1/39 in Little Falls (3-5/9)

RUSTIN, Lydiaette, about 1 yr., youngest dau. of Richard, d 8/10/49 in Saugerties (8-8/18)

RUTENBER, Maria L. - see SAVAGE, Edward N.

RUTGERS, Anthony, Esq., 27, late of Belleville, NJ d 6/24/36 at Poughkeepsie (6-6/30)

RUTGERS, Nicholas S., 22, second son of Nicholas G. Rutgers of NYC, d 12/27/25 in East Florida (6-2/7)

RYAN, Lucy M. - see CATLIN, Samuel

RYCKHAM, Lydia - see VANDENBURGH, Maria

RYDER, Jesse of Mount Pleasant m 3/24/40 Mary J. Conklin of New castle, both of Westchester County, in NYC; "by His Honor the Mayor" (12-3/31)

RYDER, Paul m 10/10/39 Jane Williams; Rev. Dr. Westbrook (all of Cortlandtown) (11-10/22)

RYDER, Willett m 4/3/39 Mary Foshay, both of Mount Pleasant; Rev. Van Deusen

(12-4/9)

RYERSON, Sophroni - see GIDNEY, Edward E.

RYKER, Mary, 35, wf of John Jr., d 3/7/39 in NYC (long and painful illness) (12-3/12)

RYKER, Sarah Jane - see MALLORY, James H.

RYNDERS, Cornelia - see TARR, John B.

RYNUM, Maria, wf of Hon. James A., representative in Congress from North Carolina, d 9/15/36 at Halifax, NC (6-10/12)

RYTHER, E.M. (Miss) - see HUGH, L.R.

SABIN, Anna (Mrs.), 78, d (date not given) at Franklin (7-8/2/09)

SABIN, Joseph, Esq., 66, d 4/27/41 at his home in Salisbury (was many years Crier of the Herkimer County Courts travelling 17 miles to Herkimer on foot (clerk of the court there) (member of the Presbyterian Church) (3-4/19)

SACKETT, John B. of Holland Patent m 10/12/44 Mary Lincoln of Marcy, Oneida County, in the Episcopal Church in Rome (1-10/15)

SACKETT, John, Esq. m 7/22/39 Amanda K. Kissam in West Greenfield; Rev. Theophilus Redfield (3-7/25)

SADLIER, Frances, 27, dau of John Sadlier, d 8/20/35 in Johnstown (6-9/5)

SAFFORD, Anna, 52, wf of Darius, d 8/9/39 (3-8/22)

SAFFORD, Sarah B - see CROSBY, O. (Dr.)

SAGE, Catherine - see LUTE, John

SAILOR, Morris, 22, son of Daniel of Fort Plain, d (date not given) at Union Centre (consumption) (4-6/20)

SALISBURY, Caroline, 37, wf of Clark Salisbury, late of Stillwater, d 6/18/38 at the home of her father, Raymond Taylor, in West Troy (was buried in Stillwater - funeral service by Rev. Babcock, Episcopal minister at Ballston Spa, of whose church she had long been a member) (5-7/4)

SALKELD, William (his age not given), youngest son of General Salkeld, Esq., formerly his Britanic Majesty's Consul at New Orleans, d 9/15/37 at New Orleans "of the prevailing epidemic" (6-9/28)

SALLES, Emilie Laurencine - see VAIL, Aaron

SALTER, John S., formerly a merchant in Albany, d 1/12/37 at his father's home in Elizabethtown, NJ (6-1/18)

SAMMONS, Huldah, 33, d 4/21/43 in Rome (1-4/25)

SAMPSON, Sanford T. of Western m 12/9/40 Ruby Ann Savery of Annsville in A.; Elder William A. Brunson (1-12/15)

SAMPSON, William, 72, counsellor at law, d 12/27/36 in NYC (6-1/2/37)

SAMSON, George W. m 7/11/41 Eliza Murdock in Vernon; Rev. R.C. Brisbin (1-7/20)

SAMSON, Ichabod, Esq. of Boston, Mass. m 1/22/49 Sarah B. Hutchinbson, dau. of Dr. Zenas Hutchinson of Western, NY in W.; Rev. A.H. Corliss (1-2/7)

SANDERS, Catharine - see NELLIS, Horatio

SANDERS, Henry of Danube m 3/8/38 Gitty Ann Dingman of Minden in M.; Rev. J.D. Hicks (3-3/22)

SANDERSON, Luther m (date not given) Abigail Hall in Boston (6-5/8/16)

SANDFORD, A.C. of Canandaigua m 4/16/49 Eunice H. Whipple, eldest dau. of J. Whipple, Esq. of Chittenango, in C.; Rev. James Abell (1-4/18)

SANDFORD, Alfred, Esq., of firm of A. & A.C. Sandford, publisher of the Madison Democrat, Chittenango, m 4/12/46 Susan Hayden, dau. of late

Henry, of Rome, in R.; Rev. H. Mattison (1-4/14)

SANDFORD, Elizabeth, 6, only dau. of Henry and Lavina, d (date not given) in
    Dansville (scarlet fever) (1-9/5/49)

SANDFORD, Henry of Madison County m 7/27/42 Lovina Barnes of Vernon in V.;
    Rev. Brisbin (1-8/2)

SANDFORD, Hezekiah (Rev.) - see LYON, Betsey

SANDFORD, James S., Esq. of Marshall, Michigan m 9/5/36 Ann Eliza Porter, dau
    of Dr. Samuel of Skaneateles, at S.; Rev. C. Johnson (6-9/15)

SANDFORD, Lucy A. - see DANA, Lorenzo D.

SANDFORD, Sarah - see SCHUYLER, Montgomery

SANDS, David (Mrs.), age not clear, d "this morning" in Newburgh (funeral 2/6/
    from his home on Smith Street) (9-2/5)

SANDS, Robert, Esq., 27, late of NYC, d 7/30/35 at home of his father, john Sands,
    of Cow Neck (consumption) (6-8/8)

SANDS, Stephen T. m 1/23/42 Elizabeth Ferris in North Castle; Rev. Wilcox (all of
    North Castle) (11-2/15)

SANDS, William G., M.D., m 10/26/37 Eliza Mygatt, dau. of Henry, at Oxford;
    Rev. Bush (all of Oxford) (6-11/3)

SANFORD, Caroline - see REEVES, James

SANFORD, Eliza - see LE BRETON, John

SANFORD, Eliza M. - see MARVELL, Alfred

SANFORD, Hugh, 69, d 3/13/36 in Johnstown (6-3/21)

SANFORD, James F. m 9/27/41 Julia Ann Henderson, both of Oriskany Falls, in
    Clinton; Rev. Dr. Clowes (1-1/11/42)

SANFORD, Josephine - see COLLYER, William

SANFORD, Lyman, Esq., counsellor at law of NYC m 11/1/37 Ann Eve Bouck,
    dau. of Hon. W.C. Bouck of Fultonham, Schoharie County, at F.; Rev.
    Lintner (6-11/3)

SANFORD, Mary E.M., wf of Hon. Nathan Sanford, d (date not given) in NYC
    (6-5/25/16)

SANFORD, Nathan (Hon.) - see LE BRETON, John

SANFORD, Rodney (Col.) m 4/10/36 Catharine Mix in Warren; Hon. Jonas Cleland
    (3-4/21)

SANNAY, Edmund m 8/18/42 Cornelia E. Hoffman in Newburgh; Rev. John
    Brown, D.D. (9-8/20)

SANXAY, Edmund of Newburgh, 46, d 9/4/35 (consumption) (6-9/12)

SANXAY, John, formerly of NYC, m 7/15/09 Nancy M. Stow of "Winstead",
    Conn.; Rev. Reed (7-7/19)

SARETT, (?) E.R. of Volney m Sevilla Ismell(?) of Westmoreland; Gardner (?) C.
    Rudd (1-1/17)

SARLES, Hannah Maria - see SMITH, S.H.

SARLES, James, 28, d 1/10/39 in Cortlandt (12-1/15)

SARLES, Maria, 18, wf of William, d 4/7/42 in Bedford (11-4/14)

SARLES, Unis - see KNIFFIN, David

SATTERLFE, Oscar Adelbert, 2 months, son of J.K. and Hannah, d 9/22/46 in
    Vernon (1-10/13)

SATTERLEE, Valentine W.R., 45(?), d 7/11/37 (6-7/15)

SAULPAUGH, Charles E. m 11/5/50/ Esther Downer, both of Utica, in U.; Elder
    Thomas Hill (1-11/20)

SAUNDERS, Col. - see SHERWOOD, Charlotte M.

SAUNDERS, Edward D. of Plattsville, Wisconsin Territory m 12/22/41 Mary J. Loomis, youngest dau. of late John Loomis of Westmoreland, at W.; Rev. Dr. Clowes (1-1/4/42)

SAUNDERS, P.H. - see WHITIN, James F.

SAUNDERS, Samuel, widower, 97, m "lately in Connecticut (date not given) Miss Susannah Bollard, 85, "who have never seen each other; and probably never will." (7-5/10/09)

SAVAGE, Catharine - see BENHAM, Asahel

SAVAGE, Edward N. m 4/19/40 Maria L. Rutenber, both of Bennington, VT, in West Troy, NY; Jonathan Hary, Esq/ (5-4/22)

SAVAGE, Elizabeth Ann - see SELLOCK, Richard

SAVAGE, Hiram F. of West Troy m 9/30/49 Sarah Bainbridge of NYC in NYC; Rev. T. Bainbridge (5-11/7)

SAVAGE, R.W., 52, wf of Hon. John Savage, late Chief Justice, d (date not given) (her remains...removed to Lanesborough, Mass.") (6-4/17)

SAVER, Joseph, 49, d 9/13/35 at Warwick (6-9/19)

SAVERY, Hosea C. m 2/9/49 Nancy L. Hartwell, both of Rome, at the Franklin House in Utica; Rev. H.C. Clark (1-2/14)

SAVERY, Mary Adaline, 21, eldest dau. of Phineas, d 10/7/40 at Annsville (1-10/13)

SAVERY, Phineas, 22 months, son of R.G. and C.D. Savery, d 3/7/48 in Rome (1-3/24)

SAVERY, Ruby Ann - see SAMPSON, Sanford

SAWTELL, Edmund, 65, of Erie, NY d (date not given) (6-11/21/26)

SAWYER, Harriet Virginia - see SELYE, Louis

SAWYER, Jude, 93, a Rev. War soldier, d (date not given) at Gardner, Maine (5-1/17/44)

SAWYER, Nathaniel - see ROBINSON, Edward

SAYLES, George M., Esq., of firm of J. & G.M. Sayles, merchants, of Albany m 7/31/36 Harriet Liffingwell, dau of late Jesse Story, Esq. of Athens, at Jersey City; Rev. Lusk (6-8/13)

SAYLES, Harriet Leffingwell, 21, wf of George M. Sayles of Albany, d 10/19/36 at Sandlake (funeral at 31 Jay Street) (6-10/21)

SAYLES, John Mason, 2, son of John, d 10/29/36 (funeral at 4 o'clock from 28 Jay St.) (6-11/1)

SAYLES, Mary W. - see BISHOP, William S.

SAYLES, Welcome (Dr.), 74, d 12/6/50 in Vernon (1-12/18)

SAYRE, Edmund I., 1, son of Henry and Sarah C. of NYC, d 7/3/42 at the home of Capt. Uriah Lockwood in Newburgh (9-7/9)

SAYRE, William of Bethlehem m 3/15/42 Elvira Munell of Newburgh in N.; Rev. John Forsyth, Jr. (9-3/19)

SCHEGMIER(?), Susan E., 5 months, dau. of Andrew E. and Elsey, d 9/23/49 in Kingston (8-9/29)

SCHENCK, Adeline, 31, wf of Dr. T.P. and dau of late Cortland Van Beuren, d 6/2/35 at Matteawan (severe and protracted illness) (6-6/8)

SCHERMER, John E., 51(?), d 4/21/49 in Kingston (8-4/28)

SCHERMERHORN, Julia - see TREAT, Alfred

SCHERMERHORN, P.A. m 12/9/35 Adeline Coster, dau of late Henry A., of NYC;

Rev. Wm. Sherwood of Hyde Park, PA (sic) (6-12/14)

SCHERMERHORN, Samuel m 8/31/37 Catharine Davis, dau. of Daniel L. Davis in Manheim; Rev. Swackhamer (3-9/14)

SCHERMERHORN, Uriel, 46, d 8/12/43 in Little Falls (3-8/17)

SCHIEFFLIN, Thomas, 31, d 1/8/35 in NYC (6-1/12)

SCHLEY, Sarah G. - see NAFEW, David B.

SCHMELZEL, George, Senior, d (date not given) in NYC (6-5/2516)

SCHOFIELD, Chester, Esq. of Utica m 3/31/43 Renett Reese of Western at the Northern Hotel; Rev. Ninde (1-4/4)

SCHOOLCRAFT, Mary Catherine, 50, wf of John, Esq., d 2/15/26 in Guilderland ("...a devoted wife and affectionate mother") (6-3/24)

SCHOONMAKER, Charlott - see FREER, Richard

SCHOONMAKER, Cornelius m 8/27/49 Ann Eliza Bennett, both of Rochester, Ulster County; Rev. C.I. Van Dyck (8-9/1)

SCHOONMAKER, Dolly, 29, wf of John, d 4/22/26 (6-4/25)

SCHOONMAKER, John, merchant, m (date not given) Sarah Staufe in Albany; Rev. Stephen Ostrander (6-1/23/35)

SCHOONMAKER, Maria - see WILBUR, Gaston

SCHOOT, Phillip, 1, son of Florence (sic) and Amina, d 8/17/40 at Salisbury (3-9/3)

SCHOTT, Louis P., only son of Florence (sic) and Aramina Schott, d 11/9/42 in Salisbury (3-11/17)

SCHRAM, Jacob d 1/22/37 suddenly at St. Johnsville (3-2/2)

SCHULTZ, Joachim O. m 10/22/39 Hannah Maria Ward, dau. of Thomas, Esq. of Ramapo in Ramapo Valley; Rev. Day (12-12/17)

SCHUYLER, ---- (Mrs.), 77, wf of Dr. Reuben Schuyler, d 4/20/38 in West Troy (5-5/2)

SCHUYLER, Angelica - see CROSBY, Clarkson F.

SCHUYLER, Catharine - see CASLER, Nicholas R.

SCHUYLER, Catharine - see MARTIN, Harvey

SCHUYLER, Catherine E., 30, wf of Stephen R., d 5/21/49 (funeral 5/23) (5-5/23)

SCHUYLER, Catherine E., youngest dau. of Thomas H. and Angelica G., d 12/8/49 in West Troy (5-12/19)

SCHUYLER, Cornelia S. - see VAN RENSSELAER, Schuyler

SCHUYLER, Elizabeth A. - see CHASE, H.G.

SCHUYLER, Harriet, age 1, dau of William Cushing Schuyler, Esq., of Roxbury, Delaware Co., d 7/28/35 in Albany (6-7/29)

SCHUYLER, Lovina - see HELMER, Joseph W.

SCHUYLER, Mary - see MILLS, Lyman

SCHUYLER, Montgomery, Esq. of Marshall, Michigan m 9/7/36 Sarah Sandford, dau of Dr. Jared Sandford of Ovid, at Lodi, Seneca County; Rev. T. Lounsbury of Ovid (6-9/15)

SCHUYLER, Nancy, 46, wf of John, Jr., Esq. of Watervliet, d 11/21/15 (6-12/6)

SCHUYLER, Nicholas - see HELMER, Joseph W.

SCHUYLER, Philip J., Esq., 66, eldest surviving son of the late Gen. Schuyler, d 2/21/35 in NYC (6-3/4)

SCHUYLER, Phillip Capt. d 5/14/44 in Boonville ("fit of apoplexy") (was sitting in his store in conversation and fell from his chair) (he was one of the oldest and most requested residents of Boonville) (1-5/21)

SCHUYLER, Richard, 27, brother of T.H. of West Troy, d 3/18/49 at Brasos, Santiago (cholera-sickness of six hours) (5-4/18)

SCHUYLER, Ruth - see OGDEN, Thomas

SCHWARTSENBERG, Jacob m (date not given) Rachel Ann Romer, dau of Ardeois(?) Romer; Rev. Dr. Westbrook (11-10/15/39)

SCISSON, Ruth - see HAVILAND, Roger

SCOFIELD, Daniel, 20, d 5/7/42 in Bedford (11-5/19)

SCOFIELD, William A. m 11/20/39 Jane Green in Poundridge; Rev. Oldrin (all of Poundridge) (12-12/3)

SCOFIL, Ezekiel of Camden m 1/1/48 Harriet Scofil of Litchfield, Conn. at the American Hotel (presumably in Rome); H.C. Vogell (1-1/7)

SCOFIL, Harriet - see SCOFIL, Ezekiel

SCOTT, ---- "the Lady of Sir Walter Scott", d (date not given) in Scotland (6-6/27/26)

SCOTT, Abigail (Mrs.), 75, wf of William, d (date not given) at Wilton (7-6/13/10)

SCOTT, Ann Eliza - see SHERMAN, Shadrick

SCOTT, Catharine - see COBB, Lucius J.

SCOTT, Charles, Esq. of Waterford m 9/6/38 Catharine Reid of Lansingburgh in L. (5-9/12)

SCOTT, Eleanora, 25, wf of Samuel B. of Toledo, Ohio, and only dau. of Israel Seymour of Troy, d 2/22/39 at Toledo (5-3/20)

SCOTT, Elizabeth, 57, wf of William H. of Waterford d 8/31/49 at the home of her son, Samuel B. Scott in Southport, Wisconsin (5-9/19)

SCOTT, Frances Cordelia - see HEARTT, Philip T. (Dr.)

SCOTT, George E., Esq. m 10/1/45 Virginia Horton in Waterford; Rev. Reuben Smith (all of Waterford) (5-10/8)

SCOTT, Jennett - see VOSBURGH, William H.

SCOTT, John, Esq., 63, attorney at law, late of Ogdensburg, d 11/24/39 in Peekskill at the home of Isaac Seymour (11-11/26)

SCOTT, Margaret, 9 months, dau. of John D., d 6/13/42 in Newburgh (9-6/18)

SCOTT, Martha Jane - see VASEY, George

SCOTT, Mary - see WOOD, James

SCOTT, Moses Y. of NYC, for past 3 years attached to Mr. Caldwell's Theatrical corps of NYC, d 4/21/26 at New Orleans (6-5/26)

SCOTT, Olive A. - see BEAGS, Samuel

SCOTT, William H. m 6/5/33 Elizabeth Spock; Rev. Kirkwood (all of Cortlandtown) (11-6/11)

SCOVEL, Jane, 26, wf of Dr. J.B., d 6/7/36 at Stuyvesant (friends of her husband and Mrs. Stillwell invited to her 10 o'clck funeral from home of Ashley Scovel, 46 Lydius St.) (6-6/9)

SCOVELL, Charles m 5/7/35 Anna Wait, both of Albany; Rev. Campbell (6-5/9)

SCOVELL, Jared, merchant, of Albany m 3/13/36 Jane Page late of Montreal; Rev. Dr. Ferris (6-3/16)

SCOVILL, Alfred C. m 4/11/43 Mary Eliza Pratt, both of West Troy at W.T.; Rev. Benjamin L. Lane (5-4/19)

SCOVILL, Betsey - see WOLF, David

SCOVILL, David, 65, d 11/10/42 in West Troy (5-11/16)

SCOVILL, Delia, 14, d 9/17/43 (5-9/20)

SCOVILL, Ebenezer K. m 12/30/41 Katharine Derby in West Troy; Rev. J.F.

Scovill (all of West Troy) (5-1/5/42)

SCOVILL, H.W., Esq. of Whitehall m 3/13/50 Sarah C. Sinnott of West Troy in
    W.T.; Rev. J.C. Burroughs (5-3/27)

SCOVILL, James, 2 years, only son of Robert and Eliza, d 1/26/45 in West Troy
    (5-1/29)

SCOVILLE, Lois Ann - see WIGGINS, J.

SCRANTON, Alonzo L. d 12/19/41 at Kirkville (1-1/11/42)

SCRANTON, Henry m 9/25/50 Margaret Mc Keen of Augusta in Herkimer; Rev.
    J.H. Harter (double ceremony - see KIMBERLY, Horace) (1-10/2)

SCRANTON, William (Rev.), formerly of Clinton, NY, d in September, 1941 in
    Michigan (1-1/11/42)

SCRIBA, George, 84, d 8/14/36 at Constantia, born at Langrave of Hesse
    Dermstadt, Germany, was in mercantile business in Amsterdam. Received
    "Scriba's Patent" and made the first two settlements there - one at Constantia
    on Oneida Lake, NY. " Ranked among the most successful and extensive
    merchants" in that region. (More detail included in this obituary) (6-9/2)

SCRIBNER, Caroline M., 36, consort of Dr. William A., d suddenly 9/29/39
    (12-10/1)

SCRIBNER, David m 2/5/42 Charody Tice at the American Hotel in Sing Sing;
    Rev. Sidney A. Corey (all of Cortlandt) (11-2/15)

SCRIBNER, Jonathan F., merchant, of Buffalo m 1/28/36 Mary Sheldon, dau of late
    Elisha of Troy, at St. Paul's Church, Troy; Rev. Dr. Butler (6-1/30)

SCRIVNER, Belphamer - see BOVEE, James (Capt.)

SCUDDER, Eliza Ann - see FROST, Theodore

SEABURY, Helen, 18, eldest dau. of Ahymen and Sarah, d 3/9/47 at Waterville
    (1-3/19)

SEAGE, Lydia Creber, 5, dau. of John and Mary Ann, d 3/17/38 in West Troy
    (5-3/21)

SEAGE, Sarah - see DONAN, John

SEALLYBRASS, Martin of Hamilton, Upper Canada m 10/16/36 Elizabeth Dove,
    dau. of Thomas Thompson of Little Falls, at Herkimer; Rev. H.S. Attwater
    (3-10/20)

SEALY, Thaddeus W. of Ithaca m 5/21/41 Phidelia H. Gibson of Rome in R.; Rev/
    H.C. Vogell (1-6/1)

SEAMEN, ----, a child of William Seamen, d 11/18/09 in Catskill (7-11/19)

SEAMON, Mary, 76, d 6/6/39 at the home of her son, Jesse Seamon, in Bedford
    (she a member of the Society of Friends) (12-6/18)

SEARLES, Caroline F. - see GRISWOLD, Rufus W. (Major)

SEARLES, Sarah Jane - see ARNOLD, Samuel G.

SEARS, Francis m 2/15/10 Susan Taylor; Rev. David Porter (all of Catskill)
    (7-2/21)

SEARS, Herman S., Esq. of NYC m 1/1/40 Almira Raymond, dau. of John, Esq. of
    Patterson, in P.; Rev. Benedict (12-1/7)

SEARS, Hetty, 100, d "sometime in April, 1845", at Greenwich, Mass. "leaving 4
    children averaging 80 years each; 68 grand children; 138 great
    grandchildren; and 13 of the 5th generation making a progeny of 219!"
    (5-6/4)

SEARS, James m (date not given) Elizabeth Gregory at Ballstown (6-6/1/16)

SEARS, William of West Troy m 10/16/45 Judith Adams of Albany in A.; Rev.

William B. Sprague (5-10/22)

SEATON, Augustine F. (Lieut.), 25, of the US Army, d 11/19/35 at Fort Gibson, Arkansas Terr. (eldest son of William W., Esq. of Washington, D.C.) (6-1/18/36)

SEATON, James W., editor of the Fotosi Republican, m 6/16/50 Amanda F. Busher in Cassville; C.A. Lagrave, Esq. (all of Fotosi) (1-7/3)

SEATON, William L. of Rome m 1/17/49 Roxana Parker of Mc Connelsville in M.; Rev. A. Adams (1-1/24)

SEAWELL, Henry (Hon.), 62, a judge of the Superior Court of North Carolina, d 10/6/35 at his home near Raleigh, NC (6-10/14)

SEBLES, C, Maine, Esq. of Little Falls m 9/18/43 Julia C. Stevens, dau. of late Caleb of Pittston(sic), at Gardiner, Maine; Rev. William S. Bartlett (3-9/21)

SECKNER, Nancy - see WELLS, Nathan

SECOR, Catharine - see MARSHALL, Richard

SECOR, Gilbert, 75, a Rev. soldier, d 11/5/38 in Greenburg (12-11/27)

SECOR, John H. m 9/30/37 Sarah Holenbeck in Bern; Lyman Dwight, Esq. (6-10/4)

SECOR, Mariam - see LENT, Augustus

SECOR, Tamer, wf of Floyd, d 11/20/39 in NYC (12-11/26)

SEDGFIELD, John, Esq. m (date not given) Mrs. Ellen Ludlow in NYC (6-5/15/16)

SEDGWICK, Frances Adeline, 6, youngest dau. of Parker Sedgwick, M.D., d 12/16/41 in Andover (1-12/28)

SEDGWICK, Mary Debia, 41, consort of Dr. Barker Sedgwick, d 12/18/41 in Westmoreland (a short illness) (1-12/21)

SEDGWICK, Mary Delia - see GOODWIN, Jeremiah

SEDGWICK, Theodroe, Jr., Esq. m (date not given) Sarah Ashburner at Stockbridge, MA (6-10/12/35)

SEE, Coles C. m 7/17/39 Emeline Gardner, dau. of Elihu, Esq., of Cortlandt, at C.; Rev. S. Van Deusen (12-7/23)

SEE, Elmira - see SEE, John A.

SEE, John A. of Mount Pleasant m 1/19/42 Elmira See of Tarrytown in T. at the Reformed Protestant Duth Reformed Church; Rev. Dubois (11-2/1)

SEEBER, Abram W., 38, son of William H., Esq. of Canajoharie, d 11/23/50 at Newkirk's Mills, Fulton County (consumption) (buried in his father's burying ground in the town of Canajoharie) (4-11/28)

SEEBER, Sarah C. - see WEMPLE, A.H.

SEEKER, John m 10/19/43 Agnes Maria Lowry in Little Falls; Rev. C.W. Leet (3-10/26)

SEELEY, Jeremiah H. of Patterson m 12/23/38 Sarah A. Requa of Yorktown in Y; Rev. Thompson (12-2/12)

SEELEY, P---- - see CLEETON, Samuel

SEELY, Columbus W. m 8/25/42 Emily Dickenson in Bedford; Rev. A.W. Partridge (all of Bedford) (11-9/22)

SEELY, James m 3/6/33 Mary T. Merick, dau of Samuel S. at the Elephant Hotel in Somers; Rev. Benedict (all of Carmel) (11-3/19)

SEELY, Samuel W. (Capt.) of NYC d 5/29/42 at Bedford (11-6/9)

SEELYE, Ambrose m 1/19/42 Sarah Allen, dau. of Samuel, in Westmoreland; Elder Alcott (all of Westmoreland) (1-2/8)

SEELYE, Sally - see THOMPSON, Archibald

SEGAR, Nelson, merchant, m 1/5/43 Elizabeth Petrie, both of Crains Corners; Rev.

Vanvalkenburgh (3-1/19)

SEGUR, J.W.B. of Taberg m 9/21/42 Mary Lany, dau. of Esquire lany of Lee, in Lee; Rev. John Barton (1-9/27)

SEGUR, Lucy - see BRAINARD, A. H.

SELDEN, C.F. - see GILLETT, Margaret (Mrs.)

SELDEN, Joseph D., 73, father of Dudley Selden of NYC, d 4/6/37 at his home in Troy (6-4/13)

SELDEN, Matilda, 82, d 10/6/50 in Rome (emigrated with her husband Thomas Selden from Vermont in 1797 and settled on Canterbury Hill when this region was almost an unbroken wilderness. Mother of 11 children, 8 surviving her death; as a widow lived in the home of her eldest son, Thomas Selden, Esq.) (1-10/23)

SELKREG, John B. of firm of Wells and Selkreg, publishers of the Ithaca Journal m 5/11/42 Clarissa M. Turner, dau of William of Poughkeepsie, at P.; Rev. Dr. Reed (11-6/9)

SELLEK, Ann - see THOMAS, Edward

SELLICK, Ezra, 77, d (date not given) at Salisbury (7-5/31/09)

SELLOCK, Richard m 1/5/39 Elizabeth Ann Savage in Haverstraw; Rev. Canfield (all of H.) (12-1/29)

SELYE, Louis of Rochester m (date not given) Harriet Virginia Sawyer of Wilkesbarre, Penna.; Rev. Robert Mc Kee (6-6/23/37)

SEMAN, Martha - see MILLER, Gerrit

SERAM, Jacob m 12/10/25 Catherine Groff at Oppenheim, Herkimer County; Rev. Devoe (6-1/3/26)

SERANTON, Harriet - see FISK, ---- (Dr.)

SERGEANT, Elizabeth, 71, widow of Dr. Erastus Sergeant, d 12/18/15 at Stockbridge, Mass. (6-12/30)

SERVIES, William of firm of Servies & Hotaling of Albany m 1/14/35 Athallah Young, dau of Peter, Esq. of Florida, Montgomery Co., in F.; Rev. Stevenson (6-1/18)

SESSFORD, Jefferson, 34, clerk of the General Post Office, d 11/23/35 at Washington City (apoplexy) (6-11/28)

SESSIONS, Harriet - see TEMPLE, Harvey

SETON, John C., 45, d (date not given) in NYC (a lingering illness) (6-1/6/16)

SETTLE, Jacob D. m 11/15/26 Margaret Marcellus, dau. of Garret N. Marcellus, in Berne; Rev. J.H. Van Wagenen (6-12/5)

SETTLE, Jacob D., merchant of Bern m 7/29/37 Elizabeth Havelet of Middleburgh in M.; Rev. R.D. Van Kleeck (6-8/5)

SETTLE, Margaret, 31, wf of Jacob D., d 11/24/36 (consumption) (6-11/26)

SEWALL, J. (Hon.) - see HUMPHREYS, Trevor

SEWARD, Benjamin J., 45, eldest brother of the Governor of this state, d 2/24/41 in Florida, Orange County, NY (he died at the home of his father, "Judge Seward") (1-3/9)

SEWARD, Cornelia, only dau. of William H., Esq., d 1/14/37 at Auburn (6-1/28)

SEWARD, Governor - see CANFIELD, Louisa Cornelia

SEWART, Robert G. of Rochester m 9/6/43 Hannah J. Hosford of West Troy in W.T.; Rev. Z. Phillips (5-9/13)

SEWELL. Frances Georgiana - see HUMPHREYS, Trevor

SEWELL, Louisa, relict of late Robert, Esq. and second daughter of Hon. William

276

Smith, d 2/21/37 at Quebec after a severe illness (6-3/4)

SEXTON, Frederick, Esq. of Sherburne m 5/20/50 Huldah Coley of Rome in R.; Rev. James Erwin (1-5/22)

SEXTON, John, about 35, d 5/23/38 in Waterford (5-5/30)

SEYGUE, ----, 52, wf of John Seygue, d 3/2/09 (7-3/8)

SEYMORE, Emory Tyler of Westmoreland m 1/21/49 Charity Goodrich, dau. of Isaac, Esq. of Verona; H.C. Vogell (1-2/7)

SEYMOUR, Adelaide - see HOWARD, James

SEYMOUR, Alice - see SMITH, Shubael

SEYMOUR, Catharine - see INGERSOLL, Edward

SEYMOUR, Charles E., 24, late treasurer of the Young Men's Association of Troy, d 9/29/35 in Troy (6-10/1)

SEYMOUR, David L., Esq., of Troy m 7/27/37 Maria L. Curtiss, dau. of late Sheldon C. Curtiss, Esq. of Lanesborough, Mass. (6-7/28)

SEYMOUR, Edward D., about 24, formerly of Herkimer, NY, d 1/12/36 at the home of Dr. A.G. Wendell near New Orleans (consumption) (3-2/9/37)

SEYMOUR, Frederick J., 2, son of D.L., d 4/26/41 in Peekskill (scarlet fever) (11-5/4)

SEYMOUR, H.C., Esq., engineer on New York and Erie railroad, m 2/9/36 Mary Sherill, dau of Augustus, Esq., of Ithaca at the Dutch Church in Ithaca; Rev. Mann (6-3/2)

SEYMOUR, Hannah - see REMINGTON, John W.

SEYMOUR, Horatio of Utica m 5/28/35 Mary Bleecker, dau of John R. of Albany; Rev. Vermilyea (6-5/30)

SEYMOUR, Isaac - see SCOTT, John

SEYMOUR, Israel - see SCOTT, Eleanora

SEYMOUR, Leverett - see REMINGTON, Hannah S.

SEYMOUR, Leverett, 73, father of Eri, d 6/9/48 in Westmoreland (1-6/16)

SEYMOUR, Louisa - see BEEBE, Abijah

SEYMOUR, Lucy H. - see MASON, Ezra

SEYMOUR, Mary Ann - see DAVENPORT, Lewis

SEYMOUR, Mary Louisa, 3 1/2, only dau of Capt. George E. and Julia, d 3/9/35 at Hudson after a few days illness (6-3/13)

SEYMOUR, Mary, 15, dau. of James of Rochester, d 12/24/36 at St. Croix, West Indies (6-2/16/37)

SEYMOUR, Milla - see ALDEN, Enoch

SEYMOUR, Sarah M. - see FITCH, J.P.

SEYMOUR, Truman (Rev.) - see TAYLOR, H.R.

SEYMOUR, William (Hon.) - see DAVENPORT, Lewis

SEYMOUR, William m 4/3/16 Jane Brady, both of Albany; Rev. Dr. Bradford (6-4/6)

SHAD, Frances Ann, age 2, youngest dau of John R. and Eliza B. of Chatham County, GA, d 8/12/35 (6-8/17)

SHADBOLDT, Jane - see BONCE, William

SHADBOLT, Lafayette of West Troy m 11/21/48 Susan M. Angevine of Pleasant Valley in P.V.; Rev. E.C. Ambler (5-12/13)

SHAEFER, Catharine - see VEEDER, Frederick

SHAFER, Martha Elizabeth - see KRAZENBERG, Jacob

SHAFER, Mary A. - see PLACE, William

SHAFER, Peter m 2/8/44 Elizabeth Foster, both of West Troy, in W.T.; Rev. O.H. Gregory (5-2/14)

SHAFFER, Emelie, 3, dau. of Charles W. and Caroline, d 8/25/49 in Kingston (8-9/1)

SHAFT, Mary - see METCALF, Francis P.

SHAKELARD(?), Margaret - see MOTT, Peter

SHALL, Richard m 12/20/41 Mary Ann Featherly in Stark; C.T.E. Van Horne (3-1/13/42)

SHANKLAND, Rachel Ann - see KELLOGG, Palmer V.

SHARER, William Mark, 10, son of Christian and Catherine, d 11/11 in Little Falls (3-11/16)

SHARP, Eliza (relict of Col. Solomon Sharp who was murdered by J.O. Beauchamp in Nov., 1825) d 1/26/44 at Frankfort, Kentucky (a member of the Presbyterian Church) (11-1/30)

SHARP, John W. m 6/12/50 Anna Bortle, both of West Troy; Rev. J.C. Burroughs) (5-6/26)

SHARP, Peter G., (age blurred), d 7/18/49 at Kingston (congestion of the lungs) (8-7/28)

SHARP, Phillip of Little Falls m 11/15/41 Charity Heath of German Flats in G.F.; Rev. J. Loveys (3-11/25)

SHARPLEY, Julia Ann - see HATCH, James M.

SHATTUCK, Ira A. of NYC m 6/15/49 Rachel Baker of Hudson in Saugerties; Rev. C. Van Santvoort (8-6/23)

SHATTUCK, Jethro m 11/25/40 Betsey Walker at Durhamville, both of D.; Rev. D.D. Ransom (1-2/23/41)

SHAUL, Eve - see DE VOE, John, Jr.

SHAUL, James m 7/23/37 Mary Thrall in Little Falls; Rev. J.W. Olmstead (3-7/27)

SHAVER, Clarissa - see SMITH, Philip P.

SHAVER, Frances Carolyn - see SHEARMAN, James B.

SHAVER, Mary - see YOUKER, Lodwick

SHAVER, Sarah - see FREDENRICH, Philip

SHAVER, Sophia - see GROOM, Richard

SHAW, Ann, 48, widow of William Shaw, M.D., d 10/31/40 in West Troy (5-11/4)

SHAW, Charity (Mrs.), 62, d (date not given) in NYC (6-11/7/26)

SHAW, Isaiah, 53, formerly from Montgomery County, d 5/23/26 in Albany (lingering illness) (6-6/2)

SHAW, Jane - see WARD, Ferdinand

SHAW, Jane A.W. - see CUSHMAN, Charles T. (Dr.)

SHAW, Lavanda - see PADDOCK, Alexander

SHAW, Maria, dau. of late John Shaw, d 1/21/37 (6-1/26)

SHAW, Marietta - see WALSH, John A.

SHAW, Mary Ann - see DANIELS, Levi

SHAW, William S., Esq., founder of the first Athenaeum in the United States and formerly private secretary to the late President Adams, d (date not given) at Boston (6-5/5/26)

SHEAR, Catherine, 26, d (date not given) in Beekman (6-5/15/16)

SHEAR, Sarah A. - see WASHBURN, Albert

SHEAR, Wallace B. m 10/15/49 Elizabeth N. Brooker; H.C. Vogell (all of Floyd) (1-10/24)

SHEARMAN, Abraham of Penn Yan m 2/18/36 Elizabeth Cole of Benton at B.
    (6-3/5)

SHEARMAN, James B. m 3/6/44 Frances Carolyn Shaver, both formerly of
    Greenville, South Carolina, in Greenville, SC; Rev. A.M. Mood (1-4/2)

SHEARMAN, Stukely B., 13, son of Willitt H., d 5/6/50 at Vernon (typhus fever)
    (1-5/15)

SHEARS, John of Carmel m 12/20/38 Maranda Boroughs of Paterson in P.; Rev.
    Mc Leod (12-1/1/39)

SHEATHER, John (Capt.) an aged Rev. War veteran, d 6/19/35 in Geneva (from
    Geneva Gazette) (6-7/1)

SHED, Dyer, 52, d 2/6/49 in Westmoreland (1-2/21)

SHEFFER, Catharine E. - see WOODWORTH, Montgomery

SHELBURGH, Andrew, 32, d (date not given) in NYC (6-2/21/26)

SHELDEN, Lois - see WINTON, Benjamin

SHELDON, Alexander (Hon.), 70, d 12/19/36 at his home in Charleston,
    Montgomery Co., NY (heart condition resulting from past heavy exertion in
    hay-making in hot weather) (6-12/28 also 12/30)

SHELDON, Amelia, wf of Seth, of Shreveport, Louisiana and dau. of Andrew A.
    Fink, Esq. of Little Falls, d 8/17/41 on the packet schooner "Maria" from
    New Orleans bound for NYC in passing the Gulf of Mexico (yellow fever
    after illness of four days) (she was a member of the Presbyterian Church at
    Little Falls) (she was buried at sea) (3-9/9)

SHELDON, C.P. (Rev.) pastor of the Baptist Church at Hamilton m 4/24/45
    Charlotte Gold(?) of Rome in Rome; Rev. H.C. Vogel (1-4/29)

SHELDON, Frances A. - see TRASK, Wyman

SHELDON, Jane - see PEEBLES, Tolbert

SHELDON, John of Delta m 12/31/40 Rosanna Hawley, dau. of Crandall Hawley,
    in Rome; Elder H.C. Vogle (all of Rome) (1-1/5/41)

SHELDON, Julia - see LOOMIS, Charles

SHELDON, Mary - see DAVIS, Seymour C.

SHELDON, Mary - see SCRIBNER, Jonathan

SHELDON, S.H. m 2/18/41 Ruth Ann Glass, dau. of Alexander, in Rome; Rev.
    H.C. Vogell (all of Rome) (1-2/23)

SHELDON, Sally Ann - see PRESTON, Shandoney

SHELDON, Samuel J., only son of Alexander of Albany, d 8/12/37 at the home of
    Samuel Jackson in Florida, Montgomery County (6-8/18)

SHELDON, Susan M. - see SQUIRE, George F.

SHELDON, Urania E. - see NOTT, Eliphalet, D.D.

SHELLEY, C.B. (Miss) - see JOHNSON, H.

SHELLEY, George O., 17, d 6/4/44 at Oneida Castle (1-6/11)

SHELLEY, Henry S. of Lowville m 7/10/48 Jane E. Orton of Rome in R.; Rev.
    W.E. Knox (1-7/14)

SHELLMAN, Anna P. - see CLARKE, William, Jr.

SHELLY, E.H. of Rome m 4/23/46 C.A. Rowley of Utica in U.; Rev. D. Corey
    (1-4/28)

SHELLY, Lucretia - see SYLVESTER, Reuben

SHELTERS, Henry of firm of Shelters and King, d 7/19/26 in NYC (6-7/25)

SHEPARD(?), Mary C. - see PARKS, John J.

SHEPARD, Caroline Matilda - see JOHNSON, Jesse W.

SHEPARD, Catharine Ann, 31, wf of Charles E., Esq. and dau. of late Glen Cuyler, Esq., d 8/28/37 at Aurora, Cayuga County (6-9/9)

SHEPARD, Charles O., Esq., member of the Assembly of Arcade, Genesee County, m 12.20.36 Rhoda H. Lymon, dau. of late William, D.D., formerly of East Haddam, CT, at Mount Morris, NY; Rev. H. Goodrich (6-1/7/37)

SHEPARD, Charles, M.D., m 12/20/36 Lucinda Putnam, dau. of Alfred, Esq. of Herkimer, in H.; Rev. H.S. Attwater (3-12/15)

SHEPARD, Edward of Richmond m 10/6/36 Helen E. Thompson of Catskill, NY at St. James Church; Rev. J.T. Eaton (6-10/24)

SHEPARD, Elizabeth - see TAYLOR, Charles J.

SHEPARD, George F. m 10/30/48 Catharine Beardsley, dau. of Dr. Levi of Verona; Rev. H. Kendall (1-11/2)

SHEPARD, Jane Elizabeth, 18, dau. of Emily, d 9/29/48 in Rome (consumption) (1-10/6)

SHEPARD, Lucretia Cynthia, 20, formerly of Watervliet and late assistant in the Female Seminary of Natchez, Mississippi, d 1/3/40 at Utica, NY (at time of her death she was visiting relatives in this state and was to have been married in a few days (5-1/22)

SHEPARD, Mary M. - see TRENAM, Octavus F.

SHEPARD, Mary S. - see PAIGE, James H.

SHEPARD, Moses (Capt.), d (date not given) at Newton (7-6/20/10)

SHEPARD, Wealthy, wf of Thomas "and also two of his children all within 57 hours of each other" d at Wintonbury, Conn. (spotted fever) (dates of deaths not given) (7-2/1/09)

SHEPHERD, ---- (Mrs.) - see STEELE, Abby (Miss)

SHEPHERD, James (Rev.), 32, d 1/8/45 at home of his father (not named) in Warrensburg ("graduate of Union Theological Seminary in NY and preached...a short time in Bridgewater, NY...compelled to abandon the Lord's work by severe disease which rendered him blind the last two years of his life") (1-2/11)

SHEPHERD, Jane Maria - see KIDD, James

SHEPHERD, Jane, 88, relict of William, d 7/20/26 in Bethlehem (6-7/25)

SHEPHERD, Phebe, Widow, d (date not given) (her friends and those of her sons-in-law, G. & S. Bleecker and William Smith invited to her funeral, 12/3/36 from her late home, 92 South Pearl St.) (6-12/2)

SHERBURNE, Silas of Sherburne m 12/12/35 Eunice Brown, adopted dau of Luke Metcalf, Esq. of South Oxford in S.O.; Rev. Nelson Doolittle (6-12/19)

SHERMAN, ----, 1, son of John, d 9/11/49 in Carmel (10-9/19)

SHERMAN, A. Jennett - see SHERMAN, Benedict

SHERMAN, Alonzo m 3/27/42 at the Methodist Episcopal Church in Halfmoon, Jennett Clow, dau. of Henry, Esq., of Clifton Park; Rev. Williams (all of Clifton Park) (5-4/6)

SHERMAN, Benedict of Fairfield, Vt. m 10/10/48 A. Jennett Sherman, dau. of James S., Esq., of Floyd; H.C. Vogell (1-10/13)

SHERMAN, Charles (Rev.), 40, d 3/10/44 in Troy (5-3/13)

SHERMAN, Cynthia Robertson, eldest dau. of the late Dr. Abel Sherman of Albany, d 5/16/37 (6-5/20)

SHERMAN, Ebenezer m 11/29/42 Sarah Thompson at Crawford; Rev. Leggett (9-12/3)

SHERMAN, Emma Jane - see CLEAVELAND, Theodore N.

SHERMAN, Helen Louisa - see COLFAX, Ebenezer

SHERMAN, Mary - see KELLOGG, R.F.

SHERMAN, Sarah - see WEAVER, Jacob

SHERMAN, Shadrick of Little Falls m 1/21/40 Ann Eliza Scott of Danube in
    Minden; Rev. J.A. Myres (3-1/23)

SHERMAN, Sheldon, d 2/19/10 (7-2/21)

SHERMAN, Watts, cashier of the Albany City Bank, m 2/26/35 Sarah L. Tierner,
    niece and adopted dau of Hon. Erastus Corning; Rev. Dr. Sprague (6-2/27)

SHERRILL, Laura - see CATON, John

SHERRILL, Mary - see SEYMOUR, H.C.

SHERWOOD, Amos G., Jr. m 2/23/42 Jane C. Smith, both of Fairfield, at F.; Rev.
    William Baker (a double ceremony - see MARKELL, John, Esq.) (3-3/3)

SHERWOOD, Caroline - see MARKELL, John

SHERWOOD, Charlotte M. (Miss), 23, only dau. of Nathan D., formerly of
    Waterford, NY, d 7/24/44 at the home of Col. Saunders near Selma,
    Alabama (5-8/21)

SHERWOOD, James M. (Rev.), pastor of the Presbyterian Church in New Windsor
    m 9/8/35 Amanda Malvina Carpenter, dau of Joseph, Esq. of Newburgh
    (married in the Presbyterian Church); Rev. John Johnston (6-9/12)

SHERWOOD, James, 77, d 2/10/39 in Phillipstown (a long term resident there)
    (12-2/19)

SHERWOOD, James, 77, d 2/10/39 in Phillipstown where he had lived many years
    (11-2/12)

SHERWOOD, Juliet - see KELLOGG, Chauncey P.

SHERWOOD, Mary Jane - see TICE, Lewis

SHERWOOD, Rhoda Ann (Miss), 27, d 3/4/39 at Fairfield (funeral sermon by Rev.
    William Baker "of the P.E. Church") (probably P.E. signifies Protestant
    Episcopal - F.Q.B.) (3-3/14)

SHERWOOD, Samuel Augustus, Esq., 20, d 2/29/36 in NYC (a short illness)
    (6-3/5)

SHERWOOD, Samuel Augustus, Esq., 20, d 3/8/36 in NYC (3-3/17)

SHERWOOD, William, 65, of Fairfield d (date not given) in Copenhagen, Lewis
    County at the home of his son-in-law, A Davenport, Esq. (3-4/13/37)

SHERWOOD, Winfield Scott, Esq., of Glens Falls m 9/7/41 Sarah Worthington of
    Rome in R.; Rev. S. Haynes (1-9/14)

SHIELDS, Daniel, 69, d 9/20/35 ("one of the few surviving soldiers of the
    Revolution") (funeral at 4 o'clock from his late home, corner Washington
    and Swan Sts.) (6-9/21)

SHILL, Mary C. - see ROLLER, John, Jr.

SHIPMAN, Eliza - see ROGERS, John

SHIPMAN, Emma, 9 months, dau. of Horace, Esq. d 5/13/48 in Frey's Bush
    (4-5/18)

SHOEMAKER, Christiana, 7, dau. of Daniel, d 7/13/37 at Stark (3-7/20)

SHOEMAKER, Henry m 11/8/15 Elizabeth Lasher, both of Bethlehem; Rev. J.
    DeWitt (6-11/11)

SHOEMAKER, Joanna - see COUNTRYMAN, David

SHOEMAKER, Matthew m 9/13/36 Catharine Bellinger, eldest dau. of Frederick,
    Esq., in Mohawk; Rev. Attwater (3-9/15)

SHOEMAKER, R.M., Esq., engineer, m 12/25/39 Mary C. Skinner in Tifflin, Ohio (3-1/30/40)

SHOEMAKER, Randolph J. & Robert - see DEXTER, Gertrude

SHOEMAKER, Richard L., widower, m Sunday 11/7/41 widow Nancy Cristman in the Stone Church at German Flats "during divine service" (3-12/2)

SHOEMAKER, Robert - see DEXTER, Gertrude

SHOEMAKER, Robert, Esq., 55, d (date not given) at his home in Juliet, Illinois (formerly of German Flats, Herkimer County, NY where he had served as county sheriff and as a representative to the state assembly) (3-5/3/38)

SHOEMAKER, Salina - see PICKARD, James

SHOKELTON, ---- (Mrs.), d 7/8/42 in Newburgh (9-7/16)

SHOLL, William N. m 1/29/50 Mary F. Coney, both of Canajoharie, at C.; Rev. Steele of NYC (4-1/31)

SHOLTUS, George H. m 1/21/50 Barbara Rupert, both of Sammonsville, in S.; Rev. Dr. Eyster (4-1/17)

SHONTS, Anna - see MACK, William

SHORLEY, Mary - see EVANS, David

SHORT, Elizabeth Ann - see BISHOP, Hosea E.

SHRIMPTON, Thomas (Deacon), 77, d 2/16/48 in West Troy (apoplectic attack) (5-2/23)

SHRIVER, Ellen - see WILLIAMS, John H.

SHRIVES, Thomas of Hoosick, NY m 2/15/47 Mary Parker of Pownal, VT in P.; Rev. Josiah Matteson (5-2/24)

SHUB, Peter S., about 39, d 7/5/49 in Saugerties (8-7/7)

SHUFELDT, William F. of NYC m 6/6/49 Erin A.A. Mullany, youngest dau. of late Col. James E., at St. Mary's Cathedral in Albany; Rt. Rev. Bishop Mc Clusky (8-6/16)

SHULL, Josiah m 1/26/43 Sally Maria Stafford, both of Danube, in Newville; Bishop S. Ottman (3-2/2)

SHULL, Zena - see SMITH, Abraham

SHULTIS(?), Matilda - see SMITH, James

SHULTIS, Hiram W. m 5/17/49 Elizabeth Yerry, both of Woodstock, at Shandaken; William Risely (8-5/26)

SHULTIS, Irena - see VERRY, William

SHULTUS, Catharine - see SPALDING, Asa

SHUMWAY, G.R.H. (Rev.), pastor of the Presbyterian Church at Palmyra, m 1/17/35 Emily C Ford, dau of Hon. James Ford of Lawrenceville, PA, at L.; Rev. E.D. Wells (6-3/2)

SHURS, Robert m 6/11/37 Sarah M. Burnop, youngest dau. of Philip; Rev. Thomas W. Pearson of the Methodist Protestant Church (all of Albany) (6-7/12)

SHUTTERS, John m 6/7/37 Rachel French, both of Albany; David Russell, Esq. (6-6/9)

SIBLEY, George A., 26, d 1/1/36 at the home of Gen. Hubbard in Rochester (6-1/12)

SIBLEY, Harriet Larned, wf of Lieut. E.S. Sibley of U.S. Army, d 4/23/35 at Detroit, Mich. Territory (6-5/13)

SICKLER, Christopher (Col.) - see SICKLES, James

SICKLER, Christopher (Col.) m 4/4/37 Ann Winne; Rev. John M. Pease (all of Coeymans Landing) (6-4/17)

SICKLER, William of Halfmoon m 4/3/41 Mary Jane Alexander, dau. of Joseph
    and Rebecca of Lansingburgh, at L.; Rev. Selah Ireland (5-4/7)

SICKLES, George m 2/24/39 Eliza Waldrone(?), dau. of Richard, in Danube; Rev.
    Thomas Towell (all of Danube) (3-2/28)

SICKLES, Harriet L. - see CRAWFORD, Richard H.

SICKLES, James - see SICKLER, Christopher (Col.)

SICKLES, James m 4/11/37 Rebecca Winne; Rev. John M. Pease (all of Coeymans
    Landing) (6-4/17)

SIERINE, William of Shrub Oak, Yorktown, m 11/14/43 Elizabeth Tompkins of
    Putnam Valley at Shrub Oak; Rev. W.F. Collins (11-11/21)

SIEUS(?), John Aaron, 3, son of Elizabeth M. and George W.H., d 7/31/49 at
    Flatbush (8-8/18)

SIGNOR, Catharine, about 45, wf of Jacob I., d 7/23/49 at High Falls (8-8/4)

SIKES, Emily - see HALL, John

SILKMAN, Polly, about 60(?), wf of John, d 2/11/42 in Lewisboro (11-2/22)

SILKMAN, Polly, about 60, wf of John, d 2/11/42 at Cross River (11-3/15)

SILL, Eliza, 58, widow of late General Theodore Sill, of Whitesboro, d 4/28/49
    (1-5/2)

SILL, Henry G. (Lieut.) of US Army d 12/1/35 at Washington City (6-12/8)

SILL, Rensselaer N. of firm of Thorn and Sill of Bethlehem m 9/6/36 Frances
    Livingston, dau of Moncrief Livingston, Esq. of Livingston, at L.; Rev. Van
    Waggaman (6-9/14)

SILL, Rensselaer of firm of Sill and Thorn, Cedar Hill, Albany County m 9/6/35
    Frances Livingston, youngest dau of Moncrief, Esq. of Livingston Manor;
    Rev. Van Wagoner(?) (6-9/8)

SILLIMAN, Carolina (Mrs.), 74, d 1/27/40 in West Troy (funeral at 10 o'clock from
    the home of Charles Easton) (5-1/29)

SILLIMAN, Levi, 58, d 6/20/44 at Cohoes (5-7/3)

SILLIMAN, Sarah A., 26, wf of Seneca M. and dau. of John and Hannah Urane, d
    11/11/46 in West Troy (5-11/18)

SILLIMAN, Sarah M. - see FINCH, Henry

SILSBURY, Samuel W. m 8/31/48 Sarah Stevens in Ames; Rev. C.H. Harvey (all
    of Ames) (4-9/14)

SIMMONDS, Mary - see CLARKSON, Paul

SIMMONS, Calista - see WRIGHT, Oren

SIMMONS, Daniel m 5/16/35 Anna Osterhout, dau of Francis, Esq., by L. Dwight,
    Esq., all of Bern (6-5/20)

SIMMONS, Emma, 15, only dau. of John and Caroline C., d 8/11/49 in Saugerties
    (8-8/18)

SIMMONS, Emma, 3, only dau. of John, Jr. and Caroline C., d 8/11/49 in
    Saugerties (8-9/1)

SIMMONS, John, Jr. - see CAMPBELL, Emma

SIMMONS, John, Jr. - see CAMPBELL, Lucy Ann

SIMMONS, Joseph A. m 11/5/45 Julia Ann Dodge, both of Cohoes, at Brunswick;
    Rev. J.Z. Senderling (5-11/12)

SIMMONS, Joseph, 67, a Rev. War pensioner, formerly of Gardiner, d (date not
    given) in Westminster (His participation in specific Rev. War battles is
    defined here) (6-12/1)

SIMMONS, Justin Bowman, 9 months, son of Andrew and Sally A. Simmons, d

11/20/49 in West Troy (5-11/28)

SIMMONS, Margaret - see ----, Elias

SIMMONS, Sarah Maria - see BABCOCK, Samuel

SIMMONS, Zebre, a Rev. War pensioner, d 3/24/26 (was knocked overboard and drowned from the sloop, "Martin Wynkoop" of Kingston, NY) (6-4/7)

SIMMS(?), Isaac m 1/23/40 Catherine Maria Emery(?) both of Greenburgh, in the village of Irving; Rev. George Walker (12-2/4)

SIMMS, ----, 7 months, "a child of Roger Simms", d 5/5/42 in Newburgh (see SIMMS, Roger (Mrs.)) (9-5/14)

SIMMS, Robert, 29, d 6/19/42 in Newburgh (9-6/25)

SIMMS, Roger (Mrs.), d 5/5/42 in Newburgh (see SIMMS, ----, 7 months)(9-5/14)

SIMONS, Agatha Gardner - see ALLEN, Russell

SIMONS, Eliza A. - see KINSLEY, Alonzo W.

SIMONS, George m 5/15/36 Cathrine Brady; Rev. C.P. Clarke (all of Albany) (6-5/19)

SIMONS, Maria - see STEWART, Henry

SIMONS, Nelson H. m 12/8/33 Henrietta Hait, dau of William, formerly of Peekskill, at the Bowery Church in NYC; Rev. Dr. Woodbridge (11-12/17)

SIMPSON, ---- (Col.) - see HARRIS, Thomas K. (Gen.)

SIMPSON, Elizabeth - see BENTLEY, H.C.

SIMPSON, Rachel, 36, wf of John, d (date not given) at her residence near Cohoes (6-9/11)

SIMS, William P. of Troy m 8/23/47 Margaret A. Lansing, dau. of Jacob T., Esq., of West Troy, in Watervliet; Rev. Anderson (5-9/1)

SINCLAIR, John P. m 9/12/46 Mary Ann Fennell at the Methodist Parsonage in West Troy; Rev. Houghtaling (bride and groom of West Troy) (5-9/16)

SINGLE, Eliza - see ACKERMAN, Thomas Jefferson

SINGLETON, Richard - see VAN BUREN, Abraham (Major)

SINGLETON, Sarah Angelica - see VAN BUREN, Abraham (Major)

SINK, Nancy - see CLARK, John R.

SINK, Robert of Utica m 9/11/43 Caroline Meggs(?) of Little Falls in L.F.; Rev. C.W. Leet (3-9/14)

SINNOTT, Maria - see VROOMAN, Adam

SINNOTT, Sarah C. - see SCOVILL, H.W.

SINSABAUGH, George W. of Troy m 11/11/45 Catharine Quackenbush of West Troy; Rev. Dodge (5-11/19)

SIPPELL, Eretta M. - see HILLMAN, Elisha

SIPPERLEY, Finetta - see EVERTSEN, John H.

SIPPLE, Jane, 25, wf of Peter B. d 11/17/50 at Boonville (survived by her husband and an infant child (not named)) (1-11/27)

SISSON, Joseph, 47, d (date not given) at New London (7-6/13/10)

SISTORE, Frances Elizabeth - see BALL, Henry

SISUM, Catherine - see CURTIS, Asa G.

SITTS, Mary, about 22, consort of Nicholas, d 6/2/39 at St. Johnsville (3-6/13)

SKADAN, Cornelia - see FOSTER, Horsa

SKINNER, Albert, 8, son of G.L. Skinner, d 12/3/38 in Little Falls ("this is the second child of S.L. to die within a month's time") (3-12/6)

SKINNER, Ann - see KNAPP, Tracy S.

SKINNER, Charlotte A. - see RICHMOND, Ira D.

SKINNER, David, Esq. - see RICHMOND, Ira D.

SKINNER, James of Little Falls m 1/23/39 Mary Bell of German Flats in G.F.; Rev.
James Murphy (3-2/7)

SKINNER, Lucy Ann - see JOHNSON, Joseph R.

SKINNER, Mary C. - see SHOEMAKER, R.M.

SKINNER, Sarah Maria, 4 months, youngest child of G.L. Skinner, d 5/29/39 in
Little Falls (3-6/6)

SKINNER, Thompson J., Esq., late treasurer of Massachusetts Commonwealth, d
1/20/09 in Boston (7-2/1)

SKINNER, W.H. of Vernon m 12/18/49 Jane Cole of Verona at Verona;
(clergyman's name blurred) (1-12/26)

SKINNER, Warren Lansing, 1, son of Garret L., d 11/14/38 (3-11/22)

SKINNER, William H. m 10/6/40 Elvira S. Wetmore in Vernon; Rev. J.P. Simmons
(all of V.) (1-10/13)

SLACK, Thomas W. of Albany m 11/23/36 Eliza D. Park, youngest dau of late
Deacon John of Framingham, in F.; Rev. Barry (6-11/26)

SLACKT (sic), Elizabeth - see CASE, Newel M.

SLADE, Thomas, 34, d 5/10/35 at Carlyle, Illinois (after a short illness), son of late
James Hemphrey, Esq. and brother to the late member of Congress from
Illinois (6-5/29)

SLALY, ____ - SEE GODDEN, David Jr.

SLATER, Almira - see WILLIAMS, Charles

SLINGERLAND, Augustus M. of firm of W.J. and A.M. Slingerland of Albany m
11/18/35 Antoinette A. Schuyler, dau of John G., Esq. of Amsterdam, at A.;
Rev. Koonz (6-11/20)

SLOAN, Horace m 12/28/45 Miss Slocum, both of Rome; Benjamin P. Johnson,
Esq. (1-12/30)

SLOAN, James of Bern m 12/18/46 Mrs. Ellen Maria Snyder of NYC at the
Methodist Parsonage in West Troy; Rev. Houghtaling (5-12/30)

SLOAN, Samuel, 50, d 12/8/26 in Albany (consumption) (6-12/22)

SLOANE, Harriet D., dau of Douglas W. d 8/12/35 at Cleveland, Ohio (from the
Cleveland Herald) (6-8/21)

SLOAT, Daniel H. m at Peekskill 4/25/41 Mary Conklin, both of Cortlandt Town;
Rev. William H. Johnson (11-4/27)

SLOCUM, Catherine M., wf of Giles J. and only surviving dau. of Judge Harvey
Granger of Saratoga, d 5/30/43 at Cohoes (buried in Saratoga) (5-6/7)

SLOCUM, Charles M, merchant of Philadelphia m 7/20/35 Mary B. Robinson, dau
of John S. of NYC, in NYC; Hon. Cornelius W. Lawrence, Mayor of the
City (6-8/6)

SLOCUM, Miss - see SLOAN, Horace

SLOCUM, William (Capt.), 57, d (date not given) in NYC (6-5/15/16)

SLOSSON, Augustus D. of North Salem m 3/15/40 Hannah Burton of Ridgefield,
CT in R.; Rev. Burton (12-3/24)

SLUYTER, ---- (Rev.) - see DICKIE, John H.

SLUYTER, Alfred, merchant, m 7/4/49 Martha Ellen Richey, dau. of James, Esq. at
Salem; Rev. H.N. Wilbur (all of Salem) (8-8/11)

SLUYTER, Ellen - see DICKIE, John H.

SMALL, Mary J. - see COTRILL, Peleg

SMALL, Melchior - see HATTER, Peter

SMALL, Souan - see HATTER, Peter

SMALL, William m 2/23/43 Fanny Folts in Herkimer; Rev. J.P. Spinner (all of Herkimer) (3-3/2)

SMALLEY, George C., merchant, of NYC m 12/3/40 Susan Maria Bartlett, recently of Buffalo, at Salisbury Centre; Rev. William S. Bartlet (3-12/10)

SMALLEY, Harriet, consort of the Sheriff of Putnam County, d 4/6/50 in Kent (10-4/10)

SMEAD(?), Timothy H. of Argus, Ohio m 8/15/36 Mary E. Herrick in Utica; Rev. Savage (6-9/19)

SMEDES, Abraham W. of Hurley m 2/8/49 Belinda Davis of Marbletown in M.; Rev. W. Bloomer (8-2/24)

SMITH(?), A.M. (Mrs.) - see GAYLORD, Chester, Jr.

SMITH, ---- (Mrs.), 79, d 10/6/41 in Newburgh (9-10/9)

SMITH, ----, 64, wf of Col. John, d 8/30/40 in Camden (1-9/1)

SMITH, A., 40, d 5/4/48 in West Troy (5-5/10)

SMITH, A.R. (Miss) - see TAYLOR, A.Z.

SMITH, Abby Jane (Mrs.), 30, dau. of Cornelius Hollister, late of Rome, d 8/1/50 at Portland, Ohio (Funeral services were conducted by the Rev. S. Haynes, her former pastor in Rome, NY, who arrived at Portland while she was dying) (1-8/21)

SMITH, Abigail Louisa - see JOHNSON, Abigail

SMITH, Abner, 54, d 12/7/46 in New London (billious pleurisy) (1-1/1/47)

SMITH, Abraham m 12/4/25 Zena Shull at Danube (6-1/3/26)

SMITH, Adam m 6/12/36 Mrs. Anna Eliza Getman, both of Manheim, in Little Falls; Rev. Burtis (3-6/16)

SMITH, Allen B. d suddenly 4/7/34 in Phillipstown (11-4/15)

SMITH, Alonzo G. of New London m 12/30/47 Miranda Humiston, dau. of C.F. Humiston of Camden, in C.; Rev. F.H. Stanton (1-1/7/48)

SMITH, Amanda, 24, wf of Daniel of St. Joseph's, Florida (late of NY), 2nd dau of Cornelius Crawford, Sr., d 1/5/39 in Phillipstiwn (consumption) (11-1/15)

SMITH, Amanda, 29, wf of James, d 9/2/39 in Little Falls (3-9/5)

SMITH, Angeline, 26, wf of Henry Smith and dau of Benjamin Heart, Esq. d 3/8/35 in Troy (cunsumption) (6-3/13)

SMITH, Anson m 10/14/41 Elizabeth Snell, both of St. Johnsville; Rev. W. Olmstead (3-11/4)

SMITH, Armona P. - see CARPENTER, Edward

SMITH, Aseneth, 32, consort of Hiram, d 7/28/39 in Warren (3-8/8)

SMITH, Barnard (Colonel), 59, Register of the Land Office at Little Rock, Arkansas, d 7/16/35 at his home near Little Rock (a native of New Jersey) (6-8/17)

SMITH, Benjamin B, Bishop of Kentucky m 9/2/35 Harriet L. Douglas, dau of Seth P. Staples of NYC, in NYC; Right Rev. Bishop Onderdonk (6-9/7)

SMITH, Calvin W. (Dr.), 60, d 8/21/39 in Little Falls (illness of several months) (funeral 8/23 from his late residence) (3-8/22)

SMITH, Carolien Amelia (Miss), 22, d 6/30/50 in West Troy at the home of her brother, G.B. Smith (5-7/3)

SMITH, Caroline A. - see BOWEN, James H.

SMITH, Caroline L. - see BOUGHTON, Joseph

SMITH, Caroline, 23, wf of V.W. Smith, Esq., editor of the <u>Onondaga Standard</u> and only dau of Jonas Earl, Jr., Esq., d 4/10/35 at Syracuse (a lingering illness) (6-4/15)

SMITH, Catharine - see FETCHER, Joseph

SMITH, Charles of Norway, NY m 3/12/39 Emma Farmer of Little Falls in L.F. (3-3/14)

SMITH, Charlotte - see BOOTH, Wheeler

SMITH, Charlotte - see MASON, John

SMITH, Charlotte D., 32, wf of Solomon A., d 12/25/49 in Saugerties (8-12/27)

SMITH, Chauncey m 3/16/36 Lucretia Carpenter, dau. of Samuel, Esq., late of Norway, NY in N.; Rev. Weber (3-3/24)

SMITH, Clark, 81, one of the earliest settlers in Fairfield, d 8/25/41 at Fairfield (3-9/9)

SMITH, Clotilda - see MASON, Frederick

SMITH, Cordelia E. - see VANOSTRAND, A., M.D.

SMITH, Daniel G. m 2/11/45 Susan Stewart, dau. of John, Esq., at Waterford; Rev. R. Hatch (all of Waterford) (5-2/19)

SMITH, David, M.D. of NYC m Sarah Ann Van Norden, eldest dau of G.P., Esq. of Nova Scotia at St. Clement's Church; Rev. L.P. Bayard (6-9/7)

SMITH, E.K. (Lieut.) of US Army m 9/30/35 Mary Jerome, dau of late Isaac, of Onondaga; Rev. Coryell (6-10/19)

SMITH, Edward of firm of Smith & Harrington (booksellers and publishers) m (date not given) Julia Ann Thomas at St. Paul's Church, Burlington, VT; Rt. Rev. Bishop Hopkins (6-3/10/36)

SMITH, Edwin, Esq., of NYC m 9/1/36 Amelia O. Mc Intyre, oldest dau of John, Esq., of Fort Edward, at F.E.; Rev. Thomas E. Vermilye (6-9/7)

SMITH, Elijah m 6/8/43 ---(?) Eliza Elmer, both of Ashford, Mass., in West Troy; Rev. C.H. Hasken (5-6/21)

SMITH, Eliza - see STODDARD, Benjamin

SMITH, Eliza S. - see SPENCER, John C.

SMITH, Eliza, 22, wf of Samuel, d 11/12/41 in Newburgh (9-11/20)

SMITH, Elizabeth - see COOK, Joseph L.

SMITH, Elizabeth - see WALRATH, Henry

SMITH, Elizabeth, 84, relict of William, d 4/8/43 in Verona ("editors of the Barre Gazette please copy") (1-5/2)

SMITH, Ephraim, Esq., 84, d at Gorham, Maine (date not given). "He was a native of Truro, Cape Cod and was one of the daring 'Tea Boys'" (6-1/24/35)

SMITH, Erastus B., merchant, m 4/21/35 Margaretta C. Henry, eldest dau of John D. Henry, M.D., in Rochester, Rev. Tryon Edwards (all of Rochester) (6-4/28)

SMITH, Ester (Mrs.), age blurred, d 10/7/41 in Newburgh (9-10/16)

SMITH, Esther - see GIBSON, De Witt C.

SMITH, Esther - see HULSE, Andrew

SMITH, Esther K. - see CARTER, Joseph A.

SMITH, Esther L. - see KIMBERLY, Hoarce

SMITH, Ezekiel, merchant of Barre Center m 12/1/35 Clarinda Almy of Farmersville, Seneca Co.; Rev. U.B. Miller (6-12/16)

SMITH, Fanny Ellen, 48, widow of Caesar Smith, colored, d 5/12/49 in Kingston (8-5/19)

SMITH, Fitzhugh, 12, only son of Gerrit of Petersboro d 7/9/36 in Utica (6-7/15)

SMITH, Frances A. - see BURCH, H.M.

SMITH, Frances M. - see RAWSON, Packard

SMITH, Gaylord (Mr.), 32, d 11/21/38 in Little Falls (3-11/29)

SMITH, George G., 77, d 8/23/35 in Glen, Montgomery Co. (formerly of Claverack) (6-8/31)

SMITH, George H., 26, d 2/11/43 in Vernon (1-2/28)

SMITH, George Henry, 7 weeks, only son of John and Catharine, d 10/20/44 in West Troy (5-11/6)

SMITH, George m 10/25/48 Betsey Maria Van Alstyne, both of Frey's Bush at F.B.; Rev. Alexander E. Daniels (4-11/2)

SMITH, George of Ballston Spa m 2/23/50 Catharine Jane Levings of Watervliet; S. Ireland (5-3/6)

SMITH, George of Coeymans m 11/25/37 Charity Davis of Westerlo in W.; Rev. Elbert Osborn (6-12/22)

SMITH, George of West Troy m 10/5/43 Emily Cook of Lansingburgh in L. (5-10/18)

SMITH, Gilbert Livingston (Rev.), 22, (son of William M. Smith and grandson of Hon. John Cotton Smith) of Sharon, CT d 11/8/35 in NYC (6-11/11)

SMITH, Gilbert of NYC m 12/20/41 Phebe Ann Wood of Newburgh; Rev. Vanderveer (9-12/25)

SMITH, Hannah - see ALLEN, Stephen

SMITH, Hannah, 74, relict of late Philemon Smith, d 3/27/34 in Phillipstown (11-4/1)

SMITH, Harriet - see GRANGER, James Harvey

SMITH, Harriet N. - see GOODMAN, Noah W.

SMITH, Helen M. - see KINGMAN, Michael

SMITH, Henry E. m 11/7/49 Hannah Perkins in Camden; Rev. F. Graves (all of Camden) (1-11/21)

SMITH, Henry Kendall of Buffalo m 5/12/35 Sarah Ann Voorhees, dau of Henry P, of Fultonville, at F.; Rev. Wheeler (6-5/23)

SMITH, Henry Randall of Buffalo m 5/12/35 Sarah Ann Voorhees, dau of late Henry of Fultonville at F.; Rev. Wheeler (6-5/18)

SMITH, Hester Ann, 6 months, dau of Noah, d 4/9/42 in Whitlockville (11-4/14)

SMITH, Hiram of Newport m 3/1/40 Statira Cross of Warren (3-3/12)

SMITH, Horace, 5, son of James T., d 7/24/41 in Little Falls (3-7/29)

SMITH, Horatio Hale, Esq., of Union City, Mich. m 11/1/48 Maria A. Lacey of Scottsville, NY in Rome at the home of Alva Mudge, Esq.; Rev. W.E. Knox (1-11/2)

SMITH, Ira (Dr.) - see BOWEN, James H.

SMITH, Ira (Dr.) - see VANOSTRAND, A., M.D.

SMITH, Isaac S., Esq., of the house of Smith and Macy in Buffalo m 1/6/37 Mrs. Olivia Congdon of Poughkeepsie in P. (6-1/10)

SMITH, J. m 7/10/36 Clarissa Myers in Fairfield; Rev. William H. Waggoner (3-7/21)

SMITH, Jacob of High Falls m 9/29/49 Hannah De Puy of Marbletown; Rev. E. Du Puy (8-10/20)

SMITH, James of Wilbur m 10/18/49 Matilda Shultis(?) of Woodstock in Woostock; Rev. H. Wheeler (8-10/27)

SMITH, James, 20, brother of the proprieter of the <u>Ohio Monitor</u>, d 10/28/35 at

Mount Holly, NJ (consumption) (had completed 3 years at Dartmouth College and had engaged to spend a year at Princeton College preparing for the ministry) (6-11/27)

SMITH, Jane Ann - see ORCUTT, Charles A.

SMITH, Jane C. - see SHERWOOD, Amos G., Jr.

SMITH, Jane Elizabeth - see GRIDLEY, Sylvester

SMITH, John (Rev.), D.D., professor of the Learned Languages in Dartmouth College, d (date not given) at Hanover (7-5/24/09)

SMITH, John Dugald, Esq., 22, one of the editors of the <u>Sunster Gazette</u> d 5/29/36 at Sunster, SC (Born in Maine grad. from Bowdoin College in 1836) (student of divinity) (6-6/23)

SMITH, John H. (Col.), 42, clerk of Westchester County, d 11/24/39 at Bedford (11-11/26)

SMITH, John H. (Col.), 43, Westchester County Clerk, d suddenly 11/17/39 at Bedford (12-11/26)

SMITH, John m 1/1/39 Tamer Ann Tillotson, both of New Castle, in Sing Sing; C. Yoe, Esq. (12-1/8)

SMITH, John m 11/13/49 Susan Ann Totten, both of Somers, in Carmel; William A. Dean, Esq. (10-11/21)

SMITH, John W., (age not given) infant son of William H. and Harriet, d 7/27/44 in West Troy (5-7/31)

SMITH, John(?), 71, d 7/26/42 in Poundridge (11-8/4)

SMITH, Jonathan (Capt.), 48, d (date not given) in NYC (6-5/8/16)

SMITH, Jonathan, 66, d (date not given) in NYC (6-5/8/16)

SMITH, Joseph G. m 9/23/47 Hannah Akin at the American (Hotel perhaps intended); Rev. Gillet (all of Rome) (1-9/24)

SMITH, Joseph, 80, d (date not given) at Brookfield (7-8/29/10)

SMITH, L.A. (Mrs.) - see POTTER, Platt

SMITH, Leland of Norway, NY m 1/30/40 Emeline West of Fairfield in F.; Rev. Brown of Newport (3-2/6)

SMITH, Leonard m 3/19/39 Mary Ann Carpenter, dau. of Walter, Esq., of Yorktown, in Y.; Rev. J. Youngs (12-4/2)

SMITH, Leonard m 3/19/39 Mary Ann Carpenter, dau of Walter, Esq. of Yorktown, in Y.; Rev. J. Youngs (11-3/26)

SMITH, Lewis L. m 11/29/42 Mary Ann Moore, only dau. of Justin, Esq.; Elder G.G. (surname blurred) (all of Union Ville) (9-12/10)

SMITH, Lewis R. of Bedford m 12/18/38 Ann Augusta Craft, dau of John M. of Yorktown, in Y.; Rev. Louree (12-1/15/39)

SMITH, Louisa - see MURRAY, Patrick

SMITH, Lucy, 17, d 4/6/42 in Bedford (11-4/7)

SMITH, Luke D. (Hon.) m 5/12/50 Mrs. Anna H. Chandler at Mexico, Oswego County; Rev. A. Weed (all of Mexico) (1-6/5)

SMITH, Lydia M. - see HACKSTAFF, John L.

SMITH, Lyle S.H., M.D. m 2/28/26 Isabella Weyman, oldest dau. of W. Weyman, Esq., in NYC at the Roman Catholic Cathedral; Rev. Thomas C. Levius and afterward at Christ Church (6-3/7)

SMITH, Lyman m 3/1/40 Orsaville Fuller in Columbia; Rev. David M---(?) (3-3/5)

SMITH, Margaret - see MC LEE, James P.

SMITH, Maria - see ANDERSON, David

SMITH, Maria - see KENT, Phineas

SMITH, Maria C. - see BOOTH, Thomas H.

SMITH, Martha Matilda, 32, consort of Norman, d 7/14/42 at Newport (consumption) (3-7/28)

SMITH, Mary - see BURRELL, Oscar

SMITH, Mary - see GYPSON, William

SMITH, Mary - see LITTLE, Levi P.

SMITH, Mary - see SMITH, Palmer

SMITH, Mary Elizabeth - see MONELL, John J.

SMITH, Mary, 57, relict of late William I., d 11/22/41 in Newburgh (9-11/27)

SMITH, Matthew, Esq. m 1/30/50 Ann Yoran, both of Minden, in Mindenville; Rev. W.G. Anderson (4-1/31)

SMITH, Millicent, 40, wf of Elijah of Tolland, Conn., d 5/22/10 at Worcester, Mass. (7-6/13)

SMITH, Nancy (Mrs.), about 60, d 11/21/42 at Middle Hope (9-11/26)

SMITH, Nancy Jane, 33, d 11/2/42 at the home of her brother in West Troy (5-11/9)

SMITH, Nelly (Mrs.) - see BURHANS, Nelson H.

SMITH, Nicholas J. of Canajoharie m 6/5/49 Catharine Morrell of Mapletown at M; Rev. Carroll (4-6/21)

SMITH, Palmer m 10/14/47 Mary Smith of Stockbridge; H.C. Vogell (1-10/22)

SMITH, Phebe A. - see HASCALL, Asa

SMITH, Phebe Ann - see THOMPSON, William

SMITH, Phebe, 66, wf of Daniel, d 10/19/39 in North Salem (she was a member of the Society of Friends) (12-10/29)

SMITH, Philemon, 72, d 2/21/34 in Philipstown (11-2/25)

SMITH, Philip P. of Western m 1/1/50 Clarissa Shaver of Rome ar Syracuse; R. Woolworth, Esq. (1-1/16)

SMITH, Phillip T. of Steuben County m 9/26/39 Amee Dean of Mattawan, Dutchess Co., NY, in M; Rev. N. Robinson (11-10/1)

SMITH, Platt, 91, of NYC d 9/22/35 at Kingston (6-9/28)

SMITH, Prudence Ann - see BANKS, George W.

SMITH, Prudence, 37, wf of Hon. Squire Smith of Norwich, Chenango County, d 7/11/37 (6-7/15)

SMITH, R. (Rev.) - see GOODMAN, Noah W.

SMITH, Richard, formerly of Goshen, d 6/25/33 at the home of E. Corwin, Esq., at Jefferson Valley. (11-7/2)

SMITH, Robert m 5/11/48 Margaret Burke; Rev. C.G. Mc Leod (4-5/18)

SMITH, Ruby Ann, 33, consort of Elisha, formerly of Litchfield, d 4/10/43 in Middleville (3-5/25)

SMITH, S.H. of Bedford m 3/11/40 Hannah Maria Sarles, dau. of Amos of Poundridge in P.; Rev. Oldron (12-3/24)

SMITH, Sally - see BRISTOL, Ira

SMITH, Saily S. - see HUNTER, William, Jr.

SMITH, Samuel (Hon.), one of his Majesty executive council and late President of Upper Canada, d 10/26/26 at York (6-11/21)

SMITH, Samuel C., M.D., m 12/6/41 Mary Crist, dau. of Henry, Esq.; Rev. R.P. Lee (all of Montgomery) (9-12/11)

SMITH, Samuel F., 25, d 3/3/47 in Rome (funeral at Zion's Church 3/4/ at 2 o'clock) (1-3/5)

SMITH, Samuel, 45, d 5/14/50 near Lake Mahopac, Carmel (spotted fever) (10-5/15)

SMITH, Samuel, 64, of Little Falls, d 3/6/42 at Nachitoches, Louisiana (born in Mendon, Mass. and youngest son of Col. Calvin Smith, an officer in the Rev. War) (lived 40 years in Herkimer County and more than 30 years in Little Falls) (was postmaster in Little Falls) (3-3/31)

SMITH, Samuel, 77, d 11/20/39 at Cross River (12-11/26)

SMITH, Samuel, Esq. (Capt.) m 11/30/40 Angeline Brothers of Utica in Vernon; Rev. J.P. Simmons (1-12/15)

SMITH, Sarah - see GRAY, Alexander

SMITH, Sarah Ann - see PEET, H.P.

SMITH, Sarah Ann, 23, wf of Henry V., Esq. and dau of Henry P. Voorhees of Fultonville, d 4/21/36 at Buffalo (6-5/2)

SMITH, Sarah Louisa - see HURLBUT, George

SMITH, Seth, Esq. of Hartford, Cortland County m 11/22/42 Sylvia Heath, dau. of Benjamin, Esq. of Locke, Cayuga County, in Locke (marriage after 19 years of courtship, he now age 61, she age 51; "he had visited the bride once a month covering 20 miles. His 232 visits, thus covered 9280 miles which occupied 464 days, a cheap wife" from Cortland Democrat) (5-12/14)

SMITH, Sheldon, Esq., 46, counsellor-at-law and formerly alderman of the 5th ward d 6/1/35 in Buffalo (6-6/8)

SMITH, Shubael of Palmyra m 10/3/50 Alice Seymour of Western in W.; Rev. J.S. Kibbe (1-10/9)

SMITH, Sidney T., merchant, of Pulaski m 9/1/35 Harriet Wood, dau of John of Richmond, Oswego Co., in R; Rev. E.B. Fuller (6-9/11)

SMITH, Sophronia, 22, d (date not given) at Truxton (6-1/20/26)

SMITH, Susan - see LIVINGSTON, Hiram

SMITH, Susan (Mrs.), 72, formerly of Sing Sing, d 9/11/39 in NYC (12-9/17)

SMITH, Thomas (Deacon), 67, d 3/5/42 very suddenly in Little Falls (born in Orange County. Moved to Little Falls more than 40 years ago) (one of the founders of the Presbyterian Church at Little Falls) (3-4/7)

SMITH, Thomas G. (Rev.), pastor of the Presbyterian Church in Tarrytown, d 4/10/37 at his home in Tarrytown (held the Gospel ministry nearly 50 years)(from the Westchester Herald) (6-4/20)

SMITH, Thomas H., Sr., 71, d (date not given) in NYC (6-8/22)

SMITH, Thomas m 8/22/36 Mrs. Elizabeth Doud in Little Falls; Rev. D. Martin (3-8/25)

SMITH, Thomas of West Troy m 5/20/48 Jane Stewart of Albany in A.; Rev. I.D. Williamson (5-5/24)

SMITH, Thomas S. of firm of Latham, Smith & Mc Callum of Albany m 12/1/36 Mary Caldwell, dau. of James of Constantia, Oswego Co., in Canajoharie; Rev. D. Scott of Albany (3-12/15)

SMITH, Thomas S. of firm of Latham, Smith & Mc Collum m 12/1/36 Mary Caldwell, dau of james of Constantia, in Canajoharie (Rev. David Scott of Albany) (6-12/7)

SMITH, Thomas(?) of North Castle m 1/13/40 Maria Woodruff of Southeast in S.; (Elder Warren) (12-1/21)

SMITH, Vernelia - see MATTESON, Harleigh J.

SMITH, W.P., Esq., late of Hudson, m 6/21/44 Elizabeth Russell of Utica in Rome;

Rev. Beecham (1-7/9)

SMITH, William - see SHEPHERD, Phebe

SMITH, William (Hon.) - see SEWELL, Louisa

SMITH, William C. m 9/12/50 Celestine L. Noyes, dau. of Peleg; Rev. Dr. Huntington (bride and groom of Watervliet) (5-9/18)

SMITH, William H. m 5/12/42 Harriet Lorman, both of West Troy; Rev. D. Starks (5-5/18)

SMYTH, Harriet Maria, 25, wf of William Smyth, merchant, of Cleveland, Ohio, d 8/12/35 in Cleveland (6-8/22)

SMYTH, John W m 9/9/35 Mary Ann Goggill, eldest dau of George, at St. Luke's Church; Rev. J.M. Forbes (all of NYC) (6-9/12)

SMYTH, Joseph - see GIBSON, Esther

SMYTH, Susannah - see GIBSON, Esther

SNEDEKER(?), Edward of Brooklyn m 11/14/39 Mary Elizabeth Allison of Haverstraw at H.; Rev. Mulford Day (12-11/26)

SNEDEKER, John, about 60(?), d 4/21/39 in Clarkstown (12-4/30)

SNELL, Aaron m 6/2/36 Catharine Timmerman, both of Manheim, in M.; Rev. David Morris (3-6/9)

SNELL, Catharine - see K-----(?), Robert

SNELL, Eliza N. - see CASE, Henry R.

SNELL, Elizabeth - see SMITH, Anson

SNELL, J.P., Esq. - see BEEBE(?), Hiram

SNELL, Jacob (Hon.), 77, d "lately" at Stone Arabia (distinguished for bravery in the Battle of Oriskany in the Revolutionary War and for his creditable discharge of civil trusts) (3-10/18)

SNELL, Marietta - see BEEBE(?), Hiram

SNELL, Mary Ann, 20, d 3/18/37 at the home of her father in Manheim (consumption) (3-3/23)

SNELL, Reuben of Minden m 2/13/39 Mary Bellinger, dau. of Henry of Herkimer, in H.; Rev. Swackhammer (3-2/21)

SNELLING, Caroline, 4, dau. of John and Elizabeth, d 4/3/49 at Rondout (see also - SNELLING, William Henry)

SNELLING, William Henry, 6 months, son of John and Elizabeth, d 3/28/49 at Rondout (see also - SNELLING, Caroline) (8-4/14)

SNIDER, John m 3/3/36 Susan Keefer, dau of Major John, in Coeymans; Rev. H. Jolly (all of C.) (6-3/10)

SNIFFIN, Elizabeth - see DASKUM, Charles A.

SNIFFIN, Reuben, about 38, d 3/11/39 in Sing Sing (12-3/19)

SNOWDEN, Charles W., 34, son of Col. Charles Snowden of Sing Sing, d 10/19/39 in NYC (12-10/22)

SNOWDEN, J. Bayard, merchant, of Nashville, TN m 2/26/35 Aspasia S.J. Bogardus, dau of Gen. Robert Bogardus, in NYC; Rt. Rev. Bishop Onderdonk (6-3/4)

SNYDER, ---- (Mrs.), 33, wf of Dr. Abraham Snyder, d 10/4/42 in Danube (3-10/6)

SNYDER, Abram G. m 1/6/42 Eliza A. Williams; Rev. O.H. Gregory (all of West Troy) (5-1/12)

SNYDER, Amelia - see ROVER, Charles

SNYDER, Ann Christina - see FINGER, Henry L.

SNYDER, Elias of Unionville m 8/30/49 Eliza Lasher of Saugerties; Rev. N.H.

Cornell (8-9/1)

SNYDER, Elizabeth, 77, widow of Henry, d 4/13/47 in West Troy (5-4/21)

SNYDER, Ellen Maria - see SLOAN, James

SNYDER, Henry of firm of Johnson & Snyder, m 7/13/36 Elvira F. Engs, dau of
P.W., Esq., Rev. William D. Strobel (all of NYC) (6-7/18)

SNYDER, Henry W. of Albany m (date not given) Margaret Arcularius of NYC in
NYC; Rev. Samuel Mervin (6-1/10/16)

SNYDER, Jacob of Saugerties m 11/6/49 Christina C. Brink of Kingston; Rev. V.
M. Hulbert (8-12/1)

SNYDER, Joseph R., 82, d (date not given) at Geneva (6-9/26/26)

SNYDER, Marilla - see MOORE, Horatio

SNYDER, Moses m 1/1/50 Ann Maria Kinter, both of Van Hornesville, in V.H.;
Rev. A.E. Daniels (4-1/10)

SNYDER, Nancy - see GUSTIAN, Daniel W.

SNYDER, Nathan M. m 10/25/48 Lucy Ann Diefendorff, both of Frey's Bush, at
Salt Springville; Rev. Alexander E. Daniels (4-11/2)

SNYDER, Simon, 67, d 3/23/48 in West Troy (formerly a resident of Troy) (5-3/29)

SNYDER, William - see MC CRACKEN, Elizabeth

SNYDER, William, late of Albany, d 9/21/26 at Schenectady on his return from
Utica (funeral from home of H.W. Snyder, 106 North Market Street, Albany
(6-9/26)

SOARE, Susan - see FULTON, Thomas

SOLEY(?), Samuel d (date not given) in Charleston (6-6/5/16)

SOLICE(?), R. Ann - see BLINDBURY, Charles

SOLISS, Elizabeth - see ARMSTRONG, James

SOLOMON, Phebe - see TOWNSEND, Alonzo

SOLUS(?), Benjamin of Schoharie-kill m 3/18/10 Mary Bortles of Jefferson in J.;
Wilhelmus Schuneman, Esq. (7-3/21)

SOPER, Asahel m 1/18/49 N. Adaline Farquarson, both of Rome; Rev. F.H. Stanton
(1-1/24)

SOPER, Charles C. m 11/9/41 Eunice Bowers in Rome; Rev. Haynes (1-11/16)

SOPER, Elizabeth, 1 year, 2 months, youngest dau. of Albert and Esther, d 3/8/50 in
Rome (1-3/13)

SOPER, Hiram m 9/8/42 Roxyann Jacobs, both of Rome, in R.; H.C. Vogell
(1-9/13)

SOPER, Jerusha, 53, wf of Philander, d 8/14/44 in Rome (1-8/27)

SOPER, Philander, about 60, d 1/12/49 in Rome (1-1/17)

SOPER, Treadwell m 10/14/47 Mrs. Edwards of Rome; H.C. Vogell (1-10/22)

SOULDEN, William M., 19, only son of William d 10/23/35 (funeral (10/25) at half
past 4 o'clock from 23 Ferry Street) (6-10/24)

SOULE, Henry m 4/24/49 Katharine M. Burnette at Rondout; Rev. Still (8-4/28)

SOUTHALL, Ann - see TUNNINGTON, John

SOUTHARD, Chastine(?) Augusta, 2, only dau. of Eben and Sarah, d 3/30/45 in
West Troy ("Massachusetts and New Hampshire papers please copy.")
(5-4/2)

SOUTHARD, Eben G., 36, d 10/20/47 in West Troy (5-10/27)

SOUTHWICK, Enoch M. merchant, of Albany m 11/26/15 Armanda Parsons of
Baltimore at B.; Rev. Livingston (6-12/6)

SOUTHWICK, Henry C m 12/28/25 Mary Parkinson, both of Albany; Rev. Lacey

(6-1/3/26)

SOUTHWICK, Sarah W. - see MC GUIGAN, Francis

SOUTHWICK, Wilmarth, 64, brother of late Solomon, Esq., d 8/19/43 in Albany (5-8/23)

SOUTHWORTH, Frances Helen, 2, dau. of D.H. Southworth, d 3/11/37 "very suddenly" in Little Falls (3-3/16)

SOUTHWORTH, Henry O., Esq. of New Berlin, Chenango Co, m 7/1/40 Mary Ann Rhodes, oldest dau. of James A., Esq. of Bridgewater, in B.; Rev. Davis (1-7/7)

SOUTHWORTH, Mary (Mrs.), 80(?), relict of Samuel W., formerly of Stratford, CT., and mother of John Southworth of Newburgh, d 12/24/42 (9-12/31)

SPAFFORD, Delilah - see CARPENTER, William

SPAFFORD, Thomas N., 27, d 6/29/38 in Manheim (consumption) (3-7/5)

SPALDING, Alexander, Esq. of Vernon m 8/25/48 Maria L. Buttrick of Clinton in C.; Rev. Seth P.M. Hastings (1-9/15)

SPALDING, Angeline W. - see SPEAR, John W.

SPALDING, Asa m 6/2/42 Catharine M. Shultus, both of West Troy, in W.T.; Rev. C.H. Hoskins (5-6/8)

SPALDING, Edwin of West Troy m 5/23/43 Almira Arnold of Albia in A.; Rev. C.H. Hosken (5-5/31)

SPALDING, Lucy - see MARTIN, George

SPALDING, Rowland E. m 7/3/45 Susan Brickell; Rev. Dodge (all of West Troy) (5-7/9)

SPANABLE, Catharine - see WIRES, Daniel

SPARHAWK, Andrew, merchant, of Albany m 7/6/36 Martha A. Phelps, dau of late John, Esq. of Granville, MA, at Blandford, MA; Rev. Hinsdale (6-7/9)

SPARKS, Frances Ann, 19, wife of Jared and dau of William Allen, Esq. late of Hyde Park, d 7/11/35 at Hyde Park (consumption) (6-7/18)

SPARLING, Elizabeth - see VAN HOUVENBURGH, Abraham

SPARLING, George m 7/26/49 Maria Krum, both of Saugerties; Rev. H. Ostrander, D.D. (8-8/4)

SPARROW, William m 3/20/39 Eliza Wheeler; Rev. S. Van Deusen (all of Sing Sing) (12-3/26)

SPAULDING, Adeline, consort of Dr. John S. and dau. of late Dr. Todd of Salisbury, Herkimer County, d 9/22/37 in Claremont, NH (typhus) (survived by a husband and "a young and interesting family") (3-9/28)

SPAULDING, E.G., Esq. of Buffalo m 9/6/37 Jane Antoinette Rich, dau. of G.B. Rich, Esq. at Attica; Rev. James B. Shaw (6-10/4)

SPAULDING, George W. of Herkimer m 11/18/41 Louisa Pearl, dau. of Hiram of Schuyler, at Frankfort; Rev. Houston (3-12/9)

SPAULDING, Nathan m 10/25/38 Mary Clapsaddle, dau. of Denas Clapsaddle of Columbia, in C.; Rev. Slocomb(?) (3-11/8)

SPEAR, Catharine - see RING, Thomas C.

SPEAR, John W. of Williamstown, Mass. m 1/1/46 Angeline W. Spalding of West Troy, NY in W.T.; Rev. Dodge (5-1/7)

SPEAR, William of Syracuse m 2/23/49 Caroline Hope of Rome in R.; A.B. Blair, Esq. (1-2/28)

SPEARY, Jannet S. - see VANDEWERKEN, Elbridge

SPEED, Susan W., wf of William P., Esq., d 6/27/35 in Caroline, Tompkins Co.

(6-7/8)

SPENCE, George of Sing Sing m 1/31/39 Mary Hambrook of New Castle; Chauncey Smith, Esq. (12-3/26)

SPENCER, A.C. of Cazenovia m 9/2/44 Mary Tibbitts, dau. of Henry of Rome, at the home of her father (1-9/3)

SPENCER, Ambrose, Esq. m (date not given) "Mrs. Norton" relict of Samuel who was a brother of Burridge Norton, late husband of the late Mrs. Spencer, former wife of His Honor Ambrose Spencer - both ladies being sisters of DeWitt Clinton (7-10/18/09)

SPENCER, Amy G., 26, wf of Archelus, d 1/17/41 in Rome (1-1/19)

SPENCER, Caroline - see ROY, James

SPENCER, Catharine, 59, wf of Hon. Ambrose Spencer, formerly Chief Justice of NY, dau. of General James Clinton and sister of late Governor De Witt Clinton, d 8/20/37 in Albany (funeral from her husband's home, 111 Washington Street, 8/22 (in newspaper dated 8/22)) (6-8/21)

SPENCER, David of Syracuse m 10/13/36 Julia I. Dodge, dau of Col. William Irving Dodge of Syracuse at Syracuse; Rev. Taylor (6-10/17)

SPENCER, David, 59, formerly of Waterford, d 2/19/46 at the home of his son-in-law, James Roy, in West Troy (apoplexy) (5-2/25)

SPENCER, Dewitt Clinton, 7, youngest child of John C., Esq., d 4/18/35 in Canandaigua (6-4/25)

SPENCER, Edward H., 22, d 5/16/42 at Western (consumption) (1-5/24)

SPENCER, Esther - see WILLSON, Esther

SPENCER, F.A. of Verona m 7/2/40 Lucia Whiting of Guilford in G.; Rev. Waterbury of Gilbertsville (1-7/7)

SPENCER, George W. m 10/24/49 Orissa A. Raymond, both of Camden, at the parsonage in Rome; Rev. James Erwin (double ceremony - see JEWELL, Merrett) (1-10/31)

SPENCER, Harriet - see PORTER, Edwin W.

SPENCER, J.B. of Frankford m 9/8/42 Hannah Pratt of Rome; Rev. W.W. Ninde (1-9/13)

SPENCER, John C., Esq., of Albany m 5/20/09 Eliza S. Smith of Catskill in C.; Rev. John Reed (7-5/31)

SPENCER, Joseph O. of Jefferson County m 11/17/50 Lydia A. Morse of Annsville in A.; Rev. Carr (1-12/11)

SPENCER, Laura O. d (date and place not given) (funeral at home of her brother, Alex. O. Spencer, at 2 o'clock at Greenbush (6-12/3/35)

SPENCER, Levania Maria - see BISHOP, George

SPENCER, Lorenzo D., 2, only son of Munson Spencer and grandson of John and Mary West of Rome, d 7/26/50 at Sand Lake (his mother, Mary West, has died 4/7/40) (1-8/7)

SPENCER, Malvina D., 22, dau. of Rev. E. Spencer, d 3/5/41 in Vernon (1-3/9)

SPENCER, Maria Louisa - see NEWTON, Ezra, Jr.

SPENCER, Mary A. - see HITCHCOCK, John V.

SPENCER, Rachel, 57, wf of David, Esq., d 10/7/42 at Waterford (5-10/19)

SPENCER, Sidney of Chittenango m 11/16/46 Lydia Ann Vickers of Cohoes in West Troy; Rev. O.H. Gregory (5-11/18)

SPENCER, Susan - see MISSON, Moses

SPENCER, William H. of Utica m 8/10/48 Sarah A. Pond of Rome in R.; Rev.

William H. Spencer of Utica (1-8/11)

SPERRY, Elizabeth - see ROBERTS, Benjamin

SPICER, Peter W. (Gen.) of NYC d 9/18/33 at Springfield, Ill. (bilious fever) (Taken ill while examining land offices, he was taken to home of William L. May, Esq., where he died) (11-10/22)

SPIER, Joseph, 72, father of Mrs. Dr. Hammond of West Troy, d 8/27/45 at Northville (5-9/10)

SPILMEIER, Henry of Westchester m 1/16/47 Mary Jamison of NYC; Rev. Houghtaling (ceremony perhaps at West Troy, where Rev. Houghtaling served) (5-1/20)

SPINDLER, Daniel m 8/12/49 Louisa Rembaldt, both of Kingston, at Rondout; Rev. C.H. Siehks (8-8/25)

SPINNER, Catherine - see BURRELL, Jacob

SPKES (sic), Mary Jane - see MILES, Oliver C.

SPOCK, Cornelia Ann - see TOMPKINS, Purdy

SPOCK, Elizabeth - see SCOTT, William H.

SPOONER, Hannah (Mrs.), 20, d 1/1/36 in Wampsville (24 hour illness) ("her surviving partner, the physician of that place") (6-1/8)

SPOOR, Gilbert m 11/3/39 Nancy Link, both of Newville, in N.; Rev. S. Ottman of Starkville (3-11/14)

SPORE, Lydia - see EIGHMY, Albert

SPRAGUE, John (Capt.), A.D.C., m 6/3/43 Mary Worth, dau. of Gen. W.J. Worth, US Army and formerly of West Troy, at St. Augustine, Florida; Rev. A. Mc Clure (5-7/5)

SPRAGUE, Mary L., wf of Rev. Dr. William B. Sprague and dau. of Hon. Samuel Lathrop of West Springfield, Mass., d 9/16/37 in Albany (6-9/18)

SPRAKER, ---- (Major), 83, d (date blurred) at his home in Palatine (Major Spraker and his father served from the Palatine District in the Rev. War. His wife (not named) was the dau. of an early Scotch settler in Johnstown) (a long obituary is included) (4-9/7/48)

SPRAKER, John, 81, a Rev. War soldier, d 6/13/37 at Palatine, Montgomery County (6-6/20)

SPRING, Edward, M.D., m 10/18/36 Rlizabeth Riker, dau of Richard, Esq., in NYC; Rev. Dr. Spring (all of NYC) (6-10/21)

SPRING, Susan (Mrs.) - see MOUNTFORD, Henry

SPRINGER, Daniel m 9/10/37 Eliza Ostrander; Rev. John D. Hicks (all of Springfield) (3-9/28)

SPRINGER, Elizabeth - see SPRINGER, Martin

SPRINGER, Harriet - see SPRINGER, Martin

SPRINGER, Henry - see SPRINGER, Martin

SPRINGER, Lovina - see OSTRANDER, Alexander

SPRINGER, Martin of Brunswick, Rensselaer County buried four of his seven children within the period 6/4 and 7/10/1845 as noted below: Springer, Philip Martin, 24, d 6/4/45 in Brunswick (typhus) (he had married Caroline Ensign "Christmas-time" 1844) Springer, Harriet, 22, d 7/6/45; Springer, Henry, 20, d 7/10/45 (typhus); Springer, Elizabeth, 27, wf of Manning Vanderheyden and mother of 2 children, d 7/10/45 (from <u>Troy Whig</u>) (5-8/20)

SPRINGER, Philip Martin - see SPRINGER, Martin

SPRINGSTEAD, Daniel m (date not given) Hannah Jane Cudney in Somerstown; Rev. Hunt (11-1/25/42)

SPRINGSTED, John m 11/15/38 Emily Knapp, dau of James, in Haverstraw, all of H. (12-11/20)

SQUIRE, George F. m 12/25/38 Susan M. Sheldon of Russia, NY in R.; Rev. Waters of Trenton (3-1/3/39)

SQUIRES, Mary Ann, about 29, wf of Orlando, d 1/30/42 in Utica (1-2/8)

ST CLAIR, John m 12/19/26 Eliza Lloyd in Albany; John Bell, Esq. (6-12/26)

ST JOHN, Abijah m 4/9/39 Altie Clark, both of Pound Ridge, in P.R.; Rev. Paterson (12-4/23)

ST JOHN, Ancel, 7 yr, 7 mo., and Howard, 2 yrs, 10 mo., sons of A. St John, cashier at the Bank of Ithaca, d 1/27/35 at Ithaca (6-2/13)

ST JOHN, Erastus, 22, d 8/8/37 in Albany (6-8/10)

ST JOHN, George m 9/6/42 Frances Lockwood, dau of Sidney E., Esq., in Lewisboro; Rev. Frame (all of L.) (11-9/15)

ST JOHN, Harriet Elizabeth - see ALLEN, Otis

ST JOHN, Horace m 5/26/35 Christina Mary Humphrey, dau of late James, Esq.; Rev. Vermilyea; all of Albany (6-5/29)

ST JOHN, Margaret - see FOOTE, Thomas

ST JOHN, Solomon, 47, formerly of Geneva and Albany, d 1/23/35 at Buffalo (6-1/31)

STAATS, Henry of Manheim m 1/30/40 Elizabeth Newman, dau. of Henry, Esq. of Albany, in A.; Rev. Maiser (3-2/6)

STAATS, Jane - see VAN VALKENBURGH, John Taylor

STAATS, Phillip m 4/12/35 Caroline Taylor; Rev. J.D. Williamson; all of Albany. (6-4/14)

STAATS, William S. - see EVERTSON, ____

STACY, John of Little Falls m 7/9/41 Mary Ann Van Driesen of German Flats in G.F.; Rev. J.P. Spinner (3-7/15)

STAFFORD, (the Lord) m 6/26/36 Elizabeth Caton, dau of Richard, Esq., and grand dau of Charles Caroll, Esq., of Carrolton, both of Maryland, and sister to the Marchioness of Wellsley and Marchioness of Carmarthey; at the Church of Roch in Paris and afterwards at the British Embassy (6-7/23)

STAFFORD, Ann Eliza, 36, consort of Brown Stafford and dau. of J.C. Young, d 10/13/49 in Canajoharie (4-10/18)

STAFFORD, Sally Maria - see SHULL, Josiah

STAFFORD, Susan (Miss), 19, dau. of John, d. 7/11/48 at Palatine Bridge (4-7/13)

STAGE, Emeline, 28, wf of John M., of Newburgh, d 3/4/42 (9-3/12)

STAGE, John (Rev.), tutor, of Geneva College, m 5/2/26 Sophia Adams of Rochester in R.; Rev. F.H. Cuming (6-5/19)

STAGG, John of NYC m 10/14/35 Louisa Caroline Ten Broeck, dau of Richard of Albany, at St. Paul's Church; Rev. J.H. Price (6-10/15)

STAGG, Rachel, wf of Absum Stagg, d (date not given) in NYC (6-11/3/26)

STAINER(?), Jane (Mrs.), 39, d 6/21/42 in Poughkeepsie (9-6/25)

STANCEL(?), Oliver m 9/18/36 Fanny Burt in Stark; Rev. Sparry (3-10/13)

STANFORD, Emely - see MATTESON, Silas

STANFORD, Rebecca, 62, widow of Robert, d (date not given) at Windsor (7-6/20/10)

STANFORD, Richard, 47, representative in Congress from North Carolina, d 4/9/16 at his lodgings in Georgetown (erysipelas originating in the common cold) (was the oldest member of the House where he had served nearly 20 years) (6-4/17)

STANLEY, Matthew, formerly of Lower Canada, m 2/18/45 Eveline Cones(?) of West Troy in Watervliet; Rev. Z. Phillips (5-2/26)

STANSEL, Lydia - see VAN HORNE, Abraham R.

STANTON, Egbert m 2/15/37 Jane Clement; Rev. John M. Pease (all of Coeymans Landing) (6-2/20)

STANTON, Jane M. - see HOLLISTER, Frederick

STANTON, Lucy, 65, consort of Elijah, a native of Brooklyn, Conn., d 4/21/36 in Fairfield (a lingering illness) (3-4/28)

STANTON, Mary (Mrs.) - see EDWARDS, David G.

STANTON, Moses, Esq. of Coeymans m 10/20/36 Elizabeth Weed of Fulton at F.; Rev. David B. Collins (6-11/5)

STAPLES, Seth P. - see SMITH, Benjamin

STARIN, Delancy D., Esq. of Fultonville m 6/17/50 Emeline F. Wagner, dau. of Joseph, Jr. of Fort Plain, in F.P.; Rev. Dr. C.G. Mc Lean (4-6/20)

STARING, Charles m 2/7/39 Clarinda Dygert, both of Little Falls, in L.F.; Rev. J.W. Olmsted (3-2/14)

STARING, Peter, 48, d 12/26/41 at his home in Little Falls (funeral sermon by Rev, John P. Spinner at the Presbyterian Church) (3-12/30)

STARK, John W., Esq., eldest son of Hon. Caleb and grandson of late General Stark, d 1/3/36 "at his father's seat in Dunbarton, NH" (6-1/13)

STARK, Samuel Gager, 24, d 10/6/48 in Fort Plain (4-10/12)

STARKS, Dyer (Rev.), 90, d 9/1/41 in Rome (was first pastor of the Baptist Church in Rome) (1-9/7)

STARKS, Henry (age not given) father of the Rev. H.L. and D. Starks of the Troy Conference of the Methodist Episcopal Church, d 6/4/44 in Canaan, Columbia County (was a member of the M.E. Church 46 years) (5-6/19)

STARKWEATHER, David - see EASTON, Sophronia

STARKWEATHER, Rufus m 1/6/42 Elizabeth Loomis; Rev. Pepper (all of Warren) (3-1/13)

STARR, John R. of Verona m 7/4/44 Helen M. Parkhurst of Oneida County in Verona; Rev. Israel Brainard (1-7/9)

STARR, Juliette - see DANA, Richard P.

STARR, Mary Clarissa, 16, only dau. of John, d 6/18/41 in Verona (1-6/29)

STARR, Sarah, consort of Rev. Peter Starr, d 7/7/09 at Warren, CT (7-7/26)

STARRING, Nancy - see STEEL, John

STARRING, Susan, 7, youngest dau. of late Peter Starring, d 4/23/42 in Little Falls (3-4/28)

STARS, David (Hon.) - see CROWNINGSHIELD, George Casper

STARS, Harriet Elizabeth - see CROWNINGSHIELD, George Casper

START, Amy L. - see OVERSET(?), P.L.

START, Daniel Shattuck, 2, son of Noah, d 6/6/38 in Little Falls (3-6/14)

START, Emily - see THOMPSON, Henry

START, Noah - see THOMPSON, Henry

START, Noah, Esq. - see OVERSET(?), P.L.

START, Sarah W. (Mrs.), 28, d 4/3/41 in Troy (3-4/8)

STAUFE, Sarah - see SCHOONMAKER, John

STAUNTON, George W., Esq. - see HULL, William C.

STAUNTON, Matilda - see WILCOX, Alonzo

STAUNTON, Sally M. - see HULL, William C.

STAURAN(?), John, about 50, of Deerpark, d (date not given) in Newburgh (9-2/26/42)

STEADMAN, Eliza Ann - see BROWN, John N. (Rev.)

STEADMAN, Willard of Unidilla m 9/28/49 Maria Church of Westernville in Utica; Rev. Beckwith (1-10/10)

STEARNS, Mary Almira, 1, dau. of Ransom and Sally Margaret, d 7/20/45 in West Troy (5-7/23)

STEARNS, Ransom S. m 6/20/42 Margaret S. Sturgess, both of West Troy; Rev. H.L. Starks (5-6/29)

STEARNS, William of Phelps m 12/15/46 Hannah Wadsworth of West Troy; Rev. O.H. Gregory (5-1/6/47)

STEBBINS, Alice, infant dau. of Edward and Lydia S., d 10/4/50 in Clinton (1-10/23)

STEBBINS, Ann - see JONES, Cyrenus

STEBBINS, Benjamin, 58, d 8/26/39 in Bedford (12-9/17)

STEBBINS, Bethuel, 71, d 1/22/40 in West Troy (5-1/29)

STEBBINS, Catharine - see EATON, Allen

STEBBINS, David - see CORNING, Edward

STEBBINS, Elizabeth Cowdry - see CORNING, Edward

STEBBINS, John Pierpont, 1, youngest child of Osman (?) L. and Eunice H., d 3/19/42 in West Troy (5-3/30)

STEBBINS, Ormyn L., 50, d 3/7/48 in West Troy (5-3/15)

STEDMAN, David of Oneida Valley m 12/12/48 Mrs. Elizabeth H. Frisbie of Newville, Oneida County at Newville; Rev. P.S. Talmage (1-12/22)

STEEL(?), Mary Ann - see ZOLLER, Isaac

STEEL, John m 4/4/36 Nancy Starring, both of German Flats (3-4/14)

STEEL, Lemuel, 73, father of Levi and Lemuel of Albany, d (date not given) at Hartford, Conn. (6-1/6/16)

STEEL, Rudolph N. m 12/4/39 Jane Pomeroy, dau. of Charles, at German Flats; Rev. J.P. Spinner (3-12/12)

STEELE, ----, son of Oliver, d (date and age of deceased not given) (note: since friends and relatives are invited to his funeral probably he died in Albany - F.Q.B.) (6-1/10/37)

STEELE, Abby (Miss), d 5/15/37 (her three sisters: Mrs. Shepherd, Mrs. Guest and Mrs. Webster are mentioned with the funeral from the home of Mrs. Webster at 83 State Street) (6-5/15)

STEELE, Atwood m 7/19/42 Charlotte Ives, dau. of Ambrose, Esq., both of Albany, in West Troy; Rev. C.H. Hosken (5-7/27)

STEELE, Daniel, bookseller, m 11/20/26 Mrs. Mary Warner, both of Albany, in Waterford; Rev. Dwight (6-11/21)

STEELE, Elvira - see LOW, Addison

STEELE, Joseph (Rev.) of Castleton, VT m 2/13/35 Harriet B Hopkins of Great Barrington, MA, in G.B.; Rev. Burt (6-2/19)

STEELE, Oliver of Albany m 5/12/26 Mary Augusta Livingston, dau. of M. Livingston, Esq., at Livingston's Manor, Columbia County; Rev. Kittle (6-5/19)

STEELE, Robert H., infant son of Roswell, d 2/8/37 (funeral from 29 Division St.) (6-2/9)

STEELE, Samuel, Esq. - see LOW, Addison

STEELE, Tempe (Miss) d (date not given) ("friends of Mrs. Guest and of Dr. P. Mc Naughton are invited to the funeral ...at 3 o'clock from 73 North Pearl Street") (6-10/7/36)

STEENBURGH, Henry m 9/20/40 Amy Cookingham, both of Waterford, at Cohoes; Rev. O. Emerson (5-9/30)

STEENBURGH, Jane Eliza - see LUFFMAN, John D.

STEER, Caroline - see LANSING, Cornelius

STEPHENS, Abel - see GREEN, J.

STEPHENS, archibald (Hon.) - see GREEN, J.

STEPHENS, Archibald, 59, d 10/14/36 in Coeymans (representative in state legislature in 1824) (at time of death he was a democratic elector of the President and Vice Pres. of U.S.) (6-10/17)

STEPHENS, Archibald, Jr. m 10/18/26 Harriet Haines, dau. of Stephen and Katy Haines, in Coeymans; Rev. Jolley (see COPLAND, Alexander) (6-11/7)

STEPHENS, Benjamin, 58, d 8/26/39 in Bedford (12-9/10)

STEPHENS, Joseph (Capt.), 30, late Sailing Master in the US Navy, d 4/17/16 in Philadelphia (typhus pleurisy) (6-5/8)

STEPHENS, Mariah - see GREEN, J.

STEPHENS, Thomas L., 55, d (date not given) in NYC (6-2/21/26)

STERLIN, Jacob M. m 3/1/26 Mary Howard, dau. of Robert H.; Rev. Buck (all of Guilderland) (6-3/14)

STERLING, John C. of Watertown m 6/12/44 Anna Brayton, dau. of late George Brayton, at Westernville; Rev. Isaac Brayton (1-6/18)

STERLING, Oliver, 45, formerly editor and proprietor of the Connecticut Herald, d 4/2/26 in New Haven, Conn. (6-4/7)

STERLING, William, Esq., 61, d 10/23/42 in Newburgh (9-10/29)

STEVENS, Belinda - see HOLDEN, Alvah

STEVENS, Caleb - see SEBLES, C. Maine

STEVENS, Charles of Holland Patent m 2/2/42 Cynthia T. Ball, dau. of Capt. Thaddeus Ball of Trenton, at T,; Rev. T.C. Hill (1-2/15)

STEVENS, Elizabeth - see CHRISTLER, Sylvester

STEVENS, Ellen J. - see KING, Salem T.

STEVENS, Frances H. - see BOWMAN, Jabez P.

STEVENS, Frederick m 2/26/50 Catharine Hyde, both of Coonradt Settlement, in Rome; H.C. Vogell (1-2/27)

STEVENS, G.B., Esq., merchant, of Hamilton, Oneida Co., m 5/20/35 Mary Imogine Wheeler, dau of Dr. Gamaliel Wheeler of Upper Red Hook, at U.R.H.; Rev. Pardee (6-6/3)

STEVENS, George D. m 11/19/50 Elizabeth E. Wales, both of Westmoreland, in W.; Rev. Graves (1-12/11)

STEVENS, Horatio d 3/25/46 at Oneida Castle (1-3/31)

STEVENS, Jacob m 2/17/42 Lucretia Larkin, dau. of Ephraim, in Rome; Rev.. W.W. Ninde (all of Rome) (1-2/22)

STEVENS, John A., Esq. m 9/13/26 Amelia Ackley of Montreal in Canandaigua (6-9/22)

STEVENS, John A., Esq., 53, formerly of Canandaigua d 4/14/36 in Brighton (from

the <u>Ontario Messinger</u>) This entry contains precisely the same citations as
for the death of Juan S. Stevens. (6-5/5)

STEVENS, Joseph, 80, d (date not given) at New Canaan (7-6/13/10)

STEVENS, Juan S, 69, d 4/13/36 at the poor house near Rochester (was one of the
first printers in western New York - published the <u>Genesee Messinger</u> as
early as 1805; state assemblyman from Ontario County 1818-19) (6-4/29)

STEVENS, Juan S. - see STEVENS, John A.

STEVENS, Julia C. - see SEBLES, C. Maine

STEVENS, Mary, 63, d (date not given) at Lima, NY (6-1/20/26)

STEVENS, Ozias, Esq., 44, d 4/27 in Broome, Schoharie County (7-5/2)

STEVENS, Phebe, 61, consort of Benjamin who was born in Saybrook, Conn., d
(date not given) in Fairfield ("an affectionate wife and parent.") (3-3/31/36)

STEVENS, Richard (Dr.), 43, d 8/22/35 at Hoboken, NJ (a protracted illness)
(6-8/25)

STEVENS, Sarah - see SILSBURY, Samuel W.

STEVENS, Seth, Esq. of Hartford, Cortland County m 11/22/42 Sylvia Heath, dau.
of Benjamin, Esq. of Locke, Cayuga County, in Locke; Levi Henry, Esq.
(Mr. Stevens, age 61; the bride, age 51) (3-12/22)

STEVENS, Susan, 69, relict of Truman Stevens, formerly of Western, d 11/29/49 at
Delta (1-12/5)

STEVENS, Thomas Holdup (Commodore) of the US Navy, d (date not given). Born
in South Carolina, entered teh US Navy in 1808 (from the <u>National
Intelligence</u> with an obituary) (3-1/28/41)

STEVENSON, Anne - see WATSON, Steward

STEVENSON, Eben J. of Little Falls m "lately" Almira M. Howard, dau. of John, in
Cornishville, Maine (3-5/18/37)

STEVENSON, James - see WATSON, Steward

STEVENSON, Martin m 1/13/49 Hannah Jane Henderson, both of Eddyville, in
Rondout; Rev. B.T. Phillips (8-1/27)

STEVENSON, Matthew, M.D., of Cambridge, NY m 5/18/42 Agnes Lander, dau.
of late John Auchinhaus of Baltimore, MD, at the Union Church in
Newburgh; Rev. John Forsyth (9-5/21)

STEVENSON, Nancy, 16, youngest dau. of Mrs. Stevenson, d 5/1/37 (funeral from
41 Colonie Street) (6-5/2)

STEWARD, Mary (Miss), 18, dau. of Alexander of Winfield, d 4/19/36 in Utica
(3-5/5)

STEWART, A.L., Esq. - see WEBB, Stephen H. (Capt.)

STEWART, Ann, 6, dau. of Daniel, d 12/5/38 (3-12/13)

STEWART, Content, 76, wf of General Samuel Stewart, d 11/11/48 at Waterford
(5-12/13)

STEWART, Cornelia, 24, wf of Samuel H., d 6/12/35 in Albany (6-12/15)

STEWART, Delia Tudor - see PARNELL, James Henry

STEWART, Henry of Summer Hill, Cayuga County m 11/15/37 Maria Simons of
Geddesburg, Onondaga Co. at Bethlehem; D. Russell, Esq. (6-11/18)

STEWART, J.J. of NYC m 8/6/35 Eliza Hunter, dau of late John, Esq., of
Greenville, Greene Co., in NYC at St. John's Church; Rev. Bishop
Onderdonke (6-8/10)

STEWART, James W of Jackson m 1/15/35 Mary Willard, sister of Hon. John
Willard of Salem, in Salem; Rev. Dr. Proudfit (6-1/24)

STEWART, James, 46, d 1/5/40 In Ossining (12-1/14)

STEWART, Jane - see DUBOIS, Jacob

STEWART, Jane - see SMITH, Thomas

STEWART, Joram N. m 10/22/26 Martha Cannon in Rutland, VT (from the Rutland Herald) (6-10/27)

STEWART, Mary - see NIXON, Jonathan

STEWART, Mary (Mrs.), 84, d 11/7/37 (her sons-in-law, Timothy and Amos Fassett are mentioned). Funeral 11/8 from Amos' home, 209 State Street (6-11/8)

STEWART, Mary Ann, about 37, wf of Robert, d 5/29/36 in Little Falls (consumption) (3-6/2)

STEWART, Mary J. - see WEBB, Stephen H. (Capt.)

STEWART, Mary Jane, about 4, d 12/27/38 in Little Falls (scarlet fever) Her siblings Elizabeth, 13, and David, 8, died during the night of Jan. 1 - Jan. 2, 1839 - all of them children of Robert Stewart of Little Falls (3-1/3/39)

STEWART, Mary, dau of A.L. Stewart of Kingston, d (date not given) at the home of D.P. Marshall in Albany (funeral at his home, 308 South Pearl St. 3/25/36 at 4 o'clock) (6-3/24)

STEWART, Samuel (Gen.), 83, (born in Voluntown, Conn., Feb 1767, and moved in 1797 to Waterford, NY where he engaged extensively in business as a merchant. At beginning of War of 1812 entered military service in the rank of Major and was stationed at Sackets Harbor - served 4 years in the NY State Senate (5-10/16)

STEWART, Samuel F. m 12/24/43 Catherine Deyo of Watervliet; Rev. S. Ireland (5-12/27)

STEWART, Sarah E., 25(?), formerly of West Troy, d 12/16/50 at Herkimer (5-12/18)

STEWART, Susan - see SMITH, Daniel G.

STEWART, William C., 26, d 11/1/40 in West Troy (5-11/4)

STICKNEY, E.B. - see DRAKE, William Henry

STIDELL, Alexander of US Navy m 9/29/35 Catherine Alexander, dau of Morris Robinson, Esq., in NYC; Rev. Dr. Turner (6-10/3)

STILES, Francis, 27, d 10/18/36 in Maumee, Ohio (3-11/24)

STILL, Charles H. (Rev.), pastor of the (name blurred) Church of New Paltz m 5/23/49 Margaret Acken of New Brunswick, NJ at N.B.; Rev. George Schenck (8-6/16)

STILLMAN, Mary Jane - see CLEVELAND, James T.

STILLMAN, Phebe Josephine, 4 months, dau. of Erastus B. and Julia A., d 8/8/46 in Newport (1-10/13)

STILLWELL, Eveline - see TILLOTSON, Matthew

STILLWELL, Eveline - see TILLOTSON, Matthew

STILLWELL, Mrs. - see SCOVEL, Jane

STIMSON, Cynthia - see BENNETT, James

STIMSON, Emily - see BOYD, James A.

STOCKDALE, William m 4/22/46 Mary Mc Guire; Rev. T.F. Wyckoff (all of Watervliet) (5-4/29)

STOCKER, George of Phillipstown m 9/26/35 Elizabeth Wilson of Peekskill in P.; Squire Purdy (11-9/29)

STOCKING, John Jr., Esq, Mayor of Mobile, d 2/4/35. Born in NY, emigrated to

Alabama in 1830 in commercial pursuits in Blakely and in Mobile. Twice elected mayor of Mobile. (6-2/27)

STOCKING, Joseph (Deacon), 60, d 9/4/35 in Buffalo (6-9/12)

STOCKTON, Richard G. of firm of Stockton and Stokes (for many years among the most extensive and efficient mail contractors), d 11/2/37 at Baltimore (6-11/8)

STODDARD, Benjamin, 2nd, m 6/2/36 Eliza Smith, all of Salisbury Center; Rev. Evan Eustis (all of Salisbury Center)(3-6/9)

STODDARD, Edwin L. of West Troy m 10/12/43 Mary H. Montgomery of Rochester in R.; Rev. Eighenbrot (5-10/18)

STODDARD, Rufus (Rev.), 25, d 7/29/36 at his home in Pickney,m Lewis Co. (consumption) (6-8/15)

STODLAR, Julia Ann - see TOWN, Oliver W.

STONE, ----, wf of John, formerly of Kent, England, d (date not given) in Lenawee County, town of Rome, Mich. (1-8/4/40)

STONE, Adelaide - see MERCEBEAU, Lawrence (Rev.)

STONE, John, formerly of Acrise, county of Kent, England, d (date not given) in Rome, NY (1-8/4/40)

STONE, Joseph L. m 9/25/50 Frances Vredenburgh of Rome in R.; Rev. W.E. Knox (1-10/2)

STONE, Joseph Scribner, 2, youngest son of Zar and Caroline, d 6/3/50 in West Troy (5-6/12)

STONE, Mary - see WILLIS, N.P.

STONE, William H. of Marcy m 4/27/48 Elizabeth Green, dau. of Joseph B. of Rome, in R.; Rev. M.H. Nogus (1-5/6)

STONELL, Harriet, 2, and Mary Jane, 3, children of Corbet Stonell, d 2/4/39 in Little Falls (3-2/28)

STORER, Clarissa Ann, 52, wf of Capt. Isaac Storer, d 9/23/49 at 6:30 p.m. in Lansingburgh (see STORER, Isaac (Capt.)) (5-10/3)

STORER, Isaac (Capt.), 64, d 9/23/49 at 4 p.m. in Lansingburgh (see STORER, Clarissa Ann) (5-10/3)

STORES, Hiram M. of Moriah, Essex County, m 11/8/49 Harriet P. Lamb of Lansingburgh in L.; Rev. Hewes (5-11/14)

STOREY(?), Orvilla W., civil engineer, m 4/15/45 Caroline E. Eames, dau. of Simeon E., Esq., of Lee, at Lee; Rev. Robert Qu---(?) (1-4/22)

STOREY, William m (date not given) Lydia Morehouse in Norwalk, Conn. (7-8/1/10)

STORM, James, Esq., clerk of Columbia Co. m 5/14/35 Susannah Paddock, dau of Laban Paddock, Esq.,; Rev. Purdy; all of Hudson (6-5/23)

STORMS, Abraham of Greenburg m 11/21/38 Margaret Lent, dau of Isaac, Esq. of Teyckeyhoe (perhaps intended Tuckahoe) at T.; Rev. George Walker (12-12/11)

STORMS, Eliza - see DIGGS, Henson

STORMS, Eliza - see HOSIE, John

STORMS, Hannah - see ODELL, Valentine

STORMS, Jane Elizabeth, infant dau. of James & Jane, d 11/16/39 in Sing Sing (12-11/19)

STORMS, John of Southeast m 2/9/42 Rebecca Jane White in Somers; Rev. Clark Fuller (11-2/22)

STORMS, Sarah - see MIX, Eli H.

STORRS, Catharine M. - see WELLS, Robert H.

STORRS, H. (Dr.) - see WELLS, Robert H.

STORY, A.G. - see MORSE, James O. (Hon.)

STORY, A.G. - see MORSE, James O. (Hon.)

STORY, Albert G, Esq., cashier of the Herkimer County Bank at Little Falls, m 5/4/35 Sarah Morse, dau of Hon. James O. Morse at Cherry Valley; Rev. Lochead (6-5/18)

STORY, James Otis Morse, infant son of A.G. Story, Esq., d 7/28/38 (3-8/2)

STORY, Jesse - see SAYLES, George N.

STORY, John m 9/3/48 Miss Phillips (her given name lacking) of Cherry Valley; Rev. C.H. Harvey (4-9/14)

STORY, Julia, 22, dau. of late William, Esq., of Cherry Valley, d 3/28/42 at her mother's home in Little Falls (3-3/31)

STORY, Susan B. - see WINCHESTER, Jonas

STOUGHTON, Don Thomas, 72, His Catholic Majesty's Consul for the State of New York for 30 years, d 3/19/26 in NYC (6-3/24)

STOUGHTONBURGH, Jane - see DEWITT, Richard

STOUSE(?), Margaret - see COLMITZ, George

STOUT, Catherine, 18, wf of E.S. Stout and dau. of William Throp, d 10/11/49 in Rondout (8-10/20)

STOUTENBURGH, Tobias, Jr. m (date not given) Betsey Traver in Rhinebeck (6-5/22/16)

STOW, Daniel B., 3rd, m 8/19/49 Emily B. Delanoy, both of Rondout, at Glasco; Rev. P.C. Oakley (8-8/25)

STOW, Nancy M. - see SANXAY, John

STOWITS, Jacob J. of Troy m 10/5/26 Pamelia Ann Wynants, dau. of Josiah of Albany, in A.; Rev. Howard (6-10/10)

STRACMAN(?), Mary - see WALSH, Jonathan

STRAIN, Henry (Major) m 1/29/42 Alida V. Bridges, both of Albany, at West Troy; Rev. O.H. Gregory (5-2/2)

STRAIN, Marietta, 28, wf of James, Jr., d 3/26/36 in South Westerlo (gangrenous eresipalas and typhus) (6-4/18)

STRANAHAN, Farrand, late a senator from Otsego County, d 10/27/26 at Cooperstown (6-10/31)

STRANG, Alsop H., Esq., m 10/16/39 Jane Eliza Ferris, dau of Jonathan, Esq., deceased, at home of late Judge Ferris; Rev. Dr. Westbrook (11-10/22)

STRANG, E.J. m 11/23/42 "Miss Marion H. Marion, daughter of David Marion, Esq.", at Grassy Point; Rev. J.P. Hildreth (11-12/1)

STRANG, Fowler m 12/18/39 Catherine Lee, dau. ofr Abijah, Esq.; Rev. R.G. Thompson (bride & groom of Yorktown) (12-12/24)

STRANG, John m (date not given) Harriet Pinkney in Yorktown; Rev. Dr. Westbrook (11-12/31/39)

STRANG, Josephine, 6 months, dau of Joseph, Esq., d 2/20/42 (11-2/21)

STRANG, Josephine, 6 months, dau of Joseph, Esq., d 2/21/42 in Peekskill (11-3/1)

STRANG, Juliet - see BASSETT, Benjamin

STRANG, Mary Ann - see HAZELTON, William B.

STRANG, Samuel - see TOWNER, Elizabeth

STRANG, Sarah, 77, relict of late Underhill Strang, d 3/14/39 in Peekskill (11-3/19)

STRANGE, Elizabeth, widow of Maxwell Strange, d 12/4/26 in Albany (6-12/8)

STRATTAN, John H. m 5/20/49 Miss Wyanhauver; Rev. S.T. Phillips (all of Rondout) (8-6/2)

STRATTON, Ann - see POWELL, Thomas

STRATTON, Austin S. of Albany m 2/27/42 Ann Eliza Miller of Watervliet; Rev. H.L. Starke (5-3/9)

STRATTON, Rebecca C. - see VAN LOON, James S.

STRATTON, Roxy L. - see WARNER, Seth H.

STREET, Willaim, 15 months, d 9/12/37 and Jennette, 3, d 9/7/37 (both are children of William and Elizabeth Street), at Cold Spring (West Point Foundry), Putnam County ("malignant sore throat" the cause of the death for each child) (6-9/13)

STREETER, Angeline - see MATTESON, Jesse

STREVEL, Joseph m 9/30/37 Polly Northrup in Bern; Lyman Dwight, Esq. (6-10/4)

STRICKLIN, John m 10/12/39 Ruth Youmans, both of Haverstraw, at H.; Henry Beebe, Esq. (12-10/15)

STROAD, Sarah - see CORSON, John O.

STRONG, Cornelia K. - see FORSYTH, William W.

STRONG, Elizabeth, 44, wf of Joseph, Esq., d 2/12/35 at Albany (6-2/23)

STRONG, Emily - see GREEN, Harvey

STRONG, Henry P., pastor of the Presbyterian Church in Rushville d 9/4/35 at Rushville (typhus) (he was formerly of Vienna, Ontario Co.) (6-9/7)

STRONG, John m 10/23/37 at Rutland, VT. Lucy Jane Williams, dau. of the Chief Justice of Vermont; Rev. Hicks (5-11/1)

STRONG, mary - see BRAYTON, Wales

STRONG, William N. of Albany m 6/9/47 Sarah Adelaide Knox, dau. of John J., Esq. of Augusta, in Augusta; Rev. O. Bartholomew (1-6/18)

STROPE, Cornelius of Troy m 12/18/41 Mary Root of Sand Lake in Troy; Rev. D. Starks (5-12/22)

STROUGH, Catharine, 18, wf of Baltus, d 4/16/37 in Manheim (3-5/4)

STROUGH, John - see DAVIS, John P.

STROUGH, Lovina - see DAVIS, Moses

STROUGH, Lucinda - see DAVIS, John P.

STRYKER, Harriet, 56, mother of John, Esq., d 4/2/43 in Rome (funeral procession from the home of John, Esq. at 3 o'clock to the 2nd church at 3:30 pm, April 4) (1-4/4)

STUART, Mary - see NORTON, John. Jr.

STURGESS, Margaret S. - see STEARNS, Ransom S.

STURTEVANT, G.A. of West Troy m 3/6/39 Jane L. Viele, dau. of S.L. Esq., of Fort Miller, at F.M.; Rev. Joseph Perry of Sandy Hill (5-3/13)

STUYVESANT, Margaret - see VAN RENSSELAER, Robert

STYLES, John of NYC m 2/21/39 Letta Maria Onderdonk of Nyack at N.; Rev. Doing (12-3/5)

STYLES, Robert S., printer, of Kingston m 5/13/49 Philura Adeline Hatch, dau. of Warren Hatch of Burlington, VT; in B.; Rev. J.E. Converse (8-5/26)

SUITS, James N. m 7/7/47 Delia H. Sullivan, in Verona; Elder C.M. Lewis (all of Verona) (1-7/16)

SULLIVAN, Cornelia - see COOPER, Charles

SULLIVAN, Delia H. - see SUITS, James N.

SULLIVAN, Mary - see JOB, Thomas

SUMMERS, Jameson C. m 2/23/36 Susan M.P. Myer, dau of late Peter T.B. Myer, at St. Stephen's Church in NYC; Rev. W. Jackson (6-3/2)

SUMMERS, Samuel, 72, d (date not given) in Stratford (7-7/4/10)

SUNDERLAND, James (Rev.), rector of Zion Church, Rome, NY m 12/8/35 Rosetta Maria Perry, dau of Rev. Marcus A. Perry at the Zion Church in Rome; Rev. Marcus A. Perry (6-12/22)

SUPPELL, William M., 24, d 2/11/42 at home of his father (not named) in Boonville (was a student at the Black River Library and Religious Institute preparing to preach in a missionary field) (1-2/15)

SUPPLY, F. Wilson, merchant, of Cohoes m 10/25/36 Cornelia Caroline Clute, dau of Nicholas of Waterford, in W.; Rev. Slingerland (6-11/17)

SUTHERLAND, Daniel P. m 1/14/50 Hannah M. Carey, both of West Troy, in W.T.; Rev. O.H. Gregory (5-1/16)

SUTHERLAND, Edmund G. of Sing Sing m 5/8/39 Ann Eliza Felter, dau of Capt. Edward of Haverstraw, in H.; Rev. T.E. Witsell (12-5/14)

SUTHERLAND, Harriet, about 46, widow of John, d 9/25/39 at Middle Patent (12-10/8)

SUTHERLAND, Jane M. - see LIVINGSTON, V. Rensselaer

SUTHERLAND, Judith (Miss) d 1/1/1835 at home of her relative, Gen. James Talmadge of Waverly Place, NYC (6-1/10)

SUTHERLAND, Silas G., 19, printer, late of Albany and brother of Edmund G. of Haverstraw, d 11/28/35 in Haverstraw (6-12/4)

SUTHERLAND, William B. m 12/22/35 Sarah Murray, dau and only child of Rev. D. Limerick. She died 12/24/35 at Steubenville. This couple planned to spend the holidays with friends in Steubenville (from Wheeling, VA. Times)(6-1/12/36)

SUTLIFF, John of Rome m 9/24/50 Sarah Whitaker of Halifax, England at Utica; Rev. Perry (1-10/2)

SUTTER, John, 80, d 12/14/39 in Haverstraw (12-12/24)

SUTTON, Daniel B. of North Castle m 1/29/42 Martha Hall, dau of Isaac of Mount Pleasant, in M.P.; Rev. J.L. Dickinson (11-2/15)

SUTTON, Elizabeth (Mrs.), 52, d 4/28/39 suddenly in Peekskill (11-4/30)

SUTTON, Henry m 7/23/33 Mary Ann Haight; Squire Lent (all of Cortlandtown) (11-7/30)

SUTTON, Henry of Croton Valley m 9/16/35 Hannah Weeks, dau of Joshua of Peekskill, at Friends Meeting House in Peekskill (11-9/22)

SUTTON, Jane - see FLEWWELLIN, Barnabas

SUTTON, John m 11/20/42 Catharine Forman in Peekskill; Rev. Dr. Westbrook (all of Peekskill) (11-12/1)

SUTTON, Leonard of Yorktown m 1/16/39 Jane Haviland, dau of Park Haviland of Quaker Hill, Dutchess Co., at Q.H. (12-1/29)

SUTTON, Phebe Ann - see CUNNINGHAM, Edward

SUTTON, Purdy m 1/28/42 Sarah Waterbury, both of North Castle, in White Plains; Rev. Buck (11-2/15)

SUTTON, William m 3/23/39 Catharine Lynt, both of Greenburg, at G.; Rev. George Walker (12-4/2)

SWADE, Catharine A. - see GLATT, Anthony

SWAIN, Margaret M. - see MYERS, P. Hamilton, Esq

SWAN, Emily M. - see BENJAMIN, Joseph L.

SWART, Benjamin, about 50, d 8/10/49 in Saugerties (cholera) (8-8/18)

SWART, Chancy M. m 5/6/49 Catherine Lasher in Saugerties; Rev. N.H. Cornell
(all of Saugerties) (8-5/12)

SWART, Jacob N. m 1/31/16 Catharine Groat at Shenectady; Rev. Cumming
(6-2/7)

SWART, Jacob Van Loon, 2, youngest son of Cornelius L., d 11/3/36 (funeral at 3
o'clock from 294(?) Washington St.) (6-11/4)

SWARTOUT, Betsey, youngest dau. of Cornelius of Utica, formerly of Herkimer
County, d 5/11/37 at Michigan City, Indiana (3-7/13)

SWARTOUT, Margaret, 49, wf of Gen. Robert Swartout, d 7/12/35 in NYC
(6-7/18)

SWARTOUT, Matilda - see LILLYBRIDGE, Harrison

SWARTWART, John m 9/20/49 Mary E. Ketch in Olive; Martin Schutt, Esq. (all of
Olive) (8-9/29)

SWATLING, Mary Rebecca - see POLOCK, John

SWEATLAND, Lucy Ann - see KETCHUM, J.T.E.

SWEET, Benjamin G., 28, d 3/5/49 in West Troy (funeral 3/7 from the Methodist
Episcopal Church, funeral sermon by Rev. Jacob Leonard (5-3/7)

SWEET, Henry L. m 4/15/48 Phebe A. Earl, both of West Troy; Rev. Houghtaling
(5-4/19)

SWEET, Martin D. of Ann Arbor, Mich. m 7/25/44 Destamonia S. Higgins of
Rome; Rev. Haynes (1-7/30)

SWEET, Martin L. of Ann Arbor, Mich. m 7/25/44 Desdamona S. Higgins of Rome
(1-8/6)

SWEET, Orlando J. m 12/9/50 Mary M. Collins, both of West Troy; Rev. T.W.
Pearson (5-12/11)

SWEET, Rachel, 70, consort of Benjamin, d 5/1/39 (town not stated - possibly
Warren) (3-7/18)

SWEET, S.N., Professor of Elocution, m in Jefferson County 8/25/46 Emily Webb
of Rutland; W.H. Shumway, Esq. (1-9/8)

SWEET, Sarah Jane, 6, dau of Davis Sweet of Peekskill, d 9/16/33 (11-9/17)

SWEET, Stephen V.R., 52, d 8/8/46 in West Troy (for many years a West Troy
resident - survived by a widow and several children) (5-8/19)

SWEET, Stephen V.R., about 55, d 8/8/46 in West Troy (5-8/12)

SWEETLAND, Samuel E., merchant of Salina, Onondaga Co., m 9/28/35 Julia
Hall, dau of Jeremiah of Elmira in E. (6-10/17)

SWEZEY, Jane, 39, wf of the editor of the Independent Republican and dau. of late
Josiah Kitchel, Esq., d 11/7/42 at Goshen (9-11/12)

SWEZEY, Sarah E., 32, wf of William W., merchant, d 10/10/41 at Newport
(consumption) (3-11/4)

SWEZEY, William W., merchant, of Newport, Herkimer County m 10/11/42 Phebe
W. Crowell of St. Andrews, Orange Co., at the Theological Seminary in
Newburgh; Rev. James B. Ten Eyck (9-10/15)

SWIFT, Achna - see DALLIDA, James

SWIFT, Benjamin G. m 1/3/42 Elmira Pruyn, dau. of Francis H., Esq.; Elder
Richards (3-1/13)

SWIFT, Isaiah, 88(?), d 12/20/38 in Kent (12-12/25)

SWIFT, Lemuel D., 22, son of Philip of Little Falls, d "lately" at Clinton, Mich.

(3-10/12/37)

SWIFT, Maria - see VAN VRANKEN, S.A. (Rev.)

SWIFT, Melissa - see JONES, John

SWIFT, Nancy E. - see REMINGTON, Asa

SWITS, Jacob (Gen.), 75, d 11/21/35 at Schenectady (6-11/27)

SWITZ, Susan - see BOYLE, Matthias

SWORDS, James Davidson, 25, son of James, d 7/16/26 in NYC (6-7/21)

SYKES, Angela, 1, youngest dau of Asaph(?), d 11/22/36 (funeral at 3 o'clock from 23 Patroon St.) (6-11/23)

SYKES, Asaph, merchant, m 12/4/26 Lydia A. Phelps, both of Albany; Rev. Dr. Chester (6-12/8)

SYKES, Charlotte Dwight - see HAWS, Elvin

SYKES, John, 87, a Rev. War soldier, d 7/26/39 in Herkimer (3-8/1)

SYLVESTER, ---- (Mrs.), about 40, wf of William, d 12/18/41 at Cold Spring (11-12/28)

SYLVESTER, John R., senior proprietor of the Catskill Recorder, m 12/10/37 Urania C. Knapp, dau. of Edwin G. Knapp of Catskill, in NYC; Rev. Dr. Ferris (6-12/22)

SYLVESTER, Reuben m 12/9/39 Lucretia Shelly of Bedford in Bedford; Elder Fountain (12-12/24)

SYMONDS, Charlotte L. - see BEAUGRAND, Isedore D.

SYPHER, John m 8/4/39 Widow Hendricks; Rev. Lucky (all of Sing Sing) (12-8/20)

SYPHER, John, about 63, d 8/16/39 ("we are compelled to notice his marriage and his death in the same paper.") (12-8/20)

SYPHER, Mary, 59, wf of John, d 11/20/38 in Sing Sing (12-11/27)

TABALD, Jacob m 11/11/47 Mary Ann Wofful, both of Ava, Oneida County; George Riggs, Esq. (1-11/26)

TABER, Silas m 3/10/36 Rheua Waterbury, both of Nassau; Rev. W.F. Hurd of New Lebanon (6-4/1)

TABER, William m (date not given) Elizabeth Ann Vandenburgh in Albany; Rev. I.D. Williamson (6-2/13/36)

TABRAM(?), William G. m 4/23/46 Emma G. Glass; Rev. Dodge (all of West Troy) (5-4/29)

TABRAM, Emma Elizabeth, 9 months, dau. of William G. and Emma E., d 8/4/47 in West Troy (5-8/18)

TAFT, Elizebeth - see TREDWAY, Alfred

TAFT, James of Lee m 3/17/39 Margaret Vaughn of Frankfort in the Baptist Church, Frankfort; Rev. T. Houston (3-4/4)

TAFT, Mary A. (Mrs.) - see COPPINS, Richard

TAGGART, Samuel, member of Congress, m 3/23/16 Mary Ayres of Washington in Washington; Rev. Dr. Hunter (6-4/3)

TAHASH, Isaac m 6/3/49 Nancy Louisa Jones (both of Danube, Herkimer County) in Frey's Bush; Rev. John I. Wendell (4-6/7)

TAIT, Hannah - see MURDEN, Talbot

TALCOTT, Clarissa J. - see KENEY, Nathaniel

TALCOTT, Enoch B., Esq. of Oswego m 7/6/43 Mary Doolittle, dau. of Dr. Harvey Doolittle of Herkimer, in H.; Rev. Dr. Murphy (3-7/13)

TALCOTT, Jonathan - see HOUSE, ---- (Mrs.)

TALCOTT, Jonathan, 2nd, of Rome, NY m 9/29/46 Mary L. House of Glastonbury, Conn. at G.; Rev. Anton Snow (1-10/6)

TALCOTT, Jonathan, 93, d 7/28/47 in Rome (among the first settlers in Rome; member of the Presbyterian Church for more than 40 years) (1-8/6)

TALCOTT, Lucy Ann, 32, wf of Jonathan Talcott, 2nd, d 4/20/45 in Rome (1-4/29)

TALCOTT, Matthew, Esq., 56, brother of late Samuel A., d 10/1/37 in Utica (6-10/5)

TALCOTT, Noah - see WYCKOFF, Emily

TALCOTT, P.W. m 10/17/50 Mary E. Patten, dau. of Adam, Esq. of Rome, in R.; Rev. H.C. Vogell (1-10/23)

TALCOTT, Sally - see TANNER, William

TALCOTT, Samuel Austin, 45, late Attorney General of New York State, d 3/19/36 at NYC (6-3/24)

TALCOTT, Samuel Austin, 45, late attorney general of NY State, d 3/19/36 in NYC (3-3/31)

TALCOTT, William H. - see JENNINGS, Nancy

TALCOTT, William H., engineer of the Albany and West Stockbridge railroad, m 7/27/36 Harriet Williams, dau of Thomas of Vernon, at V.; Rev. H.P. Bogue (6-8/1)

TALLER, Rebecca Mrs., 68, d (date not given) at Windsor (7-6/20/10)

TALLMADGE, Betsey, 16, dau. of Seymour Tallmadge, Jr., d (date not given) at New Canaan (7-6/13/10)

TALLMAN, Effie, 52, wf of Isaac W., d 2/22/48 in West Troy (5-3/1)

TALLMAN, Horace of Providence, RI, m 2/24/42 Rebecca Guinn of Newburgh, NY; Rev. E.E. Griswold (9-3/12)

TALLMAN, Isaac W., 50, d 1/7/48 in West Troy ("long term member of the Methodist Episcopal Church) (5-1/12)

TALLMAN, John m 4/29/50 Caroline Rowe, both of West Troy; Rev. Houghtaling (5-5/1)

TALMADGE, Gen. James - see SUTHERLAND, Judith

TAMMANY, Mary C., 10, dau. of James, d 11/29/42 (9-12/3)

TANNATT, Margaret Gilmour, 7, dau of James S., d 6/20/39 in Cortlandt town (11-6/25)

TANNER, Lucina - see GRAY, Willard A.

TANNER, William m 1/23/43 Sally Talcott, dau. of Samuel, Esq., in Salisbury; Rev. Devendorf (3-2/2)

TAPLEY, Elizabeth, 59, wf of Daniel, formerly of County of Kent, England, d 6/27/42 in Westmoreland, NY (1-7/12)

TAPPAN, Sarah Harriet - see BRADLEY, Henry

TARBELL, Martha D. - see ROBERSON, William H.

TARBOX, Hepzibah - see LEWIS, James

TARBOX, Lydia (Miss), 25, dau. of Jonathan d (date not given) at Coventry (7-6/13/10)

TARR(?), Marianne Josephine - see CLARK, George

TARR, John B., formerly of West Troy m 2/24/46 Cornelia Rynders of Waterford at W. (5-3/4)

TATE, David S. m 7/25/41 Catharine Henry, dau of John Henry, all of Verplanck; Rev. Dr. Westbrook (11-7/27)

TATTERSELL, James, about 70, "a foreigner", d 5/15/09 in Catskill (7-5/17)

TAVER, John W. m 5/28/43 Orselia M. Clark, both of Stephentown in West Troy; Rev. Z. Phillips (5-5/31)

TAYLOR, ---- (Lieut.) of US Army and son of Hon. John W. of Ballston, NY, drowned (date not given) enroute from Fort Towson to Washington, Arkansas (6-12/7/35)

TAYLOR, A.z. of Lisbon, Kendall County, Illinois m 10/31/47 Miss A.R. Smith of Vernon Center at V.C.; Rev. R.A. Avery (1-11/5)

TAYLOR, Austin, 24, d 11/20/49 at Franklin, Delaware County (typhus fever) (4-12/6)

TAYLOR, B., Esq. - see WILSON, David W.

TAYLOR, Caroline - see STAATS, Phillip

TAYLOR, Charles J., merchant, of Albany m 8/7/26 Elizabeth Shepard of Brooklyn in Cleveland, Ohio; Rev. Bradstreet (6-8/22)

TAYLOR, Cornelia - see BRIGHAM, Lucius

TAYLOR, Cynthia - see AUSTIN, Milo S.

TAYLOR, Dorcas - see MATTICE, Joseph

TAYLOR, E.L. (Miss) - see HART, Gilbert B.

TAYLOR, Eliza - see WILSON, David W.

TAYLOR, H.R., merchant, of Apalachicola, Florida m 11/11/47 Ann Eliza Hochstrasser, dau. of Rev. Truman Seymour, at the Methodist Episcopal Church in West Troy; Rev. Truman Seymour (5-11/17)

TAYLOR, Hannah Jane - see LEE, John

TAYLOR, Hannah Mary, 17, dau. of Robert and Mary, formerly of West Troy, d 10/27/44 in Henry County, Illinois (5-11/20)

TAYLOR, James m 10/11/37 Maria Post in Little Falls; George Petrie, Esq. (all of Little Falls) (3-10/12)

TAYLOR, Joseph (Major), 67, d 1/16/36 at Hartford, Washington County ("was standing in his yard and died instantly") (6-1/20)

TAYLOR, Julia A. - see MILLS, Seth D.

TAYLOR, Lydia Ann - see GREENMAN, Adley

TAYLOR, Maria, 31, wf of M.L., d 7/29/43 in West Troy at the home of her father, James Lobdell (5-8/2)

TAYLOR, Morgan L. of Apalachicola, Florida m 9/22/42 Maria Lobdell, second dau. of James, Esq. of West Troy in W.T.; Rev. W.H.A. Bissell (5-9/28)

TAYLOR, Moses, Sr., 86, d 4/27/26 at Mount Pleasant near Newark, NJ (an old inhabitant of NYC) (6-5/5)

TAYLOR, Raymond - see SALISBURY, Caroline

TAYLOR, Robert W. m 12/15/35 Jane H. Woodruff, dau of Thomas T., Esq., at NYC; Rev. Dr. Broadhead (6-12/23)

TAYLOR, Sarah P. - see FEARING, George B.

TAYLOR, Sarah, only dau. of Richard, d 7/7/37 (funeral 7/8 from her father's home at 26 Washington Street) (6-7/8)

TAYLOR, Susan - see SEARS, Francis

TAYLOR, Sylvester of NYC m 5/20/45 Louisa A. Matteson of Rome in R.; Elder H.C. Vogell (1-5/27)

TAYLOR, William of firm of Chapman, Shields & Taylor m 12/31/35 Mary E. Barber; Rev. Vermilye (all of Albany) (6-1/1/36)

TAYLOR, William, Esq., 57, d 9/24/36 in Charlton (survived by his wife, 8 sons, and 2 daughters) (from the Ballston Spa Republican) (6-9/30)

TEACKLE, Elizabeth M., 5 years, youngest dau of James H. Teackle, Esq. and grand dau of Elisha Williams, Esq., formerly of Hudson, d 6/4/35 at Waterloo (scarlet fever) (6-6/8)

TEALE, Sidenus m 12/11/40 Sarah Ann Kempton at Fairfield; Rev. William Baker (3-12/24)

TEED, Nelson m 12/31/38 Jane Wilson, both of Somers, in S.; Rev. Leadbetter (12-1/8/39)

TEED, Sarah - see CULVER, Edward

TEEDS, Charles, about 35, d 9/3/42 in Somerstown (11-9/8)

TEESDALE, John of Philadelphia m 11/22/48 Isabella Patterson of West Troy in W.T.; Rev. T.F. Wyckoff (5-12/6)

TEETSELL, Hannah, about 58, wf of John, d 3/20/49 in Saugerties (8-3/24)

TEFFT, L.K., merchant, of Little Falls m 1/21/40 Frances P. Ames, dau. of Silas of Syracuse, in S.; Rev. Whiting (3-1/23)

TEFFT, Levinson, 40, wf of Daniel Tefft, Jr., d 4/13/43 in St. Johnsville (3-4/20)

TEFT, John of Minden m 10/10/49 Catharine Degarmo of Van Hornesville in V.H.; Rev. John D. Hicks (4-10/18)

TEFT, John, 81, a Rev. War soldier, d "lately" in Winfield, Herkimer County (3-2/16/37)

TELL, Elizabeth - see LANE, Savrin

TELLER, De Witt C. of Fort Plain m 1/1/50 Caroline Clark of Cooperstown in Minden (4-1/10)

TELLER, Eliza - see OLCOTT, James H

TELLER, Jacob V.B. m 6/17/35 Martha T. Akin, dau of William, at Greenbush (6-7/2)

TELLER, James W. m 4/10/33 Fanny Lee; Rev. William A. Hyde (all of Yorktown) (11-4/16)

TELLER, John A. of Hamptonburgh m 1/6/42 Sarah E. Hays of Montgomery in M.; Rev. Lee (9-1/15)

TEMPLE, ----, wf of Sir Greenville Temple and widow of late Hon. Thomas Russel of Boston, d (date not given) at Rome (7-2/7/10)

TEMPLE, Almira - see CONGER, Samuel

TEMPLE, Harvey of West Troy m 1/1/50 Harriet Sessions of Cohoes; Rev. O.H. Gregory (5-1/9)

TEMPLE, Mary - see PEER, Stephen H.

TEN BROECK, Christina C. - see IRELAND, Francis

TEN BROECK, Christina C. - see VAN RENSSELAER, Nicholas B.

TEN BROECK, H.W.B., Esq., formerly of Albany, NY, m 9/8/35 Eliza F. Clark of Mercer, PA at M; Rev. Isaac Beggs (6-9/15)

TEN BROECK, John C. (Major), 80, d 8/10/35 (funeral from home of late Thomas Hillhouse in Watervliet (6-8/11)

TEN BROECK, Louisa Caroline - see STAGG, John

TEN BROECK, Samuel S. m 3/16/36 Maria Parke, dau of Samuel, Esq., at Livingston; Rev. Van Waggenen (all of Livingston) (6-3/25)

TEN EYCK, Abraham, Jr., 68, d suddenly 2/14/46 at his home in West Troy (5-2/18)

TEN EYCK, Andrew, former assemblyman from Albany, m 2/4/36 Elizabeth Gay, dau of John of Coeymans, In C.; Rev. S. Kesam (?) (6-2/9)

TEN EYCK, Anthony, Esq., 66, of Schodack d 1/4/16 in Albany at the home of his son (not named) on Hamilton Street, Albany, ("where he had come for the benefit of his health")(in 1787 was a member of the Convention which ratified the Constitution) (6-1/13)

TEN EYCK, Anthony, Esq., counsellor at law, of Detroit, Mich, m 8/23/36 Harriet Elizabeth Fairchild, only dau of Rev. J.H. of Boston, at B.; Rev. J.H. Fairchild (6-9/3)

TEN EYCK, Catharine J. - see FOSTER, Jabez, Jr.

TEN EYCK, Catharine L. - see possibly COX, Stephen

TEN EYCK, Edward, 13, grandson of Abraham R., d 7/20/36 in Albany (6-7/23)

TEN EYCK, Elizabeth Ann - see YEARSLEY, George J.

TEN EYCK, George m 5/19/41 Huldah Maria Pratt, dau. of Job, in Salisbury; Elder H.N. Loring (3-5/27)

TEN EYCK, H.H., Esq., 42, postmaster of Leesville, Schoharie Co., d 12/3/36 at Leesville (6-12/10)

TEN EYCK, Harriet - see GAINS, John (Capt.)

TEN EYCK, Isaac - see possibly DENIKE, Jacob

TEN EYCK, Isaac, Sr. - see possibly, DENIKE, Isaac Sr.

TEN EYCK, Jacob - see DOUW, Lyntie

TEN EYCK, Jacob - see possibly DENIKE, Jacob

TEN EYCK, Jacob m 11/7/35 at Albany (see possibly DENIKE, Jacob m 11/7/35)

TEN EYCK, Robert - see possibly DENIKE, Jacob

TENNANT, Eliza C. - see HAIKES, Joseph M.

TENNANT, R.R. m 2/15/49 Eve Eliza Young, both of Van Hornesville, in V.H.; Rev. Jesse S. Robinson (4-2/22)

TENNEY, Martha Maria, 15 months, d 12/23/48 in West Troy (5-12/27)

TEPP, Edward, 45, d (date not given) in NYC (6-11/28/26)

TERRY, Adrian E., M.M., Professor of Chemistry at Bristol College, m 7/25/36 Louisa Gillingham of NYC in the Church of the Ascension in NYC; Rev. Professor Good. (6-7/29)

TERRY, Ann, 49, wife of Seth, Esq. and mother of Mrs. Daniel Gardiner of Troy, d 10/22/35 in Hartford, CT (6-10/29)

TERRY, Anne - see GARDNER, Daniel

TERRY, Daniel of River Head, Long Island m 9/18/42 Jane Eliza Carpenter in Yorktown; Rev. D. Devinne (11-9/29)

TERRY, George of Coeymans m 11/15/36 Phebe Harkes of New Baltimore at N.B.; Rev. John M. Pease (6-12/30)

TERRY, Gilbert, 15 months, son of David, d 2/17/26 funeral from 3 Maiden Lane (6-2/21)

TERRY, Sarah Ann - see CARRINGTON, Edward

TERWILLIGER, Isaac m 6/30/49 Miss H. DuBois, both of New Paltz; Rev. B.F. Wile (8-7/21)

THALHIMER, Elizabeth - see CROWNER, William

THATCHER, Henrietta M. - see HYDE, George C.

THAYER, Electa A. - see LEVETT, J.C.

THAYER, Eliza C. - see BALDWIN, Lyman M.

THAYER, Emily - see PARDEE, Bela

THAYER, Ezra, 72, d 8/15/37 (funeral 8/16 from "the second house south of the Rail Road on the Delaware turnpike") (6-8/16)

THAYER, Frances E. - see CRONK, Stephen A.

THAYER, George James Warren, only son of Mrs. Caroline M. Thayer, principal of the Female Academy at Clinton, Mississippi, d "in March last near Goliad, Texas (of a wound received in the cause of Texas")(was educated at Maysville College, Kentucky, served aboard the US ship "Vandalia" about two years and had returned recently to his mother's home in Clinton. Was in the Alamo about a month before the Fort was taken (more detail in this obit.) (6-8/13)

THAYER, George m 10/1/44 Frelove R. Whipple, both of West Troy; Rev. Dodge (5-2/9)

THAYER, Jenette - see HARRISON, William

THAYER, Joel E., Esq. - see LEVETT, J.C.

THAYER, Stephen Van Rensselaer of Rome m 2/1/42 Phebe Calista Carroll, dau. of Davis Carroll, Esq., of Springfield; Rev. S. Bowdish (1-2/8)

THERWILLAGER, Frederick of Whitestown m 1/6/47 Harriet Griswold of Kirkland at K.; Rev. Long

THOMAS, Abigail - see AMBLER, John V. (Rev.)

THOMAS, Amery, Esq., attorney at law m 7/4/36 Flora Butler, dau of Dr. A.R.R., in Alexander; Rev. J.S. Flagler (all of Alexander) (6-7/12)

THOMAS, David - see JONES, John (Capt.)

THOMAS, Edward m 11/29/41 Ann Sellek, both of Troy, in West Troy; Rev. D. Starks (5-12/1)

THOMAS, Elizabeth (Widow), 106, d 1/1/16 in Howe (6-1/10)

THOMAS, Emily Elizabeth, 3 months, dau. of James S. of Whitesboro, d 8/8/46 at Vernon Center (1-8/18)

THOMAS, Gilbert of Lee m 9/3/46 Lovina E. Champlin of Rome; Rev. G.S. Boardman (1-9/8)

THOMAS, Hiram m 12/8/35 Susan Winslow at Stamford; Rev. Fenton (all of Stamford) (6-12/22)

THOMAS, James P. m 3/15/37 Mary Carow, dau. of Isaac, Esq., in NYC; Rev. Dr. Milner (6-3/20)

THOMAS, Jeremiah, 49, d (date not given) at Salisbury (7-8/29/10)

THOMAS, John Alexander - see COLE, Thomas

THOMAS, John m 7/5/41 Mary Ann Evans, dau. of John, at Frankfort; Rev. Thomas Houston (all of Frankfort) (3-7/15)

THOMAS, Julia Ann - see SMITH, Edward

THOMAS, Mary A. - see LANGFORD, Philip B.

THOMAS, Mary Elizabeth - see BROWN, William

THOMAS, Mary R. - see WHITBECK, John

THOMAS, Rachel - see JONES, John (Capt.)

THOMAS, Sarah Elizabeth - see HANCY, Nelson

THOMPSON, ---- (Mr.), "the celebrated steam doctor", died (date not given), "under the operation of one of his own prescriptions", in Fairlee, VT (6-11/21/26)

THOMPSON, Alexander, M.D., m 12/24/34 Eliza M Burnham, dau of Eliazer, Esq., at Aurora, Cayuga Co.; Rev. C. Cook (6-1/16/35)

THOMPSON, Archibald J. m 3/29/37 Sally Seelye in Albany; Rev. C.P. Clarke (all of Albany) (6-3/31)

THOMPSON, Arietta M., wf of Gilbert L. and eldest dau. of late Daniel D. Tompkins of NYC, d 10/3/38 at Opelousas, Louisiana (6-11/21)

THOMPSON, B. Esq., counsellor at law, of Buffalo m 8/17/35 Esther Haviland, eldest dau of Grant Haviland of Glens Falls, in G.F.; Hon. Judge Barber (6-8/22)

THOMPSON, Benoni, Esq., of Buffalo m 8/17/35 Esther Heaveland of Queensbury in Q.; H. Barber, Esq. (6-8/21)

THOMPSON, Catharine - see RICE, Hamilton

THOMPSON, Edward, 25, son of Judge Thompson, d 1/2/26 in NYC (6-1/10)

THOMPSON, Electa - see FLEUR(?), Andrew

THOMPSON, Elizabeth Dove - see SEALLYBRASS, Martin

THOMPSON, Elizabeth W. - see HAND, Edward

THOMPSON, Helen E. - see SHEPARD, Edward

THOMPSON, Henry, merchant, of Little Falls m 6/10/39 Emily Start, dau. of Noah in Little Falls; Rev. Blodget (3-6/13)

THOMPSON, Jane H. - see EVERITT, Thomas T.

THOMPSON, John W, Esq., surrogate of Saratoga Co., m 3/29/35 Augusta Isabella Lee, dau of Joel Lee, Esq.; Rev. Babcock (all of Ballston Soa) (6-5/6)

THOMPSON, Joseph of NYC m 8/23/50 Ellen Milward of West Troy; Rev. Joshua Weaver (5-9/11)

THOMPSON, Lucy - see GAY, Horace

THOMPSON, Martha Ann - see RANSOM, Nicholas Huntley

THOMPSON, Nelson of Pen Yan m 7/15/39 Renette C. Miller of Newark, Wayne County in Little Falls; Rev. Thomas Towell (3-8/22)

THOMPSON, Richard S., 38, formerly of Peru, Mass., d 10/16/38 in Little Falls (a short illness) (3-10/18)

THOMPSON, Sarah - see SHERMAN, Ebenezer

THOMPSON, Sarah, 35, wife of Hon. Smith Thompson, d 9/22/33 at Poughkeepsie (11-10/1)

THOMPSON, Smith (Hon.) m 11/2/36 Eliza D. Livingston, dau of Henry, Esq., at Poughkeepsie; Rev. Thomas (6-11/7)

THOMPSON, Thomas - see SEALLYBRASS, Martin

THOMPSON, Thomas Jefferson, merchant, m 7/23/35 Elizabeth E. Dingman, both of NYC, at Galway, Saratoga Co.; Rev. Jenkes (6-7/30)

THOMPSON, Thomas S. of Saugerties m (date not given) Louisa Weaver of Hudson; Rev. Gosman (8-4/14/49)

THOMPSON, William of Troy m 2/24/41 Phebe Ann Smith of West Troy in W.T.; Rev. Crandall (5-3/10)

THOMPSON, William, 27, d 4/19/35 (funeral from his late home, 47 Columbia St.) (6-4/21)

THOMSON, Smith, formerly of NYC, m 6/18/44 Lavenia D. Dimmick, only dau. of late J.U.H. Dimmick of Savannah, Georgia, in Savannah; Rev. L.G.R. Wiggs (1-7/9)

THORN, James Harvey, 14 months, son of William, d 10/12/36 (friends of his father and of his mother-in-law, Mrs. Gager, invited to the funeral at 3 o'clock from 36 South Lansing Street) (6-10/14)

THORN, Sarah - see OSTRANDER, ---- (Mr.)

THORN, Sarah - see OSTRANDER, Matthew

THORNDIKE, Olive (Widow), 66, d (date not given) in Dunstable, Mass. (6-5/15/16)

THORNDIKE, William (Hon.), late President of the National Insurance Company of Boston, d in Beverly, MA (consumption) (6-7/23)

THORNE, Nicholas - see GASTON, Louisa S

THORNE, Sarah, 73, widow of Stephen, d (date not given) in NYC (6-12/26/26)

THORNLEY, Anthony of Philadelphia m 6/15/46 Alice Rawnsley of Trenton,
formerly of Lee, in Philadelphia (1-7/7)

THORNTON, Alvira - see WAKEMAN, Zalmon B.

THORNTON, Hester T. - see LORD, Edmond J.

THORNTON, Jane - see HUNTER, George

THORNTON, Lucy Ann - see MANCHESTER, James T

THORNTON, Mr. - see CHRISTIAN, John

THORP, Henry of NYC m 12/25/41 Rachel Lent of Peekskill in P.; Rev. William H.
Johnson (11-1/4/42)

THORP, Mary - see MC PARSONS, A.

THORP, Minerva, 10, dau. of Peter, d 2/14/10 in Catskill (7-2/21)

THORP, William of the firm of Thorp and Sprague m 6/3/35 Mary Powell; Rev.
Potter; all of Albany (6-6/4)

THRALL, Mary - see SHAUL, James

THROOP, Christina, 25, relict of Hamilton Throop, d 2/7/35 in Schoharie (6-2/20)

THROOP, Origin B. m 11/1/37 Mary Laura Michaels, dau. of William G., in
Schoharie; Rev. Dr. Lintner (all of Schoharie) (6-11/10)

THROP, William - see STOUT, Catherine

THUM, Laura - see HYSER, Aaron

THUMMEL, Elizabeth M., 19, wf of the Rev. C. Thummel and eldest dau of Henry
F. Cox, Esq., late of Canajoharie, d 12/15/35 at Clinton (6-1/4/36)

THURBER, Dr. Abner - see POND, Eveline E.

THURSTON, Thirza A. - see WENDALL, Gilbert A.

THURSTON, William - see WENDALL, Gilbert A.

TIBBETS, Charlotte C. - see HARTER, James

TIBBITS, Henry W m (date not given) Abby Ann Vradenberg in Rome (1-3/11/45)

TIBBITS, Julia M. - see DOIG, Daniel

TIBBITS, S.B. m 10/25/48 Mariette Clark 10/25/48 in Verona; H.C. Vogell
(1-11/2)

TIBBITS, Sally, 44, relict of the late Elisha Tibbits, Esq. of NYC, d suddenly
7/25/35 at Troy (6-7/28)

TIBBITS, Sarah, 48, wf of Jacob, d 1/2/41 in Rome (both of Rome) (1-1/5)

TIBBITTS, Cynthia - see BRILL, John

TIBBITTS, Sarah, 79, wf of George, d 7/31/46 in Troy (5-8/5)

TICE, Abraham, 52, d 7/23/39 at his home in Cortlandtown (11-7/30)

TICE, Charody - see SCRIBNER, David

TICE, George H., 55, d 1/10/42 suddenly in Newburgh (9-1/15)

TICE, Lewis m 9/1/41 Mary Jane Sherwood, both of Peekskill, in P.; Rev. William
H. Johnson (11-9/6)

TICE, Mary Jane - see LOUD, Samuel

TICKER, Joseph m 2/16/43 Mary Ann Ostrander in Stark; James Winegar, Esq.
(3-3/2)

TICKSON, William James, 23, late editor of the Livingston Journal, d 12/22/36 in
Covington (6-1/10/37)

TIEMAN, Nicholas of the firm of A. Tieman & Co. of NYC m 7/28/35 Mary Ann
Rothgangal of Rochester in R.; Rev. Dr. Whitehouse (6-8/3)

TIERNER, Sarah L - see SHERMAN, Watts

TIFFANY, L.F. of Buffalo m 4/27/37 Maria L. Patchen of Albany at St. Peter's Church; Rev. Alonzo Potter (6-4/28)

TILDEN, Barnard m 8/5/36 Mary Ann Mc Corie, both of Troy, in Albany; Rev. C.P. Clarke (6-8/8/36

TILDEN, Elam, Esq. - see PELTON, William S. (Dr.)

TILDEN, George Frederick, 18, son of Elam Tilden, Rsq. of New Lebanon, d 7/14/35 at New Lebanon (6-7/17)

TILDEN, Mary B. - see PELTON, William S. (Dr.)

TILLETSON, Gardner d (date not given) (his friends and those of Green Hall invited to his funeral at 3 o'clock from the home of Amos Fish, 26 South Pearl Street) (6-5/4/36)

TILLEY, Charlotte - see MONTROSS, Ambrose

TILLEY, James, 73, d (date not given) in New London (6-5/8/16)

TILLEY, William m 10/8/44 Mary Fild (sic), both of Augusta; Rev. S.H. Battin (1-10/15)

TILLINGHAST, Amelia C - see GASTON, N.B.

TILLINGHAST, Sylvanus, 71, d 3/9/43 in Little Falls (3-3/16)

TILLINGHAST, Thomas m 1/13/41 Nancy Ives in Norway, NY; Rev. L.O. Lovell (3-2/4)

TILLMAN, Lewis T., Esq., 53, d 3/26/36 in Troy (6-3/30)

TILLOTSON, Abigail (Mrs.), 88, dau. of late Ezra Backus, d 3/6/48 in Cazenovia where she had lived for more than 50 years (she was born in Norwich, Conn.) (4-3/16)

TILLOTSON, Matthew W., Esq., senior editor of the Ogdensburgh Republican, m 2/15/36 Eveline Stillwell, dau. of Hon. Smith Stillwell, at Ogdensburgh; Rev. Savage (3-3/17)

TILLOTSON, Matthew W., one of the editors of the St. Lawrence Republican, m 2/17/36 Eveline Stillwell, dau of S. Stillwell, Esq. of Ogdensburgh, at O.; Rev. J.A. Savage (6-3/5)

TILLOTSON, Tamer Ann - see SMITH, John

TILLOTSON, William of Geneva, Cayuga County m 10/17/37 Louisa Ouden of Jerusalem, NY at the home of Hon. Mordecai Ogden in Jerusalem; Rev. Thomas J. Champion (6-10/27)

TILMON, Emanuel L., 5 months, only son of Rev. L. Tilmon, d 3/19/50 in Rome (funeral service 3/21 at the home of Rev. Tilmon in Canal Village) (1-3/20)

TIMERMAN, Mary (Miss), 46, d 10/9/49 in Minden (a deaf mute) (4-10/11)

TIMERMAN, Nancy, 73, widow of late John D., d 2/9/50 in Frey's Bush (4-2/14)

TIMESEN, Eldert m 7/3/45 Elizabeth Groat in West Troy; Rev. T.F. Wyckoff (5-7/9)

TIMMERMAN, Catharine - see SNELL, Aaron

TIMMERMAN, Levi, 18, oldest son of Rev, Jacob and Elizabeth, d 6/27/48 in Frey's Bush (4-6/29)

TINKER, Abel m 3/6/42 Elizabeth Dearnsley, both of Mattewan; Rev. J. Johnston (9-3/26)

TINKER, Philander P. of Utica m 12/27/42 Mercy Ann Vincent of Little Falls; Rev. C.W. Leet (3-1/5/43)

TINKHAM, Deborah Jane - see COON, Van Rensselaer

TINNEY, Lumira S. - see WHEELER, William G.

TINNEY, Susannah (Miss), 45, d 9/20/47 (5-10/13)

TIRNEY, Peter m 5/22/41 Mary Ann Blevens, both of West Troy, in Albany; Rev. Kelly (5-5/26)

TITTARINGTON, David m 8/20/48 Elizabeth Gibson, both of Oriskany, at Rome; Rev. William E. Knox (1-8/25)

TITTLER, George, nearly age 90, d 3/27/39 in Sing Sing (a Rev. War soldier and pensioner) (born in Ireland) (12-4/2)

TITUS, Delana B. - see DOOLITTLE, Henry

TITUS, Susan, about 76, widow of John, d 4/28/39 in North Salem (12-5/7)

TOBIAS, Phoebe (Miss), 24, d 11/7/41 in Cornwall (9-11/13)

TODD, Abraham H. of South Salem m 1/9/39 Mary A. Horton, dau of Daniel of South East, in S.E.; Rev. Atwater (12-1/15)

TODD, Albert, Esq. of St. Louis, Missouri m 10/27/42 Jane Wilson, eldest dau. of Gould Wilson, Esq., in Little Falls, NY; Rev. Livermore (3-11/3)

TODD, Anna - see MC CORD, Samuel

TODD, Bede(?), 66, widow of late Dr. Stephen Todd of Salisbury, d 2/3/42 at the home of her son-in-law, Hon. A. Loomis in Little Falls (3-2/10)

TODD, Caroline W. - see GRIDLEY, G. Thomson

TODD, Dr. - see SPAULDING, Adeline

TODD, Eli M., Esq., about 55, d 11/12/45 in Waterford (5-11/19)

TODD, Elizabeth - see HALSTED, James D.

TODD, Elizabeth S. - see HALSTED, James D.

TODD, Horatio N. of Jersey City m 9/11/35 Jane Bennett of Brownville, Jefferson Co.; Rev. Price (6-9/15)

TODD, Susan A. - see INGHAM, Silas A.

TODD, Thnakful, 17, wf of Charles H. d 2/12/39 in Southeast (12-2/19)

TODD, William A. of Sawpit m 5/8/39 Angeline R. Mead of Bedford in B.; Rev. Varnard (12-5/21)

TODRIO, F.T. (Rev.), rector of St. John's Church in Ithaca, m 9/22/36 Louise Norton, niece of Chester Griswold of Utica, in Trinity Church, Utica by the Rector, the Rev. P.A. Proal (6-10/3)

TOLL, Maria, 23, dau. of Simon I. Toll, late of Schenectady, d 12/13/25 at Oppenheim (funeral sermon by Rev. David Devoe) (6-1/10/26)

TOLLEY, William, 49, Judge of the Greene County courts, d 10/10/36 at Athens (6-10/20)

TOMBLING(?), Mary Louisa - see NOONAN, Josiah A.

TOMBLING, Abijah (Dr.) - see NOONAN, Josiah A.

TOMPKINS. C.L. - see CAULKINS, Abby

TOMPKINS, Caroline - see DINGEE, Roswell

TOMPKINS, Daniel D. - see THOMPSON, Arietta M.

TOMPKINS, Eliza - see CONEY, Joseph

TOMPKINS, Elizabeth - see SIERINE, William

TOMPKINS, Elizabeth Ann, about 13, inly dau. of Gilbert H., d 3/16/40 in New Castle (12-3/24)

TOMPKINS, Joseph, 57, d (suddenly) 1/3/42 in Somers (11-1/18)

TOMPKINS, Miss - see WARD, Thomas

TOMPKINS, Nathaniel, 45, of Dutchess County, d 9/19/43 (typhus) (11-9/26)

TOMPKINS, Purdy m 3/6/33 Cornelia Ann Spock, dau of Stephen; Rev. Bartlett (all of Cortlandt) (11-3/12)

TOMPKINS, Susan - see BROWN, Daniel

TOMPKINS, Thomas, Esq., 75, d 8/28/42, suddenly, in Yorktown (11-9/1)

TOOMAS, Emily - see VANN, James

TOPMKINS, Amer - see CHAPIN, Josiah

TOPP, Sophia - see PORTER, John K.

TOPPING, Elizabeth, 21, wf of Henry, d (date not given) in NYC (6-11/28/26)

TORANCE, Lemuel m 8/26/40 Sylvinia Wright in Lee; Rev. Robert Dunn (all of Lee) (1-9/8)

TORRANCE, Jared S., Esq. of Buffalo m 10/7/42 Helen Wilson of Vernon; Rev. R.C. Brisbin (1-11/15)

TORREY, Elijah of Albany m 3/3/16 Arethusa Hall, dau. of Elias, Esq., of Hardwick, VT; in H.; Rev. Rawson (6-3/16)

TORREY, Joseph W., attorney at law of Detroit m (date not given) Caroline Collins, oldest dau. of Charles Collins, Lieutenant Governor of Rhode Island, at Newtown, Long Island (6-10/10/26)

TOTTEN, James G. (Lieut. Col.) of the US Engineers m (date not given) Oxiline Pearson, dau. of George Pearson at Waterford; Rev. D. Coe (6-2/17/16)

TOTTEN, Susan Ann - see SMITH, John

TOULAU, Maria - see GREEN, Robert

TOURTELOT, Augustus C., M.D., of US Army, d 12/8/37 at Washington City (formerly of Herkimer County and received appointment of Assistant Surgeon in US Army in 1836) (3-1/18/38)

TOURTELOT, Catharine, about 60, wf of Isaac, d 9/10/40 in Herkimer (3-9/17)

TOUSON, (General) - see JENKINS, Elisha (Col.)

TOWELL, Charles Hubert, 1, son of Rev. T. Towell, Pastor of Emmanuel Church in Little Falls, d 9/19/38 at Fairfield (where the infant had been carried for its health) (3-9/27)

TOWER, Charlemagne of Waterville m 6/14/47 Almmelie Malaina Bartle, dau. of late Lambert Bartle of Orwigsburgh, Schuylkill County, Penna., at Orwigsburgh; Rev. John A. Hoffmeir (1-7/2)

TOWN, Maria - see HOLMES, John W.

TOWN, Oliver W. m 3/10/36 Julia Ann Stodlar at Cohoes; L.V.K. Van Doren, Esq. (6-3/15)

TOWNER, Elizabeth, wife of James O. and dau of late Samuel Strang of Peekskill, d 10/28/41 at Ithaca (11-11/23)

TOWNER, Richard, 35, of firm of R. Towner & Co., lumber merchants of West Troy, and formerly of Peekskill, d 6/20/44 in West Troy (5-6/26)

TOWNSEND(?), Nancy, age blurred, wf of Joseph, d 5/18(?)/49 near Ellenville (8-6/2)

TOWNSEND, Alonzo m 12/23/38 Phebe Solomon, both of Patterson, in P.; Rev. Benedict (12-1/8/39)

TOWNSEND, Anna - see MARTIN, Henry H.

TOWNSEND, Daniel J. of Peru, Illinois m 9/26/37 Jane M. Porter, youngest dau. of Hon. Augustus Porter, at Niagara Falls; Rev. Harris (6-10/3)

TOWNSEND, Hannah H. - see MARTIN, George B.

TOWNSEND, Harriet C. - see HENRY, Peter Seton

TOWNSEND, James B. of Washington County m 8/6/39 Cordelia Dunning of Fairfield in F.; Rev. James B. Townsend (3-8/22)

TOWNSEND, John P., M.D., m 9/8/36 Catharine Louisa Douw, dau of late John

D.P. Douw, Esq., in Albany; Rev. Vermilyea (6-9/10)

TOWNSEND, Laura - see DANIELS, John

TOWNSEND, Maria, 47, wf of Dr. Charles D., d 11/12/35 (6-11/13)

TOWNSEND, Mary - see PECKHAM, John

TOWNSEND, Samuel of the firm of Townsend and Shields d 7/16/35 (illness of 4
    weeks) (funeral from his late residence 5 o'clock, 27 Dean Street) (6-7/17)

TOWNSEND, Stephen - see PECKHAM, John

TOWNSEND, William H. m 12/3/35 Sarah Ann Austen, dau of David in NYC;
    Rev. Wheeler (6-12/5)

TRACY, Avery, d 3/14/36 at his home in Watervliet ("left a wife and 7 children")
    (6-3/15)

TRACY, Charles, Esq. of Rome, NY m 8/31/37 Louisa Kirkland, dau. of Gen.
    Joseph, in Utica (6-9/16)

TRACY, Content, 30, wf of Dr. L.M. Tracy, formerly of Cohoes, d 11/29/43 at
    Mechanicville, Saratoga County (5-12/6)

TRACY, Elizabeth - see FIDLER, Nathan

TRACY, Emma - see MYERS, Philip A.

TRACY, Frederick J., 29, son of Jabez, d 10/26/48 in Lee (consumption) (1-11/2)

TRACY, George H., Esq. of Troy m 4/20/36 Helen E. Woodruff, dau of James Esq.
    of Albany, in Albany; Rev. Professor Yates of Schenectady (6-4/27)

TRACY, Hannah, 64, wf of Nathaniel, Esq., d 8/18/44 in Rome (1-9/3)

TRACY, Julia Frances - see VAN VALKENBURGH, Daniel (Rev.)

TRACY, Maria - see MYGATT, Henry R.

TRACY, Mary H. - see MOREY, John H.

TRACY, Philemon (Dr.), 79, father of the Hon. Albert H. Tracy, d 4/30/37 in
    Norwich, Conn. (from the Norwich Currier) (6-5/8)

TRACY, Susan - see BAGG, Moses

TRACY, Uriah - see ROBBINS, Caroline

TRACY, William Baldwin, 4, son of Dr. I.M. Tracy, d 8/6/36 in Cohoes (6-8/8)

TRASK, Israel E. (Col.) of Springfield, MA d suddenly 11/25/35 at the home of his
    brother (name not given) near Woodville, Mississippi (6-12/29)

TRASK, Sally, 42, wf of James, d 11/9/42 in Russia, NY (3-11/17)

TRASK, Wyman of Little Falls m 12/25/42 Frances A. Sheldon of Norway, NY at
    Grace Church in Norway; Rev. Baker of Fairfield (3-12/29)

TRAVER(?), Amanda - see COBOT, William H.

TRAVER, Betsey - see STOUTENBURGH, Tobias

TRAVIS, Aaron m 5/25/41 Sarah Beedle, both of Peekskill; Rev. Marshall (11-6/1)

TRAVIS, Adeline - see MERRITT, Solomon

TRAVIS, Elijah, about 90, d 7/28/39 in Cortlandt (a short illness) (11-8/6)

TRAVIS, Henry m 1/30/39 Emeline Hopkins, dau of Joseph, in Carmel; Rev.
    Warren (all of C.) (12-2/5)

TRAVIS, Hinman N., 8, son of Capt. Hiram, d 3/19/42 in Peekskill (11-3/21)

TRAVIS, John m 2/17/42 Eliza Hains in Southeast; Elder John Warren (11-2/22)

TRAVIS, Lewis of Yorktown m 3/3/42 Elizabeth Wright in Carmel; Elder John
    Warren (11-3/15)

TRAVIS, Mary - see WILLIAMS, George

TRAVIS, Nathaniel of Peekskill m 11/30/47 Ellen Eliza Billings of West Troy; Rev.
    Houghtaling (5-12/15)

TRAVIS, Robert, 82, d 4/15/39 in Somers (12-4/23)

TRAVIS, Sarah, 21, widow of late Joseph, Esq., d 1/15/35 in Peekskill (11-1/20)

TRAVIS, Silas, 29, d (date not given) in Somers (12-2/18/40)

TRAVIS, Stephen m 4/2/45 Caroline M. Urann, dau. of Charles L. of Peekskill, both formerly of West Troy, in Peekskill at the home of Mr. Hall; Rev. Dr. Westbrook (5-4/16)

TRAVIS, William T. m (date not given) Betsey Reynolds, both of Somers, at the Friends Meeting, Croton Valley. (12-3/26/39)

TREADWAY, Sarah W. - see LAKE, Isaac

TREAT, Alfred A., m Julia Schermerhorn, dau of Casper, at Roxbury; Rev. David Mead (6-8/13)

TREAT, Richard S., Esq., 87, d 5/22/37 (funeral 5/23 from his late home on North Market Street) (6-5/23)

TRED, Richard of Somers m 9/11/49 Julia (surname blurred) of Carmel in C.; Rev. Henry G. Livingston (10-9/19)

TREDWAY, Alfred m 9/30/46 Elizabeth S. Taft, dau. of Newell, Esq., in Lyons (all of Lyons) (1-10/6)

TREDWAY, John - see BILL, Mary Ann Tredway

TREDWAY, John, 63, d 5/5/47 at Western (funeral at his home in Western 5/7/ at one o'clock) (1-5/7)

TREDWAY, Lydia B. (Mrs.) - see HAYDEN, Orange

TREMPER, Gertrude (Mrs.) of Kingston d 8/20/36 in Albany at the home of her sisters, "the Misses Cantine", in Albany (6-8/24)

TRENAM, Daniel m 4/19/46 Lydia Cristy, both of Whitestown in W.; Elder Paddock (1-4/21)

TRENAM, Octavus F. m 5/28/49 Mary M. Shepard, eldest dau. of Noble, Esq., in Rome; Rev. F.H. Stanton (bride and groom of Rome) (1-5/30)

TRENHAM, ____ - see ADSIT, Sylvanus

TRIP, Hannah - see DEAN, Bradford C.

TRIP, Salome - see GLASS, H. Samuel

TRIPP, Jacob, 21, son of Samuel, d 12/4/39 in New Castle (12-12/24)

TRIPP, Margaret - see WILLIAMS, Cyrus

TRIVETT, Sarah Jane, 35, wf of James and dau. of Joseph I. Jackson of Fishkill, d 8/19/49 in Poughkeepsie (8-8/25)

TROTTER, Anna Maria, 12, d 12/2/15 (funeral 12/7 from 438 South Market St.) (6-12/6)

TROTTER, Jane (Miss), d (date not given) (funeral from home of John Trotter, 20 North Market St. at 3 o'clock) (6-11/29/36)

TROUP, Robert R., eldest son of late Robert, Esq., d 11/27/36 in NYC (6-12/1)

TROWBRIDGE, ----, 4 months, son of Orson(?) and Elizabeth, was "found dead in his mother's arms in Southeast... on the morning of the 12th of January"(1840) (12-2/4)

TROWBRIDGE, James, 21, (son of Samuel of Sing Sing), late of firm of Gelston, Ladd & Co. of NYC, d 9/9/39 in NYC (buried in Sing Sing) (12-9/17)

TRUAX, Catharine W., 26, dau. of Henry, d 7/12/26 in Albany (6-7/21)

TRUESDALE, Jane - see MC DOUGALL, Peter

TRUESDALE, Sybil, 71, relict of Samuel, d 11/18/39 in North Salem (12-11/26)

TRUMBULL, Alonzo of Ithaca m 2/8/41 Lucy Ann Chidney of Florence in F.; Calvin Dawley, Esq. (1-2/16)

TRUMBULL, George m 1/23/35 Charlotte Bailey; Rev. Dr. Sprague (6-3/3)

TRUMBULL, J. Abner of Ephratah, Montgomery Co. m 1/28/35 Rosiana Hanay of Schenectady in Schen.; Rev. J. Trumbull Backus (6-1/31)

TRUMBULL, Jonathan, Esq., 69, governor of Connecticut, d 7/7/09 at his home in Lebanon (7-8/16)

TRUMBULL, Mary Ann - see BROWN, Edwin

TRUMPBOUR, ---- (Mrs.) - see ACKER, John

TRUMPBOUR, Mrs. - see ACKER, John

TRYON, Anna - see HULSEY, William

TRYON, Josiah, 61, d (date not given) at Lewiston (6-1/20/26)

TUBS, Hannah (Mrs.), about 65, formerly of Cambridge, NY, d (date not given) at Colchester ("Editors of the Northern papers are requested to publish the above for the information of an absent husband") (7-6/27/10)

TUCKER, Dunton (Capt.) of Little Falls m 2/15/38 Ann Eliza Wooleber, dau. of Nicholas of Herkimer, in H.; Rev. Spinner (3-3/1)

TUCKER, Floyd of Bedford m 10/21/39 Ann Baker of Wilton in Bedford; Rev. Jacob Timberman (12-11/5)

TUCKER, Harriet E. - see FRANCIS, John M.

TUCKER, Mary Ann Richardson - see HOPKINS, William

TUCKER, Mary, 31, wf of J.M.T. Tucker, Esq., assistant editor of the Troy Whig, d 10/20/48 in Syracuse (5-11/1)

TUCKER, Rhoda - see MAIN, Thomas

TUCKER, Sarah - see BALCH, Lewis H.

TUCKER, Sarah (Mrs.), 78, d 12/20/47 in West Troy (long term member of the Methodist Episcopal Church) (5-12/22)

TUCKER, William A., 5, son of William and Lucenia, d 7/22/45 in West Troy (funeral 9/24 at 10 o'clock at the Methodist Episcopal Church) (5-9/24)

TUDOR, Edmund H., 23, son of Henry Tudor of Newburgh, NY, d 9/8/41 at Napoleon, Arkansas (yellow fever taken at Vicksburgh, Mississippi) (9-12/25)

TULFURD, Charles Philips, 1, son of Alexander, d 6/16/42 in Newburgh (scarlet fever) (9-6/18)

TULLY, William, Esq., judge of Greene Co. court, d 10/18/35 in Athens (6-10/15)

TUNNECLIFF, William, 59, merchant, d 8/3/36 at Warren (apoplexy) (6-8/8)

TUNNINGTON, John m 2/2/42 Ann Southall in Sing Sing; Charles Yoe, Esq. (all of S.S.) (11-2/15)

TUNSTALL, Stephen m 1/17/44 Delia Lunt; Rev. J. M. Pease (all of Peekskill) (11-1/23)

TUPPER, James m 1/5/41 Prudence M. Bronson of Lee Center at L.C.; Rev. H.C. Vogell (1-1/19)

TUPPER, Mary Esther, 2, dau. of George O. and Mary Ann, d 6/25/38 in West Troy (5-6/27)

TURK, Katharine Livingston - see BLOORE, J.

TURNBULL, Robert J. of South Carolina m 2/16/47 Cornelia P. Van Rensselaer, dau. of late Stephen of Albany, at NYC; Rev. Cortlandt Van Rensselaer (5-2/24)

TURNER, Amanda M. - see MYER, Abraham J.

TURNER, Amelia - see CRONK, Thomas P.

TURNER, Clarissa M. - see SELKREG, John B.

TURNER, Mrs. - see CROOK, Almina

TURNER, R.B. of Hamilton, formerly of Verona, m 5/30/44 Catharine A. Havens, youngest dau. of Joseph of Westmoreland, at W.; Rev. Isaac Swart (1-6/18)

TURNER, Thomas, Esq., accountant of the Navy department, d 3/15/16 at his seat in Georgetown (6-3/27)

TURTELOTT, Catharine, 50, wf of Isaac, d 9/9/40 in Schuyler (3-9/24)

TUSKER, John, 74, mechanic, d 8/2/37 in Little Falls (an early settler there - "father of a numerous family") (3-8/3)

TUTHILL & MOORE - see MOORE, Emmet

TUTHILL, Baldwin m 1/20/42 Lucy Barnes at Camden; Rev. Barton (1-1/25)

TUTHILL, Betsey, 68, wf of Daniel, d 8/12/47 in Lee (1-8/20)

TUTHILL, Charles E. m 12/23/49 Sarah Lincoln, both of NYC; Rev. James Erwin (1-1/2/50)

TUTHILL, Julia Ann - see DEWING, Jared

TUTHILL, Martha, 9 months, dau. of Samuel, d 11/29/41 in Newburgh (9-12/4)

TUTTLE, Adah M. - see REES, Ambrose

TUTTLE, Alanson of Fairfield m 3/9/43 Elmina Bowen of Manheim in M.; Rev. B.I. Devendorph (3-3/30)

TUTTLE, Ann - see AYRES, Hiram

TUTTLE, Chauncy of Salisbury m 3/16/43 Phebe J. Fuller of Fairfield in F.; Rev. Howard (3-3/23)

TUTTLE, Eliza C. - see GRAVES, Albert

TUTTLE, Harriet - see IVES, Chauncey

TUTTLE, Henry B. of firm of A. Groesbeck & Co. m 10/10/37 Emeline Reed in Lansingburgh; Rev. P.F. Phelps (all of Lansingburgh) (5-10/25)

TUTTLE, Jacob m 2/20/41 Margaret Conklin, both of Cortlandtown; Rev. William H. Johnson (11-2/23)

TUTTLE, John - see LOCKWOOD, Clarissa

TUTTLE, Stephen of U.S. Army, a native of Hanover, N.J., d 1/22/35 at St. Augustine, FL (6-2/23

TUTTLE, William, 12, drowned (date not given) (the ice broke as he attempted to cross a pond on his way to school in Nottingham, NH) (6-12/29/26)

TUTTLE, Zophis M., Esq., 61, d 4/21/42 in Salisbury (3-5/19)

TUYKE, Margaret (Mrs.) - see WALDRON, Resolved

TWIGGS, John (Major General), d (date not given) near Augusta (6-5/8/16)

TWING, A.T., rector of Trinity Church, Lansingburgh m 10/13/45 Amelie E. Barker, dau. of late Calvin Barker of Lansingburgh; Rev. Bissell (5-10/22)

TWING, Lavonia P., 37, wf of Rev. A.T. Twing, rector of Trinity Church, Lansingburgh and formerly of West Troy, in Lansingburgh (5-6/28/43)

TWITCHELL, William, 20, son of David, Esq., d 8/19/41 in Lee (1-8/24)

TYLER, Eliza May (Miss), 23, dau. of Moses, d 8/10/41 in West Troy (members of the Reformed Dutch Church) (5-8/18)

TYLER, Eliza, 33(?), wf of Moses, d 11/28/41 in West Troy (5-12/1)

TYLER, Martha D. - see BENEDICT, Lewis

TYLER, Mary - see CORNELL, Robert

TYLER, Moses m 12/31/35 Eliza Alger; Rev. Bronk (all of Watervliet) (6-1/7/36)

TYLER, Olive S., 60, wf of Daniel, d 12/19/41 in West Troy (5-12/22)

TYMESON, Cornelius m 10/28/35 Sarah Ann Van Benthuysen, dau of V. Van Benthuysen of Watervliet, in W.; Rev. Chittington (6-10/30)

UDELL, Adelaide M., 1 yr, dau. of William C. and M. d 3/4/45 (1-3/11)

UDY, Dolly, d (date not given) in Concord, North Carolina "by hanging herself with a bandana handkerchief (tied) to the limb of a tree") (she had been left an orphan while very young) (7-7/4/10)

UFFORD, Daniel of Lee m 1/26/48 Sylvia J. Higgley of Western in Rome; Rev. F.H. Stanton (1-1/28)

UHLE, Irving, 1 year, son of Henry Uhle, d 7/7/38 in Little Falls (3-7/12)

UHLE, James H. of Little Falls m 1/1/43 Lana M. Phillips, dau. of Col. George W. Phillips of Fairfield, in Herkimer; Rev. John P. Spinner (3-1/5)

UNDERHILL, Abraham S., 77, d 5/5/41 at his home in Yorktown (11-5/11)

UNDERHILL, Ann V., about 27(?), wf of Jesse H., d 3/27/40 in New Castle (a member of the Society of Friends) (died of "hasty consumption") (12-4/14)

UNDERHILL, Harriet - see WATERMAN, Andrew Jackson

UNDERHILL, James, 81, d 9/3/49 at West Branch (1-9/12)

UNDERHILL, Maria - see CARPENTER, Job

UNDERHILL, Mary - see LEPAREUX, Alexander

UNDERHILL, R.L. m 8/25/36 Frances Minerva Howell, dau of Hon. Edward, in Bath; Rev. Bostwick (6-9/5)

UNDERHILL, Robert L. m 8/25/36 Frances Minerva, dau of Hon. Edward Howell, at Bath; (all of bath) Rev. Bostwick (6-9/13)

UNDERHILL, Sarah Ann, 2, dau. of G.W., d 12/22/41 (9-12/25)

UNDERHILL, Sarah, 74, wf of Daniel, d 11/24/38 in Bedford (12-12/11)

UNDERHILL, William m (date not given) Elizabeth Kissam at Cow Neck, Long Island (6-5/22/16)

UNDERWOOD, Flora Virginia, 11 months, only dau. of John C. and Maria G., d 9/18/41 in Herkimer (3-9/23)

UNDERWOOD, John C., Esq. of Herkimer m 10/24/39 Maria Gloria Jackson, dau. of late Hon. Edward B., at Valley View, Fauquier County, Virginia; Rev. George Lentman (3-11/14)

UNDERWOOD, Joseph, 55, formerly of Massachusetts, d 7/30/35 at Cohoes (6-8/6)

UPFOLD, George, 64, formerly a schoolmaster in Albany, d 11/3/26 in NYC (6-11/7)

UPHAM, Timothy, M.D., 37, d 8/7/43 in Waterford (5-8/16)

UPPHOR, George P. (Lieut.) of US Navy m Margaret Eyre, dau of Gen. Severn E. Parker; Rev. Jackson (all of Northampton, VA) (6-7/13)

UPSON, Charles, Esq., 57, of Waterbury, d (date not given) at East Haven (7-5/24/09)

URANE, John - see SILLIMAN, Sarah A.

URANN, Caroline M. - see TRAVIS, Stephen

URANN, James R. of West Troy m 3/2/48 Catharine Ferrell of Troy in T.; Rev. Baldwin (5-3/8)

URTICK, Stephen C., 63, (brother-in-law to the late editor of the New York Gazette, J. Lang, Esq.) d 11/11/37 near Cincinnati, Ohio (6-11/27)

USHER, Martha M. (Mrs.) - see MILLS, Samuel

USHER, William, about 22 months, d 8/17/40 in Little Falls (3-8/20)

UTLEY, David, Esq. of Rome m 4/24/50 Catharine Marsh of New York City; Rev. Dr. Price of NYC (1-5/8)

UTLEY, H., M.D., of Western m 5/1/48 Caroline S. Butler, dau. of Ezekiel, Esq., of Rome; H.C. Vogell (1-5/12)

UTTER, Agatha, 11, dau. of Abraham and Eliza, d 12/2/47 at Canajoharie (5-12/8)

UTTER, Harriet - see CREGO, Paul

UTTER, Joel, about 70, d 2/26/42 in Bedford (11-3/15)

UTTER, John (Capt.), 45, d 1/17/37 at Duanesburgh (6-1/23)

VAIL, Aaron, Esq., Charge' d'affairs of the US at the British Court, m 8/24/35 at
Paris Emilie Laurencine Salles, dau of late Laurent Salles, Esq. of NYC, at
the Legation and in the presence of the Charge' d'affairs and Consul of the
US. (6-10/12)

VAIL, David M., 31, d 6/5/49 in West Troy (5-6/6)

VAIL, Kate, infant dau. of David M. and Elizabeth, d 5/2/49 in West Troy (5-5/9)

VALCK(?), Abraham F. m 11/3/49, between 8 and 9 P.M. on board the steamboat
"Robert L. Stevens", Maria Hummel; Rev. H. Ostrander, D.D. (all of
Saugerties) (8-11/10)

VALCK, Betsey Adaline - see JOY, Tjerck

VALENTINE, Maria - see MORGAN, Sarah

VALENTINE, Mathias, 41, d 9/13/33 at Westchester (11-10/1)

VALENTINE, Rev. - see MC DOWELL, Margaret

VALLEAU, Peter R. m (date not given) Eleanor Houseworth in NYC (6-6/5/16)

VAN ALEN, John A., about 63, d 1/26/36 in Albany (formerly of Columbia
County) (firends and members of the Mechanic's Benefit Society invited to
his funeral at 3 o'clock from 73 Hamilton Street) (6-1/28)

VAN ALEN, Samuel m 2/6/40 Catharine E. Horton, both ofMount Pleasant, in Sing
Sing; Rev. J. Luckey (12-2/11)

VAN ALEN, Teunis, about 80, d 5/17/35 at Kinderhook (6-5/23)

VAN ALLEN, Jane A. - see CARVER, Richard

VAN ALSTINE, C.N. (Gen.) - see FINK, Henry

VAN ALSTINE, Catharine - see FINK, Henry

VAN ALSTINE, G.P. - see DEAVENBURGH, P.W. (Rev.)

VAN ALSTINE, Mary, 38, wf of Peter, d 3/25/36 at Troy (a lingering illness)
(3-3/31)

VAN ALSTINE, Mary, 39, consort of Nicholas N., Esq. and dau. of late John
Beardslee, Esq. of Manheim, d 1/25/37 at Canajoharie (3-2/2)

VAN ALSTINE, Sarah M. - see DEVENBURGH, P.W. (Rev.)

VAN ALSTYNE, Betsey Maria - see SMITH, George

VAN ALSTYNE, Eliza J. - see LANSING, A.Y.

VAN ALSTYNE, Eliza J. - see LANSING, A.Y.

VAN ALSTYNE, Mary, 38, wf of Peter, d 3/25/36 at Troy (6-3/29)

VAN ALSTYNE, Nicholas S., Esq., 40(?), d 1/6/49 in Canajohjarie (4-1/18)

VAN AMBURGH, Anna - see DRAKE, Jolen J

VAN ANTWERP, Isaac m 12/22/42 Catharine Hartman, both of Little Falls; Rev.
C.W. Leet (3-1/5/43)

VAN ANTWERP, James, 33, merchant, d 12/7/36 in Herkimer (survived by a wife
and a son) (3-12/15)

VAN ANTWERP, Maria - see VAN DER CARR, Abraham

VAN ARDEN, Gertrude - see VAN VECHTEN, Abraham

VAN ARNAM, Catharine - see CURTIS, Daniel

VAN ARNUM, Martha A. Wescot, 32, wf of Newcomb J. Van Arnum, formerly of
West Troy, d 1/31/50 in new Orleans (consumption) - "Albany papers
please copy" (5-2/13)

VAN ARNUM, William H. m 6/14/46 Mary Dewey, both of West Troy, in W.T.; James M. Barnard, Esq. (5-6/17)

VAN BENTHUYSEN, James P, 62, d 5/8/35 (a "lingering illness") (funeral at 4 o'clock from home of his brother, O.R. Benthuysen, 85 Lydius St.) (6-5/11)

VAN BENTHUYSEN, Sarah Ann - see TYMESON, Cornelius

VAN BENTHUYSEN, Sarah, 52, wf of O.R. Van Benthuysen, d 11/9/37 (funeral 11/11 from her late home, 94 Lydius Street (6-11/10)

VAN BENTHUYSEN, Sophia, formerly of Schenectady, d 11/23/42 at home of Rev. Samuel Phinney in Newburgh (9-11/26)

VAN BENTHUYSEN, Susan (Mrs.), 52, d 6/22/37 (her husband, Benjamin and her son-in-law, Thomas Mc Mullen, are mentioned - funeral from her late home at 85 Herkimer Street) (6-6/24)

VAN BERGEN, ----, wf of Peter. Her funeral 7/11/37 from 11 Van Schaick Street, Albany (6-7/11)

VAN BEUREN, Cortland - see AYMAR, Benjamin

VAN BEUREN, Cortland - see SCHENCK, Adeline

VAN BEUREN, Elizabeth - see AYMAR, Benjamin

VAN BOSKERCK, John L. - see possibly VAN ROSKERCK, John L.

VAN BOSKIRCK, Simon of Glensville m 6/23/49 Mary A. Mosley of Rome in R.; Rev. W.E. Knox (1-7/4)

VAN BRAMER, ----, 73, widow of Thomas, d 1/8/49 in Kingston (8-1/27)

VAN BROECK, Delia, about 64, wf of Nicholas and mother of "numerous children", d 1/27/37 in Danube (3-2/2)

VAN BRUNT, Sarah - see JACKSON, Joseph H.

VAN BUREN, A., Esq. m (date not given) Catherine Hogeboom in Claverack (6-5/18/16)

VAN BUREN, Abraham (Major) eldest son of the President of the United States m 11/27/38 Sarah Angelica Singleton, youngest dau. of Richard Singleton, at her father's home in Sampler District, South Carolina; Rev. Converse (3-12/20)

VAN BUREN, Elizabeth - see COCKBURN, William

VAN BUREN, J. m 6/4/49 Miss M.L. Ruff, both of Albany, in A.; Rev. T.F. Wickoff (5-6/6)

VAN BUREN, Jane, 58, sister of the President of the U.S. d 6/19/38 at Kinderhook (5-6/27)

VAN BUREN, Louisa - see HARRISON, William

VAN BUREN, Mary Fisher - see WILSON, John, M.D.

VAN BUREN, Peter - see WILSON, John, M.D.

VAN CAMP, David of Jefferson County m 3/15/48 Elmira J. Elliot of Fort Plain; Rev. Dr. Mc Lean (4-3/16)

VAN CLEVE, Horatio P. (Lieut.) of the US Army m 3/22/36 Charlotte Ouisconsin, dau of late Major N. Clark of the Army, at Fort Winnebago; Rev. Henry Gregory (6-4/29)

VAN CORTLAND, Pierre, Jr. of Peekskill m 6/14/36 Catharine Elizabeth Beck, dau of T. Romeyn Beck; Rev. Dr. Campbell (6-6/16)

VAN CORTLANDT, Catharine - see FORSHAY, Schuyler

VAN CORTLANDT, Philip, 70, d 4/9/40 at Syracuse (12-4/14)

VAN DALFREN, Sarah (Miss), 26, d 9/19/35 at the home of her brother-in-law, Col. Abraham Verplank in Coeymans (6-9/22)

VAN DER BECK, James J. m 9/26/49 Elizabeth Fiero, dau. of Christian, deceased; Rev. H. Ostrander, D.D. (all of Saugerties) (8-9/29)

VAN DER CARR, Abraham of Middletown m 11/10/36 Maria Van Antwerp of Waterford; Rev. Slingerland (6-11/17)

VAN DERVOORT, Ida - see JOHNSON, Andrew J.

VAN DEUSEN, Gertrude, 56, relict of Francis, d 11/29/37 (her brother-in-law, Jacob Brinkerhoff is mentioned - funeral from home of J. and T. Brinkerhoff on Hudson Street, west of Eagle Street) (6-11/30)

VAN DEUSEN, Lucina, (her age not given), dau. of William J., Esq., d 9/4/48 at Union Centre in the town of Canajoharie (illness of two days) (4-9/14)

VAN DEWATER, Robert J. of NYC m 1/31/37 Ann Sophia Hurd, dau. of General J.N. Hurd of Albany; Rev. Joseph H. Price (6-2/1)

VAN DRIESEN, Mary Ann - see STACY, John

VAN DUSEN, Angeline, consort of Dr. Harlow A., d 4/3/48 at Mapletown (4-4/6)

VAN DUSEN, Catharine - see WAIT, Benjamin

VAN DUZEN, Isaac R. (Hon.), about 42, attorney, d at his himne in Newburgh (from the Goshen Republican) (9-12/4)

VAN DYCK, Ann - see REED, Newton

VAN DYCK, Elsie - see DE WITT, Clinton

VAN DYKE, Henry of Oswego m 9/11/50 Charlotte Case of Utica in U/; Rev. Dr. Proal (1-9/18)

VAN DYKE, Sarah - see BLAKE, Robert, Esq.

VAN EPS, Herman of Schenectady m 1/21/36 Agnes Johnson of Albany; Rev. James R. Boyd (6-1/22)

VAN ESS, Sarah C., widow of late William C., Esq., and dau of William Radcliff, Esq., d 9/9/35 at home of her brother Edward Radcliff in Lower Red Hook (6-9/12)

VAN EVEREN, (Miss) d 5/8/36 (her friends and those of her sister, Mrs. Huff, invited to her funeral at 3 o'clock from 73 Hamilton Street) (6-5/9)

VAN GAASBEEK, Christopher Jr., 53, d 8/23/49 in Kingston (8-9/1)

VAN GAASBEEK, Eliza C. - see PARSON, Elijah

VAN GORDEN, Abraham, Jr., of Catskill, d 8/19/09 (very suddenly) (7-8/23)

VAN HORNE, Abraham R. m 11/25/49 Lydia Stansel, dau. of Paul of Van Hornesville, at V.H.; Rev. A.E. Daniels (4-11/29)

VAN HORNE, Fredus m 5/31/37 Harriet Peters, both of Albany; Rev. Williamson (6-6/2)

VAN HORNE, Mary Ann - see PAINE, Cornelius B.

VAN HORNE, Nancy, 29, wife of F. Van Horne, d 10/26/35 (6-10/31)

VAN HOUSEN, Thomas of NYC m 5/19/39 Jane M. Horton, dau. of Wright Horton of Yorktown, in Y.; William Clements, Esq. (12-5/21)

VAN HOUVENBURGH, Abraham m 11/24/49 Elizabeth Sparling; Rev. M.L. Schenk (all of Saugerties) (8-12/1)

VAN INGEN, Eliza - see BANKER, Isaac

VAN INGEN, Margaret - see HOOK, Thomas I.

VAN KLEECK, C. (Mrs.), her funeral "this afternoon at 3 o'clock" from the home of B. Knower, Esq., 132 State St., Albany (her death date not given) (6-10/14/35)

VAN KLEECK, C., 85, relict of late Laurence Van Kleeck of Dutchess Co., d suddenly 10/12 (funeral 10/14 from 132 State Street, Albany.) (6-10/13)

VAN KLEECK, Elizabeth E. - see BALDWIN, John Abeel (Rev.)

VAN KLEECK, Lawrence L. - see BALDWIN, John Abeel (Rev.)

VAN KLEECK, Mary - see RAYNES(?), Willit

VAN LOON, Barent, 41, d 9/22/35 (funeral from his late residence at 86 Washington Ave. at 4 o'clock) (6-9/23)

VAN LOON, Esther - see CATY(?), Elisha W.

VAN LOON, Isaac - see KIERSTED, Maria

VAN LOON, James S., Esq., of Albany m 11/29/48 Rebecca C. Stratton of West Troy in W.T.; Rev. J.C. Burroughs (5-12/6)

VAN NESS, Abijah, 26, d 2/2/45 in West Troy (5-2/5)

VAN NESS, Augustus Edward, d suddenly (date not given) at the home of Edward Radcliff in lower Red Hook from an injury received when run over by a cart. (youngest son of Mrs. Sarah C. Van Ness) (6-11/2/35)

VAN NESS, Henry m 3/11/41 Hannah Cronkhite, dau. of John C., Esq.; Rev. Hathaway (all of Danube) (3-3/18)

VAN NESS, John m 1/9/50 Maria House; Rev. N. Van Aletlan(?) (all of Minden) (4-1/17)

VAN NORDEN, Sarah Ann - see SMITH, David

VAN NORT, John, 42, formerly a merchant of Salina, Onondaga Co., m 9/28/35 Julia Hall, dau of Jeremiah of Elmira, in E. (6-10/17)

VAN O LINDA, P. (Dr.) - see RUSSELL, Charles

VAN OESTRAND, Almina - see CLARK, Adam A.

VAN OLINDA, Cornelius of Montgomery County, m 12/8/41 Cornelia Campbell of Danube; Rev. Loveys (3-12/16)

VAN OLINDA, Mary Ann - see MILLER, Martin

VAN OLINDA, William T., 27, (brother of late Capt. Abram Van Olinda, who was killed in the storming of Chapultiepec) d 6/29/48 in Watervliet (5-7/12)

VAN ORDEN, Benjamin - see VAN RENSSELAER, Nicholas B

VAN ORDER, Lucinda - see FRENCH, M. Holly

VAN PATTEN, Adaline - see HILLS, Ira

VAN PATTEN, Simon S. m 10/30/46 Frances Reed, both of Glenville, in West Troy; Rev. Houghtaling (5-11/4)

VAN PLANK, Isaac of Westerlo m 9/3/35 Charlotte Elizabeth Mc Carty, dau of Hon. John of Coeymans at C; Rev. Slingerland (6-9/7)

VAN RANST, Eleanor - see GIFFORD, George

VAN RENSSELAER, Cornelia P. - see TURNBULL, Robert J.

VAN RENSSELAER, Cornelius G. m 10/25/26 Catharine W. Bleecker, dau. of John, Esq.; Rev. Ludlow (6-11/3)

VAN RENSSELAER, Cortlandt (Rev.) of Albany m 9/13/36 Catharine Ledyard, dau of late Moses(?) P. Cogswell, M.D., at Hartford, CT; Rev. Dr. Hawes (6-9/17)

VAN RENSSELAER, Elizabeth Ann - see VAN RENSSELAER, Richard

VAN RENSSELAER, Elizabeth wf of Richard Van Rensselaer, d. 1/1/35 (funeral 1/4 at her late residence, 19 Steuben St., Albany) (6-1/3)

VAN RENSSELAER, Jacob Rutsen, Esq., 68, d 9/21/35 in NYC (former Columbia Co. member of the bar and for many years represented this county in the legislature) (6-9/26)

VAN RENSSELAER, Jeremiah, M.D. m 7/16/35 Anne F. Waddington, Eldest dau of Joshua, Esq., at St. Thomas' Church, NYC; Right Rev. Bishop

Onderdonk (6-7/21)

VAN RENSSELAER, John S., Esq. of Albany m (date not given) Ann Dunkin, dau. of late Robert H. Dunkin, Esq. of Philadelphia, in P.; Rev. Dr. Wilson (6-3/20)

VAN RENSSELAER, Margaret Schuyler - see DOUW, John DePeyster

VAN RENSSELAER, Nicholas B. m 5/3/36 Christina C. Ten Broeck (dau of late Jeremiah, Esq.), both of Albany, at Catskill in the home of Benjamin Van Orden; Rev. Thomas Lane (6-5/14)

VAN RENSSELAER, Richard, Esq. m 11.1.26 Elizabeth Van Rensselaer, dau. of Gen. Solomon, in Albany (all of Albany) (6-11/3/26)

VAN RENSSELAER, Robert m 2/5/35 Margaret Livingston, dau of the late Nicholas W Stuyvesant; Rev. Dr. Creighton (all of NYC) (6-2/10)

VAN RENSSELAER, Schuyler of Albany m 9/9/35 Cornelia S. Schuyler, dau of Alexander H., of Barton, Tioga Co., at Ithaca; Rev. Carpenter (6-9/15)

VAN RENSSELAER, Schuyler, formerly of Albany, d 5/5/36 at Huron, Ohio (6-5/12)

VAN RENSSELAER, Stephen - see DOUW, John DePeyster

VAN ROSKERCK, John L. m (date not given) Eliza H. Webb in NYC (6-6/5/16)

VAN SANDFORD, Catherine - see MC COLLUM, Robert

VAN SANTVORD, _____, wf of Anthony Van Santvord, d (date not given). Friends of her husband invited to attend her funeral from his home (209 North Market Street) at 3 o'clock (6-3/11/35)

VAN SCHAACK, Asa D. of firm of Van Schaack & Noyes m 6/2/36 Mary Heyer, dau of Cornelius, Esq.; Rev. Dr. Matthews (6-6/4)

VAN SCHAACK, Nicholas of firm of J. & N. Van Schaack, merchants, m 12/21/26 Margaret Ann Linacre, dau. of Thomas; Rev. Ferris (all of Albany) (6-12/26)

VAN SCHAACK, Stephen m 3/19/16 Harriet Dunnel, both of Albany; Rev. Webb (6-3/27)

VAN SCHAICK, ----, widow of late Abraham, d 8/10/49 in Rondout (see VAN SCHAICK, Abraham) (8-8/25)

VAN SCHAICK, Abraham, about 20, son of late Abraham, d 8/15/49 in Rondout (cholera) (see VAN SCHAICK, ----) (8-8/25)

VAN SCHAICK, John B. (Col.), 35, late editor of the Albany Daily Advertiser, d 1/3/39 at his home in Albany (5-1/9)

VAN SCHAICK, Sybrant G. - see CONINE, Mary

VAN SCHOONHOVEN, Ebenezer m 11/15/42 Mrs. Eliza Green in West Troy; John Hastings, Esq. (all of West Troy) (5-11/23)

VAN SCHOONHOVEN, Louisa, widow of John, d 10/13/36 in Albany (funeral 10/16 at 5 o'clock from her late home, 73 North Market St.) (6-10/15)

VAN SCHOONHOVEN, Sarah, 75, formerly of Waterford, d 5/16/48 at West Point, NY (5-5/24)

VAN SCHUYLER, Joseph of Rochester m 2/26/37 Almira Brown, dau. of James of Columbia, at C.; Rev. David Devoe (3-3/2)

VAN SECY, William C. m 12/24/39 Sarah Egleton at Caldwells; Rev. Dr. Westbrook (11-12/31)

VAN SICE, ---- (Mrs.), wf of Gilbert, d 2/18/26 in Schenectady (6-2/21)

VAN SICE, Harriet - see WHALLON, Daniel M.

VAN SICE, James - see WHALLON, Daniel M.

328

VAN SICE, John P., 42, printer and former publisher of the <u>Oneida Republican</u> published in Rome, d 3/1/43 in NYC (consumption) (1-3/14)

VAN SLYCK, Anthony m Sarah S Dollars, both of Kinderhook (see marriage of George Lainhart, adjacent in same newspaper, same date) (6-1/17)

VAN SLYKE, John of Mohawk, m 12/15/41 Sarah A. Wellis of Winfield, in W.; Rev. Holcomb (3-12/16)

VAN SLYKE, Louisa - see DYGERT, Joseph

VAN SLYKE, Mason of Little Falls m 1/27/42 Nancy G. Elbridge, dau. of Nathaniel of Herkimer, in H.; Rev. Dr. Murphey (3-2/3)

VAN SLYKE, Richard, 69, d 7/13/39 in Mohawk (3-7/18)

VAN STEENBERGH, John, about 50, d 9/4/49 in Kingston (8-9/8)

VAN TASSELL, Catherine, 42, wf of Peter, d 12/17/26 very suddenly in Albany (6-12/26)

VAN TASSELL, Sophia - see MC CRACKEN, Samuel

VAN TINE, Esther, 78, d 9/27/42 at the home of her son, Theodorus Van Tine in New Windsor (9-10/1)

VAN VALKENBURGH, Catherine - see RUSSELL, William

VAN VALKENBURGH, Daniel (Rev.) of East Richfield, Otsego County m 5/6/38 Julia Frances Tracy, formerly of Norwich, Conn., in Mohegan Chapel, Montville, Conn.; Rev. A. Gleason (3-5/17)

VAN VALKENBURGH, J.Q. of Cherry Valley m 11/1/39 Miss C.J. Gardner of Little Falls in L.F.; Rev. J.W. Olmstead (3-11/14)

VAN VALKENBURGH, Jane C. - see CLARK, Samuel H.

VAN VALKENBURGH, Jerorakim A. - see CLARK, Samuel H.

VAN VALKENBURGH, John - see RUSSELL, William

VAN VALKENBURGH, John P., 85, d 7/16/37 (funeral from his late home in Greenbush) (his sons, J. and B. Van Valkenburgh, are mentioned) (6-7/17)

VAN VALKENBURGH, John Taylor of Little Falls m 1/8/39 Jane Staats of Danube in D.; Rev. L.P. Blodget (3-1/17)

VAN VALKENBURGH, Mary, about 31, consort of Rev. Daniel Vam Valkenburgh, pastor of the Presbyterian Church in East Richfield, Montgomery County, d 11/16/37 in E.R. (3-11/23)

VAN VALKENBURGH, Peter, 53(?), d 2/8/37 at Greenbush (6-2/13)

VAN VECHTEN, Abraham of Schenectady m 5/27/35 Gertrude Van Arden, dau of Abraham, Esq. of Albany; Rev. Jacob Van Vechten of Schenectady (6-6/1)

VAN VECHTEN, Abraham, 74, d 1/6/37 (funeral from his late home at 220 North Market St.) (6-1/9)

VAN VECHTEN, John - see CHEW, Elizabeth Anna

VAN VLIERDEN, Margaret - see FULLER, Henry

VAN VOAST, ---- (Mrs.), mother of John and Richard, d 9/12/26 in Schenectady (she died "at an advanced age") (6-9/19)

VAN VOLKENBERG, Rebecca - see HARDING, Ira

VAN VOLKENBURGH, James, about 82(?), d 9/10/36 in Chatham (was a Whig and militiaman in the Rev. War) (had 12 children) (from Kinderhook Sentinel) (6-9/19)

VAN VOORHIS, Charles m 10/22/39 Mary Ann Rikeman, dau of Cornelius, Esq.; Rev. Dr. Westbrook (all of Peekskill) (11-10/29)

VAN VOORHIS, William R., 23, son of late Major William R., of Fishkill, d 7/16, suddenly, at Fishkill (11-7/23)

VAN VORST, Elizabeth B. (Miss), 21, d (date not given) at the home of her uncle, James Baker, Esq., at Norfolk, Virginia (from the Norfolk and Portsmouth Herald (6-5/10/37)

VAN VORST, James, about 75, d 1/27/37 in Little Falls (had been a long term resident of Schenectady County moving to Little Falls about a year prior to his death) (3-2/2)

VAN VOST, James m 12/4/47 Eliza Rainbow, both of Glenville; Rev. J.C. Burroughs (5-12/8)

VAN VRANKEN, Lyman m 1/20/48 Margery Graham; Rev. C. Pomeroy (all of Watervliet) (5-2/2)

VAN VRANKEN, Margaret - see HILLS, Samuel

VAN VRANKEN, S.A. (Rev.) of Reformed Dutch Church, m 5/6/35 Maria Swift, dau of Henry, Esq, both of Poughkeepsie; Rev. J.B. Hardenbergh of Rhinebeck (6-5/14)

VAN VRANKEN, William m (date not given) Sally Disbrough in Schenectady; Rev. Montieth (all of Shenectady) (6-8/22/26)

VAN VURSTE, Catherine - see PALMER, James

VAN WAGENER, John H. (Rev.) m 5/23/26 Catherine E. Cooke, dau. of Richard Cooke, merchant, of Schenectady, at S.; Rev. Murphy (6-6/20)

VAN WART, Henry, a Rev. War soldier and pensioner, d 9/25/33 in NYC (interred in Westchester County) (11-10/1)

VAN WINKLE, Albert of NYC m Jemima C. Willis, eldest dau. of John, 10/29/39 in Mount Pleasant; Rev. Henry (12-11/5)

VAN WYCK, Philip Cortlandt, 26, of the US Navy d 1/12/42 at the home of his father, Philip G., in Sing Sing (11-1/25)

VAN WYCK, Theodorus, Jr., 22, d 4/4/37 in Fishkill village (6-4/20)

VAN YORX, Sarah Louisa, 28, wf of Matthew, d 2/3/35 in New York City (a lingering illness) (6-2/7)

VAN ZANDT, John G. (Dr.), 78, d 4/14/41 at his home at Lisha's Kill in the town of Watervliet (5-4/21)

VAN ZANDT, John, 31, d suddenly 12/17/35 (funeral at 3 o'clock from his home at 125 Lydius Street) (6-12/18)

VAN ZANDT, Sarah (Miss), 74, d 3/26/35 in Albany; her funeral at 5 p.m. from house of Jonathan Kidney, 62 Hudson St. (6-3/27)

VANCE, John m 4/25/36 Eliza Hardick; Rev. Kirk (all of Albany) (6-4/27)

VANCLEVE, Louisa Elizabeth - see DAVIES, C.C.

VANDEMARK, Alida Jane - see LAVENDER, Thomas

VANDEMARK, L.V.K., Esq., 33, d 3/26/41 in West Troy (5-3/31)

VANDENBERGH, John H. m 10/28/49 Sophia Burnett in Saugerites; Rev. P.C. Oakley (all of Saugerties) (8-11/10)

VANDENBERGH, Lyda - see MORGAN, Thomas C.

VANDENBURG, Julia - see WHITE, James

VANDENBURGH, Elizabeth Ann - see TABER, William

VANDENBURGH, Gilbert, 80(?), d (date not given) at his home in Greenbush (6-9/13/36)

VANDENBURGH, Hannah Maria - see LYON, Charles

VANDENBURGH, Maria, 101, d 7/4/36 in Albany (her friends and those of her sister, Lydia Ryckman, invited to her funeral at 4 o'clock from her late residence, 15 Liberty St.) (6-7/7)

VANDERBERG, Peter of Manchester m 8/14/40 Margaret Dockstader, dau. of
    Frederick of Herkimer at H.; Rev. J.P. Spinner (3-9/3)

VANDERBILT, Jane Ann - see GOETSCHUS, Henry

VANDERBILT, John, late coroner of NYC, d 6/19/26 in NYC (6-6/27)

VANDERBURGH, Frederick H. of Beekman m 2/19/35 Caroline Williams,
    youngest dau of late David R. Esq. of NYC; Rev. C.G. Semmurs (6-3/7)

VANDERCOOK, John F. of Watervliet m 1/1/47 Cornelia Fonda of Halfmoon;
    Rev. E. Stover (5-1/13)

VANDERHEYDEN, Ann (Mrs.), 87, d 7/22/44 in Rome (1-7/23)

VANDERHEYDEN, Elizabeth (Mrs.) - see SPRINGER, Martin

VANDERHEYDEN, Manning - see SPRINGER, Martin

VANDERHOFF, David, son-in-law of Dr. Drake of Peekskill, d 10/25/41 at Fort
    Pierce, Florida ("of the prevailing fever") [typhus perhaps - FQB]
    (11-11/30)

VANDERHOOF, Jane Ann - see GOETCHIEUS, Henry

VANDERLIP, George R., friends are invited to attend the funeral at 5 o'clock "this
    afternoon" of his deceased mother-in-law at his home, 9 Montgomery Street
    (6-6/5/35)

VANDERLIP, S.S. - see ADAMS, Louisa (Miss)

VANDERLIP, Wheeler, 23, d 12/19/44 in West Troy at the home of his brother,
    Mr. E. Vanderlip (5-12/25)

VANDERPOEL, Harriet Gates, wf of Hon. Aaron Vanderpoel, (he late a member of
    Congress from NY) d 4/8/37 at the home of her father (he not named) in
    Newark, NJ (6-4/11)

VANDERPOEL, Leo Fidelis (Rev.), superior of Phillips College and "an exemplary
    divine of the Catholic Church", d 1/22/37 in Detroit, Mich. (He was born in
    Flanders and arrived in the US in 1833) (6-2/28)

VANDERPOEL, Rebecca G., wf of Hon. Aaron Vanderpoel, congressional
    representative from New York, d 9/8/37 at the home of her father. Jesse
    Baldwin, Esq., in Newark, NJ (6-4/17)

VANDERPOEL, Sarah Ann - see FRENCH, James M.

VANDERPOOL, David, son-in-law of Dr. Drake, d 11/25/41(?) at Fort Pierce, East
    Florida (of the "prevailing fever") (11-12/7)

VANDERWACKER, Nancy - see MILLER, Thomas

VANDERWARKEN, Martha - see HIMES, James, Jr.

VANDERWERKEN, Tunis, 70, d 10/23/37 in Waterford (illness of 8 months)
    (5-11/8)

VANDERWERKER, Eliza - see CLARK, Sidney

VANDERZEE, Gitty, 84, widow of Teunis Vanderzee and mother of Storm T
    Vanderzee, Rsq. of Troy, d 3/17/35 at home of John Vanderzee in
    Greenbush, Rensselaer Co. (6-3/25)

VANDERZEE, Margaret - see MC ALISTER, Charles

VANDEWERKEN, Elbridge m 6/23/36 Jannet S. Speary, both of Albany; Rev.
    A.L. Covall (6-6/30)

VANDUSEN, Maria - see MAC CLATLIN, James

VANDUZEN, Elen - see RAYNES, Henry

VANN, James A. m 7/20/44 Emily Toomas, both of Clinton; Rev. Whaley (1-7/30)

VANOSTRAND, A., M.D. of Philadelphia m 10/19/43 Cordelia E. Smith, dau. of
    Dr. Ira Smith, formerly of Little Falls, at Evan's Mills, Jefferson County;

Rev. Armstrong (3-10/26)

VANSANTFORD, Maria (Miss), 39, d 9/6/47 in West Troy (5-9/22)

VANSCOY, Abagail, about 41, wf of Timothy, d 10/20/38 in North Salem (12-11/6)

VANSTEENBURG, John, 22, son of Abraham T., d 6/10/49 in Kingston (8-6/16)

VANSTEENBURGH, Elizabeth, 9, dau. of late John H., d 11/2/37 (her uncle, Hugh Humphrey is mentioned - funeral 11/3 from her late home at 30 Maiden Lane) (6-11/3)

VANZANDT, Joseph R., 64, merchant, d 3/9/36 (a lingering illness) (funeral at 3 o'clock from his home, 407 South Market St.) (6-3/10)

VARK, Gertrude, 82, relict of John and mother of Hon. Aaron Vark of Yonkers, d 10/13/39 in NYC (12-10/22)

VARLEY, Catharine Matilda, 5, eldest dau. of Stephen and Enid(?), d 8/26/44 in West Troy (5-8/28)

VARLEY, John, about 43, d 10/17/40 after a lingering illness caused by the accidental discharge of a cannon on the 4th of July (5-10/21)

VARNEY, ---- (Judge) - see INGHAM, S.A. (Dr.)

VARNEY, Alfred E. (Dr.) of Middleville m 2/3/41 Ann Maria Willard, dau. of Col. Charels Willard, in Fairfield; Rev. William Baker (3-2/11)

VARNEY, Anna - see INGHAM, S.A. (Dr.)

VARNEY, Edward (Hon.) - see INGHAM, Anna

VARNEY, Freelove, 28, consort of A.E. Varney, M.D., and dau. of Thomas and Amey Arnold, d 3/12/39 in Middleville (scrofulous consumption) (3-3/21)

VARNEY, M.G. (Col.) of Russia m 10/9/39 Jane R. Carpenter, dau. of Hazel of Norway, NY in N.; Rev. Baker of Fairfield (3-10/17)

VARNUM, John, 63, recently of Washington, DC, but formerly of Massachusetts, d 7/23/36 at Niles, Mich. (was representative to Congress and held many offices in state government) (6-8/29)

VASEY, George m 12/22/46 Martha Jane Scott, both of Oriskany; Rev. B.J. Diefendorf (1-1/1/47)

VAUGHAN, Nancy - see READ, William S.

VAUGHAN, Nancy's friends "are requested to attend her funeral at 3 o'clock from 34 South Lansing Street" (6-1/9/35)

VAUGHAN, Samuel K. m 6/6/44 Luvinna Wandell in West Troy; Rev. Z. Phillips (all of West Troy) (5-6/12)

VAUGHN, Margaret - see TAFT, James

VEAZIE, Henry of Rome m 4/20/43 Lydia Ann Hayden of Annsville in A.; Rev. Mason

VEAZIE, Mary - see HAYDEN, Cyrus

VEDDER(?), Herman of St. Johnsville m (date not given) Catharine Nellis of Oppenheim at St. Johnsville (3-9/5/39)

VEDDER, Albert of Glenville m 11/22/26 Susan Veeder of Rotterdam; Rev. J. Searle (6-12/5)

VEDDER, Ann - see PIERCE, Richard

VEDDER, Ann M. - see DAVIS, John J.

VEDDER, John E. of Broadalbin m 2/3/26 Sarah Robison of Schenectady in S.; Rev. Prost (6-2/21)

VEDDER, Samuel A., Esq. - see PIERCE, Richard

VEEDER, Frederick m 9/22/36 Catharine Shaefer in Oppenheim; Rev. Martin

(3-9/29)

VEEDER, Garett S., (Hon.), 84, d 2/18/36 at his home in Rotterdam, Schenectady Co. (was ill just 2 or 3 days) (was a Captain in the "regular army" during the Rev. War) (6-3/5)

VEEDER, Henry, Esq., postmaster at Fonda, m 9/28/37 Rachael Lansing, dau. of James, Esq.; Rev. A. Amerman (all of Fonda) (6-10/2)

VEEDER, Jemima - see LEONARD, Jacob

VEEDER, Susan - see VEDDER, Albert

VENZIE, Polly, 68, wf of Thomas, d 10/10/50 at Dresden, Yates County (1-10/23)

VERDON, Margaret - see possibly ROGERS, David H.

VERMILYE, Robert G. m 3/31/36 Anna Maria Mc Carty, dau of Richard, Esq., in NYC; Rev. Dr. Mc Cartee (6-4/5)

VERMULE, Cornelius (Rev.) m (date not given) Sarah Post in NYC (6-5/22/16)

VERNAN, Frances A. - see LAWRENCE, Lewis H.

VERNON, William - see OAKEY, Sarah

VERPLANCK, Augusta Maria, 34, wf of Philip of Verplanck's Point, d 9/13/35 (11-9/15)

VERPLANCK, Harriet, 6, dau of Col. Abraham, d 9/30/36 (inflammation of the bowels from eating wild plums) (6-10/4)

VERPLANCK, Isaac D (Major), 77, formerly a judge of the court of common pleas of Albany Counry; d 2/4/36 at Coeymans (last survivor of the Coeymans Patent); (with six townsmen built the Reformed Dutch Church ar Coeymans) (funeral from his brick mansion at Achquctuc 2/6) (6-2/5)

VERPLANCK, William Beekman, 34, d (date not given) at his late home, Woodlawn, Verplanck's Point (11-7/16/39)

VERPLANK, Abraham - see VAN DALFREN, Sarah

VERPLANK, David, 15, son of Col. Abraham, d 4/2/36 at Coeymans ("organic affliction of the heart") (6-4/5)

VERPLANK, Sarah A. - see MILLER, M.C.B.

VERRY, William m 10/18/49 Irena Shultis(?); Rev. H. Wheeler (all of Woodstock) (8-10/27)

VERVALEN, Catherine - see LOZIER, George

VESTON, Darcas - see HICKS, Gerardus

VIALL, Job G. m 10/25/38 Fanny Fellows at Mechanicville, Washington Co.; Rev. Lockwood (12-10/30)

VIBARD, Rebecca - see POTTER, Abel

VICKERS, Lydia Ann - see SPENCER, Sidney

VIELE, Augustus, M.D., of Trot m 10/8/39 Mary Ann Kenyon, dau. of V.S. Kenyon, at Middleville; Rev. Baker (3-10/10)

VIELE, Jane L. - see STURTEVANT, G.A.

VIELE, Louisa - see WINNE, Charles

VIELE, Maria E. - see WHIPPLE, J.E.

VIELE, Mrs. John L., 45, d 9/15/37 in Albany (6-9/18)

VIELE, S.S., Esq., attorney at law, m 12/20/36 Catharine E. Dewey, both of Seneca Falls, at S.F.; Rev. A.D. Lane (6-1/7/37)

VINCENT, Mercy Ann - see TINKER, Philander P.

VINCENT, Samuel, 36, son of John d 5/21/33 in Greenburg (11-6/4)

VISCHER, Elizabeth - see MIX, James

VISSCHER, John Van Schaick, youngest son of John V.S. Visscher, d 11/18/35 in

Albany (funeral 11/19 from his home, 131, North Market St., Albany) (6-11/19)

VOGEL, Augustina - see GOODING, William

VOGELL, Elder - see DAVIS, Nathaniel S.

VOORHEES, Cornelia - see POMEROY, Theodore (Dr.)

VOORHEES, Henry P. - see SMITH, Sarah Ann

VOORHEES, Inez, 5 months, dau. of Francis C. and Ann Maria, d 6/22/49 in Kingston (8-6/30)

VOORHEES, John - see MARCELLIS, Maria

VOORHEES, Sarah Ann - see SMITH, Henry Kendall

VOORHEES, Sarah Ann - see SMITH, Henry Randall

VORHIS, Ann Loomis - see QUINBY, Underhill

VORIS, Elizabeth Louise - see CHURCHILL, Marlborough

VORY, Frances - see BILLINGS, Hamilton

VOSBURGH, Eliza Ann - see WAGER, Paul

VOSBURGH, Henry of West Troy m 1/14/45 Adaline Bunnel of Troy in Troy; Rev. S.G. Spees (5-1/22)

VOSBURGH, Isaac W, m 3/30/36 Maria Pitcher, dau of Joseph Russell, Esq.; Rev. Professor Yates of Union College (6-4/1)

VOSBURGH, Mary E., about 26, wf of Peter, deceased, d 12/18/37. (See VOSBURGH, Peter) (3-12/28)

VOSBURGH, Peter of Schuyler m 10/12/37 Eveline E. Hagen of Little Falls at L.F.; Rev. Whipple (3-10/19)

VOSBURGH, Peter, 26, d 12/3/37 in Schuyler (see also VOSBURGH, Mary E. This couple were married in October 1837) (3-12/28)

VOSBURGH, William A, 46, d 3/5/35 in Albany (funeral at 3 o'clock at his father's home, 13 North Market St.) (6-3/6)

VOSBURGH, William H. m 8/13/48 Jennett Scott, both of West Troy, in W.T.; Rev. J.C. Burroughs (5-8/16)

VOUGHT, Henry Christian, about 84, d 11/7/42 at Annsville, Cortlandt Town (a Rev. War soldier throughout the war - his obituary is included in this death report with details of his military funeral service) (11-10/13)

VOUGHT, Isaac C. m 10/30/39 Martha Mc Carty of Fishkill at Annsville, Cortlandt town; Rev. William H. Johnson (11-11/12)

VOUGHT, Jane C., 30, dau of John C., d 3/26/42 in Peekskill (lingering illness of 4 years) (11-3/29)

VOUGHT, Jane C., age indecipherable, dau of John C., d 3/28/42 in Peekskill (a lingering illness) (11-3/31)

VRADENBERG, Abby Ann - see TIBBITS, Henry W.

VREDENBURGH, Frances - see STONE, Joseph L.

VROMAN, Rachael - see ACKER, John

VROOMAN, Adam m 2/16/42 Maria Sinnott of West Troy in W.T.; Rev. C.H. Hoskins (5-2/23)

WABEN (or WAREN?), Joseph H. of Troy, NY m (date not given) Elizabeth Phelps, dau of Walter, Esq., of Hartford, CT at Christ's Church in Hartford; Rev. Bishop Brownell (6-9/16/35)

WADDELL, John d (date not given) (funeral at 3 o'clock from his late home, Green and Johnson Sts.) (6-4/29/36)

WADDELL, John, Esq. of Louisana m 7/25/35 Lucia Chauncey Porter, dau of late

Capt. John Porter of US Navy, in Christ Church, Alexandria, D.C.; Rev. C.E. Dana (6-8/31)

WADDINGTON, Anne F. - see VAN RENSSELAER, Jeremiah

WADE, Virgil B. of Rome m 2/1/48 N. Marian Kinney, only dau. of Ebenezer of Westmoreland, in W.; Elder Denison Alcott (1-2/18)

WADLEY, E.S., printer, m 3/11/35 Margaret Anna Cahill; Rev. B.T. Welch; all of Albany (6-3/13)

WADLON, George W. m 11/4/36 Elizabeth Johnson, both of Staten Island in Albany; Rev. Marshall (6-11/7)

WADRATH, Elizabeth - see WILSON, Nelson

WADSWORTH, Hannah - see STEARNS, William

WADSWORTH, Mary - see BENTON, Catherine

WADSWORTH, Roger, 55, d 5/29/10 in Catskill (7-5/30)

WAGER, Harriette - see CURTIS, ---- (Mr.)

WAGER, Paul of Troy m 5/19/36 Eliza Ann Vosburgh of Albany; Rev. E. Holmes (6-5/21)

WAGER, Philip (Major) of 4th infantry, US Army, d 11/28/35 at Philadelphia (6-12/4)

WAGGONER, Eleanor - see BURHANS, John H. (Col.)

WAGNER, Chauncey of Palatine m 10/2/49 Emeline Foster, eldest dau. of Auston Foster of Stone Arabia at S.A.; Rev. A. Rumpf (4-10/4)

WAGNER, Edward, 27, son of Charles, d (date not given) in Aurora, Kane County, Illinois (4-7/27/48)

WAGNER, Eli, about 30, son of William P., d 10/25/50 at Natural Bridge, Jefferson County (was formerly of Fort Plain) (survived by a wife and aged parents) (4-10/31)

WAGNER, Emeline F. - see STARIN, Delancy D.

WAGNER, Lavina - see GUTWITZ, David

WAGONER, Catharine W. (Mrs.), 23, d 9/1/49 in Danube (4-9/13)

WAID, William, 25, son of Charles Waid, d 11/16/49 in Lee (spent the last winter in Florida hoping to improve his health; returned to Lee in early summer, 1849) (1-11/21)

WAIT, Anna - see SCOVELL, Charles

WAIT, Benjamin m 2/26/43 Catherine Van Dusen in Fairfield; Rev. Loveys (3-3/2)

WAIT, Daniel W. of Jonesville, Saratoga County m 1/7/38 Fanny Richerson of Troy; A.W. Richardson, Esq. (5-1/10)

WAIT, George m 3/29/35 Minerva Hinckley; Rev. J.S. Campbell (all of Albany) (6-8/1)

WAIT, Josiah, 76, d 8/25/50 in West Troy (5-9/4)

WAIT, Juliet - see ADAMS, Franklin

WAIT, Richard, Esq., d 6/16/10 at Lyme, Conn. (7-6/27)

WAIT, Samuel C., M.D., of Somerville, St. Lawrence Co., late of Fonda's Bush, Montgomery Co., m 9/22/35 Electa S. Keyes, only dau of Daniel Keyes of Governeur, in G.; Rev. Laurence (6-10/5)

WAKEMAN, Esther, 67, wf of Daniel, d 4/1/42 in Herkimer (3-4/21)

WAKEMAN, Hugh B., 4, youngest son of John B. and Mary, d 7/13/42 in Little Falls (3-7/28)

WAKEMAN, Zalmon B. of Herkimer m 10/9/37 Alvira Thornton, dau. of Stephen, in Richfield; Rev. Chauncey E. Goodrich, pastor of the Presbyterian Church in Winfield (3-10/12)

WALBRIDGE, Ann - see MERCHANT, George W.

WALBRIDGE, E.W., Esq. - see MERCHANT, George W.

WALBRIDGE, Henry T. of Lansingburgh m 5/29/45 Margaret Knickerbacker, dau. of John, Esq. of Waterford at Grace Church in Waterford (5-6/4)

WALBRIDGE, Romeo, 35, stage proprietor of the firm Baker & Walbridge, d 4/7/35 in Troy (6-4/15)

WALCOTT, Irene E. - see HASLEHURST, James

WALCOTT, Proctor m 2/14/41 Hannah Russell, dau. of Daniel, at Vienna; Rev. Bronson (1-2/16)

WALDRING, Emma - see BALDWIN, Ebenezer

WALDRON, Resolved, a bachelor age 63, m 4/23/39 Margaret Tuyke, a widow, age 30, in Clarktown; Rev. Quick (12-6/4)

WALDRONE, Eliza - see SICKLES, George

WALDRONE, Richard - see SICKLES, George

WALES, Elizabeth - see STEVENS, George D.

WALES, Permelia (Mrs.), 36, d (date not given) at Windham, Conn. (7-5/10/09)

WALKER, Eliza (Mrs.) - see CARDY, Joseph

WALKER, Betsey - see SHATTUCK, Jethro

WALKER, Eunice U. - see POTTS, Jesse C.

WALKER, Frances, about 4, dau. of Rev. Joseph B. Walker, d 1/11/40 at Delhi, Delaware Co. (12-3/3)

WALKER, Lucy - see ROCKWELL, Julius

WALKER, Margaret - see BURNS, Thomas

WALKER, Margaret, 27, dau., of late Oliver, d 1/5/48 in Lee (1-2/11)

WALKER, Mary, 3, youngest dau of Willard, d 8/16/35 (funeral 4 o'clock from her father's house, 76 Division St.) (6-8/18)

WALKER, Simeon, 72, d 3/24/47 in Waterville (1-4/2)

WALKER, Thomas R - see JOHNSON, Louisa

WALKER, Willard H., 28, of firm of Gilbert, Walker & Co., merchants, NYC, and eldest son of Willard, Esq., of Albany, d 3/11/36 on the Island of St. Croix where he had gone for his health (6-4/26)

WALKER, William F (Rev.) of NYC m 7/2/35 Alida Ritzma Bogert of Geneva at Trinity Church in Geneva; Rev. Seabury (6-7/13)

WALKER, William, 70, d 7/29/46 in Lee (apoplexy) (1-3/31)

WALLACE, Andrew (Sgt.), 105, a Rev. War veteran, d 1/21/35 at Water St., NYC (born at Inverness, Scotland in 1730; arrived in America in 1772; remained in the army nearly 30 years; assisted in rescuing Lafayette when the latter was wounded. (from NY Journal of Commerce) (6-1/26)

WALLACE, Frances L. (Mrs.) of the Camp Street Theatre, d suddenly 4/10/36 at New Orleans (6-4/28)

WALLACE, George, 68, d 10/9/41 in Newburgh (born in Aberdeenshire, Scotland but lived in Newburgh and vicinity since 1817) (9-10/16)

WALLACE, Hannah R. - see LOW, Francis S.

WALRAD, Fanny - see BABCOCK, Nathan

WALRADT, Charles m 10/24/26 Jane Bortle, dau. of Richard, at Palatine; Rev. Wack (all of Palatine) (6-10/31)

WALRATH, Alfred m 6/28/49 Hellen H. Hall, both of Fort Plain, at F.P.; Dr. C.G. Mc Lean (4-7/5)

WALRATH, Catherine (Mrs.), 44, d 6/11/50 in Stark ("She was a kind mother, an affectionate sister and beloved neighbor") (4-6/27)

WALRATH, David H. m 6/20/48 Maria Nellis, dau. of Garret, in Palatine (bride & groom of P.); Rev. A. Rimpf (4-6/22)

WALRATH, Henry of Minden m 1/18/49 Elizabeth Smith of Danube; Rev. N. Van Alstine (4-1/25)

WALRATH, Lysander, 27, d 11/29/48 in Oswego, Illinois (arrived in Oswego about 18 months prior to his death (obituary from the Platform published at Aurora, Ill.) (4-1/4/49)

WALRATH, William J. m 10/25/49 Lucinda Dunckel at Frey's Bush; Rev. James Diefendorf (all of Frey' Bush) (4-11/22)

WALSH, Dudley, Esq., 54, late President of the Bank of Albany, d 5/24/16 (6-5/29)

WALSH, James d 10/23/35 (funeral at 4 o'clock from home of his brother, John S. Walsh) (6-10/24)

WALSH, John A. m 10/29/35 Marietta Shaw; Rev. B.T. Welch (bride & groom both of Albany) (6-11/4)

WALSH, John m 10/15/42 Deborah M---- (surname illegible), both of Peekskill, in P.; Rev. Luckey(?) of Sing Sing (11-10/20)

WALSH, Jonathan m 4/28/42 Mary Stracman(?) in Newburgh; Rev. John Forsyth (all of Newburgh) (9-4/30)

WALSH, Thomas d (date not given) in NYC (6-2/21/26)

WALSH, William m 5/17/36 Mary Bay, dau of Dr. William Bay; Rev. F.F. Vermilye (all of Albany) (6-5/19)

WALSWORTH, Jesse - see RUSSELL, Bartlett

WALTER, Henry, Esq., 59, d 5/17/33 at his home in Sing Sing (11-6/4)

WALTER, Jane E. - see HAWLEY, Charles

WALTON, Harriet N. - see WING, Halsey R.

WALTON, Mary - see WAYNE, W. Clifford

WALTON, Octavia V. - see LEVERT, Henry S.

WALTON, William - see DUANE, William R

WALTZ, Gashere m 12/27/49 Diana Miller in Frey's Bush; Rev. Joseph I. Timmerman (all of Frey's Bush) (4-1/10/50)

WALTZ, Mary Elizabeth - see BROWER, Heshel

WALWORTH, Ann Eliza - see BACKUS, J. Trumbull

WALWORTH, Aphelia (Mrs.), 79, surviving parent of Hon. R.H. Walworth, chancellor of the state, d 2/15/37 at the home of her son-in-law, D.J. Matteson, Esq. of Fredonia. She was formerly of Hoosac, NY (from the Geneva Gazette) (6-2/28)

WALWORTH, Chancellor - see BACKUS, J. Trumbull

WANDELL, Eleanor, 70, wf of Capt. Daniel T., d 6/20/44 in West Troy (5-6/26)

WANDELL, Emma Louisiana, 18, only dau. of Stephen S., d 3/3/47 at the home of her father in West Troy (painful illness of 18 days) (5-3/10)

WANDELL, Esther, 4, youngest dau. of Stephen S., d 2/20/38 in West Troy (scarlet fever) (5-2/28)

WANDELL, James Halsted, 3 months, son of Stephen S., d 4/16/38 in West Troy (5-4/18)

WANDELL, Luvinna - see VAUGHAN, Samuel K.

WANDELL, Rosanna M. - see BEEMAN, Philip

WANDS, James W, 43, d 1/15/35 at New Scotland ("of a lingering illness")

(6-1/21)

WANDS, James, 2nd, 64, of New Scotland d 9/2/36 in Albany (6-9/3)

WANZER, David, 53, d suddenly 3/14/40 in Herkimer (formerly of Connecticut) (3-3/19)

WARBURTON, John, 38, d (date not given) at East Windsor (7-8/29/10)

WARD, Ann (Mrs.), 30, d 11/29/48 at the home of her brother, John Perrigo, in West Troy (pulmonary consumption) (5-12/6)

WARD, Benjamin, Esq., 42, d 2/26/42 in Peekskill (lived always in Peekskill) (11-3/1)

WARD, Benjamin, Esq., 44, d 2/26/42 in Peekskill (survived by wife and 3 children) (11-3/1)

WARD, Calista Ann - see CAREY, Josiah W.

WARD, Caroline, infant dau of Caleb of Peekskill, d 2/15/34 (scarlet fever) (11-2/18)

WARD, Catharine D. - see HIGGINS, Morris R.

WARD, Edward of Fishkill Landing m 12/6/42 Sophia Rankin, dau. of Alexander Rankin of NYC; Rev. Dr. Case (9-12/17)

WARD, Emily, 21, wf of Samuel and dau of William B. Astor, d 2/13/41 in NYC (11-3/2)

WARD, Ferdinand D.W. (Rev.) of Rochester m 9/21/36 Jane Shaw of NYC; Rev. Asa D. Smith (6-9/24)

WARD, Hannah - see HOXIE, H.C.

WARD, Hannah Maria - see SCHULTZ, Joachim O.

WARD, James A. of Schenectady m 2/2/50 Elizabeth Cole, eldest dau. of Dr. John Cole of West Troy, in W.T., Rev. J.C. Burroughs (5-2/20)

WARD, James, 77, d (date not given) at Torrington (7-1/31/10)

WARD, Jane - see MARKS, Edwin

WARD, John of Utica m 7/12/45 Joannah Perrigo of West Troy; Rev. Dodge (5-7/16)

WARD, John P., 17, son of Stephen, Esq., d 12/30/49 in Rome (1-1/2/50)

WARD, Jonathan (Hon.), 71, d 9/22/42 at White Plains (11-9/29)

WARD, Mary - see BRAKEFIELD, Thomas

WARD, Mary (Mrs.), 87, d 1/20/49 in Adams (1-2/7)

WARD, Mary Ann - see HOLMES, William

WARD, Thomas of White Plains m 2/9/42 Miss Tompkins, dau of U. Tompkins of Greenbirgh, at G.; Rev. Francis (11-2/22)

WARDEN, Satterlee (General) of Auburn m 7/19/37 Harriet E. Randall, dau. of George Roswell Randall, in Cortland village; Rev. John C.F. Horn of Ithaca (6-7/24)

WARDEN, Seymour m 2/16/42 Frances Cummings in Pound Ridge; Rev. Sizer (11-3/8)

WARDWELL, Abby M. - see DOXTATER, E.R.

WARE, Richard, 45, d 11/4/41 in Westmoreland (1-11/9)

WARFIELD, Lott (Rev.) Episcopal Church minister, d 5/25/33 at Easton, MD (paralysis of his limbs and speech while delivering a sermon a week previous) (11-6/4)

WARFORD, Charles Ignatius, 10 months, son of Capt. James and Elizabeth, d 10/8/47 (5-10/13)

WARFORD, Charles, 61, d 5/24/46 in West Troy (5-5/27)

WARFORD, James P. m (date lacking) ---- T. Dumont, both of West Troy (This record partly cut out from the newspaper) (5-1/1/45)

WARFORD, Joseph m 5/28/48 Hester A. Carey, both of West Troy; Rev. O.H. Gregory (5-5/31)

WARING, Eliza - see MC CORD, Henry T.

WARNER, Bingham m 3/2/37 Pamela Klock, both of Oppenheim, in Little Falls; Rev. H.S. Attwater (3-3/16)

WARNER, Ezra T. of NYC m 6/13/47 Catharine M. Horner of West Troy; Rev. Houghtaling (5-6/16)

WARNER, John - see HILL, Susan

WARNER, John Jost, 95, a Rev. War soldier, d 9/6/50 in Schoharie (father of 14, grandfather of 101 and great grandfather of 98 children) (5-9/18)

WARNER, Leonard R. m 9/16/41 Eliza Knox at Cohoes (5-9/29)

WARNER, Louisa - see AVERY, Charles H.

WARNER, Mary (Mrs.) - see STEELE, Daniel

WARNER, Seth H. of Kirkland m 6/29/47 Roxy L. Stratton of Columbus (late of Vernon); Rev. S. Green (1-7/16)

WARNER, william, 17, son of Aaron, d (date not given) at Wethersfield (7-5/10/09)

WARRELL, James of Poughkeepsie m 3/2/42 Sarah Ann Gardner of Newburgh; Rev. Dr. Ferris (9-3/5)

WARREN, Anna C. - see INGERSOLL, Edward

WARREN, Catherine Louisa, 8 weeks, dau. of George T. and Catherine, d 4/4/42 in Newburgh (9-4/9)

WARREN, Frances - see RUSH, George

WARREN, George B - see BOWERS, Sarah Stewart

WARREN, Phebe (Mrs.), age 80 yrs, 10 mo, 12 days, d 1/17/35 at Troy (6-1/19)

WARRING, Eliza, 22, wf of Burr Warring d 12/30/41 in Ridgefield, CT (11-1/18/42)

WASHBURN, Albert of Annsville m 3/8/49 Sarah A. Shear of Lee in Rome; Rev. F.H. Stanton (1-3/14)

WASHBURN, David C. m 2/17/48 Matilda M. Miles, both of Lee, in L.; Rev. F.H. Stanton (1-2/25)

WASHBURN, George E. m 10/16/49 Emeline N. Merrill, both of Carmel; Rev. H.G. Livingston (10-10/17)

WASHBURN, Lydia - see MC CALL, James

WASHBURN, Morgan of Mount Pleasant m 12/25/38 Mrs. Deborah Carpenter of New Castle in Sing Sing; Rev. P. Van Deusen (12-1/1/39)

WASHBURN, Sarah - see MILES, Marcus W.

WASHBURN, William of Sing Sing m 11/14/38 Mrs. Richard Curtiss of Haverstraw in H.; Rev. James Sherwood (12-11/20)

WATERBURY, Eliza, about 42, wf of Drake Waterbury, Esq., d 12/23/39 at North Castle (12-12/31)

WATERBURY, Elizabeth - see JONES, William

WATERBURY, Holly, 22, son of Joseph, d 1/20/39 at Pound Ridge (consumption) (12-2/12)

WATERBURY, Jane - see CARPENTER, C.

WATERBURY, Rheua - see TABER, Silas

WATERBURY, Sarah - see SUTTON, Purdy

WATERMAN, Andrew Jackson of Ballston m 1/18/37 Harriet Underhill of

Waterford in W.; Rev. Reuben Smith (6-1/23)

WATERMAN, Eliza Ann - see DE WITT, Thomas

WATERMAN, Frances E. - see BRIGHAM, Oragen S.

WATERMAN, Henry P. m 11/7/40 Sarah Emma Mead of Frankfort at F.; Rev. T.H. (blurred) (3-11/26)

WATERMAN, Isaac V. m 1/24/46 Mary E. Burleson, both of West Troy, in W.T.; Rev. J. Frazer (5-2/4)

WATERMAN, Jeremiah, 45, merchant, d 8/21/35 in Albany (6-8/24)

WATERMAN, Lucinda B. - see HILLS, Russell D.

WATERMAN, Sophia, 56, widow of F.Y. Waterman, Esq., d 2/13/40 at Cohoes survived by "a large family of children" (not named) (5-2/26)

WATERS, Catharine, wf of John, d (date not given) at Quarryville (cholera) (8-9/8)

WATERS, Chester W. m 1/3/49 Helen Maria Mansfield, youngest dau. of D. Mansfield, Esq. in Westmoreland; Rev. F.A. Spencer (all of Westmoreland) (1-1/17)

WATERS, Elizabeth, 17, dau of Michael of Peekskill, d 7/16/42 (11-7/19)

WATERS, Elizabeth, 17, dau of Michael of Peekskill, d 7/16/42 (11-7/21)

WATERS, Lucy, 75, wf of Elijah, d 2/17/45 in Westmoreland (1-3/25)

WATERS, Polly, 47, wf of Samuel, d 6/3/44 in Rome (1-6/11)

WATERS, Russell, Esq., 48, d 5/11/35 at Coventry (illness of 7 weeks) (from Chenango Telegraph) (6-5/23)

WATERS, Sylvanus J. m 2/27/37 Catharine M. Petrie, dau. of Jacob, Esq.; Rev. H.S. Attwater (all of Little Falls) (3-3/2)

WATERS, Sylvester m 7/15/39 Elizabeth Romer; Rev. Dr. C.D. Westbrook (all of Peekskill) (11-7/16)

WATKINS, Alvan m 1/10/26 Abigail Weaver, both of Westerlo, in W. (6-1/20)

WATKINS, D.C. m 4/11/50 Eliza Maddock at Vienna; Elder Beckwith (all of Vienna) (1-4/24)

WATKINS, Eliza, 30, wf of Isaac, d 1/3/37 at Schoharie after a lingering illness (6-1/9)

WATKINS, Mary Augusta, 18, wf of Alfred, M.D., of Troy d 10/10/47 in Schenectady (had left previously for the West in ill-health and had hoped to go South for the winter to regain her health. Reached West to Buffalo and returned through Rochester to Schenectady where she died) (5-10/13)

WATKINS, Susan A. - see HOOKER, James, Jr.

WATLEY, Experience, wf of John, d 7/20/26 in Albany (funeral from 7 North Market St.) (6-7/21)

WATROUS, Rachel - see POST, O. Rollo

WATSON, Agnes Martha - see ESPIE, James

WATSON, Elkanah, Esq. - see LARNED, George

WATSON, Emily M. - see LARNED, George

WATSON, G.C. (Mrs.), 27, d 1/18/26 (Friends of the deceased and of George C. Watson are invited to her funeral from her late home "in South Pearl Street" (6-1/20)

WATSON, Isaac of Floyd m 1/1/45 Emily Bryan of Rome; Rev. G.M. Boardman (1-1/7)

WATSON, Mary E. - see PRATT, Z. (Col.)

WATSON, Mercy, 90, widow of Captain Titus Watson, a Rev. War pensioner, d 5/14/38 at Cohoes (5-5/23)

WATSON, Persis, about 79, d 6/2/41 at Frankfort (a short but severe illness)
(3-6/17)

WATSON, R.J. formerly of Troy but now of Glenville, Schenectady County m
2/27/40 Sarah Ann Wood of West Troy in W.T.; Rev. Pomeroy (5-3/4)

WATSON, Sarah Ann, 30, wf of R.J., d 2/3/44 in West Troy (5-2/7)

WATSON, Steward, portrait painter of NYC m 6/15/37 Anne Stevenson, dau. of
James, merchant of Edinburgh; Rev. Smedes, Rector of St. George's Church,
Schenectady (6-7/26)

WATSON, Uriah C. (Dr.), d 8/2/42 at Mohawk (3-8/25)

WATTERS(?), William S. of Fulton County m 9/16/40 Mary Catharine Gismer(?)
of Little Falls in L.F.l George Petrie, Esq. (3-9/24)

WATTS, Judge - see COUNHOVER, Emma C.

WAYNE, W. Clifford (Gen.) of Georgia m 11/16/36 Mary Walton, dau of late
Lewis Morris, at Morrisania; Rev. Hart (6-11/22)

WEARE, John m 9/29/37 Lucy White, both of Albany; D. Russell, ESq. (6-10/2)

WEATHERHEAD, Thomas, 35, d 4/4/42 in Newburgh (9-4/9)

WEATHERWAX, Charlotte C., 3 months, d 3/8/42 in Little Falls (3-3/17)

WEAVER, Abigail - see WATKINS, Alvan

WEAVER, Catharine - see BOWE, Obadiah A.

WEAVER, Catharine (Mrs.) - see KELLS, John

WEAVER, Jacob, 17, m 3/7/46 Sarah Sherman, 13, in West Troy; John Cather, Esq.
(5-3/25)

WEAVER, John G. (Gen.), 58, d. (date not given) in Deerfield (long term resident
in D.) (6-9/12/35)

WEAVER, Louisa - see THOMPSON, Thomas S.

WEAVER, Maria - see GERMAN, William P.

WEAVER, P.C., 28, late of Utica, d 11/14/44 at Geddes (a member of the Oneida
Lodge of the Independent Order of Odd Fellows. About 80 members from
Rome and Utica "came up on Sunday to [attend] the funeral service.") (from
the Syracuse Journal) (1-12/3)

WEAVER, Philanda C., 35, wf of Stephen, d suddenly 12/24/35 (6-12/28)

WEAVER, Philo C. (Major) of Frankfort m 10/4/41 Robah C. Willard of
Chittenango; H.C. Warner, Esq. (1-10/12)

WEBB, ----, 10 months, only dau. of Benjamin, d 7/27/39 in Warren (3-8/8)

WEBB, Ann - see BLASHLY, Selah

WEBB, Anna - see EATON, Thomas H.

WEBB, Catharine Adelia, about 6, dau. of William, d 12/13/38 at New Castle
Corners (12-12/25)

WEBB, Charles Henry, 8, son of William, d 12/23/38 at New Castle Corners
(second child of William to die within a space of two weeks) (12-1/1/39)

WEBB, Elizabeth, 77, widow of Salvene Webb, d 12/10/39 in Bedford (12-12/24)

WEBB, Emily - see SWEET, S.N.

WEBB, Jane - see BRIGGS, Alfred

WEBB, Joseph, Esq., 68, father of John Webb of the house of Webb and Dummer
of Albany, d (date not given) at Weathersfield, Conn. (6-1/6/16)

WEBB, Stephen (Capt.) of US Army m (date not given) Mary J. Stewart, dau. of
A.L. Stewart, Esq., in NYC; Rev. William Parkinson (6-2/24/26)

WEBBER, Arsenal of Cazenovia m 6/26/44 Patience Richardson of West Troy in
W.T.; Elder O. Dodge (5-7/10)

WEBBER, Clement, 42, d 4/15/48 at New Woodstock, Madison County (consumption) (for many years he lived in West Troy and was a member of the Baptist Church there) (5-4/26)

WEBBER, David W. m 11/7/40 Margaret Dygert, both of Bridgewater, in Herkimer (1-11/17)

WEBBER, Dorcas, 76, wf of Edward, d 5/19/50 at Vernon (1-6/5)

WEBBER, Emergene A., about 17, dau. of late Edward D. and Harriet and grand-dau. of Edward, d 1/18/42 in Vernon (consumption) (1-1/25)

WEBBER, Mertercia A., 19, dau. of Edward D. and Harriet and grand dau. of Edward Webber d 10/29/41 at Vernon (consumption) (1-11/9)

WEBBER, Samuel (Rev.), President of Harvard University, d (date not given) at Cambridge (7-8/1/10)

WEBBERS, David D, late sheriff of Westchester Co., d 5/20/33 at Pinesbridge, Yorktown (11-6/4)

WEBER, Almira - see LYMAN, Harvey W.

WEBER, James m 7/7/40 Mrs. Elizabeth Morse in Little Falls; Rev. J.W. Olmstead (3-7/16)

WEBSTER, ---- (Mrs.) - see STEELE, Abby (Miss)

WEBSTER, Charles W., Esq. of Fort Plain m 6/19/50 Julia Pellet of Norwich in N.; Rev. Hansen Cox of Oxford (4-6/27)

WEBSTER, David (Rev.), formerly of Saugerties, d 1/6/49 in Groveland, Mich. (8-1/20)

WEBSTER, Esther M. - see POTTER, William S.

WEBSTER, George B. of Buffalo m 2/22/36 Hannah Joy, dau of Thaddeus, Esq. of Albany, at St. Peter's Church; Rev. Potter (6-2/23)

WEBSTER, Henrietta - see HUDSON, Franklin A.

WEBSTER, Horace B., Esq., 30, City Attorney, d 12/8/43 in Albany after a severe illness (5-12/13)

WEBSTER, Joseph m 4/30/39 Amelia Esther Greenly, eldest dau. of William, in South Salem; Rev. Frame (bride & groom of South Salem) (12-5/14)

WEBSTER, Levi, 80, m Mrs. Mercy Robinson, 86, at Colchester, Conn. He had been a widower about 3 weeks and she a widow about six weeks (7-11/8/09)

WEBSTER, Lewis d (date not given) in NYC (6-5/22/16)

WEBSTER, Lydia - see ADAMS, Roland

WEED, Catherine M. - see HOVEY, J.P. (Rev.)

WEED, Chauncey, 8, son of Seth, Jr., d (date not given) at New Canaan (7-6/13/10)

WEED, Cornelia - see MURPHY, G.S.

WEED, Cynthia - see PRATT, Lucius

WEED, Elizabeth - see STANTON, Moses

WEED, Emily - see BARNES, William

WEED, Levi, 73, d 10/2/46 in Vernon (more than 40 years a member of the Church of Christ) (survived by a widow and two daughters) ("Will the Northern (Lowville) Journal copy?") (1-10/13)

WEED, Lucretia - see MINN, David S

WEED, Mary L. - see READING, Joseph

WEEKS, Ann G., 12, dau of James, d 2/28/42 in Peekskill (11-3/8)

WEEKS, Ard of Penfield m 4/16/43 Marilla Boughton of Little Falls at the Baptist Church in L.F. (3-4/20)

WEEKS, Benjamin E., 19, son of Caleb, Esq., d 3/1/42 (9-3/5)

WEEKS, Hannah - see SUTTON, Henry

WEEKS, Samuel of Fishkill m 5/12/41 Sarah Parks of Peekskill; Rev. Richard
Wymand (11-6/1)

WEEKS, Susan - see GREEN, Jered

WEEKS, William, Esq. m 8/30/38 Anny Gilyee(?) of New Castle in N.C.; Thomas
Vale, Esq. (12-11/13)

WEELS, Lemuel, Esq., 79, d 2/11/42 in Yonkers (11-2/21)

WEIST, Abram V. m 7/15/49 Wealthy A. Blake, both of Kingston, in K.; Rev.
Shook (8-7/21)

WELCH, Emily - see BUTTS, Henry

WELCH, James m 8/30/49 Elizabeth Delanoy(?); Rev. V.M. Hulbert (all of
Saugerties) (8-9/15)

WELCH, William m 6/29/26 Maria Harris, both of Albany; Rev. Alburtis (6-6/30)

WELDEN, Mary, 44, d 10/17/35 in Albany (a lingering illness) (6-10/21)

WELLER, Gideon, Esq., late editor of the Hartford Times, and now Comptroller of
the State of Connecticut, m 6/16/35 Mary Jane Hale at Lewiston, Mifflin
Co., PA (6-7/25)

WELLER, Joseph, d (date not given) in Rochester (6-6/5/16)

WELLER, Sarah Authelda - see ENGLISH, Horace

WELLES, Ashbel, Esq., clerk of Tioga County, d 5/4/09 at Chenango Point
(7-5/10)

WELLINGTON, Eli, printer, 83? or 63?, formerly publisher and proprietor of the
Morning Mail, d 3/16/39 in Troy (5-3/20)

WELLIS, Sarah A. - see VAN SLYKE, John

WELLMAN, Charlotte A. - see CHITTENDON, George W.

WELLS, Abigail, 85, d 2/28/26 at Shakers Village, Watervliet (for many years a
member of the Shaker's Society) (mother of 8 sons and 2 daus. - all living)
(6-3/7)

WELLS, Almeda - see BROWN, Henry H.

WELLS, Almeda - see CUNNINGHAM, Edward

WELLS, Benjamin m (date not given) Catherine M. Green at Kingston (6-6/5/16)

WELLS, Edwin (Col.) of Sherburne m 9/27/35 Rachel Arnold of New Berlin in
Norwich; Perez Randall, Esq. (6-9/29)

WELLS, Hannah (Miss), 27, adopted dau. of George Russell of Salem, d 10/23/50
in West Troy (5-10/30)

WELLS, J.D., merchant, m 6/13/49 Maria D. Manning at Middleburgh; Rev. J.
West (all of Middleburgh) (4-6/28)

WELLS, J.H. - see AGAN, Cornelia Ann

WELLS, John A., Esq., cashier of the Mechanics and Farmers Bank in Detroit, m
10/14/36 Henrietta Hall, dau of Ebenezer, Esq., at Canandaigua; Rev. O.
Clark of Detroit (6-10/28)

WELLS, Lemuel, Esq., 82, d 2/11/42 at Yonkers (11-2/22)

WELLS, Leonard m 10/17/39 Eliza Allen at White Creek, Washington Co.; Rev.
E.H. Newton (12-10/22)

WELLS, Letitia(?), 2, dau. of John A., d 9/22/42 in Newburgh (9-9/24)

WELLS, Margaret Amelia, 15, youngest dau. of Joseph and Sophia, d 7/7/41 in
Rome (1-7/13)

WELLS, Mary - see BAKER, Ichabod C.

WELLS, Mary J. - see BROWN, Edwin C.

WELLS, Nathan m 1/3/39 Nancy Seckner in Little Falls; Rev. Thomas Towells (all of Little Falls) (3-1/10)

WELLS, Robert H., Esq. of Albany m 9/13/43 Catherine M. Storrs, dau. of Dr. H. Storrs, deceased, formerly of Utica, in Little Falls; Rev. Mc Ilvaine (3-9/21)

WELLS, William A., 69, d 9/24/35 at Albany (6-9/25)

WELTON, Charity - see KITTRIGE, George

WELTON, Clarinda J. - see HAVENS, George F.

WEMPLE, A.H. of Mohawk m 4/28/50 Sarah C. Seeber of Canajoharie at Fonda; Rev. G. Simmons (4-5/9)

WEMPLE, Walter V m 1/27/35 Sarah Cox; Rev. McMaster. all of Schenectady (6-1/31)

WENDALL, Gilbert A. m 11/28/39 Thirza A. Thurston, dau. of William, in Herkimer; Rev. Simeon Osborn (3-12/12)

WENDELL, A.G. (Dr.) - see SEYMOUR, Edward D.

WENDELL, Alida - see MC MULLEN, Andrew

WENDELL, Anna Mary - see MINTERN, Robert B.

WENDELL, Charles Albert, 1, son of Jacob, Esq. and Margaret E., d 8/19/50 in Fort Plain (4-8/22)

WENDELL, Ellen B. - see BOYCE, Daniel D.

WENDELL, H.C. (Mr.), 56, d 7/6/37 (funeral from his late home at 23 North Pearl Street) (6-7/7)

WENDELL, Harmanus H., d (date not given) (his funeral at 3 o'clock from his late home in Greenbush) (6-9/7/36)

WENDELL, Jane, 49, wf of E.G. Wendell, formerly of West Troy, d 5/2/49 in NYC (5-5/9)

WENDELL, Laura Ann, 6, dau. of Jacob and Margaret, d 7/22/50 at Fort Plain (4-7/25)

WENDELL, Louisa - see BURRELL, Thomas S.

WENDELL, Rufus of Canajoharie m 8/14/50 Charity Mosher of Duanesburgh at D.; Rev. Thomas Armitage of NYC (4-8/22)

WENTWORTH, A.E. (Capt.) m 2/23/48 Julia Garnryck in Vernon; Rev. Pomeroy (all of Verona) (1-2/25)

WENTWORTH, Elizabeth - see ROCKWELL, J.S.

WENTWORTH, Elizabeth (Mrs.), 53, d 7/15/49 in Rome (1-7/18)

WENTWORTH, Oliver, 60(?), d 3/23/41 in Lee (1-3/30)

WESCOTT, John (Col.), 70, d 10/12/47 at Verona (lived many years in Rome; was formerly commandant of the 157th Regiment, NYS militia - marched with his regiment to Sackets Harbor in 1814; was buried in the village cemetery in Rome) (1-10/22)

WESSCHER, John H. of Orange, Ohio m 11/30/44 Margaret M. Lewis of West Troy, NY in W.T.; Rev. John Fraser (5-12/4)

WESSELLS, Henry W. (Lieut.) of the US Army m 9/21/35 Mary T. Griswold, dau of Chester, Esq. of Utica, at Trinity Church in Utica; Rev. Dorr (6-9/26)

WESSELS, Eliza - see LOUD, Samuel

WEST, Charhille - see RAYNOR, Reuben

WEST, Cornelia A. - see KING, Robert P.

WEST, Daniel D. of Fairfield m 8/10/40 Adaline Clemence of Herkimer at H.; Rev. John P. Spinner (3-9/3)

WEST, Emeline - see SMITH, Leland

WEST, G.L. of Rome m 1/3/50 Margaret E. Brooker of Floyd in F.; Rev. W.E. Knox (1-1/9)

WEST, George of Giles, Virginia, 106, m 11/20/15 Mary Gartner of Munroe, 30, (place not given); Rev. Jacob Cooke (6-1/6/16)

WEST, Hannah - see HOLLAND, Robert

WEST, John - see SPENCER, Lorenzo D.

WEST, John Jr., attorney at law m (date not given) Mary Ingraham in Bristol, RI (6-5/15/16)

WEST, John m 7/4/42 Sarah Mills; W. Stillman, Esq. at Verona (all of Verona) (1-7/12)

WEST, Manton(?) of Fairfield m 2/5/40 Nancy Brown of Herkimer at Bridgewater (3-3/5)

WEST, Mary (Mrs.) - see SPENCER, Lorenzo D.

WEST, Salome (Miss), 46, d 8/22/43 in Fairfield (consumption) (3-8/31)

WEST, Sarah - see COLE, Lemuel

WEST, Thomas F. m 9/15/41 Abby S. Kenyon, both of Vernon, at V.; Elder C.M. Lewis (1-9/21)

WESTBROOK, Isaac Van Wyck, 28, 2nd son of Rev. Dr. Cornelius D. Westbrook, pastor and founder of the New Reformed Dutch Church in Peekskill, d 11/24/43 (11-11/28)

WESTBROOK, Jane - see DECKER, Apollas

WESTBROOK, John F. Jackson, infant son of Frederick E. & Catherine E. Westbrook and grandson of the Rev. Dr. Westbrook, of Peekskill, d 12/23/39 at NYC (11-12/31)

WESTCOTT, Amos - see PAINE, John

WESTERVELT, Sarah - see COLBY, Moses

WESTERVLET, John J., 80, of NYC d 7/26/36 in NYC (6-7/29)

WESTFALL, Catharine - see COX, Henry M.

WESTFALL, Sarah - see MARTIN, William M.

WESTMACOTT, John d 10/18/44 in Rome (1-10/22)

WESTON, Harriet M. - see MILLER, James A. (M.D.)

WESTON, William, 72, "an honest man", d 8/13/35 in Albany (6-8/21)

WETHERWAX, John M.B. of Little Falls m 3/14/36 Eliza Lotts, eldest dau. of John of Shelby, Orleans County, in S.; Rev. S. Gilbert (3-3/17)

WETHERWAX, Sebastian of Watervliet m 1/1/39 Sally Conklin of Sand Lake, at S.L.; Rev. D. Starks (5-1/16)

WETMORE, Alphonso (Major), 49, son of late Seth, Esq. of Ames and brother of Solomon H. and Pythagorus Wetmore of Canajoharie, d 6/13/49 at St. Louis, Missouri (was a US Army officer for 21 years and lost his right arm in the last war with Great Britain) (4-6/28)

WETMORE, Alphonzo of Canajoharie m 9/16/48 Mary Pegg of Palatine in P.; Rev. Pegg (double ceremony - see WETMORE, Justus, Esq.) (4-9/21)

WETMORE, Amos - see WHITE, Alice

WETMORE, Charles P. of Rome m 10/10/44 Harriet C. Butler of New Hartford; Rev. M.C. Searle (1-10/15)

WETMORE, Elvira S. - see SKINNER, William H.

WETMORE, Enos, 72, d 6/1/45 at his home in Whitestown (funeral 6/4) (1-6/3)

WETMORE, Francis of Rome m 9/22/41 Abigail Maria Norton of Troy in T.; Rev. N.S.S. Beman (1-9/28)

345

WETMORE, Justus, Esq. of Fort Plain m 9/16/48 Rhoda Baily(?) of Canajoharie in
    Palatine; Rev. Pegg (double ceremony - see WETMORE, Alphonzo)
    (4-9/21)

WEY, Jane Grosvenor - see GROSVENOR, Seth Heacock

WEYMAN, Isabella - see SMITH, Lyle S.H., M.D.

WEYMAN, W. , Esq. - see SMITH, Lyle S.H., M.D.

WHALLON, Daniel M, m 7/22/26 Harriet Van Sice, dau. of James, at Schenectady;
    Rev. John Cooper (all of Schenectady) (6-7/25)

WHEAT, Lydia A. - see FRENCH, Samuel

WHEATON, Julia Ann - see CLARK, Lewis

WHEATON, Lucy - see HOUSE, Charles

WHEELER, Adams, 26, d (by hanging himself) 5/22/35 at Lodi (6-6/5)

WHEELER, Alfred, 6 months, son of Dr. James Wheeler, d 12/9/39 in Little Falls
    (3-12/12)

WHEELER, Augusta Sophia - see LEGGETT, John N.

WHEELER, Baron Haller, 6, son of David, Esq. formerly of West Troy, d 3/3/44 at
    Blackberry, Kane Co., Ill. (scarlet fever) (see also WHEELER, Edward
    Warren) (5-4/24)

WHEELER, David G. of Rome m 7/22/46 Sarah Jane Clark of Verona in V.; Rev.
    H. Kendall (1-7/28)

WHEELER, David G. of Rome m 7/22/46 Sarah Jane Clark of Verona in V.; Rev.
    H. Kendall (1-8/4)

WHEELER, Edward Warren, 9, son of David, Esq. formerly of West Troy, d
    2/27/44 at Blackberry, Kane Co., Ill. (scarlet fever) (see also, WHEELER,
    Baron Haller)(5-4/24)

WHEELER, Eliza - see SPARROW, William

WHEELER, George M. m 11/22/38 Elmina J. Hitchcock, dau. of Isaac, Esq., in
    West Troy; Rev. Gregory (5-11/28)

WHEELER, John R., printer, d (date not given) at Sempronius (6-11/28/26)

WHEELER, Kenneth May, 2, son of George M. and Almina J., formerly of West
    Troy, d 3/6/44 at Blackberry, Kane County, Illinois (scarlet fever) (5-4/3)

WHEELER, Laura J. - see COLE, James P.

WHEELER, Mary Ellen, 1 yr, dau. of Asa and Lavinia, d 3/31/45 in Rome (1-4/8)

WHEELER, Mary Imogine - see STEVENS, G.B., Esq.

WHEELER, Olive - see FRAME, Solomon V.

WHEELER, Phineas, 67, d 8/5/49 in Rome (pleurisy) (1-8/8)

WHEELER, Priscilla - see FARQUARHANSON(?), William

WHEELER, Robert B. m 2/25/36 Hannah Doolittle at Branchport; Rev. T.J.
    Champion (all of Penn Yan) (6-3/5)

WHEELER, Samuel, 86, a Rev. War soldier, d 9/10/42 at Collaburg (11-9/22)

WHEELER, Susan - see MC KNIGHT, George

WHEELER, Walter m 4/10/43 Mary Mabie, both of Danube, in Little Falls; Rev.
    C.W. Lee (3-4/13)

WHEELER, William G. m 10/9/50 Lumira S. Tinney; Rev. T.F. Wyckoff (all of
    West Troy) (5-10/16)

WHEELER, William of Rutland, VT m 1/29/43 Almira Cronkhite of Little Falls in
    L.F.; Rev. C.W. Leet (3-2/2)

WHEELOCK, Daniel, 60, d (date not given) at Wilton (7-6/13/10)

WHEELOCK, Eliza M., 24, dau. of William and Harriet, d 2/9/45 in Swanzy, New

Hampshire (1-3/25)

WHILPLEY, Almyra, about 45, wf of Ebenezer, d 10/7/42 in Bedford (11-10/13)

WHIPPLE, Allen of Ingham County, Mich. m 7/10/41 Clarissa G. Collins of Rome in R.; Rev. S. Haynes (1-9/14)

WHIPPLE, Eunice H. - see SANDFORD, A.C.

WHIPPLE, Frelove R. - see THAYER, George

WHIPPLE, J.E., Esq. of Lansingburgh m 12/1/41 Maria E. Viele of Albany in West Troy; Rev. Gregory (5-12/8)

WHIPPLE, J.W. m 5/29/41 Margaret Jane Dorras of Lansingburgh in L.; Rev. S. Ireland (5-6/2)

WHIPPLE, Joshua, 60, d (date not given) at Norwich, Conn. (7-8/2/09)

WHIPPLE, Malachi, an elderly resident of Bern, Albany County, d 12/13/36 at his home in Bern (apoplexy) (6-12/17)

WHIPPLE, Malachi, Esq., 67, d 12/12/36 at Bern (survived by "a numerous family") (6-12/19)

WHIPPLE, Solomon m 12/20/26 Caroline Churchill, dau. of Roswell Churchill; Rev. Romeyn (6-12/26)

WHIPPLE, Susan L. - see HILL, Zacheus

WHITAKER, Abm. D. m 2/2/49 Sarah Maria Yates, both of Flatbush, in Kingston; Rev. C. Shook (8-2/24)

WHITAKER, Olive - see BOUGHTON, E.H.

WHITAKER, Sarah - see SUTLIFF, John

WHITAKER, Thomas V.L. of Kingston m 4/14/49 Nelly Ann Osterhout of Saugerties in Flatbush; Rev. J.M. Bulbert (8-4/28)

WHITALL, Ann - see LOUNSBERRY, James

WHITALL, Anne - see LOUNSBERRY, James

WHITALL, Jane H.W. - see WILLIAMS, John (Col.)

WHITALL, Matilda - see RICE, M.M.

WHITBECK, Henry R. of Root, Montgomery County m 12/12/48 Ann Humiston of Vienna in V.; Rev. A. Adams (1-12/15)

WHITBECK, Jane Helen - see CAULKINS, Russell (Dr.)

WHITBECK, John of firm of J. & H.M. Whitbeck of Livingston m 6/1/37 Mary R. Thomas of Albany; Rev. Holmes (6-6/2)

WHITBECK, Peter - see CAULKINS, Russell (Dr.)

WHITBECK, Storm m 2/24/36 Margaret Ouderkirk, dau of Peter of Westerloo, in W.; Rev. E. Slingerland (6-3/14)

WHITCALL, Jane H.W. - see WILLIAMS, John (Col.)

WHITCOMB, Ann Maranda - see GIFFORD, Joseph

WHITE, Abby, 29, wf of Roswell, d (date not given) at East Granville, Mass. (7-6/13/10)

WHITE, Albert Le Roy of Rutland, Jefferson County m 12/23/35 Almira White, dau of Henry, Esq., of Athens at Trinity Church, Athens; Rev. Thibatt (6-1/1/36)

WHITE, Alice, 25, wf of James of Utica, d 5/4/45 at the home of her father, Amos Wetmore, at Whitestown (1-5/6)

WHITE, Almira - see WHITE, Albert Le Roy

WHITE, Calvin, 23, son of Daniel, d (date not given) "at Coventry (Andover Society)" (7-5/24/09)

WHITE, Campbell B., Esq. of Baltimore m 1/31/16 Harriet Banyer LeRoy, dau. of late Jacob, Esq., at NYC; Rev. Dr. Romeyn (6-2/7)

WHITE, Canvass, Esq., about 46, formerly of NY State, d 12/18/34 at St. Augustine, FL shortly after arrival there. Was chief Engineer of the Delaware Eritan (sic) Canal. (6-1/13/35)

WHITE, Caroline - see FRAZER, C.E.

WHITE, Caroline - see LEACH, James S.

WHITE, Delos (Dr.), about 50, d 3/18/35 at Cherry Valley "after a long illness." (6-3/24)

WHITE, Elijah, Esq., 54, formerly of West Springfield, MA, d 8/8/36 at his home in Amboy, Onondaga Co. (6-8/23)

WHITE, Elisha Putnam, youngest son of William White, d 5/18/35 (funeral at 4 o'clock at his father's home at North Dean St.) (6-5/19)

WHITE, Ellen - see MC ELROY, Peter

WHITE, Eve, 98, relict of Harry, Esq., formerly a commissary of the British government, d in NYC (Mrs. White of the family of Van Cortlandt, one of the oldest and most respected of New York") (detailed obituary from the Cooperstown Journal) (6-9/6/36)

WHITE, George, 50, printer, formerly of Albany, NY, d 4/19/26 in Philadelphia (6-4/25)

WHITE, Hannahette - see MILLS, Dwight

WHITE, Horace T., one of the publishers of the Vermont Statesman at Castleton m 3/24/35 Lydia Lorraine Fay, dau of the editor of the Rutland Herald, at Rutland; Rev. William Mitchell (6-3/28)

WHITE, Howard H., Esq of NYC m 9/19/36 Emma Hart of the Seminary at the Troy Female Seminary; Rev. Judah (6-9/22)

WHITE, Howard H., Esq., formerly Surrogate of Putnam County, d 4/4/40 in Danbury, CT (12-4/14)

WHITE, James (Dr.) of Buffalo m 12/6/36 Mary Elizabeth Penfield, dau of Henry F., Esq., in Penfield, Monroe Co.; Rev. Orange Clark of Rochester (6-12/14)

WHITE, James m 11/4/41 Mary Ann Mills; Rev. E.D.G. Prime (all of Wallkill) (9-11/6)

WHITE, James of Goshen m 12/1/42 Mary Nelson of Newburgh in New Windsor; Rev. Ira Ferris (9-12/7)

WHITE, James of Kingston m 3/19/40 Julia Vandenburg of West Troy in W.T.; Rev. George Phippen (5-3/25)

WHITE, John, 79, d (date not given) in Hartford, Conn. (7-6/20/10)

WHITE, Levina - see JOHNSON, Daniel

WHITE, Lucinda - see FORT, Jacob

WHITE, Lucy - see WEARE, John

WHITE, Lyman - see JOHNSON, Daniel

WHITE, Margaret - see CHATFIELD, Clinton

WHITE, Mary - see JOHNSON, F.M.

WHITE, Michael, d (date not given) in NYC (6-5/15/16)

WHITE, Rebecca - see MARTIN, James (Rev.)

WHITE, Rebecca Jane - see STORMS, John

WHITE, Robert of Lansingburgh m 12/4/39 Mary Jimiltson of Troy in West Troy; John Hastings, Esq. (5-12/11)

WHITE, Solon H., Esq., of Cold Spring, NY m 4/8/43 Margaret Randall of Bowdoinham, Maine, at B.; Rev. C. Quinnum, D.D. (11-5/9)

WHITE, Willard D. of Ames m 5/31/49 Eliza A. Duffin of Cherry Valley in C.V.; Rev. C.H. Hervey (4-6/14)

WHITEALL, Anna E. - see CARRINGTON, T.

WHITEHOUSE, Henry D.D. m 11/7/36 Harriet Bruen, dau of M. Esq., at Brighton House, Perth Amboy, NJ; Rt. Rev. Dr. Onderdonk (6-11/11)

WHITFIELD, Georgiana Frances - see DE PEYRONNET, Lewis Jules

WHITIN, James F., Esq., of Whitinsville, Mass. m P.H. Saunders of Providence, RI at St. Stevens Church in Providence (1-7/26)

WHITING, Catherine M. - see JOHNSON, Horace H.

WHITING, Lucia - see SPENCER, F.A.

WHITING, Mary - see BRAINARD, Thomas (Rev.)

WHITMAN, Catharine (Miss), 63, formerly of Keene, NH, d 9/20/39 (for many years a member of the Methodist church) (3-9/26)

WHITMAN, Mary, 91, relict of John Whitman, d 10/23/36 in Little Falls (she was born in Germany but from an early age has lived in Massachusetts and New Hampshire having been brought from N.H. by her friends a few weeks since) (3-10/27)

WHITMAN, Rebecca, wf of John, d 10/25/38 in Fairfield (3-11/8)

WHITMASH, Joseph of Mass. m 8/8/40 Elizabeth Wilkes of Rome, NY in R.; G. Wadsworth, Esq. (1-8/11)

WHITMORE, Annette Madeline, 2, dau. of John and Lucretia, d 5/13/44 in Rome (1-5/21)

WHITMORE, Richard, 48, formerly of Fairfield, VT, d 12/20/39 in Waterford, NY ("Printers in Vermont will please copy...") (5-2/12)

WHITNEY, Abigail, 9, dau. of Samuel, d 9/20/44 in Westmoreland (1-10/15)

WHITNEY, Angelina - see BROOKS, I. Lloyd

WHITNEY, Catherine M. - see JOHNSON, Horace H.

WHITNEY, Eliza H. - see OSBORN, Daniel

WHITNEY, Emma, only dau of William Alvord, d 7/23/36 at DeFreetsville (6-7/26)

WHITNEY, Nicholas B. (Rev.), 64, d 11/26/35 at Hamilton, MA (in 35th year of his ministry) (6-12/4)

WHITNEY, R.M. of Albany m 2/22/37 Miss Nancy Flagg, dau. of Capt. Aaron Whitney of Harvard, Mass. in H.; Rev. Washington Gilbert (6-3/3)

WHITNEY, Richard J. m 11/10/41 Margaret Elder in Newburgh; Elder George Phippen (all of Newburgh) (9-11/20)

WHITNEY, William Wallace, 26, d 10/12/37 in New Orleans (from the prevailing fever)(born in 1810 in Broome County, NY, son of Gen. Joshua Whitney of Binghamton - survived by a wife and 2 children)(arrived in New Orleans "about three years ago for prosecuting the claim of his wife, legal heir of the late Daniel Clark to a very large estate pending in the US Dictrict court)(from New Orleans Commercial Bulletin) (6-10/24)

WHITON, Sarah A. - see YEARSLEY, Henry

WHITTEMORE, Annette Cordelia, 6 months, dau. of James and Seraphina, d 3/20/48 in Rome (1-3/24)

WHITTEMORE, Thomas H. - see CUSHING, Helen M.

WICK, Henry, Esq., merchant, of Little Falls m 9/17/37 Russilla Mc Credy of Warren in W.; Rev. Lewis (3-9/28)

WICKSON,. Alva m 12/20/38 Charlotte Mead in South East; Rev. George D. Sutton (12-1/1/39)

WIER, Susan Emily, 4, dau. of Edward and Susan, d 12/28/41 in Newburgh (9-1/1/42)

WIGGINS, Catharine - see HENDERSON, J.E.

WIGGINS, Charles E., 28, son of Benjamin, d 7/12/50 in Rome (typhus fever) (1-8/7)

WIGGINS, Don C. of Rome m 3/16/42 Sarah A. Woodworth of Florence at F. (1-3/22)

WIGGINS, Harriet - see ROGERS, --- (Mr.)

WIGGINS, J. of Rome m 8/17/50 Lois Ann Scoville, dau. of H. Scoville of Camden, in C.; Rev. E.G. Townsend (1-8/28)

WIGGINS, John, 71, d 7/6/46 in Rome (1-7/21)

WIGGINS, Mineva (sic) - see WOODWORTH, James B.

WIGGINS, Sarah - see CHASE, Stephen C.

WIGHT, Jabez of Rome m 6/27/44 Hannah P. Munson of Paris in P.; Rev. Allen of Bridgewater (1-7/2)

WIGHT, Mary - see DUNN, John

WIGHTMAN, Jane I. - see DONALDSON, James C.

WIGHTMAN, Silas, 79, d 8/4/47 in Rome (1-8/13)

WILBER, Gaston m 10/9/49 Maria Schoonmaker, dau. of Peter D., in Saugerties; Rev. C. Van Santvoord (all of Saugerties) (8-10/13)

WILBER, Jasper of Lee County, Iowa m 4/15/49 Martha Pilkington of West Troy, NY in W.T.; T.F. Wyckoff (5-4/18)

WILBUR, Amanda - see CRESSEY, E.H.

WILBUR, John W., Esq., of West Troy m 4/11/49 Ellen Clute of Saratoga in Albany; Rev. W.W. Clapp (5-4/18)

WILBUR, Solomon B. m 8/3/43 Fanny Randall, both of Troy, in West Troy; Rev. Z. Phillips (5-8/9)

WILCOX, ---- (Mr.) m (date not given) Honora Griffing, dau. of Augustus, Esq., at Oyster Bay, Suffolk County (3-7/21/36)

WILCOX, Alonzo m 11/24/36 Matilda Staunton in Eatonville; Rev. William H. Waggoner (3-12/1)

WILCOX, Benjamin, 76, a Rev. War soldier, m 2/17/41 Mrs. Briggs, 56, of Durhamville at D.; Rev. D.D. Ransom (1-2/23)

WILCOX, Clarissa Ann, 12, eldest dau. of A. Wilcox, d 9/29/36 in Danube (3-10/13)

WILCOX, Daniel ("his funeral 1/20/36 at 3 o'clock from his late home, 27 Dallius Street, Albany") (6-1/20)

WILCOX, Daniel, 40, merchant, of Albany, d 1/18/36 (funeral at 3 o'clock from his late residence, 27 Dallius St.) (6-1/19)

WILCOX, Henry W. m 7/2/50 Mary Eliza Jones, dau. of R.H.; Rev. William E. Knox (all of Rome) (1-7/10)

WILCOX, Lucy, 55, wf of Sylvester, d 12/13/35 in Albany (funeral from his residence at the Western Hotel) (6-12/15)

WILCOX, Nancy, 74, d 8/25/43 in Danube (married 1/7/1788 Nathan Wilcox at Westerly, R.I. Her husband d 1839 (she was mother of 10 children, 67 grand children and 26 great grand children) (member of Baptist Church) ("Herkimer Journal will please copy") (3-9/7)

WILCOX, Peleg, 35, d suddenly 3/6/40 at his home in Norway, Herkimer County (an obituary is included) (3-3/19)

WILDER, Alfred of NYC m 11/9/35 Lydia E. Babcock of New Lebanon Springs at
    N.L.S.; Rev. Churchill (6-11/11)

WILDER, Elijah (Deacon), 84, d 7/9/36 near Geneva (6-7/18)

WILDER, James L. of Lowville m 7/5/47 Nancy Ann Eddy of Rome in R.; H.C.
    Vogell (1-7/9)

WILDER, Simon Hulbert, 15, youngest son of Abel and Asenath, d 4/9/43 at
    Verona (1-5/2)

WILEY, William M., 5, son of John, d 12/3/42 in Newburgh (9-12/10)

WILGUS, Ann Elizabeth - see BOWEN, Henry L.

WILHILMI, Ernest, 84, d 3/26/36 in the parish of Lachenaye (?), Lower Canada
    ("came to America in 1776 as a lieutenant in the Hessian Chauseurs")("the
    last of the Hessians")(6-3/29)

WILKES, Elizabeth - see WHITMASH, Joseph

WILKESON, Eli H. of Buffalo m 2/13/37 Julia Allen, dau. of late Ethan B., Esq. of
    Batavia, at B.; Rev. Whitney (6-2/21)

WILKESON, Sarah, wf of Hon. Samuel Wilkinson, mayor of Buffalo, d 4/21/36 at
    Buffalo (6-4/28)

WILKIE, William m 12/19/36 Susan Byce, both of Little Falls, in L.; Rev. Petrie,
    Esq. (3-12/29)

WILKIN, James A., Esq., about 45, d 4/30/42 in Montgomery (9-5/7)

WILKINSON, Adelia D - see OLMSTEAD, Charles A.

WILKINSON, Cornelia - see COTRELL, J.G.

WILKINSON, Hannah - see MINK, Stephen G.

WILKINSON, Maria - see LELAND, David Warren

WILKINSON, Robert, Esq., 51, d 8/13/49 at Poughkeepsie (8-8/18)

WILLARD, Ann Maria - see VARNEY, Alfred E.

WILLARD, Betsey - see HILDRICK, Thaddeus

WILLARD, Charles (Col.) - see VARNEY, Alfred E.

WILLARD, Charlotte M. - see YOUNG, Glover S.

WILLARD, Elias (Dr.) - see FOSTER, William

WILLARD, Elias (Dr.) - see MORRIS, Walter R.

WILLARD, Elizabeth - see MORRIS, Walter R.

WILLARD, Jane - see LOOMIS, Dyer, M.D.

WILLARD, Mary - see STEWART, James

WILLARD, Mary, 57, widow of Dr. Sylvester Willard, d 2/11/43 in Little Falls
    (member of the Methodist Episcopal Church for 22 years) (funeral service
    preached by Rev. George Gary at Eatonville where she was buried) (3-2/23)

WILLARD, Robah C. - see WEAVER, Philo C. (Major)

WILLARD, Sarah - see JOHNSON, Chauncey

WILLES, Mary - see ELLIOT, Jesse (Rev.)

WILLIAMS, Aleina - see LARKIN, J.W.

WILLIAMS, Amos, 9, son of Jesse, d 1/13/39 in New Castle (12-1/22)

WILLIAMS, Ann Eliza - see EMERSON, Oliver (Rev.)

WILLIAMS, Anna Maria - see JONES, John R.

WILLIAMS, Anna, 67, widow of late Robert, formerly of Buttermilk Falls, d
    10/24/41 at Peekskill. (11-10/26)

WILLIAMS, B. Whitman m 1/17/49 Cynthia Peggs, dau. of R. Peggs, Esq.; Rev.
    F.H. Stanton (all of Rome) (1-1/24)

WILLIAMS, Beliah (Mrs.), 83, d (date not given) at New Haven (7-1/31/10)

WILLIAMS, Betsy - see LEROW, John

WILLIAMS, Brown H. m 11/10/41 Maria Farmer, dau. of John, Esq. of Herkimer, in H.; Rev. Williams of Utica (3-11/18)

WILLIAMS, Caleb, about 55, d 9/28/42 at his home in Peekskill (11-9/29)

WILLIAMS, Calvin C. m 5/11/26 Morana Aurelia Winants, dau. of Josiah; Rev. Leonard (all of Albany) (6-5/15)

WILLIAMS, Caroline - see VANDERBURGH, Frederick

WILLIAMS, Charity - see MYERS, Joseph

WILLIAMS, Charles m 10/4/49 Almira Slater at Oak Ridge, Warwarsing; H.B. Taylor, Esq. (8-10/20)

WILLIAMS, Charlotte Augusta, 8 months, d 2/20/38 and Mary Wells Williams, 3 years, d 2/21/38 (both are the only daughters of Albert and Elizabeth Williams) (both scarlet fever) (5-2/28)

WILLIAMS, Charlotte, about 9 months, dau. of Robert, d 2/20/38 in West Troy (5-2/21)

WILLIAMS, Chauncey P. of Albany m 9/21/42 Martha A. Hough of Whitesboro at W.; President Green (sic) (1-9/27)

WILLIAMS, Cornelia - see MARTIN, E.T. Throop

WILLIAMS, Cyrus F. m 5/21/44 Margaret Tripp, both of Rome, in Floyd; Rev. Haynes (1-5/28)

WILLIAMS, David - see MEAD, David

WILLIAMS, Delia - see PROUDFIT, Alexander (Rev.)

WILLIAMS, E. Esq., of Auburn m 8/23/36 Helen L Leonard, dau of Rev. Joshua Leonard of Geddes, at G. (6-8/29)

WILLIAMS, E., Esq., editor of the Jacksonville Courier, d 11/3/35 at Jacksonville. (6-11/28)

WILLIAMS, E., Esq., of Auburn m 7/23/36 Helen L. Leonard, dau of Rev. Joshua Leonard of Geddes, at G. (6-9/2)

WILLIAMS, Elias L. m 3/17/46 Caroline M. Bill, dau. of Amos of Lebanon, at Colchester, Conn.; Rev. Dr. Strong (1-4/7)

WILLIAMS, Elijah, 34, editor of the Jacksonville Courier, d 11/3/35 in Jacksonville, FL (6-12/7)

WILLIAMS, Elisha - see TEACKLE, Elizabeth M.

WILLIAMS, Eliza A. - see SNYDER, Abram G.

WILLIAMS, Emeline - see MARSH, Moses P.

WILLIAMS, Emeline - see MARSH, Moses P.

WILLIAMS, Francis Wells, 4, son of Robert and Elizabeth, d 5/28/44 in West Troy (funeral 5/29 at 2 o'clock from his parents home on Erie Street, first door north of James Lobdell's home, 4th Ward) (5-5/29)

WILLIAMS, George m 12/19/41 Mrs. Mary Travis in Carmel; Absolon Austin, Esq. (11-12/28)

WILLIAMS, George of Rome m 6/3/49 Annie S. Rudd, dau. of B. Rudd, Esq., of Delta, in D.; Rev. B.J. Drefenderf (1-6/13)

WILLIAMS, Gibson T., merchant, of Buffalo m 10/12/41 Harriet Cordelia Howard, dau. of Capt. Rufus Howard of Frankfort, in F.; Rev. Thomas Houston (3-11/4)

WILLIAMS, H.C. (Major) of the treasury department, Washington City m 11/17/35 Frances A. Chapman, dau. of late George, Esq., at Thoroughfare, Prince William County, Virginia; Rev. Slaughter (6-11/28)

WILLIAMS, Harriet - see TALCOTT, William H.

WILLIAMS, Henry B. m 12/4/39 Hannah Golden; Rev. J. Youngs (all of Peekskill) (11-12/10)

WILLIAMS, Henry of Schenectady m 9/12/36 Eleanor Lansing of Salisbury in S.; Rev. L.C. Rogers (3-9/15)

WILLIAMS, Hugh m 9/1/49 Elizabeth Edwards, both of Rome, in R.; Rev. W.E. Knox (1-9/5)

WILLIAMS, Isaac H., 57, d 7/8/38 in West Troy (5-7/11)

WILLIAMS, Jane - see RYDER, Paul

WILLIAMS, Jared, 42, Mayor of Hartford, CT, d 11/22/35 in Hartford (a short illness) (6-11/28)

WILLIAMS, Jehiel, 77, d (date not given) in Middletown (7-7/4/10)

WILLIAMS, Jerome D., 2, son of Cyrus F. and Margaret, d 8/28/49 in Rome (1-8/29)

WILLIAMS, John (Col.) of the Eagle Hotel in Peekskill m 11/17/39 Jane H.W. Whitall, dau of late George of Pennsylvania; Rev. Cooly (11-11/19)

WILLIAMS, John (Col.) proprietor of the Eagle Hotel at Peekskill, m 11/17/39 Jane H.W. Whitcall, dau. of late George Whitcall of Pennsylvania; Rev. Cooly (12-11/26)

WILLIAMS, John Chandler - see NEWTON, Sarah Thorndike

WILLIAMS, John H., Esq., editor of the Political Examiner, m 11/17/36 Ellen Shriver, dau of Abraham, judge of the 5th judicial district, in Frederick, Maryland (6-11/29)

WILLIAMS, John m 12/31/34 Mrs. Harriet Pinkerton; Rev. Hiram Meeker (all of Albany) (6-1/3/35)

WILLIAMS, John, 69(?), d 1/11/43 at Westmoreland (1-1/17)

WILLIAMS, John, 73, born in Westchester County, for past 20 years a resident of Ossining, d 3/14/40 at Hyde Park (12-3/24)

WILLIAMS, John, Esq. - see MARTIN, E.T. Throop

WILLIAMS, John, Jr. of Salem (Washington Co.) m 9/9/35 Harriet S. Martin of Auburn at A.; Rev. Bethune (6-9/15)

WILLIAMS, Louriett, 4, dau. of William, d 9/19/49 in Kingston (8-9/29)

WILLIAMS, Lucy - see LAW, Edward

WILLIAMS, Lucy Jane - see STRONG, John

WILLIAMS, Martha A. - see GAY, James Porter

WILLIAMS, Mary - see BRAYMAN, Mason

WILLIAMS, Mary Ann (Mrs.), 46, d 3/19/46 in West Troy (5-4/8)

WILLIAMS, Mary E, 17, dau of John Williams of Utica d (date not given) at Sand Beach near Auburn (was at the school of Miss Benners at Sand Beach for her studies and...her health) (6-1/8/35)

WILLIAMS, Mary Wells - see WILLIAMS, Charlotte Augusta

WILLIAMS, Mary, 22, d (date not given) "at Wethersfield, Miss." [Perhaps intended for Wethersfield, Conn. - FQB] (7-5/10/09)

WILLIAMS, N., M.D., m 7/3/41 Mary Ann P---- (surname blurred) in the Methodist Chapel in Little Falls; Rev. J. Loveys(?) (surname blurred) (all of Little Falls) (3-7/8)

WILLIAMS, Nancy, 14, dau. of Jesse and Amanda, d 5/8/47 in Rome (hydrophalus) (1-6/4)

WILLIAMS, Nathan (Hon.) d 9/24/35 at his home in Geneva (a protracted and painful illness) (clerk of Supreme Court of NY; for many years circuit judge and vice chancellor of Fifth Judicial District, he "until recently lived in Utica") (6-10/2)

WILLIAMS, Nathan (Hon.), clerk of the Supreme Court of NY and Vice Chancellor of the Utica District d 9/24/35 in Geneva (long obituary included) (from Utica Observer) (6-10/3)

WILLIAMS, Otis P. of Greenfield, Saratoga County m 4/16/43 Margaret Ladd of Fairfield at F.; Rev. William Baker (3-4/27)

WILLIAMS, Robert M., merchant, d 6/12/40 in West Troy (5-6/17)

WILLIAMS, Rufus O. (Rev.) of Hartford, CT m 10/1/35 Jane Maria Burr, dau of William G., Esq. of Mount Pleasant, Westchester Co., in M.P.; Rev. S.J.H. Byer (6-10/9)

WILLIAMS, S. Ann, 35, wf of Benjamin S. and dau. of Edward Webber, d 5/18/44 in Vernon (1-6/4)

WILLIAMS, Samuel m 6/8/35 Eliza Graham in Little Falls; Rev. H.S. Attwater (3-6/15)

WILLIAMS, Sophia W. - see GARDNER, James V.P.

WILLIAMS, Thomas, 100, "a colored man and formerly a slave", d 1/21/44 at Saratoga Springs (6-2/7)

WILLIAMS, Thomas, 80, d (date not given) in Yorktown (a member of the Society of Friends) (12-2/18/40)

WILLIAMS, Thomas, Jr. of Vernon m 7/27/36 Eliza A. Knox, dau of Gen. John J. Knox of Augusta, NY at A.; Rev. H.P. Bogue (6-8/1)

WILLIAMS, Warren B. m 1/15/45 Lydia Clemons ("each measuring six feet") in Lee; Daniel Twichel, Esq. (1-2/4)

WILLIAMS, William (Retired General), late Senator of Stockbridge, Mass. m 7/5/43 Mrs. Mary B. Everill of Salisbury, Conn. in Salisbury, Conn.; Rev. Adam Reid (3-7/13)

WILLIAMSON, Howard J. of Troy m 5/21/50 Helen G. Greenwood, dau. of George, of West Troy; Rev. Joshua Weaver (5-6/5)

WILLIAMSON, James m 9/17/49 Jane Powell, both of Saugerties; Rev. H. Ostrander, D.D. (8-9/29)

WILLIAMSON, Jason m 12/20/26 Letetia Armstrong in Albany; Joseph Bell, Esq. (6-12/26)

WILLIAMSON, Jedediah (Mr.), age blurred but possibly 59, d 1/9/37 at Stony Brook, Suffolk County (6-1/18)

WILLIAMSON, Sarah Ann - see LOCKE, Frederick Augustus

WILLIAMSON, William J., Esq. m 12/30/41 Altaline Wood in NYC; Rev. R. Gilbert (all of NYC) (11-1/18/42)

WILLINK, John Abraham, Esq. of Amsterdam m (date not given) Cornelia Ann Ludlow in NYC (6-5/8/16)

WILLIS, Jemima - see VAN WINKLE, Albert

WILLIS, N. Judson of Columbia, Herkimer Co. m 10/30/49 Jannette Briggs of Rome in R.; Rev. H.C. Vogell (1-11/7)

WILLIS, N.P. of the United States and one of the editors of the New York Mirror m (date not given) Mary Stone, dau of William, Esq. of the Royal Arsenal, at Plumstead, England (11-11/17/35)

WILLIS, Sarah S. - see HUNN, Jacob

WILLMARTH, John L. of Stanford, VT m 2/27/39 Mrs. Annah H. Brown of

Fairfield in F.; Rev. A Gross (3-3/14)

WILLOUGHBY, Benjamin Larned, M.D., 24, d 4/18/35 at Newport, Herkimer Co. (consumption) (6-4/27)

WILLOUGHBY, Bridget (Mrs.), 77, d at Canterbury (7-6/13/10)

WILLOUGHBY, Sarah, 58, wf of Westel Willoughby, M.D., d 12/14/38 at Newport (3-12/20)

WILLSEY, Catharine - see LAWPAUGH, Solomon

WILLSON(?), Mary Ann - see RATHBUN, William

WILLSON, Esther, 55, d 10/25/42 at the home of David Spencer, Esq. in Waterford (5-11/2)

WILLSON, Richard H. m 11/14/41 Orpha Burgett in West Troy; Rev. D. Starks (5-11/17)

WILSON, ----, wf of Stephen Wilson (her funeral at 3 o'clock from her husband's home at 49 Hudson Street) (6-1/21/36)

WILSON, Alfred, dentist, of NYC m 8/28/39 Mary Elizabeth Denison of Little Falls in Herkimer; Rev. J.P. Spencer (3-8/29)

WILSON, Banjamin F. of Westmoreland m 3/7/49 Susan F. Brewster of Verona in V.; Rev. M. Johnson (1-3/14)

WILSON, Calvin, 54, d (date not given) at Windsor (7-6/20/10)

WILSON, Catharine - see IRWIN, James

WILSON, Catharine Amelia, 33, wf of William, d very suddenly 3/13/42 in West Troy (5-3/23)

WILSON, David W. of Boston m 7/15/26 Eliza Taylor, dau. of B. Taylor, Esq. of NYC, at St. Mark's Church in NYC, Rev. Creighton (6-8/8)

WILSON, Deborah B., wf of John A., d 7/3/36 (consumption) (6-7/7)

WILSON, E., Jr. - see COOPER, William

WILSON, Elizabeth - see MEADE, Orlando

WILSON, Elizabeth - see STOCKER, George

WILSON, Emily - see EVSTAPHIEVE, Alexis Alexander

WILSON, Eva - see CASE, Everett

WILSON, George S. (Rev.), 27, formerly a pastor in Utica, d 5/17/41 at Gouverneur (1-6/1)

WILSON, George S. of Windsor, VT m 8/16/35 Julia R. Preston of Rupert, VT at R.; Rev. W. James of Albany (6-9/8)

WILSON, Gould - see TODD, Albert

WILSON, Hannah H., 33, wf of Joseph, d (date not given) at Cohoes (consumption) (6-3/4/37)

WILSON, Harriet H - see FAWBY, William

WILSON, Harrison, 13 months, son of Kniffin Wilson, d 1/24/39 in Carmel (12-1/29)

WILSON, Helen - see TORRANCE, Jared

WILSON, Henry of Middletown m 6/5/42 Ann Elmira Embler of Newburgh; Rev. William Hill (9-6/11)

WILSON, James - see IRWIN, James

WILSON, James J m 6/3/35 Ann Read Gill, dau of Bennington Gill of NYC, in NYC; Rev. Dr. Sprague (6-6/8)

WILSON, James, about 50, d 5/27/10 at home of Elijah Parsons at Enfield (deceased was "a transient person whose name from papers in his possession was supposed to be James Wilson (who) had the appearance of a foreigner")

(7-6/27)

WILSON, James, Esq., late of Murray shire, Scotland m 10/7/43 Mary Garet Clark of West Troy in Albany; Rev. Dr. Wyckoff (5-10/11)

WILSON, Jane - see TEED, Nelson

WILSON, Jane - see TODD, Albert

WILSON, John, 45, d 6/12/38 in Newport (3-6/21)

WILSON, John, M.D., m 5/1/37 Mary Fisher, dau. of late Peter Van Buren of Johnstown; Rev. Dr. Sprague (6-5/2)

WILSON, Margaret - see BUERLEY, Daniel

WILSON, Mary Elizabeth - see HAIGHT, R. Stewart

WILSON, Mary J. - see JESSUP, William B.

WILSON, Mary Louisa, infant dau. of Abram F. Wilson, d 8/3/37 (funeral 8/4 from her father's home corner of North Market and Wilson Streets) (6-8/4)

WILSON, Moses of Fairfield m 12/28/42 Adeline Parkhurst of Schuyler in S.; Rev. Jones (3-1/19/43)

WILSON, Nancy - see BAUM, Jacob H.

WILSON, Nehemiah (Capt.), 81, a Rev. War soldier, d (date not given) while chopping down a tree which fell on him at Greenwich, Conn. (from the New York Times) (6-8/16)

WILSON, Nelson m 8/18/40 Eizabeth Wadrath, both of Little Falls, at Herkimer; Rev. J.P. Spinner (3-9/3)

WILSON, Rebecca - see LANCASTER, Cyrus

WILSON, Samuel, 25, son of Daniel, d 4/29/41 in NYC (a lingering illness) (11-5/4)

WILSON, Samuel, Jr., about 43, d 5/1/ 39 in Somers (12-5/7)

WILSON, Sarah, 62, wf of Joseph, (long a resident of the Colonie), d 2/26/35 in Albany (funeral 2/29 at home of Mr. Wilson, 163 North Market St.) (6-2/28)

WILSON, Thaddeus D. d 7/15/49 in Saugerties (8-7/21)

WILSON, Wilford L. of Cazenovia m 9/16/40 Ann H. Perry of Newport in N.; Rev. H.H. Kellogg of Clinton (3-10/15)

WILSON, William, 21, only son of John and Susan, d 11/3/42 in Lewisboro (11-11/10)

WILTSIE, ----, infant child of Charles Wiltsie, d 1/16/39 in Sing Sing (12-8/20)

WILTSIE, Robert, Esq., agent of the Mount Pleasant Prison, m 8/10/36 Mary Bard at Sing Sing; Rev. Edward N. Mead (all of S.S.) (6-8/12)

WILTSIE, Susannah, 81, widow of John, d 8/14/49 in Kingston (8-8/25)

WILTSIE, Susannah, 84, widow of John, d 8/14/49 in Kingston (8-8/18)

WINANS, Henry, Esq., 57, father of W.H.S. Winans, editor of the Cohoes Advocate, d 4/17 in Cohoes (consumption) (5-4/21)

WINANS, Jane, 55, wf of Henry, Esq. for many years a resident of West Troy, d 8/24/46 at Valatie (5-9/2)

WINANS, Ursula, 25, wf of William H.S., late editor of the Cohoes Journal, d 8/15/48 in Troy (5-8/23)

WINANTS, Josiah - see WILLIAMS, Calvin C.

WINANTS, Morana Aurelia - see WILLIAMS, Calvin C.

WINCHELL, Alex. (Prof.) of Amenia m 12/10/49 Julia F. Lines(?) of Utica in U.; Rev. W. Wyatt (1-12/12)

WINCHESTER, Jonas of firm of H. Greeley & Co., publishers of the New Yorker,

356

m 11/19/35 Susan B. Story; Rev. Dr. Cutler (all of Brooklyn) (6-11/24)

WINDHAM, ---- (Mrs.), member of the House of Commons, d (date not given) in England (7-8/1/10)

WINDSOR, Thomas (Capt.), 73, formerly of Rhadishland (sic), and for many years a resident of Little Falls, d 5/1/36 (3-5/5)

WINEHOOP, Jacob m 1/19/26 Helena Carhart at Bethlehem; Rev. Kissam (6-1/24)

WING, Angeline - see PECK, Reuben

WING, D. Smith of Fort Edward m Sarah A. Heath, dau of Sidney, Esq. of Arkinsaw, Washington Co., NY; Rev. Babcock (6-5/13)

WING, Halsey R., Esq., attorney at law, of Brockport, NY, m 8/31/35 Harriet N. Walton, dau of General E.P. Walton of Montpelier, VT, in M; Rev. Chester Wright (6-9/8)

WING, Mary, 45, wf of Dr. Joel A. Wing and dau. of Matthew Gregory, Esq., d 9/6/37 (illness of several months) (6-9/7)

WINN, T. - see ELLIS, Eliza R.

WINNE, Aerian of West Troy m 6/9/45 Mary Grant of Albany in Troy; Rev. S.L. Stillman (5-6/18)

WINNE, Alida, 61, widow of Daniel I., Esq., d 12/17/36 (friends of the deceased and her son, Isaac, invited to her funeral at 3 o'clock at her late home, 286 North Market St.) (6-12/19)

WINNE, Ann - see SICKLER, Christopher (Col.)

WINNE, Catharine - see HUMPHREY, James

WINNE, Charles, M.D. of Buffalo m 9/30/35 Louisa Viele, dau of late John L. Esq., at Lansingburgh; Rev. Vermilyea (6-10/2)

WINNE, Daniel I. - see HUMPHREY, James

WINNE, John D., Esq., 78, a Rev. War soldier, d 4/30/37 (funeral from his former home in Bethlehem) (6-5/2)

WINNE, Luvinius L., Esq., 33, d 2/11/16 in Albany (6-2/21)

WINNE, Rebecca - see SICKLES, James

WINSLOW, Anna, 1 yr, dau. of Henry and Sarah, d 2/28/45 in Rome (see WINSLOW, Frances Louisa) (1-3/11)

WINSLOW, Erasmus, 4, son of Pascol Paoli and Mary Winslow, d 5/16/39 in Yorktown (12-5/21)

WINSLOW, Frances Louisa, 4, dau. of Henry and Sarah, d 3/4/45 in Rome (see WINSLOW, Anna) (1-3/11)

WINSLOW, Henry, 32, formerly of Rome, NY, d 3/16/47 at Barnard, VT (1-4/2)

WINSLOW, Mary, 1, only dau. of Henry and Sarah, d 1/15/47 at Barnard, Windsor County, VT, (whooping cough) (1-4/2)

WINSLOW, R. (Mrs.) - see CORNING, Asa

WINSLOW, Susan - see THOMAS, Hiram

WINTERS, Abigail, 52, wf of Isaac, d 5/8/42 in Newburgh (9-5/14)

WINTERS, William m 5/18/39 Rebecca Foster, both of Somers, in S,; Elder Warren of Southeast (12-6/18)

WINTHROP, Francis B., Jr. m 2/2/16 Elizabeth Woolsey, dau. of William W., Esq., at New Haven; Rev. Dwight (6-2/7)

WINTON, Benjamin m 12/30/41 Lois Shelden, both of Rome in R.; Rev. Ninde (1-1/4/42)

WIRES, Daniel m 1/11/49 Catharine Spanable, both of Minden; Rev. N. Van Alstine (4-1/25)

WIRT, Peter R., M.D., m 6/29/36 Lydia M. Wood, dau of late William of Albany, at
Waterloo; Rev. Hays (6-7/6)

WIRT, William (Hon.), 61, formerly attorney general of US, d 2/18/34 in
Washington (11-2/25)

WISE, ----, wife of the Hon. Henry A. of Virginia, d "a few days since" at the home
of her husband in Accomac County. "Mr. Wise, it is said, will visit
Boston...in the present summer" (from the Boston Globe. The Boston
Advocate's detailed obituary reflecting mutiple family tragedies is here
included also) (6-6/14)

WISMER, Henry G., Esq., about 60, d 2/19/42 in Goshen (9-2/26)

WISNER, Frances - see MURRAY, Ambrose

WISWALL, Ann, 67, wf of Ebenezer, Esq. of Watervliet, d 2/26/49 in Watervliet
(5-2/28)

WISWALL, Catharine Amelia, 2, youngest dau. of Ebenezer and Catharine, d
10/18/47 in West Troy (5-10/27)

WISWALL, Thomas (Capt.) m 8/18/36 Mrs. Ann Maria Denison of NYC in NYC;
Rev. Dr, DeWitt (6-8/22)

WISWALL, William, 5, son of James Wiswall, d 3/10/38 (3-3/22)

WISWELL, nancy - see BOYER, Leonard

WITBECK, F.M. of West Troy m 10/6/42 Almira Grawbarger of Schaghticoke in
S.; F.M. Witneck (5-10/19)

WITBECK, Isaac F., son of Lucas J., m 3/7/49 Jane U. Cobee, dau. of Lawrence J.;
Rev. William Pitcher (all of Watervliet) (5-3/14)

WITBECK, James A. of Coeymans m 2/8/45 Catharine Evan of Bethlehem in West
Troy; James M. Barnard, Esq. (5-2/12)

WITBECK, Lucas G., Esq., 66, of Watervliet d 1/11/44 (5-1/17)

WITBECK, Mary A. - see KIRK, Andrew B.

WITBEECK, Peter, 18, son of Andrew, d 3/28/37 in Coeymans (6-3/30)

WITMARSH, Rebecca - see LINSLAY, William

WITT, Hannah, 57, widow of John, Esq., d 3/4/40 in West Troy (she was formerly
of Hubbardston, Mass.) (5-3/11)

WOFFUL, Mary Ann - see TABALD, Jacob

WOKES, George, Jr., 31, d 11/19/41 in the town of Ramapo, Rockland County
(9-12/4)

WOLCOTT, Ellen M - see BATES, George C.

WOLCOTT, Frederick (Hon.), 69, d 5/27/37 at his home in Litchfield, Conn.
(6-6/16)

WOLCOTT, John P. m 12/2/46 Jane Ann Mc Harg in Rome; H.C. Vogell (1-12/15)

WOLENCE(?), Nicholas m 9/24/36 Harriet Angell in Little Falls; William Brooks,
Esq. (3-10/13)

WOLF, David of Verona m 1/8/45 Betsey Scovill of Rome in Verona; Rev. Wetzell
(1-1/14)

WOLF, Eliza - see GRANT, Gerdon

WOLFE, Rebecca - see LANSING, Stephen

WOLFE, William H., 38, d 7/26/35 in Troy (6-7/30)

WOLVEN, James E. m 11/7/49 Nelly Hendricks of Saugerties; Rev. M.L. Schenck
(8-12/1)

WOOD, Abraham, 82, d 8/23/42 at St. Andrews in Montgomery (9-9/3)

WOOD, Altaline - see WILLIAMSON, William

WOOD, Ancel, son of Col. Aaron Wood of Rensselaerville m 8/26/35 Jane Carter, dau of Judge Carter, formerly of Freehold, Greene Co., at Rensselaerville; Rev. Samuel Fuller. (6-8/31)

WOOD, Ann - see MC CHAIN, Lewis

WOOD, Ann Marie - see MAXON, George G.

WOOD, Ann Matilda - see AUSTIN, John

WOOD, Caroline Martha, 8 months, dau of Bradford R., d 2/20/36 (funeral at 4 o'clock from 149 Washington St.) (6-2/25)

WOOD, Charlotte Augusta - see LITTLE, William Coffin

WOOD, Daniel, 71, d 4/13/36 (friends of his son, R.W. Wood, and his son-in-law Mayell are invited to his funeral 4/17 at his late home, 61 Hudson St.) (6-4/16)

WOOD, Daniel, Esq. - see DUSENBURY, Richard J. (Dr.)

WOOD, David, Esq., 48, president of the Canal Bank, d 11/20/41 at Albany (11-12/7)

WOOD, Dorleson A. - see LOOMIS, William G.

WOOD, Edward d (date not given) in Rochester (6-6/5/16)

WOOD, Elizabeth Ann - see PECK, Abraham

WOOD, Elizabeth Ann, 17, dau of Samuel S., d 12/16/38 in Peekskill (12-12/25)

WOOD, Enoch H., 23, d 8/29/48 in Fort Plain (4-10/5)

WOOD, George of Haverstraw m 1/22/34 Mary Brown of Tarrytown at T. (11-2/4)

WOOD, Gilbert m 1/1/42 Alma Furman in Newburgh; Rev. E.A. Griswold (all of Newburgh) (9-1/8)

WOOD, Gilmon of Brownville m 12/31/34 Harriette Keyes, dau of late Hon. Perley Keyes, at Watertown, Jefferson Co.; Rev. Tredway (6-1/16/35)

WOOD, Gursham of Westmoreland m 3/11/47 Mary Churton of Vernon; Rev. John Barton (1-3/19)

WOOD, Harriet - see SMITH, Sidney T.

WOOD, Hezekiah, about 80, a Rev. War soldier, d 12/30/41 in Pound Ridge (11-1/18/42)

WOOD, Jacob m 12/24/38 Mary Peterson at home of John Peterson of Cortlandt; Rev. Benjamin Curry of Shrub Oaks, Yorktown (a double ceremony, see also marriage of Thomas Peterson) (12-1/15/39)

WOOD, Jacob m 12/24/38 Mary Peterson at the house of John Peterson of Cortlandtown; Rev. Benjamin Curry of Shrub Oak (a double ceremony - see marr. of Thomas Peterson same date) (11-1/8/39)

WOOD, James G. of NYC m 8/18/42 Mary Scott of Newburgh; Rev. T.F. Drake (9-8/20)

WOOD, Jethro - see FOOTE, Jeremiah

WOOD, John, about 60, d "very suddenly" 5/20/39 at Haverstraw (12-6/4)

WOOD, Juliett - see HUNT, Robert S.

WOOD, L. Sprague m 6/11/43 Mary S. Johnson in Lowville, Lewis County; Rev. T.H. Batten (3-6/29)

WOOD, Louisa - see RANDALL, P.N.

WOOD, Louisa H. - see HASTINGS, Heman J.

WOOD, Lydia - see MAYELL, John

WOOD, Lydia M. - see WIRT, Peter R.

WOOD, Maria - see FOOTE, Jeremiah

WOOD, Maria, 16, dau. of William E., d 9/29/41 at Fairfield (3-9/9)

WOOD, Mary - see PRESCOTT, Daniel

WOOD, Mary and Adaline, ages 2 and 4, daus of William and Rosetta, d 1/17 and 1/18/42 in Cortlandtown (scarlet fever) (11-1/25)

Wood, N.B. - see DAY, E. Bennet

WOOD, Phebe Ann - see SMITH, Gilbert

WOOD, Robert m 2/3/39 Lucinda Freeman, both of Danube, in D.; Rev. Covill (3-2/7)

WOOD, Rosanna - see METCALF, Lorenzo D.

WOOD, Ross W., merchant, m 1/9/26 Ann Dunn, both of Albany; Rev. Lacey (6-1/10)

WOOD, Sarah - see COOPER, William

WOOD, Sarah - see DUSENBURY, Richard J. (Dr.)

WOOD, Sarah Ann - see WATSON, R.J.

WOOD, William m 6/16/36 Ann T. Hooker at Watertown; Rev. George Boardman (6-6/27)

WOODALL (?), Nancy Catharine, 3 months(?), dau. of Rev. John I. Woodall, d 4/4/48 at Frey's Bush (4-4/6)

WOODARD, Caleb G. m 12/6/48 Jane A. Damf(?), both of West Troy, in Troy; Rev. G.C. Baldwin (5-12/20)

WOODARD, Sarah M. - see COON, William H.

WOODBRIDGE, Frances Ann - see QUARLES, Francis

WOODCOCK, David, Esq., 50, d 9/18/35 at Ithaca (had been an invalid for many years) (members of the Bar of Ithaca held a special memorial service for him) (6-9/26)

WOODCOCK, Mary - see CUSHING, S.B.

WOODFORD, O.P. of firm of Robinson, Pratt & Co. of NYC m 8/24/36 Elizabeth Burnell of Cazenovia at C.; Rev. C.W. Rogers (6-8/31)

WOODHOUSE, Abijah, 48, d (date not given) at Wethersfield (7-6/27/10)

WOODHULL, John (Gen.), 51, of Brookhaven, Long Island d 7/21/37 after a protracted illness (6-7/29)

WOODRUFF, Andrew m 10/6/42 Sarah Jane Priest, dau. of Eli, in Little Falls; Rev. S. Northrup (bride and groom of Little Falls) (3-10/13)

WOODRUFF, Ann - see HAZLEHURST, William

WOODRUFF, Elias, formerly of Coldenham, Orange County, m 1/20/42 Anna Eddower(?) of Galena, Illinois in G.; Rev. Kent (9-2/19)

WOODRUFF, Elizabeth - see BLAKE, James R.

WOODRUFF, Helen E. - see TRACY, George H.

WOODRUFF, J.L. m 9/8/36 Julia Bacon, dau of late Rev. David Bacon, at Canandaigua; Rev. Thompson (6-9/20)

WOODRUFF, Jane H. - see TAYLOR, Robert W.

WOODRUFF, Lauren C, cashier of the Lockport Bank, m 8/25/36 Ann M. Allen, dau of Samuel of Lockport, at L.; Rev. Wheeler (6-9/10)

WOODRUFF, Maria - see SMITH, Thomas(?)

WOODRUFF, Mary, 24, wf of Sylvester of Cairo, d (date not given) at Bristol, Conn. (a short illness) (7-6/6/10)

WOODRUFF, Samuel M., Esq., of Albany m 10/25/36 Leona Deforest, dau of Lockwood Deforest, Esq., of Bridgeport, CT at B.; Rev. Dr. Hewett (6-11/1)

WOODRUFF, Theodore, 3, son of Silas, d 7/4/42 in Newburgh (scarlet fever) (9-7/9)

WOODRUFF, Wealthy - see BUEL, Francis

WOODSULL(?), Margaret (Mrs.), about 70, d 3/13/42 in New Windsor (9-3/19)

WOODWARD, J.M., m 11/18/35 Sarah Ann Ackerman, dau of late Gilbert, Esq.;
Rev. Horatio Potter (all of Albany) (6-11/21)

WOODWORTH, Adeline, 10 weeks, only dau. of Montgomery and Catherine, d
6/20/47 (5-6/30)

WOODWORTH, Benjamin L. m 12/31/48 Mary A. Osborn in Delta; F. Tracy, Esq.
(1-1/17/49)

WOODWORTH, James B. of Florence m 3/15/42 Mineva (sic) Wiggins, dau. of
David, Esq., of Rome, in R.; Rev. H.C. Vogell (1-3/22)

WOODWORTH, Jane E. - see MURRAY, Andrew J.

WOODWORTH, Maria, 19, d 2/20/36 in Albany (eldest dau of David) (6-2/24)

WOODWORTH, Montgomery m 9/1/46 Catharine E. Sheffer, both of Watervliet, in
Kansingburgh; Rev. Griffin (5-9/9)

WOODWORTH, Samuel, printer, m 9/14/10 Lydia Reeder, dau. of Widow Julia
Reeder, in NYC; Rev. Dr. Moore (all of NYC) (7-10/3)

WOODWORTH, Sarah A. - see WIGGINS, Don C.

WOOLEBER, Ann Eliza - see TUCKER, Dunton (Capt.)

WOOLEBER, Nicholas - see TUCKER, Dunton (Capt.)

WOOLLEY, Nathaniel C. of New Paltz m 1/10/49 Cornelia Miller of Middletown,
Orange County; Rev. H. Lounsbery (8-1/27)

WOOLSEY, Benjamin M., 23, of the house of William M. Woolsey & Co. of
Albany, d 4/4/16 at Havanna ("whither he went for his health") (6-5/8/16)

WOOLSEY, Elizabeth - see WINTHROP, Francis B., Jr.

WOOLSEY, Jonathan Carter, 9, son of Levi D. and Margaret, d 2/10/42 in
Newburgh (9-2/12)

WOOLSEY, Melancthon B. (Lieut.), of the US Navy m 10/8/50 Mary L. Morrison
of Wheeling, Virginia at Christ Church, Baltimore; Rev. C.W. Bolton
(1-10/16)

WOOLSEY, Thomas m 8/11/42 Harriet Amelia Anthony, both of Ulster County, at
the Orange Hotel in Newburgh; H.Armstrong, Esq. (9-8/13)

WOOLSEY, Thomas, about 70, d 12/5/39 in Bedford (12-12/24)

WOOLSEY, William W. - see WINTHROP, Francis B. Jr.

WOOLSEY, William W., Esq. m 12/20/15 Sarah Chauncey, dau. of Hon. Charles
Chauncey, at New Haven; Rev. Dr. Dwight, President of Yale College
(6-12/30)

WORDEN, Frances A. - see CHESEBRO, Henry O.

WORDEN, Julia - see LEONARD, Asaph D.

WORDER, Savannah, 108, dau. of one of the black servants of William Penn,
proprietor of Pennsylvania, d (date not given) in Philadelphia (7-7/26/09)

WORDON, Henrietta K. - see MANCHESTER, Lester A.

WORTH, Dorothy - see REEVES, J.

WORTH, Elizabeth - see CURRAN, Horace D.

WORTH, Mary - see SPRAGUE, John (Capt.)

WORTHINGTON, Sarah - see SHERWOOD, Winfield Scott

WRIGHT, Benjamin, Esq., 72, formerly of Rome d 8/24/42 at the home of his son-
in-law, T.S. Nelson in NYC (1-8/30)

WRIGHT, Catharine - see CHRISTIAN, Truman

WRIGHT, Charles M., 5 months, son of G. and Hannah R., d 9/15/49 in Rome

(1-9/26)

WRIGHT, Eleanor, 85, widow of late Silas of Weybridge, VT and mother of
    Governor Wright, d 12/20/46 at Weybridge. Her husband Silas, died at age
    85 and they were married for 61 years (1-1/8/47)

WRIGHT, Elizabeth - see TRAVIS, Lewis

WRIGHT, Francis, merchant, of Utica d 1/2/45 at Philadelphia (1-1/14)

WRIGHT, Isaac m 8/4/37 Catharine Deck in Starks; Henry Wick, Esq. (3-9/28)

WRIGHT, James C., Esq., attorney at law, Oswego, m 7/16/46 Adeline F. Gay,
    eldest dau. of C.B. Gay, in Rome; Rev. Haynes (1-7/21)

WRIGHT, Jane L. - see CRANE, W. Carey

WRIGHT, John, 107, d 1/16/16 (6-1/20)

WRIGHT, Joseph (Dr.), 69, d (date not given) in NYC (6-5/15/16)

WRIGHT, Joseph, 73, d 7/17/47 in Rome (1-7/23)

WRIGHT, Louise - see EDWARDS, Churchill

WRIGHT, Lovina M. - see MALTAY, Norman

WRIGHT, M----(?) of Westchester Co. m 11/13/39 Sarah Jones of Haverstraw in
    H.; Rev. Mulford Day (12-11/26)

WRIGHT, Mary, 7, eldest dau of Thomas of Albany, d 9/5/35 (6-9/7)

WRIGHT, Oren, 49, M.D., d 7/28/36 in Pittsfield, MA (for 20 years a physician at
    P.) (Pittsfield Sun) (6-8/12)

WRIGHT, Oren, Esq. of Stockbridge m 9/15/41 Calista Simmons of Madison in M.;
    Rev. Black (1-9/21)

WRIGHT, Phebe, 13, dau. of Benjamin, d 2/7/39 in Somers (12-2/12)

WRIGHT, Phineas, d 4/28/26 in Albany (6-5/5)

WRIGHT, Sally - see BECK, Fayette S.

WRIGHT, Sarah - see COUCH, Franklin

WRIGHT, Sarah Jane - see BOND, William Grant

WRIGHT, Silas, 83, d 5/13/43 in Weybridge, Addison County, VT, (after a five
    year illness with extensive paralysis). He was father of Hon. Silas Wright,
    Jr. of St. Lawrence County (3-6/1)

WRIGHT, Sylvinia - see TORANCE, Lemuel

WRIGHT, Timothy of Parma, Monroe Co., m 9/21/35 Mary Ann Almond, eldest
    dau of William of Hartland, at H.; Rev. Halsey (6-9/28)

WRIGHT, William G., 18 months, only son of William E., d 1/19/41 at Akron,
    Ohio (1-2/2)

WYANHAUVER, Miss - see STRATTAN, John H.

WYBOURN, John O. of Bethlehem m 1/8/37 Matilda Bush of Troy; Rev. R.C.
    Brisbin (6-1/10)

WYCKOFF, (Rev. Dr.) m 10/9/49 Cornelia Reed, dau. of late Roswell Reed of
    Coxsackie; Rev. P.D. Van Cleef of Coxsackie Landing, her present pastor,
    presided and the Rev. I. Searle, her former pastor, asked the benediction
    (5-10/17)

WYCKOFF, Emily M., 23, wf of William H. and dau. of Noah Talcott of NYC, d
    7/8/39 at West Bloomfield, NJ (12-7/16)

WYCKOFF, J.K., wf of Rev. Dr. Wyckoff, d 1/29/48 in Albany (5-2/2)

WYCKOFF, Mary La Grange, 15 months, dau. of Rev. T.F. Wyckoff of West Troy,
    d 7/18/49 at Somerville, NJ (5-7/25)

WYCKOFF, Samuel B., formerly of Illinois, m 11/23/48 Orpha Lyman of
    Deansville, Oneida Co. in D. (both deaf mutes) (4-1/4/49)

WYCKOFF, Theodore F., pastor of the South Reformed Dutch Church in West Troy m 5/12/47 Elizabeth La Grange Elmendorf, dau. of Peter Z., Esq. of New Brunswick, NJ; Rev. Dr. Wyckoff of Albany (5-5/19)

WYGANT, Martin (Capt.) of NYC d 5/21/35 (6-5/26)

WYLIE(?), Margaret - see DICKINSON, Abel

WYLIE, ----, 12, youngest dau. of late Charles of Rome, d 6/8/41 at Rochester (scarlet fever, ill just 3 days) (1-7/13)

WYLIE, Charles (Hon.) - see KEITH, Eliza D.

WYLIE, Clarissa B., 34, wf of Allen G., formerly of Rome, d 8/2/47 at Marcellus (1-8/20)

WYLIE, John m 12/29/47 Frances Montgomery in Westmoreland; Rev. Dunham (all of Westmoreland) (1-1/7/48)

WYMAN, Henry C. of Lee, m 8/28/50 Jerusha Preston of Ava in Rome; Rev. James Erwin (1-9/11)

WYMAN, Samuel of Lee m 8/25/48 Irene Preston, eldest dau. of Ezekiel of Ava; Samuel T. Jones, Esq. (1-9/15)

WYNANTS, Josiah - see STOWITZ, Jacob J.

WYNANTS, Pamelia Ann - see STOWITS, Jacob J.

WYNKOOP, John I., about 40, d 12/25/48 in Saugerties (8-12/30)

WYNN, James, about 45. d 6/20/49 in Saugerties (8-6/23)

YALE, Charlotte M. - see FRANE(?), Lawrence

YALE, T.G. of Boonville m 4/6/43 Mary Ann Eaton of Little Falls in L.F.; Rev. E.D. Towner (3-4/20)

YATES, Angelica, 15, youngest dau of Samuel S. Baldwin, Esq., d 3/24/35 at her father's home in Lafayette, Onondaga Co. ("a lingering disease") (6-4/15)

YATES, Catherine L. - see BRISTOL, David E.

YATES, Eliza - see OLCOTT, Theodore

YATES, Garret - see COOPER, Caroline (Miss)

YATES, Henry F. - see PREVOST, William (Dr.)

YATES, Isaac, 2, youngest son of Gen. Isaac L. Yates, d 2/12/36 in Schenectady (3-2/18)

YATES, J.M. (Rev.) of West Troy m 6/26/49 Susan Northrup, dau. of late Enos of Greenbush, in G.; Rev. E. Phillips of Troy (5-7/4)

YATES, Jane Anna - see BUEL, Charles

YATES, John G., 46, son of Garret, Esq., d 3/7/37 at his home in Greenbush (funeral from his late home) (6-3/9)

YATES, Joseph (Dr.), brother of Giles F. Yates, Esq., d 6/12/37, suddenly, in Schenectady (6-6/20)

YATES, Joseph C., 69, late Governor of NY, d 3/19/37 (funeral 3/21 from his home in Schenectady (6-3/21)

YATES, Mary Ann - see RASBERRY, Maxim

YATES, Richard m 9/30/35 Margaret Mancius, youngest dau of late Jacob Mancius, in Albany; Rev. A. Potter of Schenectady (6-10/2)

YATES, Sarah Maria - see WHITAKER, Abm. D.

YATES, William m 5/30/48 Helen Jane Calwell, both of West Troy, in W.T.; Rev. J.C. Burroughs (5-6/7)

YATES, William, Esq. m 10/26/37 Maria Hicks, both of Troy, in Troy; Rev. N.S.S. Beman (5-11/1)

YEARSLEY, George J. of West Troy m 10/12/37 Elizabeth Ann Ten Eyck, formerly of Chicago, in Watervliet; Rev. Mann (5-10/18)

YEARSLEY, Henry m 5/5/42 Sarah A. Whiton, eldest dau. of Lyman, in the Methodist Episcopal Church in West Troy; Rev. D. Starks (all of West Troy) (5-5/11)

YEARSLEY, Margaret Maria - see CARY, John

YEARSLEY, Maria Ann (Miss), 28, d 9/30/43 in Watervliet (5-10/4)

YEARSLEY, Silas Wright, 10 months, son of George J. and Elizabeth Ann, d 8/6/47 in West Troy (5-8/11)

YEATMAN, Jane - see BELL, John

YERDON, John Peter, 83, d 8/9/50 in Frey's Bush (4-8/15)

YERDON, Margaret - see ROGERS, David H.

YERKS, Henry, 71, d 11/17/38 in Mount Pleasant (12-11/27)

YERRY, Elizabeth - see SHULTIS, Hiram W.

YERRY, Henry m 6/21/49 Mary Happy, both of Woodstock; Rev. Alexander Goulick (8-6/30)

YOEMANS, Epenetus, about 80, d 8/19/50 in Carmel (10-8/22)

YOEMANS, Moses, 71, d (date not given) at Kingston (6-6/5/16)

YORAN, Ann - see SMITH, Matthew

YORK, Elizabeth (Mrs.), 69, d 9/15/49 in Saugerties (8-9/22)

YORKE, Ann, 55, widow of John, d 8/15/50 at North Bay, Vienna (1-8/21)

YORKE, Samuel, an eminent merchant of Philadelphia, d (date not given) in Philadelphia (6-5/22/16)

YORKES, Phebe - see HANES, Henry P.

YORKS, Eliza - see REYNOLDS, Enos

YOST, Jacob S. - see COFFIN, George M.

YOUKER, Lodwick m 6/2/36 Mary Shaver, both of Oppenheim, in Little Falls; Rev. Atwater (3-6/9)

YOUMANS, Ruth - see STRICKLIN, John

YOUNG, Alexander, 43, d (date not given) in NYC (born in Perthshire, Scotland) (6-12/26/26)

YOUNG, Alvin, 35, d 2/4/47 in Florence (billious fever) (1-2/19)

YOUNG, Ann - see HALSTED, Ira

YOUNG, Athallah - see SERVIES, William

YOUNG, Catharine - see DAVIS, Leander

YOUNG, Charles C., Esq., of NYC m 8/4/36 Elizabeth Huntington, dau of Henry, Esq., of Rome, NY, at R. (6-8/8)

YOUNG, Coe F., merchant of Barryville, Sullivan County, m 1/17/49 Mary A. Cornell, dau. of Peter, Esq. of Rosendale, at Eddyville; Rev. W.S. Mikels (8-1/27)

YOUNG, David H. m 5/14/48 Ann Mc Cormick, both of Fort Plain, in the Fort Plain Methodist Church; Rev. B. Isbell (4-5/18)

YOUNG, David S. m 5/9/41 Mary Parke, dau. of William, Esq. in Lee; Rev. Hodges (all of Lee) (1-6/15)

YOUNG, De Witt C. m 10/20/39 Eliza Marshall, dau. of Ira E. Marshall, in New Castle; Rev. Travis (all of N.C.) (12-11/5)

YOUNG, Emma N. - see ROOF, John I.

YOUNG, Eve Eliza - see TENNANT, R.R.

YOUNG, Ezeriah m 1/1/50 Ada Carl, both of Chittenango; H.C. Vogell (1-1/9)

YOUNG, Glover S. m 11/30/43 Charlotte m. Charlotte M. Willard; Rev. C.W. Leet

(3-12/7)

YOUNG, Harriet - see KNIFFIN, Alanson

YOUNG, Henry G. m 12/25/48 Phebe A. Robinson, both of Van Hornesville, in V.H.; Rev. A.F. Daniels (4-12/28)

YOUNG, J.C. - see STAFFORD, Ann Eliza

YOUNG, Jacob P., 25, formerly of Stark, Herkimer County, d 3/5/40 in Utica (3-3/19)

YOUNG, Joseph, 81, d 5/10/37 in Little Falls (was born in Southhold, Long Island and at an early age moved to Killingworth, Conn. - lived in his latest home more than 40 years. He had 15 children) (3-6/1)

YOUNG, Maria - see RUE, Stephen D.

YOUNG, Mary - see BEACH, John G., Esq.

YOUNG, S. (Hon.) - see BEACH, John G.

YOUNG, Samuel - see BURWELL, Catherine

YOUNG, Samuel - see BURWELL, Catherine Ann

YOUNG, Thomas Y. m 2/8/38 Elizabeth M. Minor in Columbia; Elder Wightman (3-2/15)

YOUNG, Truesdel of Bedford m 10/22/39 Eliza Brown, dau. of Jesse of New Castle, in N.C. (Rev. Travis) (12-11/5)

YOUNG, Zeruah, 68, widow of James Young, Esq., of Lee, d 5/14/49 in Lee (dropsical consumption for several years) (1-5/16)

YOUNGS, Barney, 83, a Rev. War soldier, d 6/9/42 at German Flats (3-6/23)

YOUNGS, Emily - see CAPRON, Nelson

YOUNGS, Isaac S., M.D., m 9/15/37 Hannah F. Best at Tonawanda; Rev. A.T. Hopkins (all of Tonawanda) (6-9/23)

ZANDT, Henry, 20, son of William, d 9/18/36 (funeral at 3 o'clock from his father's home, 79 Liberty Street) (6-9/19)

ZEBULON, Maria - see POWERS, Daniel

ZEIDER, George C. m 11/18/49 Mrs. Hannah Jones in Saugerties; Rev. John Hendricks (8-12/8)

ZIEGLER, Frederick, widower, m 12/5/41 Christina Krause, both immigrants from Bavaria of Middle Franconia in Germany, in the Stone Church at German Flats (they settled "in Jacksonburgh of Little Falls") (Rev. J.P. Spinner performed the marriage ceremony) (3-12/9)

ZIELMAN, Mary Ann - see LUTHER, Jeremiah

ZIMMERMAN, John m 12/4/25 Nancy Klock at Oppenheim (6-1/3/26)

ZOLLER, Charlotte - see HORDICK, Jeremiah

ZOLLER, Isaac m (date not given) Mary Ann Steel(?) in German Flats (3-9/5/39)

ZOLLER, Josiah m "lately" Catharine Moyer in Minden (3-2/2/37)

APPENDIX

Posted below is a list of the books and articles I have published in the genealogical field within the time span 1982 through 1997 inclusive. Items 2, 3, 4, 6, 8 and 12 reflect cumulatively more than 46,000 vital records (all dated prior to 1851) drawn from the marriage and death columns found in newspapers published in various sections of New York State.

Books:
    Landholders of Northeastern New York, 1739-1802 (228 pp.). Baltimore:
        Genealogical Publishing Company, 1983.
    10,000 Vital Records of Western New York, 1809-1850 (318 pp.). Baltimore:
        Genealogical Publishing Company, 1985.
    10,000 Vital Records of Central New York, 1813-1850 (338 pp.). Baltimore:
        Genealogical Publishing Company, 1986.
    10,000 Vital Records of Eastern New York, 1777-1850 (356 pp.). Baltimore:
        Genealogical Publishing Company, 1987.
    New York's Detailed Census of 1855 - Greene County (277 pp.). Rhinebeck, NY:
        Kinship, 1988.
    8,000 More Vital Records of Eastern New York State, 1804-1850 (287 pp.).
        Rhinebeck, NY: Kinship, 1991.
    Directory to Collections of New York Vital Records, 1726-1989, with Rare
        Gazetteer (91 pp.). Thomas J. Lynch, co-author. Bowie, MD: Heritage
        Books, Inc., 1995.
    7,000 Hudson-Mohawk Valley, New York, Vital Records, 1808-1850 (368 pp.).
        Baltimore: Genealogical Publishing Company, 1997.

Articles:
    "Redding Grandsons of Thomas[1] Redding" (New England based). The
        Genealogist, Volume 3 (1982).
    "Vital Records Listings of an Indian Missionary in Western New York, 1832-
        1879. "The New York Genealogical and Biographical Record, Volume 117
        (1986).
    "John[1] Horsington of New England." The New England Historical and
        Genealogical Register, Volume 141 (1987).
    "1,100 Vital Records of Northeastern New York, 1835-1850." Thomas J. Lynch,
        co-author. The New York Genealogical and Biographical Record, Volumes
        118, 119 (1988-1989).
    "Towns and Families of Ontario County, New York, 1790." Heritage Quest, Issue
        #46 (1993).

The seventh book above (Directory to Collections...) is divided into three sections. Part 1 identifies several hundred collections of newspaper-published vital records and specifies in which of five large genealogical libraries each of these collections is available. Part 2 in gazetteer form identifies 6710 New York cities, villages and hamlets (some communities obsolete) showing present-day counties and towns (called townships in some states) within which each lies or formerly lay if obsolete. Part 3 identifies the formation and origins of New York's present-day sixty-two counties.

Fred Q. Bowman

www.ingramcontent.com/pod-product-compliance
Lightning Source LLC
Chambersburg PA
CBHW070544270326
41926CB00013B/2192